THE SUDAN
IN ANGLO-EGYPTIAN
RELATIONS

THE SUDAN
IN ANGLO-EGYPTIAN
RELATIONS

A CASE STUDY IN POWER POLITICS

1800-1956

L. A. FABUNMI

GREENWOOD PRESS, PUBLISHERS
WESTPORT, CONNECTICUT

Library of Congress Cataloging in Publication Data

Fabunmi, L   A
   The Sudan in Anglo-Egyptian relations.

   Reprint of the 1960 ed. published by Longmans,
Green, London.
    Bibliography: p.
    1. Sudan—History—1820-   2. Egypt—
Foreign relations—Great Britain. 3. Great
Britain—Foreign relations—Egypt. I. Title.
[DT108.F3 1974]   327'.11'09624   73-15242
ISBN 0-8371-7165-2

First published in 1960 by Longmans, London

Reprinted with the permission of Longman Group Limited

Reprinted in 1973 by Greenwood Press,
a division of Williamhouse-Regency Inc.

Library of Congress Catalogue Card Number 73-15242

ISBN 0-8371-7165-2

Printed in the United States of America

Of revolutions and intrigues
The war, its causes, course and crime,
The ups and downs of pacts and leagues,
And wounds as yet unhealed by time,
Such are the themes you treat, who dare
(A risk which many a heart dismays)
To stir hot ashes, which may flare,
At any moment to a blaze.

—HORACE, *Odes*, II

It is an undertaking of some degree of delicacy to examine into the cause of public disorders. If a man happens not to succeed in such an enquiry, he will be thought weak and visionary; if he touches the true grievance, there is a danger that he may come into persons of weight and consequence, who will rather be exasperated at the discovery of their errors, than thankful for the occasion of correcting them.

EDMUND BURKE: *Thoughts on the Cause of the Present Discontents*

To the Memory of
MY MOTHER
who instilled in me a love of mankind and who died at home in Nigeria just before I finished my studies at Hope College, Michigan, where I received my first challenge in the field of international relations.

CONTENTS

Part Three
The War and Post-War Developments in the Dispute

Part Four
The Final Stages of the Dispute and the Re-Emergence of the Sudanese, 1948–56

PLATES

MAPS

PREFACE

OURS is an age of great technological achievements, but one that is sociologically distressing. It has failed to strike a balance between the rapid advance in science and technology on the one hand, and, on the other, the skill (plus the will) to live and work together in harmony. And so we are faced with tensions here and frictions there; one race is pitted against another, and nations bicker with nations. In December 1955, in the course of the customary Christmas Day Message to the world, Queen Elizabeth focused on this human behaviour:

We have still to solve the problems of living together as peoples and nations.[1]

Two such nations in conflict were Britain and Egypt, and the major bone of contention between them was the Sudan.

The Sudan Question in its local and wider significance, is an example of the struggle for power, so common in the world today. With its twin issue of the Suez Canal Zone, the Sudan has been a source of mixed pride and anxiety to Britain, and a painful thorn in the flesh of Egypt —an ever-present memento of foreign occupation and national weakness. It nearly involved Great Britain in war with France at Fashoda. In short, as we shall show, pragmatically, the Anglo-Egyptian Sudan Question vividly reflects certain poisonous elements, intrigues and conflicting vested interests which are at work at various levels, in the relations between States, particularly in the relations between 'Eastern' and 'Western' Governments—even between Europe and the United States; and especially between great powers and small ones. Certain aspects of the Sudan Question are similar to other situations in, say, Nigeria, Uganda and other colonial territories.[2] Therefore, a presentation of the Anglo-Egyptian dispute over the Sudan may have 'a special value as a case study of the breakdown of common sense and good faith which affects, in a greater or less measure, the behaviour of political leaders and the conduct of political affairs in many parts of the world today'.[3] Like an anti-toxin, the study of these poisonous elements could

[1] See 'The Queen's Broadcast', in *The Times Weekly Review*, London, 29 December 1955.
[2] Some parallels are given (in parenthesis) in the appropriate sections of this study. Many others will occur to the reader.
[3] Gibb, Professor H. A. R., 'Anglo-Egyptian Relations', in *International Affairs Magazine*, Vol. XXVII, No. 4, October 1951.

be employed either in a curative or a preventative way. Its worth, I hope, resides in the use of the knowledge thus gained—one of the means of avoiding mistakes is to anticipate them. This is not to suggest that Anglo-Egyptian relations were bedevilled only with 'poisons' and errors. Such a study would also reveal, of course, values and high principles concomitant with the drive for power.

International relationships are a complex of open and hidden phenomena; these phenomena are not only directly or obliquely inter-related, but are in several dimensions. This being the case, I may have been compelled to touch on points which, at first sight, might appear to be outside the theme. But such points have been dealt with in order that a full-faceted picture might be gained. I have, therefore, endeavoured to deal with the complex and inter-related phenomena observable in the Anglo-Egyptian dispute over the Sudan and yet to maintain singleness of subject and unity of thought.

'Objectivity' in the study of international affairs as a whole and particularly in matters of dispute between vested interests, or in Power Politics, is not to be had by failing to give verdicts or by avoiding indications of preference. The multiplicity of groups to which peoples can belong, by chance or by choice, enriches world civilization. There might be much gain but perhaps also some loss were English students discouraged from taking an English view of the Black Hole of Calcutta; a member of the Society of Friends from looking at the Reformation through the eyes of a Quaker; or a Black African from having a Negro reaction to the doctrine of 'White supremacy'; and each side of the Atlantic from having its own version of the American War of Independence. I ought to add that in power-political encounters such as the Sudan dispute, statesmen and politicians should be distinguished from philosophers and scientists, not so much by the degree of intelligence or scholarship possessed by statesmen and politicians, but by the nature of their responsibility and their accountability to the communities which they represent.

I am not an Englishman; I hope therefore to be excused if I am found wanting in the traditional zeal for perpetuating the British Empire at whatever cost.[1] Nor am I an Egyptian, so I have not experienced the

---

[1] Professor Toynbee observes that Universal States 'are possessed by an almost demonic craving for life' and that if we look at them through the eyes of their 'own citizens we shall find these are apt not only to desire with their whole hearts that this earthly commonwealth of theirs may live for ever, but actually to believe that the immortality of this human institution is assured '.—*A Study of History*, Vol. VII, London, 1954, p. 7.

type of 'British Occupation' complex which often makes the Egyptian excitable and anti-British. I am a West African, born and bred in Nigeria, and so I lack the characteristics of a dissatisfied Sudanese 'Effendi', obsessed with the Sudanese viewpoint. I have worked at the matter, not as a politician who is responsible to an electorate, but as a critical student. This is not to claim, however, that I have succeeded—where others have failed—in solving the problem of objectivity in the recording of history, especially the history of conflicts of interests, or in the interpretation of facts. I am only too aware of the gibe that the history of the Arabs has been written, in Europe, mainly by historians who knew little Arabic, or by Arabists who knew little history; and that in any case, Negroid Africans are academically and politically babes in the wood. Nevertheless, I have honestly endeavoured to follow the example set by Spinoza:

> When I have applied my mind to politics so that I might examine what belongs to politics with the same freedom of mind as we use for mathematics, I have taken my best pains not to laugh at actions of mankind, not to moan over them, not to be angry with them, but to understand them.[1]

Therefore, while conceding my fallibility, I would stand by my findings. But I am, at the same time, possessed of the desire to understand other students—especially in Great Britain, Egypt, and the Sudan —who might be so placed as to see the problem in a different light altogether. Perhaps in this way, we can each make our contribution to mankind's total vision of truth and reality.

[1] *Tractatus Politicus*, Chap. I, Sect. 4.

ACKNOWLEDGMENTS

It is difficult to mention all who have aided in one way or another. I can only refer to a few.

I want to thank Sir James Robertson (for thirty years in the Sudan Service before his new assignment as the Governor-General of Nigeria since April 1955) for finding the time to peruse Chapter 8—British Stake in the Sudan—and for his valuable criticism. I ought to mention here his main objection; he pulled me up for appearing to 'impute Machiavellian motives to people who were honestly trying to rescue a nation from poverty and misgovernment'. Sir James did not see other chapters, especially the one on 'British Legacy to the Sudanese. . . .' In any case I want to assure him publicly (and all others—dead or alive—who have helped to shape the course of events in the Sudan) of my good faith. Philosophy and scholarship, at which I am a most average amateur, aim at perfection in the overall interests of mankind. But as perfection is not easily, if ever, attained, one way of pursuing it is by trying to discover and understand the imperfections in other people's achievements.[1]

I am indebted to the Egyptian Education Bureau, London, and the Ministry of Education, Cairo (especially Dr. A. Ateek), for co-operating as much as possible with me in my visit to Egypt to collect first-hand information and general impressions about the subject. In Cairo I received much factual assistance from the Sudanese Affairs Department of the Ministry of National Guidance, from the Ministry for Foreign Affairs and from the British Embassy. I am particularly grateful to Mr. J. K. Drinkall, First Secretary, British Embassy, and Mr. Mohammed Said, Second Secretary, Egyptian Ministry of Foreign Affairs, both of whom read my draft chapters on the negotiations leading to the Anglo-Egyptian Agreements of 1953 and 1954. At Aswan, His Excellency Abdel Aziz Abdel Hai, Governor of the Aswan Province of Egypt

---

[1] Sir James has since read the whole work. In a letter dated (Cholsey, Berks.) 3 July 1957, he generously comments: 'I have read these two volumes with much interest and congratulate you on your research and also on the very interesting way in which you have set out your thesis. I don't agree with it all by any means, and presumably you would not expect me to do so—but of course those in the thick of things do not see everything with the same outlook as those on the outside, who make their judgments from documents. . . .'

together with his Deputy—Col. Amin Abdel Aziz—contributed much to my understanding of certain aspects of Egypto-Sudanese relations; they also gave me official escort to the Aswan Dam; and Mr. Mahghoub El Mahi, Agent of the Sudan Railways at Aswan, kindly offered me generous hospitality during my stay. In Khartoum, the Prime Minister's office made quick arrangements for me to meet most of the public personages connected with the various aspects of the subject.

I am also grateful to all Librarians who have aided and tolerated me, indeed a troublesome reader, at the following institutions in London: The London School of Economics and Political Science, The Royal Institute of International Affairs (Chatham House), the Public Records Office, and the British Museum; the Sudan Agent, the American and the Egyptian[1] Embassies; and also at the Public Libraries in the Boroughs of Islington, Hornsey, Westminster and Hampstead.

This book has evolved from work done for the Degree of Doctor of Philosophy in the Faculty of Economics (International Relations) of the University of London. I must thank Professor Manning, my official Supervisor, who suggested this intriguing subject in the first place; Dr. F. S. Northedge, Lecturer, Department of International Relations; Miss Hilda Lee, Lecturer, Department of International History, both of the London School of Economics and Political Science; and Miss Marjorie Nicholson of the Fabian Society, all of whom gave me much of their valuable time. The moral support of several British and Nigerian friends was a constant source of inspiration.

The London School of Economics
  and Political Science,
London, October 1958.

[1] Mr. Mustafa El-Dib Benshi, First Secretary to the Egyptian Embassy, was particularly helpful.

1

INTRODUCTION:

THE SUDAN—THE LAND, ITS PEOPLE AND PROBLEMS

This book 'Egypt and the English' was written . . . to remind him [the British reader] of the delights of travel which await him in Egypt and the Sudan.[1]

DOUGLAS SLADEN, 1908

We reach now the Sudan itself, one of the most fabulous countries of the world. . . . Politically, Sudan is, I think, the most exciting country we saw in all Africa with the possible exception of Nigeria.[2]

JOHN GUNTHER, 1955

IN order to supply some background to a picture of the Sudan, it is necessary to give a brief geographical and ethnographical survey of the country which was the bone of contention in Anglo-Egyptian relations for over half a century. For our present purpose this survey need not be comprehensive, but we shall also discuss in this chapter some of the socio-political problems of the country.

'Sudan' is part of the Arabic phrase 'Bilad-al-Sudan' meaning 'The Country of the Blacks', and is, properly speaking, the whole area which corresponds approximately to the section of Negro Africa north of the Equator and mostly under Mohammedan influence.

The Sudan proper can be divided roughly into four political areas: the Western area, or that part lying west of the Niger River, i.e. Senegal, French West Africa, etc.; that area between the Niger and Lake Chad —within the Northern sector of Nigeria; the central area between Lake Chad and the Nile basin, e.g. the French Congo or Equatorial Africa, and the area within the Upper Nile Valley.

The last area is the part with which we are concerned in this work: they are the Sudanese states conquered during the nineteenth century

---

[1] Sladen, Douglas, *Egypt and the English*, London, 1908, p. xi.
[2] Gunther, John, *Inside Africa*, British Edition, London, 1955, pp. 223–4.

by the modern Egyptians. Hence, before the revolt of the Arabic-speaking inhabitants under Mohammed Ahmed el-Mahdi in 1896-8, it was brought under the joint rule of Britain and Egypt, and that accounts for its new name of Anglo-Egyptian Sudan (until 1 January 1956, when it became an independent and sovereign republic).

This vast country is the biggest territory in the north-eastern quarter of Africa and its shape on the map resembles something like a human thigh. It lies between north latitudes 22° and 3° and between east longitudes 22° and 38½°, having an area of about one million square miles. This is more than double the size of Egypt; or almost one-quarter of the area of Europe; or about the size of Britain, France, Portugal, Italy, Belgium, Norway, Sweden and Denmark put together; or about eleven times the area of the United Kingdom of Great Britain and Northern Ireland; or about one-third the size of the United States of America. The population, however, is only about nine million—nearly that of New York City or London. (A new census was still in progress in February 1956, when the writer visited the country.)

The country is bounded on the north by Egypt and Libya, and on the north-east by the Red Sea; Eritrea and Ethiopia lie on its south-east whilst British Kenya, British Uganda and the Belgian Congo are on its south. It is bounded on the west by French Equatorial Africa. Its length from the Egyptian border at Wadi Halfa in the north to Uganda in the south is about 1,300 miles and the breadth is between 1,000 and 500 miles.

The area lies within the Tropics, and too far removed from the Ocean to enjoy sea breezes; it is also less than 1,500 feet above sea level. Consequently, the climate is too warm, particularly for those Europeans who have not yet become used to the Tropics. The mean annual temperature is above 80° F. January is the coldest month, and June the hottest. When the writer visited Khartoum in February 1956, it was too warm, even for a Nigerian; the highest maximum temperature recorded in Khartoum during February is 110° F. However, the dryness of the air makes the climate healthy.

For descriptive (and administrative) purposes the Sudan is conveniently divided into three sectors; the Northern, Central and Southern Zones. The transition is gradual, with no precise limits in climate and vegetation.

The Northern Zone runs roughly from the Egyptian frontier near Wadi Halfa through some 350 miles; it is partly desert and bare hills. But the monotonous scenery of the Atmour desert, which is a continuation of the Sahara, leads on to Karima, where some green vegetation and scattered palm trees appear by the Nile Valley. Owing to the dryness and poverty of this area, it is very thinly populated, but there are farmers along the Valley who are described as 'peaceful folk, very much like the Egyptian fellaheen (peasants); but (unlike the fellaheen) crime is almost unknown among them'.[1] Mekki Abbas states that magistrates of the Wadi Halfa district may go for about twenty years without having to try any case of murder or grievous bodily hurt, but that litigation is frequent.[2]

In the desert area to the west of the Nile are some nomadic Arabs who rear cattle, camels and horses, seeking pasture from place to place for their herds. The very striking similarity in physical appearance and in general folkways, together with the geographical proximity of this section to Upper Egypt, lends some strength to the Egyptian claim of common cultural and ethnic ties with the Sudanese. One of the Egyptian sources asserts:

> As for the Northern Sudan, there is no doubt that its early history and civilisation were intimately connected with those of Ancient Egypt. Nubia and adjacent Sudanese territories have been throughout the ages, recorded in history and even in prehistoric times as almost inseparable from Egypt.[3]

Some British sources also express in one form or another this Egypto-Sudanese affinity. In his archæological review, Edison calls it 'the total Egyptianisation of the region now comprising the provinces of Halfa and Dongola'.[4] Dr. Mekki Shebeika, himself Sudanese, supports this view.

The chief town of the region is Port Sudan. With about 47,000 people, it lies on the Red Sea which forms a passage for most of the country's external trade. A railway line connects the port with Atbara and Khartoum, both in Central Sudan.

The central zone of the Sudan extends approximately 600 miles from Atbara to Malakal, and occupies roughly the area between the 18th and 10th parallels of north latitude. South of Malakal, the main river line splits into several branches flanked by several marshes. The river banks in this area present, by and large, living conditions similar to those prevailing in the northern zone. But this is the nerve centre of the country—the most active, the richest and most thickly populated part

[1] The British Society for International Understanding: The British Survey—Popular Series No. 100, *The Anglo-Egyptian Sudan*, p. 3.
[2] Mekki Abbas, *The Anglo-Egyptian Sudan*, p. 3.
[3] Egypt/Sudan, Press Section, Cairo, 1947, p. 69.
[4] Sudan Govt., *The Anglo-Egyptian Sudan from Within*, London, 1935, p. 21.

of the Sudan. It contains the great Gezira cotton area and the gum forests, which together provide most of the country's exports and revenues. Seven-eighths of the world's supply of gum-Arabic is shipped from Port Sudan, the biggest buyers being the United States and the United Kingdom.[1] The chief towns of the Sudan are found here: Khartoum (82,673 inhabitants), Omdurman (125,300), El Obeid (70,000), Wad Medani (57,000) and Kassala (36,000). Khartoum means 'Elephant's Trunk', so named, it is said, because of the narrow tongue of land on which the town stands at the confluence of the White and Blue Niles. It is the political and commercial capital of the country, with an airport lying at the point where the Cape to Cairo airline cuts across the route from West to East Africa. It was replanned by Lord Kitchener on its old site, its streets set out in the pattern of the British Union Jack. Khartoum has become a pleasant garden city with low houses, green lawns and flower beds carefully irrigated from the river on each side. It is a cosmopolitan town where East and West appear to meet and mingle culturally, politically and sometimes socially. Most of the signposts on the streets are in three languages: English, Arabic and Greek.

On the Western side of the Nile, near the junction of the two rivers, lies the native city of Omdurman, the centre of Sudanese cultural, political and religious life. To Mekki Abbas and other Sudanese, it is the most interesting town in the Sudan. The population—125,300—is 'almost a hundred per cent Sudanese and a visitor from any part of the Northern Sudan can find relatives to accommodate him'.[2] Omdurman is well known for its bazaars of native handicrafts of gold, silver, ivory and leather. Geographically, Khartoum and Omdurman, joined by the 'Blue-White River' Bridge, are like Lagos and Ebute Meta (in west Nigeria) joined by the Carter Bridge. But in certain other respects nothing could be more different from Lagos than Khartoum; Lagos is basically an African town ('the Liverpool of West Africa'), whereas Khartoum strikes one as a dominantly European intrusion; the psychological impact is considerable and emphasized by the proximity of Omdurman. Compared with Ebute Meta, Omdurman, though possessing such amenities as one tramway, electric lighting and water supply, is very suburban.

[1] Sudan Govt., *1001 Facts about the Sudan*, Khartoum, 1952, p. 14.
[2] Mekki Abbas, *op. cit.*, p. 6. On about 3 February 1956, when the writer was sightseeing in Omdurman, a youngster from whom he merely asked directions invited him home to dinner, within about ten minutes of their meeting! He accepted the spontaneous invitation.

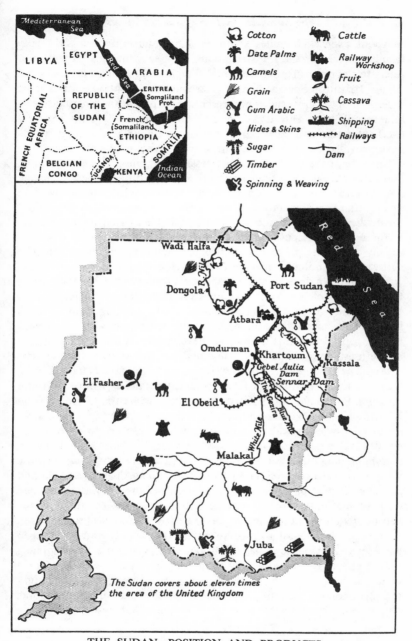

Cotton   **Cattle**

Date Palms   **Railway Workshop**

Camels

Grain   **Fruit**

Gum Arabic   **Cassava**

Hides & Skins   **Shipping**

Sugar   **Railways**

Timber   **Dam**

Spinning & Weaving

The Sudan covers about eleven times the area of the United Kingdom

THE SUDAN—POSITION AND PRODUCTS

(Adapted from a Crown copyright map, by permission of the Controller, H.M. Stationery Office)

About twenty-five miles south of Khartoum stretches the fertile farming district of Gezira Mesopotamia. 'Gezira' means 'Island' and refers to the peninsula between the White and Blue Niles. Here lies the Gezira Irrigation Scheme, which is so much talked about. It is a joint enterprise of the Government representing the public, the tenant farmers, and the management. It has helped thousands of farmers to grow excellent cotton and other crops on about a million acres, and its yields have provided about fifty per cent of the Government's revenue.

It is one of the world's most successful examples of irrigation work and agricultural technique, perhaps next to the Tennessee Valley Authority Scheme in the United States. It sets Mekki Abbas, now one of the Managing Directors of the Scheme, dreaming: 'Indeed, should the civilisations which rose in the Mesopotamia of Iraq and other parts of the Fertile Crescent have any future parallel in the Sudan, it will be mainly due to the prosperity contributed by this Mesopotamia when its cultivable two million acres are fully developed.'[1]

The Southern zone of the Sudan extends over some 350 miles from the branching of the White Nile above Malakal to the Belgian Congo, Uganda and Kenya. Here the rainfall is good, ranging from 30 to 50 inches. This makes the region vary from grassy plain to marsh and nearly tropical forest. It is an under-developed part of the country, one of the most acute needs here being means of transport and communication. The Nile steamer takes twelve days to cover the 600 miles from Kosti to Juba in Equatoria Province and the railway from Khartoum or from Port Sudan does not go south beyond Kosti, 150 miles from Khartoum. The mineral resources of the South include surface and solid deposits of iron ore, copper and some gold. However, owing partly to the difficulties of transport and communication, the mining and processing of minerals have not been developed. But for a long time the inhabitants used charcoal and clay furnaces to smelt iron, and worked the deposits of copper, especially for rings. But this art was abandoned during the Mahdia, probably as the result of a misinterpretation of the Muslim religion, in the same way as the early Christian missionaries in Nigeria urged converts to forsake their works of art, which were then considered as evidence of paganism, but are now universally acclaimed.

Ethnologically, opinions vary about the peoples of the Sudan. Three main schools of thought are discernible. First, there are those we might call the 'Atomistic School', to which many British administrators, some Arabs and a few Sudanese (especially Southern Sudanese under British

[1] Mekki Abbas, *op. cit.* p. 8.

influence) belong. This school generally speak of the Southern Sudan as the home of 'numerous Negroid tribes'. They submit that in the Upper Nile and in a great part of Bahr El Gazal Provinces the majority of the people belong to one of the three most famous of the groups: the Dinka, the Nuer and the Shilluk. (But anthropologists group all of them together as Nilotics.) Continuing this process of atomization, members of the school state that in Equatoria Province alone, 'there are not less than forty different tribes'.[1] And they conclude that the peoples of the Southern Provinces, because they 'were almost untouched by the impact of civilisation, whether Arab or European, . . . are therefore one of the most primitive peoples in the world'.[2] But they say, at the same time, that 'there is no evidence that the Southern Sudanese is either of inferior intelligence or notoriously lazy'.[3]

The next group of opinion we might describe as the 'Amalgamate' School, or 'Euro-Africanists'. To this belongs, I venture to suggest, E. E. Evans-Pritchard, sometime Professor of Sociology at the Egyptian University, Cairo, now at Oxford. Writing for the Anglo-Egyptian Administration in the Sudan, he stresses that two main 'racial types' have contributed to the racial characters of the Anglo-Egyptian Sudanese— namely, the Negro and the Caucasian, or the Black and the White. 'We must regard the peoples of the Sudan as variations between the two ideal poles, the pure Caucasian and the pure Negro types', he asserts.[4]

There is a third school of thought which we shall call political 'Unitarians'. Its members recognize that the Sudan (or any country for that matter) can be divided into several geographical and administrative units or ethnic groups. They accept the fact that the Northern Sudan, itself by no means wholly homogeneous, is predominantly Arab by orientation and Islamic by religion, whilst the South is on the whole different in vernacular and Pagan in religion (though there are Christians of many denominations and Muslims also). They would contend that since no nation or state is ethnically, religiously or culturally homo-geneous *per se*, it is not impossible to administer the whole Sudan— North or South—as one political unit, provided, of course, that there is the will to do so through the use of such instruments as education, communication and administration to promote the concept of oneness —common nationality or citizenship. I am myself inclined to agree more with this school of thought than with that of atomicism; as

[1] Republic of the Sudan, *Southern Sudan Disturbances*, August 1955; *Report of the Commission of Enquiry*, Khartoum, October 1956, p. 4.
[2] *Ibid.*   [3] *Ibid*, p. 7.
[4] Sudan Govt., *The Anglo-Egyptian Sudan from Within*, p. 81.

everyone knows, Britain and Egypt have each, in spite of their respective internal diversities, established and maintained a unitary state. The estimated population of the whole Southern Sudan, it must be remembered, is under three million and that of the North about seven million; the total maximum population of the whole Sudan is estimated to be eleven million—half the number of people in Egypt and only about one-fifth of those in the United Kingdom. On the question of 'backwardness', no country is evenly developed—absolutely. In any case, the core of the relative backwardness of the Southern Sudanese is due mostly to the fact that, as a Commission of Enquiry has discovered, 'he has simply not had the same opportunity as other members of the [Sudanese] community'.[1] Several forces of cohesion, such as the Mahdia in the 19th century together with the better means of communication and better education in the 20th century, have increased the advantages of the Northerner over the Southerner.

At any rate, the admixture of various groups of Africans, Arabs and even Europeans has been going on for a long time through marriage or concubinage. As a result, the Sudanese are a blend of all these groups of humanity. There may not be anything approximating to what race or tribe enthusiasts call 'pure types'. For many of the people commonly referred to as Arabs are in fact Negroid physically, e.g. the Baggarra and the Islamic people of Darfur. Also, among the 'black-skinned' peoples are individuals displaying some Caucasian features; this is so even as far south as Northern Nigeria, particularly among the Fulanis.

This brings us to an important factor in the domestic politics of the Sudan and, indeed, in those of most parts of British Africa—namely, sectional frictions. There has existed a good deal of fear, suspicion and sometimes open hostility, between the Southern and the Northern Sudanese. For the light which such an attempt might throw on our main subject—a study of the interplay of power or influence over a people—we propose to examine some of the major causes of the problem of friction between the North and the South. The major factors underlying the misunderstanding include first, the arbitrary political demarcations and groupings by Europeans during the great scramble for Africa. A Briton, Professor Harlow, declares: 'Most African territories south of the Sahara (and north of it) were demarcated by historical accidents—the outcome of the scramble.'[2] As a result, several groups of

---

[1] The Republic of the Sudan, *Southern Sudan Disturbances*, p. 7.
[2] Harlow, Professor Vincent, 'Tribalism in Africa', *The Colonial Review*, Vol. VIII, No. 8, London, December 1954, p. 241.

peoples of different political and cultural orientations or emphasis became lumped together. National feeling or the sense of common citizenship on a country-wide scale is often lacking amongst native inhabitants; and the Imperial Power should not be blamed for not cultivating, consciously and actively, nationalism or collective feeling for one another through the process of education. To do so might lead, too soon, to a united front against the occupying Power. Second, there is the British sense of chivalry—i.e. the desire to protect the 'weak' (the South) from the 'strong' (the North). This may be a genuine human love for the 'underdog'; but it is also interwoven with the well-known imperial formula of 'divide and rule'. In the Sudan this has become notorious as the Southern Policy. (In Nigeria, by the way, it is the Northern Policy.) In pursuit of this policy, several artifices were used, especially an appeal to the memory about slavery, an unpleasant past in the life of mankind; racialism, and religion—The Bible and the Flag. I must elaborate on these.

Many writers, mostly British, attribute the source of friction to the events of slavery during the 18th and 19th centuries, when the Southerners were the chief victims of Arab, Sudanese and Egyptian slave traders from the North. Today Northern Sudanese accuse the British administrators and Christian missionaries in the South of winning Southern converts at the expense of the Northern Muslims, by labelling the Northerners as slave traders and by giving undue prominence in Christian schools to the history of the slave trade. The influence of these schools predominates in the South.

Undoubtedly, there was slavery. But many Britons often put the whole blame on the Northern slave hunters, the pashas of Egypt and the Egyptian governors of the Sudan, who either permitted or condoned this human traffic. But, while many of the slaves were employed internally in the Sudan and Egypt, quite a few passed into European hands, and the Northern Sudanese and Egyptian merchants were merely middlemen for the European market. Indeed, the whole of mankind, in a way, must be blamed—including the African kings, chiefs, and middlemen who sold their own people for a handful of silver, some drops of gin, or a few grains of gunpowder. In fact, as everyone knows, Britain herself not only encouraged the slave trade through seafarers like John Hawkins and his cousin, Sir Francis Drake, but actually made treaties with other European nations to carry it on in most parts of Africa—including the whole of the Sudan, North and South, where she employed the services of middlemen. The current standards of the 16th and 17th centuries conveniently ignored the moral issues of slavery (involving the selling and buying of the Black or the White) and concentrated on the material profits and the display of human vanity—the glorification of the subjugation, by force, of one man by another. Accordingly, such English ports as Bristol and Liverpool waxed prosperous on the slave trade. By the Treaty of Utrecht, concluded in 1713, the British secured a thirty-year monopoly of the trade, thus supplanting all the other European nations—the Danes, Swedes, Portuguese, French and Dutch, etc. who all participated in the rape of Africa. During the debate on the emancipation of slaves, the Duke of Wellington emphasized the importance of slaves to Britain in these words:

> I say that . . . the country itself will suffer if the abolition is to be total and immediate . . . a very large revenue is derived from the trade which is carried on with these colonies. . . . Here is a commerce which gives employment to 250,000 tons of shipping, independent of 100,000 tons belonging to His Majesty's North American Colonies—making in the whole 350,000 tons by shipping employed in the trade.[1]

It was, therefore, 'a chapter in the world's history', to quote a British Colonial Office report, 'on which England, in common with other nations, now looks back with distaste, only mitigated by memories of the earnest efforts made to remedy as far as possible the wrong which has been done'.[2]

Britain recognized the fact that slavery and the slave trade had the effect of creating very strong feelings of hatred against northerners, but was perhaps also motivated by 'earnest efforts' to rectify the wrong which the slave trade had done. Therefore, when the Condominium regime began, at the end of the 19th century, slavery was prohibited; the Government (i.e. the British Administration) built up 'a protective barrier against northern merchants, which later crystallized into what is called the Southern Policy'.[3]

On 25 January 1930, the then Civil Secretary (the equivalent of Chief Secretary in Nigeria and other British Territories), Mr. Harold MacMichael (as he then was), issued a directive to the Governors of the Southern Provinces. This explains, *inter alia*:

> The policy of the Government in the Southern Sudan is: to build up a series of self-contained racial or tribal units with structure and organisation

[1] *Mirror of Parliament*, Vol. II, 2 May 1830, p. 1553.
[2] Colonial Office, Colonial Reports, *Nigeria 1951*, H.M.S.O., London, 1953, pp. 94–5.
[3] Sudan Govt., *The Sudan—A Record of Progress*, Khartoum, 1947, p. 12.

based, to whatever extent the requirements of equity and good government permit, upon indigenous customs, tribal usage and beliefs.[1]

Certain measures were immediately introduced: practically all Northern officials serving in the South were transferred to the North. Northern traders, who were already in the South, were refused licences to trade; this was because, in the words of the British Administration, it was: 'The aim of the Government to encourage Greek and Syrian traders rather than the Gallaba type'.[2]

The Administration made the Southern Provinces 'closed areas', allowing no Northerner to go there without special permit. The purpose of this was said to be to prevent illegal slave trading.[3] Administratively, the South was separated from the North. Subsequently, this policy aroused the suspicion of the Sudanese nationalists who feared that the British meant to cut the South, politically, from the North and attach it to the British Protectorate of Uganda,[4] or to incorporate it in a proposed federation of British East Africa. On this point, the Sudan Government (British) commented in 1947:

> These parallel activities have tended to create a division between the North and the South which has been accentuated by the use of English instead of Arabic in the Southern schools and the Northern Sudanese fear that the ultimate result may be to split the country in half, and even to attach the southern part of the South to Uganda. The arguments whether such a course would be to the ultimate advantage of the South or to the rest of Africa are many on both sides and the whole question might at some date form a proper subject for consideration by an international commission.[5]

While this statement appears to present a middle-of-the-road attitude, it also indicates that the Government at least did toy with the idea of annexing the Southern Sudan to Uganda, a British Protectorate, where no other external power, like Egypt, existed as a rival to Britain.

In disagreeing with the 'Southern Policy', Mekki Abbas, himself a Northern Sudanese, points out that if the sole aim were the protection of the Southerners the policy would be justified, if the present Northerners had wished to enslave Southerners. But, he submits, there can be no justification for the policy of barriers or separation

> when the danger of slavery has gone for ever. The Sudan is not the only place which experienced slavery and the slave trade in the eighteenth and nineteenth centuries. The greatest and most civilised countries of the world

---

[1] The Republic of the Sudan, *Southern Disturbances*, p. 16.   [2] *Ibid.*
[3] British Society for International Understanding, *op. cit.*, p. 7.   [4] *Ibid.*
[5] Sudan Govt., *Record of Progress. 1898–1947*, pp. 13–14.

today, including Britain, have been guilty of these inhuman practices on a much larger scale. Those countries have given up the practice and none of their present day policies towards the old homes of slaves bear any relation to the history of slavery. The Sudanese have also gone a very long way towards dismissing the idea of slavery and inequality among men.[1]

To this comment one may add that the Sudan Government made some statements suggesting that the South was stronger than the North until the introduction of some modern weapons of war into the country during the 19th century. One such pronouncement runs thus:

> It took much longer to re-establish public security in the South. . . . The fighting tribes, like the Shilluk, had held the North successfully at bay until the introduction of firearms in the nineteenth century, during which they were in a constant state of warfare against the Government[2] and the slavers.[3]

If this is correct, then the argument about protecting the South against the North becomes weak.

Mekki Abbas informs us that there is a second British argument of which he became more fully aware at a Sudan Administrative Conference; it is that the South lags far behind the North. He agrees with this view only in part, to the extent that higher education in the South was almost non-existent. But the level of elementary and intermediate education, prepared from official records, shows that the South compares favourably with the North. He concludes that if political advancement is measured by the incidence of education and by experience in the art of government 'then it will not be true to say that the South lags far behind the North'.[4] Mekki Abbas would perhaps agree further that people with higher education participate more effectively in the overall administration of a country than those with a mere elementary education. Mekki Abbas's book was published in 1952; but even in February 1956 when I visited the Sudan there were seventeen secondary schools in the North, apart from the University of Khartoum. But there were only two secondary schools for the whole South. The remedy therefore should be sought not in isolating the North from the South (as the British did) but partly in producing programmes for education and development in the South to catch up with those in the North.

Another argument is the appeal to racial differences. The British Society for International Understanding asserts that the South is hostile to the North because of the slave trade 'combined with the

---

[1] *The Sudan Question*, Appendix C, p. 179.
[2] That is, the Condominium Government.
[3] Sudan Govt., *A Record of Progress*, p. 12.
[4] Mekki Abbas, *op. cit.*, pp. 178–9.

obvious differences of race and religion',[1] which led the British to declare the Southern provinces as 'closed areas'. To this I would say that the differences of 'group' feeling and of religious attitude do exist in the Sudan as indeed they do in most other parts of the world (including Britain) but they need not be unduly stressed.

As already stated, the peoples of the Sudan, North and South, are in varying degrees, a blend of Negro, Arab and Caucasian 'tribes' or 'races'. That Khartoum is a kind of melting pot is evident from, for instance, the international character of the Roman Catholic Secondary School (Comboni College), which the writer visited in February 1956. According to the official census of the school in January 1955, there were 396 Sudanese, 115 Egyptians, 59 Syrians, 58 Greeks, 33 Israelis, 29 Italians, 28 Armenians, 19 Saudi Arabians, 15 Ethiopians, 4 British, 3 Yemenis, 3 Jordanians, 2 Maltese, 2 Pakistanis, 2 Somalis, 1 Dane, 1 Spaniard, and 1 Nigerian. They represent ten main religions.[2]

Race or nationality by itself, does not necessarily lead to antagonism; it is miseducation that often does. The proper perspective seems to have been maintained at the Comboni Secondary School:

> From the top of the Secondary Building stood out two great flags (the British and the Egyptian) fluttering joyfully together with the other 18 flags representing 18 different nations to which our 800 pupils belong.[3]

But in the power politics of the Nile Valley, the question of race and nationality of the North and the South and of the Sudanese and the Egyptians, became one of the serious points of disagreement in various Anglo-Egyptian talks (which we shall discuss more fully in another part of this work).

Whatever the merits of the racial argument, political annexation of the Southern Sudan to British Uganda would not have changed the 'race' of the Southerners; furthermore, it has not been proved, even in this context where the word 'race' is loosely applied, that the peoples of Uganda and those of the Southern Sudan are racially homogeneous. Therefore, at best the race argument is valid only in part. Common citizenship rather than race determines nationality. 'Most people are ignorant of the fact that each nation is composed of different racial elements and that the composition changes in the course of time.'[4]

However, as a result of the incessant criticism of the 'Southern

---

[1] *British Survey*, p. 7.
[2] Comboni College, *Year Booklet*, Khartoum, 1955, p. 40.
[3] *Ibid.*, p. 6.
[4] Hertz, Frederick, *Nationality in History and Politics*, London, 1944, p. 52.

Policy' on the part of the politically conscious elements of the Northern peoples, who participated in the Juba Conference of 1947, the Sudan Government began in 1948 to adopt a new policy, or orientation. In that year, the Administration, with the support of the British Government in London, made provisions for the representation of the three Southern Provinces in a legislative assembly for the whole country—both North and South. Sir James Robertson, commenting on the change of policy which the British arrived at in 1944 to 1947, informed me in July 1957, that after a beginning by the late Sir Douglas Newbold (who preceded Sir James Robertson as Civil Secretary of the Sudan):

> 'I, against quite a lot of local opposition, decided after the Juba Conference to bring Southern members into the Legislative Assembly—on the grounds that the days of Southern separation must be ended and that the South must be integrated with the North, with which its economic and political future must continue.'[1]

In 1950, a policy of cultural integration of the North and the South was also established by a decision of the Executive Council and the Legislative Assembly. The teaching of Arabic in all Government, private and mission schools above the elementary stage was introduced. Some of the few 'Southerners' who qualified for higher education started to go to Gordon Memorial College in Khartoum in place of Makerere College in British Uganda. These were part of the measures calculated to promote a common outlook and common feeling of citizenship between North and South.

But in spite of this new orientation, the problem of the South became one of the points of difficulty between Egypt and Britain in their talks over the 1953 Agreement, when Britain sought special powers of 'protection' over the South, and in August 1955, when the Southern Corps mutinied against the North. One might wonder what the attitude of the Southerners themselves was in these matters before the mutiny. John Hyslop, once editor of the *Sudan Star*, supplies an answer in his brief account of a Press conference by a group of American newspapermen with some Southern spokesmen who submitted a written statement, accepting the principle of self-government for the whole Sudan but on two main conditions: first, that the South should have an autonomous status within the self-governing framework until a more perfect union between the two parts of the country is attained, and second, that the British Governor-General should remain head of the state until the

[1] Letter from Sir James Robertson to L. A. Fabunmi, dated (Cholsey, Berks) 3 July 1957.

future status of the country be decided and a satisfactory system of parliamentary rule established.

Mr. Hyslop reports that during the discussion which followed, a young Shilluk in an eloquent speech in English told the pressmen:

> We have been neglected. The North has gone ahead, but we have been retarded. If a few of us are educated we can thank the missionaries. It is only in recent years that the Government has shown any real interest in spreading learning among our people. . . . The British gave us protection, but still we are ignorant. The North is up, and we are down, and we should stay under British trusteeship until we are on the same level as the North.[1]

This speech is similar to those often made by Northern Nigerians, whose situation *vis-à-vis* the Southern Nigerians is comparable to that of the Southern Sudanese *vis-à-vis* the Northern Sudanese. Whilst the British administration in the Sudan pursued a 'Southern Policy', in Nigeria it has been a 'Northern Policy'. But in Nigeria, the so-called 'backward' North is Muslim and the South 'pagan' as in the Sudan. This policy of encouraging sectionalism in Nigeria has led to 'regionalization', creating federation out of the one-time semi-unitary state (built by the British themselves before the demand for self-government).

On 9 January 1954, self-government began in the Sudan, followed by increasing 'Sudanization' of the Administration. It seems relevant therefore, to indicate the attitude of the new administration to the problem of the South. In November 1954, the Prime Minister of the Sudan, Ismail Azhari, paid a state visit to Britain, and the 'African and Middle East Discussion Group' of the Royal Institute of International Affairs (Chatham House) London, received him on the eve of his return to the Sudan. After the Prime Minister's address, some members of the audience, particularly those who had served in the British administration in the Sudan, expressed concern about the 'backward' Southern Sudanese. The Prime Minister remarked that, as a person, he was by birth a combination of both North and South (Arabic and Negroid) and that officially he was the Prime Minister of the whole country. Therefore, he could not condone any discriminatory practices jeopardizing the interests of his own flesh and blood, whether in the North or South.

Mohammed Yassein, first Sudanese Governor to take over from the British administrator of the Upper Nile Province in the South, accompanied the Prime Minister and he informed Chatham House of the various development and welfare programmes for the South. Later, in

[1] Hyslop, John, *Sudan Story*, London, 1952, pp. 70–1.

response to the writer's private question, Mr. Yassein commented significantly:

> To me the question of North and South is a hackneyed one. It becomes the more so when the last British administrator leaves the country towards the end of this year. I was the first Governor to take over his Province from the British and I can assure you that the much publicised differences between North and South are more imaginary than real. It is true that the Nilotes are not of the same stock as the Arabs; but the same applies to the Hadendowa in the East, the Nulis in the North, the Nubas in Kordofan and to the Fur in general. When the question of the future of Eritrea was discussed, the British thought of creating a Hadendowa Kingdom or state to embrace the Hadendowa and Beni Amer in Eritrea and in the Sudan.
>
> If you want to apply feudalism to the nascent countries of Africa then there is no end to the theoretically feasible Kingdoms you may build up. But the foundation will be so shaky that you will soon have to give it up and allow the melting pot of insurgent nationalism to unify the various elements and weld them together. [In this connection, might one recall, for instance, the social and structural basis of Ethiopia, religion and all?]
>
> The British Administrators and missionaries have in the past done much to sow the seeds of dissension and hate between the North and South. But they failed ignominiously to achieve any lasting success. (I wish the missionaries had produced real Christians.)
>
> The Sudanese of the new Sudan are determined to live as equals in civil and property rights and that is what really matters. The present Administration allocates £3,000,000 every year as a subsidy, and more is to come as capital expenditure in the South.

Mohammed Yassein here underlines the contribution of missionaries, perhaps without active consciousness on their part, to the imperial policy of 'divide and rule' in the Sudan; and this brings us to the fifth artifice listed above—namely, religion. In this connection Mekki Abbas, too, criticizes with evidence missionary activities in the Sudan.[1] This charge against missionaries—of collaboration with colonial administrators—is a common one amongst colonial peoples. For instance, Dr. F. O. Onipede (a Nigerian) writing on a proposal to build three separate religious chapels at the University College, Ibadan, Nigeria, complained (from Columbia University, New York, where he was then a student) that:

> The point at stake is that the Christian Missions in Nigeria are trying hard to make Nigeria appear as a Christian nation to the outside world. In doing this they are introducing the intolerance of (Missionary) Christianity into Nigeria. Even in the United States of America, quite a few universities . . . have a common religious centre for all faiths.[2]

[1] *The Sudan Question*, p. 21.
[2] Onipede, F. O., Letter to the Editor, *West Africa*, No. 1972, London, 11 December 1954, p. 1167.

'pure' Negro South

The 'pure' Negro and the 'pure' Caucasian types. Two Southern blacks and a European playfellow at Lainya, Southern Sudan

The matter, being thus a part of the problems of the Sudan, seems to deserve some elucidation. Christian Missionary societies were established in the Southern Sudan as far back as 1848, before the Condominium; but their activities increased after the reoccupation of the Sudan in 1898. There are now both Protestant and Roman Catholic Missionaries, and each of them 'is given spheres of influence to the exclusion of the other'.[1] They are accused, as we have mentioned, of aiding imperialism in the Sudan.

Now, in the Sudan as in most other dependencies, the position of missionaries is a trying one. In the first place, many unsophisticated 'natives' regard them as benefactors. But to the politically conscious, missionaries and colonial administrators are agents of the same power— the former propagate religious, and the latter administer political imperialism. A missionary may disagree, or even detest, certain aspects of imperial policy; but such clash is seldom, if ever, allowed to come into the open. This point, together with the fact that the missionary shares with the administrator the same absence of skin pigmentation (popularly called 'White'), the same general folk (European cultural) ways of behaviour, the same social intercourse (in the territory), makes the difference between the two somewhat unreal to the native.

In the second place, the missionary often depends upon the administrator's recommendation to the Government for financial aid for educational endeavours such as building grants, maintenance of teaching staff, etc. In addition, the missionary looks up to the administrator for ultimate protection of life, church and personal property.

The third point, which may be influenced by the second, is that administrators often put pressure on the missionary to conform to their political and social programme. A current example exists in South Africa, where the State has been using various means to make the Church comply with the State's policy of 'Apartheid', especially with regard to 'native' education.[2]

Fourthly, apart from the religious rivalry among the Protestant denominations, there still exists a sort of cold war between the Protestant missions on the one hand and the Roman Catholic on the other. Writing soon after the reconquest of the Sudan in 1889, Felkin urged

[1] *The Southern Disturbances*, p. 5.

[2] The *News Chronicle*—London, 11 December 1954—contained an editorial captioned 'AFRAID'; it says about the Bantu Education Act: 'They are afraid, these South African Nationalists with their grim-visaged legislation. . . . They force one after another missionary school to abandon efforts, long devotedly pursued, to impart to Africans the knowledge of humanity's purposes and possibilities.' See also 'Apartheid Plan ', in *African Affairs* (published by the Royal African Society) No. 214, London, January 1955, p. 16.

the British Government 'to make it impossible for Catholics and Protestants to plant their Missions in close proximity to each other. . . . By such a wise provision, a repetition of the discord and bloodshed which have taken place in Uganda may be prevented'.[1] This religious rivalry and separation extend to the native converts.

In the fifth place, there has been over the centuries a strong religious rivalry—amounting almost to cut-throat competition—between the followers of the Cross and those of the Crescent. Wherever Islam is already professed, Christian missionaries find it difficult to propagate the Gospel effectively. Northern Sudan is predominantly Islamic, and missionaries have made many fewer converts there than in the South. The Diocese of the Sudan declares its policy in the South: 'We must put all our strength and energy into Christianising the Southern Sudan. The Dinkas, the Baris, the Zandes, etc., must be brought to the feet of God. Our evangelical, educational, and medical work must be strengthened. This can be done in two ways: (i) by the sending out of more and more recruit missionaries, (ii) by co-operation with the various Government services.'[2] Thus, in their campaign to win the South, missionaries might have contributed to the Southerner's suspicion of the Northerner. Indeed, they have been described as regarding the Muslim influence of the Northern Sudanese as a sort of challenge to their own work, or competition in their own trade—religion.

However, the New Sudanese Government appears to be devoted to the policy of unification of the whole Sudan, of its even development, and of one common citizenship and equality of opportunity in both North and South. To implement this might not, of course, be easy in view of the difficulties created by the previous policy of sectionalism as well as the 'human casualties of change'. But the Sudanese of the 'new Sudan' say, significantly, that they 'are determined'; they have not yielded to the pressure of tribalism. The Sudan Parliament has Southern members in it. In spite of the Southern Mutiny in August 1955, the causes of which we shall examine in chapter 15, the whole Sudan—North and South—remains at the time of writing a unitary state, though there has been a Southern pressure for a federal constitution. The new Sudanese seem to have evolved a philosophy out of the Southern situation.

'New' states often have their own sense of mission. Soon after

[1] Felkin, Robert W., 'The Sudan Question', in *Contemporary Review*, Vol. LXXIV, 1898, pp. 496–7.

[2] The Church Missionary Society, *Introducing the Diocese of the Sudan*, London, 1946, p. 67.

independence, the United States of America became committed to the idea of becoming 'the land of the free and the home of the brave'. Today, India assumes the role of mediator between the Capitalist West and Communist East. Similarly, the new Sudanese are becoming imbued with the idea of playing a great role. They feel that the political integration of the Negroid South with the Arabic North makes the whole country a link between the Middle East and Central Africa, between the Arab world and the Negro world.[1]

[1] 'The Sudan', Special Edition of the *Diplomatic Bulletin*, No. 23, London, November 1954, p. 5.

Part One

THE HISTORICAL BACKGROUND AND
FOUNDATIONS OF THE
ANGLO-EGYPTIAN DISPUTE

2

BRITAIN, EGYPT AND THE SUDAN:
EARLY RELATIONS

In those distant days it was thought right and noble for a civilized country to take charge of an uncivilized country, to clean it up and help it on. Today that process is called 'Imperialism' and is regarded as very wicked indeed.

SIR HAROLD NICOLSON

FOR more than half a century—for fifty-seven years, to be precise—Britain and Egypt disputed; they bickered one with another, each claiming the right of control over the Sudan. There are hardly any of the recent and most familiar features of the Sudan Question which can be fully understood or appreciated without some knowledge of, or reference to, the past. We consider it relevant and necessary, therefore, to show briefly the beginning and development of the early relationships between Egypt and the Sudan; how Britain occupied Egypt; and how she subsequently extended her control over Egypt to the Sudan.

1. EGYPT'S CONTACT WITH THE SUDAN

The main source for most of the knowledge available about the early history of the Sudan, especially the Northern Sudan (or ancient Kush), are the ancient Egyptian records. About 2800 B.C., Egyptians of the Old Kingdom carried out frequent raids into the Sudan. Subsequently, that is about two hundred years later, the Egyptians, according to the 1956 official handbook of the Republic of the Sudan, were carrying on peaceful trade with the Dongola area. During the Middle Kingdom of Egypt, from about 2000 B.C., the Egyptians colonized the Sudan as far south as modern Merowe of the Fourth Cataract of the Nile; they established at Kerma a governor, 'whose large fortified residence can still be seen'.[1]

This Egyptian occupation lasted about three hundred years. But, possibly owing to the invasion of Egypt by the Hyksos from Asia in about 1700 B.C., the Egyptian administration in the Sudan collapsed.

[1] *The Sudan Almanac*, An Official Handbook, Khartoum, 1956, p. 27.

When the Hyksos were expelled from Egypt in 1580 B.C., the Egyptians were soon able to reassert their dominion over the Sudan.

Beginning from the reign of Ahmose I, the Egyptians built many temples in the Sudan—e.g. at Buhen, near Wadi Halfa, and as far south as Jebel Barkal. Rameses II, who, during his sixty-seven years' reign, practically filled Egypt and Nubia with his own monuments, built a rock temple at Abu Simbel. I visited this temple in January 1956. It is situated at a choice spot, facing the sunrise and overlooking the Nile, between Eneba and Wadi Halfa. It is, as John Gunther correctly describes it, 'the most isolated, time-worn, and immovably serene of all temples, a sublime sight'.[1]

At the entrance of the temple—below the colossal statues of Rameses —I saw on the walls two rows of captives in ropes on either side of the gate. Those on the right (north) side have long hair, thin lips and sharp noses; evidently, they are Asiatics and/or Europeans. Those on the left (south) are shown with thick lips, curly hair and sturdy physique; these are characteristic features of Nubians, Sudanese or Negroes.[2]

At the end of the 2nd millennium B.C., the Egyptian Empire declined; with that fall, the Egyptians disappeared once more from the face of the Sudan for a period of about three hundred years. But in 1750 B.C., a Sudanese kingdom arose at Napata, near what is now known as Merowe. Sudanese kings conquered Egypt, and their successors, among whom Tirhaka (688–663 B.C.) was most famous, formed the 25th dynasty of Egypt. But in about 660 B.C., the Sudanese rulers were finally removed from Egypt by the Assyrians.

Later, the Arabs conquered Nubia, and subsequently established their rule there in A.D. 651. In the 16th century, the Turks occupied Egypt and nominally extended their rule to the Sudan. But Turkish sovereignty became effective in the Sudan only when Mohammed Ali became Viceroy of Egypt and subdued, by force of arms, the peoples inhabiting the Sudan. He began in 1820 to enforce the sovereign powers conferred on him, by the Sultan of Constantinople, over the provinces lying south of Egypt. These sovereign powers were set out in a firman to him dated 13 February 1841, as follows:

> Whereas, as by our previous Firman, we have confirmed you as Viceroy of Egypt with hereditary rights on specific conditions and within

---

[1] Gunther, *op. cit.*, p. 227.

[2] But this great and vivid evidence of the power of the ancient Egyptians over the Sudan will soon disappear, together with the whole neighbouring town of Wadi Halfa, if and when the gigantic high dam, proposed by the contemporary Revolutionary Regime in Egypt (President Nasser's Government) becomes a reality.

well-defined limits, we hereby confer upon you the additional vice-regal rights upon the provinces of Nubia, Kordofan and Sennar and all dependencies beyond the frontiers of Egypt proper. . . . The exercise of such rights does not, however, confer any hereditary prerogatives.

By the experience and wisdom of which you have given proof you are to administer such provinces and manage their affairs in accordance with my wishes to justice and with a view to ensuring the welfare of the inhabitants. You shall send to our Sublime Porte an annual statement of all the revenues of the above-mentioned provinces.[1]

In an address to the notables of Sennar, who gathered to meet Mohammed Ali, the Viceroy informed his audience that peoples in other parts of the world were formerly savages, who by instruction, labour and perseverance civilized and enriched themselves. The people of Sennar, too, could do just that. 'Nothing is wanting for this purpose,' he assured them; 'you have a great quantity of land, cattle and wood: your population is numerous, the men strong and the women faithful. Up to the present time you have had no guide. You have one now: it is I.'[2]

But despite the above indication of good intention, most of the sixty years of Egyptian rule amounted to inefficient administration because of the inferior quality of the administrative officers posted to the Sudan. Just as Britain sent out what some colonial administrators considered to be the scum or the ne'er-do-wells of British society to her American and Australian colonies, during the opening up of those settlements, some of the Egyptians sent to the Sudan were there in effect as a punishment for crimes committed in Egypt, or for incompetence at home; they lacked public spirit.

However, the Egyptians of today point out that their administration of the Sudan at that time was not so bad as it is often represented by British critics. They say that the Egyptians were no more cruel and no less kind than most Europeans at the end of the 18th and the beginning of the 19th centuries. They, too, fought slavery, maintained law and order and did well enough in the Sudan to attract the attention of Samuel Baker, himself an Englishman, who wrote in 1861: 'European tourists can now travel alone throughout the vast expanse of the Soudan with the same feeling of safety as Londoners have in Hyde Park in the evening.'[3]

---

[1] Agence France-Presse, *Information et Documentation*, Paris, 14 and 21 June 1947 (English translation 'The Sudan Question'), p. 4. See also Nourdonhian, *Recueil d'Actes Internationaux de l'Empire Ottoman*. See Appendix I below.

[2] Mekki Abbas, *op. cit.*, p. 30.

[3] Agence France-Presse, *op. cit.*, p. 4.

Judged by the standard of the British administration of the Sudan in the 20th century, when select men from Oxford and Cambridge were sent out, the Egyptian administration at the time of Mohammed Ali in the 19th century might have been worse. Egyptian inefficiency at that time was probably due to the fact that the Sudan venture was the first colonial experiment embarked upon by Modern Egypt.

Partly on account of this inefficiency, and the unpopularity of the Turko-Egyptian officials, and partly on account of religious inspiration, a wind of rebellion swept the Sudan in 1882–3. Like the ancient Jews of the Bible expecting the Messiah, the Muslims of the Sudan had been waiting for a Saviour—the 'Mahdi'—that is, the 'Guided', to deliver them from political domination by foreigners from the North, and to save their religion from the inroads of European infidels, whose ambition in Africa was beginning to manifest itself. A brilliant man, Mohammed Ahmed, who could recite the Koran by heart at the age of twelve, presented himself as the Messiah, and he succeeded in getting the headman in the territory to acknowledge him as the elect who was to eradicate evil and corruption not only from the Sudan but, like other inspired Saviours of the world, from the face of the earth. Mohammed Ahmed defeated all the forces sent against him, became the ruler of the country, and embarked upon certain reforms.

Pressed by the Mahdist forces, the British, who had occupied Egypt since 1882, asked Egypt, through Sir Evelyn Baring, later Lord Cromer, who was then the British diplomatic and consular agent in Cairo, to withdraw from the Sudan. The Egyptian Prime Minister, Sherif Pasha, in a letter dated 21 December 1883, declined to comply for five reasons: Withdrawal on the part of Egypt would be tantamount to the cession to the rebels of the Eastern Sudan, Berbera and Dongola provinces with the whole course of the Nile down to Southern Egypt. The Administrative Order (Firman) of 7 August 1879, from the Porte, categorically denied the Khedive the right of surrendering any part of the Egyptian territory, controlled by Turkey. Such a step would strengthen the prestige of the 'false prophet' and undermine loyalty to Egypt. It would strip Egypt of her natural frontiers, which were essential to the security of Egypt; and despite alleged Egyptian inefficient administration, the territory had 'become part of the civilized world and Egyptian efforts had enabled European firms to operate in the Sudan, helped organized expeditions to be carried out and Christian missions to settle there'.[1]

---

[1] *Ibid.*, pp. 5–6.

But Sir Evelyn Baring was adamant and warned the Khedive that Ministers who refused the instructions of Her Majesty's Government must resign. Sherif Pasha preferred giving up his office to yielding.[1] However, the succeeding Cabinet ordered the withdrawal of Egypt from the Sudan. For about ten years, therefore, the Sudan was administered by the Mahdi and his successor until the country came, after the reconquest in 1898, under the Anglo-Egyptian Condominium of 1899.

2. BRITISH CONTACT WITH EGYPT

The British hold on the Sudan came about as a result of their domination of Egypt. Both logically and historically, the British administration of the Sudan can be understood only in the light of British occupation of Egypt.

MAHMOUD FAHMY NOKRASHY PASHA
in the U.N. Security Council, 1947[2]

British interest in Africa dates as far back as the time of Vasco Da Gama, who discovered for Portugal the sea-route to India at the end of the 15th century, bringing the riches of the Orient to the attention of Europe. Vasco Da Gama's discovery had the eventual result of bringing about the colonization of the East by opening its commerce to the Western Nations through the Mediterranean. With the subsequent establishment of the British Indian Empire, and the opening of the Suez Canal in 1869, which linked Europe with the Orient and thus increased the amount of trade through Egypt, Egypt became increasingly important to Britain. From about 1862, however, a new element, not connected with the location of Egypt as one of the world's highways, began to be infused. Egypt became financially dependent on European speculators, and a commission of public debt was created in 1876. For our purpose, British contact with Egypt became more vitally important again from about 1880.

However, the stage for British action in Egypt, and later in the Sudan, had been set by the mood which overtook Britain before the end of the 18th and the beginning of the 19th centuries. Following the Tudor period of great ambition and grand adventures, 'when men dreamed great dreams for England and set out to realize them',[3] the 18th and 19th centuries were an era of British expansion and consolidation

---

[1] Compare the Wafdist Cabinet which, in 1951, unilaterally abrogated the 1936 Anglo-Egyptian Treaty and the Neguib Revolutionary Government, which upheld it, in 1952.
[2] U.N. Security Council, *Official Records*, 175th Meeting, Lake Success, 5 August 1947.
[3] Rose, J. H., *et al.*, *Cambridge History of the British Empire*, Vol. I, 1929, p. v.

overseas. The 19th century witnessed the European scramble for Africa, with Britain, France and Germany as the chief contestants, and the Anglo-French intrigue for control over Egypt and the Sudan. At the close of the 18th century, Egypt, weak and bankrupt, lay at the mercy of any power strong and enterprising enough to grab it from Turkey, its weak master. Against this background we should set the history of the British occupation of Egypt, and eventually of the Sudan.

The British realized that the possession of Egypt by the French was a threat greater to themselves than to the Turks. Bonaparte's possession of Egypt was well assessed in Britain: 'As he could not take India, the great spring of British wealth and naval power in London, he conceived the design of flaunting it out from England by the possession of Egypt.'[1] Henry Dundas, the British Minister of War, wrote to Lord Granville, then Foreign Secretary, warning him that the possession of Egypt by any independent power would be a circumstance fatal to the interests of Britain.[2]

With this assessment of the situation in mind, British diplomacy and military strategy went into swift action. Barely a week after the French occupation of Cairo, a British squadron, under Sir Horatio Nelson, was despatched; it attacked and destroyed the French fleet at anchor in Abuquir Bay. In December 1798, a Russo-Turkish Alliance, encouraged by Britain, was concluded, and about a month later (January 1799) an Anglo-Turkish Alliance followed as part of the grand strategy of war against the French. The forces of the allied powers rendered the French position hopeless; and Menou, the French Commander-in-Chief, surrendered in 1801, after about three years of French occupation. France having evacuated Egypt, the British Government set up a kind of native administration, amounting to British indirect rule (as was the case in Nigeria, subsequently). However, because Anglo-Turkish negotiations about this problem broke down, the British forces, like those of the French, had to be withdrawn in March 1803—after two years of occupation. As a result, Turkey was able to make another effort to reassert her sovereignty over Egypt. But the British were gone, only to be back again. Like an organism which lives, grows and eventually dies, the Ottoman Empire was becoming too weak to carry on with effective zeal and vitality, and the Turkish dominion of Egypt was drawing to a close.

It often happens that during a critical period in the life of a nation,

---

[1] *The Annual Register*, London, 1798, p. 135.
[2] Marlowe, John: *Anglo-Egyptian Relations 1800–1953*, London, 1954, p. 15.

a suitable saviour emerges. During the American War of Independence, George Washington was the man. For the Soviet revolution, Lenin rose to the stage, and during the Second World War, Winston Churchill became the man of the hour in Britain. Similarly, during that time in Egypt, one, Mohammed Ali, grappled with the situation and endeavoured to rescue the Egyptians. He was an illiterate, but in the words of Lt.-Col. Elgood, himself a high British official, for about fifty years the history of Egypt is the history of Mohammed Ali, 'one of those commanding figures who from time to time pass across the World's stage. . . . Such was the natural genius that he would have established a reputation in any environment. . . . He had repelled the Englishman, he had ousted the Turk, and there remained but the remnants of the Mamelukes to contest his supremacy in Egypt.'[1] He became the undisputed ruler of Egypt, and like his contemporaries in Europe, he too became possessed with territorial ambitions and dreamed of a great empire reaching out far beyond Egypt. Consequently, in 1820 (the year in which George III, the protagonist of the British policy of expansion in America, died), he sent an expedition to the Sudan. He also made imperialistic adventures in the Eastern Mediterranean, which brought him into open conflict with Britain.

Turkey having become weakened, Mohammed Ali felt that he had acquired enough power to make loyalty and subordination to the Sultan no longer essential; he therefore rebelled against Turkey and showed signs of extending his power to Asia Minor. This again caused uneasiness to the Great Powers—Britain, France and Russia—who calculated Mohammed Ali's move to be against their own position and interests. Britain was so much alarmed about the territorial ambitions of Mohammed Ali that Palmerston instructed Col. Campbell, on 28 March 1838, to warn the Pasha 'of the consequences to himself, which will follow any attempt on his part to extend his authority, by force of arms, in any direction. You will point out to the Pasha that his talents and energies, great as all the world know them to be, will find ample scope . . . in establishing good local administration in Egypt.'[2]

Meanwhile, Britain's commercial and strategic interests in Egypt itself were growing. Because Egypt and South Africa stood prominently on the only two routes to India (where the East India Company had been consolidating the British Empire) and because of their respective

---

[1] Elgood, P. G., *The Transit of Egypt*, London, 1928, pp. 45–7.
[2] 'Communications with Mehemet Ali, 1838', in *Parliamentary Papers*, Vol. I, London, 1839, p. 316.

strategic locations on the continent of Africa (where the European penetration was taking shape), these territories were the two most important links in the British imperial strategy. It is convenient to add here Britain's later interests in Egypt at the time of Ismail Pasha.

Apart from commercial and strategic interests, Britain had, within Egypt itself, financial stakes. Ismail Pasha inherited a substantial debt when he became the Khedive of Egypt, and British speculators raised loans for him in 1862, 1864 and later. He indulged in borrowing without taking thought about the political consequences. A debt of about £90,000,000 was subsequently imposed upon Egypt by European speculators, in consideration of which only about £45,500,000 was nominally received.[1] He became 'a dupe of his friends and advisers, Egyptian and European, who turned his good nature, his ambitious purposes, his generosity to their own ends'.[2] This financial imbroglio eventually led to Anglo-French control of the fiscal policy of the Egyptian Government.

Slowly but surely, Egyptians began to lose control of their own affairs. By a system of treaties called the Capitulations the most vital privileges were conferred on foreigners in Egypt; these privileges included: (1) exemption from taxation; (2) inviolability of domicile, and protection from arbitrary arrest; (3) exemption from the jurisdiction of the native courts; and (4) the Mixed Tribunals, established in 1876, which demanded, in effect, that no legislation applicable to foreigners could be enforced without the consent of the Capitulatory Powers.[3]

Thus, Britain's interests in Egypt were becoming increasingly considerable and important, under the direction of Lord Palmerston.

But in 1882, dissatisfied Egyptians responded, under Arabi Pasha, to the cry of 'Egypt for the Egyptians'. The Egyptians revolted against the Khedive, the foreign bankers and powers, and many Europeans were massacred. This time the Austrians, French and Germans, who had previously lent their aid in similar circumstances, declined to support the British against this revolt; naturally, Turkey stood aside with a chuckle and watched. Consequently, Britain had to 'go it' all alone; and in September 1882, the British Government sent a force to Egypt. It broke the nationalist resistance and thus brought Egypt under British military occupation.

Britain henceforth became the absolute and undisputed possessor of Egypt, through which she later maintained her interests in the Sudan and

---

[1] Keay, Seymour J., *Spoiling the Egyptians. A Tale of Shame*, told from the Blue Books, 4th ed., London, 1882, p. 1.
[2] Feis, Herbert, *Europe: The World's Banker, 1870–1914*, New Haven, 1931, p. 383.
[3] H.M.S.O., *Egypt No. 2* (1921), p. 12.

in the Suez Canal—a twin problem with the Sudan in Anglo-Egyptian relations. The link was established by Granville in a memorandum, dated 6 January 1882, in which he speculated:

> Should the occupation of Egypt be necessary to secure our highway to the East the question at once presents itself, viz. the occupation of the entire Delta—Lower Egypt, and the occupation of such points as would give us command of the Canal, for the real way of quartering the Canal is to hold Lower Egypt and Cairo.[1]

Another connection was made by Ramsay MacDonald 42 years after Granville. In an official conversation with Zaghlul Pasha in London MacDonald maintained that Egyptian aspirations in the Sudan 'do conflict too hopelessly with our irreducible requirements regarding the defence of the Canal'.[2]

Therefore, apart from political considerations, communicational, strategic and the general requirements of the Empire, three factors prompted the Gladstone Government to occupy Egypt in 1882: the bond holders, the Suez Canal, and the Sudan.

By a dual system now known in British Colonial Organization as 'Native Administration', the Khedive of Egypt and his Cabinet continued to function, whilst the virtual and ultimate ruler of the country became the British Government in London, through its agent in Cairo. As time went on, British Control was stretched to reach Egypt's dominion—the Sudan—in accordance with the policy approved by the British Government for adoption in the Nile Valley, namely that of 'a gradual advance' within and beyond Egyptian borders.[3] This brings us to a presentation of Anglo-Sudanese relations.

3. BRITISH PENETRATION INTO THE SUDAN

Before her occupation of Egypt, Britain had no 'direct political or commercial dealings with the Sudan. In the 18th century, the British people and Government had no specific knowledge of that country which was to them just a part of 'darkest Africa'. Some reports, like those of J. L. Burckhardt who travelled in Nubia in 1819, caused British nationals in Egypt to begin collecting information on the Sudan from European traders and officials in the service of Mohammed Ali Pasha. These reports, particularly about the slave trade, captured the

---

[1] Despatch No. 2, dated 6 January 1882, from Granville to Malet: P.R.O. F.O. 141/152.
[2] Foreign Office Despatch, 3 April 1924. Mr. MacDonald—Zaghlul Conversations, under Chapter IV below.
[3] P.R.O. W.O. 32/132/7700/7661.

interest of the British Government and the British Anti-Slavery Societies. Sir John Bowring went to Nubia under the auspices of the British Government with a view to establishing trade connections, but he saw enough of slavery, a stumbling block to peaceful trade, to make him protest to the Pasha. (Though once the leading nation in this human traffic, Britain had succeeded, by this time, in abolishing the slave trade.) Influenced by pressure groups, based partly on humanitarian principles and partly on the fact that slave labour was no longer economic, certain influential persons, headed by the Archbishop of Canterbury and some organizations such as the Aborigines Protection and the Anti-Slavery Society,[1] Britain and Egypt signed, on 4 August 1877, a convention repudiating slavery and the slave trade.

The Egyptians, under Ismail, Mohammed Ali's grandson and second successor, dreamed of including the whole of the basin of the White Nile (from the source to the confluence) within the dominion of Egypt. Perhaps in an attempt to win the British to this territorial project, Ismail took two major steps: he publicized a proclamation to abolish the slave trade (about which Britain had expressed concern) in the Sudan, and in 1869 he appointed a British explorer and big game hunter, Sir Samuel Baker, as Governor of Equatoria Province of the Sudan.

Ismail's instructions to Baker would justify the British suggestion today that Egypt's ambition is to replace Britain as the imperial power in the Nile Valley, if not in the whole of Africa. (See chapter 7 (3) below.)

According to these instructions, Baker was to extend Egyptian annexation as far as the Equator; suppress the slave trade; introduce a system of regular commerce; open to navigation the great lakes of the equator; and establish a chain of military stations at intervals of about three days' march throughout Central Africa, using Gondokoro as the base of operations.

Of his motivation and purpose in Egypt, Baker wrote: 'My chief endeavour was to work for the interest of Egypt, at the same time that I sustained and advanced the influence of England. General Gordon who succeeded me, was actuated by the same desire and died in the hope that England would reach Khartoum.'[2]

Having formally proclaimed Gondokoro as part of the Egyptian

[1] The Anti-Slavery Society still exists, with its office now in Denison House, Victoria, London.
[2] Murray, T. D. and Silva, A., *Samuel Baker, A Memoir*, London and New York, 1895, p. 353.

Kingdom, and accomplished much of his mission, Baker left the Sudan in 1873, and returned to occasional travel and game hunting in various parts of the world.

The Egyptians of that time would seem to have pursued the policy of picking unique men of character, from abroad, to help them administer their territory, probably in the same way as the present-day West Africans and Sudanese tend to seek and retain the services of trusted Europeans, Americans and others with ability, desirable temperament on racial issues and of a political outlook, healthy, and compatible with national aspirations. Nubar Pasha, at that time Prime Minister of Egypt, and General Charles Gordon (popularly called 'Chinese' Gordon for his previous life and work with the Chinese) had met in Constantinople. As a result of this meeting, Gordon was offered, and he accepted, the post of successor to Baker. He arrived in Gondokoro, as Governor of Equatoria Province, early in 1874, with Colonel Charles Chaillé-Long,[1] an American already employed by the Khedive. This, with the presence of persons of several other nationalities, gave the Egyptian civil and military services a somewhat international appearance. In 1876 Gordon was promoted Governor-General of the Sudan, but he had to resign three years later in protest against the deposition (by the British Government) of Ismail, his chief employer and friend; in a private letter, Gordon wrote about him: 'It pains me what sufferings my poor Khedive Ismail has had to go through.'[2]

Although he did not succeed in improving the Egyptian administration overmuch, Gordon left the Sudan nominally an Egyptian territory much larger than what came to be the Anglo-Egyptian Sudan; at that time it included Massawa (now in Eritrea), Berbera and Zeila (both now part of British Somaliland), Tadjoura (now in French Somaliland) and Harra and Bogos (now Ethiopian provinces). Today, in their hope for the 'Unity of the Nile Valley', and apparent desire for territorial expansion in Africa, the Egyptians are reminding the Sudanese of these lost bits and pieces of territory. (See chapter 7 (3)—Egypt's Visionary Extension in Africa.)

In 1881—two years after the resignation of Gordon—the Mahdi, one of '*The Three Prophets*'[3] emerged in the Sudan and led the revolt to

---

[1] A graduate of Washington Academy, he was first appointed an officer in the Egyptian Army in 1869. *Dictionary of American Biography*, Vol. III, New York, 1929, p. 591.
[2] Lord Elton, *General Gordon*, London, 1954, p. 262.
[3] In 1884, Colonel Chaillé-Long published in New York *The Three Prophets*. Its theme was that the religious fanaticism of three men—Arabi Pasha, the Mahdi and Gordon—had made them useful tools for the British Government's imperial interests in the Sudan.

which we have already referred. Although Britain had then practically taken over the direction of Egyptian policy, she declined Egypt's request for help and decisive action against the Mahdi, whose forces were increasingly successful in the Sudan. Granville underrated the Mahdi and dismissed him as 'The false Prophet'.[1] Egypt had lost to Britain the substance of her own power, both at home and abroad. She therefore had to use what was left—the mere shadow of power—to resist alone the Mahdist revolt.

Egypt's precarious situation was reinforced when, in May 1883, Granville instructed the British Consul-General to inform the Egyptians that:

> Her Majesty's Government are in no way responsible for the operations in Sudan which have been initiated on the authority of the Egyptian Government.[2]

This instruction was further elaborated in November of the same year when the British Government warned the Egyptian Government that:

> H.M. Government can do nothing in the matter which would throw upon them the responsibility of operations in the Sudan. This responsibility must rest with the Egyptian Government relying on their own resources. . . . The Egyptian Government would be right to restrict their action to defensive operations.[3]

This advice was based on the point that ineffectual efforts to secure the Egyptian position in the Sudan would only endanger Anglo-Egyptian success and prestige.

In due course, the rebellion succeeded against all the feeble attempts to suppress it, and the Mahdi became virtually master in the Sudan. Sherif Pasha, the Egyptian Prime Minister, pleaded with the British against abandonment, giving the reasons already cited above. Britain's reaction to his appeal was a directive to the British Representative in Egypt (Evelyn Baring) to the effect that British policy must prevail during the Occupation of Egypt, and that only those Egyptians who would co-operate with the British in this respect must be appointed to office. This instruction read:

> It is essential that in important questions affecting the administration and safety of Egypt, the advice of the British Government should be followed

---

[1] From Granville to Barry: Despatch No. 387 of 30 October 1882 in P.R.O. F.O. 141/153.
[2] From Granville to Cartwright: Despatch No. 99 of 7 May 1883, P.R.O. F.O. 78/3550.
[3] From Granville to Baring: Despatch No. 302, dated 25 November 1883, P.R.O. F.O. 78/3551.

for as long as the present occupation continues. Ministers and Governors must carry out this advice or forfeit their posts. The appointment of British Ministers would be most objectionable, but it will no doubt be possible to find Egyptians who will execute the Khedive's orders under British advice. The Cabinet will support you.[1]

This directive of putting weaklings into power still forms a cornerstone of the British Colonial Policy of Indirect Rule.

However, Sherif Pasha refused to be a mere stooge. Rather than accept the British orders, he resigned; but as the British Government had estimated, it was possible to find pliable Egyptians. Nubar Pasha (a political rival of Sherif Pasha) agreed with the British Government to form an Egyptian Cabinet pledged to the policy of abandonment of the Sudan.

In addition to the British Representative and his staff, the British Government required an able and qualified British official with full military and civil powers to conduct the Sudan evacuation scheme. Baring, influenced by personal knowledge and goaded by Press opinion in Britain, regarded General Gordon as the best man for the job. In a letter to *The Times* Samuel Baker, ex-Governor of Equatoria Province, asked: 'Why should not General Gordon be invited to assist the Government? There is no man living who would be more capable or so well fitted to represent the justice which Great Britain should establish in the Sudan.'[2] But 'Chinese' Gordon—a soldier saint, a 'heroic, eccentric and other-worldly genius',[3] appeared too independent and too unorthodox for a British Government accustomed to well-disciplined conventional civil and military servants. Whilst the British Government aimed at subduing the natives of Africa and Asia through the process of 'civilizing' them, Gordon was convinced that his own country and people had no divine right to do so. In a letter to Florence Nightingale (his close friend), Gordon said: 'To me they [the British Government] are utterly wrong in the government of the subject races; they know nothing of the hearts of these people.'[4]

Perhaps quite understandably, therefore, the Cabinet considered him somewhat of a risk; but none of them had as much knowledge about the Sudan and its people as Gordon, and the Press was campaigning for him. The Cabinet found a way out of their dilemma by appointing him to the Sudan, but with severely restricted powers. He was to go to

---

[1] Despatch No. 210, dated Foreign Office, 4 January 1884, in *Correspondence Respecting the Affairs of Egypt—Egypt No. 1* (1884), p. 176.
[2] London, 1 January 1884, p. 4b.
[3] Elton, *op. cit.*, p. 367.   [4] *Ibid.*, p. 295.

Suakin, report on the general military situation in the Sudan with a view to evacuating the remaining Egyptian garrisons and return immediately. A proviso which would discourage a most patriotic Colonial Governor of today was included, namely: 'Government not indebted beyond passage money and £3 *per diem* travelling expenses.'

Gordon, in Belgium at that time, had accepted an offer to serve King Leopold in the Congo; but turning this down, he accepted the British appointment in January 1884, and returned to the Sudan again as the Governor-General. The feeling of mistrust and uneasiness against the personality of Gordon, underlying the appointment, was evinced in the following British memorandum sent nine months later through Tewfik Pasha, the Khedive of Egypt:

To His EXCELLENCY GORDON PASHA,
   Governor-General of the Sudan.

Lord Wolseley has been appointed by H.M. Government to command the British expedition to the Sudan, and full powers and necessary instructions have been given to him by H.M. Government. On the arrival of H. L. in the Sudan it is necessary that you should obey his orders in order that he may accomplish his mission with success, which is our desire. I have addressed this letter to you for your information in order that you may comply as directed.

(Signed) L. S. MOHAMMED TEWFIK,
   The Khedive.
   26 September 1884.[1]

From the British viewpoint, General Lord Wolseley, who had fought most desperately but successfully against the Ashanti people in West Africa, would be more qualified temperamentally and militarily than Gordon, who was more a humanitarian than a soldier.

Soon after Gordon's arrival in Khartoum, the Mahdist rebellion spread as far as north of that city; and it was becoming so strong as to alter the character of Gordon's mission from mere reporting to military defence. This he could not fulfil without more aid and succour than the British Government had grudgingly granted. Consequently, both the British and the Egyptian Commanders-in-Chief, with Sir Evelyn Baring, recommended that the force under General Graham, which was then in the Eastern Sudan, should be instructed to aid Gordon in repelling the Mahdist pressure on the north of Khartoum. The British Government declined. Gordon's difficulties were increased by a form of guerrilla

[1] P.R.O. W.O. 32/124/346.

warfare with Europeans in Egypt who objected to his sympathizing with Ismail and the natives, with Egyptian slave dealers who opposed his crusade against the trade, and with the officials of the British Foreign Office who had never fully trusted him but had nevertheless commissioned him to the Sudan. The Foreign Office employed the well-tried tactics of evasion and inactivity to wear down even the fiercest protests from Gordon, whose honesty, sincerity and humanitarian principles appeared too much for those dedicated to the intrigues of empire-building. In a private letter to Lady Burton, Gordon complained against the Foreign Office:

> I must say I was surprised to see such a thing. A Government like ours governed by men who dare not call their souls their own. . . . I have written letters to the Foreign Office that would raise a corpse; it is no good; I have threatened to go to the French Government about the Sudan; it is no good. . . .[1]

However, when the regular communication between Cairo and Khartoum was blockaded by the Mahdists, thus isolating Gordon and other Europeans in Khartoum, the British Government became alive to the necessity of despatching a force to relieve them. *The Times*, generally cautious in expressing decided views, ejaculated: 'The Crisis is becoming so serious, and the complications with which this country is beset in different parts of the world are so menacing, that the incapacity displayed by the Cabinet in its external relations is becoming a national danger.'[2]

The strong campaign in the Press, and the Opposition in Parliament forced the hand of the Government to belated action. The news was flashed to other parts of the British Empire, and the Government used the Colonial Office to mobilize forces from the Colonies. On 20 August 1884, the Governor of Canada (Lord Lansdowne) received a telegram from the Colonial Office in London requesting a supply of manpower to assist in the Nile (Sudan) Expedition. As a result, Canada mobilized five hundred men, including 'Indians and a certain number of men of a better class'.[3] Before sailing on the S.S. *Ocean King*, the Governor-General addressed the men, explaining among other things the object of the expedition. It had been undertaken 'not for wanton aggression or selfish conquest, but for . . . the rescue of a religious man—General

---

[1] Elton, *op. cit.*, p. 269.
[2] *The Times*, London, 3 January 1884, p. 9.
[3] Lord Melgund, Military Secretary of the Canadian Government: Copy in the Public Records Office (W.O. 32/124/7700/495).

Gordon'.[1] The *Sydney Herald* in Australia also carried a feature article on 'The Sudan Expedition'. After rebuking those British politicians who had hitherto regarded colonies as a drag upon, and a source of weakness to the mother country, the article went on: 'Our men[2] have the proud pre-eminence—in the matter of which every good and true man in the other Colonies will envy—of being the first selected to strike a blow for the old country in her hour of need in Africa.'[3]

Thus, toward the end of 1884, General Wolseley led Australian, Canadian, English, East Indian and other Colonial troops to rescue General Gordon and save Khartoum. The Sudan campaign thus became memorable as one of the first occasions on which the English and the Colonial forces participated jointly (as the recent Korean War was the first in which many members of the United Nations became collectively involved). But meanwhile, the Mahdists were gaining more ground and Gordon was making heroic efforts to hold out until the arrival of the British Empire troops. There was much fuss in the Press and in the British Colonies about saving Gordon; but in a letter, dated Khartoum, 4 November 1884, and addressed to 'The English', Gordon said with calmness and sardonic humour: 'Your expedition is for relief of garrisons which I fail to accomplish. I decline to agree that it is for me personally. . . . All the [European] captives with the Mahdi are well; the nuns, to avoid an Arab marriage, are ostensibly married to Greeks. . . .'[4]

The imperial expedition, having set out too late, and equipped with inadequate means of transport and communication, found it impossible to reach Khartoum in time to save Gordon. At about 3.30 a.m. on 26 February 1885, a determined attack was made from the Southern front by the Nationalist forces on Khartoum and soon the town was at the mercy of the Mahdists.

It is difficult, from the confusing accounts, to make out how General Gordon was killed. But all the evidence, especially that of a Syrian merchant named Ghalli, tends to show that the incident happened at the Palace or nearby. Ghalli was at Khartoum during the siege and he claimed to be an eye-witness. He had, hitherto, been employed by the Mahdi to supply cloth; he lived with him for a short while, during which time he was compelled to take the usual oath to the Mahdi: not

---

[1] *The Quebec Morning Chronicle*, Quebec, 16 September 1884. Copy in the Public Records Office (W.O. 32/124/495).
[2] Mainly from New South Wales.
[3] *Sydney Herald*, 11 March 1885.
[4] Copy in Public Records Office (W.O. 127/7700/309–20).

to steal; not to commit adultery; not to drink or smoke; not to run away from the holy war; 'I have given you my soul and blood and whatever property I possess, and my property for the sake of God.'[1]

According to this Syrian, the only people who had the strength to fight when the Dervishes entered Khartoum were the 'Blacks who fought well; the other soldiers were too exhausted.' Gordon was upstairs in the palace when he heard the noise in the street and in the palace yard. He came down saying to the Dervishes: '. . . You have entered the town at last just as the English are coming [but] you have outwitted them.'[2]

No sooner had he finished the last sentence than several of the Dervishes struck him with swords and cut off his head, which they carried to the Mahdi. He, however, rebuked the assassins because it was his intention that Gordon (for whom he probably had a personal regard as another 'prophet' like himself, though of a different religion) should not be killed; he meant to exchange Gordon, if he had been delivered alive, for Arabi.[3]

According to a letter from M. de Billing, formerly French Envoy in Egypt, to M. Rocheforte, the Mahdi had numerous agents in Paris, Berlin, London, etc., who kept him well informed on European affairs, particularly British military plans. Some of these agents (Europeans) called on de Billing before the fall of Khartoum asking him to use his good offices to inform the British that the Mahdi had undertaken to deliver Gordon safely for a ransom of 50,000 francs.[4] This was promptly conveyed to the British authorities, but Lord Granville turned down the offer.[5]

What followed the death of Gordon and the fall of Khartoum was looting and cruel massacre; however, the 'black troops'[6] and the women —especially the European women—were spared.

General Wolseley, leader of the relief expedition to the Sudan, sent

[1] Correspondence No. 1884, dated Cairo, 22 June 1885, from General Lord Wolseley to the Secretary of State for War, P.R.O. W.O. 32/130/7700/2812.

[2] *Ibid.*

[3] Arabi, as we have noted, led, like the Mahdi, a revolt against foreign occupation of Egypt; for this he had been deported by the British to perpetual exile in Ceylon. Accepting his fate philosophically, he considered himself 'greatly honoured in being sent to the last resting place of the Common father of all men' (Adam) because, according to Muslim legend, Ceylon (or somewhere nearby in the Orient) was the Garden of Eden. See *The Annual Register*, London, 1883, p. 381.

[4] Sayed Abdel Rahamen-el-Mahdi (the Mahdi's surviving son) has, it is understood, in his possession in Khartoum, a letter in the Mahdi's handwriting addressed to Gordon a short time before the fall of Khartoum and denying that he wanted any ransom for him.

[5] *The Times*, London, 13 July 1885, p. 5e.

[6] *The Times*, 3 October 1885.

a despatch to the Secretary of State for War, the Marquis of Hartington, and gave a report on the general situation prevailing in the Sudan at that time. He said:

> We . . . have no party here in our favour. . . . They look upon us with hatred as infidels and invaders who have come here for our own selfish ends, and who intend, if we succeed, to place in power some foreign ruler, who will tax and oppress them as the Egyptian Pashas did.[1]

As a result of this anti-British feeling, the British Government seemed to make only a half-hearted attempt to yield to the pressure from the British public to avenge the death of Gordon and to 'smash the Mahdi'.

The Mahdi is a very significant figure in the history of the Sudan, and we should give a brief indication of his personality and family. He was named Mohammed Ahmed, a native of the Province of Dongola. Lt.-Col. Stewart, British Military Official in the Sudan, described him to the British Government as tall and slim, with a black beard. He received little or no formal education; his father, Abdullahi, was a carpenter, like Joseph, the father of Jesus of Nazareth. But whilst Jesus was a religious and moral philosopher—the Messiah who conquered men's hearts by the force of persuasion, patience and love, and whose kingdom was not of this world—the Mahdi, though aiming to establish a universal equality, a universal religion and 'a community of goods', was a political saviour; he wanted to dominate not only the Sudan, but most parts of the world. 'All those who did not believe in him should be destroyed, be they Christian, Mohammedan, or Pagan.'[2]

The Rev. Father Joseph Ohrwalder, Priest of the Austrian Mission Station at Delen, in Kordofan Province of the Sudan, from 1880 until his capture by the Mahdists in 1885, gives a physical picture and some mannerisms of the Mahdi. His outward appearance was 'strangely fascinating'; he was strongly built, very dark in complexion, and 'his face always wore a pleasant smile', under which gleamed a set of singularly white teeth, and between the upper middle ones was a V-shaped space, which in the Sudan was considered a sign that the owner would be lucky. His mode of conversation was exceptionally pleasant and sweet.[3]

His courtyard, observed Ohrwalder, was full of women (possibly

[1] General Wolseley, Despatch No. 78, dated 6 March 1885, P.R.O. W.O. 32/127/7700/1772.

[2] Lt.-Col. Stewart, enclosure No. 3, dated 27 December 1882, to despatch from Lord Duffering, in *Egypt No. 13*, p. 6.

[3] Father Joseph Ohrwalder, *Ten Years' Captivity in the Mahdi's Camp*, edited by Major F. R. Wingate, London, 1892, p. 13.

protegées)—from little Turkish girls of eight years old to the pitch-black Dinka Negress or copper-coloured Abyssinian.[1] However, though a much married man, he kept within the limit of four wives allowed by Islamic law, according to Stewart's observations. His principal wife was called 'Aisha' or 'Om el Muminin', meaning the Mother of the Faithful. It would not seem likely, therefore, that he left 150 widows, as reported by a Cairo correspondent of *The Times*, London. Another wife, El Magbula, mother of Sir Abdel Rahman el Mahdi, was still alive in Omdurman till about 1950, when Mr. Langley visited the Sudan.[2]

The Mahdi's Descendants: It is also interesting to note that the Mahdi's own posthumous son, Sir Abdel Rahman, has 17 children— 11 daughters (most of them now married) and 6 sons. The eldest son, Sayid Siddik (42 years old) was President of the Umma Party; El Hodi (32) was in the cotton business; Yahya (24), whom the writer met in Khartoum in February 1956, read Modern Greats at Oxford, and was then Assistant General Manager of his father's cotton firm; Ahmed (21) was a 2nd year Law student at New College, Oxford (all in 1956).

As the British could not 'smash the Mahdi', the Sudan was administered by him until his natural death, and by his successor (the Khalifa) until 1896, when British interest in the country was revived; then Anglo-Egyptian forces reconquered the country, thus bringing Britain nearer to her political objective: 'The Power holding Khartoum would practically hold Egypt.'[3]

With this historical background of the first phase of the Anglo-Egyptian dispute—the struggle to reconquer the Sudan—up to the death of Gordon, we may now proceed to the second phase—the reconquest of the Sudan—in the next chapter.

---

[1] Ohrwalder, *op. cit.*, p. 157.
[2] Langley, *No Woman's Country*, London, 1950, p. 196.
[3] *The Times*, editorial, London, 3 March 1885.

3

THE RECONQUEST OF THE SUDAN AND THE CONDOMINIUM AGREEMENT OF 1899

The Emperor of Constantinople to oppose his neighbours, put 10,000 Turks into Greece, who after the War would not go away again, which was the beginning of the servitude of Greece to the infidels.

NICCOLO MACHIAVELLI: *The Prince* (1532)[1]

THE year 1896, noted at the end of the last chapter, ushered in the second phase of the Anglo-Egyptian dispute. Before that date, however, some major incidents occurred, bringing in certain elements influencing the issue either direct or obliquely. These were British reaction to the death of Gordon; the death of the Mahdi; the European scramble for Africa; the emergence of the United States of America, and the allocation of the Nile Waters for irrigation and other purposes.

1. THE REACTION TO THE DEATH OF GORDON

As we indicated in the last chapter, General Gordon was sent to the Sudan mainly for the purpose of expediting the British Government's policy of abandonment; while on this mission, the forces of the Mahdi stormed Khartoum, killing Gordon on 25 January 1885: Gordon's death affected the British nation deeply.

The general reaction to the fall of Khartoum was mixed with, and overshadowed by, the death of Gordon. In Germany and especially in France, the news was received with indignation. The French (casting aside, at least momentarily, their territorial ambitions in Africa, and their competition with Britain in Egypt and the Sudan), suddenly became pre-occupied with one thought—the fate of Gordon, whom they considered to be one of the most remarkable men of the 19th century and a fellow-citizen in many nations.[2] In Britain, public opinion

---

[1] The World's Classics Edition, London, 1952, p. 61.

[2] This is apparently a tribute to Gordon as a well-travelled man, able to associate closely with the natives and assimilate their cultures. He was a member of an international Commission appointed to delimit the boundary between Russia and Turkey in Bessarabia. While on a similar mission to Asia Minor, Gordon studied the Armenian language and

and all interest was swiftly transferred from home affairs to foreign policy. The Cabinet was accused of indecision and vacillation; the War Office for having stinted men and materials; and Wolseley for acting too late in despatching forces to rescue Gordon and defend Khartoum. *The Times*, in an editorial, summed up the British people's reaction, saying that the shock caused by the news of the fall of Khartoum had no parallel in the experience of that generation.

The biting tone of the British Press incited the Government. The *Morning Post* set the mood and indicated a policy: the British could not turn their backs upon the Mahdi and 'his hordes' without sacrificing Egypt and uprooting the foundations of the British Indian Empire. 'Having entered on this struggle, we must go on with it; having gone to the Sudan we can only quit as victors.' The *Manchester Guardian* was convinced that the British people would grudge no sacrifice which might be needed to save their military pride and to complete the task of stemming this general tide of insurrection. *The Times* complained: 'gambler fashion, we had staked everything upon desperate chances and had lost.'

But, as in most public issues, there were minority views. Leonard Courtney and John Morley (Radicals) protested, almost alone, against the whole Sudan venture. Speaking at Torpoint on 5 February 1885, Courtney declared in effect that the Sudan should be left for the Sudanese, who were doing nothing wrong but fighting for their own liberty, and be it remembered that the British had proclaimed themselves lovers and champions of freedom. 'If I stood alone, I would protest against the notion of waging war against the Mahdi . . . simply for the purpose of showing our might.'[1] Speaking in accord with Courtney, Morley said in a public speech at Glasgow that if once Britain sanctioned extended operations merely for the purpose of revenge, to break up the power of the Mahdi, it would all end in permanent occupation. 'If we remain in the Sudan one day or one hour longer than necessary for the safety of the expedition, we shall remain in the Sudan for ever.'[2] The advocates of revenge and war, he continued, would first say that honour demanded the flying of the British flag in Khartoum. That done, honour would again demand that the flag flew there for ever.

On Saturday afternoon, 16 February 1884, there had been a public

geography. In China he served first the British cause and then a Chinese Emperor, who promoted him to the rank of *Titu*, the highest rank in the Chinese Army. Hence, he became 'Chinese' Gordon, before going to Egypt and then to the Sudan. (*Encyclopædia Britannica*, Vol. X, 14th ed., London, 1929, pp. 525–8.)

[1] *The Annual Register*, 1885, pp. 22–3.   [2] *Ibid.*, p. 23.

demonstration against the Government's policy in Egypt and the Sudan. It was at the Princes Hall, Piccadilly, which was overcrowded that afternoon. There, Lord Randolph Churchill, father of Sir Winston Churchill, moved:

> that in the opinion of this meeting, Her Majesty's Government are solely responsible for the anarchy which prevails in Egypt and the bloodshed which has occurred and which is imminent in the Sudan and that the vacillating pusillanimous policy of the Ministers deserves the severest censures of the country.[1]

The motion was carried unanimously. A similar meeting in Guildhall under the Chairmanship of the Lord Mayor and summoned in consequence of signed petitions to him, also passed similar resolutions disapproving Government policy in Egypt and the Sudan.[2]

The defence of the Government's policy in reply to the various criticisms, was put forth in several speeches made by members of the Government, particularly Gladstone. The Government stand could be summarized as follows. There was fear of objection by the other European powers, with whom Britain was competing in Africa. Gladstone was afraid that to attack the Sudan would be 'a gross breach of the public law of Europe'. This is correct, because the Sudan was virtually a Turkish territory; but the Government did flout, at any convenient and opportune time, the public law of Europe. As we shall see later, they by-passed the 'law' and took possession of the Sudan. Also, the Cabinet was trying to avoid the problem of Christians governing Mohammedan peoples. True, there has been constant friction between Christianity and Islam, but this did not prevent Britain from occupying Egypt and India, where there were Muslims. Again, Gordon, said Gladstone, had not asked specifically for British soldiers, had not stated he could not leave Khartoum; and had never stated that he was in serious danger.

But we must point out here that Gordon, on 8 February 1884, had got a message through to Sir Evelyn Baring, in Cairo, in which he had said:

> I do not see the fun of being caught here to walk about the streets for years as a dervish with sandalled feet; not that (D.V.) I will ever be taken alive. It would be the climax of meanness after I had borrowed money from the people here, and called on them to sell their grain at a low price, etc., to go and abandon them without using every effort to relieve them, whether those efforts are diplomatically correct or not, and feel sure (whatever you may

[1] *The Times*, 18 February 1884, p. 12b.   [2] *The Times*, 16 February 1884.

feel diplomatically) I have your full support—and every man professing himself a gentleman—in private.[1]

Intervention, furthermore, would involve great military costs and risks, with a relatively small advantage in return. This argument is perhaps the crux of the Government's policy of non-intervention. They would prefer to await such conditions as would make the occupation of the Sudan easier, less risky, and more profitable. It was the duty also of the Government to consider the economic interests, the blood and honour of Britain in connection with the circumstances of the time. Conscious of their obligations, the Cabinet had endeavoured to act in the best interests of Britain and would continue to do so, in spite of criticisms.

There were certain other factors which would seem to have influenced the actions of the British Government in these matters: Britain had advised Egypt to withdraw from the Sudan, but Egypt did not comply. The Army, under General Hicks, was defeated by the Mahdists, and the British Government were probably cautious not to incur a similar loss of prestige through a British commander. When Turkey was expressing uneasiness about British intentions in Egypt and the Sudan, Granville had told the Turkish Ambassador in London, Musurus Pasha, that Britain was merely assisting 'in maintaining order in and defending Egypt proper', and that Britain 'had no intention of sending troops to undertake the reconquest of the Sudan'.[2] The British Government depended much upon the reports and recommendations from their accredited representatives in Cairo. These officials, though very capable and perhaps unimpeachable, were, being human, none the less fallible; a critic pointed out: 'officials are themselves the best judges as to how much of their conduct should be submitted to public scrutiny',[3] and thus they often misled the Government. 'Our officials in Egypt have systematically deceived the Home Government as to the real state of national feeling in that country.'[4] Joseph Chamberlain, himself a member of the Gladstone Cabinet, admitted in his *Memoirs*: 'There is no doubt throughout this period that the Government had no settled policy but adopted its decisions from time to time without attempting to look forward into the future. Harcourt strongly advocated what was

[1] Gordon's letter reproduced in *The Times*, London, 17 January 1885, p. 8a.

[2] Despatch No. 213, dated Foreign Office, 4 January 1884, from Granville to Dufferin, in *Further Correspondence Respecting the Affairs of Egypt—Egypt No. 1* (1884), p. 177.

[3] Keay, Seymour J., 'Spoiling the Egyptians: A Rejoinder', in *Contemporary Review*, Vol. XLII, 1882, p. 765.

[4] Keay, Seymour J., *Spoiling the Egyptians: A Tale of Shame*, 4th ed. London, 1882, p. ii.

known as the "policy of scuttle" and on several occasions threatened resignation if any definite steps were proposed to carry assistance to Gordon or to the garrisons.'[1] The religious and moral rectitude of Gladstone might have influenced him and his Cabinet against the military campaign against the Sudanese, who were, he once pointed out, fighting for their own freedom. Gladstone endeavoured to apply conscientiously the principles of Christianity to the business of public life and foreign policy. Cardinal Manning was reported to have said: 'Gladstone was nearer being a clergyman than I was. He was, I believe, as fit as I was unfit.'[2]

However, the Government, which appeared to have been immune to pressure from all quarters, found it politically desirable to give the impression of making posthumous amends for what looked to the public as the betrayal of Gordon. Public regard (particularly among the Christians) for Gordon was indicated by the various memorial services held, on 13 March 1885, at nearly every church in England—at St. Paul's Cathedral, Westminster Abbey, Canterbury, Durham, Winchester, etc.[3] Thirteen years later, even the Government paid tribute to him by establishing the Gordon Memorial College at Khartoum, with a fund raised largely in England in response to an appeal by Lord Kitchener in 1898—soon after the battle of Omdurman.

In their plan to recapture the Sudan, Government spokesmen used the slogan of preserving Western civilization. Speaking in Liverpool in reply to Courtney and Morley, who had pleaded that the Sudan should be left alone for the Sudanese, in 1885 Goschen said: 'We should remember that in the interests of Western civilization we have a duty to perform to a country we have engaged to protect.'[4] The expedition for the relief of Gordon was therefore expanded into a campaign for the reconquest of the Sudan. The Secretary for War, Lord Hartington, instructed General Wolseley to pursue a military policy based upon 'smashing the Mahdi'. But as soon as public feeling had become less passionate and articulate about Gordon and Khartoum, the British Government reverted, in April 1885, to the policy of evacuation. The reason for this step might be the dislike by Gladstone, a disciple of Richard Cobden (1804–65) for the acquisition of new territory.[5]

[1] Chamberlain, Joseph, *Political Memoirs, 1880–92* (Batchworth Press) London, 1953, p. 83.
[2] Russell, George, 'W. E. Gladstone's Theology', in *Contemporary Review*, Vol. LXXIII, 1898, p. 778. See also Norman Hampgood, 'Mr. Gladstone' in Vol. LXXIV, 1898, p. 34.
[3] *The Times*, 14 March 1885.   [4] *Annual Register*, 1885, p. 24.
[5] Russell, Bertrand, *Freedom and Organization (1814–1914)*, London, 1934, p. 460.

2. THE DEATH OF THE MAHDI

In June, the Liberal Government, headed by Gladstone, collapsed. The acceptance of their resignation by Queen Victoria was announced in Parliament on 10 June; soon after, the Mahdi died in the rosy glow of victory. The element of relief brought to the British Government by his death was conspicuous in the Queen's Speech from the Throne: 'The death of the Mahdi will probably enable me to perform with less difficulty the duties towards the ruler and people of Egypt which events have imposed upon me. . . .'[1]

But the Queen's hope for fewer difficulties in Egypt and the Sudan after the death of the Mahdi did not immediately materialize. In the first place, his successor, called the Khalifa, was determined both to put a finishing touch to the Mahdi's victory and to push ahead his own schemes. Most of the Egyptian garrisons in the Sudan had either surrendered or been destroyed. In the second place, and more important, the fall of the Gladstone Government[2] and the victory of the Conservatives in 1886, ushered in a new outlook in Britain, for, to quote Bertrand Russell, 'from that year until the end of the century, the passion for empire continually grew, taking forms which were sometimes criminal, often ridiculous and always disgusting'.[3] The new epoch intensified the European scramble for Africa; it therefore became clear that the Sudan would not remain for long as an independent African State.

3. THE SCRAMBLE FOR AFRICA

The European scramble for Africa at this time brought in the third element influencing the Anglo-Egyptian issue. In about 1890, Britain became uneasy at the French penetration in Africa. By an Anglo-German Convention in 1885, Germany had recognized the whole of the Nile Valley as a British sphere of influence. France objected to this, arguing that the Sudan was under Turkish sovereignty. A year earlier, Belgium had ceded to Britain the Lado Enclave—a strip of land now part of the Anglo-Egyptian Sudan. Soon after, Belgium also ceded to France a route through the Lado Enclave to the Nile. Britain protested, saying that the French route ran through the Egyptian Sudan, embracing

---

[1] *Parliamentary Debates*, Vol. CCCI, 14 August 1885, pp. 31–2.

[2] According to Lord Winterton, the attitude of the Liberal Party to the position of General Gordon in the Sudan was the prime cause of the fall of the Gladstone Government, and one of the principal reasons 'why for such a long time afterwards the Liberal Party were not entrusted with an adequate majority for the Government of this country' —*Parliamentary Debates*, 10 July 1924; *Official Reports*, Vol. CLXXV (1924), p. 2506.

[3] Russell, *op. cit.*, p. 460.

the whole of the White Nile. Furthermore, the President of the French Republic was quoted as saying that: 'The time has come to raise the Egyptian question. We must occupy part of the Egyptian territory (the Sudan) so that Britain will protest. The *Big Powers* will intervene and force her to withdraw her troops from the Nile Valley.'[1]

Also, French columns were at this time pushing their outposts beyond the British frontiers in Nigeria; and aiming to link up the French territories from West Africa to East Africa, they were within striking distance of the Sudan. The British Cabinet, realizing that the French move might oust the British and endanger their proposed Cape to Cairo route, their imperial lines of communication and particularly their position in the Sudan, decided upon the re-conquest of the Sudan.

4. THE EMERGENCE OF THE UNITED STATES OF AMERICA

At that time, the adventurous and energetic nations plunged into the contest for the possession of the only markets left open for absorbing surplus manufactures (as they still do today), because they were all forced to encourage exports for self-preservation. In the United States, the ideals of Washington and Jefferson, with the American tradition of neutrality to European power politics had begun to lose their hold upon the Americans; something else was filling up the vacuum. It was 'multimillionarism'. With it went marriage alliances of European peerage with American aristocracy (e.g. the Anglo-American parents of Sir Winston Churchill); very high commercial speculations; and the arrival of the American age of inventions. All of these gave rise to a desire in America to have a place in the sun together with the Powers of the Old World. Writing during that period, an American said: 'Whether we like it or not we are forced to compete for the markets of international exchanges or, in other words, for the seat of empire.'[2] It was a period of the revival of the 'Manifest Destiny', when Josiah Strong wrote his book[3] *Our Country: Its Possible Future*, in which he urged that American civilization should be extended to the 'backward' nations; because 'the American excels all the others in pushing his way into new countries'.[4] In short, the sceptre of industry had begun to pass from the Old World to the New.[5] As we have seen, Chaillé-Long,

---

[1] Agence France-Presse, *op. cit.*, p. 8.
[2] Adams, Brooks, 'The New Struggle for Life Among Nations', reproduced in the *Fortnightly Review*, Vol. LXV, London, 1899, p. 283.
[3] New York, 1885 and 1891.
[4] Quoted in *The Making of American Democracy: Readings and Documents*, Vol. II, 1950, by Billington and others, p. 258.
[5] 'American Competition in Europe', *The Times*, 25 March 1885, p. 4e.

the American (who was later to become American Ambassador in Korea), had been in the Sudan with Gordon in the service of the Khedive.

During the peace negotiations which began at Paris in October 1898, four commissioners representing the U.S. definitely and openly committed their country to a large policy of imperialism and expansion.[1] The U.S.A. was, furthermore, one of the Capitulatory Powers with influence in Egypt and the Sudan. The uneasiness felt by Britain about the rise of America during the period was expressed by Samuel Baker who was an adviser to the British Government of the day. In a letter written at Bath on 4 April 1890, Baker recommended (through Moberly Bell, *The Times* Correspondent in Egypt) the construction of railways and irrigation projects which 'would make the Sudan a mine of wealth: because it would bring an area of thirty million acres of the most fertile soil (Moroe, etc.) under cultivation and supply England with cotton, *thereby making her entirely independent of America*'.[2]

Britain was, therefore, anxious to forestall in the Sudan not only the French and other European powers but also the United States of America which was then suspected by European powers in a way somewhat similar to the watchfulness of the Western Powers with regard to the U.S.S.R. today. Writing on 1 January 1898, *The Times*, in its leading editorial, sounded a warning to the British: 'The New Year opens with ambiguous omens. In several parts of the world this country is confronted by the organised and determined rivalry of other powers', which by their better equipments appeared more able than Britain to control the markets of 'uncivilised or undeveloped regions'. The emergence of America did, in this way, act as the fourth element influencing the British decision to reconquer the Sudan.

5. THE ALLOCATION OF THE NILE WATERS FOR IRRIGATION AND OTHER PURPOSES

To Egypt, the Sudan was a dominion lost while she was herself under British occupation, and Britain had given an undertaking to help Egypt regain the lost territory. On the other hand, Egyptian interests in the Sudan became more intensified by the development of irrigation works on the Sudan sector of the Nile, which was and still is the source of life

---

[1] Morrison and Commager, *The Growth of the American Republic*, Vol. II, New York, 1942, p. 336.

[2] *Samuel Baker: A Memoir*, p. 354; the italics are the writer's.

to Egypt. We shall discuss this in greater detail in Part III, under Egyptian Interests in the Sudan.

Driven by the above circumstances and each with different motives, Britain and Egypt agreed to reconquer the Sudan as soon as this became possible from the point of view of Egyptian finance and Anglo-Egyptian military preparations.

Sir Michael Hicks Beach, Chancellor of the Exchequer, speaking about the task of reconquering the Sudan, said in the House of Commons in February 1897: 'it was obvious that in the first place, partial reconquest of the Sudan was not beyond the military and financial resources of England'; but little inclination was for some while shown both by successive Governments and by public opinion to employ these resources in order to attain that objective. The problem, which apparently had to be faced, was how the Egyptian Government, with very little or no British help, could reassert their authority in the Sudan.

Before any thought of reconquest could be entertained, the British felt that two conditions had to be fulfilled. In the first place, the Egyptian Army had to be made efficient. Secondly, not only had the solvency of the Egyptian Treasury to be assured, but funds had to be provided for the extraordinary expenditure which the assumption of an offensive policy would certainly involve.

But, owing to the defeat of the Italians by the Ethiopians at Adowa (near the Sudan frontier) in 1896, and their call for British help, the British Government suddenly changed their former attitude and decided on the re-occupation of Dongola in March 1896. Behind the friendly aid to Egypt, the British policy, says Lord Cromer, 'was in some degree the outcome of the rapid growth of the Imperialist Spirit which about this time overtook England'.[1]

The Egyptians opposed the British expedition which was, it seemed to many Egyptians, planned in the interests of the Italians, manned by British troops, and commanded by Kitchener. In this connection, Cromer remarked that the Khedive apparently had no clear ideas of what he wanted either in Egypt or in the Sudan, 'but in this particular case he cannot get over the feeling that any advantage now gained in the Sudan constitutes an English rather than an Egyptian success'.[2] It all led to anti-European feeling in general and Anglophobia in particular.

Nevertheless, 'Kitchener's expedition was a joint Anglo-Egyptian

---

[1] Cromer, *Modern Egypt*, Vol. II, p. 83.
[2] Cromer to Salisbury, No. 57, Secret, 12 April 1898, F.O. 78/4956. Also Mekki Shibeika, *British Policy in the Sudan*, London, 1952, p. 404.

undertaking in which Egypt provided the title, about two-thirds of the armies, and paid by far the greater share of the expenses. Britain provided the leadership, about one-third of the army and an insignificant part of the funds necessary for the initial Dongola expedition.[1] Accordingly, Anglo-Egyptian forces, comprising Egyptians—fellaheen and 'Blacks'—under Lord Kitchener, captured Dongola in 1896. In 1898, Kitchener crushed the followers of the Mahdist movement at the battle of Omdurman; and later in the same year, he scared away, at Fashoda, the French forces led by Marchand.

Like the Mahdists during the previous fall of Khartoum, the Anglo-Egyptian soldiers, overcome by the spell of glory of conquest, became atrocious. As a symbol of their triumphant power and perhaps in an attempt to avenge the beheading of Gordon, and to weaken the morale of the subdued Sudanese to whom the Mahdi was a source of religious and national inspiration, the British Commander desecrated the tomb of the Mahdi. He ordered the embalmed body of the dead to be turned out of the grave; the head was wrenched off, 'and the trunk cast into the Nile'.[2] Thus the reconquest of the Sudan was accomplished. Salisbury communicated to Cromer the policy to be adopted in the Sudan henceforth. First, the Cabinet did not contemplate any further military operations on a large scale, or involving much expense; and while not yielding any recognition of territorial rights to France or to Ethiopia in the Nile Valley, the British representatives in the valley must recognize 'the necessity of avoiding, by all possible means, any collision with the forces of the Emperor Menelek'[3] of Ethiopia.

The Sudan had been conquered. However, a new problem arose—that of the British position alongside that of Egypt in the Sudan. Lord Kitchener hoisted the British and Egyptian flags side by side in Khartoum as emblems of the concurrent dominion of Egypt and Britain over the Sudan. However, the Marquess of Salisbury, in a letter to Lord Cromer on 2 August 1898,[4] gave indications of Britain's intentions of being the senior partner in the joint-stock holding of the Sudan. The Marquess declared:

> You will, however, explain to the Khedive and his Ministers that the procedure I have indicated is intended to emphasize the fact that Her Majesty's

---

[1] The total strength of the army was 25,000 men, made up of 8,000 British and 17,000 Egyptians and Sudanese; Agence France-Presse, *op. cit.*, p. 8.

[2] Bennett, Ernest N., 'After Omdurman', *Contemporary Review*, Vol. LXXV, London, 1899, p. 295.

[3] Confidential Despatch No. 109, dated 2 August 1898, from Salisbury to Cromer: P.R.O. F.O. 78/4955.

[4] F.O. 78/4955. (The italics are the writer's.)

Government consider that they have a *predominant voice in all matters connected with the Sudan and that they expect any advice which they think fit to tender to the Egyptian Government in respect to the Sudan will be followed.*

6. INTERNATIONAL REACTIONS TO THE CONQUEST

The reaction of most of the European Powers to the British military success could be illustrated by the Belgian, German and French attitudes. Sir F. R. Plunkett, British Envoy Extraordinary and Minister Plenipotentiary in Brussels, informed Lord Salisbury that the heads of the Belgian and of the Congo State Governments had warmly congratulated the British Government on their military success under Kitchener, and that 'in all leading organs of the Brussels Press, this brilliant feat of arms and strategy has been commented upon in terms highly flattering to Great Britain'.[1] The Germans saw in the success, the restoration of European prestige in Africa. Reporting to the British Government from Berlin, Frank C. Lascelles quoted the *Cologne Gazette* as saying that the task of rehabilitating European and especially English prestige had been reserved to 'Sir Kitchener, a more practical man than Hicks Pasha and Gordon'.

Sir E. Morson reported to London his conversation with the French Minister for Foreign Affairs who congratulated the British, notwithstanding the differences between the two Governments. In spite of the formal greetings of the Government, the French reaction was, however, more mournful of their own loss than joyful for the British success. *Le Matin* of 29 June 1898, contained an article entitled 'The Egyptian Question and French Interests'. It stated that the fall of Khartoum to the British marked the end of French illusions; that the British success in the Sudan provided Britain with an admirable base for expansion farther south—beyond the Equator. The question of evacuation which Britain had been promising for the past sixteen years was now improbable. The time had therefore arrived for France to demand from the British compensation for her loss in the Nile Valley.

Probably the majority of the British people were, quite naturally, pleased with their military success in the Sudan. But there were minority opinions, and one of the dissenting voices was that of Lord Farrer. He agreed that the suppression of the Mahdists was a chivalrous act,

but one which loses much of its chivalry when it is effected by England not at her own cost, but at the cost of Egypt and with the sacrifice of Egypt's

[1] Despatch dated 16 April 1898, in P.R.O. F.O. 141/332.

most important interests. . . . In Africa as in Asia we are extending our borders with the blood and money of the subject races.[1]

Britain had to look for a fresh policy. Two avenues were now open to the British under the international law then in practice: either the Sudan could be returned to the Sultan of Turkey and the Khedive of Egypt as a former dominion, or it could be annexed to the British Empire. The first would satisfy Egypt, Turkey and the European rivals, among whom France was conspicuous, but such a course would not satisfy Britain, who had helped to bring down the prey. Although annexation of the Sudan to the British Empire would be in British interests, it would enrage Egypt in whose name the campaign had been carried on; it would also open the door to political intrigues from France; and it might incite the other European powers to rally against such British covetousness.

But somehow luck favoured Britain. In more or less the same way as the international situation was favourable to the Anglo-Egyptian Agreement of 1954, on the Suez Canal Base (see chapter 14 below) the tide was likewise favourable to Britain in reaching some agreement with Egypt on the Sudan at the end of the last century. The year 1899 was relatively quiet and politically passive in Egypt. The relations of the Khedive with his English advisers were fairly friendly; representatives of French interests in the country became less hostile and irritating to the British. The scurrility and bitterness of the Egyptian and/or French Press against the British diminished. Economically, Egypt was relatively prosperous, particularly in the cotton trade with Lancashire. The only significant cause for disquiet was the failure of the Nile flood—'the lowest ever recorded'.[2] Above all, the insurrections in the Sudan had been smashed jointly by Britain and Egypt; Turkey was truly the 'Sick Man of Europe'. The time was, therefore, opportune and the mood favourable for Britain and France to secure their interests in the Upper Nile Valley; and for Britain to reach with relative ease an agreement with Egypt, on the Sudan question.

The only problem was to find a solution by which the Sudan could be, at one and the same time, Egyptian to such an extent as to satisfy equity and political exigencies; and yet effectively British to prevent the administration of the Sudan from being hampered by the international character of Egyptian political existence. It became clear that these conflicting requirements needed a unique form of agreement and adminis-

---

[1] Lord Farrer, Letter to *The Times*, 7 January 1898.
[2] *The Annual Register*, 1899, p. 366.

trative machinery seldom used, if at all, in international jurisprudence. A 'hybrid' form of government was, therefore, adopted for the Sudan by Cromer; and it was named the 'Condominium'—the Anglo-Egyptian Agreement of 1899 which made the Sudan constitutionally a slave with two masters: Britain and Egypt.

The Condominium can be summarized as a formula devised, in its wider effect, to achieve seven major objectives: namely to placate France; to offset Ottoman interference; to exclude other European powers (and the United States of America); to give Egypt a subordinate role in the administration of the Sudan; to establish British paramountcy in the country; to establish British influence on better-defined and less anomalous conditions than those in Egypt; to provide a substitute for the annexation of the Sudan to the British Empire, from which course Britain had hitherto been hindered by various considerations.

A full text of the convention is appended below[1] but in order better to understand its *raison d'être* it seems desirable to annotate it, article by article.

The Preamble explains the need for the Agreement, namely, that those provinces in the Sudan which were in rebellion against the authority of Egypt having now been reconquered, new forms of administration and of legislative procedure became necessary, and it became desirable to effectuate British claims accruing from her part in the conquest, and share in the present and future administration of the Sudan.[2]

Article I defines the frontiers of the Sudan for the purpose of the Agreement. This would seem necessary because Wadi Halfa and Suakin remained in Egyptian hands throughout the Mahdiya administration; to exclude these areas from the new (Condominium) administration, leaving them in the hands of Egypt, might create certain problems sooner or later. Cromer therefore discovered a way out. He argued that these provinces would have been lost to Egypt during the rebellion were it not for the defensive action of British troops. Consequently, for the purpose of the Agreement, he divided the Sudan into three categories: (*a*) the territories which remained consistently under Egyptian administration since 1882, (*b*) those under Egyptian administration before the Mahdist

[1] Copy in *State Papers*, Vol. XCI (1898–9), H.M.S.O., London, 1902, pp. 19–22. See Appendix 3 below.
[2] The rights of the British were given more prominence because the rights alone constituted the real justification for setting up a political and administrative status in the Sudan, different from that in Egypt (Cromer, Memo. marked 'Confidential', P.R.O. F.O. 78/4957).

insurrection, but not reconquered jointly by Britain and Egypt; and (c) those that might be conquered at any subsequent time jointly by Britain and Egypt, but excluding any extensions from any part of the adjacent British territories (e.g. Uganda).

Article II. To hoist the British flag at Suakin would arouse severe criticisms and protests, especially because the jurisdiction of the Mixed Tribunals extended to that town. This article therefore provides for British and Egyptian flags to fly jointly in the Sudan except at Suakin where the Egyptian flag alone should be used. When still anticipating the occupation of Khartoum, Salisbury had communicated with Cromer on 2 August 1898, on the subject of British policy in the Sudan. 'In view of the substantial military and financial co-operation which has recently been afforded by Her Majesty's Government to the Khedive, Her Majesty's Government have decided that at Khartoum the British and Egyptian flags should be hoisted side by side. This decision will have no reference to the manner in which the occupied countries are to be administered in the future.'[1] Earlier in the year (while on leave in Britain) Cromer had sent a memorandum to the British Government in which he referred to the hoisting of flags in the Sudan: 'The Khedive knows perfectly well that neither in Egypt nor in the Sudan can he take any important step without the consent of Her Majesty's Government'.[2]

Nevertheless, hoisting the British and Egyptian flags jointly would serve four main purposes: it would bring the political theory of the Condominium into harmony with reality; it would emphasize the point that the Khedive could not act in the Sudan without the consent of his senior partner in London; it would serve as a statutory warning to the Sultan in Turkey; and it would indicate clearly to the French and the Ethiopians that the Sudan 'is more an English than Egyptian question'.[3]

Articles III and IV form the crux of the Agreement. They spell out the process of exercising authority, and specifically invest the supreme military and civil power and command in the hands of one single officer —the 'Governor-General of the Sudan'—who shall be appointed by the Khedive on the recommendation of 'Her Britannic Majesty's Government', and shall be removed only with their consent. Cromer recommended in his explanatory memorandum that specific mention should be made of obtaining the sanction of the British with regard to

[1] Despatch No. 109, marked 'Confidential' and 'Printed for the use of the Cabinet', dated 2 August 1898, F.O. 78/4955.
[2] Memorandum by Lord Cromer, printed for the use of the Cabinet, 27 July 1898, P.R.O. F.O. 78/4956.
[3] *Ibid.*

the appointment and removal of the Governor-General, even though such a course might not appear altogether necessary, because 'the Khedive is under obligation to follow English advice in all important matters so long as the occupation lasts'.[1] This explains in part why all the Governors-General of the Sudan since the signing of the Condominium were always British, and never Egyptian. This article is perhaps an extension of the 54th Article of the Law of Liquidation which provided that the Controller of Dairah in Egypt should be appointed by the Khedive on the recommendation of the British Government.[2]

Article V prohibits the application of Egyptian law in the Sudan.

Article VI seeks the right to impose conditions under which foreigners might trade or become domiciled in the Sudan. Cromer considered this article as a necessary evil. 'We are in possession and shall be able to assert our rights even although we may not be able to convince others of the regularity of our position or the validity of our arguments.' To encourage all those desiring to come to the Sudan might precipitate international rivalry and hostility over the country.

Article VII gives to Egypt preferential treatment about import duties (somewhat similar to the British imperial trade preference) which shall be free on exports from Egypt to the Sudan. Technically, this could be stretched to imply that the Sudan is Egypt's domestic sphere of influence.

Article VIII limits the jurisdiction of the International ('Mixed') Tribunal only and specifically to Suakin, where the 'Mixed Courts' in Egypt had been exercising authority for many years. Naturally Britain was anxious not to allow other powers to interfere in what now appeared to be her domestic jurisdiction, in somewhat the same way as the United Nations Charter under Article 2, Section 7, prevents member states from interfering in the 'domestic' problems of the others. Suakin, it seems, became a sort of 'trust' town as Trieste was at the end of the Second World War until 1954.

Article IX puts the whole Sudan, excepting Suakin, under martial law. This action was taken for three main reasons: first, to get away from the system of 'capitulations' which had existed in Egypt and 'which gravely hindered', to quote Sir James Robertson, 'the ordinary process of law and gave foreigners a privileged position';[3] second, to assure, also, that the Sudan would be free from the control of the 'Mixed Courts', which had no control over the territories in which

---

[1] Public Records Office, enclosure with F.O. 78/4957.
[2] Granville to Malet, Despatch No. 96, 7 May 1883, F.O. 78/3550.
[3] Letter to L. A. Fabunmi from Sir James Robertson (Governor-General of Nigeria), formerly Civil Secretary of the Sudan Government, dated Cholsey, Berks., 3 July 1957.

martial law prevailed; and third, to give the Governor-General ample powers of maintaining 'law and order'—the right to expel from the country any such Europeans and Sudanese who might be stumbling blocks to the new Government in the Sudan. However, Cromer pointed out that his intention was that the extreme powers invested in the hands of the Governor-General should be used only in exceptional cases, until such times as Civil Law could be introduced.

Article X conceded to Britain alone (not both Britain and Egypt) the right to grant or withdraw recognition to any accredited representative of any nation.

Article XI prohibits slave trading in the Sudan.

Article XII puts the manufacture or importation of arms and alcoholic drinks under the Brussels Act of 2 July 1890.[1]

The Agreement was signed on 19 January 1899, by Boutros Ghali, then Minister of Foreign Affairs for Egypt, and Lord Cromer, for Britain. Soon afterwards, however, another Convention was signed—on 10 July 1899—abrogating all the provisions of the January Agreement by which the town of Suakin was excepted from the regime of the Sudan. Thus Suakin, formerly under the jurisdiction of the Mixed Courts, became absorbed into the Sudan, because, the British argued, the Mixed Tribunals were too expensive for Suakin.

The Agreement attracted much attention when it was published. A foreign diplomat, addressing Baring, remarked that he understood what British territory meant, so also an Ottoman territory, but that he found it difficult to understand the new status of the Sudan, which was now neither British nor Ottoman. Baring, in response, said that the most precise definition of the new political status of the Sudan could be found in the Agreement of 19 January 1899. As it was, and still is, customary for nations to keep, as far as possible, a general record of their citizens abroad, foreign nationals in the Sudan consequently became anxious about the provisions of Article X of the Agreement, which provided, in effect, for the removal of foreign Consuls or other accredited agents in the country. Cromer was asked what, in the absence of any Consuls, was to happen to Europeans who were married or buried in the Sudan? He could only reply that any European who considered it essential that his marriage or burial should be attested by a Consular representative of his country, would do well to remain in the territory lying North of the 22nd parallel of latitude. In other words, foreigners would be better advised to stay out of the Sudan. The Sultan

---

[1] *State Papers*, H.M.S.O., Vol. XCI, London, 1898–9, pp. 6–12.

of Turkey, the nominal owner and absent landlord of the Sudan whom Britain was successfully outmanœuvring, protested, but without effect. As is often the case today, the splutter of amazement and general indignation caused by the Agreement soon died away amongst all the Powers; they found some compensation in Article VI of the Agreement, which provides equal opportunities and privileges to the citizens of all the Powers trading with or residing in the country.

In Egypt and the Sudan, however, the weapons of opposition were merely stored, not buried; the inhabitants sooner or later became more and more conscious of the injustice done to them, and they fought tooth and nail for 54 years to undo it, until the Anglo-Egyptian Agreement of 1953; and until January 1956, when the Sudan became an independent republic.

The validity or otherwise of the Agreement has been subjected to much discussion. Naturally, the British (who gained much by it) would maintain its validity, just as the Egyptians (who felt cheated because of their minor role) and the Sudanese (who, having no voice in the matter, felt that they were regarded in this affair as a mere commodity for bartering) would oppose it. Mekki Abbas, a Sudanese, suggests that any attempt to give a ruling on the validity or otherwise of the Condominium is engaging in 'a sterile academic discussion'. Even so, he argues, conclusively, that it is valid, and his reasons are: it was not questioned by the Sultan; it has never been denounced by the various foreign governments having intercourse with the Sudan Government, to which the Agreement gave birth; and it was recognized by the Mixed Tribunal in Cairo on 2 April 1910.[1]

On the first point above, it is difficult to agree entirely with Mekki Abbas. The Sultan did protest. The British Government was certainly aware of the feeling of Turkey in this matter, and Baring admitted it: 'It is true that the Sultan murmured some few words of ineffectual protest.'[2] If the Sultan murmured instead of shouting protests, it was probably because he was aware of his helplessness. Britain, France and Turkey had competed vigorously for many decades; France won the heats, but Britain won the finals. But Turkey had become relatively powerless; she had been reduced to the status of the 'Sick Man of Europe', and the protesting voice of the Sultan became correspondingly ineffectual. In April 1899, even a Turkish official declared: 'Turkey (European, African and Asiatic) is doomed to die. England's share in her succession will be the undisputed possession of Egypt and the

---

[1] Mekki Abbas, *op. cit.*, pp. 55–6.   [2] Cromer, *op. cit.*, p. 118.

annexation of Arabia up to Baghdad.'[1] In any case, the validity or nullity of an Agreement is not necessarily measured by the strength of applause for it or the amount of murmur against it.

As to the second point about many Governments dealing with the Government in the Sudan without denouncing it, it is essential to remember that once a form of government has been established 'de facto' within a nation, other Governments often consider it desirable to recognize—whether or not they approve—such a form of government. Communist China, recognized by many Capitalist countries such as Britain, which at the same time dislike its Communistic form, is a good example today. In other words, there is a difference between recognition (for the purposes of trade and other forms of beneficial intercourse) and approval. It must be remembered also that in any case, most of the other Powers, in spite of their jealousy and rivalry, were in league with Britain. There was, among the European powers, a gentlemen's agreement not to interfere destructively in each other's spheres of influence. In addition to the Agreements reached at the various Berlin Conferences on the scramble for Africa, the International Convention at the Hague recognized 'the solidarity which united the members of the society of civilizations'.[2] The Convention was signed on 29 July 1899—just within six months after the Anglo-Egyptian Condominium Agreement and was ratified by 23 nations, including the U.S.A. and Russia but not Turkey.[3] Furthermore, the Anglo-French Agreement of 1904 provided for French recognition of the British position in Egypt (and the Sudan) in return for British recognition of the special position of France in Morocco.[4] Temperley asserts that the status of the Sudan is important not only to Egypt and Britain, but also to Foreign Powers, 'and that is one of the reasons why foreign states are recommended not to question these matters in which the rights of the British Empire are so vitally important'.[5] In a despatch to the Governors-General of the British Dominions, Lloyd George, as Secretary of State for the Colonies, said emphatically: 'We will regard as an unfriendly act any attempt at interference in the affairs of Egypt (and the Sudan) by another power.'[6]

---

[1] 'A Turkeyish official, The Future of Turkey', in *Contemporary Review*, Vol. LXXV, 1899, p. 541.
[2] The Pacific Settlement of International Disputes: *Treaty Series*, No. 9 (1901), p. 19.
[3] *Ibid.*, p. 36.
[4] *Treaty Series*, No. 6 (1905), 'Egypt and Morocco', signed in London on 8 April 1904.
[5] Temperley, H. W. V., *A History of the Peace of Paris* (published under the auspices of the British Institute of International Affairs), London, 1924, p. 204.
[6] Telegram dated 27 February 1922, from Lloyd George to the Governors-General of the Dominions, Cmd. 1592—*Egypt No. 1* (1922), p. 31.

As for Mekki Abbas' third argument concerning recognition of the Condominium by the Mixed Tribunal, here again, the Mixed Courts could recognize without approving (as indicated above) the Sudan Government. Secondly, the Mixed Tribunal in question was originally set up by and included the capitulatory powers, i.e. Great Britain, France, U.S.A., Germany, Austria-Hungary, Belgium, Denmark, Russia, Spain, Greece, Italy, Portugal, Sweden and later Norway.[1] With Britain as a most leading member, and in view of the Hague Convention mentioned above, it should not be difficult to see how the Mixed Tribunal could condone or 'recognize', at their sitting in Cairo in 1910, the Condominium Convention, in more or less the same way as the U.S.A. now often manages to bring the majority of the United Nations members to support her actions.

Egyptian sources oppose the validity of the Agreement on many grounds which could be summarized as follows. They say that it was signed under duress by Boutros Ghali (the Egyptian Foreign Minister) and ratified under the same circumstances by the Egyptian Cabinet. After quoting the directive of the British Government demanding the Egyptian Government to conform to 'all and any advice which will be given by the British Government concerning Soudan affairs', it is said in support of this argument that 'the Council of Ministers were advised, or, to be more strictly correct, ordered to approve an Agreement which was submitted to them. Accordingly, they had to conform to this British advice, and this Agreement was duly signed'.[2] They maintain further, that its nature is abnormal, unconventional in international customs, and a shock to the diplomats of the time; that Egypt, and the Sudan, being then protégés of the Ottoman Empire, had no right to make political treaties or agreements with other Governments without the approval of the Sultan of Turkey; that the Sultan protested against such an aggression. But Great Britain, who had occupied the whole Valley of the Nile, took no notice of such protests. Moreover, they maintain that it was an Agreement between a 'trustee' and a 'minor' because the occupation of Egypt by British forces since 1882 put Egypt completely under British tutelage—a protectorate with whom Britain could not, legally, contract an international compact. Thus, they conclude that being in fact nothing but 'a legal screen to conceal British

[1] Marlowe, *op. cit.*, p. 109.

[2] The Ministry for Foreign Affairs: *The Soudan Question*, based on British documents and compiled by Abdel-Moneim Omar, Librarian, Egyptian National Library, Cairo, 1952, p. 67.

imperialism' the Agreement is 'no longer in accordance with the spirit of the age'.[1]

The Egyptian arguments deserve some comment. Many treaties or agreements are made under some form of duress, especially those concluded between the very strong and the very weak. At the time, Egypt was certainly not equal to Britain. There is sufficient evidence to show that the Egyptian Government was coerced; but the Big Powers who make international law or custom provide a loophole: 'Coercion invalidates a treaty if it is applied against the persons of the state negotiators, *but not if it is applied against a state.*'[2]

It would be difficult to prove, in the eyes of the law, that coercion was used against the person of Boutros Ghali, who signed the Agreement on behalf of the Egyptian Government.

We may also remark that the principle of Condominium was not then so new as the Egyptians and the Earl of Cromer have suggested, though its application to the Sudan situation might be unique. The word 'Condominium', meaning literally joint domination or collective rule, seems to have been applied by the Romans. It certainly formed the subject of many Latin treatises during the 17th and 18th centuries, often by Germans; for instance *Frommanus De Condominio Territoriali* (Tübingen, 1682). The *Saturday Review* (of New York), 16 September 1882, contained the idea of the 'establishment of a new Condominium with all Europe'.[3] Therefore, though the word might be unfamiliar to some diplomats of 1899, it had long been in use. In any case, we live in a changing world with new situations and problems demanding new solutions. Consequently, the validity of an agreement need not necessarily depend upon the conventionality or novelty of its form.

Further, the parties to an Agreement must be legally competent to contract one in order to make it legally binding upon the signatory states. Dr. J. C. Hurewitz, Professor of International Affairs, Columbia University, questions the validity of the Agreement because 'the Ottoman Sultan had expressly forbidden the Egyptian Khedive from entering into political arrangements with foreign powers'.[4] True enough; but if this point is pressed far enough, Egypt would also seem to have violated the rules of her status with the Sultan by asking for and accepting military aid from Britain. Another weakness of this argument

---

[1] Professor Al Sayed Sabri, 'The 1899 Convention is Null and Void', in *Egypt/Sudan*, published by the Press Section (of the Egyptian Information Department), Cairo, 1947, p. 23.

[2] Schuman, F. L., *International Politics*, p. 161.

[3] *Oxford Dictionary*.   [4] *Foreign Policy Bulletin*, New York, 15 March 1950.

is the fact that there are precedents to the Egyptian situation *vis-à-vis* Turkey and Britain. For instance, on 6 February 1778, France signed treaties of alliance and trade with the United States representatives at Paris, when Britain was still actively engaged in subduing these Americans (then her rebellious colonials), though Britain legally resorted to declaring war against France as a result. Another example is that the United States recognized the independence of Mexico and the other Latin American Republics in 1822 and 1823, when Spain was still claiming them as part of her empire.

The fourth Egyptian argument against the validity of the Agreement rests on the point that the occupation of Egypt by Britain as far back as 1882 renders Egypt a British protectorate, thus reducing the status of Egypt to that of the 'domestic' jurisdiction of Britain. For all practical purposes this is true, but it is not wholly foolproof technically. It is a fact that in a memorandum signed by Milne Cheetham, the British Government 'regard themselves as trustees for the inhabitants of Egypt, and His Majesty's Government have decided that Great Britain can best fulfil the responsibilities she has incurred toward Egypt by the formal declaration of a British protectorate'.[1] But this formal declaration of the protectorate did not take place until 19 December 1914—about fifteen years after the signing of the Condominium Agreement.

The last Egyptian point is based on the evils of imperialism under which the Agreement was made. Granted: but Egypt's adventure in the Sudan, too, was 'imperialistic'. The writer would agree with Professor Sabri that it is 'against the Spirit of the Age'—i.e. our present generation. But imperialism was the order of the day and was still in its glory in 1899 when the Agreement was signed.

Thus, the validity of the Agreement is debatable. Moreover, that it is in many respects unjust there is no doubt—unjust to the Sudanese, who were given no voice in the matter, and to the Egyptians, who were relegated merely to a symbolic role. But in this world of power politics, with so much emphasis on military might and on the philosophy of the 'survival of the fittest', states just and honest are rare. The Egyptian case has many lessons: one which needs stressing, at this juncture of our study, is that foreign auxiliaries and general aids (whether in the nature of the Anglo-Egyptian military combine of 1898 or the Egyptian arms deal with the Soviet bloc in the summer of 1954) should be sought with caution; because 'Only those defences are good, certain and durable, which depend on yourself alone and on your own ability'.[2]

[1] Elgood, *op. cit.*, p. 323.   [2] Machiavelli, *The Prince*, p. 110.

4

THE BEGINNING OF EGYPTIAN PRESSURE
AND BRITISH RESISTANCE

*To win the loyalty of the conquered is difficult so long as national
aspirations for self-determination are denied. To induce ac-
quiescence by distributing material benefits is equally difficult
since benefits are costly and are often received with resentment
rather than with gratitude. . . . To grant genuine independence
to the victims of the game tends to make the game itself quite
pointless.*

FREDERICK L. SCHUMAN, *International Politics*[1]

*To their claim for the possession of the Sudan our refusal should
be uncompromising.*

The Times, editorial, 1924[2]

IN the preceding chapters we have presented the Sudan—the land, its
peoples and certain of its problems; we have given an account of the
expansion of Egypt into the Sudan, of the occupation of Egypt by
Britain, and of the re-conquest of the Sudan by an Anglo-Egyptian
army which culminated in the Anglo-Egyptian Condominium over the
Sudan, beginning from 1899. During most of the period, the interests of
Britain in Egypt and of the Egyptians in their own country were, to all
appearances, more or less the same. With regard to the Sudan, Britain
had given the impression of acting as Egypt's adviser and trustee. But
the Condominium Agreement brought effectively into focus the fact
that Britain did have interests in the Sudan. In theory, the Condominium
made Britain and Egypt co-partners in control of the Sudan. But after
some years it became clear to the Egyptians that Britain was in fact
determined to be permanent master not only in the Sudan but in Egypt
as well. Naturally, Egypt made great efforts to resist British domination
in Egypt as well as in the Sudan. The British, on the other hand, were
unwilling to yield. We may now proceed, therefore, to deal with Egyptian
pressure and British resistance.

[1] 'Cries for Freedom', p. 540.
[2] London, 3 September 1924, p. 13a.

1. EGYPT'S INITIAL CLAIMS FOR THE RESTORATION OF THE SUDAN
(1900–1924)

The period between 1900 and 1919 witnessed economic, educational, political, and other developments both in Egypt and in the Sudan. But it was relatively a calm period in so far as the Anglo-Egyptian dispute over the Sudan itself was directly concerned. There were, however, certain incidents which slowly but surely coalesced and matured to affect the subsequent negotiations for an agreement about the status of the Sudan. These incidents could be arranged under two major and interrelated headings, the general relations between Egypt and Britain, which became strained (over the status of Egypt itself), and the problems arising from the Condominium Agreement when put into practice.

During this period a number of social and political events within Egypt continued to affect adversely Anglo-Egyptian relations in general. These included the effect of Education in Egypt; the declaration of a British Protectorate over Egypt; the Denshawaii Incident; Egypt's Post-War Nationalism; the Decline of British Virtues; and the Deportation of Egyptian Leaders.

When asked to compare the educated with the uneducated, Aristotle once said that one was as much superior to the other as the living was to the dead. Again, J. Horne Tooke (1736–1812) defined the use of education: 'to give us confidence, and to make us think ourselves on a level with other men. An uneducated man thinks there is magic in it, and stands in awe of those who have had the benefit of it.'[1] This definition would apply to the situation in Egypt, in the Sudan, and in colonial territories where demands for national interests often increase with the spread and rise in the general standard of education among native populations.

In the field of education British policy in Egypt was aimed at spreading among the population (mostly among the males) 'a simple form of education' consisting mainly of elementary knowledge of Arabic, Arithmetic and English, and at forming an educated class, suitable for the bare needs of the Government Service. In effect this policy limited the number of the educated class in the population. Free places in the Europeanized schools were abolished, age restrictions were imposed and examination standards set high, etc. 'The idea was that that kind of education turns out a large number of youths unfit for manual labour,

---

[1] Powell, G. H., *Reminiscences and Table Talk of Samuel Rogers*, 1903.

or good only for subordinate positions of which there were not enough to go round.'[1]

Even the British officials themselves were conscious of the limitations of their education policy in Egypt. Lord Cromer's report for 1906 said: 'The Government system of schools, as has been frequently explained, was not conceived and cannot be regarded as a complete expression of the ultimate needs in the matter of education. A national system of education remains to be developed.'[2] Informed opinion in Britain, also, observed that British authorities did not give a 'decent' education to the Egyptians; at a discussion in Chatham House, London, following a Lecture given by Professor Gibb under the auspices of the Royal Institute of International Affairs, a member declared, as late as 1936: 'What Great Britain should have done, and had not done, was to give the Egyptians a decent English education.'[3]

Ineffectual and deliberately limited as the British policy of Egyptian education might have been, it did ultimately produce certain elements among the educated class, who were becoming confident and thinking of themselves as 'on equal level with other men'—even with the British. This consciousness was strengthened by two Egyptian Ministers of Education—Zakki Abu's-Sa'ud Pasha and Ali Mahir Pasha—who committed themselves to making at least elementary education both universal and free; to improving primary and secondary education, to feed institutions of higher learning both in Egypt and abroad; and by Egyptians who studied in continental Europe, of which there were 446 in European countries in 1918. In 1920 Allenby reported that 'an unprecedentedly large number of Egyptian youths are leaving Egypt at the present time for Europe, principally for Berlin and Vienna'.[4] He attributed this to lack of accommodation in the higher colleges in Cairo; to the great difficulty of obtaining admission to the universities in Britain; and to political motives—a belief in the excellence of German and Austrian education and the reports in the Egyptian Press about the warm welcome extended to Egyptian students in Berlin where student life was financially cheap and socially gay. In May 1924, 280 students financed by the Egyptian Government, and 1,204 students at their own expense, were in different European countries.[5]

[1] *Note of Educational Development in Egypt*, before and after the British Declaration of 28 February 1922, communicated to Professor Arnold Toynbee, *Survey of International Affairs for 1925*, Vol. I, London, 1927, p. 583.

[2] Egypt: Report for 1906.

[3] Gibb, Professor H. A. R., 'Situation in Egypt', *International Affairs*, May–June 1936, p. 372.

[4] *Egypt No. 1* (1920), p. 57.   [5] Toynbee, Arnold, *ibid.*, p. 190.

The broad effect of education and travel abroad, added to literacy at home, was to increase the Egyptian national consciousness, which gave impetus to political agitation in Egypt and in the Sudan during the First World War, when Egypt became a protectorate.

Before Egypt became a protectorate there was already considerable political frustration. Whilst Egypt was occupied and administered by Britain, she remained nominally a Turkish province, even though the Porte had lost all practical control. Furthermore, theoretically the Government of Egypt was in the hands of the Khedive, who chose the Ministers and legislated by decrees. But his power was limited externally by the Turkish, if not British, suzerainty. And, above all, the Khedive's authority belonged in practice to the British Agent. He exercised his authority direct by his active interference in the details of administration.[1] The key positions in most of the military and civil departments of the Government were manned by British, either as direct executives or as effective 'backstage' hands. In other words, 'the British advisers were the heads and the Egyptian officials the hands'.[2]

Pressed partly by war-time exigencies and partly by the age-long political desire (the full attainment of which had been made somewhat difficult by the international interests), Britain took certain steps in Egypt—some essential, some just desirable and others seemingly avoidable—during the First World War. At the outbreak of the War, Abbas II (described by the British as the 'notoriously Anti-British Khedive') was at Constantinople as the guest of the Sultan, and Lord Kitchener, who had then become British Agent and Consul-General in Egypt, was home on leave in England. Up to that time, the affairs of Egypt appeared to have been relatively normal, for Lord Kitchener in his report for 1913 indicated that the inhabitants were prosperous and he hoped that this satisfactory state of affairs would continue uninterrupted.[3] But the Khedive did not return to Cairo at the time expected by the British Government. Also, information reaching London suggested to the British that 'agents of the enemy powers were engaged in intrigue against us in Egypt, and that emissaries of Turkey were also actively hostile'.[4] At the end of October 1914, Turkey clearly sided with Germany. A new situation therefore came about with swift and dramatic results. Martial law was proclaimed in Cairo, Germans and Austrians were interned, Turkish agents arrested, and Egyptians whose tendencies

[1] 'Egypt', *The Round Table*, Vol. I, November 1910–August 1911, p. 446.
[2] Marlowe, *op. cit.*, p. 192.
[3] *Reports on Egypt and the Sudan in 1913, Egypt No. 1* (1914), p. 1.
[4] *Annual Register*, 1914.

appeared dangerous to the British were also rounded up. Furthermore, the Foreign Office issued on 18 December 1914, a proclamation making Egypt a Protectorate. It announced: 'His Britannic Majesty's Secretary of State for Foreign Affairs gives notice that in view of the state of war arising out of the action of Turkey, Egypt is placed under the protection of His Majesty and will henceforth constitute a British Protectorate.'

The proclamation is silent as to whether or not the Protectorate was a war-time measure or whether the defence of Egypt by Britain was limited to defence in that war only.

Other drastic measures followed in quick succession. Sir Arthur Henry McMahon was appointed High Commissioner; the office of 'Agent and Consul-General' was abolished. The British Government dispensed with the services of the Egyptian Minister of Foreign Affairs and placed the Egyptian Foreign Office under the new British High Commissioner. On 19 December, the second day after the establishment of the office of High Commissioner, another proclamation was made, deposing Abbas II. This step was graver than the proclamation of the Protectorate. Moreover, Egypt was made the base for Britain's Mediterranean Expeditionary Force for the Gallipoli campaign; and in 1916, thirteen military divisions, and no less than three General Headquarters had been established in Egypt.

In his report for the war period (1914–19), Lord Allenby, with an understatement characteristic of the British, said that 'all classes of the population were, in varying degrees, psychologically disturbed' at having been made to pass under military administration.[1] The published report, 135 pages, omits the measures and proclamations mentioned above, and thus substantiates Keay, who complained in 1882 about official reports from Egypt: 'Officials are themselves the best judges as to how much of their conduct should be submitted to public scrutiny.'[2]

To Egyptians, the word protectorate had an unpleasant connotation. Locally, protection meant 'Himaya', derisively used to describe the status of Christian minorities protected by some European power. The feeling could be compared with that of some Protestants in the United States towards Roman Catholics, who are often regarded—rightly or wrongly—as owing allegiance to the Pope in Italy. The idea of a protectorate was therefore doubly humiliating to the Egyptians. As to the War, they considered themselves no party to the quarrel or to the jealousies and rivalries which had caused the outbreak. Had it been left to the Egyptian Prime Minister, he—with all Egypt—would have

---

[1] *Egypt No. 1* (1920), p. 58.   [2] *Contemporary Review*, 1882, p. 765.

proclaimed neutrality. But there was no way out; because 'at one elbow stood the cool and resourceful Milne Cheatham, temporarily in charge of British diplomatic interests; at the other Byng, commanding the forces in Egypt. Before the insistence of the two Englishmen, Rushdi yielded and signed on 5 August a decree that committed his country irrevocably to war'.[1]

In his discourse on the establishment of the protectorate over Egypt, Amine Yousef Bey, an Egyptian Minister in Washington, often described as a friend of the British, said that it aroused in the Egyptians the thought of the hated capitulations together with the long history of foreign injustices and tyrannies in Egypt. 'But', he continues, 'the essence of it went very much deeper. Egypt had never at any time regarded herself as a part of the British Empire. . . . Now, taking advantage of the generous feelings of the Egyptian people, of their acceptance of the breach with Turkey, of the imposition of martial law . . . the British Government had stolen a march on them. . . .'[2]

Shakespeare says that the evil which men do lives after them, whilst the good is often interred with their bones. This is certainly applicable to the actions of the British during the war. The Egyptians seemed to forget or overlook the good side of British policy. The war crisis brought up memories of past incidents; one of these was the famous Denshawaii incident of 1906. Some British mounted infantry were marching from Cairo to Alexandria, and five officers went off to Denshawaii to shoot pigeons. This resulted in a fight between the officers and a group of villagers with casualties on both sides. A villager died on the spot, and an officer died later. According to official reports, permission should have been obtained from the Omdeh of the village for pigeon shooting by the soldiers. It is not clear whether the hostility of the villagers was due to the shooting of their pigeons (with or without permission) or to a belief that the fire which broke out in a granary was a result of the shots fired by the officers.

In any case, the villagers were brought to trial on a charge of assault against British officers. After three days, a special tribunal passed judgment on twenty-one of the villagers. Four of those considered to be ringleaders were sentenced to death, two to penal servitude for life, one to fifteen years, and six of them to seven years imprisonment. Three were sentenced to one year and fifty lashes; and five to fifty lashes. The executions and floggings, witnessed by 'some 500 natives' were carried

---

[1] Elgood, *op. cit.*, pp. 208–9.
[2] Yousef, Amine, Bey, *Independent Egypt*, London, 1940, pp. 57–8.

out 'on the scene of the outrage and in public'.[1] Even in the House of Commons, many Liberals expressed the view that if any crime had been committed by those executed, it was done under provocation and hardly amounted to murder; and that in any case, the executions and floggings had been carried out with haste and cruelty.[2]

It is no surprise, therefore, that Egyptians should have no great love for the British particularly for this act of excessive vindictiveness; the whole matter was raked up after the declaration of a protectorate. Even as late as January 1956, an Egyptian official told the writer in Cairo: 'The name Denshawaii is still remembered and recalled whenever it is desired to arouse anti-British feeling in Egypt.' The Denshawaii affair, together with the crude methods used by British military authorities in the deeply-resented conscription of manpower, fanned the flame of Egyptian nationalism during the war. This nationalism became an important factor in the furious campaigns of 1919 and 1920, which in turn had its bearings on Egyptian claims in the Sudan.

Most Egyptians, willy-nilly, co-operated with the British in the war effort. They were expecting independence in return for the help given to Britain in her time of need. This expectation was given impetus by a Franco-British Declaration, issued to the Press on 7 November 1918, regarding British and French war aims in the East. One of the significant passages of the Declaration states:

> The object aimed at by France and Britain in prosecuting, in the East, the war let loose by German ambition is complete and definite emancipation of the peoples so long oppressed by the Turks and the establishment of National Governments and administrations deriving their authority from the initiative of the indigenous populations.

This Press release had great effect on opinion, not only in Syria, but also in Arabia, Egypt and Mesopotamia. From it, these subject nations derived a conviction that they would have a free choice in questions wider perhaps than the intentions behind the Franco-British Declaration. It stimulated the spirit of nationalism in the Arab world, and the Egyptians convinced themselves that the long-expected hour of independence had arrived. If Syria could be free, they might have asked, why not Egypt also?

President Wilson's encouraging words to the small nations of the world as embodied in his famous 'Fourteen Points' brought further good cheer to Egypt. Wilson's ideals of national freedom and self-

---

[1] *Correspondence respecting the Attack on British Officers at Danshawaii, Egypt No. 3* (1906), p. 11.

[2] *Parliamentary Debates*, 1906, Vol. CLIX, pp. 342–3; 261; 1619, etc.

determination were discussed with great optimism among the educated elements and there was hope for the dawn of brighter days. They little appreciated the fact that President Wilson was appealing, in the main, on behalf of the smaller Central European nations, many of whose emigrants had become citizens of the United States. He could hardly have imagined that his appeal would be interpreted eventually by the Egyptians and by the other non-'White' peoples of the world as proof that he was basically anti-British, or desirous of the balance of world power weighing in favour of the small nations in Africa and Asia. It came, therefore, as a shock to the Egyptians that the U.S. recognized the British protectorate over Egypt on 23 April 1919.

Egypt had other national frustrations. One was the refusal of the British authorities to grant permission to a proposed Egyptian delegation to Europe and Britain to plead the cause of Egyptian independence. The Egyptian Prime Minister, Rushdi Pasha (who allied Egypt with Britain during the war), and Adli Pasha—the Minister for Justice—also applied for passports to go to England for the purpose of discussing matters with the British Government. They were refused. Again, neither the Egyptian Government nor the delegation were given even a token invitation to the Peace Treaty meetings at Versailles, even though Egypt considered herself a loyal member of the Alliance.

The Egyptians interpreted these attitudes as indicating Britain's intentions of being false to her pledges, and of forcing Egypt permanently into the British Empire without her being allowed to consider the terms on which she was to surrender.

Although Cromer was a great administrator—perhaps greater than any other British administrator of his generation—his last years in Egypt failed to earn him the credit and reputation commensurate with his ability and worth. He was, during most of his administration, faced with a choice between political expediency and administrative efficiency. His name commanded both authority and respect, not only in Egypt but also in Britain. But, like other mortals, he became corrupted by power. 'In his last years in Egypt, Cromer displayed a certain aura of infallibility, and a certain contempt for Egyptian opinion.'[1]

He was succeeded by able but perhaps lesser men.

The war made the situation worse, for it thinned the number, the rank and the quality of British officials in the Anglo-Egyptian Civil Service. Many of the able-bodied younger officials and a few of the older ones were on active service.

[1] Marlowe, *op. cit.*, p. 193.

Furthermore, the war brought into Egypt more men and perhaps women of ordinary calibre, as soldiers, sailors or civilians who were temporarily stationed in Egypt, and whose behaviour often fell short of the standards set by the very disciplined administrators with whom Egyptians had often come into contact. Politics apart, many Egyptians seem to admire and respect the ideals and characteristics of the British people.

But owing partly to the decline in the level of moral conduct set by Cromer and perhaps equally because of the spread and rise of education to which we have referred, the Egyptians were becoming more and more critical and exacting. Their reliance on the British word and administration began to wane. Amine Yousef Bey, the admirer of the British way of life, expressed concern:

> Both in regard to ourselves and to others, the British people, in common with other European peoples, seemed to have lost their best qualities. Everywhere, we saw falsehood, self-seeking, despotism, injustice, violence, not only practised but even preached. What had become of Great Britain's ideals of justice? What right had these Europeans to accuse us orientals of so many of the faults and sins they were themselves openly and unrestrainedly committing? The pedestal on which we had placed the British people was sensibly lowered and our confidence in the good qualities of our own people raised.[1]

Marlowe, himself a loyal British citizen who served in Egypt, says that in Egypt Britain became identified with 'all those forces of reaction and oppression which it has been the aim of the earlier British administrators to eliminate'.[2]

These degenerations were concomitants of the war. Nevertheless, they left their own scars on Anglo-Egyptian relations generally, and have affected Egyptian attitudes towards the Sudan question.

Stirred by the political and psychological conditions which we have tried to explain above, Egyptian feeling became so strong and opposition by London so determined, that Allenby was forced to despatch a telegram pleading with the British Government. He wrote:

> I MUST ask your Lordship and His Majesty's Government to believe me when I state the fact that no Egyptian, NO matter what his personal opinions may be, can sign any instrument which, in his view, is incompatible with complete independence.[3]

[1] Yousef, Amine, Bey, *op. cit.*, pp. 60–1.
[2] *Op. cit.*, p. 258. See also *The Round Table*, Vol. I, 1910–11, p. 446.
[3] Telegraph dated Cairo, 11 December 1921, from Allenby to Marquess Curzon of Kedleston, in *Egypt No. 1* (1922), p. 9.

Sarwat Pasha was willing to form a Ministry only on certain conditions, among which was the item that the 'Ministry will devote themselves to taking up the burden and to directing affairs of the country solely in national interests'.[1] Meanwhile, Zaghlul Pasha, apparently a less compromising Nationalist, was prohibited from participation in politics by Allenby's imposition of Martial Law. Zaghlul reacted through a Memorandum of defiance, calling the prohibition

> a tyrannical order, against which I protest with all my power, because there is no justification for it. As I am delegated by the people to strive for their independence, no one else has any authority to free me from this sacred duty. . . . Force can do what it wishes with us individually and collectively as we are all prepared to meet what may befall us with a steady heart and a calm conscience.[2]

Zaghlul's defiance appeared too much for the British military authorities in Egypt, and some forty-eight hours later, Zaghlul and three other national leaders—members of the Wafd Party—were conducted to Port Said and from there deported to Malta. The die was cast. The news flashed through Egypt, and general revolt became inevitable. Schools and even Government officials went on strike,[3] there was rioting in Cairo and other large towns, students paraded the streets shouting for Zaghlul and for independence for Egypt. Thus, contrary to the effects desired by the military authorities, Zaghlul and the three others became, while in exile, greater menaces than when in Egypt.[4]

These and other incidents the Egyptians have perhaps forgiven, but certainly not forgotten. They seemed to bury their hatchets only to dig them up for use as occasion required. Memories of these incidents came to the surface in Egyptian minds each time they negotiated with Britain over the Sudan. When the British declared that they had moral obligations to the Sudan, the Egyptians and the Sudanese recalled unfulfilled pledges to Egypt, and then doubts cropped up. For instance, Mr. Herbert Morrison, when British Foreign Secretary in the Labour Government, made a statement in the House of Commons on 30 July 1951, in which he referred to the problem of the past still living in the present. 'Now I come to the Sudan. We are now discussing with the

---

[1] *Ibid.*, p. 11.   [2] *Ibid.*, p. 14.   [3] *Ibid.*, p. 17.

[4] Compare the more recent cases of: (i) Prince Seretse Khama of Bechuanaland, who was exiled in England, seemingly for marrying an English woman; (ii) His Royal Highness the Kabaka of Buganda, who was exiled in England for, to all appearances, his indocility or refusal to comply with certain official instructions, but who became popular in England as 'King Freddie'; and (iii) the case of His Holiness Archbishop Makarios of Cyprus, who was exiled to the Seychelles for the part he played in the nationalist movement of Cyprus.

Egyptian Government the future of the Sudan. Here, again, we are faced with certain prejudices which prevent the Egyptian Government from approaching the problem in a realistic frame of mind. . . .'

With the above situation as a psychological background, we may now proceed to give an account of Anglo-Egyptian negotiations made in an attempt to reshape the status of the Sudan.

We have shown in the last chapter that the Condominium Agreement of 1899 set up an administrative form of government in which the British assumed nearly all authority in more or less the same way as they had done in Egypt proper. Although the Agreement reduced Egypt practically to a mere symbolic role in the Sudan, she was left with certain rights expressed or implied. Yet Britain did not avoid giving the impression that she was violating these rights of Egypt in the Sudan. The first Anglo-Egyptian difficulties over the status of the Sudan arose, therefore, from a series of apparent violations. Among these were the Frontier Treaty with Ethiopia. In 1902 (just three years after the Condominium Agreement) Britain concluded an Agreement with Ethiopia concerning the frontiers between the Sudan and Ethiopia. Article V of the Treaty provides for the Emperor of Ethiopia to grant the British Government and the Government in the Sudan the right to construct a railway through Ethiopian territory to connect the Sudan with Uganda,[1] a British territory. In the first place, Britain ignored consulting Egypt about the Anglo-Ethiopian treaty affecting the Sudan. Secondly, Egypt suspected that the construction of a British railway connecting the Sudan with Uganda might be a preliminary step towards political annexation of the two territories under British suzerainty.

Then there was the making of laws unilaterally by the British. The last paragraph of Article IV of the Condominium Agreement rules that all laws proclaimed in the Sudan ought to be approved both by the British and Egyptian Governments. In his report for 1904, Cromer emphasized this point: 'Every Sudan Ordinance, before it becomes law, is submitted to the Egyptian Council of Ministers and examined by them.'[2] Britain continued this practice till 1912, when the Governor-General began to issue laws without seeking the approval of the Egyptian Government. 'In some cases', Egyptians complained, 'he went so far as to ignore even notifying the Egyptian Government of the promulgation of such laws'.[3]

Another difficulty arose over the filling of the post of Governor-

---

[1] *Treaty Series, Egypt No. 1* (1904).   [2] *Egypt No. 1* (1905), p. 110.
[3] Abdel-Moneim Omar, *The Sudan Question*, Cairo, 1952, p. 69.

General. The text of the Agreement does not provide, either by direct declaration or by implication, that the Governor-General should be either British or Egyptian. It merely, in Article III, indicates the process of appointing and removing the Governor-General of the Sudan. It would appear fair to both Governments if terms of office were held alternately by British and Egyptian nationals. But for 57 consecutive years—from 1899 until December 1955, the Governors-General were without exception British. In addition, all the high posts in the Administration were given to British officers, even though Egypt paid about five-sixths of the joint military expenditure in the Sudan. It is difficult to tell how much of this situation was due to a British suggestion that educated Egyptians prefer city life in Egypt to administrative work in the Sudan.

Next, the Sudan's national economy became increasingly prosperous. In 1913, the value of external trade—private and Government—was recorded as £E3,388,000, whilst in 1924 it was £E9,305,000—an increase of 174·6 per cent.[1] Conditions were so good as to encourage Allenby to report to Sir Austen Chamberlain that 'The economic progress of the country has been considerable, and administration has been developed, public health has been excellent, and the general condition of the people has shown material improvement'.[2] But Egypt was hindered from sharing with Britain this economic prosperity, partly because the Sudan Government gained practical autonomy by succeeding in making the Sudan financially independent of Egypt in 1913, and also because the 1922 Declaration made the Sudan one of the four points 'absolutely reserved to' His Majesty's Government. Consequently, Egypt, who contributed financially to the prosperity of the territory, became frustrated and disgruntled. In his report for 1900, for instance, Reginald Wingate, the Governor-General, thanked Egypt for the liberal financial help given, and appealed for more.[3]

Egypt, which had previously been having greater trade with the Sudan than had Britain, became decreasingly significant whilst Britain became increasingly important in this regard. For example, in 1923, Egypt imported only 21·4 per cent of the Sudan's trade whilst Britain imported 40 per cent, whereas in 1919 the shares had been 37 per cent and 26·5 per cent respectively. Another cause for Egyptian complaint was the fact that the Sudan was represented at the British Empire Exhibition at

---

[1] *Report on the Finances, Administration, etc., of the Sudan in 1924, Sudan No. 1* (1925), p. 24.
[2] *Ibid.*   [3] *Egypt No. 1* (1901), pp. 70–1.

Wembley, London, 1924. When the Egyptian Government asked the Governor-General of the Sudan why this was arranged without consultation with Egypt, Lord Allenby replied that Britain would have no objection to the Sudan participating in an Egyptian exhibition without consultation with the British Government.

For these several reasons, Egyptians appeared to conclude that the Agreement was being worked to benefit Britain at the expense of Egypt, and that Britain accepted them into the Condominium mainly because the Sudan was a financial liability at the time of the reconquest. Their position—that of a mere tool in the Sudan venture—was a wound to their pride, and a great disappointment to their expectations, for they expected that the benefits accruing from the Sudan venture would be shared equally.

Writing generally on the violation of the Agreement, Professor Toynbee asserts that Egyptian national feeling concerning the Sudan was 'further irritated by the habit into which Englishmen, even in high places, had fallen of thinking, and acting, as though the Sudan were not subject to an Anglo-Egyptian Condominium, but was an integral part of the British Empire'.[1] National feeling against the Agreement became so strong that Boutros Ghali, the Foreign Minister who signed it with Cromer, was assassinated on Sunday, 20 February 1910, though the immediate occasion was a proposal to prolong the Suez Canal concessions. According to Sir E. Gorst, who was the British Agent and Consul-General in Egypt,

> The murderer had no personal grudge against his victim, and was not acting under the influence of religious fanaticism. His deed merely repeated the accusations which have in season and out of season been alleged against Boutros Pasha, in violent and threatening language, in the columns of the Nationalist Press.[2]

In consequence of the factors we have analysed, Egypt sought ways and means to alter the *status quo*. The question of the Sudan in Anglo-Egyptian relations came up several times soon after the First World War: during the visit of the Milner Commission, 1919–20; during the negotiations on the Nile Waters, 1921; at the declaration of Egyptian Independence, February 1922; during the MacDonald-Zaghlul talk in September 1924; and when Sir Lee Stack, Governor-General of the Sudan, was assassinated, November 1924.

Before discussing these attempted negotiations, however, it is essential to give an indication of the general British attitude and feeling about

[1] *Survey of International Affairs*, 1925, Vol. I, p. 242.
[2] Annual Reports: Egypt and the Sudan, *Egypt No. 1* (1901), p. 1.

the Sudan question. It should be remembered, as indicated in chapter 2, that the Mahdist revolt came about partly as a result of what was considered to be inefficient Egyptian administration in the Sudan, and that for many years Egypt had to admit the supremacy of the Mahdists until the British Government joined Egypt in active steps to 'smash the Mahdi'. Although Sir Francis Drake and John Hawkins, perhaps the most notorious trans-Atlantic slave merchants, when Britain was the foremost slave-trading nation of the Western world, were English, William Wilberforce, perhaps the greatest advocate of the abolition of slavery (when in the 19th century Britain repented and became the emancipator) was also British. Although the British Government did not actively support the suppression of slavery in the Sudan,[1] Samuel Baker and General Gordon, encouraged by the Anti-Slavery Society and Missionary Societies, were most instrumental in stopping the slave traffic not only in the Sudan but also in Egypt itself. British control subsequently ended completely slavery in the two countries. Many British observers therefore felt that Egyptian control in the Sudan might lead to slavery. 'There is the Sudan itself,' said the Marquess of Salisbury, 'where the loss of our controlling power might bring back all those scenes of barbarism which most of us can remember and from which we saved the people'.[2]

Quite naturally, the British were proud of the constructive work accomplished in the Sudan on their initiative and under their direction since the time they assumed authority in the territory. The country was increasingly prosperous and, in the field of education, the Gordon Memorial College, established in 1899, had been opened in 1902. There was fear that Egyptian rule in the Sudan might create such uncertainties and governmental instability as to discourage capital investments from abroad, particularly from Britain.[3]

In a Foreign Office despatch to the British High Commissioner for Egypt and the Sudan, Ramsay MacDonald declared:

> Since going there [to the Sudan], they [the British Government] have contracted heavy moral responsibilities as a trust for the Sudan people; there can be no question of their abandoning the Sudan until their work is done.[4]

---

[1] In a letter, dated 1 February 1884, to Charles H. Allen, the Secretary of the British and Foreign Anti-Slavery Society, Baker complained: 'The British Government is not earnest, neither did it exhibit the slightest interest in the difficult task I undertook, nor in those of my excellent successor, Colonel Gordon.' *Samuel Baker: A Memoir*, p. 204.

[2] The Marquess of Salisbury in the House of Lords on 4 November 1920, *Parliamentary Debates* (House of Lords), Vol. XLII, 1920, p. 183.

[3] *The Times*, London, 18 July 1924, p. 13a.

[4] *Position of H.M. Government in regard to Egypt and the Sudan*, Cmd. 2269 (1924), p. 4.

Sir Ivor Jennings, speaking in February 1955 about the conflict of Colonialism with Nationalism in British Dependencies generally, stated the British case, which is applicable to the Sudan question:

> We want to hand over responsibility as soon as we can. On the other hand, we have spent a good deal of time, money and energy in building up a sound economy, an efficient administrative system, and a truly British judicial system—we do not want it to deteriorate badly when we leave; in fact, we believe, rightly, that it is not in the interests of the people that it should.[1]

A section of the Milner Report (1919) appraised British administration in the Sudan and it became an often-quoted passage by all parties in the House of Commons.[2]

With this belief, the British tended to regard the well-governed and increasingly prosperous Sudan of the 20th century as their own exclusive creation and therefore their own affair only. This British attitude and feeling is often summed up in the official and parliamentary phrase— 'Our responsibility in the Sudan'—which contains much more than is actually expressed. As a result, the British were shocked and exasperated when the Egyptians presented their claims in a manner seemingly militant and extreme. In like manner, the Egyptians were shocked when the British turned down their claims as being preposterous. Thus there existed on both sides all the elements of misunderstanding and bitterness which matured to produce violent and tragic consequences in 1924, when Sir Lee Stack was assassinated.

With this background in mind, we must now turn attention to the series of attempted negotiations. First there was the Milner Commission.

Owing to the manifestations of violence and general disorder in Egypt which had been simmering for some years as we have shown, the British Government despatched a Special Mission to Egypt, under the Chairmanship of the Right Hon. the Viscount Milner, Britain's Principal Secretary of State for the Colonies. The Mission, which arrived in Egypt in December 1919, was to enquire into the causes of the unrest in Egypt which had culminated in violence in 1919; to report on the existing situation in the country, and to suggest the form of constitution which, under the Protectorate, will be best calculated to promote its peace and prosperity, the progressive development of self-governing institutions, and the protection of foreign interests.[3]

[1] 'Making Self-Government Work', *The Listener*, Vol. LIII, No. 1355, London, 17 February 1955.
[2] *Parliamentary Debates*, 10 July 1924, Vol. CLXXV (1924), pp. 2508–9.
[3] *Egypt No. 1* (1921), Cmd. 1131, p. 1.

The terms of reference were mute on the Sudan Question, and the Commission 'deliberately excluded' them.[1] It seems, however, that the Egyptian public, if not their delegates to the Commission, had in their minds that the scope of discussions included, or should include, the status of the Sudan. In any case, Lord Milner had to write to Adli Pasha on 18 August 1920, confirming their joint conversation the previous day concerning the Sudan. The letter was 'once more to repeat' the view of the Mission that the Sudan Question lay outside the proposed agreement with Egypt, and the belief that there was a wide difference in conditions between Egypt and the Sudan. On the other hand, the letter conceded one point to Egypt, namely the Egyptian interest in the waters of the Nile: 'We fully realize the vital interest of Egypt in the supply of water reaching her through the Soudan, and we intend to make proposals calculated to remove any anxiety which Egypt may feel as to the inadequacy of that supply both for her actual and prospective needs.'

On 4 November 1920, the Egyptian question was raised in the House of Lords as a result of the Milner proposals. The Marquess of Salisbury submitted four considerations, the third of which declared that the Government of the Sudan ought to be in the hands of Britain, and the fourth referred to the position of Britain's military requirements in the Sudan. In reply, Lord Curzon informed the House that the Government was carefully considering the proposals of the Milner Mission but emphasized that the proposals, though authoritative, were not the Government's scheme, and that when matters had reached a more advanced stage, properly accredited representatives of the Egyptian and British Governments should meet to arrive at a solution.[2] Therefore, the Milner Commission reached no effective agreement with Egyptian delegates in 1920.

There followed the Adli–Curzon Negotiations in 1921. In pursuance of his statement in Parliament, Curzon received in England an Egyptian delegation, led by Adli Pasha, the Prime Minister. They met to negotiate a settlement of every aspect of the Egyptian and Sudan Questions. Lord Curzon gave an undertaking to secure for Egypt a fair share of the Nile Waters, and to guarantee that the concurrence of a Board of Conservators representing Egypt, the Sudan and Uganda, would be sought before any further irrigation works were constructed on the Nile south of Wadi Halfa. In return for this undertaking, Curzon urged on

[1] *Ibid.*, p. 32.
[2] *Parliamentary Debates* (House of Lords), Vol. XLII, 1920, pp. 179–98.

Adli Pasha the continuance of Egypt's contribution to the military expenditure in the Sudan. But Adli Pasha refused to accept any agreement which failed to 'guarantee to Egypt her indisputable right of sovereignty over that country and the control of the waters of the Nile'.[1] No settlement was reached, and Adli, with his colleagues, returned to Cairo at the end of the year empty-handed. On his arrival in Egypt, Adli and the other members of the Egyptian Cabinet resigned collectively as a result of frustrations they suffered from the failure of these negotiations.

Lastly came the Declaration of Egyptian Independence and of the Status of the Sudan. As a result of vigorous agitation for independence, the absence of any Egyptian Cabinet, and the withdrawal of effective 'native co-operation' in the administration of Egypt, Britain was forced to declare Egypt an independent sovereign state. The Unilateral Declaration, made on 28 February 1922, terminated the British protectorate over Egypt but established the Sudan as one of the 'four matters absolutely reserved to the discretion of His Majesty's Government until such time as it may be possible by free discussion and friendly accommodation on both sides to conclude agreements in regard thereto between His Majesty's Government and the Government of Egypt'.[2] The other three matters 'reserved' to Britain were: the security of the communications of the British Empire; the defence of Egypt against all foreign aggression or interference, direct or indirect; and the protection of foreign interests in Egypt and the protection of minorities.

While critical of the unilateral character of the Declaration, Egypt seized the advantage of the opportunity for which it had opened the way. In March, Sultan Fuad formally expressed the new international status of Egypt by assuming a new title—'King' (Malik) in place of 'Sultan'. In April, a commission was appointed to draft a new parliamentary constitution for Egypt. In May, Rushdi Pasha announced to the Drafting Commission an Egyptian scheme for a new Anglo-Egyptian Convention, which would, in effect, greatly increase the Egyptian and diminish the British control over the Sudan.

The Egyptian Constitution for the Sudan, became, at this stage, the subject of a question in the House of Commons, in London. On 15 May, the Prime Minister's attention was called to reports that the Egyptian Constitution Commission had declared the Sudan to be an inseparable

---

[1] *Papers respecting Negotiations with the Egyptian Delegation, Egypt No. 4* (1921), Cmd. 1555, p. 9.

[2] *Correspondence respecting Affairs in Egypt, Egypt No. 1* (1922), pp. 29–30.

part of Egypt; and would he state what attitude the British Government proposed to take in regard to the matter?[1] In reply, Sir Austen Chamberlain informed the House that Lord Allenby, British High Commissioner, had warned the Egyptian Prime Minister about the impropriety on the part of Egypt of incorporating in her new constitution any clause dealing with the Sudan—one of the specially reserved subjects.[2] The draft Constitution, however, contained, in fact, two articles about the Sudan; the first provided that the titular head in Egypt should be styled 'King of Egypt and the Sudan', and the second that the Constitution was inapplicable to the Sudan which would have a separate regime although it formed (declared the draft Constitution) an integral part of the Egyptian Kingdom. Lord Allenby, as British High Commissioner, reacted swiftly and 'demanded that the Egyptian Government should consent, within twenty-four hours, to delete all reference to the Sudan from the draft'.[3] The Egyptian Government seem to have obeyed only to complain later—the Prime Minister agreed provisionally on the understanding that final decision should be taken by the Egyptian Parliament when it resumed sitting. Without giving the British Government time to reply to the suggestion, the Prime Minister —Tewfick Nessim Pasha—resigned. No agreement was therefore reached. The Sudan, however, became the subject of parliamentary questions both in Cairo and in London, until the MacDonald–Zaghlul negotiations in 1924.

What seemed to be the main obstruction to agreement at this stage was the fact that the terms of the Declaration of the Independence of Egypt contained latent contradictions. The 'sovereign independence' granted in the first clause was potentially denied by the four reservations which followed. We must note, however, that an agreement on the four reserved points, of which the Sudan was one, was not inherently impossible.

Meanwhile, the scene of action shifted to the Sudan itself, where the seeds of discontent had germinated. The peaceful tone of the reports from the Sudan became rudely interrupted in 1924 by 'political agitation which threatened public security for the first time in the history of the Condominium'.[4] A White Flag Society, with the aim of uniting the whole Valley of the Nile with Egypt as a single independent state, was organized in Khartoum. The Society included such native Sudanese as

---

[1] Pennefather in *Parliamentary Debates*, Vol. CLIV, 1922, p. 14.
[2] *Ibid.*, p. 15.
[3] Toynbee, *Survey of International Affairs*, p. 244.
[4] From Allenby to Chamberlain: *Sudan No. 1* (1925), p. 4.

ex-students of Gordon College, ex-officials and Egyptian residents in the Sudan. Anti-British and pro-Egyptian demonstrations and disturbances took place at four main points—Atbara, Khartoum, Omdurman and Port Sudan; eventually they culminated in violence. On 9 August, Egyptian and Sudanese cadets from the Khartoum Military School marched with arms and ammunition through the streets of the town, visiting such places as the prison in which Abdul-Latif Effendi, leader of the White Flag Society, was serving a sentence of three years for sedition, imposed by the British administration. During the night anonymous notices inciting feeling against British rule were affixed to telegraph poles and houses. The notices said in part: 'We Sudanese intelligentsia, on behalf of the inhabitants of the Sudan, declare our hatred of the British Government. Long live our comrade Ali Abdul-Latif and the leaders of the military school. Down with British domination.'[1] On that day, too, some Egyptian soldiers, employed by the Sudan Government, mutinied, committing wholesale sabotage on Government property for three successive days. With the arrival of British naval and military reinforcements in Egypt and the Sudan, the unrest was quelled, and mixed Anglo-Egyptian military courts of enquiry later passed various sentences on those they considered guilty of one form of offence or another. Abdul-Latif Effendi died in exile in 1948, at Abbassia Asylum in Cairo.

On 16 August 1924, the Egyptian Legation in London handed to the British Foreign Office a Note protesting against the action of the British Government about the disturbances in the Sudan. In their Note, dated 29 August, the British replied that they were determined to maintain the occupation of the Sudan unchanged.[2] However, Egyptians continued to hope that negotiations might alter British policy. Consequently, the whole subject of the future status of the Sudan was raised during the subsequent talks in London between MacDonald and Zaghlul Pasha. To these we must now turn.

In pursuance of the decree ordering the first general election under the new Egyptian Constitution, the Egyptians went to the polls. The election results returned to power the Wafd Party, led by Zaghlul Pasha, with an overwhelming majority. Consequently, Zaghlul, formerly deported to Malta by the British, emerged in January 1924 as the first Prime Minister under the new Constitution. With the formation of a constitutional Government in Egypt, the way was prepared for re-

[1] *The Times*, 16 August 1920, p. 10.
[2] *The Times*, 2 September 1924, p. 10a.

opening negotiations between the British and Egyptian Governments on the four reserved points, among which the Sudan was the most topical.

Furthermore, a Labour Government came into power in London almost simultaneously with the Wafd Government in Cairo. The two new Prime Ministers had had friendly relations in the past, and Zaghlul expected an entirely sympathetic attitude on the part of the British Government. Some hints at the hopes aroused in his mind at the accession of Ramsay MacDonald to office in Britain were embodied in Zaghlul's speech a little before he was sworn in as Egyptian Prime Minister. He said: 'We, at any rate, are ready to negotiate in a spirit of equity, with a view to arriving at an agreement which will guarantee the independence of that we demand [for Egypt with the Sudan] while respecting such British interests as are reasonable and acceptable.'[1]

MacDonald, too, showed signs of optimism. In a telegram he sent cordial greetings to the 'newest of Parliaments' and invited the Egyptian Premier to London in these words:

I believe that Britain will be tied by a strong bond of friendship, our desire being to see this bond made stronger on a permanent basis. For this purpose, the Government of His Majesty the King is ready now and at any time to negotiate with the Egyptian Government.[2]

In the speech from the Throne at the opening of the Egyptian Parliament, the Egyptian Government answered the British invitation solemnly:

You have before you the most grave and delicate task upon which the future of Egypt depends, the task of realizing her complete independence in the true meaning of the word. . . . My Government is ready to enter into negotiations, free of all restrictions, with the British Government so as to realize our national aspirations with regard to Egypt and the Sudan.

An invitation to Zaghlul to meet MacDonald was sent in the Spring of 1924. Zaghlul arrived at Victoria Station on 23 September; he was met by an organized demonstration of Egyptian and Sudanese students in Britain who shouted 'Long live Zaghlul! Long live Egypt and the Sudan! Long live King Fuad, King of Egypt and the Sudan!'[3]

At their first meeting at Downing Street, on 25 September, the

[1] *Oriente Moderno*, IV, 2, p. 124.
[2] Egyptian Kingdom Royal Ministry for Foreign Affairs.
[3] Glasgow, G., *MacDonald as Diplomatist—The Foreign Policy of the First Labour Government in Britain*, London, 1924, p. 217.

Premiers discussed the Suez Canal problem but parted in disagreement. The second one, held on the 28th, was focused on the Sudan. Both men were uncompromising. The Egyptian Premier insisted on Egypt's complete right of control over the Sudan, whilst MacDonald maintained his earlier statement that the Egyptian aspirations 'do conflict too hopelessly with our irreducible requirements regarding the Sudan and the defence of the Canal'.[1]

The Egyptian claim over the Sudan at this time was supported by the argument that Britain had held the Sudan in trust for Egypt as a 'minor'. Now that the minor had come of age, the trusteeship should be relinquished. The metaphor might be appropriate, but perhaps it would have been more practical for Egypt to start by demanding amendments to the provisions of the Condominium Agreement, rather than to ask for complete control at a time when Egypt herself was struggling to settle down as an independent state. But perhaps Egypt, realizing the tenacity of Britain, aimed at the star to obtain the moon.

It is striking, however, and perhaps ironical, that MacDonald, personally a declared pacifist, and officially committed to the 'Principle of diplomatic pacifism' which earned for the first Labour Government a high reputation in foreign relations, should have failed in his last act about the Sudan Question as Britain's Foreign Secretary.

We may attempt to explain the paradox and give some of the underlying factors of the MacDonald–Zaghlul diplomatic failure. Both men were influenced by 'diehard' pressures from the extremists in their respective parties, and parliaments. As a person, MacDonald possessed not only a sound mind but also a kind heart devoted to peace and amity among nations.

In the House of Commons he had appealed to all concerned to be reasonable, hoping 'that Egypt and ourselves will remain friends—for each other's good and for the good of all the peoples of the countries round about us'.[2] But some M.P.s wanted it to be known that 'If Egypt refuses partnership with us, then it must be decided in regard to the Sudan that Egypt must go, because we are not going to go.'[3] Lord Parmoor, speaking in the House of Lords on 26 June, had also warned: 'His Majesty's Government are not going to abandon the Sudan in any sense whatever.' Zaghlul, too, though often described as a firebrand nationalist agitator, was a reasonable man as an individual, and also

---

[1] Foreign Office Despatch, 3 April 1924.
[2] *Parliamentary Debates*, 10 July 1924, Official Reports, Vol. CLXXV (1924), p. 2533.
[3] Col. Sir Charles Yate, *Parliamentary Debates, ibid.*, p. 2541.

when in office.[1] According to Marlowe, Zaghlul was never personally an Anglophobe. His personal relations with the Englishmen with whom he came into contact were steadily cordial. He conducted political battles against Britain with bravery and vehemence, but with no personal animosity. For instance, when in exile he won money from the British officers responsible for guarding him at Malta by beating them every night at poker.

In the words of Lord Winterton, 'The present Prime Minister of Egypt is a man of great ability and indeed a genius of whom the late Lord Cromer is reported to have said that he was the ablest and most progressive of all the young politicians.'[2] But like many other nationalist figures, he often followed and did not lead his 'wild men'.

MacDonald might have been influenced by the policy and commitments inherited from his predecessors, as well as by the advice of the permanent officials of the Foreign Office and the Press. As for Zaghlul, the memory of British war-time behaviour in Egypt, and of his own deportation to Malta by the British administration, may have haunted him.

Finally, in Britain, Governments come and go, but the objectives of the colonial and foreign policies remain essentially the same; British Labour Governments have always been as jealous and fully as capable of upholding British vital interests abroad as any other Government, Conservative or Liberal. The main difference lies in the general method of approach—Labour appears readier to obtain Britain's objectives through a degree of 'fraternization'.

Consequently, the negotiations were more nominal than real; the talks inevitably collapsed. Zaghlul's summary of his experiences during the London conference was laconic and graphic: 'They invited us to London that we might commit suicide.'[3] He returned to Egypt frustrated, and the Egyptian Government, unable to forgive what was considered the British rebuff, became more irreconcilable. The anti-British campaign was resumed with vigour by the Egyptian Press and public. The whole issue came to a head on 19 November 1924, when the Governor-General of the Sudan, Sir Lee Stack, was assassinated in

---

[1] Compare Dr. Azikiwe in Nigeria and Dr. Nkrumah in the Gold Coast, first as Nationalist 'agitators' and then as men with ministerial responsibilities. (Dr. Azikiwe is currently Prime Minister of the Regional Government, Eastern Nigeria, and Dr. Nkrumah the Prime Minister of Ghana.)

[2] *Parliamentary Debates, ibid.,* p. 2514.

[3] *The Annual Register* 1924, p. 286. For instance, during Mahatma Gandhi's struggle for Indian self-government, Mr. Winston Churchill had shewn no qualms about calling Gandhi 'the naked fakir', just as Gladstone called the Mahdi 'the false prophet'.

Cairo. The incident put the hands of the clock back for Egypt and forward for Britain in the Sudan.

2. THE ASSASSINATION OF SIR LEE STACK AND THE BRITISH ULTIMATUM, 1924

Because of their far-reaching effects on Anglo-Egyptian relations in general, and on the respective claims of the two countries with regard to the Sudan in particular, it is pertinent to discuss the circumstances surrounding the assassination of Sir Lee Stack, Governor-General of the Sudan and Commander-in-Chief of the Egyptian army; the measures taken by Britain over the incident; and Egyptian reactions thereto. In its wider aspect, the Anglo-Egyptian crisis over the assassination is of interest in the study of international relations. It raises the general question of how far a state could be held responsible for a political crime committed in its territory and of how far the state of the person against whom the crime is committed can go in taking measures of reprisal. In its restrictive aspect, it has left a lasting mark on the Egyptian. Writing in 1954, about thirty years thereafter, General Neguib complained: 'Allenby issued an ultimatum that few Egyptians of my age have either forgotten or forgiven.'[1]

The Stack incident, judged by the standard of international politics of today, would seem crude indeed. But it happened in 1924, when 'hatchet politics' was prevalent in excitable Egypt and when Britannia still ruled the waves—when Britain's policy was: 'What we have we hold.' The British policy of get-tough-with-the-Egyptians, which we shall discuss presently, must be understood in the light of the imperial fears of that day: 'Unless we can harden our hearts and turn a deaf ear to demands, however persistent, we shall lose our Empire and shall have deserved to lose it.'[2]

Before going into the Stack incident, however, it is essential to indicate some of the relevant elements preceding it. Domestic politics often have repercussions much more far-reaching than intended or expected. The collapse of the Labour Government and the return of the Conservatives by the end of 1924 had various effects in Egypt and the Sudan. In Britain the prospect of a Labour Government coming into power in January 1924 had been viewed with great alarm by large and influential sections of the community as it had been received with some feelings of hope in Egypt, the Sudan, and the British territories overseas where attention

---

[1] *Egypt's Destiny*, London, 1955, p. 63.
[2] *The Round Table*, September 1924, p. 682.

was (and still is) generally focused on political developments in the 'Mother' Country. The Liberals were accused by Labour circles of a 'plot' or 'conspiracy' to turn Labour out of office and to put the Conservatives in.

The Egyptians and Sudanese probably read with despair, if not with active alarm,[1] the editorial in *The Times* on the eve of election day, which urged the electorate to vote Conservative and warned that a Labour victory would be a 'constitutional rebellion' because the Labour Party aimed at 'a really socialist Commonwealth' which would in effect destroy the principles upon which the British State and Empire were based.[2]

In any case, as a result of the polling which took place on 29 October, Baldwin's second Conservative Ministry took office on 7 November, and a new element was at once introduced into the Anglo-Egyptian problem. Just a few days after the Conservative Government assumed office, a step was taken which confirmed Egyptian fears. The Assembly of the League of Nations had adopted the Geneva Protocol for the Pacific Settlement of International Disputes, which, by a resolution adopted on 2 October 1924, was made open for signature not only by members of the League but by all other states (including Egypt, in effect). The preamble to the Protocol announced that it was 'animated by the firm desire to ensure the maintenance of peace and the security of Nations whose existence, independence or territories may be threatened'.[3] Realizing this to be a potential weapon for Egypt whose territory—the Sudan—might be considered 'threatened', the new British Secretary of State (Sir Austen Chamberlain) quickly despatched a Note to the Secretary-General of the League on 19 November. The Note sought to prevent the League from intervening in what had then become 'the Egyptian Crisis'; it stated that as the terms of the League's resolution might suggest the communication of the Protocol to the Government of Egypt for signature, Britain would maintain her position under the *reserved subjects* in the Declaration of Egyptian Independence. The Note warned, that the British Government 'would consider as an unfriendly act any attempt at interference in the affairs of Egypt by another power. . . .'[4]

---

[1] In British dependencies (and semi-dependencies like Egypt) a Labour Government in comparison with a Conservative one, is almost always regarded as the lesser of two evils.
[2] *The Times*, 28 October 1924.
[3] *Protocol for the Pacific Settlement of International Disputes*, Cmd. 2273 (1924), p. 38.
[4] Text in *The Times*, 5 December 1924.

Egyptians may have been aware of the British intention to forestall Egypt and thwart her case before the League. In any case, by some curious and ironic coincidence, Sir Lee Stack was shot on 19 November, the very day on which the British Foreign Office Note to the League about Egypt was despatched. The incident took place in Cairo, when he was going in his car from the Egyptian War Office to the Sirdaria (the official residence of the head of the Egyptian Army) for luncheon. Near the Ministry of Public Instruction, 'seven Egyptians of the student class in effendi dress . . . all simultaneously opened fire'.[1] But the assassins eluded pursuit. Sir Lee Stack died the following day.

It should be noted that both Lord Allenby, the British High Commissioner for Egypt and the Sudan, and Sir Lee Stack were on leave in London when the military riots had occurred in August and they had both been called into conference in London about the measures to be taken.

The question of how much responsibility actually rests on the Egyptian Government in this matter has been a sore point. Evidently, the assassination of Sir Lee Stack deeply affected leading members of the Egyptian Government. Within an hour of the news of the assassination, the Egyptian Prime Minister (Zaghlul Pasha), with the Minister of the Interior, hastened to the scene of the crime and from there proceeded to carry the 'doleful news' to King Fuad, who immediately sent his Grand Chamberlain to convey to the British High Commissioner his profound regrets for the attempt on the life of Sir Lee Stack Pasha—a crime which he strongly condemned. He asked that his sympathy be conveyed to H.M. King George and to the British Government.[2]

King Fuad's Chamberlain immediately visited Lady Stack with a similar message of grief. The Prime Minister also expressed deep sorrow to the High Commissioner, assuring him that the Egyptian Government would leave no stone unturned to trace the criminals for punishment. Furthermore, he issued an appeal to the Egyptian people to help the Government in identifying the guilty persons.

According to *The Times*, in London, the Egyptian Government offered a reward of £E10,000 to anyone who could identify all the culprits or £E1,000 for each single culprit.[3] On 21 November 1924, Izzet Pasha, the Egyptian Minister in London, called at the British Foreign Office and expressed to Sir Austen Chamberlain the sorrow of the Egyptian Government and people.[4] The Egyptian Press, normally

[1] Text in *The Times*, 20 November 1924.   [2] Omar, *op. cit.*, p. 80.
[3] *The Times*, 20 November 1924.   [4] *Ibid.*, 22 November 1924.

anti-British in tone, abandoned their scurrilous tendencies at least temporarily; they unanimously regretted the crime, and vehemently denounced it.

The funeral was attended by the Grand Chamberlain as representative of King Fuad, and by the Egyptian Premier, the Presidents of the Senate and the Chamber of Deputies, as well as Ministers.

Meanwhile, the inquiry, instituted by the Egyptian Government soon after the crime, continued; the man driving one of the cars in which the assassins had fled was arrested.

But despite the sincerity evident in the condolences expressed, and the apparent adequacy of the steps taken by the Egyptians concerning this political crime, Lord Allenby, perhaps driven by indignation and the sense of personal loyalty to a friend and colleague, decided that Egypt should be taught a stern lesson.

Accordingly, at 5.0 p.m. on Saturday, the very day of the funeral, Allenby in practice carried to its logical conclusion a British belief that force is a balm for their overseas subjects. He went to the Presidency of the Egyptian Council of Ministers, 'escorted by the entire regiment of the 16th/5th Lancers, which he had captained before, and handed to the Egyptian Premier'[1] an ultimatum which Professor Toynbee describes as harsh and 'humiliating in almost every detail to the Egyptian Government'.[2]

The Ultimatum was submitted in two parts—the first, delivered by Allenby in person, accused Egypt of base ingratitude and made general demands. The second concerned specific requirements about the army in the Sudan and about foreign interests in Egypt. To avoid any misrepresentation through paraphrasing, the two documents are reproduced verbatim here.

First Communication. The Governor-General of the Soudan and Sirdar of the Egyptian Army, who was also a distinguished officer of the British Army, has been brutally murdered in Cairo. His Majesty's Government consider that this murder, which holds up Egypt, as at present governed, to the contempt of civilized peoples, is the natural outcome of a campaign of hostility to British rights and British subjects in Egypt and Soudan, founded upon a heedless ingratitude for benefits conferred by Great Britain, not discouraged by Your Excellency's Government, and fomented by organizations in close contact with that Government. Your Excellency was warned by His Majesty's Government little more than a month ago of the consequences of failing to stop this campaign, more particularly as far as it

[1] Royal Ministry for Foreign Affairs, *The Sudan Question*, p. 83.
[2] *Survey of International Affairs, 1924*, pp. 215–16.

concerned the Soudan. It has not been stopped. The Egyptian Government have now allowed the Governor-General of the Soudan to be murdered, and have proved that they are incapable or unwilling to protect foreign lives. His Majesty's Government therefore require that the Egyptian Government shall:—

(1) Present ample apology for the crime.

(2) Prosecute inquiry into the authorship of the crime with the utmost energy and without respect of persons, and bring the criminals, whoever they are and whatever their age, to condign punishment.

(3) Henceforth forbid and vigorously suppress all popular political demonstrations.

(4) Pay forthwith to His Majesty's Government a fine of £E500,000.

(5) Order within twenty-four hours withdrawal from the Soudan of all Egyptian officers, and the purely Egyptian units of the Soudan Army, with such resulting changes as shall be hereafter specified.

(6) Notify the competent Department that the Soudan Government will increase the area to be irrigated at Gezira from 300,000 feddans to an unlimited figure as need may arise.

(7) Withdraw all opposition in the respects hereafter specified to the wishes of His Majesty's Government concerning the protection of foreign interests in Egypt.

(8) Failing immediate compliance with these demands, His Majesty's Government will at once take appropriate action to safeguard their interests in Egypt and the Soudan.

Second Communication—'Further Specific Demands'. With reference to my preceding communication, I have the honour to inform your Excellency, on behalf of His Britannic Majesty's Government that their specific requirements respecting the army in the Soudan and the protection of foreign interests in Egypt are as follows:—

(1) The Egyptian Officers and purely Egyptian Units of the Egyptian Army having been withdrawn, the Soudanese Units of the Egyptian Army shall be converted into a Soudan Force owing allegiance to the Soudan Government alone, and under the supreme command of the Governor-General in whose name all commissions will be given.

(2) The rules and conditions governing the service discipline and retirement of foreign officials still employed by the Egyptian Government and the financial conditions governing the pensions of foreign officials who have left the service, shall be revised in accordance with the wishes of His Majesty's Government.

(3) Pending the conclusion of an agreement between the two Governments regarding the protection of the foreign interests in Egypt, the Egyptian Government shall maintain the posts of Financial and Judicial Advisers and preserve their powers and privileges as contemplated on the abolishment of the Protectorate: and shall respect

the status and present attributions of the European Department of the Ministry of the Interior as already laid down by Ministerial Order, and give weight to such recommendations as the Director-General may make upon matters falling within his sphere.[1]

The Egyptian Government was given notice to comply not later than 8 p.m. on the following day—the 23rd.

The Ultimatum is open to criticism on several grounds. With regard to the demands for an apology, and for prosecution, Egyptians pointed out that their Government did detest the crime and had already, quite voluntarily, instituted an inquiry resulting in the arrest of one of the accomplices, and that these British demands were therefore unnecessary. To this we might add a point that the call made by the Egyptian Minister in London at the British Foreign Office to express condolence, together with the communication from the Palace of King Fuad, and similar actions by the Council of Egyptian Ministers could be regarded as constituting enough expression of regret about the incident, though without accepting responsibility for the act.

They objected to the idea of paying a fine whilst the criminals were still being prosecuted—when the matter was yet *sub judice*. This criticism seems to be valid; also the wording of the paragraph imposing the fine does not suggest whether or not the demand was a compensation for the family of the victim. As for the evacuation of Egyptian forces from the Sudan, Egyptians asked: 'Why did the British demand that the Egyptian forces should evacuate the Sudan in twenty-four hours, when there had never been any insinuation that these forces were in any way responsible for this assassination? What right had the Governor-General of the Sudan, who owed his appointment to the Sovereign of Egypt[2] to ask the Sudanese units of the Egyptian Army to swear an oath of allegiance to him instead of to their supreme commander, the King of Egypt?'[3] While agreeing that the evacuation clause in the Ultimatum appears irrelevant, we should point out, with regard to the oath of allegiance, that theoretically at least, some of the Sudanese in the units would owe allegiance to the Sovereigns of both Britain and Egypt. Because their life is so decisively dependent upon the waters of the Nile, Egyptians reacted rather intensely against the Gezira paragraph

---

[1] Royal Ministry for Foreign Affairs, *The Soudan Question*, Omar, pp. 8–84. See also Toynbee, *Survey of International Affairs*, 1924.

[2] Constitutionally (according to the Condominium Agreement) the Governor-General is appointed by the Khedive on the recommendation of the British Government. Practically, it is a British appointment.

[3] Royal Ministry for Foreign Affairs, *The Sudan Question*, p. 85.

of the British Ultimatum. They objected on the justifiable ground that the increase in the cotton cultivation in the Sudan to an unlimited area had no relevance to the assassination. In this connection Marlowe, himself a British resident in Egypt, blames the British Government for conveying the impression that they were prepared to use their control of the waters of the Nile as a means of bringing Egypt to heel if and when desired.[1]

The demand for the vigorous suppression of all popular political demonstrations appears too vague and unspecific. It seems incompatible with constitutional government and a direct negation of the democratic principles of which Britain had always been a declared advocate. Lord Lloyd commented that the British Foreign Secretary himself saw, at the time, that the demands were unwise and somewhat irrelevant; that a full apology, the full punishment of the guilty, and the demands for measures ensuring the cessation of the outrages could have been enough.[2] Lord Lloyd admitted that the demands which Britain made in regard to the Gezira and the removal of Egyptian officers and units were tantamount to a recognition that in the present temper of Egypt, the Condominium could not be worked and that one member of it must cease to take an active part.[3] We should add that item (7) of the first Ultimatum, in which Allenby endeavoured to silence any criticism of his policy in Egypt, is against the democratic principles and practice in Britain. A British Government on foreign soil should expect from native nationalists even greater opposition than that provided in Britain by the Press, pulpit and public, or by the Opposition Party in Parliament.

Zaghlul Pasha laid the British Ultimatum before an emergency session of the Egyptian Chamber, on the very evening he received it from Lord Allenby. They decided to accept the first four and to reject the last three of the demands; they commissioned the Cabinet to convey a reply accordingly. An Egyptian Note was therefore despatched, expressing, once again, abhorrence of the crime, but repudiating the imputations in the second and third paragraphs of the British demands. It declared that:

> the only responsibility which this Government recognises and claims is that of pursuing the criminals. Rapid and effectual measures have already been taken to this effect, and the favourable results, already obtained, give us full confidence that the criminals will not escape.[4]

---

[1] *Op. cit.*, p. 270.
[2] *Egypt Since Cromer*, p. 95.
[3] *Ibid.*, p. 21.
[4] The Egyptian Kingdom: Royal Ministry for Foreign Affairs, *op. cit.*, p. 87.

Rejecting three of the demands, the Note declared that these were contrary to the existing Anglo-Egyptian arrangements or undertakings. But 'in order to show the deep regret which the crime has caused in the country and to appease the British Government', the Egyptian Government would agree to present its apologies and to pay the £E500,000. The Note expressed the hope that Britain would find the Egyptian reply entirely satisfactory because 'it is, at all events, inspired by a very sincere desire to maintain and ensure the best relations with the (British) Government, and which (relations) can, at the same time, be conciliated with the rights of Egypt'.[1]

The Egyptian Note was followed by the payment of the £E500,000 to the British Residency the next morning—the 24th. But at noon, less than an hour after the payment, Lord Allenby notified Zaghlul Pasha that, because of the Egyptian Government's non-acceptance of the seventh demand (regarding British and other foreign interests in Egypt and the Sudan), British troops had been ordered to occupy the Customs Offices at Alexandria.[2] The British fleet began to carry out naval displays in Egyptian ports.[3] Moreover, Lord Allenby suggested to London that diplomatic relations with Egypt should be broken and that 'hostages should be taken and shot in the event of any further assassinations'.[4]

Seemingly, the condemnation became too much for Zaghlul. He resigned. But he simultaneously issued a public appeal to the Egyptians to remain calm and in the words of *The Times*: 'to refrain from action which might endanger Egypt.'[5] Commenting on the crime, Amine Yousef Bey, who knew Zaghlul well, declares that it is incredible to any Egyptian that Zaghlul or any of his colleagues should have had the slightest responsibility for the crime, that though he refused to submit to intimidation, he was, by temperament and practice, a non-violent man.[6] In an interview with him by a Special Correspondent of *The Times*, London, Zaghlul confided that 'the assassination painfully affected him, not only because of Sir Lee Stack's fine qualities but especially because of the horror it inspired.'[7]

There was a wide belief in Egypt that the murder was committed by a criminal group in an attempt to embarrass and do damage to Zaghlul's Government. This belief was shared by the writer of an editorial in *The Times*, who said: 'There are those, however, in Egypt and there are others in different countries who would not be sorry to make trouble

[1] *Ibid.*, p. 88.   [2] *The Times*, 25 November 1924, p. 14e.
[3] *Ibid.*, p. 14b.   [4] Marlowe, *op. cit.*, p. 271.
[5] *The Times* editorial, 25 November 1924, p. 15a.
[6] *Independent Egypt*, pp. 126–7.   [7] *The Times*, London, 20 November 1924.

for King Fuad and for England.'[1] A current example of such a group of international trouble-makers is provided by the famous trial of thirteen prisoners, on charges of espionage, before the military court in Egypt in 1954.[2]

The Egyptian defence is acceptable; but while it does not now appear conceivable that the Egyptian Government would have planned or directly aided in the assassination of Sir Lee Stack, Egyptian nationalism and the anti-British feeling, built up both by the Egyptian Press and politicians, appear to have, without plan or intention, set the stage and the mood for potential assassins. Egyptian journalists, like most of the other pressmen of the world, may get away with many sensational, tendentious and inciting items, because newspapermen are adequately protected by the 'liberty and freedom' of the Press. Statesmen, however, enjoy less freedom; they are imprisoned by the relative dignity, responsibility and the deeper appreciation of the general state of affairs required by the office they hold. As President of the Council of Ministers, Zaghlul Pasha had made certain statements before the Egyptian Parliament which could have been left to a back-bencher to make. But on 17 May, according to information which reached the British Foreign Office, Zaghlul Pasha had stated that the fact that a foreign officer was Commander-in-Chief of the Egyptian Army, and the retention in that army of British officers were incompatible with the dignity of an independent Egypt. This was a political truism. But the British Government considered that the expression of such sentiments in an official pronouncement by the responsible head of the Egyptian Government had placed not only Sir Lee Stack as Commander-in-Chief, but all British officers in a difficult position.[3]

The Egyptians were guilty of some irresponsibility by their speeches, which could be described as inciting. Zaghlul Pasha was credited with the power of an eloquent pleader and a vivid writer. To the Egyptians he was a man with a tongue of gold, a pen of fire, and an eye

---

[1] *The Times*, London, 16 August 1924, p. 11.

[2] 'The Egyptian authorities described the thirteen persons as professional spies who received money to play mischief among nations; because, when there was every indication that Anglo-Egyptian negotiations about the Suez Canal were coming to a successful end in July 1954, a bomb was thrown at the U.S. Embassy in Cairo, and another at the U.S. Information Bureau in Alexandria. Egyptian authorities announce that the confessions by the accused show that they had committed the crimes: (i) to undermine the Anglo-Egyptian negotiations, (ii) to create a breach between Egypt and the U.S., and (iii) to instigate disturbances against the Egyptian Government.' *The Story of Zionist Espionage in Egypt*, Cairo, 1955, p. 35.

[3] From MacDonald to Allenby, *Correspondence respecting the Position of H.M. Government in regard to Egypt and the Sudan*: Cmd. 2269 (1924), p. 4.

bright as the stars. But, in the opinion of Owen Tweedy, 'he was no extremist.'[1]

The British, too, seemed blameworthy for that lack of calmness desirable for a sound judgment. They appeared unwilling to understand the situation and their counter-measures were extreme indeed. It should be remembered that the assassination of Sir Lee Stack was not the first outrage of its kind. Between September 1919 and 19 November 1924, when Sir Lee was shot, there were at least forty-six outrages— nineteen against Egyptians, among them some Ministers, eleven against British persons, and sixteen against Egyptian Ministers and officials who were for co-operation with the British. Between December 1921 and December 1922, the average was reported to be about two per month, and in the forty-six outrages, there were more than sixty victims.[2] Mohammed Said Pasha, Tewfik Pasha, and Boutros Pasha had been attacked during their respective ministries. Boutros was assassinated, as we have already noted, mainly for signing the Anglo-Egyptian Condominium Agreement over the Sudan. Zaghlul Pasha himself was shot at, just about four months before the Stack incident, on 12 July 1924, at the Cairo railway station. This attempt on his life was made by an Egyptian medical student who had just returned from Berlin; the motive was 'to stop the negotiation' (with Britain).[3]

When the Russian fleet was held responsible for the murder of some British fishermen on the Dogger Bank, the British Government's behaviour was calm and dignified. By contrast, their reaction to the political assassination of Sir Lee Stack was rash and vindictive. Lord Allenby's indignant rage can be understood. At the time of the assassination, Sir Lee was his guest at the Embassy in Cairo. He was a trusted colleague and a personal friend. The situation would rouse most mortals, and allowance should therefore be made for the emotional stress to which the British High Commissioner was subjected. In addition to this personal element, Sir Lee, as the Governor-General of the Sudan and Commander-in-Chief of the Egyptian Army, was a pre-eminent emblem of British influence and authority in the Nile Valley. Consequently, the murder was a serious threat to British power not only in the Nile Valley but in other parts of her Empire. But indignation, though often legitimate, is not always the best counsellor; loyalty to a friend, concern for the pressure from fellow-citizens on the spot, and undue apprehension about the Empire need not have been allowed supremacy over the greater

---

[1] Tweedy, Owen, 'Zaghlul Pasha', in the *Fortnightly Review*, July 1926, pp. 111–12.
[2] *The Times*, 27 December 1924.   [3] *Ibid.*, 14 July 1924, p. 14d.

responsibility for the preservation of the best relations between the Egyptian and the British nations. For the loss of temper and the excessive show of might, Britain paid, slowly but surely. To quote Marlowe:

> The memory of the threat rankled. It was a gift to unscrupulous propagandists, and it cast a shadow over Anglo-Egyptian relations for many years to come. Of all the sanctions with which we might have threatened Egypt, this was the one, above all others, which should have been left alone.[1]

In Shakespeare's *Merchant of Venice*, Shylock could be blamed for lacking mercy in his demand for the pound of flesh from Antonio; but his action was within the law of Venice. Let us consider the British reprisals in the light of this analogy. We must therefore ask the question: 'In what circumstances and to what extent is a state responsible, in the law of nations, for a crime committed against an alien on its territorial soil?'

The answer was given in general terms by a special Commission of Jurists appointed, by the Council of the League of Nations, to consider certain questions arising out of the Italian-Greek dispute over the assassination of the Italian General Tellini (in circumstances similar to those surrounding the murder of Sir Lee Stack). This Commission of Jurists had declared, on 24 January 1924, that:

> The responsibility of a state is only involved by the commission in its territory of a political crime against the person of foreigners if the state has neglected to take all reasonable measures for the prevention of the crime and the pursuit, arrest and bringing to justice of the criminal. The recognised public character of a foreigner and the circumstances in which he is present in its territory entail upon the state a corresponding duty of special vigilance on his behalf.[2]

The first criterion—i.e. the taking of all reasonable measures for the prevention of the crime—appears difficult to apply in the Egyptian situation. One could only take preventative measures if one suspected that a crime was about to be committed. It would be difficult to establish whether or not the Egyptian Government had any such suspicion. Furthermore, at the time of the assassination of Sir Lee Stack, the two officials in the Egyptian service upon whom immediate technical responsibility could be presumed to rest—that is, the Commandant of the Cairo City Police and the Director-General of the European Section of the Department of Public Security—were in fact Englishmen.[3] On

---

[1] *Op. cit.*, p. 270.
[2] League of Nations, *Official Journal*, Vol. V, 1924, p. 524.
[3] Toynbee, *Survey of International Affairs*, p. 215.

the question of bringing the criminals to justice, the Egyptian Government did pledge themselves to pursue the criminals and they undertook immediate measures to implement the pledge. However, the British High Commissioner took swift action before it was possible to judge whether or not the Egyptian Government was honouring its pledge to the full. Undoubtedly, as the Commander-in-Chief of the Egyptian Army, Stack was pre-eminently entitled to receive from the Egyptian Government special vigilance on his behalf. But at the time of the attack, he was, as usual, accompanied by his bodyguard; furthermore, the officials immediately responsible were the two Englishmen mentioned above. Besides, as the head of the Egyptian Army, he was himself part and parcel of the Egyptian Government, and he could be considered to be no longer a foreigner in Egyptian territory; he had been attached to the Anglo-Egyptian Army since July 1899, i.e. resident in Egypt and the Sudan for a total of not less than 25 years.[1]

It seems, therefore, that the Egyptian Government could not, within the terms of the international jurists quoted above, be held fully, if at all, responsible for the crime. Even a spokesman for the British Cabinet, in reply to a question in the House of Commons admitted that the British Government had no evidence connecting the murder of Sir Lee Stack with the Egyptian Ministry.[2]

Assuming, nevertheless, for the moment, that the Egyptian Government was guilty, under international law, of the crime, was Britain right in taking the coercive measures she did? This brings us to the second aspect of the legality of the Ultimatum, namely:

> Are measures of coercion which are not meant to constitute acts of war consistent with the terms of Articles 12 to 15 of the Covenant when they are taken by one member of the League of Nations against another member of the League without prior recourse to the procedure laid down in these articles?

A reply to this question was provided at the sixth public Meeting of the Council of the League held at Geneva in March 1924. According to the Commission of Jurists, coercive measures which are not intended to constitute acts of war might or might not be consistent with the provisions of Articles 12 to 15 of the Covenant. It was for the Council, when the dispute had been submitted to it, to recommend the maintenance or

---

[1] See 'Sir Lee Stack, Work for Egypt and the Sudan', in *The Times*, 21 November 1924, p. 11a.
[2] Written Answers (Murder of Sir Lee Stack). *Parliamentary Debates*, Vol. CLXXIX, 1924, p. 372.

withdrawal of such measures. The President of the Council elucidated further, and the Council agreed, that measures of peaceful coercion should be limited to reprisals of a legal, economic or financial character; that no measures of coercion . . . should be contemplated before the peaceful means for settling disputes between members of the League of Nations have been exhausted. These measures include diplomatic negotiation, arbitration, reference to the Permanent Court of International Justice or the mediation procedure of the Council.[1]

From the facts, it is evident that the British Government did not make the least attempt to meet the minimum requirements of the League's formula.

We have mentioned that the British demands regarding the Sudan were among those rejected by the Egyptian Government. However, Britain forced through the evacuation of the Egyptian Army from the Sudan between 24 November and 4 December.[2] The Egyptian artillery at Khartoum declined to leave without instructions from King Fuad, but the King was made to send the necessary order, which was obeyed. Nevertheless, the Sudanese infantry at Khartoum mutinied. They obstinately refused to return to duty; and British troops opened fire on the mutineers, who, fighting to the last man, were annihilated.[3]

With the removal of the Egyptian force from the Sudan, the establishment of a new Sudan Defence Force and the ban on the traditional Sudanese expression of loyalty (through the Friday prayers) to the King of Egypt, the assassination of Sir Lee Stack created a *de facto* change in the Sudan, detrimental to Egypt but advantageous to Britain. Be this as it may, the constitutional or juridical position of the Anglo-Egyptian Sudan remained intact; and the Declaration of 1922 still provided (under the clause reserving the four points) an instrument for peaceful negotiations. Egypt, therefore, was left with the hope of availing herself of this residual opportunity to bring about a return to her position in the Sudan before the crime against Sir Lee Stack. Egyptian endeavours towards this objective, and British conciliation dictated by the imminence of the Second World War, culminated in the Anglo-Egyptian Treaty of Friendship in 1936, which forms the subject of the next chapter.

---

[1] League of Nations, *Official Journal*, pp. 525–6.
[2] *The Times*, 5 December 1924.
[3] Toynbee, *Survey of International Affairs*, p. 251. See also, Oral Answers (Egypt and the Sudan), in *Parliamentary Debates*, 1924, Vol. CLXXIX, p. 957.

5

RECONCILIATION AND THE TREATY OF FRIENDSHIP: 1925–36

1. THE RESTORATION OF THE PRE-ULTIMATUM STATUS, 1925–34

History writes the word RECONCILIATION over all her quarrels.
GENERAL SMUTS to LORD MILNER[1]

THE first six years (1925–30) after the 1924 incident witnessed certain efforts to lessen the tensions between the two parties. Also, the years of the great world depression (1930–4) created for either disputant at home enough economic problems to cope with. In this way, the world calamity was a contributory factor to the peaceful period in Anglo-Egyptian relations. Then came expansionist Italy to arouse concern within Cairo and London: Italy's aggression against Ethiopia and Italian territorial ambitions on the continent of Africa were a threat to the safety of Egypt and to the general interests of Britain in the Nile Valley and in all Africa. This situation forced Britain and Egypt together into a treaty of alliance and friendship in 1936. Therefore, we shall deal in this chapter with two main issues: first, the reconciliatory overtures which led to the restoration of the Egyptian position in the Sudan as it was before the Stack incident of 1924; and secondly, the Treaty of Friendship and Alliance, signed in 1936.

The years 1925 and 1926 brought certain changes in Britain, Egypt and in the Sudan, which were relevant to the Anglo-Egyptian question. Lord Allenby, the British High Commissioner for Egypt and the Sudan —the force behind the British reprisals of 1924—had resigned. Lord Lloyd had succeeded him. Before Lloyd's arrival in Cairo, seven of the Egyptians accused of being implicated in the political assassination of Sir Lee Stack had been hanged, and the eighth had been sentenced to penal servitude for life. In the Sudan, the Egyptian Army, which had hitherto helped to garrison the country, had been withdrawn; and the

[1] *The Milner Papers: South Africa, 1897–9* (Vol. II, London, 1931, p. 542).

Sudan Defence Force was created as a substitute, the change being completed in January 1925. The excitement over the assassination of Sir Lee Stack therefore subsided.

In Britain, the Conservative Party was confidently in the saddle. But in Egypt, the year 1925 began with the dissolution of Parliament; the Ziwar Pasha Government which assumed office after the resignation of Zaghlul Pasha seemed to lack the full support of the people and the electorate. The Cabinet, however, managed to remain in office until May 1926, when Zaghlulists (Wafd Party) returned to power in full strength. Zaghlul Pasha, while very popular with the Egyptians, was, for obvious reasons, *persona non grata* to the British Government. Consequently, the British High Commissioner intervened and induced Zaghlul to renounce office. Zaghlul therefore nominated Adli Pasha for the premiership. However, the new Egyptian chamber indicated its wishes by electing Zaghlul Pasha its President. British interference in Egyptian internal politics provided further evidence to justify the criticism that Egyptian affairs were run according to the whims of the British Government. Speaking about British meddling in Egypt, C. F. Trevelyan had said earlier in the House of Commons, 'Owing to our actions, Ministers who suit us and not the Egyptians are in office.'[1]

There was also a change of mood in Britain and Egypt—both became relatively reconciliatory. The underlying reasons could be attributed, on the part of Britain, to the fact that her Ultimatum of 1924 had been successful in the sense that she had got what she demanded in Egypt and the Sudan.

As for Egypt, she had been out-manœuvred and overwhelmed by Britain, who, like a boxer with heavy punches, had knocked Egypt down unconscious with a blow from the reprisals following the assassination of Sir Lee Stack. Fearing further punitive measures, she had no choice but to eat hot soup by the edge and assume a conciliatory attitude in her negotiations with Britain over the Sudan. The King's Speech from the Throne at the opening of Parliament on 10 June 1926 was therefore moderate.

In spite of the apparent desire on both sides for reconciliation, there emerged real issues of friction caused by the changes in the military situation in the Sudan.

In the fifth demand of the British Ultimatum of 22 November 1924, the text of which has been quoted in the preceding chapter, the Egyptian

[1] *Parliamentary Debates*, Vol. CLXXIX, 1924, p. 651. Compare the deposition of Sherif Pasha (pp. 33–34) and that of the Kabaka (note 4 appended to p. 71).

Government had to order within 24 hours the withdrawal from the Sudan of all the Egyptian Army. Against her will, Egypt complied and a New Sudan Force was fully established under British control in 1925. These military changes in the Sudan were later followed by corresponding changes in the strength and organization of the Egyptian Army in Egypt. Those Egyptian units which had been evacuated from the Sudan, were added to the Egyptian Army stationed in Egypt. In addition, two new battalions and a new squadron of cavalry were raised in 1925 to provide employment at home for most of the Egyptian men who had lost their positions in the military units and civil administration in the Sudan. By 1926, the strength of the Egyptian Army in Egypt had risen, from 4,800 in 1923, to 10,580, all ranks. Partly as a result of transfers to the Sudan Defence Force, the British officers in the Egyptian Army fell from 172 in 1922 to nine in 1926. Britain viewed the increasing military strength of Egypt as a threat to herself and the Foreign Secretary frankly declared that any proposal to strengthen the Egyptian Army or reserves or to improve their equipment would be regarded by Britain 'as a preparation for opposition to herself'.[1]

Therefore, when *The Times* Correspondent in Cairo telegraphed, rather incorrectly, that the Egyptian Parliamentary War Committee on the War Budget had 'published' a report increasing the forces of the Egyptian Army and recommending 'unanimously the cancellation of the Credit for the Sirdarate',[2] the British Government became nervous, and was led to act rashly. The report in question turned out to be about a private and personal memorandum which had not been officially considered by the Committee of the Chamber, and which became public property only by some leakage. The erroneous report was repeated in *The Times* of 31 May 1927; and it referred to 'the decision of the Committee of the Egyptian Parliament to recommend the suppression of credits for the Sirdar'. A correction of the error does not appear to have been made in any subsequent issue of *The Times*.

Nevertheless, the British High Commissioner in Egypt quickly made representations to the Egyptian Government; and on 30 May the British Government addressed a Note to the Egyptian Government. This Sarwat Pasha received on the same day. On that very evening, three British warships left Malta for Egyptian ports—two for Alexandria and one for Port Said!

[1] Memorandum, dated Foreign Office, 13 July 1927, by Sir Austen Chamberlain, in *Papers regarding Negotiations for a Treaty of Alliance with Egypt*, Cmd. 3050, 1928, p. 5. Compare British reaction to Egypt's arms deal with the Soviet bloc in 1955.
[2] *The Times*, 25 May 1927. See also *Contemporary Review*, July 1927, pp. 112–13.

Naturally, this British action perturbed the Egyptians, and King Fuad had to change his plans about proceeding via Alexandria to Europe. He remained in Cairo.

When questioned in the House of Commons on 1 June 1927, the British Foreign Secretary (Sir Austen Chamberlain) defended the despatch of the warships as a precaution, pending an Anglo-Egyptian agreement.

An Egyptian reply on 14 June to the British Note was accepted by the British Government as satisfactory in explaining the intentions of the Egyptian Government and removing 'the cause of the recent tension'.[1]

Though the incident was thus formally disposed of, the document upon which the British based their action turned out, in fact, not to possess any Egyptian official character which the British had assumed by error or by intention. The knowledge of this error aggravated by the despatch of British warships to Egyptian ports, left an open wound in Egyptian minds.

However, the Egyptians were apparently willing to let the wound heal; and King Fuad made his intended journey to Europe, visiting London first before going to certain other capitals of Europe. In an editorial, on 4 July 1927, *The Times* prepared the way for a warm reception for the Egyptian King in Britain by describing his impending visit as a sign of recent improvement in the relations between Egypt and Britain. On 13 July, Sarwat Pasha, who had accompanied King Fuad to London, called on Sir Austen Chamberlain at the Foreign Office. The talks between them formed the nucleus of yet another attempt to reach a formal agreed settlement. Their respective attitudes in the conversations indicated that both were personally willing to make concessions, though conscious of the fact that they were not officially free agents. We should now, therefore, proceed to give some account of their efforts to reach a common ground.

Between 1927 and 1930, three main attempts were made to reach an agreement, but they all failed. The first was between Sarwat Pasha and Sir Austen Chamberlain, who agreed on a settlement of certain of the reserved subjects, but postponed the Sudan question. In this negotiation, there were two draft treaties, one Egyptian, the other British. Article 11 of the Egyptian draft agreed to defer the settlement of the Sudan question to further negotiations in which the two parties should 'have

---

[1] Statement by Locker-Lampson, Under-Secretary of State for Foreign Affairs, *Parliamentary Debates*, 16 June 1927.

complete freedom to maintain their rights', but maintained a return to the *status quo* before 1924, and demanded a determination of the quota of the waters of the Nile attributable to Egypt. Article 13 of the British counter-draft recognized the joint interests of Britain and Egypt in the Sudan; suggested continuation of the Condominium, and an adjustment in the distribution of the Nile waters, and added a clause asking Egypt to continue her contribution to the cost of the administration of the Sudan.

But as a result of the conversations between Sarwat Pasha and W. Selby (Private Secretary to the British Secretary of State for Foreign Affairs) at the British Embassy in Paris on the afternoon of 31 August 1927, the articles on the Sudan were expunged from both the British and the Egyptian drafts. According to Selby's Memorandum, while Sarwat Pasha held out no hopes of being able to carry an agreement of the kind which Britain had submitted to him (through the British High Commissioner in Egypt) he saw no reason why mention of the Sudan should not be omitted altogether and be reserved for settlement on a favourable occasion in the future.[1]

It would seem, however, that the idea of avoiding the Sudan question in the proposed treaty originated from Sir Austen Chamberlain. In his explanatory notes to the British draft, he said:

> I was careful in my draft to avoid broaching the general question of the Sudan, in which the two Governments do not see eye to eye. My object was to raise as few controversial points as possible. . . . In the British draft, on the contrary, the issue is raised squarely and a solution is provided which accords with the British policy on this matter. I do not see my way to follow the British Government in this. I prefer to leave the question for later negotiations.[2]

The second attempt was when Mohammed Mahmoud Pasha and Mr. Henderson agreed, after protracted discussions, on the restoration of the situation existing before the Stack incident of 1924—that is, that the status of the Sudan should rest on the Condominium Agreement of 1899. Accordingly, the Governor-General was to continue to exercise the power conferred upon him by the Condominium Conventions. Agreement was also reached about payment by the Sudan Government of the money (approximately £4,000,000) advanced by Egypt for the construction of Port Sudan and the building of railways between 1901 and 1909; the method whereby certain international conventions were

---

[1] Cmd. 3050, 1928, p. 15.
[2] Sir Austen Chamberlain, *Minutes on the British Draft Treaty*, Cmd. 3050, p. 26.

to be made applicable to the Sudan; and the abrogation of item 5 of the British Ultimatum of 1924, by which the Egyptian battalion was forced out of the Sudan.[1]

These were good signs of improvement in Anglo-Egyptian relations, but nothing very tangible seems to have come out of the proposals, agreed upon in England by Mr. Henderson and Mahmoud Pasha. This was partly because Mahmoud Pasha, who was described as an unpopular dictator, returned to Egypt only to be defeated in a general election. The proposals could not, in consequence, be ratified.

However, a third attempt was made. The Egyptian Delegation, led by Nahas Pasha (Minister of the Interior) included all the most important members of the Cabinet.

In this attempt, the negotiators came to terms on many disputed points but disagreed on several issues connected with the Sudan. These were: the Egyptian demand for an unrestricted Egyptian emigration into the Sudan (this had become a new issue in the dispute); the refusal by Britain to recognize the right of Egyptian sovereignty over the Sudan; the British rejection of the Egyptian demand for participation, *de facto*, in the joint Anglo-Egyptian Administration in the Sudan in accordance with the 1889 Agreement (which had not been carried out in practice since even before the 1924 Ultimatum).

As a result, the Sudan Article (Article 11) in the joint Draft Treaty was left blank,[2] and the Draft did not become a formal instrument.

In spite of the disagreement, the negotiations personally and officially ended, not with the resentment and recrimination usually characteristic of Anglo-Egyptian differences, but with apparent friendship and hope.

The cordial behaviour of the British officials and some members of the public in Britain together with the favourable impressions made by the Egyptian Delegation, did a lot to create the goodwill and mutual confidence essential to an agreement.

However, with all these appearances of friendliness, the essentials in Anglo-Egyptian relations remained substantially the same, particularly in regard to the Sudan. What seems to be true is that Britain—the dominant power—put on a conciliatory attitude about small matters, such as the distribution of the Nile Waters between Egypt and the Sudan. By doing this, Britain gave the impression of general friendliness, which helps a state to achieve her requirements in essential matters without

[1] *Exchange of Notes on Proposals for an Anglo-Egyptian Settlement*, 1929, Cmd. 3376.
[2] *Papers regarding the Recent Negotiations for an Anglo-Egyptian Settlement*, Cmd. 3575, 1930, p. 37.

creating animosity or a suspicion of intransigence. *The Round Table*, a semi-official magazine of the British Commonwealth, and Sir Austen Chamberlain had clearly put the real essential British objective.

The Round Table declared: 'Unless we can harden our hearts and turn a deaf ear to demands which, however persistent, are clearly unreasonable, we shall lose our Empire.'[1]

Sir Austen Chamberlain, as British Foreign Secretary, stated in the House of Commons: 'The policy of His Majesty's Government is to preserve the Condominium, to let it continue in the interest of this country and of Egypt, and we ask Egypt to accept, as the Government of Zaghlul Pasha would not accept, the necessary conditions of a joint rule.'[2]

Also, in his Minutes to the Draft Treaty of 1927, he had made it abundantly clear that no British Government would yield to Egypt on whatever was considered to be vital to Britain—'The fundamental requirements of British policy were common to all parties in this State and a change of Government made no alteration in them'.[3]

Therefore, during this period (1925–30) the motto for the foreign policy of each to the other could be thus laconically stated: *For Britain* —Relax (but don't yield in essentials), having won your prizes from the weak. *For Egypt*—Press on your demands, but avoid any further clash with the strong.

2. THE TREATY OF ALLIANCE AND FRIENDSHIP, 1936

After Mr. Henderson and Nahas Pasha had parted on friendly terms but without agreement about the Sudan in 1930, there followed four years which were relatively quiet both in respect of Anglo-Egyptian relations generally and the Sudan question in particular. This period of comparative peace was in part owing to the world economic depression, whose problems occupied the attention of both disputants between 1930 and 1934. But the grave political situation of the world in 1935–6 brought a very dramatic change in Anglo-Egyptian relations.

In 1935, Fascism and Nazism were becoming increasingly threatening to the world at large and to Britain and Egypt in particular. Italian craving for expansion was a threat to the security of Egypt and to

---

[1] 'Egypt and the Sudan', *The Round Table*, Vol. XIV, September 1924, p. 682.
[2] *Parliamentary Debates*, Vol. CLXXIX, 1924, p. 670.
[3] *Memorandum by the Secretary of State for Foreign Affairs*, 13 July 1927, Cmd. 3050, 1928, p. 4.

Britain's territorial interests in Africa. The Rome–Berlin Axis was considered as a potential menace to the safety of the Suez Canal and of the whole Mediterranean, which formed the British strategic, commercial and political gate to India and the Far East. Nineteen-thirty-six was a year of even greater significance, because the world was then definitely in a crisis. The League of Nations was breaking down, and general anxiety was hanging over Europe. The Five Great Powers of Europe were all playing their role of mischief-makers-in-chief,[1] there was increasing animosity between Berlin and Moscow; Spain was divided by a Civil War. In Asia, Japan was quietly but effectively penetrating China. In Africa, the Italian armies had won their objective by the middle of 1936—the Abyssinian capital had fallen and the 'Lion of Judah' had become a fugitive in Britain. In England, 1936 was the year in which Edward VIII made his 'final and irrevocable decision'[2] to abdicate.

One could have expected that the gravity of the world situation in 1935–36 would have adversely affected (as did the prelude to the First World War) the Anglo-Egyptian issue. However, the effect, great as indeed it was, was for the better, not for the worse. We must therefore examine the background of the success of the negotiations of 1936.

The Italo-Abyssinian conflict, being a common threat, brought Britain and Egypt together. In the British Parliament, the Italian ambitions were watched with concern.

'The decision of the Italian Government to annex the whole of Abyssinia is a menace to our position in Africa and the Far East.'[3]

It was obvious that Britain would defend her interests if Italy was too successful in Abyssinia.

Egypt was the key to the Mediterranean and to other areas of potential conflict of Anglo-Italian interests. In Britain, the strategic importance of Egypt in the defence of the British Empire and Commonwealth, increased by the threat from Italy, Germany and Japan, was fully realized. Britain was therefore prepared to use Egypt to her own advantage, not through force (which was characteristic of the 1924 Ultimatum) but by diplomacy and reconciliation which were the theme of Nahas–Henderson efforts in 1930. The new British approach was well put by *The Times*, in March 1936:

'If the right relations can be established, what we give away with

---

[1] George Glasgow, 'Foreign Affairs', *Contemporary Review*, No. 852, December 1936, p. 748. (U.S. policy was still 'Monrocan'.)

[2] King's Letter of Abdication: *Parliamentary Debates*, Vol. CCCXVII, 1936.

[3] *Parliamentary Debates*, 22 May 1936.

one hand we shall receive back with the other. All the privileges and influence which we need in Egypt can be had under the guise and conditions of an alliance, provided we give the Egyptians freedom to give them to us.'[1]

The Italo-Abyssinian conflict had a great impact on Egypt also, in several ways. She found herself geographically closer to the belligerent states (Italy and Abyssinia) than any other neutral nation. She was faced with a decision as a state with at least formal attributes of self-determination in external matters—in respect of war between two of her neighbours. Her strained relations with Britain increased her danger and difficulties, because the crisis evidently gave Britain a freer hand to use Egyptian soil and territorial waters for military and naval bases as indeed she did during the First World War.

Egypt could not, therefore, remain effectively neutral. Italy was a colonial power controlling Libya—a Muslim country and a close neighbour on the western frontier of Egypt. In addition, Italy was not on good terms with the League of Nations, of which Egypt had been longing to be a member. On 13 October 1935, the Council of the League of Nations declared Italy to be an aggressor. For these and other reasons, Egypt could not afford to side with Italy in the conflict with Abyssinia.

On the other hand, there were strong reasons for Egyptian sympathy with Abyssinia. In the first place, Egypt felt the natural sympathy of an African neighbour and subject peoples for any African state about to become the victim of European aggression and expansion. Economically, Lake Tana, the principal source of the Blue Nile, upon which Egyptian agriculture depends, lies in Abyssinian territory. In religion, although Egypt is predominantly Muslim, the Abuna or Patriarch of the Abyssinian Church was by long tradition chosen from amongst the Coptic monks in Egypt—a source of emotional gratification to Egyptians. Geo-politically, Abyssinia had a common frontier with Egypt, and with the Sudan.

An Egyptian Committee was therefore formed to 'defend the cause of Abyssinian independence'; and retired Egyptian officials joined the Abyssinian Army in 'large numbers'.[2] Having thus declared her sympathy, Egypt must be prepared to fight. But the strength of the Egyptian Army had been weakened by British interference and control, which Austen Chamberlain regarded as essential to prevent Egypt from constituting a threat to Britain. General Neguib complains that until 1936

[1] 'Relations with Egypt', leading article in *The Times*, 22 March 1936.
[2] *The Times*, 30 July 1935.

'the Army's British mentors had opposed every effort to make it (the Egyptian Army) an effective fighting force for fear that it might some day be used against them'.[1] The weakness of the Egyptian Army made it impossible for Egypt to feel quite equal to the responsibility of defending herself against such danger as might threaten her if the Eastern Mediterranean became a theatre of war. It therefore became apparent that, without military assistance from Britain (no other power was as qualified as Britain), Egypt could ensure the security of her frontiers. This fact, together with the apprehension that the whole situation, in any case, offered Britain an easier chance to increase her military and naval bases in Egypt, drove Egypt further into the hands of Britain. Egyptians therefore had to shelve their militant nationalism with its anti-British campaigns. Like the British, they too were in a reconciliatory mood. Early in July 1935, Egyptian newspapers began to analyse the Italo-Abyssinian conflict. A comment was:

> Italy means to fight Great Britain for Mediterranean supremacy. Egypt will become a scene of hostilities. We can either try to stand aside from the conflict, and at its end make the best bargain possible with the victors, or we can declare our sympathies now, and in return for giving every possible assistance to England, secure from her a promise that our independence shall be complete, as soon as the present conflict is past, instead of qualified by substantial reservations as it has been since 1922.[2]

Many Egyptians had realized that they were powerless to force Britain to accept their claims in the Sudan until some more powerful factor than their agitation brought its influence to bear on the British Government. In the Anglo-Italian tension the Egyptians found such a powerful factor. Therefore, while conciliatory and friendly, they were determined to exploit the dispute and Britain's consequent need of Egyptian co-operation in naval, military, economic and other fields of action, and to exact from the British Government the best possible bargain over Egyptian claims in the Sudan.

Having thus attempted to outline the principal factors underlying the 1936 Agreement, we must now turn to the negotiations resulting in that Agreement.

Owing to the external crisis, the various Egyptian politicians of whatever adherence sank most of their differences and formed a United Front. On 13 December 1935, the new body published a Note addressed to the British High Commissioner, about obstacles in the way of Egypt's

[1] Mohammed Neguib, *Egypt's Destiny*, London, 1955, p. 19.
[2] Excerpt from the Egyptian Press, quoted in *The Round Table*—'Reactions to the Abyssinian Crisis'—March 1936, p. 274.

development. Among the list of such obstacles were the absence of an adequate national defence force, the exclusion of Egypt from the League of Nations, and the absence of a regular treaty with Britain. No direct mention of the Sudan was made. The British reply was amicable; it specifically declared that agreement should be reached on the Sudan. Mr. Anthony Eden, the new Foreign Secretary, instructed Sir Miles Lampson to inform the Egyptian Government that the British Government 'were prepared to enter forthwith into conversations with the object of arriving at an Anglo-Egyptian treaty settlement'.[1]

The British Government thought it desirable to begin negotiations with the categories which had given most difficulty in 1930. If these difficulties were surmounted, they suggested, the prospects of reaching a settlement would be greater. The subjects which had constituted the greatest obstacles in 1930 were, as we have shown, military questions and the Sudan.

From the very beginning, it appeared that the negotiations were destined to succeed. The conversations took place in Cairo, not in London. There was, therefore, greater opportunity for the Egyptian delegation to keep in close touch with their own advisers and with most sections of Egyptian opinion; furthermore, it gave Egyptians a greater feeling of security and less chance for any belief that any member of their Delegation had been 'bought' by the British with lavish hospitality if not with money. The most important factors, contributing to the success of the negotiations were that the Egyptian Delegation was headed by Nahas Pasha who had brought Egypt to the favourable point where the dispute was shelved in 1930, and that the 1936 Delegation represented every important political group in Egypt. Previously, Egyptian delegations had to submit to detailed criticism of every paragraph of such terms as they were believed, sometimes erroneously, to be arranging for the conclusion of a treaty with Britain; and they often had to suffer the anxiety of threats to their lives.

There was another significant contributory factor to the success of the negotiations. The Egyptian students 'who are a far more important element in Egyptian politics than is appreciated in other countries',[2] expressed their desire for national unity (without which the treaty could not have been achieved), even through acts of violence, to which attention was drawn in the British House of Commons.[3] To this we must add,

[1] Anthony Eden, *Parliamentary Debates*, Vol. CCCVIII, 4 February 1936, pp. 55–6.
[2] Yousef, Amine, Bey, *op. cit.*, p. 244.
[3] *Parliamentary Debates*, 4 February 1936, Vol. CCCVIII, p. 56.

on the British side, the personality of Sir Miles Lampson, a comparatively popular British High Commissioner in Egypt, who injected a refreshing cordiality into Anglo-Egyptian relations, and whose initiative saved the negotiations from breaking down at a critical moment.

On 2 March 1936, before going into the Conference Chamber of the Zaafaran Palace—where the conversations were to begin, Nahas Pasha, leader of the Egyptian Delegation, and Sir Miles Lampson, leader of the British Delegation, made mutually agreeable speeches before an audience in the Palace; and the conversations and negotiations went on in an atmosphere of apparent confidence, cordiality and determination to succeed—all in greater measure than on the previous occasions. Nevertheless, it was not all smooth sailing. The conversations designed to produce a draft treaty began on 2 March but had to be suspended throughout June, and agreement was not reached until July. In Egypt, the death of King Fuad on 28 April 1936, the Egyptian Parliamentary elections on 2 May; and in Britain many matters (such as the problems of the League and the world situation as a whole) demanding the attention of the British Government, were part of the causes of the delay. But the chief factor was the real disagreement, which sprang from the influence of British technical experts, who, in advising the British Government, demanded what *The Times* in London described as 'the unattainable ideal of a perfect military security, watertight for all time and in all circumstances'.[1]

As indicated in the earlier chapters of this work, the Suez Canal is a vital link in the long chain of British imperial communications and it became the real obstacle in the treaty negotiations. It is not surprising that British military opinion should seek the fullest liberty of action in its defence, that legal advisers should urge that liberty must be clearly defined, and that political 'realists' should suggest that such liberty must be ensured by an 'agreement that left nothing to chance—but left next to nothing to Egyptian sovereignty'.[2] Consequently, the conversations were suspended at the end of May, when Sir Miles Lampson left Cairo for London to confer with the British Government both about the Sudan and the military aspects of the question of the Anglo-Egyptian problem.

The consultations, which lasted a month, cleared the way for an Agreement. On Sir Miles' return to Cairo on 1 July, negotiations were resumed. By 7 July, general agreement had been reached and a

---

[1] Editorial, 'Back to Egypt', *The Times*, 30 June 1936.
[2] *Ibid.*, 7 July 1936.

drafting Committee of ten (five British and five Egyptian) was charged with putting the proposals into formal terminology.[1] The Foreign Secretary, Anthony Eden, was able to report on 27 July in the House of Commons that the first stage in the Treaty discussions had been concluded, and that articles dealing with military matters had been initialled on 24 July.

In Egypt the Treaty was received with general satisfaction, though there were reasoned criticisms. On being put to the vote, the Treaty was ratified, on 14 November, by 202 votes to eleven.

In Westminster, the Opposition supported the Treaty in the hope that it would 'close for ever an old chapter in Anglo-Egyptian relations which was marked by misunderstandings on both sides from time to time by certain apparent conflicts of purpose'.[2] The motion for ratification of the Treaty was adopted unanimously.

The Treaty was signed in London on 26 August, and ratified in Cairo on 22 December 1936. Its essential provisions were:

1. Recognition of Egypt as a sovereign state, with all the international rights accorded to a free state (e.g. exchange of Ambassadors between the two countries).

2. Termination of the military occupation of Egypt, with the exception of the Suez Canal Zone.

3. Conclusion of an Alliance requiring both parties to establish no relations with a third party which might be inconsistent with this Alliance.

4. Limitation of the number of British troops which should be on the left bank of the Nile at the Suez Canal, and ensuring that Egypt was to pay a good deal of the necessary cost. This arrangement was to be for the transitional period leading to a return of the guardianship of the Canal to Egypt. The Treaty was to be reviewed at the end of 20 years (i.e. in 1956) and in the case of difference about the revised Treaty this should be submitted to the League of Nations.

The question of the Sudan (one of the 'reserved points' in the Declaration of 1922) and the greatest stumbling block at the negotiations, was dealt with in Article 11, according to which the Sudan was to be administered as under the Condominium Agreement of 1899, without prejudice to the question of sovereignty over the country. There was no specific reference to Egyptian participation, but 'the Governor-General shall continue to exercise on the joint behalf of the high contracting parties the powers conferred upon him by the said

---

[1] *Daily Telegraph*, 8 July 1936.
[2] 'Anglo-Egyptian Treaty', *Parliamentary Debates*, Vol. CCCXVIII, 2 November 1936, p. 268.

Agreement.'[1] However, Egypt secured the removal of the difficulties imposed upon her after the murder of Sir Lee Stack in 1924. Egyptian immigration into the Sudan was again to be unrestricted, except for reasons of public health and order; while posts in the Administrative Service were to be open to Egyptians according to qualification, but only where qualified Sudanese were not available. In either case, all appointments remained vested in the British Governor-General. Through this Article, Britain and Egypt defined, for the first time, the aim of their joint administration in the Sudan, which was that 'the High Contracting Parties agree that the Primary aim of their administration in the Sudan must be the welfare of the Sudanese'.[2] It further provided that Egyptian troops were to be under the military responsibility of the Sudan Administration. In addition to the Sudanese troops, both the British and Egyptian troops should be placed at the disposal of the Governor-General. But a proviso was contained in the agreed minutes—'As the Egyptian Government are willing to send troops to the Sudan, the Governor-General will give immediate consideration to the number of Egyptian troops required for service in the Sudan [and] the precise places where they will be stationed.'[3]

As we have already said, the Egyptian Parliament approved the Treaty by 202 votes to eleven in the Chamber (and 109 votes to seven in the Senate). The British House of Commons accepted it without a division. These reactions in Cairo and in London were indicated in November (about four months after the signing of the Treaty)—a long enough time interval for second thoughts to show themselves. The Treaty also received favourable Press comment in Britain and America. Describing its immediate effect, the writer of a special article in the *Manchester Guardian* declared with manifest jubilation: 'The air has been cleared, and with it something rather heavier than air—the British conscience.'[4]

The Round Table expressed the hope that Britain would, by the Treaty, rely henceforth on a friendly Egypt to share the burden of defending Egypt and the Sudan; but it warned that the Treaty created a new situation in which the best brains and constant co-operation of both parties would be necessary. It expressed delight at the fact that, in spite of the friction of the previous years, the new situation was 'overwhelmingly *in our* [*British*] *favour*'.[5] In an editorial comment, *The American Journal of International Law* described it as 'a masterly

---

[1] *Treaty Series*, No. 6, 1937, Cmd. 5360, p. 10.   [2] *Ibid.*
[3] Agreed Minutes, Treaty Series, *ibid.*, pp. 16–17.
[4] *Manchester Guardian*, 23 December 1936.
[5] *The Round Table*, December 1936, pp. 119–23.

solution of a serious controversy . . . a real triumph for British diplomacy (and) an extremely clever device'.[1]

Egypt accepted it as the Treaty of 'honour and independence'—the terms being in accord with what Zaghlul Pasha had in fact demanded in the first instance.[2] For the moment, at least, it brought to an end a chapter in Anglo-Egyptian relations which had begun fifty-four years earlier, with the opening of hostilities between British and Egyptian armed forces in Egyptian territorial waters and on Egyptian soil on 11 July 1882.

While it did not appreciably increase the degree of Egyptian sovereignty over the Sudan, it did eliminate the four reservations of 1922 and removed the difficulties imposed upon Egypt by the British Ultimatum of 1924.

The first tangible sign of the new relationship created by the Treaty was that the Residency in Cairo changed into an Embassy. The Foreign Office announced, concurrently with the ratifications on 22 December 1936, the appointment of Sir Samuel Miles Lampson—a chief architect of the Treaty—as British Ambassador to Egypt. Egypt, too, quickly reciprocated by appointing Dr. Hafiz Afifi Pasha (formerly a Minister in London) as the first Egyptian Ambassador to the Court of St. James's. Egyptian students, who had violently reviled Britain for many years, now acclaimed Britain as a friend.

But with the passage of time, especially when the world situation had considerably improved in 1945, and the common danger had almost disappeared, serious difficulties began to arise. The Treaty was vague in defining certain of its provisions. Egypt began to doubt whether she could regard herself truly and securely independent as long as a foreign army, maintained at her own expense, occupied some of her territory —within a short distance of Cairo, her capital city. Egyptians began to feel able to take over the military responsibility for the Canal Zone (which was interlocked with the Sudan question).

Before the first ten years were over, at the end of which the Treaty could be revised, Egyptian feeling had risen high. Anglo-Egyptian friction increased so much that the Egyptian Government despatched a Note on 20 December 1945, asking the British Government to open negotiations for a revision of the Treaty. But the clash of British and Egyptian interests led to the breakdown of the Bevin–Sidky negotiations

---

[1] *The American Journal of International Law*, Vol. XXXI, Washington, D.C., 1937, pp. 293–4.
[2] Yousef, *op. cit.*, p. 247.

which followed. The question of the revision of the Treaty was therefore taken to the Security Council of the United Nations in 1947. At the Council, the Egyptian Government charged the British Government with policies designed to sever the Sudan permanently from Egypt, or to divide the Sudan into two political units, the North and the South, with a view to annexing the South to Uganda. The Wafd Government unilaterally abrogated the Treaty in 1951, but without effective success, since a treaty can be terminated normally only with the consent of both parties.

The points of disagreement in the Bevin–Sidky negotiations and in the Security Council form the subject of another section, but it is relevant to mention them here and now to indicate the discontent which subsequently emerged some years later, in place of the apparent satisfaction immediately after the signature.

Therefore, although the 1936 Treaty was a significant landmark in Anglo-Egyptian relations, it failed to reconcile the fundamental and conflicting interests of the two countries, in the Sudan. These interests, though seldom, if ever, explicitly stated, were the invisible oxygen which kept the flame of the Anglo-Egyptian dispute in continual combustion. In the following pages, we will therefore examine Egyptian interests and British stakes in the Sudan.

Part Two

(A) THE BASIC FACTORS CAUSING THE ANGLO-EGYPTIAN TENSION

6

EGYPT'S IMMEDIATE INTERESTS IN THE SUDAN

1. THE CONTROL AND DISTRIBUTION OF THE WATERS OF THE NILE

Both are alike in their hearts, yes, in spite of their quarrels. Both seek to assuage, to no end, the old simian thirst.
CLARENCE DAY, *This Simian World*

From the dawn of history Egypt has depended on the flow of the waters of the Nile as the individual depends upon the circulation of the blood.
COLONEL SAMIR HELMY
Secretary-General of the High Dam Authority, Egypt

IN diplomatic relations it has been characteristic of national governments not to declare openly their real objectives in other countries, especially not in colonial territories. In their official communiqués and public statements, they tend to couch their policies—whether altruistic or selfish—in ideological, humanitarian or religious forms—which are capable of giving at least some satisfaction to the moral sense and feelings which often dominate public opinion. It is therefore not surprising that in their disputes and negotiations about the Sudan, neither Britain nor Egypt has openly declared her own real interests and objectives in the country. The Condominium Agreement of 1899 was silent about the objectives of the two countries in the Sudan. In the 1936 Treaty of Alliance and Friendship, they jointly declared that their main purpose in the Sudan was the welfare of the Sudanese. Later, in their disagreement, they each proclaimed it to be their intention to save the Sudan from the territorial ambitions of imperial powers. And so, Egypt proclaimed it her own desire to protect the Sudan from British imperialism; Britain, on the other hand, maintained that she wished to protect the Sudan from Egyptian political corruption, slovenliness, and territorial incursions in Africa. But beneath these altruistic declarations lay Egypt's vital interests, and Britain's stake, in the Sudan. When the anxieties about these interests and stake were acute, or when attention was focused on them, they exploded—causing sometimes mere bubbles or gusts of passion, but quite often storms of violence in Anglo-Egyptian relations.

We therefore propose to examine first the Egyptian interests and later the British stake in the Sudan.

Egypt's primary interests in the Sudan are the waters of the Nile upon which Egypt and the Sudan depend; relief for her surplus population; and her need for external markets and capital investments.

Her seemingly remote, but also important, anxiety springs from her exposure to the dangerous currents of world strategy and politics in the Mediterranean region, as we shall show in Chapter 7 below.

The mighty Nile, the longest river in Africa (4,000 miles) and the second longest of the world's rivers, which emerges in Uganda from Lake Victoria—the second largest lake in the world; the Nile which fascinated Herodotus about 2,400 years ago, stirred the poetic imagination and thoughts of Shakespeare, inspired Nelson to victory in the Battle of the Nile in 1798, and kindled the literary imagination and fighting spirit of Winston Churchill in his *My African Journey* and *The River War*; this mighty Nile which fertilized early civilization, has also fertilized the Anglo-Egyptian dispute over the Sudan.

The Nile starts at Jinja in Uganda; at Khartoum it is joined by the Blue Nile which flows from Lake Tana in Ethiopia. From Khartoum, it proceeds for about 2,180 miles to the Mediterranean—passing through several cataracts before reaching Aswan in Egypt. From Aswan to the Delta the Nile has formed (by the perennial deposit of silt at the flood seasons beginning in July) a strip of fertile land 600 miles long and about ten miles wide. The Delta region which begins below Cairo is also built up of silt from the Nile. This fertile silt, essential to Egyptian farming, is brought down to Egypt by the Nile's tributaries from the Ethiopian plateau. The tributaries provide the flood, while the White Nile contributes most of the water from January to July—the low river season. One is therefore aptly reminded of the ancient Babylonian hymn:

> O thou river, who didst bring forth all things,
> When the great gods dug thee out,
> They set prosperity upon thy banks.

Thus, owing to its economic importance to the peoples and governments in its valley, the Nile has contributed much to the politico-economic friction between Britain, Egypt and the Sudan. Both Egypt and the Sudan are in turn concerned with maintaining good relations with Ethiopia, with the Belgian Congo and with Uganda, within whose boundaries lie the mountains and lakes whence the Nile derives its waters. The control of the Nile Waters has therefore been the subject of international discussions and agreements for many years. An example of this is the undertaking by the Emperor of Ethiopia in 1902

> not to construct, or allow to be constructed, any work on the Blue Nile, Lake Tana, or the Sobat, which could arrest the flow of their waters into the Nile, except in agreement with His Britannic Majesty's Government and the Government of the Sudan.[1]

The soil productivity and economic prosperity of both Egypt and the Sudan are mainly dependent on the irrigation of the land by the waters of the Nile. Therefore, the variation in the supply of the waters at different seasons of the year is most vital to the Nile Valley—particularly to both Egypt and the Sudan. The importance attached to the flood of the Nile by Egypt is evident from the report that in Egypt the height of the Nile flood has been recorded annually as 'the chief event of the year since at least 3600 B.C.'[2] For thousands of years Egypt has looked to the South to get gold, ivory and slaves, it is true; but also, first and foremost, because of those waters which to her were and still are the main sources of life. Without them her green fields would be barren waste within the great Sahara Desert, because rainfall in Egypt is negligible and all land, except the 2½ per cent watered by the Nile, is desert. This explains why Egyptians have a kind of fearful tenderness towards the Nile: 'From the dawn of history', Egyptian water engineers reverently plead, 'Egypt has depended on the flow of the waters of the Nile as much as the individual depends on the circulation of the blood'.[3]

Most of the geographical problems of the Nile which puzzled European geographers for several centuries have been solved by British explorers. James Bruce discovered the source of the Blue Nile in 1770, with financial assistance from Ali Bey, the Mameluke ruler of Egypt; Captain John H. Speke found the source of the White Nile at Victoria Nyanza in 1862; and Sir Samuel Baker explored the Atbara and other tributaries in 1862. But, economically, the Nile continues to offer problems of great and wide interest in regard to the conservation and distribution of its waters for the purposes of irrigation and hydro-electric power, more so now than ever. Consequently, the Egyptian

---

[1] *Treaties between the United Kingdom and Ethiopia relative to the Frontiers between the Soudan, Ethiopia and Eritrea.* Treaty Series, No. 16 (1902), Article III, p. 3.

[2] *Encyclopædia Britannica,* 1947, Vol. XVI, p. 454.

[3] Sudan Govt., *The Nile Waters Question—the Case for Egypt and the Case for the Sudan,* published by the Ministry of Irrigation and Hydro-Electric Power, Khartoum, December 1955, p. 10.

Department of Public Works has carried out special studies to determine how the waters of the Nile can be used most advantageously and economically, conscious, as it was, that the control of the Nile Waters was not wholly an Egyptian question. The basin also includes parts of the Sudan, Ethiopia, Uganda, the Belgian Congo, Tanganyika and Kenya. About 84 per cent of the water reaching Egypt, comes from the Ethiopian tributaries of the Nile—that is from the Blue Nile, and the rivers Atbara and Sobat. The central African lakes supply about 16 per cent; but the water from this source is more reliable from January to June, when the White Nile with the Sobat contributes about $2\frac{1}{2}$ times as much water as the Blue Nile and the Atbara put together.[1] Egypt and the Sudan, the two big consumers of the Nile waters, contribute only a tiny fraction of the flow.

It is convenient to pause here and indicate British interests in the Nile waters. Britain started in the 19th century the contribution to the study and planning of the development of the Nile Waters. Britain has either initiated, or contributed to, most of the contemporary great projects in the Nile Valley. She has furnished part of the capital, the personnel with the necessary technical and scientific knowledge, the essential machinery and equipment for the great engineering works which have been developed in Egypt and the Sudan. Consequently, Britain has been deeply involved in, and concerned about, the technical development of the Nile Waters, as the British Central Office of Information openly admits.[2]

Egypt's interests in, and apprehensions about, the Nile Waters therefore increased when the British Administration in the Sudan embarked upon agricultural development of a large area by means of artificial irrigation from the Nile. Professor Toynbee likens the importance of the Nile to Egypt to that of the Suez Canal to the British Empire:[3] but Mekki Abbas, a Sudanese, thinks that the control of the Nile is far more important to the existence of Egypt than the Suez Canal is to the British Empire. In any case, it is evident that Egypt's anxiety about the control of the Nile Waters by any foreign power is very real. Geographically, the Nile runs through Egypt; physically, it thrusts itself upon Egyptian eyes (but to most British people it exists only in imagination); emotionally, it is deep-seated in the heart of the Egyptian. Consequently, the Egyptian Government's concern was such that they

---

[1] Wright, H.M., *Christian Science Monitor*, 5 September 1950.

[2] (British) Central Office of Information, Reference Division: *Nile Waters Development* (R 2434), July 1952, p. 1.

[3] *Survey of International Affairs, 1925*, Vol. I, pp. 234–5.

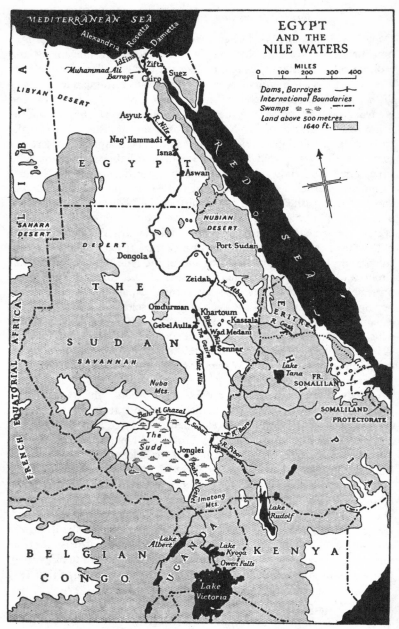

(Crown copyright—reproduced by permission of the Controller, H.M. Stationery Office)

expressed willingness in 1929 to postpone the question of settlement of the status of the Sudan in favour of a settlement about the Nile Waters.[1]

Their anxiety springs from the following factors. Egypt's livelihood has depended mainly on agriculture—over 70 per cent of the population depending upon farming. From time immemorial the Nile flood supplied Egypt's need, but during his rule, Mohammed Ali introduced summer irrigation; summer water therefore became a necessity. Today, agriculture in Egypt no longer depends on the Nile flood, but upon hydrological engineering, which artificially controls and irrigates the land. This control is becoming increasingly dependent upon the Nile Waters (e.g. the proposed Sudd El Aali or High Dam, at Aswan). The Condominium could be used by the British administration in the Sudan to promote British economic and political interests at the expense of the Egyptians, especially because Britain is the manufacturer and the Sudan a grower of cotton; also, the technical staff, capital and machinery of the great dams were partly, if not mainly, British. This fear was forcibly driven home to the Egyptians by the Nile clause of the British Ultimatum of 1924. In answer to the British Government's question as to why he included this item in the Ultimatum, Allenby explained that it 'was included to impress on Egypt the power we could wield if necessary by our control of the Sudan'.[2]

To the Sudan, also, the waters of the Nile are of vital importance. While the Southern part of the country has an annual rainfall sufficient for the cultivation of crops, the North is practically without rain, and the annual rainfall in Khartoum is below 200 mm. Consequently, the question of the Nile Waters became at least one of the main elements in the minds of Egyptian statesmen and negotiators when dealing with Britain about the Sudan question. When the Sudan Government took over in 1950 the now famous Gezira Scheme, the Egyptians considered it as a great threat to their own economic interests. They therefore opposed the Scheme because of its politico-economic consequences and they agitated for the control of the river from Cairo, insisting on full Egyptian sovereignty over the Sudan.

Egyptian opposition to the utilization of the Nile Waters for irrigation purposes in the Sudan had three interwoven roots—economic,

[1] Correspondence dated Cairo, 7 May 1929, in the *Exchange of Notes between H.M. Government in the U.K. and the Egyptian Government regarding the Use of the Nile Waters for Irrigation Purposes*, Treaty Series, No. 17 (1929), p. 2.

[2] Wavell, Field-Marshal Earl (Viceroy of India), *Allenby, Soldier and Statesman*, London, 1946, p. 337.

technical and political. Economically, it was shown that in Egypt irrigation had been resorted to only when no more cultivation could be done without its aid; but that in the Sudan the Makwar dam, for instance, was projected 'long before the growing possibilities of the Sudan had been fully exploited'.[1]

An attempt was made at the beginning of the scheme to assure Egypt that the British administration in the Sudan would not interfere with the Nile Waters to the detriment of Egypt on the grounds that Britain herself needed Egyptian cotton.

While politicians on both sides haggled, British and Egyptian engineers began a system of Nile projects to meet the water needs of the Sudan and Egypt. The projects included: the Aswan and Sennar dams; a Jebel Awlia dam (30 miles south of Khartoum); an Equatorial Lakes dam; a dam on Lake Tana; and a dam on the Nile, near Merowe in the Northern Sudan, to protect Egypt against high floods.

These projects were examined by the Nile Projects Commission appointed under the joint auspices of the Governments in Cairo and London. The importance attached to the problem is indicated by the international nature of the Commission, which was composed of a member nominated by the Government of India (Chairman), one nominated by the University of Cambridge; and another chosen by the Government of the United States.

The Commission was asked to give to the Egyptian Government its opinion on the projects, so that further regulation of the Nile supply for the benefit of Egypt and the Sudan could be made; and to report upon the propriety of the manner in which, as a result of these projects, the increased supply of available water provided by them would be allocated at each stage of development between Egypt and the Sudan.[2]

In their report, the Commission endorsed unanimously the plans set out in Nile Control, but did not agree on the matter of the allocation of waters. Hence there was a Minority Report (by the American nominee) and a Majority Report.

The Majority Report in essence recommended that Egypt be given the right to use the discharge of the Nile in low season, and the Sudan to use the flood waters for her needs. The Minority Report recommended that the vested rights of Egypt, as they then existed, should be respected and that the balance of unappropriated water (or surplus supply) should be divided equally between Egypt and the Sudan.

[1] Arthur Ransome, *Manchester Guardian*, 15 May 1925.
[2] H.M.S.O., *Report of the Nile Projects Commission*, 1920, p. 5.

In any case, the political atmosphere in Egypt and Anglo-Egyptian relations (Egyptian militant nationalism and British militant diplomacy) soon after the First World War, when the Reports came out, was not conducive to an agreement on the matter. The question was shelved until 1925, when another committee set out to examine it. Its purpose was to examine and propose 'the basis on which irrigation can be carried out with full consideration of the interests of Egypt and without detriment to her natural and historic rights'.[1] Their recommendations were based, except for some amendments, on those by the Majority Report of the previous committee; they were adopted substantially in a subsequent exchange of Notes between Lord Allenby and Mahmoud Pasha on 7 May 1929, and they formed a basis of the 1929 Nile Waters Agreement.

One of the amendments allotted a net volume of 929 million cubic metres to the Sudan, or just 1/22nd of Egypt's share. This amendment was said to be in the interests of economy and easy control of water; but in effect, the Agreement limits the amount of water which the Sudan is allowed to use between 1 January and 15 July in any year for irrigation during the low season.[2]

The 1929 Agreement guaranteed Egypt's irrigation interests, at least temporarily. In his communication of 7 May 1929, Lord Lloyd, confirming the arrangements mutually agreed upon, assured Mahmoud Pasha that the 1929 Settlement would certainly facilitate development and promote prosperity in both Egypt and the Sudan.[3] Lord Lloyd's estimation appears correct in the economic aspect only. It does not substantially meet the political considerations. The 1925 Commission foresaw the necessity, from time to time, for reviewing the questions discussed in their recommendations upon which the 1929 Agreement was based. The Commission was impressed by the fact that future developments in Egypt might require the construction of works in the Sudan and in the neighbouring territories such as Uganda, Kenya and Tanganyika. They therefore declared that neither the elaborate drafting of an Agreement nor the provision of special machinery for adjudication should be allowed to obscure the importance of mutual confidence and co-operation in all matters concerning the river and its waters.[4] The essential mutual confidence and co-operation were yet to come.

[1] Cmd. 3348. Treaty Series No. 17 (1929), p. 6.
[2] Sudan Govt., Ministry of Irrigations and Hydro-Electric Power, *The Nile Waters Question*, p. 2.
[3] H.M.S.O., *Notes in Regard to the Use of the Waters of the Nile*, in Cmd. 3348, p. 50.
[4] *Ibid.*, p. 31.

Egypt even today, fears the political aspect of the control of the Nile in the Upper Basin. Any strong power holding the control of the Nile could keep Egypt on her knees; because 'He who holds Khartoum holds Cairo', as the British often say. Sir Reginald Portall, British Delegate to Uganda, writing in 1894, declared: 'He who holds the Upper Nile, could dispose of Egypt as he likes and even destroy her'.[1]

As indicated above, the available waters of the Nile are shared between Egypt and the Sudan in accordance with the Nile Waters Agreement of 1929. As it works out even at the moment of writing, the Sudan gets about 1/23rd of the waters and the rest goes to Egypt. The Sudan asks for more than this allotment. The (British) Irrigation Adviser to the Minister of Irrigation and Hydro-Electric Power informed the writer at Khartoum in February 1956, that the Gezira Scheme, which is now the mainstay of the Sudan's economy, could certainly be expanded to 3,000,000 feddans (acres) if additional waters could be obtained.

In Egypt, on the other hand, the land problem is much more acute and the need for larger water supplies is approaching the point of desperation. Consequently, in addition to the 'Century Storage' Scheme[2] Egypt has been making other Nile projects, which include electrification of Aswan Dam, and the contribution of the Sudd El Aali (High Dam).

Since the establishment of the Revolutionary Regime in 1952, two executive agencies—the National Resources Development Board and the National Production Council—have been created in Egypt for a rapid development of Egypt's economy. It is evident therefore that Egypt hopes to make increasingly greater use of the Nile Waters.

The most recent and indeed the greatest evidence is the proposed High Dam at Aswan, situated 4 miles south of the present Aswan Dam. Its capacity is estimated at 120 billion cubic metres. It will be about 3 miles wide and 300 feet high, and will cost about £E120 million, together with a hydro-electric power station.

On Thursday, 9 February 1956, Col. Nasser, Prime Minister of Egypt, concluded discussions with Mr. Eugene Black, President of the International Bank for Reconstruction and Development (World Bank). 'Substantial agreement' was reached on the Bank's participation in the cost of the High Dam, for an amount equivalent to $200,000,000.[3] The Egyptian Government had hoped to complete the project by 1959.

[1] H.M.S.O., *Notes in Regard to the Use of the Waters of the Nile*, in Cmd. 3348, p. 29.
[2] A storage to last a long time.
[3] *Egyptian Mail*, Cairo, 11 February 1956, p. 1.

This hope may not, however, materialize so soon as envisaged. This is because, for reasons best known to the Anglo-American authorities, whose influence with the World Bank is considerable, the promise of financial assistance was suddenly withdrawn. The notorious Suez Crisis that followed in 1956–7 delayed any concentrated effort on the construction of the dam.

On the other hand, the Sudan, too, is deeply interested in, if not disturbed by, these Egyptian projects; as we have said, the Sudan already feels herself entitled to a bigger share of the Nile Waters than she now receives. In Press statements on 20 November and 1 December 1953, Sayed Ismael El Azhari emphasized that his National Unionist Party did not recognize the Anglo-Egyptian Agreement allotting 'only one twenty-third of the Nile Waters' to the Sudan. He intended negotiating a new agreement whereby the Sudan would be allowed more water with which to develop its agriculture.[1]

The National Unionist Party, which formed the first Sudanese Parliamentary Government in 1954, issued a politico-economic blueprint in April 1955. Their declared economic principles included (i) the exploitation of the resources of the Sudan 'to the possible extent and for the benefit of the whole people' of the country; (ii) expansion of agriculture and increase of land productivity by means of both natural and technical methods; and (iii) 'to work for industrialization on studied plans'.[2]

These Sudanese plans, like the Egyptian projects, will depend upon the use of the waters of the Nile. Realizing this situation, the new regime in the Sudan sought to make treaties with the Egyptian Government. The importance attached to the Nile by the Sudanese is further revealed in the fact that the Nile Policy took precedence over any other economic schemes listed in the Government's blueprint. In regard to the waters of the Nile, the Unionist Government declared its policy:

> The Nile is the main source of life for the two countries, and, as it connects Egypt with the Sudan, it also runs through other countries. So the problems relating to the Nile Waters should be defined through co-ordination of interests and through official treaties between the two Governments.[3]

The Sudan's long concern about the Nile Waters is abundantly demonstrated by the fact that the Sudan Government appointed in 1946

---

[1] Keesing's *Contemporary Archives*, Vol. IX, London, 1952–4, pp. 13, 304.
[2] Full text in *Sudan Weekly News* published by the Sudan Govt.: Ministry for National Guidance and Social Affairs, Khartoum, 19 April 1955, p. 1.
[3] *Ibid.*

a Committee—known as the Jonglei Committee—and a Team of Investigators, called 'The Jonglei Investigation Team'. The terms of reference for the team included a detailed study of the proposals about the Nile Waters 'as submitted by the Egyptian Government, and all information at present available concerning them'.[1] The Investigation Team was composed of twenty-one various experts from all Ministries and Departments of the Sudan;[2] the membership is therefore another testimony to the significance attached to the problem by the Sudan Government. The Government published the Report and Recommendations of the team at the time when the decision about the future of the Sudan in relation to both Britain and Egypt was imminent. It covers field work from 1946 to 1952 and is published in five substantial volumes, with the significant title, *Equatorial Nile Project and Its Effects in the Anglo-Egyptian Sudan.*

In December 1955, the Ministry of Irrigation and Hydro-Electric Power, Khartoum, published a 54-page brochure—*The Nile Waters Question*—which summarized the case of the Sudan and the case for Egypt, as put during the Cairo discussions of April 1955. At the time of writing no agreement has yet been reached between Egypt and the Sudan. Egypt seems to feel, rightly or wrongly, that in the negotiations the hand was the hand of the Sudan, but the voice was the voice of British advisers, and that as soon as the British were pushed out of the Sudan, agreement would be possible. The Sudan became independent in January 1956, but the attitude of the Sudanese Government was already summed up in 'The Case for the Sudan'. The Sudanese argue that the Sudan was not a party to the 1929 Nile Waters Agreement between Britain and Egypt. They state, categorically:

> The present Sudan Government considers that it was an unjust agreement because it limited the development of irrigation in the Sudan while leaving Egypt free to develop her irrigation as fast as she pleased. As a result Egypt has increased her established right in the Waters of the Nile from 40 milliards in 1920 to 48 milliards at the present time. The Sudan does not dispute rights which have been established while her hands have been tied, but she claims that the time has now come to change the Nile Waters Agreement.[3]

---

[1] Sudan Govt., *The Equatorial Nile Project and Its Effects in the Anglo-Egyptian Sudan,* Introduction and Summary, Khartoum, 1955, p. iii.

[2] *Ibid.,* see the page showing members of the team, and the 'Acknowledgements'. Its chairman was Dr. P. P. Howell, of the Sudan Political Service (1948–53).

[3] Sudan Govt., Ministry of Irrigation and Hydro-Electric Power, *The Nile Waters Question,* pp. 2–3.

Commenting on the discussion held in Cairo during April 1955, between delegates from Egypt and the Sudan, the Sudanese Government concludes:

No agreement was reached, and Egypt then resorted to public abuse of their Sudanese guests. . . . The Sudan Government wishes to place on record their resentment at the tactics adopted by the Government of Egypt.[1]

Undoubtedly, it will be a number of years before the Sudan can make full use of her share in the waters of the Nile. But, nevertheless, she is very anxious to have that share defined now. The reason is that the Sudan Government fears that 'Otherwise, Egypt would continue to acquire established rights as she has in the past, and the Sudan would be the loser'.[2]

The Sudan Government therefore insists that the full 84 milliards, being the balance of water not allocated by the 1929 Agreement, must be equitably divided between Egypt and the Sudan *before* work starts on the Sudd el Aali (High Dam). The Government asserts:

It must not be forgotten that the construction of the Sudd el Aali will drive fifty thousand Sudanese citizens (in the town and district of Wadi Halfa) from their homes and livelihoods. Under international law the Sudan Government has an unquestionable right to veto the Sudd el Aali project, and she will do so unless her interests are properly safeguarded before work starts.[3]

The stand taken by the Sudan Government is supported by certain members of the British Parliament. On 14 March 1956, Lord Killearn asked the Minister of State for Foreign Affairs whether the British Government was completely satisfied that the Sudanese Government's agreement to the High Dam project was sufficiently definite to justify British participation in the finance of the Dam.[4]

Thus, it was forcibly brought home to Egypt, once again, that a powerful and unfriendly Sudan could jeopardize Egyptian interests in the waters of the Nile. Hence, Egypt sought, before the 1952 Revolution, to achieve the Unity of the Nile Valley 'under the Egyptian Crown', and now with the Republican flag of Egypt.

But this is not all: other claimants for the gifts of the Nile have been coming up of late. In 1950, Uganda (British Protectorate) started to harness the headwaters of the Victoria Nile to provide 'the mightiest

---

[1] *Ibid.*, p. 8.   [2] *Ibid.*, p. 6.   [3] *Ibid.*, p. 3.
[4] House of Lords, *Official Reports*, Vol. CXCVI, No. 71, London, 14 March 1956, p. 389.

hydro-electric plan in the Empire',[1] and 'incomparably the largest storage reservoir in the world'.[2]

The principal works envisaged by the British are a dam across the White Nile at Owen Falls in Uganda, which will increase the storage capacity of Lake Victoria, and a hydro-electric station associated with the dam to generate power for industrial expansion in British Uganda; a smaller dam on Lake Albert, which is partly in the Belgian Congo territory; the Jonglei Canal System, which will train the river through the Sudd in the Sudan; and another dam at the source of the Blue Nile at Lake Tana in Ethiopia, to increase the storage capacity of Lake Tana and to provide a hydro-electric station.

Naturally, Egypt is deeply concerned about these projects; but she is being assured by the British, who own most of the capital investments in the projects just mentioned, that there 'would be consequential new work to be carried out in Egypt to ensure that the great new access of water brought fresh benefits only and not dangers to the flood protection system'.[3]

Consultations between the British, Belgian and Ethiopian Governments were in progress in relation to the last three stages of the Scheme as listed above. But as to the first stage—the Owen Falls Dam—work was begun after agreement on its execution between the United Kingdom and Egyptian Governments in May 1949.[4] It was formally opened by Queen Elizabeth in April 1954. Egyptian concern and British appreciation of it are indicated by the fact that an Egyptian resident engineer and his staff were at the site to represent Egyptian interests during construction; and they were responsible for carrying out instructions which regulated the water that passed through the (Owen Falls) dam. The formal agreement between the two Governments regarding the dam is embodied in the Exchange of Notes, dated Cairo, 16 July 1952, to 5 January 1953.[5]

It is most probable that, some time in the future, Ethiopia, too, will make similar claims in respect of the Blue Nile. It is clear, therefore, that the waters of the *moody* Nile will continue to be a delicate subject of negotiations in the future between the various Governments interested in the Nile Valley. Meanwhile, Egyptians and some Sudanese politicians, in search of a security formula, rest on the attractive slogan —THE UNITY OF THE NILE VALLEY.

[1] *Daily Express*, London, 27 March 1950.
[2] Central Office of Information, *Nile Waters Development*, London, 1952, p. 6.
[3] Central Office of Information, Reference Division, *Nile Waters Development*, p. 6.
[4] *Ibid.*   [5] Treaty Series, No. 30 (1954), Cmd. 9132.

For the moment, however, the control and distribution of the Nile Waters continue to cause anxiety; Egyptians who formerly agitated for the political unity of Egypt and the Sudan 'under the Egyptian Crown', continue their campaign, though more mildly, under the revolutionary flag or the Arab League, of which the Sudan became a member in January 1956. Apprehensive about the waters of the Nile and conscious of the Egypto-Sudanese consanguinity, General Neguib engaged 'in a conspiracy to unite the Egyptians and the Sudanese in an effort to free both countries from British tutelage'.[1] However, Britain's capital investments and other interests in the waters of the Nile were among the forces which govern British policy in the Sudan: it was to bring up the Sudan as an independent state outside Egypt's political control, should she fail to incorporate the Condominium in the British Commonwealth and Empire. This policy constituted, in the minds of the Egyptians, an added threat to Egypt's interests in the waters of the Nile. It drove Mohammed Fahmy Nokrashy Pasha to plead before the Security Council of the United Nations in 1947:

I have shown you that Egypt cannot live without the Sudan, and the Sudan cannot live without Egypt. Nor does the life-giving Nile alone compel our partnership. Tradition, coming down through hundreds of years, giving our people to a large extent a common language and a common culture, forging for us links which neither Egyptians nor Sudanese wish to sever; these traditions make Nile Unity a must for all the people who live upon its bounty.[2]

2. THE SUDAN: A RELIEF FOR EGYPT'S SURPLUS POPULATION

In the 19th century, the population of Europe overflowed, and occupied 'empty lands', such as the Americas and Australia. Similarly, in this 20th century, Egypt, with a greatly increasing population and inadequate means of feeding them at home, is seeking 'empty lands' for her surplus population.

In 1951, the British Board of Trade expressed alarm at the problem of Egyptian population, which tends to increase rapidly, without corresponding increase in the means of subsistence.[3]

Furthermore, the very first sentence of an Egyptian Government publication on social and economic problems, refers to the population,

---

[1] Mohammed Neguib, *Egypt's Destiny*, p. 15.
[2] United Nations Security Council, *Verbatim Records of the 197th Meeting*, Lake Success, 11 August 1947.
[3] H.M.S.O., *Overseas Economic Survey; Egypt, 1951*, p. 1.

which is 'increasing quite rapidly and causing concern to the authorities in regard to finding means of living for these extra numbers'.[1]

The density of population per square mile of cultivated land in Egypt was 1,450 in 1937—more than twice as high as that of England and Wales (672 per square mile) and ten times as high as the average population density in Europe. The average annual increase in population from 1950 to 1955 is 2·5 per cent.[2] The density has risen to 1,600 per square mile—'the highest in the world'.[3] The birth-rate in Egypt is, and may continue to be for some time, one of the highest in the world. Calculating on the 1955 population figure of 23,240,000 and the current rate of growth (2·5 per cent), Egypt would have about 581,000 more children every year. It would, therefore, become necessary for the Egyptian Government to provide food and employment for an additional two million three hundred and twenty-four thousand (2,324,000) people every four years. In any case, it is generally realized that there is a large but unascertainable surplus of rural population in Egypt, with little or no productivity. In the urban areas, over-population shows itself through under-employment.

The Egyptian Revolutionary Government is undertaking certain projects of land reclamation. Some 311,680 acres are to be reclaimed, apart from the districts of Ibis, Western Fayoum, Nubariah, Wadi El Natrun and Ras El Hekmah. Situated 80 kilometres north of Cairo and west of the Nubariah Canal is a new venture—the 'Liberation Province' —an area of about 1,200,000 acres. Here the Egyptian Government hopes to reclaim an average of 34,000 acres annually.[4]

However, these projects, imaginative and laudable though they are, can solve only a small fraction of Egypt's population and land problems. Therefore, a partial solution has been sought in internal redistribution of population to the sparsely peopled north of the Delta; and, more important, by emigration to the Sudan or Iraq, where geographical and agricultural conditions, as well as language and religion, are very akin to those of Egypt.

Two questions now arise: whether or not there are opportunities for Egyptian labour in the Sudan, and whether there is any serious objection on the part of the Sudanese to Egyptian immigration. Evidently, opportunities exist, and opposition, if there is any, does not appear to be strong.

[1] Egypt, Ministry of Social Affairs, Labour Department, Cairo, 1951, p. 7.
[2] Republic of Egypt, Ministry of Finance and Economy, Statistical Department, *Pocket Year Book for 1953*, Cairo, 1954, p. 1.
[3] Gunther, John, 'Inside Egypt,' *Reader's Digest*, May 1955, p. 68.
[4] Republic of Egypt, Information Administration, Cairo, February 1956.

The acute shortage of labour in the Sudan is met in part by immigrants from West Africa—especially from French Equatorial Africa and from Northern Nigeria; this is evident from the statistics of the picking labour in the Gezira Scheme. Picking labour there is usually drawn from three main sources: locally, i.e. from the Blue Nile Province; from other parts of the Sudan, notably the two Western Provinces of Kordofon and Darfur; and from foreign sources, especially French Equatorial Africa and Northern Nigeria (Hausa, etc.). Locally recruited labour accounts for a little over half of the total labour force at the Gezira, but non-Sudanese constitute the second biggest group of pickers—amounting, quite often, to double the number of Sudanese recruited from outside the Blue Nile Province. The following figures of picking labour for two seasons during the Second World War, two post-War, and two very recent, seasons illustrate the point:

PICKING LABOUR: SUDAN GEZIRA SCHEME[1]

Season	Blue Nile Province	Western Province	Foreigners: French Equatorial Africa	Fellata, Hausa, etc.
1941–2	75,415	19,312	21,004	18,973
1942–3	49,982	7,626	11,693	13,001
1945–6	98,244	9,832	15,857	12,669
1946–7	101,042	8,503	15,466	12,918
1951–2	98,080	23,626	24,901	11,069
1952–3	126,561	29,711	29,651	17,483

Members of a select committee of the Advisory Council of the Northern Sudan in 1947 felt very strongly 'that to encourage foreign labour is most undesirable because of the great harm it does to the Sudan'.[2] On the other hand, in February 1956, Mr. Mubarak Zarouk, Minister of External Affairs of the Sudan, informed the writer at Khartoum that 'because of the high productivity of their labour at the Gezira, the West African population there is an economic asset to the Sudan'.

However, common language, ties of relatively common folk-ways, geographical nearness and political status make it easier for Egyptians to become assimilated than for West Africans, especially in those areas

[1] Sudan Govt., Gezira Board: *Second Annual Report*, 1953, p. 33.
[2] The Advisory Council of the Northern Sudan, *Proceedings of the Sixth Session*, Khartoum, 1947, p. 42.

in the Sudan where the population is of Arab majority. But in spite of the ethnical and other factors in favour of Egyptian immigration, even some Northern Sudanese fear it. Many Sudanese regard the Egyptians with suspicion because of the personal domination of the Sudan by Mohammed Ali, the oppression of the Turko-Egyptian Government in the Sudan, and also because Mohammed Ali's conquest had the ulterior motive of the acquisition of slaves and gold in the Sudan. In addition, the Independence Front (a political party led by the Mahdi's son) suspect that if the Egyptians migrate in large numbers into the Sudan, they might form a 'fifth column' there and put up a resistance to the independence movement for the Sudan, which the Party supports.

Nevertheless, when the limit of cultivation has been reached at home, Egypt will want to send the overflow of her population to the Sudan, as the line of least resistance. After the 1927 census in Egypt, the population problem became more serious to Egyptian statesmen; consequently, the question of Egyptian immigration to the Sudan was brought up for discussion during the Anglo-Egyptian dispute in 1930 and it partly accounted for the breakdown of the negotiations between Henderson and Nahas Pasha in that year. By the Treaty of 1936, however, Egypt succeeded in obtaining British agreement to Egyptian immigration, unrestricted except by consideration of public health and order.

It is therefore understandable that in a letter published in the *New York Times* in October 1950, K. S. Selim, then member of the Egyptian delegation to the United Nations, pleaded so fervently for the unity of the Nile Valley—Egypt and the Sudan. He stressed that the two countries had common economic interests and that their separation would be harmful to both, because of the over-population in Egypt and under-population in the Sudan.[1]

It is fair to mention the fact that Egyptians endeavour not to discriminate against Sudanese labour in Egypt; indeed, Egyptian authorities consider the Sudanese as Egyptian nationals. This is evident from the fact that several Sudanese are employed in the Egyptian Civil Service, even as members of the diplomatic corps. The writer has met a few Sudanese working at the Egyptian Embassy in London and in the Civil Service in Egypt, though often in the lower grades.

In spite of the foregoing facts, the employment of Egyptians in the Sudan remains comparatively small. Out of the 'classified posts'[2] in

---

[1] *New York Times*, 5 October 1950.
[2] 'Classified posts' are those for which individual provisions are made in the Annual Budgets of the Central Government.

the Sudan Civil Service on 30 November 1950, 993 were British and 202 Egyptians.[1] In 1951, even when Sudanization had taken root, British Nationals held 10·2 per cent whilst Egyptians held only 2 per cent of the classified posts in the country.

In June 1953, of the permanent staff of the Gezira Scheme, 114 were British and there were no Egyptians; at the end of that year the number of Field Inspectors was 63 British and 44 Sudanese—again, no Egyptians.[2] As the Gezira Scheme was not part of the Administration as such, there would appear to be no constitutional obligation to employ Egyptians, but even so, the Egyptian Government would have liked to see some Egyptians employed.

What then, in view of the over-population in Egypt, is the explanation for the comparative insignificance of the Egyptian labour force in the Sudan? In supplying the answer we should note that emigrants into the Sudan could be classified into agricultural labourers, would-be peasant cultivators, and professional men and women seeking Civil Service jobs or private enterprise.

While it is a fact that Egyptians have been, on the whole, a non-migratory people, this characteristic is not sufficient of itself to explain the limited number of Egyptians emigrating into the Sudan. One reason is the fact that the demand for labour in the Sudan agriculture which could be met by Egyptian immigrants, is largely seasonal. This seasonal character suits the West African Muslim immigrants who do not come to the Sudan for permanent employment, but who, on the whole, merely use the Sudan as a stop-gap—to do seasonal work, and to earn part of the expenses of a pilgrimage to Mecca. Some do, of course, remain permanently. Egyptians, on the other hand, would naturally want permanent employment in the Sudan. But the agricultural labour available for immigrants is too seasonal to receive serious attention from the Egyptian fellaheen.

Those Egyptians, who might want to go to the Sudan and establish themselves there permanently as peasant cultivators, would find themselves up against many practical difficulties. In the first place, Sudan law prevents any non-Sudanese from purchasing land without the specific permission of the Government,[3] a permission which so far has been given very rarely, especially by the British Administration. Secondly, the Nile Waters Agreement of 1929 limits the amount of water for

[1] Sudan Govt., *1001 Facts About the Sudan*, Khartoum, 1952, p. 10.
[2] The Sudan Gezira Board, *3rd Annual Report*, Cairo, June 1953, p. 17.
[3] See *Laws of the Sudan*, Vol. III, Khartoum, 1940, pp. 1310–11 (the Natives Disposition of Lands Restriction Ordinance of 1918 and 1922).

irrigation purposes in the Sudan; naturally, the first claim on the limited amount of water goes to Sudanese applicants. The demand for trained personnel in the Sudan is unquestionably large. The share of Egypt in supplying this demand has been rather limited. This is in part due to the fact that those responsible for the recruitment of staff had tended to preserve, as much as possible, the predominantly British character of the Sudan Administration. The immigration and employment clauses of the 1936 Agreement did not adequately meet Egypt's objective—full employment for her university graduates and other qualified men and women—because, although Egyptian immigration was free, all appointments remained vested in the British Governor-General. This is not to deny that after the signing of the 1936 Treaty a number of Egyptians had been recruited to the Sudan Civil Service. But their number was rather negligible; furthermore, these officials had been largely teachers and technicians rather than administrators. Besides, Egypt—herself still under-developed—could ill afford losing a large number of her trained technicians. She could have supplied a comparatively large number of administrators—recruited from the annually increasing output of her universities (there were 27,000 students at Al Azhar and Cairo Universities alone in 1954–5), and from Egyptian overseas graduates. That possibility had not become a reality, owing to the British ascendancy in the Sudan. The consequent frustration increased Anglo-Egyptian friction.

3. THE SUDAN AS EGYPT'S EXTERNAL MARKET

Naturally, there has been trade between Egypt and the Sudan, especially in cotton. The Sudanese population wear, by and large, cotton clothes all the year round. And Egypt, in spite of competition from Japan and Lancashire, exported into the Sudan manufactured cotton worth £E63,000 in 1941,[1] rising to £E962,912 in 1947.[2]

After reaching the peak of the purchasing power of the Egyptian populace, an assured market in the Sudan would help to sustain Egyptian industries; at present, possibilities for further expansion of Egyptian trade with the Sudan are by no means exhausted.

Commercially, Egypt evidently regards the Sudan not so much as a foreign country but as a sort of semi-domestic territory. This attitude

---

[1] *Review of Commercial Conditions*, p. 22.
[2] *Annual Report*, 1947, p. 59.

is portrayed in the annual statement of foreign trade, made by the Egyptian Government, in which the following annotation appears:

Trade with the Sudan:—
  The figures of the foreign trade of Egypt do not include trade with the Sudan.[1]

However, according to the Sudan Government, Egyptian exports into the Sudan in 1952, amounted to £E4,351,722[2] and £E5,033,410 in 1954.[3]

The Sudan was, therefore, a market vital to Egypt. But Egypt's commercial strength in the Sudan was increasingly threatened by Britain's ascendancy. In 1920, for instance, Egypt's exports into the Sudan were £E3,868,335, whilst those of Britain were only £E150,679. In recent years, however, Britain has been in the lead. In 1947, the figure for Britain was £E3,888,360 and for Egypt £E3,507,553.[4] In 1954, Egypt's exports to the Sudan were less than half those of Britain. The difference was about the same in 1953, when the values were £E4,214,374 for Britain and £E2,108,193 for Egypt. We must not, however, overlook the fact that even today the Sudan needs a large variety of manufactured goods (e.g. engineering products) which Egypt, with her limited range of industry, cannot supply. To lessen, if not remove, this commercial threat from Britain, Egyptians emphasized the unity of the Nile Valley. Britain, on the other hand, endeavoured to keep and strengthen her own commercial position in the Sudan; and this competition formed part of the factors underlying the Anglo-Egyptian friction over the Sudan.

Another factor is that the Sudan, too, now competes on a different level with Egypt, at least on the agricultural if not yet on the industrial level. Egypt, being responsible for about six per cent of the world's supply of long staples, ranks second amongst the cotton exporting countries of the world.[5] Consequently, Egyptians feel that their own soil and climate are better suited for the production of cotton than those of the Sudan. They dislike the cotton competition from the South, where the Gezira Scheme—a private project—now produced large quantities of cotton which had brought profits not only to the Sudan but to British shareholders as well (until July 1950, when the Scheme was nationalized).

---

[1] Republic of Egypt, *Annual Statement of Foreign Trade for 1952*, Govt. Press, Cairo, 1954, p. 7.
[2] Sudan Govt., *Foreign Trade and Internal Statistics*, Khartoum, January 1953, p. 26.
[3] *Ibid.*, January 1955, p. 40.
[4] Sudan Govt., *Foreign Trade Report*, 1947, p. 2, Table III.
[5] International Cotton Advisory Committee, *Cotton—Monthly Review of the World Situation*, Washington, U.S.A., Vol. VI, June 1953, p. 7.

Therefore, Egyptians advocated a one-valley system based on economic co-operation rather than competition.

4. THE SUDAN AS AN OUTLET FOR EGYPT'S CAPITAL INVESTMENTS

The foreign capital investments in the Sudan belong almost exclusively to the British. The British Board of Trade announces that 'the United Kingdom remains the Sudan's best customer'.[1] But Egypt, too, is eager to invest capital in the Sudan. This desire has been well expressed by Abbas Hilmi II, a Khedive of Egypt, who wrote:

> We consider that the right of Egyptians to participate in the development of the country [Sudan] must be asserted and full equality in the opportunities of investment with those enjoyed by the British capitalists should be claimed and accorded.[2]

Apart from private Egyptian investments, there are Government financial institutions with the capacities and propensity to invest capital not only in developments at home in Egypt, but also abroad—particularly in the Sudan. There has existed, since 1931, a Farm Credit Bank, known as the Crédit Agricole d'Egypte, formed to meet the needs of small farmers and cultivators. In 1947, an Industrial Bank was created, with Government participation in both capital and management, 'to facilitate the promotion and development of industrial enterprises'.[3] Since the removal in 1937 (as a result of the Anglo-Egyptian Treaty of 1936) of the financial disabilities imposed on Egypt by the Capitulations, the general budget accounts of Egypt had shown a substantial surplus each year. These accumulated surpluses were intended by the Government for the financing of economic development plans immediately in Egypt and eventually in the Sudan.[4] Although each operated its own exchange control over all transactions outside the Egyptian monetary area, Egypt and the Sudan together formed a separate and independent monetary area, and the Sudan had a common currency with Egypt.

While it is true that 'Egyptians are still reluctant to invest in new ventures—unless there is a prospect of high and rapid returns',[5] the Egyptian Government—as distinct from a regime—has facilities and a

[1] *Sudan, Review of Commercial Conditions*, H.M.S.O., London, 1952, p. 7.
[2] Abbas Hilmi, *A Few Words on the Anglo-Egyptian Settlement*, p. 29.
[3] United Nations, Department of Economic Affairs, Financial Division: *Egypt—Public Financial Information Papers*, Lake Success, New York, 1950, p. 7.
[4] *Ibid.*
[5] Royal Institute of International Affairs: *Great Britain and Egypt, 1914–51*, Information Paper No. 19, London, 1952, p. 171.

span of life far greater than those at the disposal of individuals, and is eager to invest in new ventures.

Egypt's investment interests in the Sudan are further indicated by the fact that the President of the Board of Directors of the National Bank of Egypt devoted seven paragraphs to the economic situation in the Sudan during 1953–4 while addressing the fifty-fifth Annual General Meeting of the shareholders at Cairo, on 23 March 1955. In the address he admitted:

> We have not restricted our commercial business in the Sudan and we have thus played a large part in financing the cotton-crop. . . . Loans granted to commercial banks have increased, totalling £E1,900,000 at 31 December 1954, and have been carried forward for financing the 1955/56 crop. . . . The Bank continues to find scope for its activities in the Sudan, financing crops other than cotton, e.g. gum Arabic, and furthering import trade.[1]

To this we should add the fact that the Sudan Government is indebted to Egypt to the extent of £E5,414,525 for development advances, of which £E150,000 had been discharged by 31 December 1949.[2] Furthermore, Egyptian capital investments have been sunk in irrigation works in the Sudan, e.g. the Jebel and Awlia dams—just 30 miles south of Khartoum. Obviously, there is more room for this form of capital investment, especially when Egypt and the Sudan get down to the actual problem of harnessing more effectively the waters of the Nile.

In the light of the foregoing facts, we reach the conclusion that in an attempt to solve their internal problems, i.e. the development of the Nile Waters, over-population, trade and capital investments, Egyptians seek a merger of the Sudan with Egypt in a way somewhat similar to that by which Britain relieves herself of some of her own internal problems through the political and economic consanguinity she maintains with the British Commonwealth of Nations. Egypt's own brand of commonwealth or the hope for one, is implied in the political slogan —'Unity of the Nile Valley', which we shall fully discuss in the second part of the next chapter. In the first section of that chapter we shall now proceed to deal with the geographical (or locational) problems of Egypt in relation to her vital interests in the Sudan.

[1] National Bank of Egypt, *Report for 55th Ordinary General Meeting, 1954*, Cairo, 1955, p. 18. Also *The Times*, London, 22 April 1955.
[2] Sudan Govt., *Sudan Almanac, 1952*, p. 73.

7

THE GEO-POLITICAL AND IDEOLOGICAL FACTORS

1. THE SUDAN AS EGYPT'S 'BUFFER STATE' AGAINST THE STORMS OF MEDITERRANEAN GEO-POLITICS

The geographical position of a nation, indeed, is the principal factor conditioning its foreign policy—the principal reason why it must have a foreign policy at all.

JULES CAMBON[1]
The Permanent Basis of French Foreign Policy

WE have endeavoured, in Chapter 6, to indicate the essentials of Egypt's immediate interests in the Sudan—namely: the control and allocation of the Nile Waters; accommodation for Egypt's surplus population; and for external market and capital investments. We now propose, in this Chapter, to indicate what might be regarded as Egypt's remote interests in the disputed country—i.e. the geo-political forces urging Egypt to seek the unity of the Nile Valley: this hope for political unity has become an 'ideology' in Egypt and the logic of this ideology we shall discuss in the second part of this chapter.

At 4 p.m. on 4 December 1950, Mr. Bevin, British Foreign Secretary, with Sir Ralph Stevenson, British Ambassador in Cairo, received Mohammed Salah Eddin Bey in the Foreign Office, London. The purpose was to continue their conversation (which began at the Waldorf-Astoria, New York, on 28 September 1950), over the revision of the 1936 Treaty. Particular attention was given to the problem of the presence of the British troops in the Canal Zone. But at the end of the lengthy debate which ensued that day, Salah Eddin Bey reminded Mr. Bevin of what he considered the other important aspect of the question—namely, the Sudan. Mr. Bevin, apparently attempting, amongst other things, to discourage discussing the Sudan issue jointly with the question of evacuation of British troops, indicated that there was no prospect of Anglo-Egyptian agreement on the Sudan, except on the basis of Self-determination for the Sudanese (which is eminently contrary to Egyp-

[1] *Foreign Affairs*, VIII (1930), p. 173.

tian aspirations for Egypto-Sudanese union). At another meeting on 7 December, Salah Eddin Bey announced: 'The Egyptian Government on its part is not prepared to accept any solution which does not recognise the unity of Egypt and the Sudan in word and in practice.'[1]

The conversation dragged on until 9 December, when Mr. Bevin categorically objected to Salah Eddin Bey's linking together the question of the Sudan with that of defence—two essentially different things, he said. To this Salah Eddin Bey retorted:

> If you dislike Egypt linking the question of evacuation with that of the Sudan, Egypt on her part cannot deviate from linking these two questions together. In fact she has always done so. . . . Indeed it is a matter of life and death to Egypt. Mr. Churchill has himself depicted Egypt and the Sudan as a palm tree having its roots in the Sudan and its branches in the Delta.[2]

Salah Eddin Bey suggested that the branches could not survive if the roots were severed.

Thus, to Britain the Sudan question and the problem of the defence of the Suez Canal Zone were, on this occasion, separate and distinct issues. But to Egypt, situated on the shores of the stormy Mediterranean, both were merely two sides of one and the same coin. Britain preferred to see the Sudan as a separate political unit from Egypt, failing to absorb the territory into the British Empire or Commonwealth. But to the Egyptians unity with the Sudan was a necessity: 'it is a matter of life and death.'

How then do we account for this Egyptian sentiment—so strong and deep-rooted? It is partly because, exposed to the violent forces of the power politics in the Mediterranean, Egypt feels insecure, and therefore seeks some refuge under the amalgamation of Egypt and the Sudan. It is therefore necessary to consider Mediterranean geo-politics, which influence Egyptian attitude to the Sudan. We will indicate the geo-political chain of circumstances and forces which drove and still drives Egypt, in her insecurity, to seek unity with the Sudan.

These elements of insecurity, which we will attempt presently to unfold, are the general force of geography in international politics; the particular historical and everlasting nature of the political storms of the Mediterranean, on whose shores Egypt is located; and the economic, political and strategic interests of the major world powers in the Mediterranean and the Middle East, of which Egypt is a pivot.

Many factors condition the national foreign policy and destiny of a

[1] Ministry of Foreign Affairs, *Records*, p. 85.   [2] *Ibid.*, pp. 95–6.

nation. The four basic ones are: the geographic, the economic, the demographic and the strategic (e.g. Britain's strategic interests in Africa and the Middle East influence her policy towards Egypt and the Sudan).

One of the permanent and most fundamental factors is undoubtedly geography.

There are three main ways whereby geography influences the national and foreign policy of Egypt. These, as with other states, are:

1. *Its size*, which affects its relative strength in the struggle for power. The factor of size has been important in Egyptian affairs since the earlier periods of history. In modern times, she is still the largest, the densest in population and consequently the leader, of the Arab League countries.

2. *Its natural resources*, which influence the density of population and the economic structure.

3. (a) *Its regional location* (with regard to immediate neighbours) defines a nation's position with reference to potential friends or enemies. The regional location of Ethiopia induced Egypt to become her ally during the Italo-Abyssinian War of 1936; because of their regional location on the Nile—a common source of life—Egyptians and many Sudanese talk of themselves as 'brothers of the Valley'.

(b) *Its global location* (i.e. with regard to the world), which determines its nearness or otherwise to international routes of communication, centres of power or areas of conflict. Whether we consider the regional location of Egypt or look at her from the standpoint of her world location, Egypt's geographical importance and consequent problems stand out significantly. Indeed, as Lord Keynes once wrote: 'Egypt is the victim of her geographical situation.'[1]

In what ways, we might ask, does geography endanger Egypt?

Egypt is the terminus of the British-controlled Cape-to-Cairo air route, which passes through the Sudan. Although the Cape-to-Cairo railway or road proposed by the British many decades ago has not been built, yet it is a project which still fires the imagination of British engineers and politicians. While conscious of the economic returns and the prestige the project would bring to Egypt, the Egyptians are afraid of the concurrent political and strategic pressure which Britain might exert.

Egypt is located on the great inland sea of the Mediterranean, whose shores are the frontiers of the great continents of Asia, Africa and Europe, which between them held in the past all of the known and all of the conjectured world. Since recorded history, the shores of the Mediterranean have been the fertile soil for the germination, growth and decay

---

[1] Quoted by the Editor, *Fortnightly Review*, No. 1048, April 1954, p. 218.

of successive civilizations. The Mediterranean has also been the scene of the birth, the early battles, and the gradual 'withering away' of two of the world's most organized and most proselytizing religions—Christianity and Islam. Many of the famous naval battles of the world were fought in or near the waters of the Mediterranean. A flash of the mind to the acquisitive quarrels over the Suez Canal, and the current issues of Cyprus, for instance, would remind the reader of the 'personal' feelings which many peoples and nations, both near and far, have for the Great Sea.

The main history of the Mediterranean has been one of conflict and conquest, pillage and piracy, since the period of Homer's heroes. It witnessed the organized piracy of the Crusaders, the long conflict between Constantinople and Venice, the naval wars of Louis XIV of France, and of Cromwell and Nelson of England. Africa invaded Europe twice and advanced each time victoriously through the Mediterranean (Hannibal with his elephants and the Moors with their horses).[1] Egypt and Mediterranean waters were actively and strategically involved in the First and the Second World Wars.

Obviously, these conflicts have always exposed Egypt to external dangers. She threw off the yoke of the Assyrians only to fall to the Persians. Later, she was subject to Greek rule and became later a Roman province which ended some thirteen centuries ago; when the Ottoman Empire was established, Egypt became a vassal of the Turks. Occupied first by Napoleon, whose fleet was destroyed by Nelson at the Battle of the Nile in 1798, she became a British Protectorate in 1914. Thus, Egypt's subjection to foreign powers lasted, with brief intervals of revolt and precarious independence, for nearly three thousand years, until the Egyptian revolution of 1952 and the agreement of 1954, by which Britain agreed to evacuate her military forces from Egypt's territorial waters.

Egypt is now independent; but her geographical problems remain unchanged; and today it is as true as it ever has been that the Egyptian problem is as much an international issue for the power blocs of the world as it is national for the Egyptians themselves. The Suez Canal, which formed the subject matter of the Bevin–Eddin Bey talks in London brings the current international interests and the consequent Egyptian insecurity sharply into focus. We must therefore consider the Suez Canal and the Suez base as part of the economic and strategic interests

[1] Slocombe, G., *The Dangerous Sea: The Mediterranean and Its Future*, London, 1936, p. 13.

of the major powers of the world which forced Egypt to seek union with the Sudan.

The Suez Canal lies in Egyptian territory and cuts through the isthmus between Egypt and Sinai.[1] About 103 miles in length and 36 feet in depth, it is 'the richest ditch on earth', as American journalists often describe it. Linking the Red Sea with the Mediterranean and running through a 'sliced' portion of Africa, it unites Europe with Africa and Asia. At its entrance is situated, for better or worse, the Egyptian town of Port Said, with a population of about 300,000.

The opening of the Suez Canal has greatly enhanced the value of the Mediterranean in world commerce, and brought economic gains as well as political troubles to Egypt. The Canal, as most people know, is a product of the imagination, and pertinacity, the diplomatic and the financial foresight of Ferdinand de Lesseps, whose endeavours were supported by the friendship and encouragement of Khedive Said Pasha of Egypt, to whom he submitted the project in 1854. After many years of French technical and administrative skill, of Egyptian and French capital, the canal was opened on 18 March 1868.

The canal has since greatly facilitated the movement of goods and persons and broken down the barriers of trade and communication; over ten thousand ships from many parts of the world (mainly American and British) now go through the canal every year.

Yet at the beginning, the British Government did all they could for about twelve years to block the construction of the canal, because they were then afraid that it would make their empire in India more accessible to rival powers. Consequently, the shares were held by French financiers and the Khedive of Egypt, Ismail. But later, through the political and financial vision of Benjamin Disraeli, Britain became involved to her great advantage. How this came about is one of the most dramatic incidents in international politics.

In 1875, the increasing financial embarrassment of the Khedive reduced him to the necessity of selling his holdings in the Canal Company—about 40 per cent of the whole capital; he desperately needed £4,000,000 at once. The news reached the British Foreign Office in London on Monday, 15 November, through Frederick Greenwood, at that time editor of the *Pall Mall Gazette*. On Wednesday, Disraeli summoned the Cabinet and urged the purchase of the Khedive's shares as an imperial investment. Power to negotiate was immediately tele-

---

[1] Mount Sinai, of uncertain identity, from where the Ten Commandments were given to Moses, according to the Holy Bible, Authorized Version, Exodus, Chapter 19.

graphed to General Stanton, in Cairo. But the British Parliament was not in session, and £4,000,000 was too large a sum to tack on to the Budget without a Parliamentary vote of credit. Disraeli took a daring step: he borrowed the money from his Jewish friend, Lionel N. Rothschild, a banker and head of a group of financiers, giving the British Government as a security. Successive Governments at Westminster, who have since owned about 44 per cent of the valuable stock of the Canal Company, and who eventually maintained a military base at Suez, have acknowledged their gratitude to Disraeli as much as successive Egyptian Governments have poured their wrath on the memory of bankrupt Ismail.

The canal proper, run by an international company registered in Egypt but with headquarters in Paris, is administratively distinct from the military base in the Canal Zone, though they are adjacent and have their local head offices at Ismailia. The base lies on the western bank of the canal, between Suez and Ismailia, and stretches for about two-thirds of its length.

The Anglo-Egyptian Treaty of 1936 deals with both questions—the canal base, and the Sudan—in Articles 8 and 11 respectively; the British authorities made the two the spear-head of the Treaty. Egypt struggled to abrogate the treaty, much as Britain persisted in upholding it. What, then, was the value of the base to Britain?

Covering about 9,714 miles in area, and costing approximately £500,000,000, it had (until the Evacuation Agreement of 1954) about 283,000 British troops; 50,000 tons of ammunition; 300,000 pieces of ordnance equipment; ten airfields, thirty-eight various installations, etc.[1]

Apart from these very considerable physical assets, its greatest importance was the might and power which the base symbolized to Britain. (But to Egypt it was a Caesarian image of national paralysis.)

It was important for British imperial police purposes in peace time. Miss Elizabeth Monroe, a British expert, says: 'The speed at which it enables protective forces to move from one part of the globe to another part imparts a warm feeling of security to all those [British] who like to go about their business undisturbed.'[2]

It was helpful, during an emergency, for extra forces from the British troops in the Canal Zone to cope with war or rebellion (e.g. troops

---

[1] H.M.S.O., Cmd. 9298 (*Egypt No. 2*, 1954), Appendix A to Annex II, etc.; also the supplement, Cmd. 9466, p. 2.
[2] Monroe, Elizabeth, *The Mediterranean in Politics*, London, 1938, p. 14.

from the Zone were sent to Kenya against the Mau Mau; to Korea during the Korean conflict; and recently to Cyprus against the 'Enosis' movement: to impart security to areas of British interests, in Hong Kong and South-East Asia, and to her bases and forces along that route). During crises Britain could use the highway with no fear of the delay usually spent on formalities at foreign ports.

It served as a chain of fuelling stations and protective cruisers, strung between Aden and Gibraltar. The safe and easy passage through and the friendly access to, the fuelling stations strengthened British Commonwealth links through the confidence which the Dominion and Colonial merchants of India, Australia, New Zealand, East and Central Africa placed in businessmen in Britain.

The Suez route is second only to the North Atlantic Ocean with regard to the volume of traffic. British shipping, carrying the goods and passengers of all nations, has been by far its largest user since the end of the Second World War, that is, before U.S. ascendancy. . . . Reliable shipping is a national advertisement for Britain, and the main sea route to the West touches more lands and serves more people than any other route in the world.

Britain owned about 44½ per cent of the shares of the Suez Canal Company, which 'was a business concern, supported by the political influence of the Great Powers. . . .'[1]

The canal is very close to the British territories of Aden, Cyprus, Gibraltar, Malta and, of course, the Sudan.

However, there are other powers, besides Britain, which are active in the Mediterranean trade and politics. During the Italian Campaign of Ethiopia, in 1935, certain powers were trying to make adjustments roughly in this manner: Britain wondered whether to stay in the Mediterranean region or get out; France was looking for an opportunity to reduce her commitments in the Eastern basin so as to concentrate on the more important concerns in the West; Germany pondered on how to get into the political game in the Mediterranean; Russia looked for ways and means to break out of the Black Sea and reach the Mediterranean; Turkey was considering how best to glean advantages during these moments of uncertainty among the other powers.[2] But this is not all! There are other various stakes in the Mediterranean, which increased the Egyptian feeling of insecurity.

In times of crisis, French thoughts at once turn to the Mediterranean

---

[1] M. Mimant, *Les Corporations 1929*, quoted by Wilson, *op. cit.*, p. 161.
[2] Monroe, *op. cit.*, pp. 1 and 2.

—to Algeria, Tunisia and to Morocco—because of the large army stationed there; and also because of the fact that these French North African possessions are the nearest (to France) and the most densely populated of the French overseas territories with advantages of recruitment, and French settlement. In recent years several regimes rose and fell in France mainly on account of the unrest in French North Africa. Tunisia and Morocco have recently been declared independent; but Algeria remains a problem territory.

Italy has often aimed at achieving greatness in the Mediterranean. Italo Balbo, the Italian Governor of Libya, declared: 'Africa is the continent on which the great nations of the world must prove their right to priority.'[1] Speaking at Tripoli in 1926 the Duce declared: 'Italy has been great in the Mediterranean. I want her to become so again.' But Italy, having been subdued in the Second World War, is no longer a major power in the Eastern Mediterranean basin. In her place, the Soviet Union, even if not a riparian power, is a strong presence, in competition with the N.A.T.O. powers in the Mediteranean. (An instance is Egypt's arms deal with the Soviet bloc in 1955.)

Even the relatively far-away United States of America is increasingly active in Mediterranean commerce and politics. According to the *New York Times*,[2] the Suez Canal has become three times more important as an artery of American foreign trade than the Panama Canal. 'United States traffic through the Suez has increased tenfold in the last fifteen years', says the *New York Herald Tribune*.[3] U.S. imports through Suez include strategic raw materials such as crude oil from Arabia, manganese from India and rubber from Malaya. U.S. exports to countries beyond Suez are grain, machinery, refined petroleum, etc. Much of the trade is borne in American ships and nearly 30 per cent of the total traffic via Suez, though carried in vessels flying the Panamanian, Liberian or Honduran flag, is controlled by U.S. interests.[4]

The Suez Canal reduces by 6,700 miles the distance from New York to the manganese shipping points of the Red Sea; and the distance from New York to the oil stocks of Kuwait and Saudi Arabia by 3,500 miles. Voyaging by the way of the Suez Canal, a laden ship from, say, Boston to Karachi, saves fourteen days' sailing time or $22,000 in costs.[5]

The international character of the Charter of the Suez Canal is reflected in many other ways. Before its nationalization by Egypt in

---

[1] Quoted by Boverie, Margaret, *Mediterranean Cross Currents*, London, 1938, p. 127.
[2] 5 January 1954.   [3] 4 January 1954.
[4] *New York Herald Tribune*, 4 January 1954.
[5] *New York Times*, 5 January 1954.

1956, the Canal Company was called the Universal Suez Maritime Canal Company; the Board of Directors included five nations—France, Britain, Egypt, Holland and the United States. The personnel included representatives of nineteen nations. But these international interests were not limited to trade and commerce alone. Strategic considerations were involved. This strategic aspect, of which the British base at Suez was part, brings us to the collective interest of the North Atlantic Treaty Organization (of which Britain is a founder and influential member), in the Mediterranean as a whole and in Egypt's territorial zone in particular.

With the intensity of the cold war, the problem of the Mediterranean and the Middle East has expanded, and the military defence of the Middle East has become increasingly important 'to the security of the free world'. Speaking of the Canal Zone in May 1953, during the negotiations over the Anglo-Egyptian Treaty of 1936, Sir Winston Churchill pointed out that it was not merely an imperialist or colonial enterprise undertaken by the British; it was for purposes with which every member of N.A.T.O., as well as the countries of the Near East and the Middle East, was directly concerned.[1] The Sudan, be it remembered, is part of the Middle East in British military strategy.

Mr. John Foster Dulles, U.S. Foreign Secretary, asked during his visit to Cairo, that the Canal base 'should be available for immediate use on behalf of the free world in the event of hostilities'.[2]

Turkey, who formerly dominated Egypt and consequently is often watched with suspicion and uneasiness by Egyptians, is a member of N.A.T.O.; this increases Egypt's suspicions and insecurity.

British official sources state the aim of the Middle East strategy and the part they expect a Middle East base (or bases) to play. It is in the interest of all free nations—the Arab States and Israel as much as Britain or the United States—to prevent the area being penetrated by Communism in time of peace or being overrun in time of war. The Middle East defence was therefore organized to strengthen the southern flank of Turkey, which was 'not only one of the strongest bastions of N.A.T.O., but the kernel of the defensive system taking shape from the borders of Italy to the frontiers of India';[3] to safeguard oil resources of the Middle East area (which includes the Sudan); to ensure the

---

[1] Conservative Research Department, in *Monthly Survey of Foreign Affairs*, No. 61. 'Britain in the Middle East: The Anglo-Egyptian Treaty in Perspective', London, January 1954, p. 1.

[2] *Ibid.*, pp. 2–3.

[3] B.B.C.: London Calling—Overseas Programme; *Turkey To-Day, a Bastion of Western Defence*, London, 7 July 1955, p. 7.

security of the canal, and give confidence to the smaller countries concerned that the Western powers would be able to come to their assistance quickly (i.e. apparently against Communism); and to gain the advantage of redeploying 'the 80,000 men at present tied down in the Canal Zone at a cost of some £50,000,000 a year. The spread of British forces round the world—Korea, Malaya, Kenya, Hong Kong, Trieste and the continent of Europe—does not allow of any wastage.'[1]

U.S. official sources give broad support to the British stand in this matter.[2]

When King Hussein of Jordan dismissed Britain's General Glubb Pasha from the military service of Jordan in March 1956, as part of the revolt of Arab nationalism against Western imperial paternalism, and when at the same time the Cyprus issue was critical, the U.S. Government despatched naval forces to the Mediterranean for 'an exercise'.

In an explanatory memorandum to *Anglo-Egyptian Conversations on the Defence of the Suez Canal and on the Sudan*, 1950–51, Britain considered herself called upon to shoulder the responsibility for the defence of the Middle East. She therefore 'could not contemplate any solution of the Egyptian question which laid the area open to aggression'.[3]

The total effect of these various interests and of the possibility of aggression against Egyptian territorial waters had been to push Egypt to seek shelter under the flag of the Arab League, and to seek security in the Unity of the Nile Valley; a frightened Egyptian Government began to demand, rather increasingly from 1946, the complete and unconditional evacuation of all foreign troops from Egyptian soil.

The Military Regime which came into being in 1952, succeeded in concluding the Suez Agreement of 1954, by which Britain agreed to move her forces out of Suez. This did not remove, but merely decreased, the Egyptian feeling of insecurity. The Premier of Egypt commented on 24 March 1956, 'The great opportunity for Anglo-Arab relations created by the Anglo-Egyptian agreement in October 1954, has been thrown away. There was a brief honeymoon, and then Britain plunged into the Baghdad Pact plan, which she knew in advance was *in our opinion* a threat to our vital interests.'[4] Egypt would therefore like to have in her own military organization the agile 'Black Fighters' from the Sudan.

[1] The Conservative Research Department, *op. cit.*, p. 2.
[2] Hoskins, Halford L., 'Some Aspects of the Security Problem in the Middle East', *American Political Science Review*, Vol. XLVII, March 1953, p. 188.
[3] H.M.S.O., *Egypt No. 2* (1951), Cmd. 8494, p. 1.
[4] *Observer*, London, 25 March 1956, p. 1.

In summary, the following are some of the major points and problems which emerge from the geographical location of Egypt and which make her seek unity with the Sudan:

(1) For both good and evil it has been the geographical fate of Egypt to be the link between the Eastern and Western worlds, to be on the shores of a great artificial waterway between the Mediterranean and the Eastern Seas and thus to share the ups and downs of the British Commonwealth and the N.A.T.O. powers.

(2) Strategically, the Anglo-Egyptian dispute became far more involved —more an international than an Anglo-Egyptian affair. The international interests, especially commercial, communicational, and military, extended both westwards and eastwards; they later included not only the big powers of the West but also the newly independent states of Pakistan, India, Ceylon, Burma and Indonesia, as well as Israel, Australia, New Zealand, Japan and the Soviet bloc. (An instance is Egypt's arms deal with Czechoslovakia in 1955.)

(3) Egypt wanted Britain's hands off her territorial waters and the Suez Zone, as well as off the Sudan. She needed allies, but could not call for any effective help from the United States for fear of becoming a slave to the 'almighty dollar'. Besides, Britain and the U.S., in spite of their conflicting global interests, are allies; they are both united in supporting Israel against the Arab League. The United States is Britain's 'first ally and foremost friend in the world'.[1] For Egypt to ask the U.S.S.R. actively and directly to sponsor her cause might lead to greater dangers.

Consequently, sceptical as to offers of friendship, and uncertain about where the greater danger lay—whether with the Western democracies or with the Eastern ones—Egypt sought safety in some neutrality (the Suez invasion of 1956 pushed her towards Russia) and in the concept of the *unity of the Nile Valley*—i.e. the amalgamation of Egypt and the Sudan. These chains of circumstances constituted most of the forces which drove Salah Bey persistently to put it to Bevin (in their London conversation, in December 1950, with which we introduced this chapter), that the Sudan question and the issue of the Canal Zone were inseparable; that the unity of the Sudan with Egypt was 'a matter of life and death to Egypt'.

Perhaps one can dare to hope that in due course the world will be so ordered that small nations, whether in strategic areas or not, will have little to fear from their more powerful neighbours. The canal is Egypt's but it has also become mankind's; the time should therefore come when a conative government of the world will unify all geography and all mankind, for the common good. For the moment, however,

[1] *Manchester Guardian*, editorial, 1 May 1954, p. 4.

states are still more in the mood for power politics, regional pacts and counter-pacts, and for bickering with one another than for real peace and order.

2. EGYPT'S IDEOLOGY OF THE UNITY OF THE NILE VALLEY

> *We, in Egypt, possess neither purse strings nor the latest techniques of the propagandists' arts. But we can dispense with them all, for do we not possess in the Nile, a bond of Union which is mightier than all the works of man? The Nile has known—and has survived —all the great Empires of History.*
>
> M. SHAFIK GHORBAL,
> Late Professor of History and the Dean of the Faculty of Arts,
> Fuad I University, Cairo, 1947[1]
>
> *The Nile is Egypt; that is to say from the Mediterranean to the Sudan.*
>
> Egyptian Tourist Administration, 1956[2]

We have shown the major aspects of Egyptian interests in the Sudan —both immediate (i.e. as a result of internal needs in Egypt) and remote (i.e. springing from external pressure owing to geographical location)— which urge Egypt to seek a formula for the 'Unity of the Nile Valley'. We said at the beginning of Chapter 7 (1) that this hope for a political unity of the Sudan with Egypt became an ideology (i.e. a doctrine or political movement) in Egypt. We should, therefore, present the Egyptian thesis of this ideology, and attempt to examine the validity of each of the premises upon which it is based.

Egyptians and their Sudanese supporters used the 'Unity of the Nile Valley' in their political campaigns before independence. The slogan inspired in them emotional and political significance similar to that inspired by 'Liberty, Equality and Fraternity' among the French revolutionists; 'The Union for ever' among the Northern elements of the United States during the Civil War; the doctrine of 'Laissez-faire' among capitalists; or 'Workers of the World, Unite' among Socialists. The deep feeling and apparent confidence which the slogan aroused even among Egyptian intellectuals is illustrated in the above prophet-like quotation from the writings of Professor Ghorbal, late of Fuad University. In some Egyptian essays on the unity of the Nile Valley, the word UNITY is almost always personified and written with a capital

---

[1] Egyptian Govt., Presidency of the Council of Ministers, *The Unity of the Nile Valley*, 1947, Cairo, p. 5.
[2] Egyptian Tourist Administration, *The Nile*, brochure distributed by Egyptian Travel Offices, Cairo, 1956.

'U'.[1] When referring to the Sudan issues, Britain *reflectively* called them: *The Sudan Question*, whilst Egypt *buoyantly* ejaculated: '*The Unity of the Nile Valley*'! This magical phrase was the peg on which the Egyptians hung (and still hang) the long and short of their claims in the Sudan. Replying to some British Government proposals of 8 June 1951, concerning the Sudan, the Egyptian Government, in a Memorandum dated 6 July 1951, commented:

> *First: The British viewpoint omitted to mention the Unity of Egypt and the Sudan under the Egyptian Crown.*[2]
> This is an established fact and no agreement which fails to recognise this fact can ever be acceptable to any Egyptian Government.

Also in a conversation with Sir Ralph Stevenson, the British Ambassador in Cairo, on 6 July 1951, the Egyptian Minister for Foreign Affairs pointed out that the British Memorandum agreed that Egypt and the Sudan were interdependent economically, geographically and through the Nile Waters; he went on: 'I believe that the interdependence of Egypt and the Sudan from these aspects which you have admitted is enough in itself to concede the Unity of Egypt and the Sudan.'[3]

Professor Ghorbal also asserts: 'Nature had made the Valley of the Nile one entity. History bears witness to this supreme fact. It is true that the manifestations of this Unity have differed from age to age. But the essence of it has never varied.'[4]

The Unity of the Nile Valley being an idea so evidently strong and significant to the Egyptian, we must find and examine the bases and foundations upon which it is built. According to Egyptian sources, supported directly or by implication in several British writings, the Unity of the Nile Valley is manifested in many ways. The manifestations may be arranged under six main headings:

(1) The geographical setting of Egypt and the Sudan;
(2) The ethnical composition of the two countries;
(3) The cultural and religious practices, and the Arabization of the two peoples (acculturation);
(4) Historical ties;
(5) The economic interdependence;

---

[1] Egyptian Govt., Presidency of Council of Ministers, *The Unity of the Nile Valley*, p. 1. Here the word 'Unity' appears five times and is written with a capital 'U', even in the middle or at the end of a sentence.

[2] Italics are the writer's to stress the priority attached by the Egyptian Memorandum to the ideology of Unity.

[3] H.M.S.O., *Egypt No. 2* (1951), Cmd. 8419, p. 33.

[4] *The Unity of the Nile Valley*, p. 2.

(6) The current tendency of nations to consolidate regionally and universally.

1. *The Geographical Aspect*: The geographical claim is based mainly on physical considerations. There is no clear-cut, natural division between Egypt and the Sudan. No mass of water separates the two countries as, for instance, the Irish Sea which cuts off England from Ireland, or the Indian Ocean, which (apart from India) divides East and West Pakistan. Egypt and the Sudan present no sharp topographical differences. From the point of view of vegetation, the change from the desert, savannah and shrub in Egypt and Northern Sudan, to the swamps and the tropical forests of the Equatorial Region in the Southern Sudan presents a natural gradation and continuum—there are no thick jungles, high mountains or vast sheets of water to form a serious barrier to movement and communication.

The natural gradations or geographical uniformity of the Sahara region and the absence of any unconquerable natural physical barriers facilitate migrations and intermingling among the peoples of North Africa generally and between the Egyptians and the Sudanese especially.

Richard Wyndham remarks, though cynically, that to the majority of Englishmen the Sudan means a 'part of Egypt, you know, but a bit further down'.[1] Egyptians therefore stress that the frontiers between Egypt and the Sudan are only artificial, based on no geographical demarcation, but 'resulting from agreements imposed by force'.[2]

There is some validity in this aspect of the argument. The absence of natural boundaries has caused Brazil, for instance, a country sixteen times as large as France, to remain a single nation. But geographical uniformity does not, and need not, always coincide with political unity. It is true, though, that the former certainly enhances the latter.

The weakness of the argument lies in over-simplification. It conveniently overlooks, for instance, the first and the second cataracts at Aswan and at Wadi Halfa, which obstruct Nile navigation. There is no motorable road between Egypt and the Sudan. To travel from Cairo to Khartoum takes three stages (except by air, which takes only about six hours, but is very expensive): from Cairo to Aswan, about 879 miles, often takes (in 1956) about 20 hours by train; from Aswan (at Shallal, near the Aswan Dam) to Wadi Halfa by a steamer, takes two nights; services are twice weekly only; and from Wadi Halfa to Khartoum by train (577 miles) takes about 30 hours.

[1] Wyndham, R., *The Gentle Savage*, 4th ed., London, 1937, p. 11.
[2] Egyptian Govt., *Egypt/Sudan* (Press Section), *op. cit.*, p. 69.

The mutual dependence of Egypt and the Sudan on the Nile Waters forms one of the basic geographical aspects of the concept of Unity. Egyptians point out that: 'Five-sixths of the Nile are in the territory of Egypt and the Sudan.'[1] It is true, as we have shown, that both the Sudan and Egypt depend largely on the waters of the Nile for irrigation, hydro-electric power, etc.; without it neither can adequately survive—more so with Egypt than with the Sudan. Because of this mutual dependence of the two countries on the Nile Waters, Egypt desires political control of the Sudan or Unity of the Nile Basin.

This aspect of the ideology of Unity is open to some criticism. The Nile Basin includes other political units—Ethiopia, Uganda, Kenya, Tanganyika and part of the Belgian Congo. If Egypt claims union with the Sudan to ensure adequate water supplies, she should also, by the same logic, have a share in the affairs of the other countries within the Nile Basin. This is at least unrealistic, if not impossible.

But what Egypt seems to mean is *regional Unity* of the valley—that is, of herself and the Sudan both as the greatest users of the Nile—and not *total Unity*, involving the whole basin. In this regard, regional Unity would have the advantage of enhancing co-operation rather than competition between Egypt and the Sudan in the use of the Nile Waters, as we have suggested. But it could become, in a way, like the Condominium, an unequal partnership, in which the stronger and more experienced Egypt would be the senior. This was one of the reasons why Britain pursued the policy of creating a Sudan independent of Egypt.

2. *The Ethnical Basis of the Argument.* The Egyptian argument flows on from the geographical plane of natural gradation and uniformity to ethnical source and similarity. The geographical setting is conducive to general migrations and nomadic life; consequently, the peoples of North Africa, north of the Sahara, were able to migrate and intermarry, thus producing one *race*, or a common flow of blood. This ethnical argument is based largely on the Hamitic origin and influence, together with the Semitic element in most of the peoples of North Africa as a whole and of Egypt and the Sudan in particular.

The Hamitic waves spread to the Sudan and, as with Egypt, greatly influenced the basic ethnical formation of its inhabitants—from north to south. Consequently, there is gradation in physical features, 'Whether we study the colour of the skin, the shape of the nose, or hair texture, this fact will remain valid, as it is impossible to find an abrupt

[1] Egyptian Information Office, *The Egyptian Question—1882–1951*, Washington, D.C., 1951, p. 11.

change in any of those characteristics while crossing from one area to another.'[1]

The argument therefore submits that the line of demarcation between what certain writers call Negro Africa and Caucasian Africa,[2] dividing the Sudan into two racial parts—the Caucasian North and the Negroid South—should not be exaggerated in scientific importance. Rather should it be considered as an attempt merely to simplify matters for the general public. It admits the fact that Negroid influence becomes gradually more and more predominant as one moves' southwards; but suggests that this is because the Sudan is in close proximity to the Negroes of Central and West Africa, whose traffic to the Sudan is encouraged by the absence of natural barriers.

The findings of Professor Seligman, of the University of London, would support the Egyptian claim.[3] It is also interesting to realize that a Hamitic group spread as far as Northern Nigeria (in about the 13th century), where they are now known as the Fulani(s).

On to the ancient Hamitic heritage has been grafted the Semitic or Arab influence, which is said to have reached Africa some long time before Islam. The Arabs migrated from Arabia mainly as traders but often as mere nomads and as warriors—'defenders of the faith'.

With the coming of the Hamites and the Semites to North Africa in general and to Egypt and the Sudan in particular, acculturation and miscegenation followed; for, unlike the British, who are traditionally separatists afraid of miscegenation, the Arabs tend to intermarry with the original inhabitants of the Nile Valley. This process of fusion is encouraged by the doctrine and applied policy of the Moslems. Islam, though jealous and somewhat intolerant of other creeds, is essentially no respecter of class, colour, or race; all are equal 'servants' of Allah.

The Egyptian argument of the ethnical unity of the Nile Valley therefore appears valid, but only within certain limits. Both ethnical *fusion* and ethnical *antagonism* go hand in hand in the Valley. In the first place, the Arabs themselves could be grouped into many 'tribes', such as the classical nomads (Ahl Ibl, i.e. 'people of the camel'), the Baggara (cattle folk of the Sudan), and the sedentaries (settled folk) like the Sawaki and other town or village dwellers.

Egyptians in the Lower Nile speak Arabic, whilst the mother tongue of those in Upper Egypt is Nubian—a different language. It should be

---

[1] *The Unity of the Nile Valley*, p. 12.
[2] A straight line from Senegal, in West Africa, to about south of Khartoum, bending southwards below the Ethiopian plateau and reaching to the Indian Ocean near Mombasa.
[3] Seligman, S. G., *Races of Africa*, revised ed., London, 1939, p. 96.

noted, also, that the Egyptian Arab is relatively Caucasoid, and the Sudanese Arab Negroid. If the Egyptian argument of ethnical unity is stretched far enough it will embrace the whole of mankind. The Hamites, Semites and Negroes of the Nile Valley are respectively Branches of the Tree of Mankind. Some people take pride in tracing their family tree back several generations. 'But all of us, if we went back far enough, hundreds of generations, would arrive at the same place, the base of the human family tree, with the first *Homo Sapiens*.'[1]

Biblically, man and woman sprang from a common stock—Adam and Eve. Biologically, the unity of the human species is emphasized by the similarity of their bone structure, of their delicate internal organs, and of their complex nervous system.

Fourthly, racial or ethnical uniformity (like geographical uniformity) does not, and need not, always coincide with political unity. But it is a fact that the one may enhance the other, especially on the emotional level.

3. *The Cultural and Religious Bases.* Egyptian sources submit that there are indeed some historians of human civilization who contend that Egypt was the source of world civilization and culture. If this is correct, so goes the argument, her civilization must have affected 'all the adjacent regions and her culture spread throughout the Nile Basin. . . .'[2] They claim that around the middle of the 6th century, Egyptian priests were sent to Nubia to convert its pagan population. As a result, 'the whole country was converted to Christianity at about A.D. 600, always looking to Egypt for spiritual leadership.'[3] Following the Arab conquest of Egypt, the Christian kingdom of Nubia began to crumble in the 7th century and finally, in the 12th century, and to receive the influx of Arabs from the north and the Fung from the south. This spread of Arab culture with Muslim religion followed the Nile, the main carriers being the traders from the north (Egypt). The argument is supported by the pastoral inhabitants, especially the Shilluk, the Baggara and the Fung, of the Sudan, who have long been converted.

Passing through the historical setting, the cultural argument arrives at the modern situation. There is, it claims, a need for a compact cultural bloc of Egypt and the Sudan to induce co-operation between the two countries which can be linked effectively through the Arabic language, which is more or less the 'lingua franca' of the inhabitants; and through Islam, which is the religion of most of the peoples of the Nile Valley.

[1] U.N.E.S.C.O., *What is a Race? Evidence from Scientists*, Paris, 1952, p. 11.
[2] *The Unity of the Nile Valley*, p. 18.   [3] *Ibid.*, p. 20.

As to the question of Egyptian Christians converting the pagan inhabitants of Nubia, there is evidence of the existence of strong early churches in Egypt. According to Philip Hughes, the Church historian, the first evidence of Christianity in Africa is as late as A.D.189—the martyrdoms at Scillium. By then the churches in Africa were numerous and highly organized. In Proconsular Africa, there were seventy bishops in the 3rd century.[1]

We must now consider the Egyptian claim of cultural unity through Arabization and the Islamic religion. In a sub-chapter entitled 'Expansion of the Arab Tribes and the Arabization of the Sudanese', Trimingham says that some Arab tribes poured south and settled in Nubia after the fall of the Christian Kingdom. They were opposed by powerful black conquerors from the south, with whom they made treaties. Their nomadic habits and ability to intermarry afforded them space for settlement in this under-populated country. Many accepted the advantages of a settled life and were absorbed. For centuries there was a process of cultural revolution, resulting from 'the Arabization and Islamization of the people'.[2]

The strength of Arabic and Islamic influence in the present-day Sudan is indicated by Dr. Rashed El-Barawy. He points out that according to an official estimate (1947) the population of the Sudan was 7,547,000 persons, of whom five million were the Arab-speaking and Islam-professing inhabitants of the Northern and Central parts of the country.[3]

But whilst the Sudanese of the North have been Arabized like the Egyptians, they have at the same time remodelled some of the cultural ways to suit their own locality, their customs and even (in the case of the Nubians and the Beja, for instance) preserved their own language. Besides, there are certain Islamic sects in the Sudan—such as the Mahdiya—differing from the sects in Egypt. The Southern Sudan is still predominantly non-Islamic and non-Arabic-speaking.

In spite of these differences, however, wherever nationalism is strong in the Islamic world, it is often strengthened and united by the Islamic teaching that to die for a noble cause is to become a martyr assured of heaven; the Prophet says 'Love of Country is part of faith';[4] by the cohesive force of the legal and social systems regulating the Moslem

---

[1] Hughes, P., *A History of the Church*, Vol. I, London, 1948, pp. 152–3.
[2] Trimingham, J. S., *Islam in the Sudan*, London, 1949, p. 82.
[3] El-Barawy, R., *Egypt, Britain and the Sudan*, Cairo, 1952, p. 4.
[4] Dagher, Ibrahim, 'Religious Heritage', in *Current History, The Monthly Magazine of World Affairs*, Vol. XXVI (North Africa), No. 152, Philadelphia, Pa., April 1954, p. 214.

community; by the common fellow-feeling among subjected peoples who, otherwise divided, are aspiring to sovereignty and unity; and by the common influence of Western contact and system of education, which have produced both an intellectual élite and political plutocrats, with a common outlook.

4. *The Historical Basis.* Egypt's historical claim to the unity of the Upper Nile region is based primarily upon the various forms of unity or political control achieved since the period of the Pharaohs and particularly during the 19th century.

Egyptians argue that from the time of the Pharaohs as far back as during the reigns of Amenhotep, Thotmes and Rameses, Nubia was an Egyptian province administered by two Governors—one in the north and the other in the south. During the Ptolemaic age, Egypt extended her trade to the Red Sea. Then followed a kind of unity imposed by the Romans and subsequently by the Ottoman Empire.

The political unity was periodically broken during the Roman Era and in the Persian Conquest. But it was again realized in the 19th century—the age of national consolidation in the East and West—the century of German and Italian unity, and of the national revival of various Slavonic peoples. Mohammed Ali, Khedive of Egypt, invaded the Sudan in 1819 and political control by Egypt remained until the Mahdi's rebellion in 1885. Subsequently, the Egyptians accepted the British Government's advice to evacuate and withdraw from the Sudan. This Egyptian control lapsed until the reconquest of the Sudan through the joint effort of Egypt and Britain, culminating in the Condominium of 1899, as we have shown in Chapter 3 above. It is therefore evident that the history of the Sudan has been bound up with that of Egypt for centuries.

Thus viewing the historical manifestation of the unity of pre-Christian and Christian eras, and looking back as recently as the 19th century, when Egyptian authority over the Sudan was real, Egypt accuses Britain of usurping, by trickery, her authority over the Upper Nile. The British reaction to this charge is (apart from the aim of forestalling the French in Fashoda) the rationale that the record of the Egyptians in the Sudan during the 19th century was a history of misgovernment; that the record was so bad as to warrant the exercise of British authority in the Sudan in the name of the Condominium. Before the Mahdia, the Egyptian administration was admittedly bad. But few, if any, Colonial administrations have so far been excellent.

In any case, the British exposition of Egyptian misrule in the 19th century as a justification for taking over from Egypt her sovereignty over the Sudan could be accepted had the Sudanese asked for British protection. In fact, as we have seen, Britain could be held largely responsible for letting the Sudan lapse into about ten years of war and famine by asking for the withdrawal of Egypt from the Sudan during the Mahdia, until the reconquest of the territory. Would it be acceptable to the British, if, for instance, the more powerful United States or the Soviet Union took control of Kenya under the pretext that British misrule gave rise to the Mau Mau, or Cyprus on account of the current unrest?

On the other hand, the Egyptian claim based on discovery and historical antecedence does not appear acceptable in its totality. It could be justified on a customary precept among nations, namely: 'The general consent of mankind has established the principle, that long and uninterrupted possession by one nation excludes the claim of every other.'[1]

But considering the fact that some phases of historical events are often ephemeral, spasmodic and changeable, this aspect of the Egyptian claim is not totally tenable.

The position in international law is that a state may, as a corporate person, possess territorial and non-territorial property within its own geographical limits or beyond them.[2] Viewed in this perspective both Britain and Egypt, as colonial administrators (good or bad), may 'possess' the Sudan through any of the customary ways and means whereby imperial powers acquire territories. If the historical facts are taken into account, different reasons may be given for the exercise of sovereignty by a state (such as Britain or Egypt) over a territory (like the Sudan). Such sovereignty could come about through many means, mainly by cession, occupation, accretion, subjugation, or prescription.

If applied to the Anglo-Egyptian situation, the case is apparently like this: Egypt did occupy the Sudan even before the European partition of Africa in general and the arrival of the British Government, especially in the Sudan, during the 19th century. Egyptian occupation was interrupted by the Mahdia, but with the assistance of British military officers, supposedly in the service of the Egyptian Government but actually working consciously in the interests of the British Government, Egypt reconquered the Sudan; and Anglo-Egyptian subjugation,

---

[1] Weaton's *International Law*, 6th English ed., by A. Berriedale Keith, Vol. I, London, 1929, p. 337.
[2] Hannis Taylor, *Public International Law*, Chicago, 1901, p. 263.

through the reconquest, followed. However, Britain, by prolonged prescription, became able to elbow out Egypt.

The question therefore arises: How far could the British claim be justified by prescription? Some writers have denied the validity of title to territorial property, whilst many jurists accept it as a principle for maintaining international order and stability. But there is yet no definite time limit specified by international rule defining when a prescriptive right commences or becomes able to bar another state from proclaiming possession. It depends on the nature of the property in dispute and the circumstances of the case.[1]

But when a dispute arises, an agreement is often made by the contestants regarding the minimum period giving a prescriptive right. For instance, in the dispute between Britain and Venezuela, the Treaty of Washington (1897) specified for the guidance of the arbitral tribunal that: 'Adverse holding or prescription during a period of fifty years shall make a good title.'[2]

But neither the Anglo-Egyptian Condominium of 1899 nor the 1936 Treaty of Friendship makes any similar provision. However, British administration existed in the Sudan for about fifty-seven years (1899–1956). Even so, this period of fifty-seven years constitutes technically and legally a joint Anglo-Egyptian rule or 'prescription' in the Sudan, apart from the Egyptian historical antecedence in the country.

In any case, we are reminded by Mohammed Salah Eddin Pasha, Egyptian Foreign Minister, to appreciate the Egyptian standpoint: 'The question is a question of Unity of Egypt with the Sudan, not a question of sovereignty of Egypt over the Sudan. When you have a United Country the question of self-determination does not at all arise'.[3]

The British viewpoint, on the other hand, was clearly stated in 1924 by *The Times*, and maintained by the Government for a long time. 'In the Sudan our course is clear and simple. We are there by right of conquest since Lord Kitchener smashed the Mahdi in 1898, and under the Condominium concluded in 1899.'[4]

5. *The Economic Argument.* Dr. Abbas Ammar, of the Geography Department at Fuad I University (now Cairo University) is a paramount

---

[1] *Droit des Gens*, II, §142, quoted by Hannis Taylor, *op. cit.*, p. 266.
[2] Weaton, *op. cit.*, pp. 336–7.
[3] Conversation between H. E. the Minister for Foreign Affairs and H. E. the British Ambassador on 8 June 1951, at 12 noon. Ministry of Foreign Affairs, Records, *op. cit.*, p. 118.
[4] *The Times*, editorial, 16 August 1924, p. 11b.

spokesman on the economic unity of Egypt and the Sudan. He submits that a study of various natural factors, particularly those of agriculture, industry and commerce, river communications and transport, shows that both countries are closely interdependent.

There are similarities in the agricultural methods of Egypt and the Sudan, and their needs in this regard are interdependent. As the more experienced and wealthier country, Egypt sees economic linkage in the technical and financial assistance she can give to Sudanese agricultural development. This argument is valid. But Britain, too, took some similar steps—particularly in regard to the Gezira Scheme—to aid Sudanese agriculture. Against this British scheme (now nationalized), the Egyptians were quick to quote Elinor Burns, who charged that it was mainly for the benefit of foreign capitalists:

> In all enterprises, the Sudan Government has been used to make the profits of British Capitalists easier and more secure. But the clearest example of the use of the colonial state apparatus, both to get contracts for British firms and to help British capitalists to exploit the native population, is provided by the Gezira Scheme. . . .[1]

Since Egypt has not become a socialist or Communist state, there is no evidence that Egyptian capitalists, too, would not have exploited the native Sudanese in one way or another. Perhaps a consolation to the Sudanese would have been the feeling that exploitation of kith by kin is probably less unkindly than that by the 'foreigner'.

The economic argument goes on to suggest that over-populated Egypt can supply experienced farm labour to the sparsely-populated Sudan. This, too, is valid, because while about 99·2 per cent of the Egyptian population—approximately sixteen million—lives on about 4 per cent of the total Egyptian soil, densities are up to about 6,500 persons per square mile. But only about nine million Sudanese live in an area of about 967,500 square miles.

Egypt, the argument continues, is an important market for Sudanese products; the growth of Egyptian industry will increase the need for Sudanese raw materials. Perhaps the main advantage that Egypt has over Britain in this regard is her proximity to the Sudan. Otherwise it might be more profitable, financially, for the Sudan to trade more with Britain, which is a greater potential market herself and is in a position to secure even wider markets for Sudanese goods, especially within the British Commonwealth and Empire. However, Egypto-Sudanese

---

[1] Burns, Elinor, *British Imperialism in Egypt*, Colonial Series No. 5, pp. 41–3.

commercial and industrial unity could be strengthened by the force of the geographic proximity of Egypt to the Sudan, and the fact that the Egyptian attitude—supported by some Sudanese—is that the two parts of the Nile Valley are a single entity and that the economic welfare and fate of one is entwined with the other. Fiscally, too, the Sudan was closely linked with Egypt; their monetary system was the same, and goods passed between the two countries without customs dues. But the declaration of independence for the Sudan in January 1956, has altered these arrangements.

A third factor in the Egyptian argument of economic unity is the Nile itself, as the principal way of communication between Egypt and the Sudan. There is no road or railway. The air route is expensive. The Nile is thus a vital community link.

Whilst there is no doubt that the Nile is a waterway, its five chains of cataracts and long bends discourage navigation and thus make the desert routes by camel cheaper. Therefore, transport between Egypt and the Sudan has been a combination of both river traffic and desert caravan; we have shown the three stages at present in use between Cairo and Khartoum. The development of railways in the Sudan by the British administration detracted from the importance of the Nile as a trade route. The historic camel route from Berber, on the Nile, to Suakin, on the Red Sea, was transformed to the Atbara route to the Port Sudan railway. Egypt accuses Britain of adopting this as one of the British policies directed towards severing the Sudan from Egypt, economically. At the Security Council of the United Nations, the Egyptian representative stated: 'To weaken the economic connection between Egypt and the Sudan, the British have done their utmost to shift the natural trend of trade which is towards the North. They have deliberately diverted Sudan exports from their natural and traditional routes along the Nile to the ports of the Red Sea.'[1] But it would seem that the British found it more economical and convenient to trade via the Red Sea, which is an international route, than by the North–South route, through the Nile, which is less navigable. One reason is that the vagaries of the 'moody' Nile make river transport difficult; another is that the railway from Khartoum to Wadi Halfa and Egypt must pass through the Nubian desert, where the inhabitants could not as yet help support the cost of such lines.

But despite the railway development, and the orientation of Sudanese trade to the East via Port Sudan rather than to the North, through

[1] 175th meeting of the Security Council, 5 August 1947.

Cairo, the Egyptian claim cannot be completely denied. Trade and traffic between Egypt and the Sudan still go on both through the Nile and the open desert. Besides, Egypt–Sudan railway lines, though now considered an unprofitable project, will certainly become a necessity in the future, especially now that the Sudan is independent and an ambitious regime governs in Egypt, and thus increase the chains of unity in the Nile Basin.

6. *The Argument on the Basis of Regional Consolidation of Nations.*

> *Hard as it is to say now I trust that the European family may*
> *act unitedly as one under a Council of Europe.*[1]
>   WINSTON CHURCHILL

> *When Bad Men Combine the Good must associate, else they will*
> *fall one by one, an unpitied sacrifice in a contemptible struggle.*[2]
>   EDMUND BURKE

Having discussed the internal aspect of the argument of the Unity of the Nile Valley, we may now consider the external aspect, that is, from the point of view of the regional consolidation now taking place all over the world.

On 9 December 1950, a conversation took place at the Foreign Office, London, between Ernest Bevin (then British Secretary of State for Foreign Affairs) and Mohammed Salah Eddin Bey (Egyptian Minister for Foreign Affairs). The Egyptian Minister remarked that he had witnessed the British delegation to the United Nations exerting every effort for the realization of the unity of Eritrea and Ethiopia under the Ethiopian Crown. This unity had lately been achieved, even though the relations between these two countries were not, in his opinion, so strong as those binding Egypt and the Sudan. He asked Mr. Bevin:

> Why should the British Government make that flagrant discrimination in treatment—strive for the unity of Eritrea and Ethiopia on the one hand and work for the separation of the Sudan and Egypt on the other?[3]

A week later—on 15 December—Mr. Bevin stated at another meeting:

> As regards Eritrea, it was our view that that part of the territory where the overwhelming majority of the inhabitants wished to be re-united with Ethiopia, should be united with that country. In the event of a different solution—federation has been adopted. Here again we have complied, because in the circumstances there was no alternative.[4]

---

[1] Winston Churchill, letter to Anthony Eden, dated 21 October 1942. In 'The Hinge of Fate', *The Second World War*, Vol. IV, p. 504.
[2] Burke, Edmund, *Thoughts on the Present Discontents.*
[3] Ministry of Foreign Affairs Records, *op. cit.*, p. 94.   [4] *Ibid.*, p. 101.

Without specifying in which respects, Bevin told Mohammed Salah Eddin Bey that circumstances in the Sudan were quite different. He implied that much depended upon the wishes of the Sudanese: but they then had no means of adequately 'expressing' such wishes, except through ineffective party channels. When the idea of a plebiscite in the Sudan was mooted to decide on the question of Union with Egypt, the Egyptian Government held, before the 1952 Revolution, the view that the Sudan was a part of Egypt. Therefore, 'it is impossible for Egypt to propose a plebiscite in a part of the Fatherland. . . .'[1] But the Egyptian Foreign Minister challenged the British Government at the United Nations in these words:

> We know above all that the indivisibility of the Nile Valley cannot be validly contested. . . . Nevertheless, I do, from this rostrum of the United Nations, declare as a challenge to the United Kingdom, that for our part, we accept to withdraw our officials and our armed forces from the Sudan, on condition that the United Kingdom do the same, so as to allow the Sudanese freely to express their will through a plebiscite for which the necessary machinery, atmosphere and preparation could be provided with the co-operation of the United Nations. This is a frank, clear-cut challenge which I make to the United Kingdom, and which, I am more than sure, the British will not dare take up.[2]

The British did not actively take up the challenge to hold a plebiscite. But they did continue with constitutional developments. In any case, the 1953–4 general elections in the Sudan (see Chapter 14 below), seen in the light of this Bevin formula, or in accordance with any democratic principles, partly show that 'the overwhelming majority of the inhabitants wished to be reunited with' Egypt at that time; the Unionists, who stood for at least some sort of unity with Egypt, won that election. After independence, the Sudan did not form a union with Egypt, but she did join the Arab League in 1956.

Besides this Eritrea–Ethiopia analogy[3] we witness today the tendency of nations to consolidate for one reason or another. We shall cite three main examples in Europe and in Africa.

Paradoxically enough, Bevin was a protagonist of Unity. Presumably referring to his role for many years as a trade union leader, he reminded

---

[1] Egyptian Foreign Minister, quoted in *The Times*, London, 11 December 1951, p. 4.

[2] *Statement by H. E. Salah Eddin Pasha, before the U.N. General Assembly, 16 November 1951*, Cairo, 1951, pp. 12–13.

[3] Article I of the Federal Act, ratified on 11 September 1952, provides (in accordance with the resolution 390 (V) of the General Assembly of the United Nations on 2 December 1950) that: 'Eritrea shall constitute an autonomous unit federated with Ethiopia under the sovereignty of the Ethiopian Crown.' *Final Report of the United Nations Commissioner in Eritrea*: General Assembly Supplement No. 15 (A/2188), New York, 1952, p. 45.

the House of Commons, while presenting a case for European Unity: 'I may claim for myself, at least, that my whole life has been devoted to Uniting people and not dividing them.'[1] And in the course of the same debate, he told his colleagues: 'I believe the time is ripe for a consolidation of Western Europe'; but when Egypt preached the same philosophy of consolidation with reference to the Nile Valley, Mr. Bevin dismissed it (probably against his personal convictions) with the elusive statement that 'the circumstances in the Sudan are quite different'.

In any case, the concept of European unity is now a practical reality. Under Article I of the Treaty of Rome (signed in March 1957), 'The High Contracting Parties establish among themselves a European Economic Community'.[2] It seeks 'an indissoluble European Community of a supra-national character founded upon a union of people and states, *substituting essential interests, i.e. security, foreign policy, economic expansion*'.[3] This appears to be the type of fusion of essential interests of the Valley sought by Egypt and some Sudanese. Mohammed Salah Eddin Bey told Bevin that Egyptians and a majority of the Sudanese were both agreed on 'the Sudan having its own Government and its own Parliament in a unity represented by the Crown of Egypt, foreign policy, army, currency and other matters which Egyptians and their compatriots—the Sudanese—may agree upon'.[4] This was in tune with the declared policy of the Unionist Government in the Sudan, before the Umma Government came into power.

We witness in Africa itself, of which Egypt and the Sudan are parts, various efforts towards regional consolidation. Some, like the Union of South Africa, are already firmly established; many others, like the proposed United States of West Africa[5] are still *sub jure*. For our purpose it seems enough to take the case of the Central African Federation which was established in 1953.

The Central African Federation is the Union of three territories, namely: the British Colony of *Southern Rhodesia*, consisting of 1,900,000 Africans and 130,000 Whites—all on an area of 150,000 square miles; the British Protectorate of *Northern Rhodesia*, having an

---

[1] House of Commons, *Parliamentary Debates*, 22 January 1948.
[2] *Treaty establishing the European Economic Community and Connected Documents*, Brussels, 1957, p. 17.
[3] Branston, Ursula, *Britain and European Unity*, Conservative Political Centre, London, 1953, p. 51.
[4] Ministry of Foreign Affairs Records, *op. cit.*, p. 93.
[5] Meeting of West African political leaders (Dr. Azikiwe of Nigeria, Dr. Nkrumah of the Gold Coast, etc.) at the Gold Coast, in 1953, to discuss West African federation; West African Students' Union Constitution, Nigeria Union Summer School, at Margate, Kent, August 1954, at which the author was present.

area of 290,000 square miles and a population of 1,800,000 Africans and 37,000 Whites; and the British Protectorate of *Nyasaland*—48,000 square miles having 2,000,000 Africans and 4,000 Whites.[1]

Leaving aside the case for or against the geographical and historical dissimilarities of these territories, the inhabitants include—apart from the African and European groups numbered above—Indians, Pakistanis, Arabs and Chinese. In religion there are Christians and heathens, Buddhists and Hindus, Muslims, Animists, Atheists, etc. Racially, Central Africa (as a result of the 'White Policy') is one of the sorest spots of tensions in the World.

These differences—natural or artificial—which are evidently greater than those between Egyptians and Sudanese, did not prevent the British Government from giving their blessing to the Federation of Rhodesia and Nyasaland. Supporting the Federal Scheme, the British Government points to the advantages of federation: 'Closer political association between the three Central African territories is essential if they are to develop their resources to the full and reach their proper status in the World. Individually the territories are vulnerable. . . .'

The economics of the three territories are largely complementary: their close association is essential if they are to achieve the economic and social development of which they are together capable.[2]

This amounts to the kind of argument put forth by the Egyptians and some Sudanese to support the ideology of the Unity of the Nile Valley.

Much could be said for the Central African Federation—the need for inter-territorial machinery to co-ordinate the economic, communicational, social and other essential services of the territories. But, in comparison, the case for Egyptian-Sudanese union is much stronger. A study of the strategic, economic and other interests of Britain in the Sudan (see Part II—'Factors Causing the Tension'—of which this Chapter is part) helps one to unveil many of the misconceptions and escape the confusions which surround the legal and moral right to preserve the disunity of the Nile Valley. The 'welfare of the Sudanese', so much talked about by Britain and Egypt alike, is a mixture of sincerity and camouflage. The strategic, economic and other British needs could be satisfied by a division encouraged through the ethnic, cultural

[1] Conservative Research Department: Commonwealth and Colonial Affairs, *Central African Federation*, London, 1952, p. 1.
[2] *Report by the Conference on Federation, held in January 1953*, by Lord Swinton, Oliver Lyttelton, Lord Salisbury, G. M. Hoggins, G. M. Rennie and G. F. T. Colby, H.M.S.O. Cmd. 8753 (February 1953), p. 5.

and political orientation of the Sudanese, particularly of the Nilotic peoples of the Southern Sudan towards the British Protectorate of Uganda. Both Britain and Egypt are often very careful not to declare their real motives, except 'moral responsibility' in the Sudan. But Mr. Malcolm McCorquodale said openly in the House of Commons in November 1951, when Egypt abrogated the 1936 Treaty: 'I cannot claim to be in any way a close authority on the Sudan but I should declare my interests . . . in that I and my family have had close business relations with Khartoum and the Sudan for the last 25 years. I have also some connections with the cotton industry in this country.'[1]

Union of the Sudan with Egypt without the British power and administration in the Sudan to keep a watchful eye on all British interests might curtail the economic returns derived from such 'business relations' as Mr. McCorquodale's. Of course, not every British voter has direct interests in the Sudan, but the minority—business corporations and others who do—are powerful enough for the British Government to watch their interests. The British interests in the Sudan, which we shall discuss more fully in the next chapter, explain in part why Britain supports federation in her central African domain where her power is settled and certain and opposes similar federation in the Nile Valley, where she is in rivalry with Egypt and Sudanese nationalists.

Thus, we may conclude that Egypt's claim based on the ideology of the Unity of the Nile Valley, is valid with regard to the various manifestations examined above. But there are limits to the claim, and we have already indicated to what extent these six premises are valid; the 'Unity of the Nile Valley' is partly a slogan, which spreads part of the truth as though it were the whole truth. This tends to over-simplify the problems and aims of the Egyptians and the Sudanese. For instance, the form or nature, or the terms of the Unity have never been clearly defined. However, the fact still remains that a division of the Sudan (in part or in whole) from Egypt cannot escape the unifying forces of the Nile. If the scheme of the White Nile is controlled not by a combined but by a single power (foreign or native) there will be apprehensions either in Egypt or in the Sudan.

Apart from the unifying forces of the Nile, we live in an age of 'Collective Security' and many nations—even those big enough to stand alone, tend to seek political unions. For instance, writing in the *Pravda* in favour of the union of all Europe, I. Alexandroff declares

---

[1] House of Commons, *Parliamentary Debates*—Official Reports, 5th Series, Vol. CCCCXCIV, 20 November 1951, p. 266.

that: 'Collective Security in Europe is considered by the Soviet Union to be an important prerequisite for strengthening World peace.'[1]

Advocating the Union of Western Europe, Bevin too, told the British Parliament: 'It cannot be written down in a rigid thesis or in a directive. It is more of a brotherhood and less of a rigid system.'[2]

So it could be said of the putative brotherhood of Egypt and the Sudan.

Considering these points, it is understandable why Salah Eddin Pasha, Egyptian Minister for Foreign Affairs, should in a statement have put the question he made in the Egyptian Parliament on 6 August 1951, which sums up the Egyptian thesis: 'What historical, legal or moral right have they [the British] to interfere between Egyptians and their compatriots—the Sudanese—who have been united from time immemorial by geographical and economic unity and by ties of race, language and religion?'[3]

To lend the weight of his argument and personality to the theme of unity of the Sudan with Egypt, Egyptians and some Sudanese quote rather frequently Mr. (now Sir) Winston Churchill, who says:

> I can imagine no better illustration of the intimate and sympathetic connection between Egypt and the southern provinces. The water (i.e. the Nile) —the life of the Delta—is drawn from the Sudan and passes up the stem of the tree, to produce a fine crop of fruit above. The benefit to Egypt is obvious; but Egypt does not benefit alone. The advantages of the connections are mutual; for if the Sudan is thus naturally and geographically an integral part of Egypt, Egypt is no less essential to the development of the Sudan. Of what use would the roots and the rich soil be, if the stem were severed, by which alone their vital essence may find expression in the upper air.[4]

Sir Winston reveals that the 'plain and honest reason' of the River War (i.e. the conquest of the Sudan), in which he himself participated as a soldier, was 'to unite territories that could not indefinitely have continued divided; to combine peoples whose future welfare is inseparably intermingled; to collect energies which, concentrated, may promote a common interest; to join together what could not improve apart—these are the objects which, history will pronounce, have justified the enterprise'.[5]

[1] Soviet Embassy, Press Department, *Soviet News*, London, 28 May 1954, p. 1.
[2] *Hansard*, 22 January 1948.   [3] Ministry of Foreign Affairs, *op. cit.*, p. 142.
[4] Churchill, Winston S., *The River War*, London, 1899, p. 363.
[5] *Ibid.*, pp. 363–4. It could be said that Churchill's simile was true in 1899 when his book was first published, but in that case we would point out that it has been revised and reprinted five times since—in 1902, 1933, 1940, and 1949.

3. THE VISIONARY EXTENSION OF EGYPT'S INTERESTS FROM THE SUDAN TO
THE REST OF AFRICA

Then only will the dawn of the New Era rise on the Nile Valley,
and create of its inhabitants a unified people able to play a leading
role in the new world, which is now in course of birth, and carry
out their civilizing mission amongst other African peoples.

Egyptian Ministry of Foreign Affairs (Press Section), 1947[1]

We indicated in chapter 2 that Ismail, who succeeded Mohammed Ali,
dreamed of embracing the whole of the White Nile within the dominions
of Egypt of that time. He instructed Samuel Baker, then in the service
of the Khedive, to explore new territories in Africa with a view to
extending the Egyptian domain from the Sudan to as far south as the
Equator. That was in the 19th century; but the Egyptians of today
appear to be not entirely free from the territorial visions of Mohammed
Ali and Ismail. In a chapter entitled 'A Leap into the Dark Continent'
Mr. M. Rafaat, a former professor of History at the Higher Training
College, Cairo, and later Director-General, Ministry of Education, pays
tribute to Mohammed Ali and Ismail's expansionist policy in Africa.
'It must be remembered', he says, 'that these expeditions took place
twenty years before Speke or Grant or any other famous explorers of
the Dark Continent began their search for the source of the Nile.
Unfortunately, Mohammed Ali did not live long enough to realize his
aim.'[2] Thus, Mr. Rafaat, with other Egyptians, wants the present
Egyptians to achieve in Africa what Mohammed Ali and Ismail failed
to accomplish.

The Egyptian economic and political interests in the Sudan, expressed
in terms of the Unity of the Nile Valley, would appear to be a stepping
stone to further penetrations in Africa. Occasional statements in the
British Press and Parliament, and certain pronouncements by the
Independence (Umma) Party in the Sudan, pointed to some suspicion
that Egyptian interests in the Sudan would eventually lead to a sub-
stitution of fresh Egyptian imperialism in place of British domination.
The fear was so prevalent in 1947 that the Egyptian Government had
to announce through Nuqrashi Pasha in the Chamber of Ministers on
16 December:

I hope that the whole world will understand that I am expressing the
opinion of all Egyptians and all Sudanese. . . . There is no ground to

[1] *Egypt/Sudan*: Essay on the Unity of the Nile Valley, p. 78.
[2] Rafaat, M., Bey, *The Awakening of Modern Egypt*, London, 1947, p. 41.

suspect that we wish to colonize the Sudan, as the desire to dominate cannot exist between brothers.[1]

With the wave of nationalism, the new Irredentism in Egypt and the new interests of Egyptian leaders in the affairs of Africa, there arose some feeling among some non-Egyptians that victory in the Sudan might encourage Egypt, sooner or later, to embark upon territorial expansion in the rest of Africa. It is therefore pertinent to give some attention to the speculative interests of Egypt in Africa as a whole, where British interests too are paramount. The relevance of this to our subject is that, whilst Britain endeavours to hold the Sudan as one of the strategic strong-points for her interests in Africa, Egypt wants, it would seem, to have it as a starting point for further advances; and this situation increased Anglo-Egyptian friction over the Sudan. In a statement issued on 25 March 1956, the Foreign Office, London, complained:

> Unfortunately, in spite of the Sudan Agreement (1953), the treaty over Suez base (1954), the offer of British help for the Aswan Dam . . . Egypt has not ceased from actions of propaganda directed against Britain. . . . Such conduct has extended to areas where Egypt has no direct interests, for example, East Africa.[2]

Allowing room for the apparent 'party politics' in this matter, the apprehension about Egyptian incursions in Africa can be substantiated by historical analogy, and by the various manœuvring and overtures to the other peoples of Africa frequently made by Egyptian leaders. If we compare the present setting of Egypt in Africa with the historical setting of Japan in Asia, for instance, the fear of Egyptian incursion could be justified.

Certain aspects of current events in Egypt bear some resemblance to historical developments in Japan. In the 1930s, Japanese nationalism stirred up anti-American feelings in Asia, in the same way as Egypt now generates anti-British feeling in Africa.

Partly for altruistic motives but largely because of a desire to control these rich possessions herself, Japan began to speak of 'liberating' the subjected Asiatics from oppression by the White races. In an effort to win a large following from the masses of Asia, Japanese politicians put up the attractive slogan of 'Asia for the Asiatics', which could arouse a similar emotional response as the 'Unity of the Nile Valley' or 'Africa for the Africans' currently used by Egypt. A Japanese patriotic society, the Skiunts, which was one of the Japanese Foreign Office propaganda

---

[1] Quoted by the Royal Institute of International Affairs, *Great Britain and Egypt*, p. 98.
[2] *Manchester Guardian*, London, 26 March 1956, p. 7d.

units 'educating' the public in imperial affairs, issued a statement in 1937. It says:

> Are the British people not ashamed of, in their democratic principles and in the name of Christ, the procedure by which India, Africa, Australia and other territories are occupied? For occupying those territories the ancestors of the present British people killed many innocent and defenceless people, and it is still remembered that in extreme cases, innocent inhabitants were herded together by hunting dogs and then mercilessly killed as though they were game animals. Thus as far as the British tyranny and inhumanity is viewed from Japan's standpoint, the first nation to be judged by God and man is Great Britain herself.[1]

The internal problems and ambitions of Japan were hidden beneath the surface of the expressed desire to champion the cause of Asia. The pressure of population, the need for markets as sources of raw materials and outlets for Japan's growing industry, and the urge to dominate soon pushed Japan to adopt the same policy of territorial expansion and aggrandisement of which she accused America and the European powers. The result was that, whilst in 1850 the Japanese Empire was only about 142,270 square miles, with nearly thirty million people, by the end of 1942, the empire covered 3,285,000 square miles, with about 350,000,000 subjects—Asiatics from Mongolia to New Guinea. That area of territorial expansion compared not unfavourably with the 13,499,270 square miles of the much older British Empire, which the Japanese set out to emulate. However, the Japanese Empire crumbled to the counter-attack of the Allied Forces during the Second World War.

Like Japan, Egypt now needs an outlet for her dense population. As we pointed out in Chapter 4, she is trying to evolve from an agrarian into an industrial economy. Beside the Union of South Africa, Egypt possesses effective power and status perhaps more than any of the other 'free' states in Africa at present. Like Japan, she has been unnecessarily humiliated, frustrated and denied 'equal status' by Britain. In the past it appeared characteristic of the Egyptian to consider himself at best a European and at worst a 'Caucasoid African'. When not accepted as a European, he sought consolation as a leader among the Arab nations. But as the Arab League was not so effective against the European powers as it desired, the Egyptian now looked for a place in the African sun and a position of leadership as a liberating 'big brother' among the 'suppressed' colonial Africans.

[1] Statement fully quoted by James, David H., *The Rise and Fall of the Japanese*, London, 1951, pp. 394–5.

Formerly, the Egyptian was eager to show that his country was not a part of the 'dark continent', and was keen to differentiate himself from Negroid Africans, with whom, following European examples, he avoided association. John Gunther observes that 'most cultivated Egyptians have much closer ties to Europe than to Asia or to their own continent, Africa'.[1]

But the Sudan Question seems now to have made Egypt not only to look north-east towards the Arab bloc, but also to turn to Africa and the Africans north and south of the Sahara. Egyptians have suffered enough from such British attitudes as expressed by Douglas Sladen, who told the British public, in his book, about the Egyptian:

> He does not come of a ruling race, but of a race which has always been ruled. . . . The Egyptian must be told to do a thing; he cannot be trusted to do it of his own accord. Politically speaking, the Egyptian nationalist is not above the level of a clerk.[2]

With this, and with the fact that Britain sought to sever the Sudan from Egypt by appealing to racial differences, some people in Egypt have come to realize that imperialism is no respecter of races—not even of the Caucasoids of the Nile Valley.

Consequently, Egyptian leaders have been trying to associate themselves with the struggles of Africans in East and Central Africa, in West and North Africa. For instance, one Cairo radio broadcast on 'Africa for the Africans' stated:

> Africa is making a great effort for liberation. In the North, Egypt, Tunisia, Algeria, Morocco, Libya and the Sudan stand as a bloc in revolt calling upon the imperialists to evacuate their territory. In Central Africa, Kenya, Uganda and the Congo see in the Mau Mau movement a symbol of liberation. In the South, hatred is reaching boiling point between Whites and Negroes.[3]

Major Salah Salem established cultural relations with the naturalists (the 'primitive pagans') of the remote regions of Southern Sudan by dancing with them in his under-pants,[4] and for this he is often cynically mentioned, in the British Press, as 'the dancing major'. In 1953, a large number of Sudanese students in Egypt were receiving increased financial assistance for their studies, as well as personal attention from the head of state.

---

[1] 'Inside Egypt', *Reader's Digest*, May 1955, p. 68.
[2] Sladen, D., *Egypt and the English*, London, 1908, pp. 2, 4 and 6.
[3] *The Scotsman*, 7 April 1953.
[4] *Daily Telegraph*, 28 January 1953.

To establish contacts with peoples in other parts of Africa, Egypt adopted methods to suit the various European colonies; and she seems to have received indirect encouragement from Africans, though not co-operation.

Egyptian overtures to West Africa have been in the form of encouraging students to complete their studies in Egypt, showing hospitality to visiting West African leaders, and negotiating the establishment of diplomatic missions. When two Nigerian Ministers (Chief Awolowo and Mr. Akinloye) visited Egypt on their way back from India in 1952, they were given a royal welcome. During his pilgrimage to Mecca in 1956, the Sardauna of Sokoto (Northern Nigeria) paid a friendly visit to President Nasser. Three prominent Nigerian scholars—the late Sultan Bello of Sokoto, Dr. Olumide-Lucas in his *Religion of the Yorubas* and Dr. S. O. Biobaku in his Lugard lectures on 'The Origin of the Yorubas'—have given evidence of kinship between Nigerians and Egyptians over the ages.

In Kenya, Egyptian overtures took the form of Swahili broadcasts; an audience was given to the Secretary of the banned Kenya African Union, Mr. Joseph Murumbi. In answer to British protests, Dr. Fawzi retorted: 'Egypt's policy is against the suffocation of freedom anywhere in the world.'[1]

With regard to French North Africa, the 'Ulema' of Al-Azhar University, Cairo,'the highest religious authority in the Muslim World', issued a statement on 16 December 1952, appealing to all Muslim governments to join hands in an economic, cultural and political boycott of France, and asking all Muslims to raise funds for the support of the 'fighting patriots of North Africa'.[2] On 7 September 1953, two resolutions were adopted by the Arab League, led by Egypt, recommending 'that the Member States make every effort through diplomatic channels at their capitals and through their diplomatic missions abroad to gain support for the Arab point of view in the case both of Tunisia and Morocco'.[3]

As it was with Japan at a similar stage of her history *vis-à-vis* Asia, Egypt is now a state of nationalism and militarism; also as Korea was the starting point of the Japanese expansion in Asia, the Sudan could be considered as a spring-board for Egypt in Africa. In 1819, Japan attacked Korea, then a dependency of the Chinese Empire, and acquired

[1] *The Times*, London, 29 August 1953.
[2] Keesing's *Contemporary Archives*, Vol. IX, Bristol, 1952–4, p. 12790.
[3] Resolutions Nos. 587 and 585, quoted in *International Conciliation* (Arab League 1945–55), May 1955, p. 431.

it by conquest. A year later, in 1820, Mohammed Ali attacked the Sudan and succeeded in acquiring it some years after. Japanese expansion was thwarted by the rival Western imperialisms of Russia, Germany, France and Britain. The victory of the Japanese in the Russo-Japanese War in 1905 gave Japan a free hand in Korea and south of Manchuria, in a similar way as the political (not military) victory of Egypt over Britain in the Sudan elections of 1953 temporarily gave confidence to Egypt in the Sudan and encouraged her to look further ahead.

Egypt's kind of 'Manifest Destiny' in Africa was summed up in a semi-official organ, *Al Akhbar*:

> We look for a power which will protect Africa and play *vis-à-vis* the American continent. We see no one but Egypt. It is the greatest African power with a personality that is universally recognized. It is necessary for Egypt to pursue one African policy aiming at the enfranchisement of the continent.[1]

It is therefore evident that the suspicion about the possibility of Egyptian penetration not only in the Sudan but in other parts of Africa is justifiable. In a talk broadcast in Cairo's Sudan programme on 19 March 1955, Dr. Muhyi al Din stated: 'The Liberation of the Sudan clearly means the liberation of the neighbouring African peoples; it means the liberation of the Congo, Uganda, Kenya, and eventually the whole of the African continent.'[2]

This and similar talks have been interpreted in Britain to mean that Egypt was trying to convince the Sudan that union with Egypt will enable her to expand her frontiers and that 'eventually they can together conquer Africa'.[3] The Press revealed that the British Government was investigating these broadcasts, because they encouraged expansionist tendencies.[4]

It is characteristic of ex-colonials to champion subject nations. Having been through the mill of foreign domination herself, Egypt has, at least for the moment, genuine sympathy with Africa's colonial peoples. But to what extent can Egypt expand effectively in Africa? That Egypt will seek to become leader of Africa is obvious; that this may become her chief object is a good guess. But there are certain factors against Egyptian 'imperialism'. It will not be easy for Egypt to displace or replace British, French and Belgian, or even American influence. For a long time British authorities have been studying

---

[1] *Al Akhbar*, Cairo, 24 March 1953.
[2] B.B.C. *Summary of World Broadcasts*, Part IV—'The Arab World, etc.', 25 March 1955, p. 41.
[3] *The Scotsman*, Edinburgh, 4 April 1955.   [4] *Ibid.*

Egypt's efforts to reach the rest of Africa; the Anglo-French attack on Egypt over Suez in 1956 was partly aimed at thwarting Egypt's potential advances.

It should be remembered, also, that the African masses are awake; and they may not be eager to substitute one foreign ruler for another. Egypt may find that there are rivals—perhaps from West Africa—for African leadership. It has been widely said that Nigeria—the largest Negro unit in population—will lead Africa. In any case, to suggest that Nigerians might easily accept domination by Egyptians is to underrate the intelligence of present-day Nigerians.

Egypt may not be able to achieve a 'new order' in Africa as Japan did (for a short time) in Asia. For one thing, Tokyo's military Shintoism is not quite the same as Cairo's military Mohammedanism; and for another, Japan rose to power when imperialism was still in its glory. Furthermore, while Japan's relative remoteness from the major powers encouraged her imperial expansion, Egypt is comparatively at the centre of world power politics; and the major powers are in constant vigilance in Africa and in the Middle East. Egypt's desire to expand territorially in Africa is also limited by other factors, such as the general inertia of her own people. Unlike the Europeans—particularly the British— Egyptians seldom emigrate from their own country. Again, Egypt's internal problems appear to be of such magnitude as to be likely to diminish some of the energy she would otherwise be able to devote to influence and expansion abroad. As a corollary to this, Egypt may not be able to find enough men of high calibre to enable her to act as the leader and guardian of *both* Africa and the Arab world.

We have submitted evidence enough to justify the British suspicion that Egypt has been trying to convince the Sudan that union with Egypt will enable the Sudan to expand her frontiers and that they can together conquer certain parts of Africa. But it is safe to conclude that in the years to come many of the dangers in Africa may prove to be imaginary. Some now feared may take a surprising turn towards the good of all. On the other hand, others, not now suspected, may come to light.

Part Two

(B) FACTORS CAUSING THE TENSION

8

THE BRITISH STAKE IN THE SUDAN, 1885–1955

*It is beginning to be understood by the people that the British
Empire is not maintained to gratify aristocratic selfishness . . .
but that it is bound up with the naval, commercial and industrial
supremacy of England, on which depends the daily bread as well
as the national dignity of the toiling millions. Englishmen ought
to be shrewd enough to see that our position in Egypt (and the
Sudan) has a direct bearing upon imperial interests.*[1]

The Times, 1885

HAVING analysed in the last two chapters Egypt's various interests in
the Sudan, we must now examine the British side of the factors which
inflamed the Anglo-Egyptian friction—namely those essentials which
constitute the British stake in the Sudan.

It is difficult to enter into the motives of nations; one can only judge
from statements and events. But in relative contrast to what we might
describe as Egyptian vocal diplomacy, the British are adepts in the art
of subtlety. In our search for the motivating forces in the British policy
in the Sudan, we are faced with the comparative elusiveness of British
diplomatic papers, about which the eminent scholar, Sir Llewellyn
Woodward, mildly complained in his Stevenson Memorial Lecture on
'Some Reflections on British Policy', which he recently gave under the
joint auspices of the Royal Institute of International Affairs and the
London School of Economics. Some papers are drawn up, he warns us,
with the knowledge that they will be published almost at once, others
with the knowledge that they will remain in closed archives, and that
the 'main principles or objectives of a policy are often taken for granted
and do not receive or require explicit statement'.[2] Mr. J. Seymour Keay,
who had seen service in India as a bank manager before becoming,
in 1892, a Member of Parliament at Westminster, where he was known

---

[1] *The Times*, editorial, London, 17 November 1885, p. 9b.
[2] Sir Llewellyn Woodward, *Some Reflections on British Foreign Policy, 1939–45*, being
the Stevenson Memorial Lecture, delivered at the London School of Economics and
Political Science, 24 May 1955; advance print by the Royal Institute of International
Affairs, p. 4.

for his 'special knowledge of Egyptian affairs'[1] complained, even as far back as November 1882, about official records on Egypt:

> British officials would ever wish to suppress evidence that told against themselves. . . . They hide away evidence not to screen themselves, but from a justifiable desire to teach meddlesome pamphleteers (and research students!) a salutary lesson. Officials (and Government) are themselves the best judges as to how much of their conduct should be submitted to public scrutiny.[2]

The materials available suggest that British administrators, ministers and the Press were more vocal and expressive in the past than now; the general policy has been established and become traditional. To those in the game, it no longer requires explicit clarification; and with the Egyptians and the Sudanese becoming increasingly conscious of their respective rights, and with the greater opportunities for alert critics in this age of 'open diplomacy', the British sources tend in addition to their normal characteristics of understatement to use in their despatches and public statements fine and carefully-chosen words which leave unanswered several specific questions which a student might put about British objectives in the Sudan.

Nevertheless, there is sufficient evidence to suggest that British interests in the Sudan are either economic and commercial, political and strategic, or altruistic, and that these interests are all closely interwoven.

1. ECONOMIC ASPECTS

When analysing Egyptian interests in the Sudan, we showed that Egypt desired the Sudan as an extra territory to relieve the pressure of over-population. Like Egypt, Britain, too, is over-populated; between 1871 and 1931 an average of 56,000 British persons emigrated yearly; and between 1919 and 1930 the average annual number was 171,000.[3]

By the Empire Settlement Act, 1922 . . . 'an Act to make better provisions for furthering British settlement in His Majesty's Overseas Dominions'[4] the British Government helped the flow of emigrants. But partly for the reasons which we shall indicate presently, the population problem of Britain has been relieved mainly through emigration to the Commonwealth countries of Australia, Canada and South Africa, in addition to the annual quota to the United States. The population

---

[1] 'The New House of Commons', *Pall Mall Gazette*, London, 1892, p. 61.
[2] 'Spoiling the Egyptians', in *Contemporary Review*, Vol. XLII, November 1882, p. 765.
[3] Royal Commission on Population: *Report*, Cmd. 7695, 1949, pp. 122–3.
[4] H.M.S.O., *Public General Acts of 1922*, p. 47.

problem of Britain is emphasized by the amount of attention currently given it in Parliament. On 7 April 1955, not less than 101 Members from both sides of the House signed the motion welcoming the Annual Report of the Overseas Migration Board, and urging: 'Her Majesty's Government to use their influence to increase the flow of migration from the United Kingdom. . . .'[1]

In spite of this population problem, tropical Africa does not offer enough inducement to British settlers; they feel that the climate is too hot, and that the natives are too much of another race, with whom the British must not intermarry. Complaining about British racial attitudes in the Nile Valley, Jean Lugol says:

> The Egyptian, the Arab in general, in fact, whether Semitic or Hamitic by race, was placed . . . in the category of inferior beings. Any 'defilement' of the Aryan race by sexual or other contact with them constituted a crime entailing severe penalties. No one of Jewish, Arab, Coptic, Armenian, Circassian or Asiatic (and African) origin might ally himself by marriage with the . . . superior race.[2]

Unlike the Red Indians of America, the brown-skinned peoples of Africa are not yet considered a 'dying race', on the contrary, they are regarded as prolific, and their increasing numbers do not announce the dying state of the race; consequently, the possibility is remote of European settlers roaming alone in 'open spaces' undisturbed by the presence of the natives. The British attitude in this respect is evident in territories wherein British people have settled and possessed full political power; in the U.S.A., where they left a legacy of race tensions; in Australia with its 'White policy'; in Kenya, where this kind of rationale by the European settlers has brought about the emergence of the Mau Mau movement and in the Union of South Africa with its doctrine of 'aparthied'. However, this European attitude to African 'natives' is changing, and will perhaps continue to change for the better as a result of African resurgence and other factors in the world which now combine to challenge the *status quo*. Even so, the Sudan is in the Tropics, and although it has a sizeable population of European merchants, missionaries and civil servants, the country is not, for the above reasons, considered as a suitable outlet for British settlers. Apart from British racial attitudes, the Sudanese were difficult to subjugate. Lord Wolseley's despatches to the Secretary of State for War in 1885

[1] *Parliamentary Debates*, Vol. DXXXIX, 7 April 1955, p. 1397.
[2] *Egypt and the World War II*, Cairo, 1945, p. 142.

contain observations about the 'blacks, who fought well' in the defence of Khartoum.

While tropical Africa has not, so far, played a major role in the emigration needs of Britain, it has certainly satisfied other British economic necessities. To quote Lord Lugard, one of the architects of British penetration and control in Africa,[1] 'the tropics produce in abundance a class of raw materials and of foodstuffs which cannot be grown in the temperate zones, and are so vital to the needs of civilized man that they have in very truth become essential to civilization. It was the realization of this fact', he repeats, 'which led the nations of Europe to compete for the control of the African tropics.'[2] The Sudan products which are vital to Britain include cotton (for the cotton industries of Lancashire).

In 1863, some Americans rejoiced that cotton was a success—'a financial recognition of our independence'—and that 'cotton is king at last'.[3] In an attempt to minimize their dependence upon the American cotton, British entrepreneurs sought new sources of supply. The soil of the Sudan provided a good substitute. As we have noted earlier, Sir Samuel Baker wrote in 1890, informing the British Government about the Sudan, where he hoped that 'an area of 30,000,000 acres of the most fertile soil under cultivation would supply England with cotton, thereby making her entirely independent of America'.[4]

Sir Samuel Baker's dream did come true. Cotton now accounts for about 80 per cent of the Sudan's total value of exports. With the Trades Facilities Bill[5] was included for discussion in 1924 a British Treasury guarantee in respect of the principal and interest of the remaining £3,500,000 Sudan Government loan for the completion of the Gezira irrigation project for the production of raw cotton. Because of British interests in the cotton, some Members of Parliament headed by a Mr. Johnston, pressed that the loan should be made conditional on an undertaking that 'all cotton produced in the Gezira should be offered for sale in the first instance in Great Britain'.[6] However, the British

[1] (1) Served in the Sudan Campaign; (2) Administrator of Uganda, 1889–92; (3) Commissioner in Nigeria, 1897–9; (4) Governor-General of Nigeria, 1914–19; (5) Director of Barclays Bank, Dominion, Colonial and Overseas, etc.

[2] Lugard, Sir Frederic D., *The Dual Mandate in Tropical Africa*, London, 1922, p. 43.

[3] Morrison, Samuel Eliot and Commager, Henry Steel, *The Growth of the American Republic*, Vol. I, New York, 1942, p. 715.

[4] See Chapter 3 above for extract from Baker's letter of April 1890.

[5] See the Trade Facilities Act, 1921, in *Public General Acts*, H.M.S.O., London, 1921, pp. 558–60.

[6] *Correspondence respecting the Gezira Irrigation Project, Sudan No. 1* (1924), Cmd. 2171, p. 3.

Board of Trade to whom the Foreign Office referred the matter in February 1924, was careful not to accept this proposal as it might irritate other countries, because it was against the 'open door' policy in international trade, and because such a step would be inconsistent with 'the settled policy of the Board of Trade . . . and of His Majesty's Government to encourage in every way possible the development of cotton growing'.[1] Nevertheless, in the four years preceding the Second World War, the United Kingdom bought some 61 per cent of the Gezira cotton and British India bought 23 per cent of it. During the last War, most of the Sudan cotton was sold to the Ministry of Supply.

In the past, the Sudan cotton was controlled mainly by two British Companies—the Sudan Plantations Syndicate Ltd., and the Kassala Cotton Company Ltd.—both of which supervised the cultivation, the ginning and the marketing of cotton. These Companies, which invested a great deal of money in the Scheme, had about 20 per cent of the net proceeds of the cotton. But now, their concessions having been terminated since 30 June 1950,[2] there are three principal cotton growers in the Sudan: the Government, through the Ministry of Agriculture and Forests; the private growers; and growers under the Gezira Scheme, who are the most important of the three.

Since its nationalization, the Scheme has a Board composed of seven directors appointed by the Governor-General at the recommendation of the Council of Ministers. A Sudanese director, Mekki Abbas (author of *The Sudan Question*), became responsible for the aspect of social development. But the whole scheme had been under a British Chairman and Managing Director (formerly Mr. Arthur Gaitskell,[3] and later, Mr. G. W. Raby) until 1955 when, as a result of the process of Sudanization, Mekki Abbas became Managing Director. Another Sudanese, Sayed Abdel Hafif Abdel Moneim, was appointed Chairman.

The Scheme helped the considerable flow of Sudan cotton into British ports; in 1951 about 136,000 bales were imported in two months as compared with 247,000 bales in the previous twelve months.[4] Agreement was reached between the British Raw Cotton Commission and the Sudan Government for the purchase of the major part of the Sudan cotton crop in 1951.[5]

The Financial Times (10 October 1951) stressed that the Sudan cotton (long staple) was extensively used in British mills and warned that any

[1] Board of Trade to Foreign Office, 14 March 1924, *ibid.*, p. 4.
[2] See *The Gezira Scheme Ordinance 1950*—1950 Ordinance No. 16.
[3] Brother to Mr. Hugh Gaitskell, Leader of the British Labour Party since 1956.
[4] *Financial Times*, 19 January 1951.   [5] *Ibid.*, 19 January 1951.

cuts would be severely felt, especially because the Sudan cotton had been used to make up for the deficit in American qualities (short staple), due to the shortage of dollars.

In the past, outside India and Pakistan, Britain's biggest source of cotton supply was the Sudan, and it provided about 40 per cent of the total Commonwealth output, especially the extra long staple type for many years. Commenting (in April 1955) on the occasion of the Golden Jubilee of the British Cotton Growing Association, *The Empire Cotton Growing Review* quoted with satisfaction: 'It is no exaggeration to say that the cotton coming from the Empire territories and the Anglo-Egyptian Sudan in the last few years has proved a veritable godsend to the mills of Lancashire.'[1] Britain's stake in the Sudan cotton and the fear of Egyptian competition was one of the causes of Anglo-Egyptian friction. This fear was expressed by a special correspondent of *The Scotsman*, who, writing from Khartoum, warned the British: 'If Egypt ruled this country, she would have a virtual monopoly of the finest cotton in the world.'[2]

In 1952, as a result of negotiations in Liverpool and Khartoum, the British Raw Cotton Commission bought 'the major part (60 per cent) of the 1952 Sudan cotton crop for the use of Lancashire spinners'.[3]

However, it is currently the policy of the Sudanized Gezira Board to sell Sudan's cotton by public auction in Khartoum. But the highest bidders are still those who buy for the mills of Lancashire. The members of the Gezira Board are pleased (so Mekki Abbas, its Managing Director, informed the writer on 30 June 1955) to retain Britain as Sudan's chief customer, so long as she pays in accordance with the competitive price in the world's open market. It would seem that, because the Sudan staples help to run the wheels of Lancashire industry, Britain might continue to be Sudan's chief customer; but she appears disinclined to pay competitive prices. According to the 1954 Annual Report of the Raw Cotton Commission, 'the Commission had in previous years bought Sudan cotton by private negotiation, but after arranging one such purchase, further private treaty transactions became impracticable, as the Sudan authorities decided to offer the remainder of the crop at a series of auctions.'[4] The Commission complained that at the auctions held during the Spring of 1954 'prices rose sharply'[5]; and that 'thereafter, prices [of the Sudan cotton] would be increasingly affected by the

[1] *The Empire Cotton Growing Review*, London, April 1955, p. 77.
[2] *The Scotsman*, 26 October 1951. [3] *The Financial Times*, 25 January 1952.
[4] H.M.S.O., *The Raw Cotton Commission, Annual Report*, June 1955, p. 6.
[5] *Ibid.*, p. 7.

marketing of the Egyptian 1954 crop for which *higher prices* . . . had been fixed by the Egyptian authorities'.[1] This is inconsistent with the provision 'that these prices shall be as low as possible'.[2]

It would seem, therefore, that rather than pay the competitive price in the open market, British merchants preferred, naturally, to see the Sudan possibly join the British Commonwealth with its internal agreement of 'imperial preference' in trade.[3] During the first week of June 1955, a delegation from the Liverpool Cotton Association visited the Sudan. The delegation spent three days in Port Sudan in discussions with the Sudan Gezira Board; at Khartoum they also had discussions with the Marketing Advisory Committee to the Board, 'on matters of sales'.[4]

It is relevant to mention that the amount of cotton imported into Britain from the Sudan seems to fluctuate with the degree of self-government in the Sudan. This is partly evident from the following table of the number of bales imported into Britain from 1948 to 1954:

SUDAN COTTON: NUMBER OF BALES IMPORTED INTO BRITAIN

Year	Number of Bales
1948	200,000
1949	304,773
1950	268,581
1951	266,349
1952	363,863
1953	104,554
1954	148,667

However, although the brains and hands behind the Gezira cotton scheme are now Sudanese, British capital, guaranteed up till at least 1974, still plays a role in the scheme; he who pays the piper has the right to call the tune. But Sir James Robertson assured the writer in 1954 that as long as the Sudan pays her annual instalments, she need not fear any British interference.

Another important crop is gum-arabic, of which the Sudan produces seven-eighths of the world's supply. The Sudan also sends Britain hides, skins, oilseeds, dates and vegetable oils.

[1] H.M.S.O., *The Raw Cotton Commission, Annual Report*, June 1955, p. 7.
[2] Raw Cotton Commission, *Annual Report for 1948*, p. 16.
[3] Chapter 8 of Russell's book—*Imperial Preference: Its Development and Effect*, London, 1949, written under the direction of the Empire Economic Union, deals with 'Textile Raw Materials', and mentions the Sudan, pp. 62–4.
[4] Sudan Govt., National Guidance Office of the Social Affairs Ministry, *Sudan Weekly News*, No. 42, 14 June 1955, p. 2.

Another objective of the British control of the Sudan was the investment of capital by the British and some other Europeans. The migration of peoples, for whatever particular reasons, forms one of the major aspects of world history. Such migrations have almost always been dictated by the belief and hope that another land offers certain superior attractions. The main forces which have influenced the movement of peoples from one part of the world to another have been almost the same as those affecting migration of capital—favourable conditions. Invited especially by those lands to which the British have spread, unobstructed by law in British territorial possessions, solicited and directed by British persons, who in large numbers have sought their fortunes in the development of the resources of young countries like the Sudan, British savings have found employment abroad.

Thus, as Hobson defines them, foreign investments consist of that part of the property of a country (in this case Britain) and its inhabitants situated abroad (in this case in the Sudan) 'from which its owners expect to derive an income'.[1] A nation of shopkeepers, the British are exponents of investment in its various forms—whether as Conservatives who have for centuries promoted private investment, or in recent years as Socialists who now advocate state investment. And so, notwithstanding the fact that two world wars had considerably weakened Britain as a capital-exporting country, her investments abroad in 1953 outweighed those of all the Commonwealth countries combined.[2]

Therefore, one of the functions of the British administrations in Colonial territories is to watch the economic and commercial interests not only of the Colonial peoples, but essentially those of the mother country as well; to create and maintain general conditions conducive to financial speculations by British nationals. Investment in British dependencies is governed by the Colonial Stock Act, 1877, subject to amendments to suit changing conditions.[3] The Colonial Governments endeavour to make investment pay by helping to minimize the risks of investment. Such risks which the Sudan administration helped to control included those arising from imperfect knowledge, ignorance, or uncertainty about the prevailing conditions in the Sudan. The Administration helped all investors, but more especially and quite naturally, the British, to obtain the necessary knowledge relevant to their interests. There are also risks arising from imperfect ability to readjust business

[1] Hobson, *op. cit.*, p. 1.
[2] Grondon, L. St. Clare, *Commonwealth Stocktaking*, London, 1953, p. 295.
[3] See Report of a Committee on Investment in Colonial Stock, C.6278: *Parliamentary Papers*, Vol. LXVI, 1890-1.

arrangements to changing conditions in the country: the ability of investors or business enterprisers to meet new opportunities or emergencies is relatively weak. A specialized Department, such as the Intelligence Branch of the Central Economic Board of the Sudan Government gave guidance in this direction. The Government as a whole sought to maintain general stability—economic, political and social—throughout the country; to avoid radical changes in the *status quo*, the Administration withheld political power from local 'agitators' or 'firebrand nationalists'. (This explains in part the philosophy of gradualism about granting self-government to colonial territories, including the Sudan.) Other risks arise from the marketing of capital. In Britain there is a group of professional investors and people who have available supplies of 'free capital'. The Sudan Government was helpful to this class of people by employing their capital in Government enterprises such as railways, telecommunications, etc. (which were essential for the development of the country) and by facilitating the movement of the stream of capital from Britain to the money market or to industries and commerce in the Sudan. One of the British Commercial Companies with direct interests in Sudan Railways is the Kassala Railway Company incorporated in England on 7 December 1922. However, the concession granted to the Company was terminated on 31 December 1953, and ownership passed to the new Sudanese Government on that date.

Soon after the re-conquest of the Sudan in 1898, some British businessmen began to apply to the Foreign Office for permission to invest their capital in the Sudan. Examples of such applications are those made by W. Sherrif on 1 October 1898; by F. Balter on behalf of a proposed 'Anglo-Sudan Trading Company' on 3 November 1898, and by Reginald Vaile on behalf of 'several wealthy and influential friends' (as the applicant himself put it) on 28 November 1898.[1]

Writing confidentially to the Marquess of Salisbury from Cairo on 10 November 1898, Lord Cromer indicated that he had to deal not only with Sudanese, but also with 'numerous demands received from Europeans who wish to reside, to invest capital, to trade with and acquire real property in the country'.[2] He submitted that it would be impossible, and also undesirable, to exclude them, because British capital and assistance were needed for real progress in the Sudan. Consequently, under what might now be called Britain's Colonial

---

[1] Public Records Office: Foreign Office File No. 141/332, pp. 164, 206 *et seq.*
[2] Foreign Office 78/4957—Lord Cromer's Memorandum to the Secretary of State for Foreign Affairs, supporting his draft of the Anglo-Egyptian Agreement on the Sudan.

development and welfare scheme, or the United States Point Four Programme, both of which float abroad capital that might remain idle at home, British investors loaned to the Sudan over £15,000,000 for the construction of the Sennar dam, canals and the building of certain railways. A portion of the loan was redeemed in 1939, but another at a lower rate of interest was made, and the Sudan will continue to pay a debt service until 1974.

As we have noted whilst discussing Egyptian interests in the Sudan, British technical 'know-how', capital, etc., were and still are involved in the schemes in the Nile Valley; for instance, with regard to the Owen Falls Scheme in Uganda, the Uganda Government which is responsible to the British Government, was empowered by its legislature to raise by loan £30,000,000 for the expenditure on the scheme. By March 1954, over £2,000,000 had already been provided 'mainly by two loans raised in London and partly in (British) East Africa'.[1] The Egyptian Government was to bear that part of the costs of the dam necessitated by the raising of the level of the lake for water storage. The amount payable by Egypt was £E980,000 for the consequential loan of hydro-electric power and she would also bear the costs of compensation to lake-side interests, affected by the storage of water.[2]

Mining concessions were granted to British and European interests by the Sudan Government under 'The Mining Prospecting Licence Ordinance' of 1900; in the early part of that year, a mining expedition was sent out under Sir Rudolph Slatin, who later became absorbed into the Sudan Government.[3] In 1901 the Governor-General reported to the British Government in London that several licences 'giving exclusive rights of prospecting were granted'.[4] Among the licences were the London and Sudan Development Syndicate, Victoria Investment Corporation, etc. A well-known mining company today is the gold mining concern in Gebeit.[5]

In addition, there are still several British firms which have sunk capital in the Sudan. These companies are, undoubtedly, beneficial to the Sudan; but expatriate companies transferred their profits overseas —to Britain. The concern for British capital investment in the Sudan was expressed by Mr. Lloyd George when the independence of Egypt was declared on 28 February 1922. He demanded that any change in

---

[1] Central Office of Information, Reference Division, *Owen Falls Scheme, Uganda.* Ref. No. R2811 of 8 March 1954, p. 3.
[2] *Ibid.*, p. 3.   [3] *Parliamentary Papers, Egypt No. 1* (1901), p. 74.
[4] *Parliamentary Papers, Egypt No. 1* (1902), p. 62.
[5] *Barclays Bank and Foreign Trade*, London, 1949 (new edition March, 1953), p. 7.

the status of the Sudan which would diminish the security for the British capital in the country must not be made. Such British capital sunk in the Sudan is guaranteed by the British Treasury under the Sudan Loan Acts of 1919 and 1922.[1]

In answering the question about the use of the Sudan to the United Kingdom, Sir Harold MacMichael, himself in the Sudan Administration (Civil Secretary, 1930) says that, apart from Britain being guarantor of loans for the development of the Sudan, 'Millions of British Capital are invested there'.[2] Included under the heading of 'British Funds' by the British Stock Exchange Year Book[3] are the following:

1. Sudan Government $3\frac{1}{4}\%$ Guaranteed Stock 1954–59, amounting to £2,000,000 issued at 97% in July 1939. The outstanding sum after 1 November 1954 was £579,300.
2. Sudan Government 4% Guaranteed Stock 1974 (£1,500,000) issued at 86% in 1924 towards irrigation of the Gezira Plain, the outstanding amount after 10 November 1954 being £1,302,300.
3. Sudan Government $4\frac{1}{2}\%$ Guaranteed Stock 1939–73, amounting to £3,763,400. Of these, £3,250,000 were issued at 93% in January 1923 for the irrigation of the Gezira Scheme.

The principals and interests of 1 to 3 above are guaranteed by Government of Britain under the Trade Facilities and Loans Guarantee Act of 1922.

Although in 1955 the Azhari Government assured foreign investors that: 'Ministers have stated in Parliament their intention to encourage all investments from overseas which have no "strings" attached'[4] the general effect is that, while British capital is still welcome in the Sudan, the field since she became independent is no longer left mainly for British investors. This is evident from the fact that in May 1955, the Sudanese Council of Ministers 'discussed the many applications by Indian and Pakistani firms to operate (and invest capital) in the Sudan'.[5]

Judged by its Condominium Constitution, the Sudan was neither a British colony nor a protectorate. But in practice the broad principles of British Colonial policy were applied in the administration and in the external commerce of the country. The British Government have learned certain lessons from the American Revolution and they avoid the obnoxious elements of the past. But it is also apparent that certain

[1] *Public General Acts of 1922*, pp. 50–1.   [2] *The Anglo-Egyptian Sudan*, p. 271.
[3] *The Stock Exchange Official Year Book*: Vol. I, 1955, p. 9.
[4] Sudan Govt., National Guidance Office of the Ministry of Social Affairs, *1001 Facts about the Sudan*, Khartoum, May 1955, p. 28.
[5] National Guidance Office, *Sudan Weekly News*, No. 40, 31 May 1955, p. 2.

aspects of the Colonial policies pursued in the 17th century were applied in the Sudan (up till the 1953 Agreement), as in other territories, although with modifications. In the 17th century, the economic doctrine known as mercantilism was the major feature of British policy; it has been defined as the pursuit of economic power in defence of national self-sufficiency.

One of the outcomes of mercantilism was the Acts of Trade and Navigation. Through a series of these Acts (1660–72) an effort was made to make the British Empire an economically self-sustaining unit and to confine profits to British merchants and peoples. The Acts embodied three main principles: (i) trade between Britain and her colonies must be conducted by British-built or British colonial vessels, 'owned, manned or captained by English subjects': (ii) all European imports into the British colonies with the exception of certain perishable commodities, must first 'be laid on the shores of England'—i.e. unloaded, handled and reloaded—before being exported to the colonies through British ports. These Acts are apparently a revival of the Navigation Acts of 1381 and 1390—'ordering that no merchandise should be shipped out of the realm except in British ships on pain of forfeiture'[1]: (iii) certain products 'enumerated' in the laws must be exported to Britain and Britain only. The navigation Acts were repealed in 1849, but their ghosts still remain, haunting the British policy of today. They were implicitly, if hot explicitly, pursued in the British economic policy towards the Sudan.

This brings us to international shipping which became one of Britain's commercial stakes in the Sudan. In 1906, the first building of a new port was begun at Port Sudan, the port at Suakin being unsuitable for large ships. In 1907, two years before it was formally opened (by the Khedive of Egypt on 1 April 1909), Port Sudan handled 312,770 tons of merchandise. Traffic there has since increased more than 100 per cent. For instance, it handled 799,714 tons of cargo and was visited by 875 merchant vessels in 1949.[2] In 1953–4 it was visited by 1,188 merchant ships and 6 naval vessels.[3]

Most of the Sudan's external trade depends upon shipping facilities (it would be much more expensive to carry goods by air). In his annual report for 1915, the Director of the Central Economic Board of the Sudan Government indicated that 'the rise in shipping freights has

---

[1] Hannay, David (once British Consul at Barcelona), *The Encyclopædia Britannica*, 11th Edition, Vol. XIX, Cambridge 1911, p. 298.
[2] Central Office of Information, London, *The Sudan 1899–1953*, p. 30.
[3] Sudan Govt., *Sudan Railways, Annual Report*, 1952–4.

made it clear that better arrangements will have to be made for ginning and pressing Tokar cotton than those which exist at present'.[1] Furthermore, he complained that, 'owing to shipping and other difficulties due to the war [the First World War] steamship companies serving Port Sudan have not been accepting transhipment traffic.'[2] In previous years, however, the quantity of gum, for example, which was transported direct to Port Sudan (through the Kosti-El Obeid Railway) for shipment amounted to 44·6 per cent in 1912, 79·6 per cent in 1913 and 88·5 per cent in 1914 and 92·6 per cent in 1915, of the total for each year.

As the Sudan products became more and more dependent upon shipping, the freight rates increased. Before 1914, the rate from Port Sudan to Liverpool was £E2 per ton of cotton; in 1916 the rate rose to £E25 per ton, and the rate for cotton seed to London was also raised 'from 110 piastres to 1,000 piastres per ton',[3] without a corresponding rise in wages, fuel or overall costs, in 1916, imports from Britain into the Sudan increased by 54 per cent and the exports from the Sudan to Britain increased by more than 67 per cent.[4]

In the same year, exports to and imports from the United States decreased; but according to the Sudan Government, 'it is known that considerable quantities were shipped thither via British ports, and no doubt much of the gum forwarded to Great Britain was re-shipped to other destinations.'[5] This, in effect, is in keeping with the objective of the Navigation Acts of 1660, to which we have referred, requiring that international commerce with British colonies must be carried through British ships and ports. We may add here that the Commonwealth shipping industry is predominantly that of Britain; Britain's gross registered tonnage in 1952, for instance, represented 88⅓ per cent of the total, and nearly 91¾ per cent that of the Commonwealth sterling area (i.e. the Commonwealth minus Canada).[6]

Under the Shipping Companies Exemption Order, 1948, British shipping companies are exempt from the submission of certain information relating to resources . . . and certain details of fixed assets[7]; but the following table of shipping arriving at Port Sudan according to nationality of ship ownership, clearly shows Britain's predominance in the international maritime commerce with the Sudan:

[1] Sudan Govt., *Sudan Railways, Annual Report*, 1952–4, p. 15.
[2] Central Economic Board, *Report for 1915*, Cairo, 1915, p. 13 (Sudan Govt.).
[3] Central Economic Board, *Report for 1916*, p. 18.   [4] *Ibid.*, pp. 32 and 36.
[5] *Ibid.*, pp. 19 and 36.   [6] Grondon, *op. cit.*, p. 310.
[7] *Stock Exchange Official Year Book*, Vol. I, London, 1955, p. 1331.

TABLE OF SHIPPING ARRIVING AT PORT SUDAN[1]

Nationality of ship ownership	Net registered tonnage					Percentages of total tonnage				
	1943	1944	1945	1946	1947	1943	1944	1945	1946	1947
1. British	384,120	454,018	500,269	632,673	1,280,870	42·3	44·2	59·3	62·8	65·8
2. American	325,733	279,555	51,131	84,282	176,823	26·0	27·3	6·1	8·4	9·1
3. Norwegian	55,290	16,568	20,581	35,453	77,302	6·1	1·7	2·4	3·5	4·0
4. Greek	65,142	74,565	25,832	6,477	14,182	7·2	7·3	3·1	0·6	0·8
5. Egyptian	72,004	142,749	91,605	96,894	126,488	8·0	13·9	10·9	9·6	6·3

[1] Sudan Govt., Department of Economics and Trade, *Foreign Trade Report, 1947*, p. 22.

The percentage of British shipping is considerable if we take into account other nationalities using Port Sudan—Panamanian, Dutch, South African, Swedish, Palestinian, French, Arabian, Danish, Turkish, Belgian, Italian, etc., it was still as high as 64·1 in 1949.[1] Writing on 1 February 1954, the General-Manager, Sudan Railways, informed Minister of Communications that 'demands fully taxed the capacity of the railways, port and steamer services'.[2]

We may now proceed from merchant ships to aeroplanes. The first Imperial Airways aeroplane flew to Khartoum in 1926 to investigate a possible African service. In April 1932, this service was inaugurated, passing through the length of the Sudan. In 1936, the trans-African stage was opened from Lagos in Nigeria to Khartoum and Cairo; in 1937, the routes were included in the Empire Air Mail Scheme, of which the Sudan is an important part (in spite of the 1953 Agreement). The airport at El Fasher was an important staging point during World War II, and the relays of lease-lend aircraft refuelled there on their way to the Middle East. It has formed in post-war years, a link between West Africa, Khartoum and the air route to Mecca. The Khartoum airport has consequently become a busy centre linking the Cape-to-Cairo airway and forming an important African air junction connecting Britain and the Far East to Central and South Africa, West Africa, Eritrea, Ethiopia and Aden. In 1950, there were 16,197 aircraft movements in the Sudan.[3] By 1951 there were about ten aerodromes in the Sudan and twenty-two subsidiary permanent landing grounds, and a fully equipped international airport capable of taking jet aircraft has now been completed.[4]

The importance to Britain of the Sudan airports is emphasized by the observation of Hobson, late of the London School of Economics, on the influence of the means of communication on capital investment. In his book *The Export of Capital*, he says:

Improvements in the speed and cheapness of communication, too, facilitated the exercise of effective control of capital invested at a distance [i.e. in foreign countries—Author]. Consequently, British and European capital has been spread more and more widely over the World, and the purposes to which it has been applied have increased in diversity.[5]

---

[1] Sudan Govt., *Trade Report for January, 1950*, p. 40.
[2] *Sudan Railways Annual Report, 1952–3*, Atbara, 1954, p. 1.
[3] Sudan Govt., *Growth of a Nation*, p. 26.
[4] Central Office of Information, *Sudan 1899–1953*, p. 31.
[5] Hobson, C. K., *The Export of Capital*, London, 1914, p. xvi.

To this we may add the financial returns to people who make direct investments to the Imperial Airways, the Sudan Airways (which became a separate Government Department in 1948) and to the British Overseas Airways Corporation to which Khartoum is a regular stop on the B.O.A.C. 'Comet' service to South Africa, and the various opportunities for employment which air communications provide.

In May 1955, the Sudanese Government estimated the daily aircraft movements in Khartoum to be forty, and the annual revenue to be £E100,000.[1]

In the 19th century, the main exports of the Sudan were gold, ivory, ostrich feathers and slaves. Mostly as a result of British influence and the alterations in world economy, the Sudan has grown in economic stature. In 1949, for instance, the Sudan's exports were valued at £E26·4 million, the major part being cotton and cotton-seed (£E21 million), the others being gum-arabic, hides, skins, livestock, groundnuts and pulses. Imports were valued at £E23·8 million.[2] But quite naturally, the British influence in the Sudan has been used to promote British trade interests.

In 1915, sixteen years after the signing of the Condominium Agreement, the Director of the Commercial Intelligence Branch of the Central Economic Board of the Sudan Government was able to report a marked increase of 'British influence in trade', and that 'much of this trade has gone to Great Britain'.[3] He attributed the increase mostly to improved import of cotton goods to the Sudan and of direct exports from the country to Britain. Undoubtedly, the general improvement in the output of Sudanese products, encouraged by the British authorities and the increase of the general demand for these products in the world market had a good deal to do with the general increase of the Sudan's trade with Britain. However, there seem to be some other underlying reasons for the increase of 'British influence in trade'. One of these was the creation and composition of the Central Economic Board, which was constituted by the Sudan Government Order No. 427 of 7 June 1906. Appointment to the Board is made direct by the Governor-General and 'is not ex-officio'. All the members were top-ranking British officials only (without any Egyptian or Sudanese representatives), the Financial Secretary to the Government (who was the President), the Civil Secretary, the General Manager of the Sudan Railways, the

---

[1] Ministry of Social Affairs, *1001 Facts About the Sudan*, May 1955, p. 30.
[2] Central Office of Information, *The Sudan*, p. 37.
[3] Central Economic Board, *Report for 1915*, p. 30.

Director of the Veterinary Department, the Director of the Steamers Department, and a few other British officials. The functions of the Board, though advisory, include 'questions of policy in regard to grant of concessions, monopolies, subsidies, legislation, protection of native industries, railway development, commercial relations with foreign countries, currency, immigration, Government charges, exploitation of the country's products generally'.[1]

Naturally, the Board would seek ways and means of increasing British commercial interests and ascendancy in the Sudan. The national character of the British in such matters has been well described by Lord Salisbury in these significant words:

> Our people, when they go into the possession of a new territory, carry with them such a power of initiative, such an extraordinary courage and resource . . . that if they are pitted against an equal number—I care not what race it is or what part of the world it is . . . it will be our people that will be masters, it will be our commerce that will prevail, it will be our capital that will rule.[2]

In fact the Board worked hand-in-hand with such agencies as the Imperial Institute in London,[3] which acted as the research brain. Paragraph 28 of the Board's Report for 1916 is entitled 'The Sudan and the Empire'. Here the Board remarks:

> The new orientation of imperial policy towards the establishment of the Empire on a self-supporting basis and the consequent need for the consistent development of its unexploited economic resources is a matter of great potential meaning to the Sudan with its possibilities for the production of cotton, livestock, grain and other raw products, for all of which the need will be greatly accentuated.[4]

It seems probable that the new orientation of the imperial policy to which the Report referred, was influenced by the Paris Economic Conference of 14 to 17 June 1916. The Conference met to adopt and realize 'from now onward all the measures requisite on the one hand to secure for themselves and for the whole of the markets of neutral countries, full economic independence and respect for sound commercial practice, and on the other hand to facilitate the organisation on a permanent basis of their economic alliance'. For this purpose, the representatives of the Allied Governments, among which Britain was a major power, passed three sets of resolutions; Measures for the War period; Transitory Measures for the period of commercial, industrial,

---

[1] Central Economic Board, *Report for 1915*, Appendix IV, pp. 60–1.
[2] Debate, House of Lords, 14 February 1895.   [3] Economic Board, *op. cit.*, p. 62.
[4] Sudan Govt., Central Economic Board, *Report for 1916*, Cairo, 1917, p. 10.

agricultural and Maritime reconstruction of the Allied Countries; and Permanent Measures of mutual assistance and collaboration among the Allies.[1]

Another instrument of British influence, though to a degree less than that exercised by the Central Economic Board, is the Sudan Chamber of Commerce, whose Executive Presidents were frequently British, especially in the early decades of the century.[2]

In any case, as a result of this 'new orientation' the Sudan's trade with Britain was increased—by 54 per cent and by over 67 per cent in exports at the end of 1916.

To what we have already examined may be added the direct efforts of the British Government in London to encourage British capital investors by providing a policy of insurance to exporters to the Sudan and other parts of the world. The Board of Trade in London, for instance, is represented overseas by British Commissioners (who are in turn assisted by 'Imperial Trade Correspondents'), in Commonwealth countries, and, in foreign countries by members of the British Foreign Service. In Egypt and the Sudan, the Board of Trade was represented by a 'Minister (Commercial)' attached to the British Embassy at Cairo.[3] To encourage exporters and investors, and to delimit what the Government has described as 'the risks of the export trade', a few publications exist, which the Secretary for Overseas Trade confidently brought 'to the notice of all United Kingdom exporters in the hope and belief that in this scheme they will find a solution to many of the problems and difficulties with which they are faced in their efforts to achieve the maximum of exports both in their own and the country's interests'.[4]

Furthermore, there is the Export Credit Guarantee Department of the British Government, in London, with the Secretary for Overseas Trade as Minister in Charge. The Department 'derives its powers from the Export Guarantees Act, 1949, which repealed all previous legislation concerning the Department and extended its powers so as to enable it *to give guarantees with the object of encouraging all exports, whether visible or invisible, which will help to improve the United Kingdom's balance of payments position'.*[5] This Department worked in consultation

[1] Keith, A. B., *Selected Speeches and Documents of British Colonial Policy 1763–1917* (World Classics ed.), London, 1948, pp. 368–75.

[2] See list of Executive Officers in the *Sudan Chamber of Commerce Monthly Journal* for 1915–17, 1919–20, 1937, etc.

[3] H.M.S.O., *The Sudan: Review of Commercial Conditions*, September, 1952, p. 2.

[4] Bottomley, A. G. (M.P., Secretary for Overseas Trade), in his Foreword to *Government Guarantees for Exporters*, London, April 1950, p. 1.

[5] *Ibid.*, p. 4.

with the British Administration in the Sudan, when necessary, either by direct contact or through the British Minister (Commercial) at the Embassy in Cairo. With the Sudan on the way to full autonomy, a British Trade Commissioner's office was set up in Khartoum in March 1953, and Mr. D. M. H. Riches arrived in Khartoum on 25 March 1953, as the first British Trade Commissioner to the Sudan.

We may therefore conclude that the British Commercial ascendancy in the Sudan and Egypt's comparative decline are partly due to the activities of the British Administration in the Sudan (through the Central Economic Board, and the Chamber of Commerce) and of the British Government in London (through the Board of Trade and the Export Credit Guarantee Department). These were, of course, assisted by political instruments. The general trend of trade intercourse between the Sudan and each of the disputants—Britain and Egypt—is shown in, the following import and export percentage table, covering ten years (1945–54). The figures speak for themselves:

Year	British Imports	Egyptian Imports
1945	12·7	16·9
1946	23·9	18·8
1947	24·0	21·6
1948	30·0	21·2
1949	32·5	16·4
1950	40·0	9·3
1951	34·8	9·1
1952	34·0	7·3
1953	41·5	8·3
1954	32·5	9·6

Year	British Exports	Egyptian Exports[1]
1947	39·7	17·9
1948	62·5	13·9
1949	67·6	10·6
1950	56·1	7·9
1951	68·2	6·2
1952	56·9	7·1
1953	41·3	5·5
1954	42·3	8·8

[1] Percentages by courtesy of the Staff, Statistics Dept., Board of Trade, London. (For the figures in monetary terms, see the Sudan Government's Annual Trade Reports.)

In June 1947, the Sudan Government informed the British Board of Trade that the Sudan offered excellent prospects as a post-war market for imports, that there would also be the demands of the European population to be satisfied in high quality consumer goods from radios to refrigerators, from linen to lingerie, from cars and crockery 'to those things that ease the heated life of the tropics'.[1] Observing the general trend of external trade of the Sudan becoming increasingly favourable to Britain, Egyptians jealously complained that, economically, the Sudan was being 'exploited in the interests of British capitalists and syndicates. The great example is the Gezira Cotton Scheme.'[2]

We must mention, however, that since the Anglo-Egyptian Agreement of 1953, granting self-government to the Sudan, the Sudanese have themselves been trying to make the Sudan emerge as an effective third party in the trade of the country. The new administration places some restrictions on the establishment of foreign business in the Sudan; prospective foreign businessmen are now required to apply initially to the Director, Ministry of Economics and Commerce, now a Sudanese. In essence, the criterion for approval is (*a*) that the proposed business should show promise of being beneficial to the Sudan, and (*b*) that its scope is 'beyond the competence of the Sudanese or already-established residents'.[3]

The Sudan attracted many young British men and a few women as a field of lucrative employment with opportunities for quicker advancement than any available in Britain. Before the conquest of the Sudan in 1898 and the subsequent Condominium arrangement which brought the country under British administration, India was the chief land of opportunity for many British citizens. But by the end of the last century, the India Service was becoming 'congested', so to speak; and the door for fresh opportunities was open in the 'new' Sudan. Professor Arnold Toynbee, who (apart from being connected with the Sudan by the nature of his many-sided academic work at the University of London and the Institute of International Affairs) personally knows many of his compatriots who served in the Sudan, informed the writer that 'the Sudan Service was much sought after', and that people were recruited mainly from the Universities of Oxford and Cambridge.

Recently, in Britain, only about seventy-five persons were recruited annually for the Administrative Class of the Home Civil Service out of

---

[1] H.M.S.O., *Sudan, Review of Commercial Conditions*, London and Khartoum, 1947.
[2] *The Sudan: A Short History*: A 25-page pamphlet apparently published in 1954 by the Egyptian Government (available at the Egyptian Education Bureau, London), p. 7.
[3] Sudan Govt., *Sudan Almanac: An Official Handbook*, Khartoum, 1955, p. 86.

more than 1,500 candidates—all with at least Second Class Honours Degrees.[1] In the past men and women of this type went to the Sudan as teachers, technicians and administrators, with the opportunities for accelerated promotion for the able, and for early retirement with pension.

Apart from advertisements in British newspapers, for particular vacancies in the Commonwealth and Colonies, there are Government publications inviting interest in the Colonial Service and showing the opportunities available. In a foreword to one of such publications, M. A. Creech-Jones, Secretary of State for the Colonies, writing in 1950, told young British men and women:

> The Colonial Service demands much of those who have the privilege of belonging to it, but it also offers much to those who have given. Few careers can be so rewarding. The work is always constructive; the response to the right approach great; the results often quick and visible. The ups are more than the downs.[2]

The Sudan was not, by technical definition, a part of the British Colonial Service. But for all practical purposes, it was often regarded as a British 'Colony' or *Protectorate*. In a radio talk about 'Self-Government in the Commonwealth' published by the B.B.C. in July 1955, Sir Ivor Jennings practically classified the Sudan with Nigeria and the Gold Coast.[3] A Commonwealth Survey Officers' Conference was held in Cambridge from 15 to 24 August 1955; some Sudanese were invited to participate, and did so.[4] Thus Mr. Creech-Jones's remarks applied equally to the Sudan.

Mr. Douglas Dodds-Parker, speaking in the House of Commons on 5 November 1953, expressed great concern about the possible withdrawal by 1955, of British personnel who formed over 50 per cent of the top-level administrators. By this date the Sudanization of the Administration would have been effected by the process of self-government.

The comparative general strength of Britain and Egypt in the Sudan Government Service since 1920 is shown by the tables opposite.

In February 1954, when the new Sudanese Government practically took over the sceptre of government from the British, there were about 1,200 British officials in the Sudan Civil Service.[5] But, as a result of 'Sudanization' the decrease in their number was accelerated by the new

---

[1] Central Office of Information, *The Sudan*, p. 46.
[2] H.M.S.O., *Appointments in His Majesty's Colonial Services*, 1950, p. 3.
[3] *The Listener*, Vol. LIV, No. 1376, London, 14 July 1955, p. 51.
[4] *The Colonial Review*, Vol. IX, No. 4, London, December 1955, p. 97.
[5] J. S. Owen, 'Sudan Civil Service', letter in *The Times*, London, 17 May 1955.

(A) CLASSIFIED POSTS IN THE SUDAN GOVERNMENT SERVICE: PERCENTAGE DISTRIBUTION BY NATIONALITY

Year	Sudanese	British	Egyptians	Remarks
1920	36·8	—	—	(i) Egypt's sudden decline between 1920 and 1930
1930	50·9	20·0	22·0	partly due to withdrawal of Egyptian officials in
1939	76·2	14·2	8·5	obedience to Allenby's Ultimatum of 1924.
1947	84·9	11·0	3·7	(ii) Even with Sudanization no sudden change oc-
1951	87·6	10·2	2·0	curred in the number of British in the Service, but the change became steep after the 1953 Agreement was put into effect.

(B) DISTRIBUTION OF POSTS IN THE SUDAN POLITICAL SERVICE, 1934–52

Year	Governors, Deputy Governors and similar	Sudanese District and Assistant District Commissioners	Mamurs and Sub-Mamurs	Total
1934	nil	nil	78	78
1943	nil	7	70	77
1952	nil	41	78	119

Year	Governors, Deputy Governors and similar	British District and Assistant District Commissioners	Mamurs and Sub-Mamurs	Total
1934	20	135	nil	155
1943	nil	146	nil	146
1952	39	95	nil	134

Remarks.—(i) No Egyptians. (ii) By the end of 1955 the Service would be over 90 per cent Sudanese.

Administration; consequently, the British were, quite understandably, much concerned. Such uneasiness was expressed in the Press, as well as in Parliament. In a letter to *The Times* in May 1955, Mr. J. S. Owen complained about the acceleration of Sudanization in the Sudan Civil Service; he pointed out that only one-sixth of the British officials showed any willingness to leave the Sudan. He therefore raised objection to the new Government making 'plain its desire to replace them [the British officials] as soon as this was possible, and [having] indeed enacted legislation to remove whatever security of tenure the long-term contracts once contained'.[1] Mr. Owen, we should point out, was once a District Commissioner and later Commercial Manager, Ministry of Agriculture, which became Sudanized in about April 1955.

2. STRATEGIC INTERESTS

The real interests of the United Kingdom in the Sudan were many, local and global. Britain is a leading imperial power in the world, and her major colonial interests, particularly in Africa, are well known. As a result of her position and objectives in Africa, Britain had and still has strategic and political interests in the Sudan. As far back as about 1877, organized groups such as the British South Africa Company were seized with the idea of a 'Cape-to-Cairo' Scheme, which envisaged the ultimate link of the British territory in South Africa with the new possessions in Central Africa, Egypt and the Sudan.[2] This imperial objective is well put, in the language of the time, by W. E. Gladstone:

> Our first site in Egypt, be it by larceny, or be it by emption, will be the almost certain egg of a North African Empire, that will grow and grow . . . until we finally join hands across the Equator with Natal and Cape Town, to say nothing of the Transvaal and the Orange River of the South, or Abyssinia or Zanzibar to be swallowed by way of viaticum on the journey.[3]

Two months earlier, in June 1877, Edward Dicey had said: 'Once we had a *locus standi* in Egypt as the dominant power, we should occupy a commanding position over the whole region lying between the Red Sea and the frontiers of India.'[4] He argued that, given a strong military position in Egypt (and of course, in the Sudan), Britain could afford to be indifferent to India, and that protectorate over Egypt (and the Sudan)

---

[1] J. S. Owen, 'Sudan Civil Service', letter in *The Times*, London, 17 May 1955.

[2] Langer, William L., *The Diplomacy of Imperialism 1890–1902*, Vol. I, New York, 1935, p. 117.

[3] Gladstone, W. E., 'Aggression on Egypt', in *The Nineteenth Century*, Vol. II, August 1877, p. 158.

[4] Dicey, Edward, 'Our Route to India', in *ibid.*, Vol. I, June 1877, p. 683.

'would supply us with the means of conducting desert warfare'.[1] It is needless to prove that these objectives have since been achieved.

The present air age has rendered the Mediterranean sea-lane, being comparatively close to the centre of military operation by the major powers, too vulnerable. Therefore, the British Commonwealth life-line has shifted southwards from the Canal Zone, making the Sudan a major outpost in global defence. This new 'Equatorial Line' of defence cuts through the whole waist of Africa—from the Gold Coast, through Nigeria and the Sudan to Kenya and Tanganyika.[2] Apart from the vulnerability of the Mediterranean area, another problem was that Egypt had been asking Britain to evacuate her forces from the Canal Zone, and British experts, consequently, speculated on the Sudan as a possible alternative. 'Control of the Sudan has always been of considerable strategic importance to the British Empire, and as British authority in Egypt diminishes so does this importance increase.'[3] In a letter dated 27 June 1943, Sir Douglas Newbold, Civil Secretary of the Sudan Government, stressed that the future of the Middle East Countries—particularly Iraq, Syria, Palestine, Transjordan and Egypt—was of some concern to the Sudan. 'Officially—for military and economic purposes'—he emphasized, 'we are part, and the Governor-General [of the Sudan] is a member, of the Middle East War Council.'[4]

The visit of Field-Marshal Montgomery to Khartoum and the arrival in the Sudan of several R.A.F. squadrons and an auxiliary unit, reported in the *Egyptian Gazette* of 1 December 1947, are indications of British military interest in the Sudan.

The Sudan has been also for the British an instrument of political strategy which was succinctly expressed by a British writer: 'If we settle at the headwaters of the Nile, we command Egypt. . . .'[5] *The Round Table*, too, stressed: 'While we hold the Sudan, and we must hold it, we cannot get out of Egypt, even if Egypt ceased to be the stepping stone to India.'[6]

Also as a power in the Sudan, Britain would be able to watch the general interests of British East and Central Africa for encroachment by any alien power.

As the Senegalese have been able soldiers useful to the French, so have been the Sudanese to the British. Before the British Government

[1] *Ibid.*   [2] *New York Times*, 10 August 1947.
[3] The Royal Institute of International Affairs, *Political and Strategic Interests of the United Kingdom*, Oxford, 1940, pp. 118–19.
[4] Henderson, *op. cit.*   [5] Quoted by Langer, William, *op. cit.*, Vol. I, p. 127.
[6] *The Round Table*, Vol. I, London, 1910–11, p. 457.

formally declared Uganda a British protectorate on 27 August 1894, Sudanese mercenaries were imported as 'soldiers of the Queen' to help subdue the hostile elements and areas of disaffection.[1]

But the Sudan Defence Force was not formed until 1925, after the Egyptian Army had been forced to withdraw from the Sudan as part of the penalty for the assassination of Sir Lee Stack. Its peacetime strength was about five thousand officers and men under the British. The force was expanded in the last war to about seven times its normal size, and it served with distinction on the Sudan frontiers, in Eritrea and Ethiopia and in the North African Campaign. In his letter to which reference has been made above, Sir Douglas Newbold said that the Sudan supplied the largest combatant army to the Allies of any Middle East territory during the Second World War. Their performance was so impressive as to earn special official tribute. 'They [the Sudanese troops] deserve in the battle of Africa the same tribute as the Prime Minister paid to the fighter pilots of the Royal Air Force in the Battle of Britain.'[2]

The principle of the balance of power, as a system to maintain the independence or weakness of each unit of a state system so as to prevent any one unit from being so strong as to threaten the rest, has existed since time immemorial as a formulated or unformulated guide in state action. It has shown itself in many Western states wherein the units have struggled competitively for power. Machiavelli, writing in 1513, put it cogently: 'The Prince who contributes toward the advancement of another power ruins his own.'[3]

This principle has become recognized as an integral feature of British policy in Europe and throughout her empire. In pursuit of this policy, Britain has waged war on, and raised coalitions against, the Spain of Philip II, France at the time of Louis XIV and Napoleon I, and against Germany in the reign of Wilhelm II.

Britain supported Sudanese 'independence' (i.e. separation from Egypt) partly because she hoped that such 'independence' would keep the Sudan more attached to Britain or to the British Commonwealth than would be the case if the 'Unity of the Nile Valley' became an established fact; and partly because most of the British officials of the Sudan Government were personally anti-Egyptian and feared that the

---

[1] Turker, Alfred R., *Eighteen Years in Uganda and East Africa*, London, 1911, p. 147. See also, Pankhurst, Dr. R. K., 'Uganda: A Factual History', in *New Times Ethiopian News*, London, 6 August 1955, p. 3.
[2] *The Abyssinian Campaign*, H.M.S.O., quoted by the Sudan Govt., *The Sudan: A Record of Progress, 1898–1947*, p. 86.
[3] *The Prince*, p. 15.

Administration which they had helped to build up in the Sudan would deteriorate under Egyptian control or influence. But in this section we are concerned more with the balancing of power, which is evident in the Sudan question.

Britain struggled against the 'Unity of the Nile Valley' for fear that an Egypt-Sudanese Union might create one of the strongest power states in the Mediterranean and the most powerful in the Red Sea—a state that would include both the 22 million Egyptians and the 8¾ million Sudanese, whose high military potentiality was fully brought home to the British during the First World War, the Italo-Abyssinian War, and the Second World War. Within a short space of time, such a state might challenge British interests and authority in the Mediterranean and Africa. With a natural desire to prevent, or at least delay, the formation of such a state, Britain persistently manœuvred to maintain the Sudan under the British regime, thereby ensuring some effective influence on Egyptian policy.[1] There also appears to have been the motive of keeping the Sudan, Egypt and the Middle East as areas of influence for Britain and the other Western powers, to counterbalance the expanding territories and the growing political power of the Soviet Union.

Conversely, Egyptians struggled to achieve a merger of the Sudan with Egypt and to form a link with the Arab League States so as to ensure that Egypt might be strong enough to meet the great powers of the day on an equal footing. This has resulted in the inevitable conflict of wills and clash of interests between Britain and Egypt.

3. ALTRUISTIC MOTIVES

The Biblical maxim that man does not live by bread alone is true of the British in Africa; although it is true to say that they range the globe mainly for bread and butter, it is also true to say that they are often driven by some sense of mission—a desire to bring 'civilization' as they know it to others whom they consider to be less fortunate than themselves. By civilization they seem to mean Western values or attitude to life—a complicated web of beliefs, habits, laws, customs and traditions.[2] This altruism takes various forms of expression. In its crude

[1] On this point, Sir James Robertson, who served the British in the Sudan for thirty years before becoming the Governor-General of British Nigeria in 1955, commented to the writer: 'Not so. We persistently tried to secure its independence, and prevent it being absorbed into Egypt before the Sudanese could choose for themselves.' Sir James's *disagreement* is, it should be obvious, a confirmation of the principle of the balance of power as suggested by the writer.
[2] 'Foundation of Western Values', *The Listener*, 28 April 1955.

form it leans towards arrogance and a superiority complex; in a mild form it is paternalistic; and in its best form, as exemplified in the work and devotion of some missionaries and administrators, it is admirable.

In this respect, the British regarded their position in the Sudan as a sort of trusteeship; they believed that they were working for the best interests and general welfare of the Sudanese. They regarded themselves as 'superiors' (Sir James Robertson calls them 'elder brothers') with high responsibility for the 'minors'—socially, economically and politically. This attitude is illustrated by Major A. R. Dugmore, who says about Anglo-Sudanese relations: 'It is to the Britisher that the natives look for everything. He may try and punish the criminal and his justice is not questioned.' He feels able to conclude that such is almost 'perfect relations between the white man and the black man'.[1] Lord Lugard, the Colonial administrator, puts it another way: 'We hold these countries because it is the genius of our race to colonise, to trade and to govern.'[2]

They were in the country as a duty, so they have claimed, to bring to the Sudanese the joys of British civilization. In a speech from the Throne, it was said: 'It will be the high task of all My Governments to superintend and assist the development of these countries . . . for the welfare of the inhabitants and the general welfare of Mankind.'[3] Joseph Chamberlain put it another way: 'We develop new territory as Trustees for Civilization for the commerce of the World.'[4] It is part of the so-called 'White Man's Burden'. Mr. Ramsay MacDonald wrote on 7 October 1924 that the British Government had moral obligations in the Sudan: 'They regard their responsibilities as a trust for the Sudanese; there can be no question of their abandoning the Sudan until their work is done.'[5]

The British point, with manifest pride, to what they had achieved in the Sudan, and put out such self-praising publications as one by the Sudan Government—*The Sudan, A Record of Progress 1898–1947* and another by a former District Commissioner and later Assistant to the Governor-General's Adviser on Constitutional and External Affairs, Mr. J. R. Duncan—*The Sudan, a Record of Achievement*. In the House of Commons on 20 November 1950, Mr. Ernest Bevin told the House that the Sudan was a remarkable development and 'an example to the whole world' . . . 'we would do nothing at all to set it back and leave it to the mercy of others.' On 5 November 1953, Mr. Dodds-Parker

[1] Dugmore, Major A. R., *The Vast Sudan*, London, 1924, pp. 248–50.
[2] *The Dual Mandate in British Tropical Africa*, p. 619.
[3] *Ibid.* front page.   [4] *Ibid.* front page.
[5] Cmd. 2269, 1924, p. 4.

told the House of Commons that the Sudan had an administrative service unsurpassed by any similar service in the world. This administrative excellence he attributed to the British officials in the Sudan, whose withdrawal would, he claimed, lead to a serious set-back in the country.

This British attitude has some justification, particularly if we take into account their relative superiority in technology. But they tend to carry it to extremes. The Sudanese long demanded that they should cease to be an 'adopted son'; in their moderate mood they asked for a key to the front door; and in their intemperate moods they shouted that the most efficient of alien governments could never be an altogether satisfactory substitute for the least efficient of native administrations. In reply, they were told that they would be regarded as adults when the time comes.[1] If the Sudanese erred on the side of excessive haste, the British were just as likely to err, as they do in many other dependencies, on the side of excessive calculated gradualism, in accordance with Major A. Radclyffe Dugmore's recommendation that Britain should adhere with absolute firmness to her hold on the Sudan. 'We have taken on the White Man's Burden and we must not drop it', he advised.[2]

We could summarize British objectives in the Sudan laconically as follows: politically, to keep the Sudan as one of the outposts—for Britain's strategic and political power in the world; economically, to retain the territory as a source of cheap raw materials for British industries, as an outlet for British manufactured goods and investment, and for British skill, technical and administrative; militarily, as a source of manpower in a major war; and emotionally, to use the Sudan along with other colonial peoples as a means of satisfying the British paternal instincts and altruistic disposition, together with the ideal of the British Commonwealth (which is presented in a separate section below).

No country in our present stage of development is genuinely and purely altruistic; no imperial country is disinterestedly philanthropic towards another; even the United States of America, with the abundance of rich natural resources which she has within her own territorial boundary, is pursuing a policy of 'enlightened self-interest' abroad. It is therefore understandable that Britain, whose local resources are relatively meagre, and whose very existence consequently depends largely on foreign soil and resources, should have been so much interested in the Sudan. In the present nature of imperial powers (and of all powers for that matter), generous impulses are occasional and

[1] Mekki Abbas, *op. cit.*, p. 100.   [2] *The Vast Sudan*, p. 256.

reversible; and this is often admitted by the British themselves—'let it be admitted at the outset', says Lord Lugard, 'that European brains, capital and energy have not been and never will be expended in developing the resources of Africa from motives of pure philanthropy.'[1] But it is also true that as in the case of individuals within a society, so certain self-interests of individual states often coincide with those of the universal body. Thus, the interests and welfare of the Sudanese was very often, though not always, promoted through the promotion of certain British interests. In a personal correspondence on the subject matter of this chapter, Sir James Robertson, Governor-General of Nigeria, who had served in the Sudan for thirty years, told the writer, on 10 December 1955, that one of the aims of the British Nationals who had served in the Sudan was: 'To have an interesting and reasonably paid job in which they could feel they were serving others' [the Sudanese].

The general improvement in the country reflects the good administration which carried the Sudanese through the economic crisis of 1929, for instance; also the increasing material wealth is a result of the economic development carried out under the Condominium. Britain's legacy, bequeathed to the Sudan after the withdrawal of British power in 1956, is embodied in a separate chapter below.

However, the crux of the Sudan Question is the conflict of interests between the British and the Sudanese, Europeanization versus the Sudanization of the Administration; and between Britain and Egypt the merger of the Sudan with the British Commonwealth and Empire is in conflict with the doctrine of the Unity of the Nile Valley. Thus Egyptian interests, and British stakes, in the Sudan were at loggerheads, and each endeavoured to exercise political control over the country. It could be argued that their respective objectives in the Sudan could have been achieved without exercising political control over the inhabitants of the country. But it should be remembered that political power results in a psychological relation between those who exercise such power and those upon whom it is exercised. It gives the former control over the minds and actions of the latter.

We may conclude here on a note of optimism. Certain forces of interdependence and mutual co-operation have begun to emerge both in Africa and in Europe—as well as in the whole world for that matter —which suggest that the time may come when the resources of the earth will be used more for mutual benefit of all mankind, than mainly for sectional interests and conflicts.

[1] *Op. cit.*, p. 617.

9

THE POLITICO-PSYCHOLOGICAL FACTORS
IN THE CONFLICT

Western Minds are apt to regard their principles as self-evident truths, which must be universally accepted. And they are often astonished to find that this is not the case.

LORD LLOYD

WE have, thus far, endeavoured to present, in the main, the external or 'visible' aspects of the Sudan in Anglo-Egyptian relations. The inward and 'invisible' or psychological elements underlying some of the events or nature of the Sudan dispute cannot all be analysed in the course of general analysis or narrative without becoming confused. We have therefore chosen to treat this section separately, though it must be considered as part and parcel of Chapters 6 to 8, wherein we attempted to show the Egyptian interests and the British stakes in the Sudan as the major factors causing the Anglo-Egyptian tension. We must also emphasize at the outset that in this chapter we are leaving the firm earth for thin air; it involves, most of the way, a departure from the realm of concrete facts to the sphere of abstraction, both of which are relevant and important. It does not seem easy to draw a sharp line between the physical entity of man and the invisible soul that drives his flesh and blood. So it is with this part in relation to the previous chapters and the subsequent ones—i.e. with the Anglo-Egyptian problem as a whole.

In this Chapter, we propose to bring into focus some of the major politico-psychological factors in the dispute under the following heads: British Empiricism and Sudanese Self-government; the Conflict of General Perspectives; and the Divergent Concept about Race and Nationality.

1. BRITISH EMPIRICISM AND SUDANESE SELF-GOVERNMENT

The question of the time when the Sudanese would be ready for self-government was one of the points of Anglo-Egyptian disagreement. Mr. Bevin described it as the 'core' of the Sudan problem during his conversation with Salah Eddin Bey in London on 15 December 1950. At a previous talk between the British Ambassador and the Egyptian Foreign Minister, the latter based his estimate on the United Nations resolution in regard to Libya, which was in his view less advanced than the Sudan, and suggested two years as a transitional period to self-government, but the British insisted on 20 years as the minimum—two widely differing estimates! The British persistence in believing that the Sudanese were unripe for home rule was considered by the Egyptians, and by the Sudanese themselves, as false pretences and as an attempt to cover up wily designs. This may be so, but there is also an element of genuine, though often mistaken, psychological force based on Britain's past; there is also the driving force of a sense of mission—that is, a feeling of sympathetic benevolence towards all human beings, particularly the weak; and lastly, the ideal of the Commonwealth also seems to come into play.

The Romans arrived in Britain in 55 B.C. In his Gallic War Caesar describes Druidism, the religion of the Celtic tribes of Britain during that time; he found that the whole of the Gaulish nation was devoted to superstitious rites; they 'sacrifice human beings for victims or vow that they will mutilate themselves. These employ the Druids as ministers for such sacrifices, because they think that unless the life of man be repaid for the life of man, the will of the Gods cannot be appeased.'[1]

In nearly all their colonial territories the present-day British tend to say that they found, during their early contacts, indigenous conditions and practices similar to those described by Caesar when he occupied the territory of the Britons. But the Romans did not finally depart until early in the 5th century A.D. If it took the Britons (members of the 'Master Race') almost 500 years to become independent of Rome and centuries after that to evolve their present constitution, it would there-fore seem somewhat difficult for the British, looking back at their own past, especially since 1066, to see enough sense in the Africans and Asians (whom they so often regard as members of the 'Inferior Race') demanding self-government within only about half a century of British tutelage.

This interpretation of history by self-projection is clearly illustrated in Sir Reader Bullard's views on the British rule in the Middle East and the question of self-government in that area where he was British Minister and afterwards Ambassador (at Tehran) from 1939 to 1946. He

[1] Quoted by Marjorie and C. H. B. Quennell, *Everyday Life in Roman Britain*, London, p. 6.

claimed that 'British connection with the Middle East has been long and close', but that it has not been long enough for self-government; this is because, in his opinion, as an Englishman, 'Self-government is a difficult art, and Middle East countries have not at their disposal the centuries that Britain took to attain it.'[1]

When debating over the time limit for self-government in the Sudan, Mohammed Salah Eddin Bey persuaded Sir Ralph Stevenson to the point where the latter had to confess that 'I did not want to start this question. The reason is that we also have a sentimental approach to it. It is one of the peculiar traits of the British character.' This 'sentimental approach' has its source partly in the projection of the British past into the Sudanese present, which had led Sir Ralph to declare earlier on: 'As to the question of how far the Sudanese are capable of self-government, it is a personal opinion. We do not think the Sudanese are ripe enough for it now.'[2]

The mistake in the philosophy of gradualism, which refuses to hand over self-government to subject peoples until they pass through the centuries that Britain took to attain it, lies, we venture to suggest, in its failure to reckon fully with the changes in circumstances, in times and in society. The Britons evolved towards democratic government when the general tempo of the world and the means of communication were very slow indeed. Now we live in an age of speed never dreamed of by even the great Romans. The progressive conquest of space by science has produced a shrinking world. In the 1830s it took British envoys in Rome thirteen days to get to London, just about the time required by couriers of Julius Caesar; but the journey is now merely a matter of hours. In the Roman era it would take probably over eight weeks to go from Hatfield, England, to Khartoum—3,080 miles; but in 1950 the journey took 14 hours, and only 6 hours 24 minutes on 22 January 1954.[3]

These developments have made the rate of social and political changes extremely rapid, and tend to cause conflict in relationships between what one might term the older and the younger generations, for the younger generation (Colonial countries) is reared in an age very different from that of the older (the imperial powers). Consequently, it is natural that the latter become old-fashioned and slow to act, whilst youth is rebellious and quick to act. The British error in projecting their past into the present of their Colonial children is comparable to the

[1] Sir Reader Bullard, *Britain and the Middle East*, London, 1951, pp. 162 and 177.
[2] Egypt, Ministry of Foreign Affairs, *Records*, pp. 72–3.
[3] *Evening Standard*, London, 22 January 1954.

common error of parents who fail to realize the fact that their child-dren are growing in a world quite different from their own.

Apart from the above British characteristic of projection, there is also the force of certain moral convictions. The British, like most other peoples, are neither beasts nor gods in their psychological make-up, but a mixture of both—a weird synthesis of devilry and divinity. During the partition of Africa, Britain was driven to the scramble by the primary motive of imperial acquisition. But there was in addition a real sense of the mission to carry 'civilization' to those whom they regarded as 'backward peoples'—the obligation to shoulder what Kipling called 'The White Man's Burden'. There was a feeling of sympathetic benevolence tinged with a chivalry towards the weak. This sentiment, fostered by missionaries, often influenced British administrations overseas. Thus, the British wished to remain in the Sudan long enough to satisfy this self-appointed mission.

'We have taken on the White Man's Burden and we must not drop it. In the Sudan we have done some of the finest work in the history of our country, but that work will be only of temporary value if we forsake the country.'[1]

Undoubtedly, the British Commonwealth, like any other human institution, has several faults; Mr. R. H. S. Crossman, a Labour Member of Parliament, describes its composition as an odd collection of scattered bits and pieces.[2] The irony in the source of its authority was expressed by Chief Obafemi Awolowo, a 'Colonial' Nigerian Minister: 'We are ruled', he protested while visiting India in 1953, 'in the name of a twenty-six-year-old English girl.' As for the method of its acquisition, 'it is built up by conquest and by the imposition of British rule upon alien peoples'.[3]

At the Imperial Conference of 1926, the status and mutual relationships of member nations were described as 'autonomous communities . . . equal in status, in no way subordinate one to another in any aspect of their domestic or external affairs, though united by a common allegiance . . . and freely associated members of the British Commonwealth of Nations'.[4] Member nations were then limited to peoples of European stock.

In recent years the British have rediscovered the British Empire in

[1] Dugmore, Major A. Radclyffe, *op. cit.*, p. 256.
[2] *New Statesman and Nation*, 12 February 1955, p. 214.
[3] Schuman, *op. cit.*, p. 516.
[4] Reference Division, Central Office of Information, *The Commonwealth in Brief*, London, February 1955, p. 3.

the form of a commonwealth. They take pride in the achievement which has brought about a quarter of the world's population into a 'single fellowship'. It seems that they begin to realize that they are bound by a good deal of mutual obligation and interdependence with peoples of all colours and creeds, races and religions.

Even Mr. Nehru, formerly a political prisoner in the hands of the British administration in India, appears to be much impressed with the new phase of the British Commonwealth. At a state banquet in New Delhi (in honour of the Australian Prime Minister), Mr. Nehru remarked, on 27 December 1950, that

> We are members of the Commonwealth—that rather strange and odd collection of nations which seems to prosper in adversity. . . . Somehow it has found some kind of invisible link by seeing that practically there is no link and by giving complete independence and freedom to every part of it. . . . While member nations of this Commonwealth sometimes disagree . . . the basic fact remains that they meet as friends, try to understand each other, try to accommodate each other. . . . This [is a] rather remarkable experiment.[1]

The way self-government was granted to India and the prestige she has been bringing to the Commonwealth since her independence in 1947 seem to have opened British eyes to similar possibilities in the non-White areas of Africa. The British pride about India and hope in Africa was well-expressed by Mr. James Griffiths (formerly Colonial Secretary). In one of the General Election broadcasts in 1955, he pleaded that 'Britain must help the new nations that were coming to the front of the world's stage in Africa and were beginning to emerge in Africa'. With an air of pride in Socialist philosophy, Mr. Griffiths pointed out that ten years earlier, over eight hundred million people were living under Colonial rule; but that then, in 1955, there were less than two hundred million. 'And it is a matter of pride to us', he told the radio listeners, 'that this great change began within our Commonwealth and was taken by a Labour Government. . . . Today India, headed by its great Prime Minister, Pandit Nehru, has become a link between the East and the West. . . . What we did for Asian nations of the Commonwealth, we also began in Africa.'[2] Thus, it would seem that Britain was playing for more time during which to bring the Sudan into the Commonwealth.

The British Foreign Secretary (Mr. Eden at that time) stated in the

---

[1] *Ibid.*, pp. 4–5.
[2] The B.B.C. General Election broadcasts, *The Listener*, 12 May 1955, p. 850.

House of Commons on 12 February 1953, that the Anglo-Egyptian Agreement of 1953 (with which we shall deal later) left the Sudan with freedom to become a member nation of the British Commonwealth. General Neguib, in a broadcast from Cairo to the Sudan, rejected Mr. Eden's interpretation and retorted that any attempt to pull the Sudan into the British Commonwealth would invalidate the agreement, which provided for the two alternatives of union with Egypt or complete independence. . . . Thirty years before Mr. Eden's statement, Sir Murdoch Macdonald had said:

> I think in the future all these races in the Sudan would be very glad indeed to remain attached to the British Empire, and I see no reason at all why Egypt herself . . . should not also be glad in the future to remain attached to the British Empire as so many of our Great Dominions.[1]

2. THE CONFLICT OF PERSPECTIVES

In the course of a preliminary negotiation (conversations) on 24 April 1951, between the Egyptian Minister for Foreign Affairs, Mohammed Salah Eddin Bey and the British Ambassador in Cairo, Sir Ralph Stevenson, the former expressed his Government's 'bitter disappointment at the reply of the British Government after long discussions lasting over ten months'. He submitted a counter proposal on the evacuation of British troops from Egyptian territory and on the unity of Egypt and the Sudan. The divergent attitudes of each towards the urgency of the problem are revealed in the following remarks:

British Ambassador: I am not yet authorized to open discussions on the Sudan but as soon as I get the authorization I shall let you know.

Egyptian Foreign Minister: I am ready to discuss the Sudan question *at any time* (italics are the author's).

British Ambassador: You should not expect *a rapid answer* to these proposals.

Egyptian Foreign Minister: We indeed expect a very rapid answer.

It is evident from conversations such as this, that the question of timing was one of the stumbling blocks in the Anglo-Egyptian dispute. The British, with their network of communication apparatus, their efficient administrative staff and general machinery, were very often swift and expeditious in action; yet they moved so slowly in the negotiations over the Sudan question that their tardiness became too difficult for the

---

[1] House of Commons, *Parliamentary Debates*, Vol. CLXXV, p. 2521, July 1924.

Egyptians to appreciate. How can we account for this slow British diplomacy compared with the speed of lightning characteristic of the Egyptians?

One of the reasons is the fact that the British were thinking of the Anglo-Egyptian question mainly in terms of the imperial strategy of defence, covering the whole Mediterranean and the western half of the Indian Ocean and in terms of the whole of Africa, in which Egypt and the Sudan formed the pivot. The independence of Burma, and other South-East Asian territories formerly ruled by Britain, lessened British military and political anxieties in that area, which was linked with Egypt by a network of cables and sea and air routes. Nevertheless, British economic, Commonwealth and other interests in the South-East Asian region remained vital particularly as a result of anxieties about Soviet ideology and rivalry, not only in the Mediterranean and the Middle East, but also in Africa. Consequently, the British diplomats had to study, it would appear, the Egyptian proposals along with British designs in the whole area mentioned above. Mr. Herbert Morrison stated, for instance, that the matter was 'not now a purely Anglo-Egyptian problem. We are a power having responsibilities in the Middle East on behalf of the rest of the Commonwealth and the Western Allies as a whole'.[1] The Egyptians, on the other hand, saw the problem in the restricted and narrowed range of the 'Nile Valley', meaning Egypt and the Sudan.

Britain also had several major world problems, and she considered the Egyptian issue one of less magnitude, particularly in 1951, when the Iranian oil dispute was pressing. Being thus preoccupied with larger and more urgent problems, she preferred to delay the consideration of the Egyptian question until she was relieved of those pressures. But to Egyptian nationalists, the case was the most urgent in the world. This sense of urgency drove the Egyptian Foreign Minister to comment:

> The troubles of the British Government are endless, and their foreign policy is of a considerably wide range, and if we delay the settlement of questions pending between us on account of the troubles confronting Britain in other parts of the world, we shall never finish.[2]

The prevailing climate of domestic politics in each of the two countries was an additional influencing factor. In Britain, the Government was less subject to the pressure of public opinion in this particular issue. In Parliament, foreign policy was practically bi-partisan and there was

---

[1] Egypt, Ministry of Foreign Affairs, *Records of Conversation, etc.,* p. iv.
[2] *Ibid.,* p. vi.

no marked difference in the policy of either the Conservative or Labour Party in the matter. Britain could therefore afford to wait and play for time hoping that the high tension in Egypt might either be lessened or be discharged over another crisis there in Egypt—preferably internal in nature. This would draw attention away temporarily from the Anglo-Egyptian issues. Egypt, on the other hand, was most susceptible to pressure from many sides—from the Opposition in Parliament which did not hesitate to embarrass the party in power, giving little consideration to the wider implications and repercussions of actions arising from party divisions and hostility; from the Egyptian Press which, by the consistent use of the weapons of propaganda, whipped up anti-British feelings among Egyptians; and from the Egyptian public who pushed their Government to action by incessant riots and demonstrations, for which Egyptian College students are well-known. Hence Salah Eddin Bey was forced, as were the preceding ministers, to demand a very rapid answer, because, as he put it himself, 'The situation is becoming more difficult both in the Press, and in Parliament.'[1]

Another domestic aspect of the problem arising out of national character, is that the British Government and people, through a long series of past troubles and crises at home, in their colonies and in world affairs, have become immune to crises by 'muddling through', whereas the Egyptian Government and people have been comparatively limited in such experiences. The result is that British reaction to external or internal crises is slow, whilst that of the Egyptian is relatively fast. This British attitude affected a French author so much as to remark: 'The English people's reaction to external menace is slow and deliberate because their purse and larder are usually threatened before their heart, and there is a time lag between the first scratch and the deep thrust.'[2]

Like most physicians, who with time acquire an impersonal and detached attitude to suffering and disease, the British Colonial and Foreign Offices have developed professional immunity to Colonial and International crises, whereas the Egyptians, on the other hand, are comparatively sensitive.

In addition to all this must be added the point that, as with an experienced long distance runner, who wins by a slow but steady pace coupled with endurance and stamina, so patience has become part and parcel of the cumulative features of British diplomacy.

This characteristic British patience contrasts with Lawrence of

---

[1] Egypt, Ministry of Foreign Affairs, *Records of Conversation, etc.*, p. 114.
[2] Bounty, Emile: *The English People*, London, 1904.

Arabia's judgment of the Arabs, to which group the Egyptians belong. He says, 'The first great rush round the Mediterranean had shown the world the power of excited Arabs for a short spell of intense activity; but when the effort burnt out, the lack of endurance and the routine in the Semitic mind became evident.'[1] Aware of this assessment of Egyptian character, British diplomats used patience, it would seem, as a weapon to 'burn out' the endurance of the Egyptians, whom circumstances had forced to sacrifice long-term gains in clinging to an immediate objective.

In negotiations the man with patience can gain much more than the other party will want to grant. Egypt's perspective was short-ranged, whereas Britain's was long-ranged. Britain therefore was able to act in accordance with a Chinese proverb: 'Patience is power; with time and patience the mulberry leaf becomes silk', and this seems to account, in part, for the British ascendancy in the Sudan for about 57 years, in spite of Egyptian opposition since the Condominium Agreement of 1899.

3. DIVERGENT CONCEPTS ABOUT RACE AND NATIONALITY

> *Psychological findings often have an important bearing on political questions and controversies.*
>
> H. J. EYSENCK[2]

In writing on the subject of 'Race and Nationality' in the Nile Valley, the writer is reminded of the Negro-American version of a well-known anecdote, which indicates the perspective in which men and women throughout the world see an object, mainly with particular reference to their respective national outlook. According to the story, a German, an Englishman, a Frenchman and an American Negro were commissioned to write on the subject of elephants. The German spent ten years in research and in scientific experimentation; he produced a twenty-volume work entitled *An Introduction to the Study of the Elephant*. The Englishman, with the latest hunting equipment, went to Africa. After five years in the jungle, he produced a slick paper on *How to Shoot the Elephant*. The Frenchman, so the anecdote continues, spent one year in the Bibliothèque Nationale in Paris and wrote a spicy little work on *The Love of the Elephant*. As for the Negro, he got himself an armful of Negro newspapers, a copy of the Bill of Rights and retired to his room. The next morning, he addressed a letter to the President of the United States on the subject of *The Elephant and the Race Problem*.[3]

[1] Lawrence, T. E., *Seven Pillars of Wisdom; A Triumph*, London, 1935, p. 44.
[2] *The Uses and Abuses of Psychology*, London, 1953, p. 300.
[3] 'Prejudiced Animals', editorial in *Ebony*, Chicago, April 1955, p. 72.

In the Anglo-Egyptian conflict over the Sudan, one of the points of disagreement was based on the question of 'race'. In opposing the idea of a political union of the Sudan with Egypt and in attempting to sever the Northern part of the Sudan from the Southern, the British eventually appealed to race and cultural differences between the Sudanese and the Egyptians on the one hand, and between the Northern and the Southern Sudanese on the other.

On 8 June 1951, the British Ambassador and the Egyptian Minister for Foreign Affairs had an official 'conversation'. During this, the British Ambassador gave two papers to the Egyptian Minister—one on defence (Suez) and another on the Sudan. The Sudan memorandum contained a 'Statement of Principles'; and one of the four principles enumerated emphasized 'the wide differences of culture (and) race . . . existing among the Sudanese'.[1] But Salah Eddin Pasha submitted his own Government's Aide-Memoire at 10.30 a.m. on Friday, 6 July 1951. He commented:

> The (British) Annex referred to the wide differences of culture (and) race . . . existing among the Sudanese. Some of these differences lack actual scientific support, such as the *difference of race.* The Sudan (British) Administration is to blame for the rest of those differences for it has sought to isolate the South of the Sudan from the North. . . .[2]

The British Ambassador disagreed:

> As regards the claim of community of race it cannot be seriously maintained that there is anything of the kind between the Shilluks and the Nuers on the one hand and the Northern Sudanese on the other.[3]

Later in the course of the argument, the Egyptian Minister for Foreign Affairs insisted:

> As to the inhabitants of the South they are linked with the inhabitants of the Northern Sudan and those of Egypt by the Hamitic origin and this is what we meant when we said that your remark about the difference of race between the peoples of the Sudan lacks actual scientific discussion but suffice it to say that several anthropologists including a number of eminent British scientists admit that the Sudanese are all one race.

To this, the British Ambassador was quick to retort:

> It does seem to me, on the basis of what you have just said, that, for instance, Norwegians and Italians should be regarded as one people. But whatever the anthropological rights or wrongs may be, it is necessary to

---

[1] Egyptian Ministry of Foreign Affairs, *Records*, pp. 116–17.
[2] *Ibid.*, p. 121.   [3] *Ibid.*, p. 122.

deal with things as they are today. I cannot believe that the Egyptian Government seriously consider the primitive inhabitants of the Southern Sudan to be one people with the inhabitants of the Delta.[1]

The British Foreign Office maintains that the 'Southern parts are inhabited by peoples sharply distinguished in race, creed and culture from the Moslem North.'[2]

It is therefore evident that divergence of views, attitudes and conceptions about race constitutes a factor in the Anglo-Egyptian friction over the Sudan. The question consequently deserves examination.

Britain herself consists of several 'tribes' or races—that is, the English, the Welsh, the Scots and the Irish. But the English have fought tooth and nail (by education, language, political parties and the symbolism of the Crown) to bring them all together within a unitary form of government under the British Crown and Parliament. In addition, the Union Jack has flown over territories of many and diverse races and peoples in Asia, Africa and America. Yet Britain (and part of the Sudan) objected to a union of the Sudan with Egypt, partly on the ground that the Sudanese of the south were of another race from those of the north; and that the two were racially different from the Egyptians. What, then, could be the explanation for this British paradox or double standardization?

The reason lies partly in the place which race has come to occupy in Western European thinking and partly in various interpretations to which the *word* race can be subjected.

Extreme race consciousness, and thinking much in terms of race have become part and parcel of the European and North American way of life, which spreads to many parts of the world, and with it spread race tensions. This artifice of dividing the human race into different and conflicting races—especially for purposes of political and economic control—is of fairly recent origin. In the past, conflicts and rivalries were based upon class, caste or religion. Race consciousness as a force in European thought and behaviour became pronounced with the arrival of the industrial and technical revolution, and of the nationalism and imperialism of modern states, among which Britain has been predominant. The Industrial Revolution gave rise to specialization of functions; by widening the gap between the rich and the poor it intensified class distinctions, especially in the 19th and 20th centuries, when racial

---

[1] Egypt, Ministry of Foreign Affairs, *Records*, pp. 126–7.
[2] *Documents concerning Self-Government and Self-Determination for the Sudan, Egypt No. 2* (1953), Cmd. 8767, p. 5.

theories went hand in glove with European nationalism. 'A study of Western politics during the 19th century', says a British expert, 'reveals a very close connection between racial myths and national and imperial ambitions. Racial attitudes and antagonism can be described, therefore, as functions of the wider organization of Western society, and the product of those movements which have been shaping its development.'[1] The 'Natural Superiority' of the Saxon over the Celt was invoked to justify English rule in Ireland. Nationalism and imperialism carried the European type of class distinctions into Africa, America and Asia in the form of race and colour differentiations. A group of British scholars confessed: 'Our whole theory of imperialism was based on the assumption that there were inferior races—"lesser breeds without the law"— over whom the Europeans were called to rule.'[2]

The next problem is one of ambiguity, because the term 'race' is used rather ambiguously. In the course of time and place, perceptions of race change—even from one academic discipline to another. Social scientists, whose business it is to be precise, have used the word race in different ways and at different times. Geneticists, who are concerned with the study of heredity, might define race as a group of people, or flies or dogs, who have a large number of inherited traits. Anthropologists, on the other hand, often define race as a group of (and limits it only to) people who share a general tendency to produce certain physical types —the same kind of hair, eyes, head shape, physique, etc. Some anthropologists use the word race to refer to the major groupings of mankind —Caucasoids, Mongoloids and Negroids; others use it interchangeably with the word 'ethnic' (a sub-division of the major groupings mainly on the basis of culture difference). Writing in 1924 about what he called 'The Races of Ireland', Professor James A. Lindsay classified the 'Irish' segment of Britain into at least six 'races'. After admitting in one breath that there are no pure races anywhere in the world, he declared: 'The Irish are a more composite race than is commonly supposed. There are *not less than six races represented in Ireland*, and this may be an understatement.'[3]

The ambiguity here is clear—the Irish are *one* ('a race'), and the Irish are *six* ('races'). Another expert, Mr. A. J. Arkell, formerly an administrative officer in the Sudan Political Service and currently Reader in Egyptian Archaeology at the University of London, also

---

[1] Little, Kenneth, *op. cit.*, p. 52.
[2] Royal Institute of International Affairs, *Nationalism*, London, 1939, p. 188.
[3] Article in *The Nineteenth Century and After*, September 1924, p. 462.

seems to use the word 'race' synonymously with 'ethnic'. Writing as late as 1955, he states: *There are several sub-races of Negro* in the Sudan, in addition to what he calls the 'Mediterranean race' in the country.[1]

In recent years, however, anthropologists are obliged to be more cautious and careful, because the racial ideas they have (consciously or otherwise) helped to propagate are becoming more and more dangerous to all mankind, with forbidding counter-reaction against the protagonists of racialism. In 1955, for instance, Political and Economic Planning, London, published its enquiry on 'Colonial (Coloured) Students in Britain' because of 'a general feeling of anxiety about the problems met by Colonial students living and studying in Britain, and a *fear* that the difficulties which the students encountered might influence adversely the good relations between Britain and the Colonial peoples'.[2] Also, a group of anthropologists and geneticists met under the auspices of the U.N.E.S.C.O., 'because false ideas about race have caused so much human and social damage'.[3] They suggested that: 'It would be better, when speaking of human races, to drop the term race altogether and speak of ethnic groups.'[4] But in September 1952, another panel of physical anthropologists and geneticists stated:

> Since race, as a word, has become coloured by misuse, and by its deliberate abuse by *racialists*, we tried to find a new word to express the same meaning of a biologically differentiated group. . . . On this we did not succeed.[5]

Modern science hesitates, therefore, to draw any conclusions on the basis of race. Apart from the ambiguous usage by several anthropologists such as we have indicated, there are two broad attitudes or approaches to race, the partisan approach and the scientific method. The partisan approach is applied by the party politician or administrator who is mainly concerned with the question of race attitudes in so far as it will enable him to exploit the race prejudices of the mob to gain a party advantage. It is the method applied by Britain to differentiate the Northern Sudanese from the Southern, and both from the Egyptian. It is effective wherever there is a clash of interests between two or more groups.

The second method is the non-partisan, or scientific approach, this is comparatively free from prejudice and transcends group affiliations which are mainly transitory. It is the approach adopted by U.N.E.S.C.O. which recognizes one race only—the human race. It is the approach

---

[1] *A History of the Sudan to A.D. 1821*, London, 1955, p. 24.
[2] P.E.P., *op. cit.*, p. 4.   [3] U.N.E.S.C.O., *What Is Race?*, Paris, 1952, p. 5.
[4] *Ibid.*, p. 77.   [5] *Ibid.*, p. 82.

adopted by Britain and the U.S.S.R. to unify the 'races' within their respective states. 'The veriest novice in biology knows that racial purity is entirely non-existent among the nations of the earth and that mankind can be classified into races only in the crudest and most unscientific fashion.'[1] This is not to say that all 'scientists' are free from the popular (partisan) tenets and beliefs about race. Eysenck, in his chapter on 'Psychology and Politics' states that 'If science has its heroes, it also has its clowns; [and that] both are likely to expose their character in the conflict between science and politics.'[2]

It is quite possible for both the partisan and the scientific attitudes to operate alternately within the same individual in the same way as some elements of contradiction appear in human nature much as catabolism and metabolism, the evil and the good. This kind of dualism explains, at least in part, the British paradox or ambivalence—the tendency to emphasize ethnical synthesis when it suits them, and to indulge in racial apartheid when convenient to do so. In his despatch to the Earl of Kimberley in November 1894, Lord Cromer, realizing the precarious position of the British, then as a minority still insecure in Egypt, commented:

> I have never entertained any doubt that, if once sentiments of differences based on race and religion were evoked, the English officers of the Egyptian Army would lose their authority over their own men. . . . This view is shared by many of the most experienced officers of the Egyptian Army.[3]

But Winston Churchill, several years later when the Sudan had been conquered and Britain was more or less in the saddle of authority, drove a wedge between the Negroes and the Arabs of the Sudan. In his work about the Sudan, he says:

> The qualities of mongrels are rarely admirable, and the mixture of the Arab and Negro types has produced a debased, cruel breed, more shocking because they are more intelligent than the primitive savages. The stronger race soon begins to prey upon the simple aboriginals.[4]

Apart from the obvious self-contradiction in this remark (the 'debased quality' of the mongrels and their 'higher degree' of intelligence), we may point out that Winston Churchill is himself an admirable crossbreed; for his father was British and his mother was American. In England many, like Robert Browning, have an unsuspected Negro ancestry as a result of the importation of West African Negroes 'into

[1] Schuman, F. L., *op. cit.*, p. 438.   [2] *Op. cit.*, p. 301.
[3] Cromer to the Earl of Kimberley, Secretary of State for War, War Office File No. W.O. 32/132/7841, November 1894.
[4] *The River War*, p. 8.

Europe in the early centuries of the African slave trade (1440–1773), and . . . to-day not one of these pure blacks remains'[1]; and in the United States, biologically a melting pot of the world, Negroes often pass for Whites. Those who have passed often conceal it; or 'their children and grandchildren may often be completely unaware of their mixed origin.'[2]

We may also add that the first Prime Minister of the Sudan is a mixture of the Arab and the Negro. He openly declared in London in November 1954, that he was especially happy about this blend, which made him simultaneously one with the Negro and the Arab.

Having attempted to show part of the forces underlying the British separatist attitude in the Egypto-Sudanese Question, it is also relevant to show why it would be more psychologically congenial for the Egyptians to see themselves and the Sudanese as one people rather than two—a more difficult point for the British. The word 'race', though of Arabic origin, is 'brought to prominence in European politics by German Nazism'.[3] But the Arabic root—RAS—means head, or chief (president, for instance). In Arabic it does not have the emotive connotation it has come to assume in English. One of the Egyptian Notes to Britain, having referred to the community of race, language, religion and other sources of Egypto-Sudanese unity, declared: 'In the interest of all these strong and inseverable ties it is gross injustice to speak of two countries and two peoples instead of speaking of one country and one people, indivisible, inseparable.'[4]

Admittedly, there is much play of party politics in this statement in the sense that it was aimed in part to fraternize with and 'buy' the Sudanese. But it is also true that the Egyptian mentality, much more readily than the British, can comprehend the brotherhood of the Sudanese and the Egyptians. Egyptians, it is true, often speak scornfully of Negroes, and their artists sometimes caricature the Negro's thick lips and woolly hair. In Cairo, Negroid Africans are often referred to as 'beriberi' (barbarians), but it is also true that Egyptians are often aware of the fact that they are themselves 'mongrels', and that many of their Pharaohs were partly of Negroid ancestry. They are also aware of the fact that whilst the north of Egypt could be described as predominantly Caucasoid, the south, especially the provinces of Aswan and Nubia,

[1] Davie, M. R. (Professor of Sociology, Yale University), *Negroes in American Society*, New York, 1949, Chapter on 'Race Mixture and Intermarriage,' p. 391.
[2] *Ibid.*, p. 407.
[3] Theimer, Walter, *The Penguin Political Dictionary*, London, 1939, p. 219.
[4] Royal Institute of International Affairs, *Great Britain and Egypt*, p. 138.

could reasonably be described as predominantly Negroid. Even the townspeople of Arabia itself have been mixed with the Gallas, Ethiopians, Indians and Malayans, 'as well as with Africans'.[1] Racially, Egypt presents, says Major Boris Gussman, 'a strange spectacle' to the British mind; there are jet black men whose ancestors came as slaves or free men from Ethiopia, Nubia or the Sudan; these are in every way, he observes, as much Egyptians as the brown men of Arabic ancestry or 'the white members. . . . Every man, no matter what the colour of his skin, is accepted as an Egyptian if he is born in the country.'[2]

For an example, since 31 August 1952 the Governor of Aswan Province has been a Southern Sudanese (Dinka)—His Excellency Abdel Aziz Abdel Hai. The writer met and discussed various questions with him at his office in Aswan in January 1956. He is ebony black, of serious countenance but extraordinarily accessible and friendly; his subordinates and subjects—black, brown and white Egyptians alike—described him with fond respect as 'a complete gentleman and a good governor'. Before this appointment, he had served in the Egyptian Army for about ten years; transferred to the Police Department of the Ministry of Interior in Cairo in 1927; was promoted from rank to rank, and was a 'Lewa' (Major-General). This is certainly in contrast to the practice in Britain, where—though the British Empire and Commonwealth teems with millions of 'coloured' peoples—it is unthinkable to appoint a 'coloured' person to any responsible post commensurate with his ability and experience. In the summer of 1953, two Nigerian graduate students, including the writer, were recommended by the National Union of Students for vacation employment (as porters) at the Waterloo Railway Station in London. Though they were recommended in response to advertisement, they were refused the temporary employment for fear that a 'colour problem' might arise among the white employees. Mr. Lennox Boyd, then Minister of Transport, in response to a protest, wrote to inform the National Union of Students that the Railway official concerned acted contrary to the policy of the British Railways about the employment of 'coloured labour'. Nevertheless, the applicants were not employed at Waterloo.

Apart from the race consciousness of the Western nations, the West is more individualistic, and tends to look at things with atomic detail, whilst the Orient, or Africa, of which Egypt is a part, is more collective

---

[1] Lane, W. E., *The Manners and Customs of the Modern Egyptians*, London, 1836, Everyman's Library ed., p. 27.
[2] 'Contrasts in Cairo', in *Contemporary Review*, January 1946, p. 47.

and general in approach to human relations. The Orient has the concept of what Professor Northrup, of Yale University, calls 'Undifferentiated Continuum'—the universal and all-embracing approach to life. 'It is the one-ness provided by this immediately apprehended aesthetic continuum common to all men (of the Orient) and to all aesthetically immediate natural objects which gives . . . man his compassionate fellow-feeling for all men and his man-to-man-ness with all men.'[1] Through centuries of conditioning, the English people have, by comparison, become too individualistic even for the French, who complain that the English are contemptuous of other nations and are unable to mix with them; they do not comprehend the one-ness of the world and its peoples but are inclined to divide questions and peoples into sections and races, 'considering them bit by bit, with no thought of combining them in the harmony of a vast synthesis'.[2] But to the Egyptian Muslims, who have not separated religion from politics to the extent the British have done, all believers in the true faith of Islam are regarded as brothers; many precepts of Islam 'admirably served the purpose of welding all Moslems into a great fraternity. The brotherhood of the believers transcended the boundaries of nationality.'[3] Some British people often pay tribute to the apparent lack of race friction in Egypt. Speaking in the House of Lords in 1926, Lord Lamington said: 'In Egypt you have a kind of international atmosphere, and all the races are represented there.'[4] One can therefore conclude that the Egyptians are comparatively less addicted to racialism than the British.

But this is not to suggest that they, too, are completely free from the ambiguities associated with racial concepts or from race consciousness. This question of racialism in the politics of the Nile Valley was brought by Egypt to the rostrum of the United Nations on 5 August 1947, when Nokrashi Pasha made an explanatory statement before the Security Council.[5] He accused British officials in the Sudan of stirring up bad feeling between Egypt and the Sudan on the one hand, and between the Northern and the Southern Sudanese on the other. Pleading for the unity of the Nile Valley, he presented the following ethnical arguments that the British are not qualified to 'force themselves and their ideas on the Sudan'. He affirmed that to the Sudan the British are complete

[1] Northrup, F. S. C., *The Meeting of East and West*, New York, 1949, p. 332.
[2] Bounty, Emile, *The English People*, London, 1904, p. 314.
[3] Hertz, F., *Nationality in History and Politics*, London, 1944, p. 140.
[4] *Parliamentary Debates* (Lords), Vol. LXIV, 1926, p. 684.
[5] U.N.O. Security Council, Official Records, 2nd year, No. 70, pp. 1745–67—see Chapter XI, above.

foreigners; that they do not speak the language of the Sudanese nor share the religious and cultural traditions of the Sudan. They have no affinity with the Sudanese and are in no way qualified to guide the social development of the country. They stand in the way of developing homogeneity; they undermine unity: they cultivate minorities.' In consequence, they keep the country backward and divided.

These arguments deserve some comment:

True, compared with the Egyptians, the British are 'foreigners' to the Sudanese. But after these 57 years of control in the Sudan, the British are hardly 'complete foreigners'.

It is a fact that the British, as a rule, appear unwilling to learn the language of their overseas subjects, and that they consider speaking English as an index of 'civilized' living, but they, like any other human beings, could learn and speak Arabic or Sudanese; in fact, some Britishers do speak Sudanese or Arabic—though not with an Egyptian or Sudanese accent! In most other British territories, British officials are granted a special allowance for proficiency in the local tongue, and this applies to Sudanese. The writer has witnessed a few British nationals chatting with Sudanese in the 'native' language. Another indicator to the British endeavours in this direction is the establishment of the School of Oriental and African Studies at the University of London. Furthermore, the British Secretary of State for Foreign Affairs appointed in December 1944 a Commission of Enquiry, with the terms of reference:

> To examine the facilities offered by Universities and other educational institutions in Britain for the study of Oriental, Slavonic, East European and African languages and culture, to consider what advantage is being taken of these facilities and to formulate recommendations for their improvement.[1]

Through the age-long process of diffusion, culture is a universal heritage; as such, there does not seem to be anything particularly unique or strange about Sudanese culture which the British are incapable of sharing. This is not to deny the superiority complex or cultural pride which often hinders the majority of the British from consciously absorbing cultures other than their own.

For Egyptians to say, categorically, that the British 'are in no way qualified to guide the social development of the country' appears to be a gross exaggeration, if not a deliberate underrating of the capabilities of the British Government and people. The social institutions and

[1] Foreign Office Report of the Interdepartmental Commission of Enquiry on Oriental, Slavonic and African Studies, H.M.S.O., London, 1947, p. 5.

achievements in Britain, the impact of British social thought in the world and particularly their record in Egypt and the social legacy (such as the University of Khartoum) which they have now left behind in the Sudan, are all ample evidence of their capabilities in social development. What could be criticized is that the guide in social development which the British give overseas often tends to breed Anglicized natives with some inferiority complex about their own local heritage. But this is a common characteristic of imperial governments and institutions. The Egyptians, for instance, are not very likely to guide educational development in the Sudan with the intent to produce more Christians than Muslims.

That the ethnical orientation by the British has the effect of obstructing the development of homogeneity by creating 'minorities' is a more valid charge. Sufficient evidence of this is seen in the British orientation of the more Negroid Southern Sudanese away from the more Arabized Northern: 'our policy aims at the establishment of an autonomous regime in the South', said the Civil Secretary of the Sudan Administration, 'which could be separated from the North'[1]; and in the British policy of encouraging separation of the whole Sudan from Egypt. But the British 'undermine unity, keep the Sudan backward and divided', *not* because they are—by national mentality—'incapable' of doing otherwise, for have they not united the English, the Northern Irish, the Scots and the Welsh into a United Kingdom? It is because their major interests could be furthered by the doctrine of *divide et impera*. However, the British alone are not entirely to blame for the elements of division in the Sudan. Apart from Sudanese provincialism, one effect of the Anglo-Egyptian Condominium—competition of both Egypt and Britain to win the Sudanese—has been a split in the 'personality' of the Sudan; one part (the Unionists) leaning towards Egypt and the other (the Umma) towards Britain. This effect of the dual control on the Sudanese we shall discuss more fully in a subsequent chapter under the re-emergence of the Sudan as a third party in the dispute.

With regard to the general concept of races and nationality in the Nile Valley, we must point out that, in any case, race is not an absolute criterion of nationality. In most parts of the world, people continue, despite the wide spread of racialism, to regard themselves as Indians, Nigerians, Englishmen, Americans, Italians, Ethiopians, not as yellow men, black men, brown men or Nordics; in other words, people identify themselves with nation-states rather than with racial groups. Since race

[1] Royal Institute of International Affairs, *Great Britain and Egypt*, p. 210.

has not become the basis of a nation-state, it therefore need not form the criterion for the Sudan as a state or for an Egypto-Sudanese state, even if the Sudanese and the Egyptians were two distinct 'races'. A nation is not physically of one 'blood'. It is a geographical and mental fact, and results from common citizenship.

Each nation is composed of different ethnical elements and its composition changes in the course of time.

It is a fact, however, that even though thoughtful people have become disinclined, or even averse, to mix the notions of races and nations, the word 'race' still carries emotional associations and provokes strong responses which politicians or partisans in Britain, Egypt and other parts of the world use to their own advantage. Outside the scientists' laboratory, the word 'race' has frequently been employed to justify policies of economic and social discrimination, and of political domination. 'Even among some scientists facts have been perverted in an attempt to justify the domination of one group by another.'[1] The British ambivalence about race and nationality or Government in the Sudan is evident in such statements in Parliament as the one made by Sir Murdoch MacDonald: 'I see no reason why the races in the Northern Sudan should rule over blacks in the Southern Sudan.' Apparently afraid of the potential strength of a united Sudan (in a possible league with Egypt), he went on: 'To erect a single kingdom such as happened in the Mahdi's time in the Sudan I think would be a mistake.'[2] In the same breath, however, he recommended that the 'races' of Britain should rule not only the whole Sudan, but also both Egypt and the Sudan, under the British Empire.[3] We must therefore agree with Dr. Maurice Freedman, of the London School of Economics and Political Science, when he says, cynically but truly: 'Race relations is so called because it is the study of the relations between groups which are not races.'[4]

On the strength of our examination of all this evidence, we may conclude that conflict between Egypt and the Sudan, as well as between Britain and Egypt, sprang not so much from the variety of skin pigmentations, religious adherences or cultural levels, important though they appear. It sprang fundamentally from competitive economic and political desires which we have indicated in Chapters 6 to 8. Race, culture and religion have been used as tools to justify or achieve those economic and political objectives.

[1] U.N.E.S.C.O., *What Is Race?*, p. 6.
[2] House of Commons, *Parliamentary Debates*, Vol. CLXXV, July 1924, p. 2520.
[3] *Ibid.*, p. 2521.
[4] *The British Journal of Sociology*, Vol. V, No. 4, December 1954, p. 343.

Part Three

THE WAR AND POST-WAR DEVELOPMENTS
IN THE DISPUTE

10

THE EFFECTS OF THE SECOND WORLD WAR ON THE ANGLO-EGYPTIAN TREATY OF 1936

Like other evils, war has an insidious way of appearing not intolerable until it has secured such a stranglehold upon the lives of its addicts that they no longer have the power to escape from its grip when its deadliness has become manifest.
ARNOLD J. TOYNBEE, *War and Civilization*[1]

1. THE WAR AND THE ALLIANCE

IN almost every country, the stresses and strains of the Second World War forced violent ferments of public opinion to emerge as soon as 'peace' was won. In Britain, for example, feeling rose against the Conservative Party despite the war-time leadership of Mr. Churchill, and there was a sharp turn by the electorate to the Labour Party, which promised a better social order. In Asia and Africa, the post-war years brought waves of nationalism. Similarly, in Egypt, the strains and stresses of the war years penetrated every aspect of the Egyptian life. This led at the end of the war to a growing dissatisfaction with the Anglo-Egyptian Treaty, now denounced by an Egypt that was in a mood different from that of 1936 when her safety was threatened by Mussolini's Italy. In the following pages we shall indicate those war-time incidents which increased the stresses and strains in Egypt and the violent eruption of public opinion against the Anglo-Egyptian Treaty of 1936 in post-war years.

Between 1936 (when the Treaty of Alliance and Friendship was signed) and the outbreak of war in 1939, Britain and Egypt together made some progress towards the implementation of the Treaty; they also agreed on the allocation between themselves of the cost of the barracks for housing the British garrison on the Canal; on the cessation of Egypt's subsidy to the Sudan Government; and on the settlement of the total debt which the Sudan Administration owed to Egypt for development purposes.[2]

[1] London, 1951, p. viii.
[2] H.M.S.O., Cmd. 5361 (*Egypt No. 3*, 1936): *Agreement regarding Financial Questions Affecting the Anglo-Egyptian Sudan.*

Seemingly in an attempt to influence Egyptian feeling towards channels beneficial to Britain (and, no doubt, to Egypt) during the danger period ahead, thirty members of both Houses of the British Parliament signed a letter to the President of the Chamber of Deputies and to leaders of all political parties in Egypt. It proposed the formation of 'an Anglo-Egyptian Union to serve as an instrument for promoting closer collaboration between the peoples at all times'.[1] The gesture worked; for not only did the Wafd Party join the Union[2] but King Farouk, as was later reported in *The Times* in London, sent £1,000 for distribution 'among the British and Egyptian troops' during the Christmas and the Courban Bairam (Muslim feast) holidays.[3] In the following April the Sudanese, too, sent £2,200 for Red Cross Relief work in Britain.[4] And it seemed there was friendship all round.

But the German attack on Poland on 1 September 1939, swiftly brought to severe test the operative clauses of the Treaty. On the evening of that date, Sir Miles Lampson, British Ambassador in Cairo, saw Ali Mahir Pasha, then Egyptian Prime Minister. As a result, the Egyptian Prime Minister took the necessary steps to implement the terms of Article 7 of the Treaty, in which Egypt undertook to come, immediately in the event of war, to Britain's aid. Soon, Egypt became divided into four main military districts, and her ports, aerodromes and communications were put at Britain's disposal. A state of siege was established. The Prime Minister was appointed Military Governor of Egypt. A speech from the Throne on 18 November 1939, expressed Egypt's willingness to fulfil her treaty obligations:

> Egypt, which seeks peace and believes firmly in its benefits, has understood that its alliance with Great Britain would confirm that peace and consolidate it in the Middle East. Our ally having gone down into the arena to defend the right, Egypt could do no otherwise than fulfil her duty and she has done so without hesitation, faithful to her given word.[5]

But Egypt did not suffer directly from the consequences of the War until about the spring of 1940—the tragic year for Britain—when Germany's military achievements were at their height and the fortunes of Britain and France extremely low.

The Allied Commander-in-Chief in the Levant (General Weygand) visited Egypt; a week later Australian and New Zealand forces arrived

[1] *The Times*, 28 November 1940.   [3] *Daily Herald*, London, 15 February 1940.
[2] *The Times*, 3 December 1939.   [4] *Manchester Guardian*, 23 April 1940.
[5] Lugol, J., *Egypt and World War II*; translation from the French by A. G. Mitchell, Cairo, 1945, p. 38.

at Suez once again, 'to strike a blow for the old country in her hour of need in Africa', as the Australians had put it 56 years earlier—during the Sudan Expedition of 1884. At Suez they were welcomed by the then British Dominions Secretary, Anthony Eden, the British Ambassador in Cairo (Sir Miles Lampson) and by the British Commander-in-Chief of the Middle East (General Wavell)—all emphasizing the importance of Egypt as a strategic area, and the value of the Dominion forces. During the three months following the arrival of these forces at Suez, Italy exploited the geographical nearness of Egypt to herself and exerted some pressure on Egypt which resulted in a war of nerves. Italy's Marshal Balbo passed through Egypt in March, on the pretence of a hunting expedition to Ethiopia, and returned through Egypt again in April. The pressure from the Axis on the one hand, and Egyptian obligation to Britain on the other, caused considerable concern in Egypt —often expressed in party strife. However, Egypt made efforts at being ostensibly neutral. Double-edged statements were made in the Press aimed at obtaining reasonable sympathy from the Axis powers on the one hand and from the Allies on the other. The Egyptian journal *Al-Balagh* wrote on 24 April 1940:

> Egypt's attitude is most clear. She is a small independent state in alliance with Great Britain, but this does not prevent her from being friendly with other states.[1]

> Egypt wants to be friendly with all States. . . .[2]

At the same time, Egypt tried to put a price on her war-time assistance to Britain. Before the Press statement just quoted, Nahas Pasha, then leader of the Wafd Opposition in the Egyptian Parliament, had addressed a memorandum to the British authorities on 1 April. In this, he attempted to make Egypt's effective co-operation with Britain dependent upon assurance of a better future—some political rewards for Egypt after the war (as Indian leaders sought to make India's war effort to Britain dependent on British undertaking to grant independence to India soon after the war). In substance, Nahas Pasha stressed that the Egyptian people, having demonstrated their loyalty to Britain and to the cause of 'democracy' for which the war was being fought, expected some tangible evidence of reciprocity. Linking the Sudan Question with the issues of the Suez Canal base, the Wafd memorandum asked Britain to promise that after the war British troops should be withdrawn from Egypt, and their place taken by the Egyptian army; that Egypt should

---

[1] *New York Times*, 27 April 1940.   [2] *Manchester Guardian*, 25 April 1940.

be invited to the Peace Conference after the war; and that, soon after the signing of armistice, negotiations should be opened with a view to the recognition of Egypt's rights (of control) over the Sudan 'in the common interests of the inhabitants of the Nile Valley'.[1]

Perhaps feeling that by this memorandum the Wafd had stolen a march on them, the Party in power and their supporters suggested that Nahas Pasha had no right to address such a memorandum direct to the British Ambassador, and that his demands for Egypt should have been made through the proper channels—the Egyptian Ministry of Foreign Affairs. However, opinions in the Egyptian Press, while indicating some objection to the method of Nahas Pasha, did fully support the objectives he was trying to achieve for Egypt at home and in the Sudan.

On 10 June 1940, Italy, siding with Germany, declared war on the Allied Powers, and the situation became worse for the Egyptians. Both Britain and Italy took advantage of 26 August 1940, the fourth anniversary of the signing of the Anglo-Egyptian Treaty of Alliance and Friendship, to influence the Egyptians. On that date, the British Ambassador, in a celebration speech at Cairo assured his audience: 'Those who, like Egypt, have stood loyally by us through the storm and stress will share with us not only the blessing of a just peace, but the gratitude of the nations.'[2]

In addition, an editorial entitled 'Alliance with Egypt',[3] appeared in *The Times* on the anniversary date. It began: 'The fourth anniversary of the Anglo-Egyptian Treaty finds the British and the Egyptian Governments more closely linked than at any time.'

After warning the Egyptians, the Arabs (and the Sudanese) about 'the new Roman Imperialism in Africa', it affirmed—addressing both the Egyptians and the Italians—that 'the defence alliance between Great Britain and Egypt stands firm.'[4] As for influence from Italy on the same day, the *Giornale d'Italia* declared, also in an editorial like that of *The Times* in London, that Egypt would be regarded as an enemy should she give military support to Britain. On the 28th another Italian Journal, *Il Telegrafo*, with fewer threats to Egypt but more gestures of sympathy, announced that Italy faced a tragic and grotesque political paradox with regard to Egypt: on the one hand Italians and Egyptians were friends; on the other, Egypt was giving military accommodation to Britain. Thus, while Germany was trying to browbeat France and Spain,

[1] *News Chronicle*, London, 3 April 1940. For full text see *Oriente Moderno*—published by the Italian Institute of Oriental (Muslim) Studies—May 1940, pp. 228–32.
[2] *The Times*, 28 August 1940, p. 3c.   [3] *Ibid.*, editorial.
[4] *Ibid.*, 26 August 1940, p. 5c.

Britain and Italy were working hard especially through their respective Press and radio, on Egyptian minds. Egypt, too, continued to manœuvre her way through the dilemma. On 21 August, the Egyptian Chamber of Deputies unanimously adopted a motion expressing full confidence in the Government and supported the decision already taken in June, that Egypt 'while not harbouring enmity or hatred towards any other state, cannot but defend herself with all the means at her command if her territories are attacked'.[1]

Almost simultaneously (the following day), the Egyptian Minister of Defence (Mahmoud Pasha Khaissi) announced that Egypt would co-operate with Britain in the defence of the Sudan in the event of an attack on the Condominium. 'The defence of Egypt,' he explained, 'also involves the defence of the Sudan.'[2]

With Egypt thus practically in league with Britain, Italy decided to move from propaganda to 'cold war', and from that to actual war, against Egypt. In September her troops invaded Egypt and occupied Sollum; Italian air forces made frequent raids on Egypt and the Sudan; the British forces based in Egypt and the Sudan henceforth found themselves more intensely at war, fighting with the neighbouring Libya and Abyssinia against Italy. Martial law was declared in Egypt on 23 September 1940.[3]

Part of the effect on Egypt was increasing unemployment and rising prices and these became political issues. The Director of the National Bank of Egypt had to broadcast an appeal to the nation to face the general consequences of the War with courage. Foreign intrigues were active in Egypt; in addition, the unexpected collapse of France in June, the menace of Italy and the apparent isolation of London from Cairo were factors which caused increasing disturbance of mind and general political uncertainty in Egypt. The Prime Minister, Hassan Sabri Pasha, collapsed and died while reading the Speech from the Throne in the Chamber on 14 November 1940. This sudden loss of a man, described by *The Times* in London as 'a clearheaded and conscientious statesman',[4] intensified the political confusion and general uncertainty in the Egyptian mind.

Egyptian sensitivity became further sharpened, and offence was found in a section of the Right Hon. Winston Churchill's broadcast from

---

[1] Quoted in Keesing's *Contemporary Archives*, No. 909 (1940–3), p. 4204A.
[2] Editorial, 28 August 1940.
[3] See Chapter 4, p. 122, for a similar declaration during the First World War—when Egypt was a British Protectorate.
[4] *The Times*, editorial, 15 November 1940, p. 5c.

London, on 23 December, 1940. In this 'Call to the Italian People' the British Prime Minister, in essence, invited the Italian people to consider how they had become involved in so tragic a quarrel with the British people to whom they had been bound together by many ties of historic friendship:

> We have always been such friends [he said]. We liked each other; we got on well together. There were reciprocal services; there was amity; there was esteem. And now we are at war . . . all because of one man. One man and one man alone has ranged the Italian people in deadly struggle against the British Empire, and has deprived Italy of the sympathy and intimacy of the United States of America.[1]

The first half of the speech (from which the foregoing excerpts are made) appears to have made a most favourable impression in Egypt; in fact, the speech as a whole was welcomed. But one phrase offended Egyptian susceptibility; in his catalogue of charges against the Mussolini Government, Churchill asked: 'where was the need to invade Egypt, *which was under British protection*?'[2] Egyptians, vigilant about their own sovereignty, particularly in relation to their position and influence in the Sudan, and suspicious of the British, gave double meaning to the phrase *under British protection*. Consequently, the Egyptian Government had to ask the British Ambassador for elucidation of the phrase. A prompt reply was given, and on 28 December 1940, the Egyptian Council of Ministers were able to issue a communiqué, explaining:

> After contacting Sir Miles Lampson, we have received assurances from Mr. Anthony Eden, on behalf of the British Government, that the phrase implied nothing more than the obligation which under the Treaty is incumbent [on Britain about the defence of Egypt], *and that the phrase casts no shadow of doubt upon Egypt's independence and the hope of Sovereignty over the Sudan*.[3]

While 1941 was a year of Allied victories in North and North-East Africa (the successful campaign in Libya and the triumph of Emperor Haile Selassie of Ethiopia), 1942 was a 'dark' and crucial year during the world conflict. Both years (and the subsequent ones), had several political and economic repercussions and difficulties in Egypt, mainly as a result of Egypt's war-time collaboration with Britain. This situation increased Egypt's hope for a greater share in the control of the Sudan, as a sort of compensation from Britain quite apart from the considera- tion of Egypt's constitutional right in the country. In February 1942,

---

[1] *The Unrelenting Struggle*, War Speeches by the Rt. Hon. Winston Churchill, compiled by Charles Eade, London, 1942, pp. 27–8.
[2] *Ibid.*, p. 29.   [3] Reuter, *Daily Express*, 30 December 1940.

Italians claimed to have made a 'daring and successful raid on Alexandria harbour by naval assault troops'.[1] In June, Egypt lost 650 men and women as a result of air-raids on Alexandria, and about 300,000— almost half the population—fled from the city. There were supply crises, increased shortage of imported goods and a soaring cost of living—all of which encouraged black marketing. In the Chamber of Deputies Sidky Pasha complained that the presence of Allied troops in Egypt and their maintenance were part of the major causes of the crisis. When the situation required it, Egypt, though with her own millions of poor to feed, spontaneously supplied food to the Allied troops. Further-more, the troops consumed much outside their own barracks—about 50,000 ardebs of wheat per month or 500,000 ardebs a year when they were on leave, for instance.[2] The Egyptian Government, unused to the magnitude on Egyptian soil of such complications of global war, appeared unable to cope adequately with several of the internal prob-lems. In February 1942, the Sirry Ministry resigned, ostensibly in consequence of inability to cope with the 'heavy burden' of the War.

In consequence of this resignation, those who shaped British policy, pressed by their responsibility for the security in the rear of the armies, became apprehensive about the political situation in Cairo. Anxious that political instability in Egypt might unduly affect the war campaigns in Egypt, the Sudan and in the Mediterranean, the British Ambassador (aided by the United States Minister) on 3 February, put pressure on King Farouk to nominate Nahas Pasha to form and head a government. King Farouk, in reply, said he would consult the leaders of all parties, Nahas Pasha included, to form a government. At midday on the 4th, however, the British Ambassador gave a warning that 'unless I hear by 6 p.m. that Nahas Pasha has been asked to form a cabinet, His Majesty King Farouk must expect the consequences.'[3] On the advice of a conference of Egyptian 'elder statesmen' King Farouk rejected the British ultimatum. Like Allenby, the British High Commissioner in Egypt who went to the Presidency of the Egyptian Council of Ministers with an entire regiment to deliver his ultimatum in 1924,[4] Sir Miles Lampson, the British Ambassador, went to the Egyptian Palace with the G.O.C. British troops and an armoured escort; he insisted upon the necessity for the King to send for Nahas Pasha to form a cabinet. As in 1924, the Egyptians had to swallow their pride and yield to British

---

[1] *The Times*, London, 7 February 1942, p. 4d.
[2] Lugol, *op. cit.*, p. 301.
[3] Quoted by Royal Institute of International Affairs, *Great Britain and Egypt*, p. 7.
[4] See Chapter 4—under 'The Assassination of Sir Lee Stack'.

pressure and to their incursions in internal politics, as though Egypt were not a sovereign state. Nahas Pasha accepted office, supported by 'British bayonets', as Ahmad Mahir was reported to have said.[1]

The British made the demand for Nahas Pasha presumably because he was the Prime Minister who concluded and signed the 1936 Treaty of Alliance with Britain and as such he would be able, they felt, to fulfil the terms of the Treaty. Although he had expressed Egypt's right to modify the treaty in the light of later developments, he described it as 'an obligation which is in our own interests'.[2] It also appears that the British found it easier to work with him than with most of the other Egyptian leaders of the time.

With an apparent effort to impress Egyptians that he would be no mere puppet to the British and to get the British Ambassador to clarify Anglo-Egyptian relations, Nahas Pasha quickly addressed the following letter to the British Ambassador on the morning of 5 February, when he took office:

> I have been instructed to form a new Ministry and have accepted this responsibility on the order of H.M. the King, given in the exercise of his constitutional rights. It is understood that I take up my functions on the assumption that neither the Anglo-Egyptian Treaty nor the situation of Egypt as a sovereign and independent state allow the Ally (Great Britain) to intervene in the internal affairs of the country and notably in the formation and resignation of Ministries. I trust your Excellency will be kind enough to confirm the above and thus draw closer the ties of friendship and respect by which we are bound by the treaty.[3]

Having obtained his main objective, the British Ambassador had no difficulty in confirming, the same day, the point of view expressed in Nahas Pasha's letter, and no apparent qualms about assuring the Egyptians 'that the policy of His Majesty's Government is to ensure sincere collaboration with the Government of Egypt as an independent and allied country, in execution of the Anglo-Egyptian Treaty, without interference in the internal affairs of Egypt or the compositions of her Government'.[4] However, the British ultimatum produced a lasting effect on Anglo-Egyptian relations and on the dispute of the two countries over the Sudan. Nine years later, when Egypt was on the verge of

---

[1] *Bourse Egyptienne*, 14 February 1942.
[2] Extract from speech by Nahas Pasha in the Egyptian Chamber of Deputies on 14 November 1936, in *Egypt No. 2* (1951) Cmd. 8419, p. 7.
[3] Original text in French. Egyptian Government, Ministry of Justice, *Recueil de Lois, Décrets et Récrits Royaux*, First Term, Cairo, 1942, p. 8. See also Chicago *Daily News*, 6 February 1942.
[4] Egyptian Government, *ibid.*, pp. 8–9.

abrogating the Condominium Agreement, Mr. H. Crossman declared in the House of Commons at Westminster:

> I would remind him (Mr. Winston Churchill) that this policy [of using force] has been tried in the Middle East. Lord Killearn (British Ambassador to Egypt) did exactly what we have been told by so many people is the way to handle the Egyptians. In order to effect a change of Government in 1942, he arranged for tanks to break into the royal palace and deliberately insulted the King. We are still suffering from the appalling scar on Egyptian national honour which this piece of toughness with the Egyptians has produced.[1]

This crisis with the subsequent exchange of correspondence between the British Ambassador and the Egyptian Prime Minister becomes more relevant to the Sudan question if we realize that this interference, with the threat of force, in Egypt's internal affairs made Egyptian nationalists more conscious of the fact that the 1936 Treaty had not in practice secured them the complete independence which was their main objective. Furthermore, such experiences made the Egyptians suspect the sincerity of the British in their ostensible support of independence for the Sudanese; i.e. the Egyptians feared that nominally the Sudan would be independent, but actually dependent on Britain through various devices.

In addition to the experience just described, the constant presence of over a million British and Allied troops in and around the principal towns of Egypt, became a constant reminder to politically conscious Egyptians of the unpleasant reality of the British Military Occupation. Also the conduct of the troops left much to be desired; apart from their ignorance of the peculiar susceptibilities of the middle-class Egyptian, they became more than a public nuisance. Alex Small, an eye witness, commented:

> Swarms of unruly youngsters (belonging to the Allied Troops) would push him [the Egyptian] about day by day—showing plainly their contempt for him—and make the streets of his cities perilous by night . . .; any woman who ventured on the streets was out of her mind—or looking for trouble.[2]

Thus, while there is great truth in one of Sir Winston Churchill's war-time inspired sayings: 'It is in adversity that the British qualities shine the brightest,'[3] we must also observe that the virtues exhibited in the war had also scope in other forms of human encounter and intercourse. The Second World War demanded the utmost courage, daring,

---

[1] *Parliamentary Debates*, 30 July 1951, Official Records, Vol. CCCCXCI, pp. 997–8.
[2] *Chicago Sunday Tribune*, 2 December 1945.   [3] *War Speeches*, p. 10.

endurance and the highest scientific and technical skill. The British virtues of bravery, resourcefulness, organization and efficiency which impressed the Egyptians, often went hand-in-hand with a simultaneous exhibition of 'cruelty, rapacity and a host of other vices',[1] which also left their mark on the Egyptian mind. Consequently, their resentment of military occupation and demand for Egypto-Sudan Union increased with the withdrawal of the war from Egypt's frontiers.

Meanwhile, however, Britain and Egypt continued together in the War effort against the Axis powers. Several major incidents took place with direct bearing on the Sudan question. These were the visit of Egyptian Ministers to the Sudan in 1940 at the invitation of the British Governor-General; the constitutional changes in the evolution of the Sudan towards self-government brought about in essence by the 'liberation' struggle of the Graduates' Congress, then under the leadership of Ismail El Azhari (who later became the first Prime Minister of the New Sudan in 1954); the presentation of a Sudanese, Ali Al-Birair, who ran a newspaper—*As-Sudan*—in Cairo, as a candidate for a Cairo Constituency in the Egyptian elections; and the Yalta Conference and the Assassination of Ahmad Mahir. Each of these incidents affected the Anglo-Egyptian question in the following ways. In February 1940, Ali Mahir Pasha, then Egyptian Prime Minister, visited the Sudan, accompanied by the Minister for National Defence (probably to represent Egyptian military interests in the Sudan, where there was an Egyptian army), and the Minister for Public Works (apparently to look after Egyptian interests in the Nile Waters). Their visit was undertaken on the invitation of the then British Governor-General of the Sudan. Such a visit was the first since the 1936 Treaty had restored the pre-1924 status in the Sudan; it therefore appears to have been arranged as one of the war-time gestures to win Egypt's full co-operation in the struggle of Britain against Italy and her Allies. The British Government's policy with regard to Egyptian forces—both in Egypt and the Sudan—was, according to George Kirk, that 'they should be developed into efficient modern forces capable of co-operating with the British forces', and placed under the command of the G.O.C. British Troops in Egypt.[2] But *The Times* correspondent at Khartoum reported that the purpose of the visit was to give an opportunity 'for the visitors to see as much as possible of the country and acquaint themselves personally with the

[1] Toynbee, Arnold J., *War and Civilization*, London, 1951, p. xi.
[2] Royal Institute of International Affairs, *Survey of International Affairs 1939–46*, 'The Middle East in the War, 1952', p. 36.

Sudan and its people'.[1] However, politically conscious Egyptians shrewdly interpreted the visit as a confirmation of the nationalist (Egyptian and Sudanese) thesis of the Unity of Egypt and the Sudan,[2] though when Ali Meher visited the Graduates' Congress, it was made very plain to him that its members regarded Egypt and the Sudan as two sister countries and not as one. This interpretation of one country, one destiny was kept alive by the publication in Cairo of the statements made and the telegrams sent from the Sudan during the Minister's visit. On his return, the Prime Minister compared, in the Chamber of Deputies, his visit with that of Mohammed Ali in 1839, 'when Europe refused to give Egypt justice'.[3] Opinion in the Egyptian Press simultaneously called for a change in the status of the Sudan—this 'obscurity' in Anglo-Egyptian relations, as they called it.[4] This attitude is partly in conformity with that expressed by M. Rafaat Bey, who urged present-day Egyptians to achieve that territorial expansion, not only in the Sudan but also in Africa as a whole, which Mohammed Ali and Ismail left unaccomplished in their own time. (See Chapter 7, Section 3.)

The Sudanese Graduates' Congress conducted a 'liberation' movement, culminating in the adoption, in 1944, of a resolution which defined their political objectives—' the termination of the Condominium and the establishment of a democratic regime'. Partly because of this resolute pressure from those politically conscious Northern Sudanese and as part of the British post-war policy of gradually yielding up such attributes of power as were not vital to Britain's imperial interests, an Advisory Council for the Northern Sudan was set up as a step in the process of evolution towards eventual self-government. This step, described by the British Governor-General of the Sudan as 'the first concrete expression of a Sudanese Nation',[5] evoked Egyptian suspicion and criticism. They complained that the Advisory Council had been formed without Egypt's knowledge; that no Egyptian representative was invited to the inauguration; and that an Egyptian should have been on the Council. Consequently, agitation for the 'Unity of the Nile Valley' ensued. On 26 August—the eighth anniversary of the 1936 Treaty, Nahas Pasha stated that he had asked the (British) Governor-General of the Sudan to maintain Egyptian interests in that territory. He also emphasized that he considered Egypt and the Sudan as one

[1] *The Times*, London, 20 February 1940, p. 7c.
[2] E.g. *Al-Balagh*, Cairo, 28 December 1939.
[3] *Oriente Moderno*, April 1940, p. 173.
[4] Arthur Merton, in the *Daily Telegraph*, London, 7 May 1940.
[5] *The Times*, London, 17 May 1944.

nation with equal rights. On 6 September 1944, the Sudan Government denied the persistent allegations in the Egyptian Press that the British Administration were taking steps to separate the Sudan from Egypt.[1]

In December 1944, Ali Al-Birair, a successful Sudanese business man in Egypt who also ran a newspaper in Cairo, stood as a candidate for a Cairo constituency in the General Egyptian Elections to be held in January 1945. The Egyptian Press congratulated the Government for permitting the candidature of the Sudanese. As we have already indicated, Sudanese resident in Egypt were considered as Egyptian citizens, often employed in the Egyptian Civil and Diplomatic Service.[2] But the Egyptian Press used the occasion of the Sudanese candidature to ask whether an Egyptian would, in turn, be permitted to represent Egypt on the Northern Sudanese Advisory Council. In Khartoum some Sudanese were immediately prompted to put questions to the Sudan Government about Sudanese nationality. In reply the British administration stated that the authorities were contemplating issuing regulations on the subject. This statement was given wide publicity in the Egyptian Press, with the allegation that the British administration was attempting to separate the Sudan from Egypt. Finding that his candidature involved more in higher politics about the unity of the Nile Valley than anticipated, Ali Al-Birair decided, on advice, to stand down. In sympathy with him and in protest against Britain, large-scale student demonstrations took place on 23 December 1944.

Meanwhile, and in spite of these incidents, Egypt and Britain continued together in the struggle against the Axis. At the Wafdist Congress in November 1944, Nahas Pasha had, while enumerating the services which Egypt had rendered to Britain, paid tribute to the British effort to save Egypt from the major horrors of war. In reply to a message of warm appreciation of Egypt's services sent by the British Ambassador to the Egyptian Prime Minister, Nahas Pasha said in part:

> The Egyptian Government and people offered, as I too offered with the greatest willingness every possible assistance which did not conflict with the interests of country, and I am proud to say that every Egyptian did at that moment his duty to his country and to Egypt's ally.[3]

In 1945 when the Allied Powers were on the verge of victory, another incident occurred which increased, in the Egyptian mind, consciousness of their war-time services and sacrifices to Britain. At the Three-Power Conference at Yalta in February 1945, it was decided that, in the words

[1] *The Times* 7 September 1944. [2] See Chapter 7 (1) above.
[3] *Al-Misri*, 5 August 1942.

of Winston Churchill, only 'those who . . . have declared war on Germany or Japan by 1st March, 1945', could be invited to attend the proposed San Francisco Conference (to be founder-members of the U.N.O.). Egyptians, probably realizing that Egypt's non-membership of the League of Nations was a great handicap during the Allenby Ultimatum in 1924, and being rather eager to ascertain her 'equality' and acceptance by the 'big' Powers, were possessed with a sanguine desire to be a founder-member of the United Nations. Consequently, the Egyptian Government, having already been in the War, in actual practice if not by declaration, were ready to comply with the Three-Powers (Britain, the Soviet Union and the United States) decision at Yalta. It should be remembered that Turkey declared war on the Axis powers on 23 February. However, the Government was besieged with criticisms sprung mainly from internal party politics. On the authority of the British Ambassador, Ahmad Mahir denied, while addressing the Chamber on 25 February, the rumours that Egypt would be required to send a labour Corps to the Far East if she did declare war. On his way to the Senate to make similar statements he was shot dead by a young Egyptian lawyer, allegedly belonging to an extremist Society. This political assassination, like the case of Sabri Pasha whose energy was sapped by the War, and who died of exhaustion in 1940, increased the list of distinguished Egyptians who were victims of the Second World War, partly because of the Anglo-Egyptian Treaty of Friendship and Alliance. The loss of such public figures during the war had the effect of increasing the price (Evacuation and Unity of the Nile Valley), after the War, which Egypt attached to her collaboration with Britain.

In fact the Egyptian Government appointed a committee of experts who published in 1947 a brochure with the title: *The Contribution of Egypt in World War II*. In this it was revealed that *financially*, the Allied War cost the Egyptian Government some 200 million pounds; in *human terms*, military losses amounted to 1,125 persons dead and 183 wounded; 2,092 civilians were killed and 3,455 wounded; and war epidemics claimed over 321,000 people by typhus, and more than 20,000 Egyptians by malaria.[1]

The British Government made statements expressing appreciation for Egypt's war-time collaboration. In reply to a comment by Mr. Geoffrey Mander during the early stages of the War, Mr. R. A. Butler, at that time Parliamentary Under-Secretary of State for Foreign Affairs,

---

[1] Egyptian Govt., Presidency of the Council of Ministers: *The Contribution of Egypt in World War II*, Cairo, 1947, pp. 19 and 20.

said in the House of Commons on 6 December 1940: 'the Egyptian Government [were] carrying out their treaty of alliance [with Britain] in *every respect.*'[1]

Five years later, towards the end of hostilities, Mr. Anthony Eden, as Foreign Secretary, assured the House of Commons, on 28 March 1945, that in the view of the British Government 'Egypt [had] faithfully discharged her obligations under the Anglo-Egyptian Treaty of Alliance'.[2] In an editorial article on 8 August 1945, *The Times* commented that the years of War had thrown light upon certain matters which at the time when the Anglo-Egyptian Treaty was signed, appeared open to doubt; that 'the collaboration of Egypt extended *far beyond the mere letter of her obligations*'.[3] In April 1946, another editorial in *The Times* emphasized:

> Successive Egyptian Governments displayed constancy and firmness in the face of imminent danger [and] the confidence of the [Egyptian] masses in the ultimate triumph of the Allied Cause successfully endured every misfortune. The Collaboration afforded to the Allies went far beyond the letter of the [1936] Treaty.[4]

Consequently, Egyptians were hopeful that Great Britain, in practical appreciation of their war-time collaboration, which was far beyond, not only the letter but also the spirit of their treaty obligations, would recognize their rights in the Sudan; for similar reasons, the politically conscious Sudanese, too, were expecting Britain to yield more to them in the administration of their own country. The inhabitants of the Nile Valley must have considered themselves included in Mr. Winston Churchill's war-time promises in the address which he broadcast to the world on 24 August 1941, in which he said that 'the ordeals of the peoples will be heard; we must give them the conviction that their sufferings and resistances will not be in vain.'[5]

Towards the end of the War, Churchill said in May 1945, 'On September 3rd, 1939, we began a heroic crusade for *right and freedom*'.[6] Some Egyptians and Sudanese hoped to share this right and freedom. To come nearer home, the British Ambassador in Egypt itself, had as we have indicated, assured the Egyptians (the Sudanese included), on the fourth anniversary of the 1936 Treaty (26 August 1940) that 'those who have stood loyally by us through the storm and stress will share

[1] *Parliamentary Debates*, House of Commons, Vol. CCCLXV, 1940– , p. 1311.
[2] 409 House of Commons Debates (5th Series), 28 March 1945, pp. 1404–5.
[3] *The Times*, London, 8 August 1945, p. 5.
[4] *The Times*, leading article, 16 April 1946, p. 5a.
[5] *War Speeches*, p. 234.   [6] *Ibid.*, p. 185.

with us not only the blessing of a just peace, but the gratitude of the Nations'.[1]

But, even after the defeat of the Axis forces and the end of general hostilities, the strategic base of Lower Egypt (the Suez Canal) and the British stakes in the Sudan, which we unfolded in Chapter 8, remained vital to Britain. It was therefore difficult for Britain to accede to Egyptian expectations so soon after the war. The clash of interests and the struggle of wills over the Sudan and the Suez Canal base therefore continued after the war.

Britain's interest in the Sudan and in the Suez Canal base remained vital and the trend of events caused Egypt to fear that what she gained by the Treaty of 1936 she might lose by the Allies' victory of 1945 which she had helped to bring about.

With these considerations and with the awareness that the Treaty could be revised in 1946 (ten years after its ratification) should the two parties so agree, Egypt approached Britain for a revision of the Treaty of 1936, which embodies the Sudan Question. As a result, a committee of Egyptian elder statesmen had a four-hour meeting on Sunday night, 23 September 1945, and another the following morning. Resulting from these was a statement on the Suez Canal base and the Sudan question. It read:

> The political committee unanimously considers that the National Rights, as affirmed by the entire nation and proclaimed by the Government, are *the withdrawal of the British forces* and the realization of the unity of Egypt and the Sudan according to the will of the inhabitants of the Nile Valley. Further, the Committee esteem the present *moment most opportune to work*[2] for the realization of national aspirations and . . . to begin negotiations with our ally with the object of arriving at an accord on this basis. . . .[3]

Meanwhile, at the Annual Conference of the Labour Party held at Blackpool on 21–25 May 1945, Mr. Attlee had declared his Party's plan for a better world of peace for all, in which they would try to work out 'the greatest common measure of agreement with other countries'.[4]

It is not surprising, therefore, that the return of the Labour Party to power in the British General Election of 1945 should have given further hope to the Egyptians; they felt that the new British Government would be more amenable than a Conservative Government under the leader-

[1] Cited at p. 227 above.
[2] Opportune because the war had ended and the treaty was due for revision in 1946.
[3] *The Times*, London, 24 September 1945, p. 4e.
[4] Keesing's *Contemporary Archives*, Vol. V, 1943–6, p. 7243.

ship of Winston Churchill, who 'personally still tended to think of Egypt in terms of the former British protectorate'.[1] In fact, as an American journalist observed, Ismail Sidky Pasha heralded the Labour Party's victory as a sign of 'the new spirit prevailing throughout the world'.[2]

As against this general background, the Egyptian Government delivered a formal note, dated 20 December 1945, to the British Government, requesting that negotiations for a revision of the 1936 Treaty be opened very soon. The Cabinet was forced to take this step by the widespread public opinion in its favour.

The Official Note submitted to Britain that the Treaty was signed 'in the midst of international crisis, when the spectre of War was already appearing, and it is to these circumstances that it clearly owes its present form'; and that Egypt accepted it under the pressure of necessity and as a testimony to the loyalty which inspired Egypt towards Britain, *her* ally. 'If Egypt accepted the Treaty with all that it implied in the way of restrictions on her independence, it was because she knew that they were of a transitory character and were destined to disappear at the same time as the circumstances and events by reason of which they had been agreed to.' Further, the victory of the Allies had rendered several of its provisions superfluous and without further justification. Peace had opened the way for the adoption of fresh arrangements. Implying that the Egyptians would no longer willingly co-operate in maintaining the Treaty in its present form, the Note warned: 'It is not the letter of the text of arrangements which decides their efficacy, but rather the goodwill of the peoples in consenting to them and the spirit governing their application.'

Again, the British Government, at the time of trial, obtained from their agreement with Egypt more than what was stipulated in the text, and much more than the most optimistic British negotiators had been able to contemplate. For these and other reasons (stipulated in the Note) and in view of the urge and desire of the Egyptian people to see their relations with Britain based on an alliance and a friendship 'which will no longer be inspired by past prejudices or out-of-date doctrines, the Egyptian Government . . . [hoped] that the British Government would take steps to fix an early date for an Egyptian delegation to proceed to London to negotiate with them the revision of the Treaty of 1936'. 'It goes without saying' so concluded the Note with emphasis on the Sudan, 'that the negotiations will include the question

---

[1] Royal Institute of International Affairs, *The Middle East, 1945–50*, p. 116.
[2] *New York Times*, 3 August 1945.

of the Sudan and will be inspired by the interests and aspirations of the Sudanese'.[1]

To these proposals for changes in the existing situation between Egypt and Britain with regard to military occupation and the question of the Sudan the Arab League gave its support.[2]

The response of the British Government was delayed owing to consultations with the Dominion Governments on the Egyptian question, and to preoccupation with other international issues. Consequently, certain elements in Egypt lost patience; riots, led by 1,500 students, broke out in Cairo. It would be difficult to exhaust the list of troubles and anxieties of the Egyptian Government, even during the Anglo-Egyptian negotiations. Disorders were endemic and invariably took the form of anti-British manifestations. These disturbances were not allowed, however, to interfere much with the efforts to revise the 1936 Treaty about the military occupation of Egypt, and the Sudan.

The British reply dated 26 January 1946, was brief and careful. It avoided examining in detail the contentions in the Egyptian Government's Note. However, it admitted that the Government in London had been well aware of the desire which had been manifested in Egypt, and explained that failure to respond formally to Egyptian opinion lay in two areas: firstly, in the continuous pressure of events arising out of the termination of hostilities; and secondly, because it was necessary to examine the provisions of the Anglo-Egyptian Treaty in the light of the Charter of the United Nations, and in the light of the lessons which these hostilities had taught the British. One of the lessons was 'the essential soundness of the fundamental principles on which the Anglo-Egyptian Treaty of 1936 was based'. Nevertheless, the Note declared Britain's willingness to undertake with Egypt a review of the Treaty. The reply concluded with the assurance that instructions would shortly be sent to the British Ambassador in Cairo to hold preliminary conversations with the Egyptian Government; and that the British Government 'take note that the Egyptian Government desire that the forthcoming discussions should include the question of the Sudan'.[3]

An Egyptian delegation, headed by Sidky Pasha (the Prime Minister) was representative of all parties (except the Wafd, who refused to co-operate), and of all leading personalities as in 1935. The failure of the British Government to announce promptly the names of their own

---

[1] Full text in *The Times*, London, 31 January 1946, p. 3c.
[2] See the letter by the League Secretary-General, in *The Times*, 26 October 1946, p. 5.
[3] Full text in *The Times*, London, 31 January 1946, p. 3.

delegation caused much surprise and concern in Egypt. On Sidky's enquiry the new British Ambassador (Sir Ronald Campbell) revealed that the British delegates would be composed of Senior Military experts and Embassy officials led by himself. Sidky objected, arguing that the Egyptian delegation included several of the most distinguished figures in the political life of Egypt. They therefore expected to negotiate with British figures of the same standing. 'People in Egypt believe, and will not forget', he stressed, 'that the policy which did not leave a good impression was planned and executed by the very Embassy officials whom you now wish to have as your assistants.'[1]

Accordingly, the British Foreign Minister, Mr. Ernest Bevin, announced his intention to lead the British delegation himself but that the earlier discussions would be entrusted to the Secretary for Air, Lord Stansgate; the British Ambassador in Cairo; the Head of the Middle East Secretariat of the British Foreign Office (Sir Kinahan Cornwallis, British Ambassador to Iraq, 1941–5); and the three Commanders-in-Chief in the Middle East. Ernest Bevin, in releasing the names of the British delegation, remarked that the Labour Government were confident that their own choice to meet the distinguished delegation appointed by the Egyptian Government will be welcomed in Egypt as an earnest indication of their desire to lay a firm foundation for the future relationship between the two countries.[2]

The two delegations met in Cairo during the second half of April. However, at the negotiation table, the two Governments operated from different standpoints. The British were concerned with what was to them a new Soviet threat (made apparent in Greece even before the end of the war) to their own position in the Middle East. In dealing with the Egyptian problem, therefore, the British Government gave first consideration to what they called 'the Russian menace'. The Egyptians, on the other hand, saw the problem in relation to their national aspirations and prestige both at home and in the Sudan—all to the exclusion of Britain's power politics with the Soviet Union and other powers. The Sudan rankled most with the Egyptians who insisted on the 'Unity of the Nile Valley'. But that, however, was the point on which the British found it hardest to yield. Negotiations dragged on. Having failed after six months to conclude a new treaty with Britain, Sidky Pasha resigned on 28 September.

---

[1] Sidky Pasha, *Mudhakorati*, Cairo, Dar ul-Hilal (Sidky Pasha's Autobiography in Arabic), 1950, pp. 61–2.
[2] *House of Commons Debates*, 2 April 1946.

But, at King Farouk's request, he had to remain; he resumed office on 2 October, on which date he announced that he would go to London, as head of the Egyptian Government, to see Bevin personally. Accordingly, he and Abdul Hadi Pasha, the Egyptian Foreign Minister, arrived in London on 17 October. After lengthy conversations with Mr. Bevin and Mr. Clement Attlee, a joint Anglo-Egyptian communiqué was issued in London stating that the conversations had been carried on 'in the most cordial and friendly atmosphere'.[1]

Bevin and Sidky Pasha were able to agree *ad referendum* (subject to confirmation by the respective governments) on the whole Egyptian problem under three major heads in the Draft Treaty; the Sudan Protocol; and an Evacuation Draft.

The Sudan protocol, which is here our main concern, had two objectives. In the first place, it was designed to secure to Egypt the support of Britain in the maintenance of a Sudan friendly to Egypt, and particularly to safeguard the position of Egypt with regard to the waters of the Nile. Secondly, it was aimed at setting up a joint Anglo-Egyptian Sudanese machinery to review the progress of the Sudanese towards self-government. The draft protocol, a synthesis of those objectives, declared:

> The policy which the High Contracting Parties undertake to follow in the Sudan, within the framework of the unity between the Sudan and Egypt *under the common crown of Egypt*, will have for its essential objectives to assure the well-being of the Sudanese, the development of their interests and their active preparation for self-government and consequently, the exercise of the right to choose the future status of the Sudan. Until the High Contracting Parties can, in full common agreement, realise this latter objective after consultation with the Sudanese, the Agreement of 1899 will continue. . . .[2]

To the ordinary man in Egypt and the Sudan the phrase 'within the framework of the unity between the Sudan and Egypt *under the Egyptian Crown*' meant everything that Bevin's constitutional lawyers in the British Foreign Office did not. They knew that the operative phrase which materially qualifies the rest in the protocol is 'within the framework . . .', but the length and breadth of the Sudan picked from the context only the words '*unity*', '*Crown*' and '*Egypt*'. Police had to quell the consequent protests by the Umma Party, which demanded independence. Thus, to the regret of many Egyptians and of Sidky

---

[1] Quoted in Keesing's *Contemporary Archives*, Vol. VI, 1946–8, p. 8289.
[2] *Papers regarding the Negotiations of the Anglo-Egyptian Treaty of 1936*—Cmd. 7179 (*Egypt No. 2*, 1947), p. 4.

Pasha in particular, the agreement collapsed partly by misinterpretation, partly by accident, and finally by intention. Returning to Cairo
on 26 October, Sidky Pasha, 'an old [he was 71], sick and exhausted
man, but glowing with pleasure at his success, made an incautious and
probably misrepresented statement, as he stumbled from his aircraft
late at night. . . .'[1] A widely distributed news agency quoted Sidky
Pasha as saying: 'I said last month that I shall bring the Sudan back to
Egypt, and I say now that I have succeeded; it has been definitely
decided to achieve unity between Egypt and the Sudan under the
Egyptian Crown.' Apparently referring to those who had criticized him
for going to London 'to beg from the British', he went on: 'I made more
progress in six days when I was in direct touch with Mr. Bevin than I
made in six months in dealing with notes and memoranda.'[2]

On the following day, the anti-Egyptian Umma Party, in protest
against Sidky Pasha's statement about the Unity of Sudan with Egypt
under the latter's Crown, threatened to boycott the British-sponsored
consultative institutions which the pro-Egyptian Unionist Parties had
boycotted in the Sudan. In Britain, there was, in any case, opposition
to the Sudan protocol. Mr. Bevin, who would have been in a position
in Parliament to clarify the situation was already on his way to Lake
Success in the United States. Just three days after the Bevin–Sidky
Agreement, Mr. Attlee, as Prime Minister, made a statement in Parliament regretting the report which appeared to him as 'partial and mis-
leading'; he made it clear that the Unity of Egypt and the Sudan under
the Egyptian Crown had not been conceded.[3] Sidky Pasha, for whose
benefit the Sudan clauses appeared to have been carefully worded, was
ill and bed-ridden. He resigned on 9 December 1946. A British source
remarked: 'he had, indeed, done as much as any Egyptian could to
reconcile the Egyptian and British thesis.'[4] Nokrashy Pasha, who
succeeded Sidky, insisted on the permanent unity of Egypt and the
Sudan under the Egyptian Crown. Consequently, the Sidky–Bevin
Protocol, which brought the two Governments nearer to agreement
than they had ever been in the past and would be unable to reach about
the Sudan until 1953, collapsed.

Reading the scanty material available in the British Official papers on
this negotiation[5] one would be led to blame Egypt solely for the failure

---

[1] *The Round Table*, March 1951, p. 115.   [2] Keesing's *Contemporary Archives*, p. 8289.
[3] *Parliamentary Debates*, House of Commons, 5th Series, Vol. CCCCXXVIII,
October 1946, pp. 295–6.
[4] Royal Institute of International Affairs, *Great Britain and Egypt*, p. 97.
[5] Cmd. 7179.

of the negotiations. However, other sources, equally reliable, reveal the stumbling blocks in the way of the personal affability and agreement between Bevin and Sidky. Some of these obstacles, immediate or remote, came from the following sources: in *Egypt*—optimism before the negotiation, party-political intrigues during the negotiations, and certain interpretations of the treaty. In the *Sudan*—the Anti-Egyptian elements and the British Administration in the Sudan; and in *Britain*— the new position of Britain in the World; consultations with the Dominions; opposition by the Conservative Party; and the influence of certain officials in the Foreign Office.

Optimism in Egypt sprang from various sources. For instance, Egyptians argued with warmth that more vulnerable countries in the Middle East—countries nearer the Soviet Union about whose power and influence Britain was concerned—had recently resumed or won complete independence and sovereignty. The Egyptians were aware of Britain's insistence, immediately after the Second World War, that both British and Soviet troops should evacuate Persia.[1] Furthermore, Lebanon and Syria, which were occupied, had been evacuated by 1946. These facts increased the Egyptian hope for a willing co-operation from a grateful Britain in return for Egypt's war-time collaboration. This optimism probably overlooked the fact that Egypt's location, being so strategically important as we have shown in Chapter 7, Section 2, would permit no effective neutrality. Therefore, Egypt would have suffered from the occurrence of the Second World War in any case, whether in alliance with Britain or any other power or even, if it were possible, to be 'alone'. From the British viewpoint, the Egyptian claims were based on costs which were in fact parts of the risks involved, by both parties, in the signing of the 1936 Treaty.

The War years had left their marks on the domestic situation in Egypt; the British Ultimatum of February 1942, had left King Farouk and others bitter against Britain. During the negotiations he accepted the anti-British demonstrations as a 'healthy manifestation of the people's ambition to realise their just claims'.[2] In addition, some members of the Egyptian treaty delegation were actually opposed to Sidky Pasha's efforts to reach agreement with Bevin. In fact they did, for internal party political intrigues, try to undermine Sidky Pasha's

---

[1] In a letter to Molotov on 19 September 1945, Bevin had urged that their two Governments should agree on the withdrawal of their respective forces from the whole of Persia before the end of 1945.

[2] Quoted by the British Secretary for the Dominions in the House of Lords, 26 February 1946—*House of Lords Debates*, 5th Series, Vol. CXXXIX, p. 873.

authority, even though he was 'as shrewd and forceful a bargainer on behalf of his country as any nation could desire'.[1] Nokrashy Pasha, too, headed an uneasy coalition, inherited from his predecessor; within his own cabinet extreme opinions were at work.

In her Note of 20 December 1945, Egypt had warned the British Government that: 'It is not the letter of the text of arrangements which decides their efficacy, but rather the goodwill of the peoples in consenting to them and the spirit governing their application.'

This truism was reasserted by Egypt in order, we presume, to arouse British sympathy; but it might have appeared self-condemnatory in the sense that it implies, in effect, that Egypt will henceforth break the spirit if not the letter of the treaty. To yield to such a threat, the British might have suggested, would be flouting the sanctity of agreements—treaties once signed must be kept.

Sir Abdel Rahman el Mahdi, a son of the Mahdi of the 1880s who defeated General Gordon and the Egyptian forces, was the effective, if not official, leader of the independence school in the Sudan. The six-foot three-inch 'Black Knight', as he was nicknamed by American journalists, flew to London during the negotiations 'to tell Prime Minister Attlee that there must be a limit to concessions to the hated Egyptians'.[2] The visit to London of Sir Abdel Rahman[3] and the exaggerated reports of the Sudan administration had adverse effects on the British Government. The pro-independence Umma Party and the Sudan administration, Bevin revealed later, accused Britain of 'breaking their pledge and of selling them [the Sudanese] to Egypt'.[4]

Evidently, the Labour Government, or rather at least Mr. Bevin, the Foreign Secretary, was anxious and willing to examine the Egyptian question sympathetically and to conclude mutual agreements with Egypt. The declared policy of Bevin, with regard to Egypt, was to rely on morality as against the use of force, to make the Egyptians overcome their inferiority complex by accepting them as equals in fact and with equal status must go friendship and trust:

> I believe sincerely there is only one way to hold the association of the Arab countries with us, and that is on the basis of friendship. . . . I suggest with respect, and despite criticism of this Government [by the Conservative Opposition] that our prestige is higher than it has been for many years

---

[1] *The Times*, editorial, 1 October 1946, p. 7b.
[2] *News Week*, Dayton, Ohio, U.S.A., 9 December 1946, p. 38.
[3] *Ibid.*
[4] *Papers regarding the Negotiations for a Revision of the Anglo-Egyptian Treaty of 1936*, p. 7.

because of this decision we have taken to trust them. I am more prepared to trust than to shoot.[1]

But Mr. Winston Churchill, then Leader of the Opposition, considered the Labour Government's friendly gestures to Egypt as 'very grave'. Supported by Mr. Anthony Eden, he protested that the work of sixty years of diplomacy with Egypt and of British administration in the Sudan was about to be undone. 'Things are built up with great labour and cast away with great shame.'[2] Captain Marsden, too, warned the Labour Government against 'Scuttle and Run' in the Sudan, which 'many generations of our people have held so dear and sacred'.[3] Although these Opposition arguments were dismissed by Mr. William Gallacher (Communist M.P.) as coming from 'a few ancient Victorian Tories',[4] they had the effect of restraining the Labour Government from reaching an agreement with Egypt; it must also be remembered that many members even of the Labour Party were antipathetic to Egypt.

The Egyptian delegation discovered, and resented the fact, that the British Foreign Office were, to quote a British source, 'treating Egypt as a slippery customer who had to sign an absolutely watertight bond . . . more caution could not have been taken in dealing [even] with a defeated enemy'.[5]

Whilst the end of the War had left the United States as the universal creditor nation, in a position of economic dominance of the world without a parallel in history, it brought to Britain (in economic terms) the prospect of 'a long and stern struggle against adverse circumstances'.[6]

As one of the means of recovery, Britain was obliged to hold tightly on to her stakes in the Sudan. In addition, though there were pro-Egyptian feelings in the Sudan, the British had to consider the existence there of the pro-British (anti-Egyptian) elements. These elements were pro-British, it must be explained, not in the sense that they wanted the Sudan to remain under British rule but because they believed Britain could help them gain their independence.

Consequent on the Anglo-Egyptian deadlock that ensued, Egypt decided to appeal to the United Nations about her claim in the Sudan.

---

[1] *Parliamentary Debates*, House of Commons, 5th Series, Vol. CCCCXXIII, 24 May 1946, pp. 786–7.
[2] *Parliamentary Debates*, 7 May 1946, p. 782.
[3] *Ibid.*, Vol. CCCCXXIII, 24 May 1946, p. 720.
[4] *Ibid.*, Vol. CCCCXXII, 7 May 1946, p. 784.
[5] 'Anglo-Egyptian Relations' in *The Round Table*, March 1951 p .125.
[6] *The Times*, 'Review of the Year', 1946, p. ii.

11

EGYPT'S APPEAL TO THE SECURITY COUNCIL, 1947

I have heard speeches sometimes that suggested that all inter-
national problems could be solved if we could only get a few people
sitting round the table and discussing them. Believe me, the thing
is not as easy as that. I have just come back from San Francisco.
RT. HON. C. R. ATTLEE, 1945[1]

With all its defects, with all the failures that we can check up
against it, the United Nations still represents man's best organised
hope to substitute the conference table for the battlefield.
PRESIDENT EISENHOWER, 1953[2]

TEN months of arduous negotiations having thus failed, the next course
followed by Egypt was a decision to appeal to the Security Council of
the United Nations. This decision was urged upon the Egyptian mind
by several factors: the most important political question to many alert
Egyptians was the Sudan issue with the question of evacuation; the
Government, therefore, felt the necessity for settling this problem;
Egypt was confident that her demands were just. Their interpretation
of the high principles and ideals of the Charter of the United Nations
encouraged many Egyptians to believe that judgment would be decisively given in their favour should the case be submitted to the
Security Council. The Egyptian Prime Minister himself declared: 'We
have taken this course with full faith in the Charter of the United
Nations. We are availing ourselves of a small nation's privilege to
appeal to the Council against one of the great powers on a footing of
perfect equality.'[3] Consequently, Nokrashy Pasha, who succeeded Sidky
Pasha, announced on 26 January 1947, his Government's intention to
take the 'whole of Egypt and the Sudan' to the Security Council.

This decision gave rise to speculations not only in Egypt but in several
parts of the world as well. In Egypt public opinion was divided; there
were the indifferent, the moderates, who conceded to the Sudanese the

---

[1] *Report of the 44th Annual Conference of the Labour Party*, Blackpool, 1945, p. 107.
[2] Address on United Nations Day, 1953.
[3] *U.N. Security Council Official Records*, 2nd Year, No. 70, August 1947, p. 1746.

right of self-government, and the 'unionists', who insisted on the Unity of Egypt and the Sudan under the Egyptian Crown. The local Press expressed confidence in the righteousness of the Egyptian case, but indicated uneasiness about the probability that the Security Council might not be convinced by Egyptian arguments. Efforts were made, therefore, to prepare the mind of the public for disappointment; it was suggested that the U.N. was a lobby where unscrupulous and 'Machiavellian' great nations cheated the honest and idealistic small ones; that the Egyptian appeal was not likely to be judged on its own merits, and consequently, that Arab nations must unite for their rights.

The Wafdist (Opposition) Party declared that Nokrashy Pasha could not lead Egypt to success. Anti-British groups predicted that Britain would use the veto should the U.N. decide the case in favour of Egypt. However, opinion from reflective quarters forecast that the Security Council would uphold the Egyptian claim, but might merely urge the parties to resume negotiations.

While inter-party wranglings went on in Egypt about the composition of the proposed delegation to U.N. and while speculations continued about timing (arranging to present the case when the representative of a State friendly to Egypt would be presiding over the Security Council), Mr. Bevin emphatically declared in the House of Commons on 16 May, that there would be 'no attempt to appease the Egyptian Government at the expense of the Sudanese people . . . whether they take this to the Security Council or anywhere else, we cannot go any further than the offer we have made'.[1] Thus, Bevin's statement nipped in the bud Egypt's hope of a fresh concession from the British. Also the (British) *Daily Telegraph*, a mouthpiece of the Conservative Party, stated on 11 November 1946, that Britain would allow no alteration in the status of the people of the Sudan whatever might be the nature of further negotiations.

In the Arab-League States the President of the Syrian Republic announced, in a Press statement, that his country was determined to support Egypt's demands, 'to stand on Egypt's side to the widest limits of collaboration and mutual help'.[2]

It was rumoured that the United States and other Western Governments contemplated mediating between Britain and Egypt. Some Egyptian Press reports stated that Mr. Molotov promised to support Egypt on the Sudan Question if it came before the United Nations; but

---

[1] *Parliamentary Debates*, 5th Series, Vol. CCCCXXXVII, p. 1963.
[2] *Egypt/Sudan, op. cit.*, p. 4.

this was denied by the Tass Agency. A British Government source was reported to have revealed that on 24 March, in a review of the Anglo-Soviet alliance of 1942 during the Moscow Conference of Foreign Ministers, Stalin and Bevin had discussed Egypt's complaints against Britain; that Stalin had appeared generally to appreciate Britain's position in the Middle East and Egypt and had assured Bevin that Russia would remain neutral in the Anglo-Egyptian dispute.[1] But this, too, was denied by the Tass Agency, which stated that Anglo-Egyptian relations were, of course, a matter between Britain and Egypt only and that interference in the matter would be against the invariable Soviet policy of non-interference.

In a letter dated 6 July 1947, Egypt formally submitted her case to the Security Council under articles 33 and 37 of the Charter of the U.N. She complained that the presence of British troops on Egyptian soil without the free consent of Egypt offended Egyptian dignity, hindered her development and thereby infringed the fundamental principle of sovereignty and equality, and was therefore contrary to the letter and spirit of the United Nations Charter, and to the unanimously-adopted resolution of the General Assembly on 14 December 1946 (asking members to withdraw immediately armed forces stationed in the territory of members without free and expressed consent). She submitted that British military occupation of Egypt had since 1899 helped the British Government to force upon Egypt a kind of partnership in the administration of the Sudan and subsequently to assume exclusive authority in the Sudan. Taking advantage of this situation, the memorandum went on, Britain had adopted a policy designed to sever the Sudan from Egypt by discrediting Egypt and the Egyptians, creating discord between Egyptians and the Sudanese, and causing dissension among the Sudanese themselves by investigating and encouraging artificial separatist movements. By this policy the Government of Britain had endeavoured to impair the unity of the Nile Valley, 'notwithstanding that this unity is urged by the common interest and aspirations of its people. . . .'[2]

In the light of these, Egypt requested the Security Council to direct the total and immediate evacuation of British troops from both Egypt and the Sudan, and the termination of the British administrative regime of the Sudan.

---

[1] Royal Institute of International Affairs, *Great Britain and Egypt*, pp. 99–100.
[2] For full text see *U.N. Security Council Official Records*, 2nd Year, No. 59, Lake Success, 1947, pp. 1343–5.

In order to appreciate the difficulties that faced the Security Council in taking a decision on the matter, and because it indicates the role of the United Nations in settling international disputes, we consider it essential and relevant to present in some detail a survey of the proceedings of the Security Council on the Anglo-Egyptian dispute. Moreover, judgments on this issue pronounced by representatives of other powers in a world assembly are relevant and significant to our further understanding of the subject. In this survey we propose to present the case under four main headings, namely: the presentation of arguments by the disputants (*first stage*); the Council's discussion and search for a solution (*second stage*); the immediate reactions of Egyptians to the result of the appeal to the Council (*third stage*); and, finally, the writer's critique of the Council's decision.

The First Stage—The Disputants' Arguments. To enable the delegates of the two disputing Governments to have at their disposal expert sources of information on the Sudan, four officials of the Sudan Administration were sent to Lake Success to be available for reference by either delegation. At the same time Sudanese delegations representing the two main political parties—the Umma and the Ashigga (see Chapter 15 below)—were also despatched to Lake Success by their respective parties to lobby and report.[1] Being neither a member of the U.N. nor specially invited on this occasion, the Sudan could not participate officially. Therefore, the Sudanese representatives, though seen, were not heard at Lake Success.

The first stage began at the 175th Meeting of the Security Council held at Lake Success on Tuesday, 5 August 1947, at 10.30 a.m. Present were: the representatives of Australia, Belgium, Brazil, China, Colombia, France, Poland, Syria, the Soviet Union, Britain and the United States. The President of this sitting was Mr. F. El-Khouri (Arab-League State of Syria).

The Egyptian chief delegate Mahmoud Fahmy Nokrashy Pasha, made a supplementary statement to his letter of appeal, a copy of which had been circulated to each member. He claimed that the dispute had possible repercussions elsewhere much wider than local implications. It was likely to endanger general international peace and security, considering the touchy situation in the Middle East. He spoke slowly and deliberately for two hours, and his main points could be analysed as follows. Egypt had done all she possibly could by negotiations,

---

[1] H.M.S.O., *Report by the Governor-General on the Administration of the Sudan in 1947 —Sudan No. 1* (1949), Cmd. 7835, p. 9.

friendly gestures and other means, peacefully to settle the dispute, before appealing to the Council. The British Government had insisted on granting the Sudan the right to secede from Egypt in future. This meant that it was left for Britain to decide the duration of the Union with Egypt, the time and the terms under which such Union might be broken. But such matters, being domestic and internal, should remain with Egypt and the Sudan. Egypt and the Sudan had been one and the same country culturally, ethnically, geographically and politically. But the British were alien to the Sudanese in every respect and were, therefore, not as qualified as the Egyptians to guide the cultural, social and political developments of the Sudanese and their preparation for self-government.[1] Moreover, British officials in the Sudan 'endeavoured to stir up bad feelings between the Sudanese and the Egyptians'[2] and in anticipation of failure to separate the Sudan from Egypt they had attempted to divide the Sudan itself by severing the South from the North (where pro-Egyptian elements existed). The Egyptian advocate went on to quote the Civil Secretary of the Sudan Administration as saying, 'Our policy aims at the establishment of an autonomous regime in the South which could be separated from the North.'[3] Nokrashy Pasha also quoted Lord Cromer, who, in his Report on the Conditions in Egypt for 1900 acknowledged the unity of Egypt and the Sudan in these words: 'I observe, in the remarks of the Egyptian Legislative Council on the estimates for the current year, that it is stated that the Council approves of the proposed expenditure on the Sudan, as they consider that the country forms an integral part of Egypt. That view is substantially correct.'[4]

Economically, the British Administration had weakened the natural connections between Egypt and the Sudan, through deliberate policies.

The Anglo-Egyptian Agreement of 1899, concluded under a military atmosphere, did not deal with the matter of Sudanese sovereignty. It was an informal arrangement between the Egyptian Foreign Minister and the British Consul-General. Full powers were lacking, the text was not ratified nor approved by any legislative organ. The Condominium Agreement did not forbid the nomination of an Egyptian as Governor-General of the Sudan. But in practice the Governor-General and the high officials who served under him had always been British. It had been the practice up to 1912 and in accordance with the Condominium to

---

[1] For our arguments against this last part, see Chapter 9, above.
[2] *U.N. Security Council Official Records*, 2nd Year, No. 70 (1947), p. 1748.
[3] *Ibid.*, p. 1765.
[4] *Ibid.*, p. 1762.

submit laws promulgated in the Sudan to the approval of the Egyptian Government. But the Governor-General had, since 1912, issued legislation without even notifying the Egyptian Government.

As for the 1936 Treaty, it was negotiated under conditions that no longer existed; Egypt signed it under the stress and strain of the time, and did so on the understanding that its provisions were temporary and had been framed to meet specific circumstances. Dominated by the fear of Nazism and Fascism, Egypt yielded to the 'onerous conditions set by Britain'. He argued that Egypt was not a free party to the Treaty because British forces occupied the territory at that time and because Egyptian negotiators were warned by the British negotiators against the possible consequences of Egypt's failure to agree to British demands. In any case, the Treaty was against the spirit of the Charter, and had outlived its purpose.

The general situation formed a source of constant irritation to Egypt, poisoned Anglo-Egyptian relations, crippled the progress of 'our people'[1]—Egyptians and Sudanese—and frustrated Egyptian efforts to shoulder her responsibilities under the Charter.

In conclusion he therefore requested the Security Council to direct the evacuation of all British forces from the Nile Valley and the termination of the British administration in the Sudan. What would replace that administration was, in his opinion, for the people of the Nile Valley to decide for themselves, as it was a domestic issue. 'In frankness, we are here to challenge the basic assumptions of nineteenth-century imperialism. We ask the Security Council to affirm that in the twentieth century the world has moved on.'[2]

In reply, Sir Alexander Cadogan, British representative, made his own statement, first with regard to the letter which the Egyptian delegation had addressed to the Secretary-General of the United Nations, and then to Nokrashy Pasha's supplementary statement. He submitted first that neither the Egyptian letter nor the supplementary statement to it had offered any proof that international peace and security were in danger. Again, he stated that the Sudan Protocol made provision for the continuance of the administrative regime in the Sudan, and for certain objectives which both Egypt and Britain undertook to follow in the Sudan. These were the well-being of the Sudanese and the promotion of their interests, the active preparing of the Sudanese for self-government, and the right of the Sudanese to choose their future, eventually.

---

[1] *U.N. Security Council Official Records*, 2nd Year, No. 70 (1947), p. 1766.
[2] *Ibid.*, p. 1749.

The Sudan Protocol, he went on, was rejected because of the difference of opinion on the meaning of the third objective. The British Government understood it to mean that the Sudanese should be able, after a period of self-government, to decide freely the future of the Sudan—whether to associate with Egypt or Britain in any form they wished. But the Egyptian Government insisted on either complete union with Egypt or self-government under a common crown with Egypt. Egypt, therefore, was not prepared to accord to the Sudan the right to independence which Egypt claimed for herself and other Arab countries.

The Treaty of 1936, he went on, would remain valid till 1956, unless bilaterally revised in accordance with its provisions. The Egyptian delegation were not confident of the legal soundness of their case, hence their avoidance of the legal aspects. To the British delegation the question was a legal one: 'the extent to which treaties could be held to be invalid on *rebus sic stantibus* grounds, otherwise than by agreement between the parties themselves, is certainly very limited as well as being controversial.'[1]

Again, the Egyptian allegation that the British had adopted a policy of severing the Sudan from Egypt was not correct. The Government of the Sudan had on the contrary pursued the most complete impartiality.

In conclusion, Sir Alexander argued: 'When once it is accepted that the Treaty of 1936 is valid, it appears that the Egyptian application is one that has no justification. Egypt has no right to negotiations for revision of the Treaty now. As a matter of grace, the United Kingdom agreed to enter into them in 1946. They were in the end unsuccessful. Egypt cannot acquire a right to negotiations for revision by bringing an ill-founded claim before the Security Council.'[2]

Second Stage—General Discussion by Members of the Council. The second stage of the case was its general discussion by members of the Council. In the opinion of the Council President, at their 182nd meeting on 13 August 1947, both the Egyptian and British representatives had 'ably and deliberately presented their cases'; the floor was open for general discussion.

The Polish representative expressed sympathy with the Egyptian case. Analysing the psychological motivations of Egypt, he defined Nokrashy Pasha's case as 'proud declarations of a young nation striving for a full, free and independent life, and striving to remove every hindrance in the way of realization of its natural aspirations'.[3] While

---

[1] *Ibid.*, p. 1778. [2] *Ibid.*, p. 1784.
[3] *Ibid.*, p. 1962.

accepting that the Agreement of 1899 was valid in accordance with the international law and right of conquest then existing, he submitted that the Treaty of 1936 was *not* applicable 'today when the Charter of the U.N. excludes that right as a title at any time and at any place'.[1] Furthermore, the presence of British troops in Egypt and the general circumstances existing when the treaty was being negotiated did not 'convey a full impression of a free atmosphere and of partners negotiating as equal with equal'.[2] He suggested that the Security Council must not be limited by the legal side of the dispute, but must bear in mind the spirit of the Charter, the preservation of world peace and the maintenance of security as the duty of the Council.

Turning to Egypt's plea for the 'Unity of the Nile Valley', the Polish representative commented: 'We have full sympathy with the desire for a Union of Egypt and the Sudan, and approach the problem of the Nile Valley with full understanding.' But the interests of the Sudanese must be considered apart from the British and the Egyptian claims. The primary objective of the U.N. and the Council should be, he concluded, not the demands and interests of the Condominium powers 'but the development of self-government and free political institutions for the peoples of the Sudan'.[3]

The Brazilian representative analysed the Egyptian appeal as a request that the Council should revise the 1936 Treaty on the grounds of lack of agreement because of compulsion; and because of changes both in the situation which justified the Treaty and in the juridical setting since the promulgation of the U.N. Charter, whose general principles are contrary to the specific provisions of the Anglo-Egyptian Treaty. But, he argued, the U.N. Charter had no provisions for revising a treaty, except for chapter 14 of the Charter under which the General Assembly might recommend the revision of treaties. After submitting that the Security Council had no justification for setting aside a treaty between two governments, he maintained that both parties to the dispute had not exhausted all possibilities of agreement; hence, he asked the Council to invite both governments to resume direct negotiations. To this end the Brazilian representative submitted a resolution:

> The Security Council, having considered the dispute between the United Kingdom and Egypt, brought to its attention by the letter of the Prime Minister of Egypt, dated 8 July 1947,
> Noting that the methods of adjustment provided for by Article 33 of the

[1] *U.N. Security Council Official Records*, 2nd Year, No. 70 (1947), p. 1963.
[2] *Ibid.*, p. 1964.   [3] *Ibid.*, p. 1966.

Charter have not been exhausted, and believing that the settlement of the dispute may best be attained, under the present circumstances, through recourse to those methods,

Recommends to the Governments of the United Kingdom and Egypt:

(a) to resume direct negotiations and, should such negotiations fail, to seek a solution of the dispute by other peaceful means of their own choice;

(b) to keep the Security Council informed of the progress of these negotiations.[1]

The U.S.S.R. representative saw in the substance of the question, two related issues: first, the evacuation of British troops from Egypt and the Sudan; and secondly, the future of the Sudan. After giving substantial justification for the Egyptian case, he concluded that Egypt's request for immediate withdrawal of all British troops from Egypt and the Sudan was well founded, and supported by his delegation. As for the future of the Sudan, he said, 'We do not know what the wishes of the Sudanese people are now—what are their aspirations. Without the precise knowledge of the aspirations of the Sudanese people, it is difficult for the Security Council to make any decision on this question.'[2]

The representative of China expressed general sympathy with Egypt, and acknowledged the desire of the Egyptian Government for the Unity of the Nile Valley as natural, and the right of the Sudanese to full and free self-determination as essential. The historical, cultural and national ties between Egypt and the Sudan appeared favourable to the wishes of the Egyptian Government in the event of the Sudanese people choosing their own future (see Chapter 7, Section 2, above).

With regard to the Egyptian complaint about British separatist policy in the Sudan, 'certain British officials' he said, 'have tried to prejudice the choice of the Sudanese people' and 'The Egyptian Government seems to have a legitimate complaint'.[3] He supported the Brazilian resolution with his own amendment, in the hope that direct negotiations would bring some, if not complete, satisfaction to the Egyptian Government.

Both the Belgian and French representatives supported the Brazilian resolution (with amendments), whilst Mr. Johnson, for the United States, had 'the impression that there is genuine sympathy for the natural ambitions and desires of the Kingdom of Egypt . . .', and that

---

[1] *U.N. Security Council Official Records*, 189th Meeting, No. 80, pp. 2108–9.
[2] *Ibid.*, p. 2111.　　　　　　[3] *Ibid.*, p. 2112.

the differences between Britain and Egypt could be settled without great difficulties. It was the belief of the U.S. Government that the disputants who 'ought to be steadfast and perpetual friends', could reach agreement through voluntary means. Hence he supported the Brazilian resolution.

Sir Alexander Cadogan considered the resolution, as amended, unsatisfactory because there was no definite pronouncement on the validity of the Treaty of 1936. '*I shall have to stick to my point and ask for some declaration from the Council to the effect that the Treaty must continue to be observed until it is rendered invalid by some authoritative pronouncement.*'

Nokrashy Pasha regretted that Egypt's hope had not been realized but observed that the general discussions revealed genuine fundamental sympathy by the Council in support of the aspirations of Egypt. He objected to the resolution because, in his opinion, it set limitations which were dictated neither by the Charter nor by the submissions made to the Council in the discussion of the case; it placed a premium on the traditional methods of handling international differences—that the Council would intervene only after the old methods had failed—and would deprive the Security Council of the role assigned to it under Article 36, paragraph 1, of the Charter. The Egyptian spokesman pointed out that a party to a dispute was not obliged first to try negotiation, then that failing, to go on to enquiry; and that failing, to proceed successively to mediation, conciliation, arbitration, judicial settlement and other gradations. Should the resolution be accepted, he argued, the Council would seem to '*put a premium on violence by implying that they would not move until the planes had begun to fly and the tanks to roll*'.

Also the resolution made no specific reference to the termination of the British rule in the Sudan; furthermore, the proposal for a resumption of direct negotiation overlooked, he concluded, 'the exigent and adamant course to which the British have never ceased to cling in their dealings with Egypt'.[1]

The whole draft resolution was put to the vote, but not carried. Six members were in favour, one against, and three abstained. In favour were, Australia, Belgium, Brazil, China, France and the United States. Poland voted against the resolution, whilst Colombia, Syria and the U.S.S.R. abstained. Consequently, another formula had to be found. (To be carried, a decision requires at least seven votes.)

[1] *U.N. Security Council Official Records*, 189th Meeting, No. 80, p. 2112.

Mr. Lopez, the Colombian representative, presented another resolution calling upon Britain and Egypt

To resume direct negotiations with a view to completing at earliest possible date the evacuation of all British military, naval and air forces from Egyptian territory, mutual assistance being provided in order to safeguard in time of War or imminent threat of War the liberty and security of navigation of the Suez Canal: and to terminate the joint administration of the Sudan with due regard to the principle of self-determination of peoples and their right to self-government. Further, Britain and Egypt should keep the Security Council readily informed of the progress of their negotiations.

The Colombian resolution is similar in spirit and objective to the Brazilian. But the Colombian appears more specific on the two issues of negotiation between the two parties, i.e. the withdrawal of British forces from the Nile Valley and the cessation of Anglo-Egyptian administration in the Sudan.

Again, the Egyptian delegation could not accept the second resolution for these reasons: it made evacuation conditional by a treaty; the 'mutual assistance' clause was a departure from the principle of leaving Egypt entirely responsible for the liberty and security of navigation in her territorial waters, and the defence of her territory; and the 'mutual assistance' clause in the time of war was taken from the 1936 Treaty, the spirit of which the Egyptian Government had come to complain about before the Council.

The Egyptian representative welcomed the proposal to terminate the existing administration in the Sudan. 'We have to negotiate the termination of the present administration of the Sudan; there is no doubt about it.' But he objected to part of paragraph 2 of the resolution for conveying the impression that Egypt had to negotiate with the British the future of the Sudan. He said: 'We maintain that it is a domestic issue and that we shall solve it to the mutual satisfaction of the Sudanese and the Egyptians, with full regard to the democratic principles of the Charter.[1]

The Colombian delegate pointed out that his second clause referred specifically only to the termination of the administration in the Sudan and not to the future of the country.

Sir Alexander, too, could not accept the resolution because, in his opinion, it spelled out the actual topics of negotiation, and the termination of the British administration in the Sudan could not be immediate, because the Sudanese were yet incapable of governing themselves.

[1] *Ibid.*

On being put to the vote, the Colombian resolution, too, was not accepted by the Council.

The Council having, for lack of the necessary majority, failed to accept either of the two resolutions on the question, the Chinese representative offered a new suggestion. He explained that the key to the whole Anglo-Egyptian dispute was the problem of the evacuation of British troops; the question of evacuation was most urgent, and psychologically most important, to the solution of the Sudan dispute. He therefore proposed a resolution which he described as the 'political solution of the problem'. The draft resolution runs:

(1) The Security Council, having considered the dispute between the United Kingdom and Egypt . . .
(and)
Recognising the natural and reasonable desire of the Egyptian Government for the early and complete evacuation of British armed forces from Egypt:

Noting that the Government of the United Kingdom have already evacuated their armed forces from certain parts of Egypt:

Having confidence that the re-establishment of direct contact between the two parties will result in early evacuation of remaining British armed forces:

(2) Recommends that the parties:

    (a) resume negotiations, and

    (b) keep the Security Council informed of the progress of these negotiations and report thereon to the Council in the first instance not later than 1st January, 1948.

Asked for his opinion by Mr. Andrei Gromyko, now President of the Council, the Egyptian representative maintained that negotiations with the British Government would yield no useful result so long as their armed forces remained on Egyptian territories—which put Egypt in a position of inequality in discussing any aspect of the dispute, as the constant pressure and potential threat always remained. He had repeatedly asked without success the British Government to withdraw their troops, and it was the failure of the previous negotiations that brought him to speak to the Council; Sir Alexander Cadogan had '*told you that the United Kingdom will not comply to those requests*'.

Sir Alexander objected because the proposal emphasized and separated the Suez issue from the Sudan Question.

In my opening statement to the Council, [he warned] I think I made it clear that we wished to deal as we had done in the original negotiations, with the whole area of the dispute all together. That is still the position of my

Government, and I am afraid, therefore, that I must warn the Council that if this present text is put to the vote in its present form, my Government would not consider it acceptable.

On the question of pressure through the presence of British armed forces, he pointed out that such could not happen if the parties resumed negotiations at the invitation of the Council to which any irregularity of such a kind could be referred.

After further discussion by the United States, the Syrian, the Australian, and the Polish representatives, the Council agreed to vote on the following amendment to the last paragraph of the preamble to the Chinese resolution:

> Having confidence that the renewal of negotiations between the parties will result in the early evacuation of British troops from Egypt and also in the settlement of the other issues in dispute between the parties.

But neither the amendment nor the resolution was carried.

Thus the Security Council was unable to adopt any decision on the Anglo-Egyptian question. But Mr. El-Khouri of Syria (member of the Arab League) made a momentous appeal to the British Government to take note of the wish of the whole Security Council, which had been clearly demonstrated, and to withdraw British troops from Egypt and the Sudan. He reminded Sir Alexander of his earlier request during the debate that the British Government should make a friendly gesture by telling the Council that they did not intend to keep their forces in the Nile Valley perpetually—to say, 'We know the desire of the Security Council and the desire of the General Assembly of the United Nations that under the rule of the Charter such practice should not continue.' He hoped that the British Government would now take this step even without being invited or recommended by the Security Council. It could be done as was the case in London when Britain and France in 1946 undertook to execute the wishes of the Security Council which had failed to find any acceptable resolution with respect to the similar case of Syria and Lebanon. 'If the United Kingdom begins that action, I think the matter will be solved without difficulty.'

The British representative, in response, assured the Council: 'My Government will take note of the statement of the representative of Syria, and will, of course, study the whole of the discussion which has taken place. . . . *I cannot say anything as to what their future course of decisions may be.*'

Thus the Security Council meeting over the Anglo-Egyptian dispute about the Sudan was adjourned *sine die.* But two things were quite clear: there was general sympathy for the Egyptian aspirations concerning the withdrawal of British troops and, secondly, all the members of the Security Council unanimously maintained the right of the Sudanese to choose the future status of their own country.

When the result of the appeal to the Security Council became known in Egypt, demonstrations started in Alexandria shortly after midnight. Thousands shouted against Britain as the Egyptian Premier returned from Lake Success. Employees of the Egyptian Army workshop demonstrated, denouncing the U.N.[1] The resignation of Nokrashy Pasha, the Prime Minister, was demanded on account of what was considered his failure at the Security Council. The U.S. Consulate was stoned. 'The Egyptian Terrorist Society' wrote to the Brazilian Legation demanding a reparation payment of £5,000,000 for Brazil's 'impertinence in moving her resolution at the Security Council, and on the night of 28th–29th August two small bombs were exploded outside the legation, but without doing any damage.'[2] But the Egyptian Government tendered an apology for the behaviour of extremists.[3] About four thousand Egyptians went on strike in protest against the U.N.; and the *Egyptian Gazette*[4] reported a proposal to the Arab world to resign their membership of the United Nations.

Sanhuri Pasha declared that Egypt had won a great moral victory, but the Prime Minister announced, 'Britain is now an open enemy'[5] and Egypt's new policy was to ignore Britain.[6]

In essence, Egypt's charge against Britain before the Security Council was fourfold. Ethically, the British foothold in Egypt and the Sudan, she said, depended upon might, not on right. Further the British occupation of the Nile Valley was against the wishes of the inhabitants —a violation of international law or the principle of self-determination. There was again constant provocation from Britain, 'which might excite the Egyptian people to unleash their resentment'[7]—a danger to international peace; and lastly British penetration undermined the natural unity of the Nile Valley and the interests of the Egyptians and the Sudanese.

---

[1] *New York Times*, 21 and 22 September 1947.
[2] Royal Institute of International Affairs, *Great Britain and Egypt*, p. 107.
[3] According to the *Egyptian Mail*, September 1947.
[4] Cairo, 25 September 1947.
[5] *Egyptian Mail*, 24 September 1947.
[6] *Egyptian Gazette*, 25 September 1947.
[7] Royal Institute of International Affairs, *The World To-day*, Vol. VII, 458, 460.

The Egyptian delegation made no mention of Egypt's real claims in the Sudan—the use of the Nile waters, an outlet for Egyptian goods and population, and as a buffer territory against the geo-politics of the Mediterranean (Chapters 6 and 7).

Britain, on the other hand, submitted that the whole matter was 'indeed simply a legal question' and argued conclusively that the 1936 Treaty remained legally valid. Consequently, the Egyptian question had no legal justifications, and under the principle of *'Pacta sunt servanda'* (treaties signed must be observed) the Security Council should 'find that the Egyptian Government had failed to make its case'. The question therefore should be removed from the agenda of the Council. Like Egypt's, the British delegation refrained from giving any indication of Britain's stake in the Sudan, which we have analysed in Chapter 8.

The Council failed to adopt any decision, but retained the question on its agenda indefinitely. Several factors militated against the Council in reaching an agreement. At San Francisco in 1945, the Great Powers who set the scope of the Charter had deliberately refrained from expressly conferring upon any Agency of the United Nations the power of revising treaties.

The main question before the Council being that the Anglo-Egyptian question constituted a threat to international peace, the Great Powers might have considered that Egypt, who bore the burden of provocation, did not have the military strength to back up her 'threats'. In this sense, the Council might have agreed with Sir Alexander Cadogan's argument that the issue was not a threat to peace. Consequently, although even certain British sources had admitted earlier that the Egyptian demands were 'reasonable',[1] and although the Council did, on the whole, express sympathy for Egyptian aspirations, members of the Council were well aware of the wishes of the Great Powers, who were not without vested interests in such cases as the Egyptian issues; partly for this reason, it would seem, the cosmopolitan Powers of the Council did not seriously consider complying with the Egyptian request. Further, the members of the Council, while conceding the right of the Sudanese to determine their own future, expressed lack of knowledge about the wishes of the Sudanese; without such knowledge, they suggested, the Council could not make any decision. But Sudanese delegates, representing the two major political parties in the Sudan, were available for consultation at Lake Success. This opportunity was conveniently ignored by the Council.

More often than not, discussions in the Security Council went on in

[1] *The Times*, 15 November 1945, p. 5.

the midst of mutual suspicions. None of the Great Powers could be committed without its own consent; this was ensured at the San Francisco Conference where all the Great Powers had insisted on the right of each to use the Veto in the Security Council on any issue except procedural questions. The smaller nations, like Egypt, regarded the Veto as a means of the protection of the interests of Colonial Powers. On the other hand, delegates of the Colonial Powers and the countries supporting them believed, as they still do, that the Anti-Colonial Campaign had already gone too far, and that it was high time that it should be restrained or stopped.[1] The frequent use of the Veto, rightly or otherwise, by either side of the 'Iron Curtain' intensified the friction between the two major power blocks in the Security Council. In a preamble to the Anglo-Egyptian talks after Egypt's appeal to the Security Council, the British Foreign Office complained that 'the use of the Veto in the Security Council had made it clear that 'the free nations of the world could no longer rely on the United Nations alone for its security'.[2] This mutual suspicion, though not openly expressed, was at work when the Sudan Case was under discussion in the Security Council, and it weakened the Council's ability to reach a unanimous decision.

Again, certain British and American commentators commend and support, quite justifiably, the legal approach of the British Government. But it should be remembered that the Security Council is *not* an impartial legal tribunal. By this we mean that it is composed of representatives of Governments; its members are *not*, unlike those of the Secretariat, required by the Charter 'not to seek or receive instructions from any Government or from any other source external to the Organisation'.[3] Even a senior legal counsellor of the United Nations Legal Department, Mr. Oscar Schachter, admits that: 'only rarely has the determination of legal rules been left to an impartial tribunal.'[4]

It could be argued that the Security Council had, by its indecision, upheld the legal obligation of treaties; much could be said for this view. If, as the Egyptian argument demanded, duress were accepted by the Council as a ground on which a treaty became void or voidable, the legal basis of peace would be in a constant state of uncertainty. In consequence, the 1936 Treaty could not be made voidable on the ground

---

[1] *New York Times*, 13 December 1952, p. 1.
[2] H.M.S.O., *Egypt No. 2* (1951), Cmd. 8419, p. 3.
[3] Article 100 of the Charter.
[4] 'The Development of International Law through the Legal Opinions of the United Nations', in the *British Year Book of International Law*, Vol. XXV, London, 1948, p. 93.

of duress. But there are weak points in the legalistic approach to such political issues as the Anglo-Egyptian dispute: ethically, it is questionable whether all promises should be kept—for instance, a promise to murder or even to marry for better or for worse. Hence, Paton's observation that 'No legal system enforces all promises as such.'[1]

The British argument rests, in the main, on the legal principle of '*Pacta sunt servanda*'. With this we have expressed agreement; nevertheless, the principle has a counterpart, equally forceful—'*Pacta quae turpem causam continent non sunt observanda*'—i.e. agreements founded on an immoral consideration may not be observed.[2] One other point is the apparent tradition or 'belief', as Dessauer calls this practice, that law is, in itself, necessary and sufficient to bring about desirable social results.

> But (that) it is not necessary in the international field as long as the great (Powers) agree and it is sufficient as they do not agree. . . . It is possible to police the small fry, who might break the law; but who can and will police the great . . . and prevent them from disturbing the peace.[3]

To a student of international politics the failure of the Security Council to agree on any resolution in the Egyptian question, might, therefore, be discouraging. Legal authority (on which the British delegation rested) without enough regard for political, social and even emotional realities might eventually condemn itself, in advance, to futility. This point is supported by the apparent and increasing ascendancy of the General Assembly over the Security Council of the United Nations as an effective world forum of public opinion.

Hypothetically, to leave the dispute to the two parties who had exhausted their resources for direct negotiation (Egypt informed the Council: 'We have spared no effort to settle this dispute before appealing to the Council')[4] appears to place a premium on power and might.

Nevertheless, the Security Council served some useful ends. The decision to adjourn the consideration of the Anglo-Egyptian question *sine die*—to leave it on the list of matters of which the Council was technically 'seized'—appears to have had some effects of restraint. It kept both parties under direct, though prolonged, negotiations while the time passed and passions cooled. One of the essential values of the

---

[1] Paton, G. W., *A Textbook on Jurisprudence*, 2nd ed., Oxford, 1951, p. 359.
[2] Weaton's *Law Lexicon*, 14th ed., 1938, p. 725.
[3] Dessauer, F. E., 'Peace and Law', in *International Journal*, Vol. II, Toronto, Winter, 1946, p. 52.
[4] *U.N. Security Council Records*, p. 1746.

United Nations is that it serves as a forum of world opinions, where disputants are often in view. In this market-place, no great power would risk asserting its sovereign will and expect a small power to cringe before it. Consequently, both Britain and Egypt had to talk openly before the Council. Whilst Britain's legal argument was not challenged, general sympathy for the Egyptian aspirations was expressed, and the Council as a whole did concede to the Sudanese the right to determine their own future. Thus, eventually, some agreement, ratified by both Britain and Egypt and acceptable to the Sudanese, was reached in 1953—six years after Egypt's appeal to the Council.

Part Four

THE FINAL STAGES OF THE DISPUTE AND THE RE-EMERGENCE OF THE SUDANESE, 1948-1956

12

THE BREAKDOWN OF RESUMED NEGOTIATIONS AND EGYPT'S UNILATERAL ABROGATION OF THE 1936 TREATY

> *The West's position in the Middle East has not been based on any real appreciation of Arab sovereignty and aspirations, but on the price of oil and fear of Russia. It was in essence imperialistic and strategic.*
>
> New Statesman and Nation, 1955[1]

> *Our greatest error would be to fashion our foreign policy merely in terms of anti-Communism. We will fail miserably if we do no more than that. For then we will end by failing and ranting at the spectre of Communism but do nothing to eliminate the conditions on which Communism thrives.*
>
> JUSTICE WILLIAM O. DOUGLAS, March 1948[2]

BOTH in Britain and Egypt the burdens of leadership took their toll in the passage of time after the appeal to the United Nations in 1947. In Egypt, failure to obtain satisfaction from the Security Council had hardened public opinion; it became more difficult, therefore, for Nokrashy Pasha and his cabinet to retreat from the position they took up at Lake Success. While the British Foreign Office accused Nokrashy Pasha of being intractable, the Opposition parties in Egypt attacked him for being 'too soft' with Britain. In Britain, Mr. Bevin was pressed to consider deposing Nokrashy Pasha (by intrigue) in the hope of substituting a more pliable Egyptian. But Bevin adhered to his policy of non-interference in Egypt's internal affairs.[3] In an editorial on British foreign policy, *The Times* observed in March 1948 that 'Mr. Bevin is treading softly' in the Middle East.[4] Later, in December, Nokrashy Pasha remarked: 'The trouble with you British is that you think the only good Egyptians are those who always do what you want.'[5]

However, Bevin's policy of non-interference paid, in the long run, a good dividend for Britain: the British did not have to get Nokrashy

---

[1] Editorial, London, 22 October 1955, p. 293.
[2] From the speech made at the University of Florida on 22 March 1948. See *New York Times*, 23 March 1948, p. 24.
[3] *The Times*, 30 March 1948, p. 3. [4] *Ibid.*, 4 May 1948, p. 4,
[5] *Ibid.*, 29 December 1948, p. 4,

Pasha out of the way. He was destroyed, ironically, by the poisonous elements in the nationalism of his own people. He had just arrived at the Ministry of the Interior soon after 10 o'clock on the morning of 28 December 1948, when a man dressed as a police officer fired five shots. The Pasha, Egypt's 'wisest statesman at a moment when mounting difficulties at home and abroad made his ability and experience of uncommon worth',[1] died almost immediately.

The alleged assassin, Abdel H. A. Hassan, was a 22-year-old veterinary student and a member of the Muslim Brotherhood, which Nokrashy Pasha's Cabinet had suppressed for extremist activities.[2]

Egyptians realized, it would seem, that it was time for stocktaking. The assassination of Nokrashy Pasha increased the list of the Egyptians who had lost their lives, directly or obliquely, in the tangled web of the Anglo-Egyptian dispute. During the previous three years there had been too much heat in Egyptian feeling over the Sudan question. But the British position remained firmly established. Failing to make life effectively uncomfortable for Britain in the Nile Valley, Egypt became, in 1949, relatively calm and ready, once more, to talk with Britain. As a gesture, King Farouk invited Mr. Bevin to dinner at his Palace, on the latter's return through Cairo from a conference of the Commonwealth Prime Ministers in Colombo. Britain was touched by Egypt's gesture, and Bevin accepted. But Britain had to see the issues of the Nile Valley in the light of her wider world problems and strategy. Bevin, British Foreign Minister from 1945 to 1950, 'considered every problem in its world setting'.[3] In the event, neither Bevin himself nor Mr. Morrison, his successor, could respond satisfactorily to Egyptian overtures.[4] We shall endeavour, therefore, to set forth briefly some of the world problems which had such repercussions on the Anglo-Egyptian question from 1948 to 1951.

Before the Second World War, Britain's international status rested partly on her position as a balancing power in Europe and partly upon the authority which she could exercise as the centre of a vast Commonwealth and Empire. After the war, however, the basis of a European balance of power became dislocated by the elimination of Germany and the decline of France. Only the Soviet Union, committed to the ideology

---

[1] *The Times*, 29 December 1948, 'Egypt's Loss', p. 5c.
[2] Incidentally, Nokrashy Pasha had been himself arrested and kept in detention, but later discharged, for the murder of Sir Lee Stack, in 1924.
[3] *The Times*, 24 February 1950.
[4] Mr. Herbert Morrison, Foreign Secretary, in the House of Commons, 16 April 1951, *Parliamentary Debates*, Vol. CCCCLXXXVI, p. 1470.

of Communism, remained as a great land power in Europe. It was a time in which, under the impact of Communism, the countries of Western Europe welded themselves together, as never before in peace time: first, Western Union[1] and, subsequently, the Atlantic Pact[2] were set up. America's Marshall Plan sustained Western Europe economically. Nevertheless Britain, faced with the dollar crisis and the consequent devaluation of the pound, remained relatively weak and her dependence on Africa remained essential. The success of Communism in China increased the struggle of the major Powers for men's minds in Asia and Africa—Egypt and the Sudan included. Sentiments publicly expressed by the principal Powers were invariably distrustful and even hostile on both sides of the Capitalist and Communist worlds. In the Middle East, the reliance of the Western Powers on the oil from that area was increasing. The feeling of the Arab-League peoples against the Western bloc was exacerbated by the emergence of a new Israel in full statehood; in the eyes of the Arabs, of whom Egypt was head, the state of Israel was nourished by the West and at the expense of the Arabs. In Africa, it was a period in which Britain and France were beset with African nationalism expressed in various forms—passive resistance against apartheid in South Africa; political insurgence in Kenya (Mau Mau); animosity against the British policy in the Seretse Khama case in Bechuanaland; the demand for home rule in West Africa; and insurrections in French North Africa. In the Nile Valley, a palace revolution was being plotted against King Farouk in Egypt, and debates on self-government by 1956 had been started in the Sudan in 1949.[3]

In this context, Anglo-Egyptian negotiations were reopened, broken off and reopened again. Faced with the world situation which we have attempted to describe, the 'defence of Western economy and civilization ... was now the ostensible or underlying motive of all the external activities of the United Kingdom and its friends'.[4] It is not surprising, therefore, that a British memorandum on the Sudan and Suez question declared: 'Britain, upon whom rested the responsibility for the defence of the Middle East, could not contemplate any solution of the Egyptian question which laid that area open to aggression.'[5]

[1] H.M.S.O., *Miscellaneous No. 1* (1950), Cmd. 7868.
[2] H.M.S.O., *Treaty Series, No. 56* (1951), Cmd. 7789.
[3] *Report on the Administration of the Sudan for the Year*, 1949, Cmd. 8434, p. 9.
[4] *The Annual Register* for 1950, chapter on 'Overseas Responsibilities', London, 1951, p. 39.
[5] *Anglo-Egyptian Conversations on the Defence of the Suez Canal and on the Sudan*, Egypt No. 2 (1951), Cmd. 8419, p. 4.

With this as a background, we must now proceed to deal with the broad details of the Anglo-Egyptian encounters: firstly, Constitutional changes within the Sudan itself (1947–8); secondly, the official talks on the Defence of the Suez Canal and on the future of the Sudan (December 1950 to November 1951); and thirdly, the unilateral abrogation of the 1936 Treaty by Egypt.

1. PROPOSALS FOR CONSTITUTIONAL REFORMS IN THE SUDAN: 1947–48

At Lake Success, Britain and Egypt had failed to agree on the future of the Sudan. But it was felt in Britain that if the two countries could agree upon the practical question of a constitutional reform in the Sudan, the ultimate decision about the political status of the country might conveniently be left to the future. Consequently, the two Governments exchanged from 1947 to 1948 proposals to that end. Before dealing with the 1947–8 Constitutional reforms, however, we should briefly acquaint the reader with the evolution of Sudanese participation in the administration of their country.

In 1922, the idea of associating the Sudanese people with the central government of their country was mooted, but abandoned on the plea that 'there were not enough natives of the Sudan at the time with a sufficiently objective outlook'.[1] Under the impact of agitation by certain Sudanese, the issue continued to be raised from time to time until 1944 when an Advisory Council with some nominated Sudanese was established for the Northern Sudan; the Southern Sudan was *not* associated with the North and Southern Sudanese were *not* represented on the Council. The pro-Egyptian parties boycotted the Council for fear of becoming British stooges: but it was accepted by the Umma Party, apparently in the hope that collaboration with the British-controlled Sudan Government would eventually bring about self-government for the country. Urged by the Sudanese elements in the Advisory Council, the Governor-General set up, in 1946, an administration Conference, with a Sudanese majority, to make suggestions on further constitutional progress. Consequently, on 29 July 1947, just a week before Egypt's complaint against Britain came before the Security Council, the British Governor-General accepted the recommendations of the Conference 'at which all Sudanese parties were represented'[2]; first, that the Advisory Council for the Northern Sudan should be superseded by a Legislative Assembly, representative of the whole country—both North

---

[1] The Sudan (British) Govt., *The Sudan—A Record of Progress, 1898–1947*, p. 11.
[2] Central Office of Information, *The Sudan, 1899–1953*, p. 16.

and South; and then, that from this Assembly, Sudanese Under-Secretaries should be included in the Governor-General's Executive Council.

The recommendations were formally presented to the British and Egyptian Governments. Britain accepted them *in toto*. But Egypt submitted counter-proposals to the effect that Egypt should be represented on the Executive Council; that full electoral rights should be given forthwith to the whole population of the Sudan, instead of the limited franchise; and that the wide powers reserved to the (British) Governor-General should be curtailed, those of the Legislative Assembly extended and the right of veto granted to the Egyptian Government.

At the root of Egyptian proposals lay Egypt's perpetual fear that the Sudan Government's scheme might perpetuate British control over the Sudan, whilst further weakening Egyptian influence. But, in defence of the British case, *The Times* explained, in a leading article, that the proposed powers of the British Governor-General were 'powers which are, in fact, a familiar balancing factor in the transition from Colonial rule to Self-Government'.[1] In Egypt, on the other hand, *Al Ahram* described, rather sarcastically, the Governor-General of the Sudan as: 'His Majesty Robert Howe I, King of the Northern Sudan, the Southern Sudan and the Bahr-ul-Ghazal.'[2] British distrust of the Egyptian proposals was expressed by *The Times*, which commented that Egypt's amendments were calculated to appeal to the educated classes and that the Egyptians were making 'an attempt to outbid Britain for the support of those Sudanese who are eager to obtain a share of immediate political power'.[3]

No agreement was reached, but under the leadership of the British Ambassador in Cairo (Sir Ronald Campbell) and the Egyptian Foreign Minister (Ahmad Muhammad Khashaba) an Anglo-Egyptian Committee was set up on 10 May 1948. The Committee agreed on five main points. They were a tripartite Anglo-Egyptian Sudanese Committee to be set up to supervise the progress of the Sudanese towards self-government; an Anglo-Egyptian Committee to supervise the elections to the Legislative Assembly; inclusion in the Executive Council of two Egyptians from the Egyptian officials serving in the Sudan; the Senior Staff Officer of the Egyptian forces in the Sudan to attend all meetings of the Executive Council when defence matters were being discussed;

[1] *The Times*, 4 March 1948, p. 5c.
[2] *La Bourse Egyptienne*, Cairo, 28 February 1948.
[3] *The Times*, 9 January 1948, p. 5c.

and the administrative machinery, then in operation, to continue for three years, subject to renewal.[1]

In Egypt, the Senate Foreign Affairs Committee, to which the Campbell-Khashaba protocol had been referred, reported back on 5 June; they considered the draft agreement unacceptable to Egypt. The reasons given were, among others, that acceptance of the proposals would have made Egypt a laughing-stock, because they were in essence a continuation of the Condominium which had been repeatedly condemned by the Egyptian people; that the draft agreement overlooked the fundamental principle of the Unity of Egypt and the Sudan under the Egyptian Crown; that it would consolidate and even increase the powers of the British Governor-General of the Sudan; that it would, moreover, imply that Egypt had given Constitutional power to the British Governor-General and not to the King of Egypt and the Sudan; that Egyptian participation would be limited to two members only on the Executive Council (maximum membership eighteen); and that Sudanese participation in the administration of their country would still be inadequate compared with the powers of the Governor-General.[2]

The Commission's attitude was made public, but before receiving any official communication from the Egyptian Government, the British Under-Secretary for Foreign Affairs, Mr. Christopher Mayhew, ostensibly lost patience and announced on 14 June:

> We have received no answer from them regarding their willingness to co-operate in the proposed reforms on the basis of the proposals of the Governor-General. His Majesty's Government therefore feel that they can no longer stand in the way of the Governor-General doing as he thinks fit regarding the promulgation of the Ordinance in accordance with his duties and obligations for the good government of the Sudan under the Agreement of 1899.[3]

Whilst Egyptians interpreted the constitutional proposals as part and parcel of the question of the political future of the Sudan, the British Government attempted to draw a distinction: 'I would like to emphasise', continued the Under-Secretary, 'that these negotiations covered only the practical question of the proposed Ordinance and were never intended to reconcile the conflicting views regarding the status of the Sudan on which both Governments have previously and publicly reserved their position.'[4]

[1] *The Times*, Cairo correspondent, 7 June 1948.
[2] Royal Institute of International Affairs, *The World Today*, Chronology and Documents, Vol. IV, No. 12, London, 4–17 June 1948, p. 399.
[3] *Parliamentary Debates*, 14 June, pp. 20–1.   [4] *Ibid.*

While the Egyptian Cabinet were yet to consider the Report of their Foreign Affairs Commission, the Ordinance was officially promulgated in the Sudan,[1] five days after the announcement of the British Government.

This Ordinance had divers effects. In the Sudan, the Anglo-Egyptian debates increased political consciousness. Miss Margery Perham, who witnessed the Sudanese excitement at this time, recorded her impressions: 'In the towns, it is politics all day long, over every drink and meal in the clubs and schools and coffee shops.'[2] In the final analysis, the Ordinance increased the participation of the Sudanese in the Administration and paved the way for the first Sudanese Parliament five years later (1953). However, its immediate effect was somehow adverse. The disagreement between the two condomini caused a split in the 'personality' of the Sudan—a disunity within the country; one sector being for independence through collaboration with the British, the other working for it through Egypt. Four thousand people were involved in demonstrations organized by the pro-Egyptian Sudanese National Front during the subsequent elections which took place on 15 November 1948. In the clashes between rival parties, a few lives were lost and certain Sudanese, amongst them Mr. Mohammed Nureddin, Vice-President of the pro-Egyptian Ashigga Party and Manager of the National Bank of Egypt, Khartoum, were imprisoned for their part in an 'illegal demonstration during the Sudan elections'.[3] Whilst the pro-Egyptian unity parties declined on principle to recognize the Legislative Assembly, the pro-British Umma Party gave it full support and Abdulla Bey Khalil, General Secretary of the Umma and formerly a military officer under the British Administration, became the leader of the Legislative Assembly.

In Egypt, the Government took Britain's unilateral action in this matter as a display of *contemptuous indifference* to the views and feelings of a joint partner in the Sudan venture. The promulgation of the Ordinance without Egypt's consent was timed to coincide with the fiftieth anniversaries of the Battle of Omdurman and of the Condominium, which were celebrated in London by pointing to the importance of the Sudan to Britain and praising British achievements in the country—

---

[1] For text of the Executive Council and Legislative Assembly Ordinance, 1948, see Egyptian Society of International Law, *Documents on the Sudan, 1899–1953*, Cairo, March 1953, pp. 12–33.

[2] 'Frustration of Anglo-Egyptian Deadlock', *The Times*, 3 May 1948, p. 5.

[3] *The Times* Khartoum correspondent, 4 December 1948, p. 3d. See also *ibid.*, 15 November 1948, p. 4b.

'Britain's record in the Sudan is one in which she is entitled to take pride'.[1] It is no surprise, therefore, that the unilateral promulgation of the Ordinance became one of the Egyptian grievances which culminated in the abrogation of the Anglo-Egyptian agreement of the 1936 Treaty, three years after the Ordinance.

The Conversations on the Defence of the Suez Canal and on the Sudan (December 1950 to November 1951). We have, at the beginning of this chapter, broadly indicated the prevailing winds affecting the climate of world politics since the Second World War, which in the background, influenced the Sudan question. But we must emphasize here those world events which somehow increased the number of stumbling blocks to any Anglo-Egyptian agreement over the conversations in 1950 and 1951. During the years 1949–51, the conflict between the Soviet Union and the Western Powers, which had become manifest in 1946, continued to dominate the world scene. The cause of this conflict was, in the words of Professor Toynbee, 'not greed but fear'.[2] As a child of this fear, the North Atlantic Treaty with which Britain hoped to associate Egypt and other Middle East countries, was born on 4 April 1949. On 25 June 1950, war broke out in Korea between the Communist North and the Capitalist South; this continued as a dominant motif in the politics of the Western Powers in 1951. Because of the vital importance of the Middle East to the Anglo-Saxon Powers, especially on account of its oil and lines of communication, the Western Powers, driven by fear of the Korean incident, made determined efforts to protect their interests in the Middle East by the formation of a defensive alliance. Consequently, on 13 October 1951, the British Ambassador in Egypt presented the Four Power[3] proposals for Egyptian participation in a Middle East Command.[4] The influence on the Sudan Question of the anxieties of the Western Powers about their position *vis-à-vis* the Soviet Union was great and direct; Britain declined the supersession of the 1936 Treaty unless Egypt was 'prepared to co-operate fully in the Allied Command Organisation'.[5] Egypt, on the other hand, while not actually hostile, was together with the other Arab States suspicious of the Western Powers and was not so much impressed by any Russian menace. In fact, the Egyptian journal, *Al Misri*, which often expressed the view of

---

[1] 'Anniversary of Omdurman—50 Peaceful Years', in *The Times*, 2 September 1948, p. 3.

[2] *Survey of International Affairs*, 1949–50, p. 1.

[3] Britain, France, Turkey and the United States.

[4] *Anglo-Egyptian Conversation on the Defence of the Suez and on the Sudan*, Cmd. 8419, p. 43.

[5] *Ibid.*, p. 44.

the Government, distrusted the Western bloc and the Soviet bloc alike —both were equally a tyrant and a colonizer.[1] Consequently, the Egyptian Government aimed at neutrality between the two blocs and was not prepared to co-operate fully with the Allied Command Organization, which might lead to consequences more formidable than those of the Anglo-Egyptian Treaty of 1936. Along with these factors was the birth of Israel as a new nation mothered by Britain and the United States, but resented by the Arab states. From these prevailing winds, with so many cyclones and anti-cyclones, blew the air permeating the various conference rooms in which the Anglo-Egyptian conversations took place in 1950 and 1951 to revise the 1936 Treaty.

2. RESUMED NEGOTIATIONS AS RECOMMENDED BY THE SECURITY COUNCIL

The 1936 Treaty of Friendship and Alliance was concluded with Britain by the Wafd regime under Nahas Pasha. Nahas Pasha was also in power from 1942 to 1944, when he collaborated with the British in putting into effect the operative clauses of the Treaty against the Axis powers. It is understandable, therefore, that the return to power of Nahas Pasha with his Party in 1950 should have been hailed in Britain as evidence of better prospects in Anglo-Egyptian relations.

But the optimism in Britain seemed to overlook the new factors with which Nahas Pasha's Cabinet had to reckon. In the first place, the Coalition Governments (Saadist-Liberal) with which Britain negotiated on the issues of the Sudan from 1945 to 1950, left no stone unturned to advance Egyptian interests. With the collapse of the Bevin-Sidky Sudan Protocol, Sidky Pasha had died, partly of frustration. Because settlement with Britain eluded him in 1946, Nokrashy Pasha had arraigned Britain before the Security Council in 1947, 'but with no tangible benefit to Egypt'.[2] In spite of all the Egyptian efforts, the union of the Sudan with Egypt, which the Egyptians desired, remained unfulfilled and the Egyptian Press and politicians continued in their general accusation that Britain was preventing that union at all costs. In the second place, Nahas Pasha's new regime had to face informed public opinion in Egypt, which was well aware of Britain's post-war plans in the Sudan and the Middle East.

In February, soon after the British Foreign Secretary (Mr. Bevin) had dined in Cairo with King Farouk, Nahas Pasha and the Egyptian

---

[1] For full quotation, see *Egyptian Gazette*, 30 May 1950.
[2] *The Times*, 24 February 1950, p. 7f.

Foreign Minister, on Mr. Bevin's way back from the Colombo Conference, the Government organ, *Al Misri* commented on the Sudan:

> Egypt is not in need of the cotton of the Gezira, to suck the blood of the Sudanese for it as Britain does. Nor is Egypt in need of other Sudanese resources to exploit them for its own benefit. Egypt is only intent on securing its water resources in the upper reaches of the Nile and forcing a foreign country out of political and military positions which may adversely affect Egypt in the future.[1]

In the third place, although when the Treaty of Alliance and Friendship was signed in 1936 'Nahas Pasha and other leading Egyptian statesmen were warm in its praise', as the British Foreign Office correctly pointed out, later, in 1950,[2] Nahas Pasha accepted and signed it only provisionally. He had told the Egyptian Chamber of Deputies, on 14 November 1936:

> But this situation is only provisional and we have the possibility of arming ourselves and arriving at a state which will allow us to undertake the protection of the Canal with our own resources. . . . Our territory will therefore be evacuated either by an agreement between us or by arbitration.[3]

We should not be surprised, therefore, that in the Speech from the Throne soon after the 1950 elections, the Wafdist Government referred to the issue of the Sudan in Anglo-Egyptian relations in the following terms:

> The nation without exception has proclaimed the necessity of liberating our Valley, both *Egypt and the Sudan*, of any restrictions on its liberty and independence; so that it may regain its past glory and assume a worthy place in the concert of nations.
>
> My Government will spare no effort to hasten the evacuation of the two parts of the Valley and to protect their Unity under the Egyptian Crown against any encroachment or aggression.[4]

In March 1950, the Egyptian Foreign Minister (Mohammed Salah Eddin Bey) addressed an official Note to the British Foreign Secretary (Mr. Ernest Bevin), quoting the Speech from the Throne and proposing talks between the two Governments with a view to settling the political issues between their two countries and to reaching 'a practical settlement which would ensure the complete independence of Egypt and the Sudan as one integral whole'.

[1] Quoted in the *Egyptian Gazette*, Cairo, 15 February 1950.
[2] Cmd. 8419, *op. cit.*, Appendix A, p. 7.   [3] *Ibid.*
[4] Egyptian Govt.—Ministry of Foreign Affairs, *Records of Conversations, Notes and Papers exchanged between the Royal Egyptian Government and the United Kingdom Government*, Cairo, 1951, pp. 3–4.

Mr. Bevin replied on 17 May: he shared the Egyptian Government's expressed desire to strengthen its relations of cordiality and good understanding with all countries on the basis of equality, mutual interest and respect within the Charter of the United Nations. He felt that it was highly desirable that both parties should reach an understanding based on mutual trust and confidence. With that in view he would, at that stage, send the Chief of the Imperial General Staff, Field-Marshal Sir William Slim to 'have completely frank and informal discussion with the Egyptian Government on the military aspects in this problem before us in the Middle East'.[1] Sir Ralph Stevenson would take up the political aspects of the case, on reaching Cairo as British Ambassador in Egypt.

The Egyptian Government agreed, expressing a desire to welcome 'everyone whom the British delegate, whether civilian or military'.[2] The conversations began on Monday, 5 June 1950, between Moustafa El Nahas Pasha, President of the Egyptian Council of Ministers and Field-Marshal Sir William Slim.

In certain instances, the official conversations repeated the arguments with which we are already familiar. In other respects, however, they put new interpretations and throw more light on the viewpoint of each of the disputants. At the end of the conversations, the British Foreign Secretary said that both sides understood each other better as a result of the talks 'which had proved extremely illuminating'.[3] We therefore consider it helpful to present a summary of the official dialogues.

The problem of the Sudan was involved in Britain's military strategy in the Middle East. Sir William Slim endeavoured to persuade the Egyptian Government to accept a new interpretation of military occupation on the ground that no nation could stand alone: all had to be united and march together politically, militarily and economically—an uneasy task, because all had to give up some of their cherished rights and traditions. The British had accepted the presence of American troops and American bases in England. Britain had agreed that her troops in Germany should be under French command, just as the French, Dutch and Belgians agreed to place their troops under foreign command. Egypt could not defend herself; neither could England; and that was not a disgrace. The presence of British troops in the Nile Valley meant not occupation but allied co-operation and defence, explained Field-Marshal Slim.

Nahas Pasha pointed out that the Egyptians had suffered much from

[1] Egyptian Govt., Ministry of Foreign Affairs, *op. cit.*, pp. 3–4.   [2] *Ibid.*, p. 6.
[3] British Foreign Office, *Egypt No. 2* (1951), Cmd. 8419, p. 23.

the repeated experiences of the past; they were angry and resentful and could not depend on new promises or accept new conceptions of military occupation the result of which would not differ from that of the past. With respect to the analogy between Egypt and Britain concerning the presence of foreign troops, if Britain asked the American forces to leave, they would do so; the presence of American troops did not prejudice the sovereignty of Britain, because of the co-equality of the two states. Also, the situation in Britain was temporary and necessitated by an emergency; but in Egypt it was a continuation of sixty years of occupation.

On 8 July 1950, Sir Ralph Stevenson, British Ambassador, began talks with the Egyptian Foreign Minister and admitted that 'I fully agree that during our relation with Egypt in the past fifty years things were far from satisfactory.'[1] On the question of the unity of the Sudan and Egypt under the Egyptian Crown, nobody could separate the two countries living on the same river unless the Egyptians themselves did so by antagonizing the Sudanese.[2] However, as a result of fifty years' administration the British had a responsibility towards the Sudanese 'and we cannot divest ourselves of it whatever the legal, historical or even moral considerations may be'.[3] The Sudanese, in his opinion, could not yet govern themselves. The Egyptian demand for evacuation was unpractical, as there was not a sufficient number of Egyptians to replace the British should the latter leave the Sudan.

The Egyptian Foreign Minister submitted that the Sudan was more qualified for self-government than Libya, to which the United Nations had granted independence with effect from 1952. Britain was not guided, he was sure, by the will of the Sudanese or British obligations towards them, but by considered and premeditated imperialistic policy. The British Administration had kept the southern part of the Sudan in a backward condition to serve as an argument for delaying the progress of the Sudanese towards self-government or separating the south from the north; in the same way the British Government were trying hard to separate the whole Sudan from Egypt. Salah Eddin Bey continued: 'I am afraid that this purpose was planned by you for Egypt and the Sudan from the very beginning, otherwise fifty years would

---

[1] Egyptian Govt., Ministry of Foreign Affairs, *op. cit.*, p. 23.
[2] Sir Ralph Stevenson's observation was prophetic. In the 1953–4 election, the pro-Egyptian Party supporting the Unity of the Nile Valley won the elections. But the personality and policy of Major Salah Salem, in Egypt, antagonized the Sudanese so much that for this among other reasons they declared their independence in the summer of 1955.
[3] *Ibid.*, p. 70.

have been enough, indeed more than enough, for the Sudan to become independent and for you to be relieved of your obligations *vis-à-vis* the Sudanese.'[1]

During the meeting of the General Assembly of the United Nations in September 1950, the Egyptian Foreign Minister (Salah Eddin Bey) took advantage of the British Foreign Secretary's presence (Mr. Bevin) in New York to meet him about the Anglo-Egyptian issue. They met at the Waldorf-Astoria, New York, on 28 September. There was not enough time to discuss the Sudan Question in detail. But the Egyptian Foreign Minister, anxious for a settlement, followed up the matter and met the Secretary of State at the Foreign Office, London, on 4 December 1950 and discussion continued till 15 December. Here Salah Eddin Bey submitted that the Sudan Question depended for support not only on legal and natural rights but also on the will of the Sudanese, the majority of whom maintained, with Egypt, the ideal of the unity of Egypt and the Sudan. The will of the Sudanese, he said, was demonstrated by the election results of the Graduates Congress—the sophisticated elements in the Sudan—which supported the unity of the Nile Valley; by the municipal elections, which even though influenced by the Sudan Government, supported Egypt's viewpoint; by the boycotting of the General Assembly's election by the Unionists—the proportion of those participating did not exceed 2 per cent of the electorate; and by the most important and largest religious sects in the Sudan which supported the unity of Egypt and the Sudan. Britain, therefore, had no right to build her argument on the will of the Sudanese and to claim that she championed their interests. He declared, with apparent loss of temper:

> You keep reiterating the slogan of self-government and self-determination for the Sudanese, but when we ask you whether you are prepared to agree that a Sudanese democratic government depending upon a truly representative assembly be forthwith established, and that the present administration hand over power to this government, you try to find excuses, just as H.E. the British Ambassador did, by replying that the Sudanese are not yet mature enough for self-government. And if we ask you when in your estimation they would be mature enough for this state, you give a period of 10 to 15 years. Again, if we offer as an analogy the case of Libya, which the United Nations had found worthy of independence and self-government within a period of two years terminating in January 1952, you contended that the Sudanese have not attained the same degree of progress as the Libyans, notwithstanding the cruel condemnation of your administration over 50 years in the Sudan, which this contention seems to imply.[2]

---

[1] Egyptian Govt., Ministry of Foreign Affairs, *op. cit.*, p. 71.
[2] Ministry of Foreign Affairs, *op. cit.*, p. 93.

Mr. Bevin, with apparent calmness, agreed that the Graduates Congress and the other elements mentioned supported unity with Egypt but that, according to his own information, all the supporters taken together were a minority of the Sudanese people. The core of the Sudan problem was the granting of self-government to the Sudanese; this was largely a matter of timing. He went on: 'Both our Governments have a duty to discharge in this matter. If, setting aside our mutual suspicion, we can work together to solve this problem, we shall have achieved a great work.'[1]

Mr. Bevin concluded the talks with an expression of gratitude to Salah Eddin Bey for making the visit to London. He felt that both sides understood each other better as a result of their present conversations, which had proved very illuminating. While suggestions were being studied, he would see to it that the British Press did not give undue attention to Anglo-Egyptian relations and he hoped that in Egypt also everything would be done to create a favourable atmosphere.

At the end of their meeting on 15 December 1950, a joint statement was made in this vein:

> The discussions between the Egyptian Minister of Foreign Affairs and Mr. Bevin on the main problems affecting Anglo-Egyptian relations have been proceeding in a friendly and co-operative spirit and have resulted in a most useful exchange of ideas.

There was delay in the resumption of talks owing to many reasons. There were the increasing complexities of the wider international situation with which Britain had to cope. Mr. Morrison explained later, in the House of Commons, that the quarrel between Britain and Egypt was no longer a purely Anglo-Egyptian problem, 'We are a Power, bearing responsibility in the Middle East on behalf of the rest of the Commonwealth and the Western Allies as a whole'.[2] There was the breakdown in the health of Mr. Bevin and the need of his successor in the conduct of foreign affairs, Mr. Herbert Morrison, to familiarize himself with the details and consider all the implications of the Anglo-Egyptian problem. But in a personal message to Salah Eddin Bey, on 24 March 1951, Mr. Morrison explained his difficulties and expressed the hope that the Egyptian Government would not consider it unreasonable 'if I am not in a position to make any communication to the

---

[1] *Ibid.*, p. 102.
[2] Foreign Affairs Middle East, *Parliamentary Debates*, Vol. CCCCXCI, 30 October 1951, p. 973.

Egyptian Government until April'.[1] Further, the position of the Labour Government with regard to Egypt was weakened during their second term of office by opposition both from the right-wing Conservative members and from a group of Labour members who were eager to support the new state of Israel but seemed indifferent to the effect which their support could have on Anglo-Egyptian relations. Lastly, there was the need to summon the British Ambassador in Cairo to London for consultation about the Egyptian Question.

Anxious about this delay, Salah Eddin Bey sent a note to Mr. Morrison on 27 May 1951, remarking that the discussions had lasted longer than necessary and that they should be brought to a definite conclusion at the earliest opportunity, in the interests of both parties.[2]

Further conversation did not occur until 11 April 1951—this time in Cairo—between the British Ambassador and the Egyptian Foreign Minister. The British Ambassador submitted a statement from his Government to the effect—in so far as the Sudan is concerned—showing that it was the aim of the British Government to enable the Sudanese to attain self-government at the earliest practicable opportunity, that it would be impossible to accept any undertaking with Egypt which interfered with that objective, and that discussions of defence must take priority over that of the Sudan.

The Egyptian Government felt frustrated and expressed regret and bitter disappointment at the British reply, 'after long discussions lasting ten months during which the Egyptian side has spared no effort to explain and support its rights and to meet all the considerations with which the British side was concerned in a manner which would not be inconsistent with Egypt's rights'.[3]

The Egyptian Government rejected the British proposals *in toto* and put forward, as a basis of negotiation, counter-proposals four of which directly concerned the Sudan: first, the unity of the Sudan under the Egyptian Crown and self-government for the Sudanese, within two years, within the framework of such unity; second, withdrawal of British troops and officials from the Sudan, with the termination of the present regime in the Sudan, immediately at the end of those two years; third, an agreement between Britain and Egypt for British forces to return to places mutually accepted, if and when considered necessary

---

[1] Message from Mr. Morrison to Salah Eddin Bey, in Ministry of Foreign Affairs, *op. cit.*, p. 106.

[2] *Parliamentary Debates*, Vol. CCCCXCI, 30 July 1940, p. 107.

[3] Record of Conversation between H.E. the Minister of Foreign Affairs and H.E. the British Ambassador, on 24 April 1951—Ministry of Foreign Affairs, *op. cit.*, p. 111.

by the two parties, in the event of armed aggression; and lastly the immediate abrogation, upon the new agreement coming into force, of the 1936 Treaty, and of the two Condominium Agreements of 1899.

The British Ambassador commented that the evacuation of British officials from the Sudan in two years was impracticable, for 'the Sudan cannot get on without the British officials', and in any case he could not open discussions on the Sudan until he was authorized to do so by his Government. Meanwhile, the Egyptian proposals would receive the immediate attention of the British Government.

Conversations, proposals and counter-proposals continued in June and July, but no agreement was reached. However, the diplomatic chess continued. Mr. Morrison made a statement in the House of Commons on 30 July, informing the House that the future of the Sudan was being discussed with Egypt. He prefaced his statement on the Sudan with one on the British problems in the Middle East: Egypt was the key to the Middle East and it was nothing but a delusion, he went on, for Egypt to pretend that she could stand aside in the event of any major conflict between the Western Powers and the Soviet bloc. He realized that the stand taken by Egypt had its roots deep in the past, but 'we have tried to take in account of that fact; unfortunately, our patience and understanding have not always been reciprocated and we are still faced with uncompromising insistence on demands which bear no relation to present-day realities.'[1]

In the Sudan Question, he complained: 'We are faced with certain prejudices which prevent the Egyptian Government from approaching the problem in a realistic frame of mind.'[2] He accepted the fact that the mutual dependence on the Nile linked the destinies of Egypt and the Sudan; in due course, the Sudanese would choose the form of relationship with Egypt which best fulfilled their needs. In conclusion, he warned the Egyptians who asked for unity of the Nile Valley without appreciating the distinction between the Sudanese people and the Egyptian people.

The Foreign Minister told the Chamber of Deputies on 6 August that the possibility that the rivalries between the powers might explode into another world war should not justify Britain in asking Egypt to tolerate indefinitely a violation of her independence and interests. The possibility of another war was, according to him, mere speculation. 'Indeed, it will

---

[1] *Parliamentary Debates*, Foreign Affairs (Middle East), 30 July 1951, Vol. CCCCXCI, pp. 972–3.
[2] *Ibid.*, p. 974.

never materialise . . . if each major power respects the sovereignty and territorial integrity of smaller and weaker nations, thus setting a good example of international conduct regardless of actions taken by others.' The Egyptian Government, he maintained, were within their international rights when they gave warning, in the Speech from the Throne, about abrogating the 1936 Treaty. Referring to Mr. Morrison's statement in Parliament which we have cited, Salah Eddin Bey inferred: 'The British Secretary for Foreign Affairs has closed the door for current talks between the two Governments in his recent statement before the Commons.'[1] As to the next step to be taken because of this impasse, he announced that the Ministerial Political Committee would decide.

3. THE ABROGATION OF THE CONDOMINIUM AGREEMENT AND OF THE TREATY OF 1936

Thus, the die was cast. To save the situation, Mr. Morrison sent a personal message, delivered by the British Embassy on 17 August, to Salah Eddin Bey, assuring him of his wish to reach a settlement; he was going on a short holiday but intended to take advantage of it to consider further a new approach.[2] But simultaneously with Mr. Morrison's message, the British Embassy in Alexandria issued a Press statement defending Mr. Morrison's statement in Parliament. This step counteracted the effect of Mr. Morrison's personal message. It led to a counter Press statement by the Egyptian Embassy in London, commenting that Mr. Morrison's speech confirmed the British Government's insistence on the denial of the Unity of Egypt and the Sudan; the statement 'came as an overt conclusion of the long and arduous discussions between the two Governments lasting over fifteen months . . . during which the Egyptian Government spared no effort to reconcile British interests to Egypt's rights . . .'[3]

On 26 August 1951, the President of the Council of Ministers, Mustafa El Nahas Pasha, commented in a Note to the British Government that it was impossible to go on indefinitely with the Anglo-Egyptian talks which had begun in July 1950, without a glimpse of hope towards reaching the designed agreement. Indeed, these talks were no more than a further link in the chain of attempts made in vain by Egypt since the end of World War II. While the British Government lost nothing by long procrastination, he concluded, it was extremely diffi-

---

[1] Ministry of Foreign Affairs, *op. cit.*, p. 148.
[2] Full text in *ibid.*, p. 156.
[3] *The Times*, 23 August 1951, p. 5e.

cult for the Egyptian Government and people to continue in that state of affairs.

The British Government were well aware of the mood in Egypt; but they were pre-occupied with wider issues in the world and problems at home, which turned their minds away from the Egyptian Question. In any case, Britain's position was well established in the Sudan. She was confident in the awareness of the fact that Egypt did not possess enough power (military strength) to force her out of the Nile Valley. The British military experts calculated that 'any attempt to expel us by force would, in fact, play into our hands, as it not only would put the Egyptians in the wrong, but would justify us in taking any more steps necessary to ensure the maintenance of our position in the country'.[1] With little or no qualms, therefore, the British Government temporarily shelved the Egyptian Note and went on with more pressing issues at home and abroad; among these were a visit by the American, British and French Chiefs of Staff to Ankara to discuss Turkey's role in the proposed Middle East Command, in which the four Powers would soon ask Egypt to participate;[2] a similar meeting in London by the British Commonwealth Chiefs of Staff about their own part in the Middle East Command, in which they hopefully included Egypt and the Sudan. Then came the dissolution of Parliament. The Labour Government, from which the Egyptians had hoped to secure a fair deal, had been handicapped by the precariousness of its majority in Parliament, by the strain imposed on its leaders during the six harassing years and by the illness and death of Ernest Bevin, Foreign Secretary from 1945 until March 1951; the Labour Cabinets had faced the onset of the severest of Britain's series of financial crises (which had led to the devaluation of the English pound); in the midst of these they had worked passionately to build a 'welfare state'. Consequently Mr. Attlee, worn and weary, had obtained the Royal assent to the dissolution of Parliament, and preparations began for a general election, all of which drew away any serious attention from the Egyptian Question in September and October. Above all, the tide of world tensions had risen considerably, and caused a set-back in British policy in Egypt. British interests and objectives were such at this time as to make Britain shrink from designing a solution acceptable to Egypt. In a preface to the official document concerning 'Anglo-Egyptian Conversations on the

[1] Air Vice-Marshal Yool, W. M., in *The Spectator*, No. 6434, London, 19 October 1951, p. 498.
[2] See 'The Four Power Proposals of the 13th October, 1951, concerning Egyptian Participation in a Middle East Command', in *Egypt No. 2* (1951), Cmd. 8419, p. 43.

Defence of the Suez Canal and on the Sudan', the British Foreign Office in London explained their difficulties:

> The world situation had changed. Soviet use of the veto in the Security Council had made it clear that the free nations of the world could no longer rely on the United Nations for their security . . . [consequently] Britain, upon whom rested the responsibility for the defence of the Middle East, could *not contemplate any solution* of the Egyptian question, which laid that area open to aggression.[1]

In this set of circumstances, it was difficult for the British Government to give a speedy reply to the Egyptian Note of 26 August. Egypt could wait and hope no longer. During one of the official conversations with the British Ambassador, the Egyptian Foreign Minister had declared:

> I am aware that the British Government are occupied to a great extent with the problems confronting them in Iran but the troubles of the British Government are endless and their foreign policy is of a considerably wide range and if we delay the settlement of questions pending between us on account of the troubles confronting Britain in other parts of the world, we shall never finish.[2]

What followed was a speech to both Houses of the Egyptian Parliament on 8 October 1951, by the Prime Minister, in which he announced his Cabinet's abrogation of the Condominium Agreement and of the Treaty of 1936. In support of this decision, he reviewed, for one hour and a half, the series of abortive endeavours to reach any satisfactory agreement with Britain; he cited eighteen instances of unilateral revocation of agreements and treaties by other states as precedents for the Egyptian action. Among the examples given were the United States, which revoked in 1884 the Anglo-American Treaty of 1850 regarding the building of a canal in Central America; France, which cancelled in 1905 the Concordat with the Pope; the Irish Free State which unilaterally abrogated in 1933 the Anglo-Irish Treaty of 1921; and Japan, which abrogated in 1938 the Nine-Power Washington Agreement of 1922 about the principles to be followed and the attitudes to be taken towards China. (This seems to be the nearest example comparable to the Condominium Agreement on the Sudan.)

Nahas Pasha submitted administrative proposals for the Sudan to replace the existing regime in the country. He envisaged for the whole Sudan—North and South—'an entirely autonomous government and a

---

[1] *Egypt No. 2* (1951), Cmd. 8419, pp. 3–4.
[2] Cmd. 8419, *op. cit.*, p. 31.

genuine democratic constitution. The working of its details is being left to the Sudanese themselves.'[1]

The Egyptian action had many repercussions; various forms of reactions to the abrogation were expressed not only in the Middle East and Britain, but in most parts of the world; they reveal part of the remote forces working against an Anglo-Egyptian settlement.

In Egypt, after Nahas Pasha's statement, which was received with prolonged cheering, the leaders of all the Opposition parties pledged their full support for the Government's action; a Parliamentary Committee, set up to study and report on the legislative proposals introduced by Nahas Pasha, unanimously gave their blessing to the Prime Minister's four draft decrees, providing among other things that the King shall be titled the King of Egypt and the Sudan. This Committee, composed of legal experts and prominent members of the Senate and Chamber of Deputies, submitted that the abrogation of the 1936 Treaty was justified in view of the violations of the Treaty by the British in several ways: the number of troops in the Canal Zone had now highly exceeded the number stipulated in the Treaty; Britain had failed to provide Egypt with arms; Article 5 of the Treaty provided that Britain and Egypt would not pursue foreign policies in a manner contrary to each other's interests; contrary to this provision, the British attitude in the Palestine question, was 'flagrantly opposed' to the interests of Egypt; and Britain had persistently tried to separate the Sudan from Egypt.[2]

These accusations against Britain are justified. Even Mr. Winston Churchill admitted the Palestine question as one of 'the mistakes and miscalculations in policy which earned almost in equal degree the hatred of the Arabs and the Jews'.[3] But the British Government was pressed from many sides; from the U.S. Government, from Zionists in Britain and in Israel; from the desire to counterbalance the growing power of the Arabs with the new state of Israel, and from the demands of the Arab states with whom, said Mr. Morrison, 'we have traditional bonds of friendship'.[4]

However, the Muslim Brotherhood, formerly banned by the Egyptian Government for extremist activities but now reinstated, was of opinion

---

[1] A draft decree-law abrogating the 1936 Treaty and its annexes, and the Condominium Agreements of 1899, regarding the administration of the Sudan, in Ministry of Foreign Affairs, *op. cit.*, pp. 171–9. For a full text of the Egyptian Foreign Minister's Speech of Abrogation, see *Vital Speeches of the Day*, New York, 1 December 1951.
[2] Keesing's *Contemporary Archives*, Vol. No. VIII, 1950–2, p. 11745.
[3] *Parliamentary Debates*, House of Commons Official Records, 30 July 1951, Vol. CCCCXCI, pp. 798–9.
[4] *Ibid.*, p. 962.

that abrogation was not enough. At a conference in Cairo on 12 October 1951, the Brotherhood passed resolutions to the effect that Egypt should declare a state of war against Britain, and British forces in Egypt and the Sudan should be considered as aggressors; that the Egyptian Government should sever economic, commercial and cultural relations with Britain, and that Egypt should declare that the Governor-General of the Sudan did not represent the Egyptian Government.

Direct negotiations having failed, both Governments chose to be judge and jury of the case in their respective parliaments. Thus in England on 6 November 1951, the King's Speech to both Houses of Parliament referred to the abrogation of the 1936 Treaty and the Condominium Agreements of 1899 as illegal and invalid. The King declared that His Government was resolved to press forward with their proposals for defence arrangements in the Middle East, and to maintain their position in the Canal Zone under the terms of the 1936 Agreement; and he continued 'nothing can be allowed to interfere with the rights of the Sudanese to decide for themselves the future status of their country.'[1]

While elaborating on the King's Speech, Mr. Winston Churchill, the new Prime Minister under the new Conservative regime, intimated that the Government would maintain their rights under the 1936 Treaty 'using, of course, no more force than is necessary'.[2]

In addition the Foreign Office issued a statement re-affirming British policy in the Sudan. They would continue to give the fullest support to the British Governor-General of the Sudan in the administration of the country in accordance with the Condominium Agreements. In the United States the Secretary of State, Mr. Dean Acheson, supported the British stand; in a Press conference on 10 October, he pointed out that the Anglo-Egyptian Question was of general concern to the 'free world' which had interests in the Middle East Area. 'The U.S. Government believes that proper respect for international obligations requires that they (i.e. the Condominium Agreements and the 1936 Treaty) be altered by mutual agreement rather than by unilateral action.' Similarly, the French Government supported the British stand in this matter.

On the other hand, the Political Committee of the Arab League met in Alexandria on 9 October and gave to Egypt the absolute support of their member states. On the same day, the Syrian Parliament adopted,

---

[1] *Parliamentary Debates*, House of Commons Official Report, Vol. CCCCXCIII, H.C. Deb. 5, 1951–2, p. 51.
[2] *Ibid.*, p. 79.

with one voice, a resolution which supported Egypt's abrogation of the Treaty and the Condominium Agreements.

In the Sudan the abrogation move was received with mixed feelings and opportunism. The Umma Party which stood for Sudanese independence from both the British and the Egyptians but which was generally regarded as pro-British, sent a telegram to the United Nations and to the British and Egyptian Foreign Ministers on 11 October, asserting that the Sudan was not a party to the Anglo-Egyptian Agreements on the Sudan and had never recognized them. 'We take the opportunity', said the telegram, 'of Egypt's abrogation move to declare to the world that we have regained our sovereignty and will accept nothing short of Sudanese Government.'[1] However, on 14 October, the Executive Committee of the Party accepted the abrogation by issuing a resolution saying that it considered that the British administration based on the Anglo-Egyptian Agreements had ceased to function in view of the abrogation and added that it regarded the existing administration as a transitional government until self-determination in the Sudan. Another Sudanese reaction was the resignation of a Minority of the Commission, under the Chairmanship of a British Judge, which was set up to agree on the principles of a temporary constitution aimed at self-determination in the country. The Sudanese Minority asserted that Egypt's abrogation of the Condominium had created a vacuum in the sovereignty of the Sudan. They considered that the Sudan should, therefore, be immediately put under the umbrella of the United Nations.

H. A. R. Gibb, at that time Professor of Arabic at the University of Oxford, addressing the Royal Empire Society, stated that it was clear from the diplomatic documents which had been published on both sides that throughout 1950 and 1951, all representations by the Egyptian Government met with nothing 'but evasive and procrastinating answers from the Foreign Office'. In the circumstances, Professor Gibb explained, there was nothing left for the Egyptian Government to do but cut Egypt loose from a Treaty 'which we had ourselves destroyed as a morally valid instrument and which had become nothing more than a figment and a legal incubus'.[2]

The Abrogation of the Treaty and the Condominium Agreements was followed by incidents that temporarily worsened Anglo-Egyptian relations. The Wafdist Government endeavoured to make the position

---

[1] *The Times*, 12 October 1951, p. 4b, see also Keesing's *Contemporary Archives*, Vol. VIII, p. 1746.

[2] *United Empire*, Journal of the Royal Empire Society, London, March–April 1952, p. 73.

of the British forces in the Canal Zone untenable. Egyptian civil employees of the British forces were withdrawn by force of propaganda or police intimidation. Road and rail communications of the forces were attacked by saboteurs. The British, on the other hand, reinforced their garrison with civilian labour imported from East Africa, Malta and Cyprus. When Egyptian guerrillas, who attacked the Suez water filtration plant, used the village of Kafr'Abdu as a strong-point, it was demolished by British military action. A British observer in Cairo commented afterwards: 'If a military necessity, it was an unfortunate political set-back; if not a military necessity, it was a psychological blunder and something approaching a political disaster.'[1]

By the Egyptian Government it was bitterly denounced as an extreme atrocity. There were further clashes and several persons were killed in defending the Ismailia police headquarters against a major British assault on 25 January 1952.

The Times correspondent commented sadly: 'Nothing was more distressing to any Englishman with pleasant memories of Egypt than to experience the hatred of Britain as was then apparent in the native quarter of Ismailia.'[2] The Egyptian Ambassador was recalled from London; British employees of the Egyptian Government were relieved of their jobs. A violent mob, including incendiary squads, destroyed British property and killed a number of English persons in Cairo, on Saturday, 26 January 1952, now known as 'Black Saturday' in the history of Egypt.

Following these incidents, King Farouk dismissed the Wafdist Government, which had proved, contrary to speculation in London when they won the 1950 elections, anti- rather than pro-British; he appointed Ali Mahir to form a new Ministry. Ali Mahir resigned on 1 March and the King appointed Ahmad Nagib al-Hilali as Prime Minister. The new Prime Minister and the British Ambassador re-opened exploratory negotiations; but the British Government would make no concession without Sudanese agreement, though the Sudanese were not invited to any of the Anglo-Egyptian talks.

This was the state of affairs before the revolutionary regime came into the picture as from July 1952, when the personality and understanding of General Neguib, himself partly Egyptian and partly Sudanese, brought in a fresh atmosphere of congeniality and manœuvring, which resulted in an Anglo-Egyptian Agreement in February 1953.

[1] Royal Institute of International Affairs, *Great Britain and Egypt*, p. 184.
[2] *The Times*, 24 January 1952.

But before dealing with this Agreement, we propose to examine four of the hidden factors apart from those we have indicated, which induced Egypt to the abrogation of the Condominium Agreements and the Treaty, in 1951—a psychological moment. These were first, the post-war decline of Britain.

There was the impression, admitted by the British themselves and widespread in most parts of the world, that Britain had declined from a first-class to a third-class power. In the Middle East the belief was gaining ground that Britain had become so weak that she had only to be pressed sufficiently by one means or another to yield her position. Indeed Britain was weak, but Egypt overlooked several factors. In the first place, in a nation, as in an individual, hope springs eternal, and states are possessed of a strong desire to survive. This urge was strong enough to pull Britain through, and to make her protect her interests. In the second place, a Nigerian (Yoruba) proverb applies: 'Dada ko le ja, ṣugbọn o ni aburo ti o gbojule'—(a weak person able to count on the strength of another is strong enough).[1] If Britain was weak, her younger cousin was young, strong and willing! Americans were the first to admit that 'the United States had had to stand by Britain for the defence of the Canal and the restoration of Order.'[2]

Sir Oliver Franks, an experienced man of affairs, especially through his years of service as British Ambassador in Washington (1948–52) remarked to his radio audience on 'Britain and the Tide of World Affairs' in 1954: 'But you know how our habits of understating what we think and minimising what we feel often completely deceive people from overseas.'[3] The Egyptians must have been deceived: for the British, though strained and weakened by the last war, had not lost their hopes, their unity and their drive for power.

Again, during the six months before the Egyptian abrogation, the Iranian Government under Dr. Mussadiq had flouted British authority over the oil refinery at Abadan; and had finally forced Britain to evacuate Abadan on 1 October 1951. This adversely affected morale in Britain, whilst it encouraged confidence in Egypt. The Egyptian Government organ remarked: 'This is the example that we must follow in our struggle with the British. It is only the weak whom they oppress. Their prestige in the Middle East is finished.'[4]

---

[1] Literally, the proverb reads: 'Dada cannot fight (too weak, old, or lazy); nonetheless he has a younger brother upon whose strength he can count.'
[2] *Time* weekly magazine, Chicago, 4 February 1952, p. 17.
[3] B.B.C. Reith Lectures (1954), *Britain and the Tide of World Affairs*, London, 1955, p. 2.
[4] *Bourse Egyptienne*, 4 October 1951.

Undoubtedly the Egyptian Foreign Minister, Salah Eddin Bey, was much impressed by Dr. Mussadiq's temporary triumph over the British whom he had forced out of Abadan. (They soon returned!) The Egyptian Government not only hoped but indeed expected the British to submit to the abrogation and withdraw from the Sudan and the Suez Canal Zone with the apparent meekness with which they had withdrawn from Abadan. Obviously, this was a miscalculation. True, British interests in Iran were considerable. But in Egypt and the Sudan they were infinitely greater. Further, in Egypt Britain had more powerful forces to invoke military power, the joint responsibility with the allied powers, the Condominium Agreements, and the 1936 Treaty. She had the potential backing of her imperial armies, the Commonwealth, and an international prestige. Egypt's only weapons were faith, sacrifice, solidarity and endurance. Again psychologically, and indeed practically, Egypt felt inferior; and the abrogation was an effort to assert total independence. And Egyptian patience had been exhausted. 'We have been talking with Britain for 20 years. They know our point of view. We know theirs. Further talks only mean more British occupation' [of Egypt and the Sudan].[1] This was solid ground for the Egyptian action.

While pressed with as great a desire as the Conservatives to achieve and maintain British interests and prestige abroad, the Labour Party endeavoured to seek these objectives through a more friendly disposition towards dependencies and weaker states. Mr. Bevin's policy of relative friendship and trust towards Egypt was followed by Mr. Morrison who succeeded him. In fact, the Labour Government realized the desirability of modifying the Condominium Agreement and of revising the Supplementary Treaty of 1936. Mr. Attlee, the Prime Minister, told the House of Commons that the 1936 Treaty was unsatisfactory: 'We have to work with them [the Egyptians] at the present time on the basis of that agreement while trying to get a better one, and many times we have been pretty near getting something satisfactory.'[2]

Egyptians were therefore eager not to lose the opportunity of reaching an agreement with a relatively amenable and sympathetic regime in Britain, and not to wait till a more formidable one came into power.

Under the circumstances, and in spite of the hypothetical dangers of Communism in the Middle East and of the consequent strategic

---

[1] Salah Eddin Bey, 'Why Egypt Broke with Britain', *The U.S. News and World Report*, Washington, D.C., 19 October 1951, p. 18.
[2] *House of Commons Debates*, Foreign Affairs (Middle East), 30 July 1951, Vol. CCCCXCI, p. 1069.

interests in that area, the Labour Government might have, in the end, secured a reasonable settlement with Egypt. But the Opposition in Parliament, the British stakes in the Sudan, the pledges of self-determination repeatedly given to the Sudanese, and the hope that Britain might eventually succeed in persuading the Sudanese to join the British Commonwealth (as the Labour Government had succeeded in doing with India) were some of the concealed but effective forces against any Anglo-Egyptian settlement at this stage.

Yet, it would be correct to suggest that both the Labour policy from 1945 until the end of their regime in 1951 and Egypt's attempt to abrogate the 1936 Treaty prepared the way for the Agreement of 1953, yielding self-government to the Sudanese and making provisions for their self-determination within three years thereafter. To this we must turn our attention in the next chapter.

13

THE AGREEMENT CONCERNING SELF-GOVERNMENT AND SELF-DETERMINATION FOR THE SUDAN, 1953

I assure everyone that Egypt will always treasure the friendship of the people of England.

GENERAL NEGUIB, August 1952[1]

The outlook for the New Year (1953) is that substantial satisfaction will have to be given to the various causes of Arab nationalism, not least Egypt's evacuation claim, before the countries of the Middle East will become reliable friends and allies.

The Times, January 1953[2]

1. THE NEW EGYPTIAN APPROACH UNDER GENERAL NEGUIB; EGYPTIAN PROPOSALS OF 1952; THE AGREEMENT OF 1953

THE year 1952 was an uneasy one in the Middle East; popular discontents at the failure of governments caused eruptions in several countries. In Egypt, four successive cabinets assumed and quickly relinquished powers within six months after Nahas Pasha and his Wafdist Party had been dismissed by King Farouk. The King himself was forced by the Egyptian Army to abdicate on 26 July 1952,[3] though his infant child was immediately styled Fuad II, 'King of Egypt and the Sudan'.

The July Revolution 1952 brought into power in Egypt General Muhammed Neguib. Like the Condominium form of government, described as a 'hybrid', he was of two different lines—born in Khartoum by the Sudanese wife of an Egyptian Army officer. Educated at the Gordon Memorial College with many of the present leading Sudanese politicians, he possessed a first-hand knowledge of the Sudan and its people. Neguib's *'bridging'* personality and the Revolution's fresh

---

[1] Broadcast in Cairo, on 11 August, reported in *The Times*, London, 12 August 1953, p. 4.

[2] *The Times*, 1 January 1953, p. 6g.

[3] For the causes and the course of these eruptions in Egypt, see Dr. Rashed El Barawy's *The Military Coup in Egypt*, Cairo, 1952, and General Neguib's *Egypt's Destiny*, London 1954.

approach succeeded in bringing to the Sudanese controversy a new atmosphere and a great relief.

The 'Liberal Rally' which was the core of the July Revolution and of which General Neguib was President, had solemnly vowed to 'evacuate the usurper, without reserve or condition, from the Nile Valley; to ensure for the Sudanese the freedom of self-determination without foreign influence; to bear in mind, constantly, the unity of the Fatherland (Egypt and the Sudan); and to help Egypt to achieve her international obligations calculated towards justice, liberty and the welfare of humanity'.[1]

A British writer remarks that the story of the Anglo-Egyptian argument over the Sudan had been one of 'a succession of stupid blunders by the old guard of Egyptian politicians, aggravated, it must be admitted, by diplomatic errors on the part of Britain'.[2]

It would seem that Neguib and his colleagues were too careful to commit similar blunders. Also Neguib's policy over the Sudan Question seems to have taken note of Mekki Abbas' appeal to Egypt to understand the problems and aspirations of the Sudanese, bearing in mind that 'The bonds of language and culture should be strengthened by a forward policy imbued with the spirit of the modern age.'[3] He had a much more realistic approach than any of the previous premiers of Egypt; he was less dependent on the mass and the Press. Neguib picked his steps delicately between the political factions in Egypt, where the desire to reach agreement with the British by peaceful means was no longer popular. He seemed to approach the Sudan problem on the basis that the Condominium Agreements and the Treaty of 1936, unilaterally abrogated by the Wafdist Cabinet in 1952, were still in force until self-determination in the Sudan; that these agreements entitled Egypt, like Britain, to take, in fact, an active part in helping the Sudanese to shape their own future; that the real 'Unity of the Nile Valley' must be based on the free recognition by the Sudanese that the Egyptian and Sudanese interests in the Nile Waters were so closely interwoven that good understanding between the two countries was most essential to both. He further considered that the Sudan issue and the Canal Zone problems were closely connected; but that they should be handled separately, on the basis of one step, then another. The Unity of the Sudan with Egypt under the Egyptian Crown had greater emotional appeal to King Farouk, he said, than to the members of the Revolutionary

---

[1] *Middle East Monthly Review*, Cairo, January/February 1953, p. 22.
[2] John Hyslop, *Sudan Story*, p. 126.   [3] *The Sudan Question*, p. 154.

Council, who destroyed the Egyptian Crown by creating the Republic State of Egypt. The more active help Egypt gave towards Sudanese self-government and general progress, the more quickly would British control over the Sudan come to an end.

The general purpose of the Neguib Government and the broad effect of his approach was to inspire new hope for fruitful co-operation between Britain, Egypt and the Sudan. Consequently, the Egyptian Government based its policy on two broad principles; first, to assist the Sudanese to full self-determination, in the hope that such assistance would encourage them to choose, eventually, union with Egypt; though the risk was realized that the Sudanese, in the exercise of that right, might prefer independence to such union; and second, to ensure that Egyptian proposals should be acceptable to all or most of the Sudanese parties and to the British Government.

With these objectives in view, General Neguib invited all the Sudanese political parties, including chiefs from the Southern Sudan, to Cairo for discussions on how Egypt could best assist the Sudan to achieve self-government and full self-determination. The response from the Sudanese was such that the Cairo correspondent of *The Times* reported that General Neguib 'succeeded in assembling the largest gathering of Sudanese politicians that this city has seen'.[1] By the end of October, agreement was reached between the Egyptian Government and the representatives of the Sudanese political parties. On 10 January 1953, the agreement was signed in Khartoum by Major Salah Salem (member of Neguib's military committee), Sheikh Ahmed Hassan (Minister of Religious Foundations), on behalf of Egypt; and by representatives of the Umma, the National Unionist, the Socialist Republican and the National Parties from the Sudan. The Provisions of the Agreement, described as 'final settlement from which no one shall go back' covered the Southern Sudan and the abolition of the Governor-General's special responsibilities there; the creation of the Governor-General's Commission, as provided in the Egyptian proposals embodied in the Note dated November 1952; the Sudanization of the Sudan Administration; and the withdrawal of Foreign Troops from the Sudan.[2]

Thus armed with their own plan and with the consent of the Sudanese, the Egyptian Government were able to present a Note to the British Government on 2 November 1952, setting out Egypt's proposals for

[1] *The Times*, London, 20 October 1952.
[2] Republic of Egypt: Presidency of the Council of Ministers, *The Sudan under the New Agreement*, Cairo, 1953, pp. 6–8.

the way in which the two Governments could co-operate in the constitutional development of the Sudan. In effect Neguib reminded the British of their utterances about giving independence to the Sudan and announced his complete agreement with them. But he went further than the British. He asserted that independence and sovereignty must be granted within three years. The most significant features of the Egyptian Government's note were the following. It expressed firm belief in the right of the Sudanese to self-determination. To attain that objective there should begin immediately a transitional period to secure full self-government for the Sudanese, and to provide the requisite and free neutral atmosphere for the Sudanese to exercise self-determination. In the transitional period, sovereignty should be reserved for the Sudanese, while in the interim period, the Governor-General should be the supreme constitutional authority in the Sudan: but such authority must be exercised with the aid of a five-member commission of two Sudanese, one Egyptian, one British, and one Indian or Pakistani. An International Commission of three Sudanese members, one Egyptian, one British, one American and one Indian or Pakistani, should be appointed to conduct elections for a Sudanese Parliament and to ensure impartiality. A Sudanization Committee—a British member, an Egyptian and three Sudanese—should be established mainly to speed up the Sudanization of the Administration, the Police and Defence Force, and any other positions which might bring about the freedom of the country to exercise self-determination. British and Egyptian military forces should be withdrawn from the Sudan at least one year before the elections of the Constituent Assembly. The transitional period should not exceed three years, and a Constituent Assembly would decide on the future of the Sudan 'as one integral whole' and choose either a form of Union with Egypt, or complete independence of the United Kingdom or any other country.[1]

In the past, Britain had appeared to be a champion of Sudanese independence on the apparent assumption that the Egyptian Government would continue to oppose it for fear that an independent Sudan, if under foreign influence, might endanger Egyptian interests. The British had frequently declared their support for self-government for the Sudanese. The change of approach in Cairo made it awkward for them not to live up to their promises. As Mr. Eden told the House of

---

[1] H.M.S.O., Cmd. 8767. See *Documents concerning the Agreement between Britain and Egypt about Self-Government and Self-Determination for the Sudan*, 17 February 1953, (*Egypt No. 2*, 1953), pp. 47–9.

Commons on 12 February 1953, the Egyptian move had 'Completely changed the situation. Whereas hitherto we had been unable to find any basis for negotiations, from that moment there was good reason to hope that we could reach agreement.'[1]

Nevertheless, there arose certain difficulties in reaching agreement. The major points of difficulty during the negotiations were three, the first being what the British Government called 'the Governor-General's special responsibility for the Southern provinces'. Britain wanted to retain special powers alleged to protect the interests of the Southerners; Egypt refused, suspecting that Britain might use such powers to detach the South from the North and incorporate it in the adjacent British territory of Uganda. On 24 November 1952, Sir Ralph Stevenson informed General Neguib with the other Egyptian negotiators that he had received instructions from Mr. Eden to continue the discussion on the Sudan. 'The first thing to talk about', he suggested to the Egyptian delegates, 'is the Governor-General's powers in the South. . . . Although it is very largely psychological, it is extremely important.'[2] To this the Egyptian view, as put by Dr. Sultan, and Wing-Commander Zulficar, was that there should be no discrimination between the people of the Sudan. . . . 'It is a trust in our hands and our primary objective is to fulfil our obligation of keeping the Unity of the Sudan and working for it. . . . The real task of the present British Administration in·the Sudan is, rather than work up their distrust (in the South) to explain to them that our projected amendment of (article) 6(c) shall be an adequate safeguard.'[3] The next point of difficulty was Sudanization, the replacement of British officials by Sudanese. Whilst the British were anxious to retain as many British officials as possible in the Sudan for as long as they could, the Egyptians were eager to ensure their departure at an early date, lest such British administrative officials remaining in the country should influence the choice of the Sudanese against Union with Egypt.

The other major problem was the reference of provisions of the Agreement to the Sudanese Parliament. Because of the Egyptian concern at the likelihood of British interference in the discussions and decisions of the Sudanese, the Egyptian Government were unwilling to agree to the conclusion of protocol empowering the Sudanese Parliament to discuss the main provisions of the Agreement.[4]

---

[1] *Parliamentary Debates* (Commons), Vol. DXI (1952–3), p. 602.
[2] The Republic of Egypt, *The Sudan under the New Agreement*, p. 15.
[3] *Ibid.*, pp. 16–19.   [4] Cmd. 8767, *op. cit.*, p. 11.

However, these items were included in the signed Agreement between the Sudanese Parties—including the Umma, the Socialist Republican, and the National Unionist, at the instance of Major Salem of Egypt, who had submitted to the Sudanese these points of difference between the British and the Egyptian Governments. Besides, the Sudanese National Unionist Party had distributed written statements that they were willing and able, with the co-operation of all concerned, to complete Sudanization within three years and that the Sudanese were able to carry out effectively all the essential responsibilities of government. With regard to the Governor-General's responsibility in the Southern Sudan, the party declared: 'We accuse the Governor-General and his government of having deliberately adopted a policy of keeping the South completely secluded from the North and virtually debarred civilisation and progress. The interests of the Southerners will be more secure when the responsibility for them is assumed by the Sudanese Cabinet in which the Southerners themselves are represented.'[1] Thus faced with a united front of the Sudanese and the Egyptians, the British had to give in. But they maintained that 'Unless the Governor-General has some powers to protect the South, I [the British Ambassador] think there is going to be some trouble.'[2] (And indeed there was trouble in August 1955, when the South mutinied.)

Finally after twenty-three plenary sessions, which began on 20 November 1952, and twenty days after the Egyptian Note was presented to the British Government, Great Britain and Egypt reached accord, and an Agreement along the lines of the Egyptian proposals was signed just before 11 a.m. on Thursday, 12 February 1953. 'Thus the historic document removed the first obstacle[3] which has been the cause of conflict between Egypt and Great Britain for more than 70 years.'[4]

The main provision of the Agreement was that the Sudan should reach freedom in three stages; there were country-wide elections for a Sudanese Parliament, the formation of a Sudanese Government, and a Sudanese decision within three years, whether to join Egypt or remain independent. (The Foreign Secretary, Mr. Eden, assured the House of Commons that the Sudan could decide to join the Commonwealth.[5])

[1] Quoted by Dr. Rashed El-Barawy in *The Military Coup in Egypt*, Cairo, 1952, pp. 267–8.
[2] The Republic of Egypt, *The Sudan under the New Agreement*, p. 19.
[3] The second obstacle was the problem of British troops in the Canal Zone.
[4] *Near East Monthly Review*, January 1953, p. 2.
[5] But *Time* magazine, referring to the South African Government's objection to 'Coloured Dominions', asked, 'What about Malan?' *Time* magazine, Chicago, 23 February 1953, p. 18.

After the Agreement was signed by both General Neguib and Sir Ralph Stevenson, both exchanged a strong and friendly handshake and even embraced each other! The United Kingdom Ambassador paid tribute to General Neguib in a personal message in which he said:

> My sincere hope is that this agreement will inaugurate an era of greater mutual confidence between Great Britain and Egypt. This Agreement has been rendered possible by increasing understanding on both sides and in particular, if I may say so, by the fact that General Neguib and his Government have shown a far higher degree of statesmanship in dealing with this question than have previous governments in Egypt. His view that sovereignty over the Sudan should be kept in reserve for the Sudanese and this agreement that the Sudanese shall freely determine his own future, show that both he and Her Majesty's Government have the best interests of the Sudanese people at heart.[1]

General Neguib, in a broadcast message to the Sudan, said that the agreement was reached after unparalleled efforts and difficulties. But success was achieved through moral arms, faith in God and the justice and legality of their claims for the Unity of the Nile Valley.

On 12 February, Mr. Eden announced the agreement in the House and described it as 'a reasonable settlement of this question which has for long bedevilled our relations with Egypt and contributed so much uncertainty to the future of the Sudan itself'.[2]

2. INTERNATIONAL REACTIONS

In the Sudan, a statement by Sir Robert Howe, the Governor-General, was read at a parade of British, Egyptian and Sudanese troops in Khartoum, which was witnessed by about thirty thousand people. In it he paid tribute to the 'wisdom and statesmanship' of General Neguib and expressed satisfaction at the unity of view shown by Sudanese political leaders.

Nearly all the leading papers in the American and Arab countries, Britain, India, Pakistan and Japan devoted their editorial columns to the Agreement on the Sudan's future, stressing the favourable impact it had on international relations on a wide scale.

The Arab countries, quite naturally, were the first to receive the news with great enthusiasm. They stressed that by the solution of the Sudan problem a new atmosphere of optimism was created in the whole of the

---

[1] *Near East Monthly Review, loc. cit.*, p. 4.
[2] *Parliamentary Debates*, House of Commons Official Reports, Vol. DXI, 1952–3, pp. 602–6.

Near East region. The entire British Press (excepting the two representing opposite extremes—the *Daily Worker*, which was silent, and the *Daily Express*, which asked for the rejection of the Agreement on the basis that through it the British delivered the Sudanese to the Egyptians) were most favourably disposed to it. This disposition, however, led Miss Margery Perham, of the Institute of Colonial Studies, at Oxford, to comment that: 'General Neguib, by the refreshing contrast between his personality and methods and those of his predecessors, seems to have so captured the good opinion of the British Press and public that neither seems in the mood to scrutinise his recent memorandum on the Sudan.'[1]

In structure the Agreement was carefully planned and well safeguarded, on paper. But when the written instrument was put to work, Anglo-Egyptian difficulties began to emerge, arising from mutual suspicions and divergence of interpretations. The immediate differences were concerned with the right of the Sudanese to unite with Egypt or with the British Commonwealth; with the Governor-General's Commission (for which provision is made in Articles 3, 4 and 6 of the Agreement); with protection of the Southern Sudanese (we shall refer later to the alleged intimidation of Chief Zakaria Jambo); and with interference in the general elections to the first Sudanese Parliament.

Anglo-Egyptian wranglings arose over the right of the Sudanese to choose, eventually, after independence, either to form a union with Egypt or to join the British Commonwealth. Mr. Anthony Eden, replying to Captain Waterhouse, in the House of Commons, stated on 12 February 1953, that the Agreement left the Sudanese with freedom to enter the British Commonwealth, if desired. General Neguib, in a broadcast to the Sudan, on 16 February, rejected Mr. Eden's interpretation; he retorted that any attempt to pull the Sudan into the British Commonwealth would invalidate the Agreement which provided for two alternatives only—union with Egypt or complete independence. On the following day, Mr. Eden reaffirmed the British stand that complete independence included the right of the Sudanese to choose any form of association with any other state, on their achieving self-determination. He had instructed the British Ambassador in Cairo to explain to the Egyptian Government that the phrase 'completely independent' as used in the Agreement, stood without reference to any particular country. Later, after Anglo-Egyptian discussions in Cairo, the Egyptian Foreign Ministry announced that the issue had been settled 'in conformity with the text of the Agreement'.

[1] *The Times*, 17 November 1952.

Again, on 10 March 1953, General Neguib accused the British Government of breaches of the Agreement, particularly by delaying nominees to the Governor-General's Commission. Furthermore, he charged British administrators with 'maltreatment' of the Southern Sudanese through intimidation and imprisonment.

Another allegation was that the British officials were being transferred from temporary to permanent posts in the Sudan, such as the judiciary, contrary to the Agreement, which specified that such appointments must be made through the Governor-General's Commission. The British Minister of State denied these allegations.

But the Sudan (British) Government Agency in London stated, on 11 March 1953, that General Neguib's allegations of 'maltreatment' of the Southern Sudanese were based on exaggerated reports of some incidents in Aweil, where four Northern politicians had held a meeting attracting so large a crowd that it was regarded as likely to lead to a breaking of the peace and, in consequence, local police 'detained them for the night'. They were later released. Press correspondents commented that Neguib's attack on the British officials in the Sudan was also influenced by the position of Zakaria Jambo, a Southern Chief who had signed an agreement with Egypt but was deposed from his seat on the local council because of that agreement. He was reinstated 'pending full examination of the circumstances'.

Another difficulty arose, however, when Mohammed Salah ed Din, former Foreign Minister in the Wafdist Government, arrived in Khartoum, on 11 March, with two other members of the Egyptian Bar, on their way to the South to defend Chief Jambo. They attempted to visit the Equatorial Province in the South but were refused the necessary permits. In a message to the Governor-General, Neguib made another protest against the refusal of the permits requested by 'notable' members of the Egyptian Bar and maintained that the Governor-General had no right, in the circumstances, to prevent Egyptians from visiting any part of the Sudan. Sir Robert Howe's reply, as reported, was vague and evasive.

Chief Jambo signed the same document signed in Cairo by the Northern Sudanese Parties in 1952 which was as a prelude to the Anglo-Egyptian Agreement of 1953. For a detailed account of the incidents leading to the trial and defence of Chief Jambo, the writer is indebted to Mr. Sapana Jambo (fourth son of the accused), who witnessed the trial; he was a senior student at the American University in Cairo, where the writer interviewed him in January 1956. According to him, Chief Jambo, convinced that the Egyptian document promised self-government to the Sudan within three years, signed it 'on his own behalf' and not as an official representative of the Moru people; this was in Amadi and at the instance of Major Salem who had asked for individual signatories.

This, however, was rather disturbing to the British District Commissioner, Mr. R. P. Tripp. On Major Salem's departure, he summoned a meeting of the district chiefs and leaders, excluding Jambo; at this he accused that Jambo had acted unconstitutionally by signing the Egyptian document without consultation with the local people. Jambo was subsequently brought to trial. The Northern Sudanese lawyers who came to his defence were put under temporary arrest, but later ordered out of the district. At the same time, the Egyptian lawyers attempted to go to Amadi to defend Jambo; they, too, were obstructed.[1]

The nature of the membership of the First Sudanese Parliament, that is whether those elected were pro-Egyptian or pro-British, would ultimately affect the nature of the relationship with Egypt and Britain. Each of the two countries had therefore a natural desire to see its own favourite political party in power in the Sudan. Inevitably this led to certain forms of alleged interference by both Cairo and London in the November–December elections in the Sudan, even though these were ably supervised by an International Commission appointed in accordance with the provisions of the 1953 Agreement. Anglo-Egyptian fever rose high. Charges and counter-charges of interference appeared in the Parliaments, Press and radio of Cairo and London in the November–December elections in the Sudan. Instances of interference were cited, but these will form part of our next chapter, wherein the 1953 elections will be discussed.

But we should not be greatly surprised at the variations of, and conflicts between, the interpretations of certain clauses of the Agreement. The problems of interpretation are legion: in the first place, students of semantics recognize that the 'meaning' of a word is an elusive quality, even in the dictionary; secondly, constructions (sentences and phrases) are subject to literal, or to broad interpretations; and thirdly, an agreement may be subject to terms not expressly included —for instance, Britain interpreted the phrase 'complete independence' of the Sudan to imply freedom of choice to join the British Commonwealth. Even legal experts admit that the problem of interpretation is 'at once one of the most vital and one of the most obstinate of all the

---

[1] This account was certified by S. Jambo, Cairo, on 22 January 1956.

tasks with which lawyers are faced'.[1] Thus evidence has been submitted in English courts to show that twelve eggs means thirteen, and that 100 rabbits means 120.[2] This may be strange to the ordinary Oriental or African mind of the peoples on the Nile; but the fact is accepted in Britain.

Although these controversies tended to bend the clauses of the Agreement they did not break them. Other forces sustained the Agreement. During the 1950–1 conversations the Sudan controversy had stood in the way of Egyptian acceptance and participation in the Four-Power Scheme for military pacts against the potential threat of Communism. Britain was, therefore, now anxious to remove the Sudan as an obstacle to the Middle East Command. Furthermore, Britain had been arraigned before the Security Council on the Sudan issue, and care must be taken to avoid similar publicity in the open forum of the world, especially now that the 'strong man of Egypt' appeared popular with the United States Government. On the part of Egypt, the *coup d'état* had to produce a settlement of the Sudan Question to justify itself and to show superiority to those Cabinets which had come and gone before. There was also pressure from the Sudan: the Sudanese, bestirred by the attention given to their country and to their fight, in the Security Council in 1947, encouraged by the 1948 Constitution to demonstrate their own ability and eager not to repeat the uncertainties of the uni-lateral abrogation, worked hard on the Condominium Governments. The Sudanese were not going to lose the chance of obtaining self-government and self-determination for their country. As a result, the Agreement withstood all the superficial strains of Anglo-Egyptian wranglings; and it brought into existence the first Sudanese Parliament —a notable achievement at a time when several other parts of British Africa were in a state of crisis.

In effect, the Agreement placed on a higher plane Egypt's relations with Britain and the United States on the one hand and with the Sudan on the other. It raised the status of the Sudan itself from a mere geographical expression to that of a quasi-State *de facto* if not *de jure*: from the position of a girl arbitrarily betrothed to two suitors to that of a maiden, able to choose her own partner. It cleared the way for the Evacuation Agreement of 1954.

[1] Cheshire, G. C., and Fifoot, C. H. S., *Law of Contract*, 3rd ed., London, 1952, p. 108.
[2] *Ibid.*, p. 107.

14

THE EVACUATION (SUEZ) AGREEMENT OF 1954

The old order changeth, yielding place to new;
And God fulfils himself in many ways,
Lest one good custom should corrupt the world.

LORD TENNYSON, *The Passing of Arthur*

I have not in the slightest degree concealed in public speech how
much I regretted the course of events in Egypt. But I had not held
my mind closed to the tremendous changes that have taken place
in the whole strategic position in the World which makes the
thoughts which were well-formed and well knit together a year
ago, utterly obsolete. . . .

SIR WINSTON CHURCHILL,
Parliamentary Debates, 29 July 1954

THE years 1953 and 1954 witnessed, in relative terms, many favourable changes in world problems. In a letter dated 21 September 1953, the U.S.S.R. delegation requested, and was granted, that 'Measures to avert the threat of a new World War and to reduce tension in international relations' should be included in the Agenda of the eighth session of the United Nations General Assembly.[1] Subsequently, there was general relaxation of the 'Cold War'[2] and much talk and writing about the philosophy of 'peaceful co-existence' of the capitalist and Communist regimes in the Parliaments and Press of the great nations; the three-year-old Korean War was stopped and an armistice was signed on 27 July 1953. The East and the West, for the first time with Communist China, met, and broad agreement was reached at the Geneva Conference on the night[3] of 20 July 1954. The French Government, proverbially ephemeral, showed signs of stability: M. Mendès-France's 'diplomacy by deadline' worked successfully and there came a cessation of the seven-year-old colonial war in Indo-China. The three-year-old

---

[1] U.N. General Assembly, *Official Records*, Supplement No. 1 (A/2/26631), New York, 1954, pp. 5–6.

[2] The position was such that Sir Winston Churchill, who was said to have coined the phrase 'iron curtain', admitted in the House of Commons that: 'We have been encouraged by a series of amicable gestures on the part of the new Soviet Government.' *Parliamentary Debates*, 11 May 1953.

[3] And morning of 21 July, almost twelve months after the Korean armistice.

dispute with Persia over the Anglo-Iranian Oil Company was concluded; a tripartite treaty 'of friendship and collaboration' between Greece, Turkey and Yugoslavia was signed at Bled.

'A bear, coughing at the North Pole, stirs the Sahara', and the peaceful state of the world in 1953–4 seems to have affected—even though indirectly—Anglo-Egyptian diplomacy. Answering a question in the House of Commons on 28 July 1954, Mr. Anthony Eden stated that the whole House wanted to get a final settlement between Britain and Egypt. He put a counter-question: 'Is it not a good idea to start improving our relations with Egypt and to make that the foundation for better relations?'[1] This, in a way, set the prelude to the new Anglo-Egyptian Agreement of 1954 over the Suez Canal, which is relevant to the Sudan Question, as we shall show presently.

The Suez Canal issue might, *prima facie*, appear not connected with the Sudan Question. But we have shown in Chapter 2, that the British Government had, as far back as 1882, speculatively included the Sudan as one of 'such points as would give us command of the Canal'. Later the Sudan and the Suez became Siamese twins whose parents were the Condominium Agreement of 1899 and the Treaty of 1936. The Egyptians, until the Revolutionary Council's tactical modification, resisted the separation of the Sudan from the Suez Canal in their negotiations with Britain.

Although Sidky Pasha appears to have agreed with Bevin on a separate Sudan Protocol in 1946, the question was not separated in fact. The protocol was not signed; it died at the stage of initialling. In 1947 Nokrashy Pasha kept the two subjects together at the Security Council. In 1950, Nahas Pasha's Government regarded the Sudan and the Suez questions as integral parts. It is necessary to repeat here the Egyptian Minister for Foreign Affairs, Salah Eddin Bey's statement to the British Government: 'If you dislike linking the question of evacuation [from Suez] with that of the Sudan, Egypt, on her part, cannot deviate from linking these two questions together. In fact she has always done so. . . . Indeed, it is a matter of life and death to Egypt.' (See Chapter 7 on 'The Sudan as Egypt's Buffer State against Mediterranean Geopolitics'.) In a letter to the British Ambassador in Cairo, dated 30 April 1952, the British Foreign Secretary wrote, emphasizing that the Egyptian Prime Minister (General Neguib) 'has made it clear that he must make agreement over a formula on defence [of Suez and Middle East] dependent upon one for the Sudan'.[2]

---

[1] *Hansard*, 28 July 1954.   [2] H.M.S.O., Cmd. 8767, *op. cit.*, p. 7.

Britain, too, had never, in all seriousness, severed the two. In 1947, Sir Alexander Cadogan objected to the attempt by the Security Council of the U.N. to separate them. The Agreement of February 1953 appears to be in part a tactical move on the part of Britain to put Egypt in the mood for a subsequent Suez Agreement advantageous to Britain. The link was made by Captain Waterhouse, who, opposing any negotiations on terms of evacuation, declared in the House of Commons that the Sudan was a 'most important factor in this issue'.[1] Addressing the United Nations Society at the London School of Economics and Political Science, on 3 November 1954, Captain Waterhouse stated that Britain was interested in the Suez because he who controls the Suez controls Africa and Persia, the Water Way (Suez Canal route) and the Sudan, especially.[2]

Julian Amery, another objector to British withdrawal from Suez, put the case more bluntly, saying it would encourage the victory of the pro-Egyptian Party in Khartoum, and that Egypt would now have a free hand in the Sudan; 'for we shall have abandoned our only means of putting pressure on Cairo', he warned.[3] Sir Winston Churchill, as we have already indicated in a previous chapter, described Egypt and the Sudan as a tree with roots in the Sudan and branches in the Delta (Egypt). Strategically, the Sudan—always considered as an appendage to Egypt—is part and parcel of the Anglo-American defence arrangements in which the Suez issue was basically involved. In communications, Khartoum had become 'an absolute Clapham Junction for air lines' of the world,[4] which was, though remotely, connected with the efficient running of the Suez Canal base.

Furthermore, Cairo is the cultural, spiritual and economic centre of the Arab world, of which the Sudan is a member so close to Egypt. It seems the Sudanese consider themselves 'Sudanese' first, 'Arabs' second and perhaps 'Africans' next. At the London School of Economics and Political Science, for instance, Sudanese students are automatically and actively members of the Arab Society; they show little or no interest in the Africa Society. *The Round Table* is therefore correct in observing that in the background of the negotiations about the Canal Zone, there were 'recurrent echoes of events in the Sudan, sometimes

---

[1] *Hansard*, 14 July 1954.
[2] From notes of the address, taken by the writer, who was in the audience.
[3] Amery, Julian, 'Hold on to Suez', article in *Time and Tide*, London, 24 July 1954, p. 981.
[4] Sir Douglas Newbold, late Governor of the Sudan—see Henderson, K.D.D. *The Making of the Sudan*, London, 1952, pp. 255–6.

serving as a "leitmotif" sometimes reverberating like distant thunder'.[1] (A British Embassy official in Cairo remarked, jokingly, to the writer that he heard no sound of any 'thunder' during the negotiations.) We should therefore treat the Suez Agreement of 1954 as a significant part of the Sudan Question.

1. THE PROTRACTED NEGOTIATIONS

Both Governments have published documents about the 1954 Agreement, but neither Britain's Cmd. 9230, with subsequent papers, nor Egypt's *Grey Book*, of ninety-two pages, contains a record of the actual debates which preceded the Agreement. We have therefore to rely on outside, but equally reliable, sources.

After some false starts, negotiations on outstanding issues between the two countries opened in Cairo on 27 April 1953, soon after the February Agreement on the Sudan. Each country was represented as follows:

Britain by Sir Ralph Stevenson (Ambassador in Cairo), Gen. Sir Brian Robertson (who until 16 April 1953, was Commander-in-Chief, Middle East Land Forces), Michael Cresswell (Minister at H.M. Embassy in Cairo), Air Chief Marshal Sir Arthur Sanders (Commander-in-Chief, Middle East) and other Senior Officers; Egypt by General Neguib (then Prime Minister and later, President), Lt.-Col. Nasser (later Prime Minister), Dr. Fawzi (Foreign Minister), and other leading members of the National Revolutionary Council.

After six meetings, the negotiations were adjourned indefinitely on 6 May, when a communiqué was issued to the effect that the talks had 'reached a stage at which the date of the next meeting cannot be announced immediately'.

The British delegation issued no further statement after the suspension of the talks, but subsequently Mr. Selwyn Lloyd (British Minister of State) announced during a Foreign Affairs debate in the Commons, on 12 May, that Egypt had insisted on a number of conditions unacceptable to the British Government. Among these were a demand that all British military installations and stores in the Canal Zone should be transferred to Egypt soon after the evacuation of British forces and that any British technicians remaining should be under Egyptian control. Earlier, on 6 May, Colonel Nasser had said that the Egyptian attitude had been made clear to the British delegation at the very first meeting; he warned that the Egyptians were no longer 'prepared to waste time

[1] *The Round Table*, No. 175, London, June 1954, p. 295.

in allowing the discussions to drag on as the previous ones did for a year and a half'. In reply to Mr. Selwyn Lloyd, Colonel Nasser explained, on 16 May, that the Egyptian delegation had proposed the evacuation of British troops from the Canal Zone and the delivery of the military base, with its installations, to the Egyptian Government, though the delegation did not object to a number of foreign technicians, provided they were prepared to serve under Egyptian authority. But the British, he went on, insisted that the base be controlled from London. Further, General Neguib made a statement accusing Britain of having been an 'aggressor' in Egypt for decades; he maintained that Sir Winston Churchill had reaffirmed the British imperialist policy against the nationalist movements in the Middle East, and had tried hard 'to conceal imperialist designs under the defence of the free world'.

Perhaps in an attempt to impress on the British, as well as Mr. Foster Dulles (U.S. Foreign Secretary), who was to arrive in Cairo on 11 May,[1] the fact that Egypt was not alone in her demands, the Political Committee of the Arab League countries met in Cairo on 10 May and passed a resolution pledging their full support to Egypt in her demand for immediate evacuation of British troops from the Canal Zone.[2]

After the adjournment of negotiations, some Egyptians resorted to violent activities, apparently calculated to force the hand of the British. By counter-measures the British, on the other hand, impressed upon the Egyptians that they would not yield. What followed was a series of incidents in the Canal Zone from the second half of May (1953). On 18 May, the Egyptian Government announced that they had made three protests to Britain about attacks on Egyptians in the Canal Zone area. They declared that forty-three attacks had been made by British forces against Egyptians between 3 April and 12 May; that on 14 May, British troops fired on the village of Kafr Abdu (near Suez) where one man was wounded; and that on 17 May, British forces occupied Abdu Hammad railway station and abducted the staff.

Lt.-General Festing (General Officer Commanding British troops in Egypt) stated on 17 May that the situation in the Canal Zone was 'troublesome but not abnormal'. On 27 May, Egypt further protested against the destruction of Salak Malak village, about 10 miles from

---

[1] Mr. Dulles, accompanied by Mr. Harold E. Stassen (Director of the Mutual Security Agency), left Washington, D.C., on 10 May 1953, for a twenty-day fact-finding visit to the Middle East and Southern Asia. They stayed in Egypt from 11–13 May and had discussions with the British Ambassador in Cairo, with General Neguib and others.
[2] All the eight Arab League countries—Egypt, Jordan, Syria, Iraq, Lebanon, Saudi Arabia, Yemen and Libya—were represented.

Fayid, as a result of which three hundred villagers were left homeless. The British military authorities admitted demolishing the village, but explained that it was mainly as a precaution against disease and that, having been derelict since 1951, the village had one inhabitant only—an elderly man. Thus, both parties conveniently dodged the real reason for concern about this village: it served as a hide-out, and a secret base for guerrilla operations against the British.

In July, the situation in the Canal Zone became worse. Mr. Selwyn Lloyd informed the House of Commons, on 15 July, that a British airman, L.A.C. Rigden, had disappeared on the night of 9 July, 'under circumstances which appeared to implicate the Egyptian authorities'.[1] On 11 July, a British airman was murdered in Ismailia. On that day, General Festing sent a message to the Sub-Governor of Ismailia, protesting that he took 'an extremely serious view of Rigden's disappearance'. He gave warning that if the missing airman did not return by 9 a.m. on 13 July, he would put into force measures resulting in 'serious disruption and inconvenience to the Egyptian community'. Rigden did not return by the time appointed. General Festing felt compelled to implement his warning: he therefore established control points to search all traffic into or out of Ismailia.

General Festing's message was described as an 'ultimatum' and his measures led to protests by the Neguib Government. However, Major Salem, in a radio broadcast on 13 July, appealed to Egyptians to remain calm, as the Government would not let themselves be provoked by the British into a battle under unfavourable circumstances; but if they must fight, they would do so to the last man. Two days later, Mr. Selwyn Lloyd defended, in the House of Commons, the measures taken at Ismailia as 'entirely reasonable'. But some Labour M.P.s criticized General Festing's action as 'inflammatory' and based on 'flimsy' allegations against the Egyptian authorities.[2] Following the criticisms in the British Parliament, General Festing announced the relaxation of his measures, taken, apparently, without full collaboration with the Foreign Office in London. Later, Rigden was discovered and arrested in Paris.

Later, the situation in Ismailia improved again, and negotiations were resumed. The talks went on smoothly until October 1953, when Sir Winston Churchill, according to a critical London weekly, 'suddenly made the (apparently) trivial issue of uniforms a matter of

[1] *Parliamentary Debates*, 1952-3, Vol. DXVII, p. 2060.
[2] *Parliamentary Debates*, 15 July 1953.

principle'.[1] Agreement was reached that three thousand British technicians should be retained in the Zone to supervise the base in peace time, but the British insisted that the technicians, because they were British troops, must wear British uniforms; but this was interpreted as an effort to impress upon all concerned that the function of the technicians was to serve as a symbol of Britain's residual power and authority in the Canal Zone and probably to ensure greater protection for the men. The Egyptian Government pleaded that such insistence on the wearing of uniforms made agreement impossible. The Egyptians were strongly averse to British men appearing in military uniform, probably because of its psychological effect on them—a visual reminder to the subconscious that their territory was still in British military occupation. Furthermore, they conceived that if military uniforms were allowed on British technicians, Britain might take advantage of that situation to bring actual soldiers into the Zone and there would, in that case, be difficulty on the part of Egyptians in telling the difference between a soldier (who might attack) and a civilian technician.

This talk resulted in another deadlock, even though the 'terms for Anglo-Egyptian co-operation in running the base, which Colonel Nasser offered, were', to quote a critic of the British Government, 'remarkably reasonable'.[2]

Meanwhile, certain Governments and persons of influence tried, for different motives, to bring indirect pressure upon Britain and Egypt to reach agreement. The Arab League countries pledged their support for Egyptian demands, essentially because their own fate hangs with Egypt's. The U.S. Ambassador in Cairo, Mr. Jefferson Caffery, played the part of a 'broker'. In the words of the *New York Times*, 'Under the gentle persistent urging from the U.S., the British Government decided to make concessions'.[3] The U.S. was motivated probably by her own economic and strategic interests in Egypt and the Middle East. The Indian and Pakistan Governments (apparently because of their psychological war against 'imperialism' and a desire to extend the areas of peace in the world) also endeavoured to use their good offices in promoting Anglo-Egyptian agreement. In June 1953, on their way home from the coronation of Queen Elizabeth II and the Commonwealth Premiers' Conference in London, Mr. Nehru, the Indian Prime Minister, and Mr. Mohammed Ali, the Pakistan Premier, held in Cairo

[1] *New Statesman and Nation*, 17 July 1954.
[2] *Ibid.* See also the *Economist*, 17 July 1954, p. 181.
[3] Quoted by the *Daily Worker*, London, 28 July 1954.

a three-power conference with Egypt. Discussions on the Suez Canal and Sudan Questions took place from 22 to 25 June. At a Press conference on 22 June, Mr. Mohammed Ali revealed that he had endeavoured while in London to reconcile the British and Egyptian viewpoints. On 25 June, Mr. Nehru expressed, in a Press statement, the hope that there would soon be a peaceful settlement in terms compatible with the full sovereignty of Egypt. He suggested that settlement should not be made dependent upon Western defence of the Middle East, because it was essentially the Middle East countries who should themselves decide whether there should be a Middle Eastern military pact.

As we have seen, during previous negotiations, the Egyptians, like peoples in British colonial territories, tended to regard the Labour Party as the lesser of two evils in the British Parliament. The Labour Party, too, endeavoured to win the confidence of the Egyptians. Partly for this reason, we presume, and apparently believing that it would be better to persuade the Egyptians to concede voluntarily the presence of the British troops in the Suez Canal, certain Socialists made overtures to Egyptian leaders. During the Christmas recess of the House of Commons, Mr. Aneurin Bevan, accompanied by Miss Jennie Lee, M.P. (his wife), visited Cairo, as the guests of the Indian Ambassador, Mr. Sardar Pannikar. They visited President Neguib and had talks with Colonel Nasser, Major Salem (Minister for Sudan Affairs) and Dr. Fawzi. At a Press conference held at the Indian Embassy, Mr. Bevan declared that he was hopeful of an Anglo-Egyptian agreement; the main stumbling-block consisted in presenting an agreement which was 'sufficiently attractive psychologically to both countries. . . . I believe in military bases, provided the country in which the bases are established is agreeable.'[1]

Mr. Bevan's friendly visit to Egypt and conciliatory gestures were, however, severely criticized in the British Press and Parliament.[2] He was attacked in particular for an article of his published first in India and later in Egypt in *Gumhurya*, the semi-official organ of the Egyptian Government. The chief point criticized was his statement that: 'The presence of the troops of another nation on one's own national soil is a circumstance to be borne only when it is voluntarily conceded.'[3]

In spite of these various overtures by governments and personalities,

---

[1] Keesing's *Contemporary Archives*, Vol. IX, p. 13424.
[2] *Parliamentary Debates*, 17 December 1953, Vol. DXXII, pp. 602–3.
[3] *The Round Table* (No. 175, London, June 1954, p. 228)—a quarterly review of British Commonwealth affairs—agreed with Mr. Bevan. It said: 'The idea that we can just sit tight and ignore Egyptian protests is impracticable.'

terrorism broke out afresh in Egypt, particularly between March and May 1954. There were more assassinations, murders and kidnappings. The murder of an Egyptian police officer by a British soldier aroused violent comment in the Egyptian Press; attacks on British troops at Suez became increasingly frequent. But more than these terrorist activities, supporters from the U.S., India and other allies, together with Mr. Bevan's report of his visit to Egypt, made Britain become reconciliatory in mood: consequently, on 10 July 1954, the British Ambassador in Cairo handed new British proposals to the Egyptian Prime Minister.

Official negotiations were resumed on the very day that the British proposals were received. After a three-day break, during which the two delegations reported back to their respective Governments, Brigadier Anthony Head, British Secretary of State for War, flew out to Cairo with fresh proposals from his Government. The talks were resumed on 15 July. General agreement was reached at a conference held in the Rest House (formerly Farouk's), under the shadow of one of the Pyramids at Giza. The Accord, reached in the seventh session of negotiations, was initialled by Brigadier Head and Colonel Nasser, at 9.20 p.m. (Cairo time) in the office of Colonel Nasser. Thus began the end of the seventy-two years of British military occupation in Egypt, and of the fifty-five years of Anglo-Egyptian Condominium in the Sudan.

The terms agreed upon represented a compromise by both delegations on points that had threatened to bog down the negotiations. There was concession on the four main points for which the British had been, to quote a gibe by the Egyptian Press, 'haggling like a peanut vendor'.[1] The points were, first, concerning reactivation. The British gave up their insistence upon a twenty-year term of agreement to cover the reactivation of the base. Instead, they accepted a seven-year term to replace the 1936 treaty. Concerning evacuation, the Egyptians yielded to the British view that twenty months (as against fifteen, maintained by Egypt) was the time necessary to complete the evacuation of British combat troops and some supplies from the base. In answer to impatient enquiries in Egypt, Major Salem remarked: 'We have waited seventy-two years to resolve the Anglo-Egyptian conflict. We can wait a few days more. . . .'[2] Britain also proposed that a threat of attack on Turkey, Persia, or any

---

[1] Description of the British in the Egyptian Press, quoted by the *Spectator*, London, 30 July 1954. In the experience of the writer in Africa, America and Europe, the most persistent hagglers are the hawkers in the streets of Cairo.
[2] *The Times*, London, 20 July 1954.

Arab State would be an occasion for reactivating the base. On the other hand, Egypt, hitherto reluctant to make any commitments, agreed to engage in an 'immediate consultation' with Britain in the event of 'a threat of an attack on Egypt, on Turkey, or any other Arab State, but with the exception of Persia'. Britain also gave up her insistence on the continued maintenance, by British men in uniform, of some military installations of a technical nature. Instead, the installations would be run by 'British and Egyptian civilian technicians and personnel'.

The other Heads of Agreement are listed in a short ten-paragraph document with an annexe of six brief items. The Document of Agreement begins with the fresh and hopeful theme:

> It is agreed between the Egyptian and British Delegations that, with a view to establishing Anglo-Egyptian relations on a new basis of mutual under-standing and firm friendship, and taking into account their obligations under the United Nations Charter, an Agreement regarding the Suez Canal base should now be drafted. . . .[1]

Further negotiations on details and the drafting of the document continued for about three months after the initialling on 27 July. In its complete form, with full appendices, setting forth details, the Agreement, consolidating the 'heads' already initialled, was signed in Cairo on the night of 19 October. The main Agreement is embodied in thirteen Articles; but there are two annexes; the first concerns the withdrawal of British forces, and the second deals with the organization of the Base. There is an Agreed Minute about the interpretation of certain aspects of withdrawal, and the meaning of the expression 'outside power' used in Articles 4 and 6. In addition, there are nineteen Exchanges of Notes on many particulars.[2] Article 2 solemnly declares:

> The Government of the United Kingdom declare that the Treaty of Alliance signed in London on 26th August, 1936, with Agreed Minute, Exchange of Notes, Convention concerning the immunities and privileges enjoyed by the British forces in Egypt and all other subsidiary agreements, is terminated.[3]

The first stage of British withdrawal began on 17 August 1954, when about 2,300 British troops embarked from the Suez Canal Zone. The Egyptian Government declared 20 October a public holiday to celebrate the ending of 'occupation'. Colonel Nasser, as Egyptian Premier, now

---

[1] H.M.S.O., London, *Egypt No. 1* (1954) and Cmd. 9230, p. 2 (Appendix 8 below).
[2] The Republic of Egypt, Ministry of Foreign Affairs: *Agreement between the Republic of Egypt and the Government of Great Britain and Northern Ireland*, Cairo, 1955, pp. 1–92.
[3] *Ibid.*, p. 2.

invited the British Ambassador in Egypt and the British Minister of State to a luncheon in Cairo on 21 October 1954.

Before considering the reactions to this Agreement, it is relevant to indicate the circumstances which contributed to bringing about an agreement.

The 1936 Treaty had only two more years to run, as it was to expire in 1956,[1] and a new treaty had to be sought. A new treaty could be reached essentially by negotiation and consent; in default of an agreement the question must be submitted to arbitration. According to the 1936 Treaty, unless otherwise agreed, the question must be submitted to the Council of the League of Nations, now succeeded by the United Nations Organization. But the case had already been debated there in 1947. It is evident from the proceedings of the case in the Security Council that Britain, after escaping safely in 1947, might find it difficult to justify her position before any international body; especially because appeal had already been made, at the Security Council, to Britain to withdraw voluntarily her forces from the Suez Canal.

The Egyptians, even under the current military regime, would be wise to refrain from attacking British forces. But they certainly could continue to make the position of British forces very uncomfortable by various devices. The Suez base could not be adequately maintained without a large number of Egyptian workmen; but Egyptian workmen could not be expected to work with full co-operation and loyalty as long as their country continued to wage psychological warfare against Britain.

The Military Government in Egypt, though not at all equal to the British military power, was made up of able military men; historical evidence in the colonial world suggests that Britain, like other imperial powers, often gives way to force rather than to reason or right. Sir Harold Nicolson, himself a British diplomat of eminence, asserts that violence cannot be restrained by reason but by force.[2] Egypt's military strength and national consciousness had grown enough to be considered a greater threat to Britain than the British Foreign Secretary had feared in 1927 (see chapter 4).

Many British subjects in the Zone had been victims of political assas-

---

[1] 1956 seems a significant year in the British Colonial Empire. It marks, by a series of coincidences, some political milestones, e.g. in Nigeria, a motion in the House of Assembly, Ibadan, for self-government in 1956, when, too, the current constitution was due for revision. The 1953 Agreement on self-determination in the Sudan ended in 1956, when the Sudanese were free to unite with either Britain or Egypt, or any other nation, or stand alone.

[2] *The Evolution of Diplomatic Method*, London, 1954, p. 88.

sinations by Egyptian fanatics, without any effective counter-measure by Britain. Between 16 October 1951 and 1 June 1954, forty-seven British servicemen had been killed in the Suez Zone and seven more were missing. There was a total of 3,297 thefts of official British property by 'robbers for political reasons as well as for private gain'.[1] For this and other reasons, British servicemen in the Zone were deteriorating in morale. Writing from Ismailia, the scene of many incidents, James Cameron, a British journalist, commented during the 1954 negotiations:

> If the emotional and abusive propagandists in Cairo could only take a look to-day at these eighty thousand imperialist aggressors (as the Egyptians call the British servicemen), living in gradually deteriorating conditions up and down the disputed strip, they would realize that all the talk is bunk. We are dying to go.[2]

Without an agreement, Britain must keep a great many more soldiers in the Zone than she could economically spare, considering her other commitments in various parts of the world. Thus the base had become more a liability than an asset.

Though the development of the hydrogen bomb had not changed everything, it had tended to make the old policy of a single large base somewhat obsolete in military strategy. As long as Egypt was made to remain hostile, actively or potentially, such a concentration of troops, in the atomic age, became obviously wasteful, if not dangerous.

British common sense foresaw the folly of becoming involved in any defiance of the inevitable. 'To hold the base by force was both morally and militarily nonsense and it could only end in a climb-down far more humiliating than that of Abadan.'[3] There was, therefore, a strong feeling in Britain that the Government should come to an early settlement with Egypt because Britain's best advantage lay in a certain amount of concession. Consequently, the British Government became conciliatory to Egypt. Urging the British Government to be reasonable, the *Sunday Times* (London, 27 June 1954) observed that it was foolish to expect that the British could expect a more accommodating spirit and easier terms from the Egyptians.

Egypt, too, was under some pressure to agree with Britain. While there seemed to be prospects for greater success than in 1947, for Egypt to appeal again to the Security Council as in 1947 would involve more money, time and energy. Moreover, Egyptians were still suspicious of

[1] Mr. A. Nutting, Under-Secretary at the Foreign Office, answering a question in the House of Commons, on 16 June 1954.
[2] *News Chronicle*, London, 27 July 1954.
[3] *New Statesman and Nation*, 17 July 1954.

the great powers and their satellites in the United Nations, who would tacitly refrain from using their authority to embarrass Britain in the U.N. Again, the base could not be kept in proper order without technicians, which would include some British at least during the transitional period before complete Egyptianization of the base, and an open breach with Britain, or a derelict base, might expose Egypt to some great risks of the cold war between the Capitalist West and the Communist East. Finally, the new regime in Egypt had suffered some political setbacks as a result of internal rivalries and tests of strength—particularly between popular General Neguib and able Colonel Nasser, in the spring of 1954. An Anglo-Egyptian agreement on a national issue such as the Suez problem would strengthen the position, prestige and influence of the Revolutionary Council which had succeeded (through General Neguib) in reaching some agreement with Britain about the other twin question of the Sudan.

2. THE GENERAL REACTIONS TO THE AGREEMENT

Reactions to the Agreement in London, Cairo, Khartoum and in other parts of the world, were swift, numerous and illuminating. They indicate the various interests involved, emphasize the broad international nature of the issue, and reveal certain aspects of power politics in its wider field.

In London the signing of the Agreement was officially announced to the House of Commons on 28 July, by Mr. Anthony Eden, the Foreign Secretary, who recapitulated the 'Heads of Agreement'. He stated that it was the conviction of the Government that the Agreement would preserve

> our essential requirements in this area in the light of modern conditions. We are convinced that in the Middle East . . . our defence arrangements must be based on consent and co-operation with the peoples concerned. . . . It is our hope that it will now be possible to establish our relations with Egypt on a new basis of friendship and understanding. H.M. Government believe that this is also the intention of the Egyptian Government. The Agreement should thus contribute to a reduction of tension through the Middle East as a whole.[1]

Sir Winston Churchill, who, in 1942, declared that he had not become Prime Minister 'to preside over the liquidation of the British Empire' (to which the Canal Zone was important), sat, with bowed head, while his own Government announced the withdrawal of British troops from

---

[1] *Parliamentary Debates*, 28 July 1954.

the Suez base. Labour Members of Parliament, who had been under Churchill's taunts of 'scuttle' when they advocated withdrawal in 1946, thoroughly enjoyed Churchill's discomfiture and greeted him with sardonic cries of 'No scuttling'.[1] For Mr. Attlee, the Labour leader, it was an occasion for jubilation in the House of Commons: 'The Opposition entirely agree with the evacuation of our troops from Egypt. I can remember saying over and over again . . . how hopeless it was to try to have a base where there was a hostile population. We did not get much sympathy.'

With the air of a man triumphant after six years of arguing, he continued: 'But that is acknowledged at all events to-day'.[2]

The Times, London, commented that the Agreement should be received with satisfaction.

But there were critics. Some saw it as a surrender of British prestige and safety. Among the chief opponents were forty Conservative M.P.s —the 'Suez Rebels', led by Captain Waterhouse—who resisted any agreement with Egypt. Major E. A. H. Legge-Bourke went so far as to resign his membership of the official Conservative Party because of, in his own words: 'the Government's decision to reopen negotiations with Egypt on terms which include the total evacuation of British troops from Egyptian territory. . . .'[3] Julian Amery considered the Agreement a repudiation of the fundamental principles of the Conservative Party.[4]

However, a motion on the subject, presented in the names of Sir Winston Churchill, Mr. Eden, Mr. Crookshank (Leader of the House) and Mr. Anthony Head (Secretary for War) was debated with zest in the House of Commons on 29 July. It read: 'That this House approves the heads of agreement negotiated in Cairo on 27 July between H.M. Government and the Government of Egypt.' The motion was carried by 257 votes to twenty-six.[5]

In the United States, the *New York Times* (29 July) welcomed the Agreement, as well as the *New York Herald Tribune* (31 July), commenting that Britain had come to recognize that—in a changing world— her interests would be better served by an agreement with Egypt than by prolonging the discontent that smouldered around the Middle East, which might otherwise burst into flame.

---

[1] Sir Winston has always felt special resentment about the 'warmonger' campaign of 1951; likewise, Mr. Attlee has always taken offence at the 'scuttle' gibe, during his term of office.

[2] *Hansard*, Vol. LIII, No. 159, London, 29 July 1954, pp. 738-9.

[3] *Manchester Guardian*, 15 July 1954.   [4] *Parliamentary Debates*, 29 July 1954.

[5] The twenty-six members voting against the Government were Conservative M.P.s belonging to the 'Suez Rebels', some of whom voted for the motion.

President Eisenhower expressed, at a Press conference on 28 July, his great pleasure at the Agreement. Mr. Foster Dulles, the Foreign Secretary, stated on the same day that the Agreement provided 'a new and more permanent basis for the tranquillity and security of the Near East'.

The U.S. Government immediately released the twenty million dollars' worth of aid to Egypt 'which had been held up to force a settlement' of the Anglo-Egyptian dispute.[1]

In Australia, Mr. Casey, the Prime Minister, said that the Anglo-Egyptian Agreement was of great interest to his country, especially because 'our air and sea communications with many of our friends of the free world pass through this area. . . . Any agreements which ensure that the free world will not be excluded from this area [Egypt and the Middle East] in a possible future emergency are most welcome.'[2]

In South Africa, the Agreement was seen as Britain's complete surrender to Egypt. There was hope that if the Suez route were closed South Africa would benefit from the shipping that again—as had formerly been the case—would have to use the Cape route.[3]

In Germany, the West German Government, evidently under U.S. influence, immediately followed the United States example of economic aid to Egypt and announced its agreement to underwrite the shipment of 65,000,000 Deutsche Marks' (15,470,000 dollars') worth of industrial equipment to Egypt. The Government guaranteed repayment to private German concerns who would ship the equipment on credit.[4] A German newspaper, in an editorial, remarked that the Egyptian example was an inspiration to all countries in which coloured peoples were still under the rule of white men.[5]

In India, Mr. Nehru sent messages to Mr. Eden and Colonel Nasser and congratulated them for having 'removed another cause of tension' and thereby 'helped to turn people's minds towards peaceful progress'.[6]

In Israel, the Agreement, in its secondary aspect, evidently increased the fear of the new state of Israel. She feared that the restraint on Egypt exercised by the presence of British troops, now being removed, might lead to another Arab attack. Mr. Moshe Sharatt, the Prime Minister, explaining his country's alarm, said: 'The grant of the new position to

[1] *Time* magazine, New York, 9 September 1954.
[2] Australian News and Information Bureau.
[3] *Johannesburg Star,* 22 July 1954.   [4] *New York Times,* 22 August 1954.
[5] Hitlerite Germany was more than ever indoctrinated with the idea of 'white supremacy'. See Chapter XI of Adolf Hitler's *Mein Kampf,* published by Keynal & Hitchcock, New York, 1940.
[6] *Manchester Guardian,* 30 July 1954.

Egypt without any obligation on her part to regularise her relations with Israel, is liable to serve as a spur to aggression.'[1] However, Israel was asked to have no qualms. In London, *The Times*, in a leading article,[2] wished to convince Israel that in strengthening the Arab states, the Western powers were showing no hostility to her, and to impress it upon the Arab states that military aid was no licence for aggressive action. But the *Jewish Chronicle*[3] encouraged, in its leader, the suggestion that a subsidiary base to Suez be established in Israel, say at Haifa or at Elath, to the Red Sea.

The Turkish Press expressed the view that the Suez Agreement would lead to Anglo-Egyptian friendship in more or less the same way as the British withdrawal from India had transformed Anglo-Indian animosity into a very strong friendship.[4]

In the U.S.S.R., a Moscow broadcast in Arabic, on 17 August 1954, emphasized that the Agreement had been studied with the utmost care by the United States, Turkey and Pakistan and had been followed up immediately by American offer of military aid to Egypt. In other words, the Soviet Union regarded the Agreement as a step further in the Anglo-American military alliance—the 'imperialist conspiracy' to dominate the world. 'Little prescience is required to realize that, since the return of foreign troops to the Canal Zone is dependent upon the future of Turkey, Egypt may be dragged into U.S. military plans, encouraging not only the Middle East but territories farther afield.'[5]

In the Arab World, the feeling is illustrated by *Falastin*, a leading Arab newspaper published in Jerusalem. It considered the evacuation of British troops from the Suez Canal as 'evacuation of foreign troops from a part of the Arab world and we are happy as Egypt at the new agreement'.[6]

In Egypt, the Agreement, which terminated seventy-two years of British 'occupation', was received with nation-wide jubilation. In Cairo cafés distributed free ices, tamarind and mango syrups to the rejoicing population. Thick crowds collected throughout the city, carrying banners and acclaiming Colonel Nasser's name as the Victor. The

---

[1] *Manchester Guardian*, 30 July 1954.
[2] London, 1 September 1954. [3] London, 30 July 1954.
[4] *The Dunya*, Ankara, 29 July 1954. B.B.C. World Broadcasts, Part IV, No. 489, reading, 6 August 1954.
[5] B.B.C. Summary of World Broadcasts, Part I (U.S.S.R.), 20 and 23 August 1954, pp. 15 and 18 respectively. *The Round Table* (No. 176, September 1954, p. 324), commenting on the co-existence of the East and the West, said: 'American policy is definite—even, in British eyes, excessively so. The strategic plan is to draw a defensive ring round the whole Communist Eurasia.'
[6] *New York Times*, 30 July 1954.

Cairo stock market shared in the general spirit of jubilation 'by a flurry of buying orders that sent prices up several points on most of all the list'.[1]

Colonel Nasser described the evacuation of the British troops from the Canal Zone as a turning point in Egyptian history and 'the biggest single achievement in Egypt's national aspirations to date'. He declared that it meant a new era in Anglo-Egyptian relations, based on friendship, mutual trust, confidence and co-operation between Egypt on the one hand and Britain and the Western Powers on the other. Referring to the anglophobia generated by the British attitude for the past seventy years which had become second nature with many Egyptians, he said forgivingly: 'We want to get rid of the hatred in our hearts and start building up our relations with Britain on a solid basis of mutual trust and confidence, which has been lacking for the past seventy years.'[2]

The Egyptian Government immediately lifted the ban, imposed as a non-co-operative measure, on the food supply by Egyptian merchants to British Camps in the Canal Zone and tactfully discontinued their propaganda broadcasts in Swahili, which had encouraged the Mau-Mau movement against the British settlers in Kenya. Britain quickly reciprocated by announcing, through the British Quartermaster-General, that 'measures to lift the embargo on the export of arms to Egypt will be taken immediately'.[3]

However, in Cairo as in London, the Agreement had its critics. It was affected by the past distrust of the British who were regarded as wolves in sheep's clothing. Suspicion of the British was so deep-seated in Egypt that any agreement with Britain was often assumed to be more 'advantageous' to Britain than to Egypt. Apart from this loose assumption on the part of the general public, three main groups opposed the Agreement for different reasons: The Wafd Party, though now dissolved, and crushed by the Military Regime, sought to re-organize its scattered members and return to power. The Muslim Brotherhood opposed it because of extreme nationalism and possibly as a reprisal for the suppressive measures taken by the Government against the Brotherhood. While making a political speech at Mohammed Ali Square (now Revolution Square) in Alexandria, four unsuccessful shots were fired at Colonel Nasser, on 26 October, exactly one week after the signing of the Agreement. Mahmoud Abdel Latif Mohammed, one of the four men arrested for the attempted assassination confessed that

[1] *Ibid.*, 29 July 1954.
[2] Royal Institute of International Affairs, *Chronology of International Events*, Vol.X, No. 15, London, July/August 1954, p. 481.
[3] *Manchester Guardian*, 20 August 1954.

he acted under the ringleadership of some officials of the Muslim Brotherhood, and that he tried to kill the Prime Minister 'because the Agreement was not in the interests of Egypt'.[1] The Communists opposed it, in their traditional defiance of Capitalism represented by Britain, the U.S. and the Egyptian landlords.

On the whole, however, Egyptians received the evacuation agreement with excitement and triumphant rejoicing.

In the Sudan the reaction of the prominent Sudanese leaders to the Agreement definitely strengthened the view that the two issues of the Sudan and the Suez base are inseparable. Sayed Sir Ali Mirghani, Head of the Khatmia, a large religious sect which supports the Unionist Party in the Sudan, went to Cairo when Egypt was joyfully celebrating the occasion of the Agreement. On 12 August 1954, Cairo's Sudan transmission carried a message from Sayed Ismail Ashari, the Premier of the Sudan 'to the people of the Nile Valley'—Egypt and the Sudan. He said the Nile Valley was celebrating the anniversary of the Egyptian Revolution, and Suez Evacuation Day.[2] The Prime Minister, who had described the evacuation as a blessing to both Egypt and the Sudan, travelled to Cairo, where he hugged General Neguib, embraced Colonel Nasser and visited Sir Ralph Stevenson, the British Ambassador, congratulating them on the conclusion of the Agreement. Later, in October, he sent a telegram to the Egyptian Prime Minister, saying, 'When the British soldier leaves Egypt, Sudan will have freed herself from all foreign influence and the Nile Valley will be free.'[3]

The Sudanese Minister of Justice commented that the Agreement would help the Sudan to go ahead with greater stability and remove British troops from the Sudan.[4] To Sayed Yahya el Fadli, Minister of Social Services, the Agreement was a vital turning point in the relationship between Egypt and Britain, as well as between Egypt and the Sudan. 'It shall be a strong source of stability in Egypt and the Sudan.'[5]

Thus many peoples, not only in Britain, Egypt and the Sudan, but in other parts of the world, considered that the Anglo-Egyptian Agreement was overdue. Even *The Round Table*, a semi-official organ of the British Commonwealth, commented that the developments in Egypt and the Sudan gave 'rise to some rather sombre reflections on our own

[1] *The Times*, London, 27 and 28 October 1954.
[2] B.B.C. Summary of World Broadcasts, Part IV, No. 493, 20 August 1954, p. 34.
[3] Quoted in the *Daily Telegraph*, 21 October 1954.
[4] *The Local News*, published by the Sudanese Press Agency, Khartoum, 2 August 1954, p. 1.
[5] *Sudan Weekly News*, Khartoum, 1 August 1954, p. 2.

policies'. It had been some thirty years since the British Government, under pressure, conceded self-government to Egypt. In spite of this, remarked *The Round Table*, 'Up to the present . . . we seem never to have realized this fact, that we have continued to treat Egypt as an overseas possession—a little more than a colony, a little less than a Dominion.'[1]

Another critic of what one might call the British 'policy of post-ponement' is Duff Cooper, who had participated in the Anglo-Egyptian negotiations in the 'twenties. Cooper (later Viscount Norwich) 'cannot be suspected of "appeasement" ' (*The Round Table—ibid.*). The writer, therefore, would attach weight to his reflections in this matter (and in the whole Sudan Question). He says:

> Many of the failures of British statesmanship have been due to the reluctance of Ministers to deal with a problem so long as postponement was possible. Too often have we been forced in the end to accept an unsatisfactory and even a humiliating solution because we have refused at the beginning to agree to a far better one. Too often we have conceded grudgingly and too late much more than would have been accepted gladly and gratefully at an earlier date.[2]

In the Colonial World the British decision to evacuate the Suez was influenced, among other considerations, by a change in strategic needs. But to the dependent peoples of Africa and Asia, it does not appear to be a matter of military significance, as it is to the U.S., Britain and the Soviet Union. To them, the Egyptian example, together with the Sudanese, was a source of inspiration. They saw in it, we think, a yielding to the movement for independence—an experience which all colonial territories had been undergoing, in one form or another, since the Second World War. They witnessed the completion, in 1947, of the withdrawal of the British from India; 1950 marked the victory of the Chinese Communists over their opponents, the Nationalists, sponsored by the U.S.A.; soon afterwards came the revolutionary nationalist movement to which the Dutch yielded in Indonesia; the French, too, had just given in to the pressure in Indo-China. Now followed the Egyptian—and with it the Sudanese—'freedom'. The natural consequence of these examples was that those peoples still under imperial rule felt that the time for their own freedom had come nearer. Free, but small, powers too would feel inspired by the Egyptian example. The Anglo-Egyptian situation seems to show the subject peoples that even the traditional custodians of the great empires were becoming less able

[1] No. 175, London, June 1954, p. 234.
[2] Duff Cooper, *Old Men Forget*, London, 1953, pp. 99–100.

to stop the trends of the 20th century. But perhaps the newly-freed should be reminded that, quite often, freedom is granted so that obedience may be more perfect.

3. RELEVANT OBSERVATIONS

In spite of the facts we have just indicated, the Anglo-Egyptian Agreement of 1954 did not succeed in removing all the difficulties in the Middle East and Africa. Subsequent events suggest that the Suez issue did not die with the 1954 Agreement; it merely changed its field of operation. The main difficulties lie in Britain's real interests in the Middle East and in Africa, which the Suez base had guarded; and in the alternative bases to Suez, which the 1954 Agreement necessitated.

British policy in the Middle East is traditionally based on four propositions which have been indicated in the earlier chapters of this work: First is the necessity to hold the Middle East both as a military transit area and a nexus of imperial communications. This involves the basic strategic concept of the 'N.A.T.O. nations', which has been to deny the Soviet Union strategic access to the Mediterranean area, the Indian Ocean or Africa. Further, control of the Middle East oilfields is still accepted as of vital economic and commercial interest to Britain and the United States and as conditioning the post-war Western strategy of 'besetting the Soviet Union . . . with bases'.[1]

While the first of these considerations has become much less important than ever before, the remaining three are still vital to Britain.

Britain started to look round for alternatives to the Suez Canal base, soon after the 1954 Agreement. Cyprus is one of the alternatives; the serious unrest there led to a state of emergency and the deportation of Archbishop Makarios in March 1956. After a special investigatory trip to Israel, Mr. E. L. Mallalieu, M.P., recommended to Britain: 'It is already possible to say that the Southern Negev could be made to serve the purposes of a base for British forces and materials as an alternative to that in Egypt.'[2]

East Africa also has been considered, for the following reasons; it would enable Britain to have 'troops acclimatised to desert, jungle and mountain warfare available at all times'; it would increase the efficiency of the British colonial forces in East Africa; it would provide political stability in East and Central Africa (where there has been an open clash of African and European interests), and would speedily counteract 'any

---

[1] *New Statesman and Nation*, Vol. L, No. 1289, London, 19 November 1955, p. 648.
[2] Contemporary Review, No. 1063, London, July 1954, pp. 6–9.

threat' to the Middle or Far East. Lastly it would obviate the practice, necessary in the Suez Canal base, of separating the British serviceman from his family, because facilities exist in Tanganyika and Kenya for 'European families to be quartered'.[1]

If these or similar plans are carried through, it would be a continuation of the old battle on new soil. A base in Israel would increase Arab–Israeli suspicions and frictions; it would in no way diminish the East–West Cold War. The East African project would further aggravate the problems of emergent Africa. In fact, Mr. Tom Mboya, Leader of the African Kenya Delegation in London in July 1957, wrote in the *Observer*: 'African elected Members are completely opposed to the proposal to establish a military base in Kenya. We are concerned about the political implications that such a base might have on Kenya's colonial status.'[2]

There is another problem. Below the surface of the happiness over the Anglo-Egyptian Agreement lies apprehensiveness about strengthening the programme of the Middle East defence organization. In the past, as we have already observed, Egyptian leaders were reluctant to be a party to N.A.T.O. or commit themselves to any Western defence plan in the Middle East. The Sudan and Suez problems have now been settled and the situation has accordingly changed somewhat. The Western Democracies were now hopeful that Egypt would join and attract the other Arab countries (including the Sudan) to their Middle East defence plan against the Democracies of the East. This would obviously incite the latter—headed by the Soviet Union—to intensify their own defence plans. As things eventually turned out, Egypt tried to pursue a neutral policy, whilst the Western Powers gave military support to Israel—Egypt's traditional adversary, even since the death of the Biblical Joseph, the first and last Israeli Prime Minister of Egypt.[3] In response, Egypt purchased arms from Czechoslovakia in 1955. Consequently, the war hysteria continued, resulting in actual combat between Israel and Egypt and speculations by the two power blocs of the world.

The Sudan and Suez Agreements now jointly replaced the 1936 Treaty of Friendship. In 1936, the mutual anxieties of both countries

---

[1] C. J. M. Alport, M.P., in a letter to the Editor, *Daily Telegraph*, London, 17 July 1954.
[2] 'The Way Forward in Kenya', *Observer*, London 28 July 1957, p. 6.
[3] About Joseph, 'the dreamer', see the Bible: Genesis, Chapters 37–50. For Egypt's fear of Israel, see Exodus, especially Chapter 2, where a King of Egypt is reported to have said unto his people: 'Behold, the people of the children of Israel are more and mightier than we. Come, let us deal wisely with them, lest they multiply,' and at the outbreak of a War 'join also unto our enemies and fight against us' (verses 9 and 10).

about the territorial ambitions of Italy led to that agreement which was then received with apparent delight both in Cairo and London. Shortly after the Agreement, Egypt, the dependent, became an ally; the British Residency became an Embassy; Egyptian students took a long vacation from their usual demonstrations against the British; and diehard nationalist leaders became friendly and co-operative. But after the danger had passed with the defeat of Italy, nationalism surged up again and Egypt began to find fault with the Treaty. With Britain the storm had not totally subsided, for it re-emerged from another direction—this time from Moscow. Consequently, the treaty of friendship became one of friction. Similarly, Anglo-Egyptian difficulties did not come to an end with the Sudan Agreement of 1953, and that on Suez in 1954. Britain and the West certainly hope to maintain their spheres of influence in the Middle East. In fact, as we shall show presently, Egypt was attacked over Suez in 1956.

However, in spite of whatever faults it had, the Agreement was, on the whole, a graceful acceptance of the inevitable on the part of Britain. The process of adjusting British interests to the new developments in Asia and Africa was demonstrated by their withdrawal from India. It continued in Egypt and the Sudan and is now taking place in West Africa. This, however, has not been a voluntary process, as Viscount Norwich has indicated. In every case, it requires painful compromise between the demands of national sovereignty on the one hand, and British interests and prestige on the other.

But the continued application of processes like these, by all nations, is one of the ways of averting explosions in this increasingly inflammable world. In February 1956, when the writer visited Ismailia, formerly a trouble-spot of Anglo-Egyptian plotting and counter-plotting, of Egyptian violence and British counter-measures, it was quiet and peaceful—almost as quiet as the Hampstead Borough of London. At 5.13 a.m. on 13 June 1956, the last British soldier, Brigadier Lacey, stepped out of the Suez Canal base, bound for Cyprus. 'This is an unhappy occasion for us', he commented, 'but we agreed to withdraw.'[1]

Four months later, however, Britain tried to come back when a fresh Suez crisis exploded in October 1956. This time, the cause was the West's sudden cancellation of a promised financial loan to Egypt to build her High Dam at Aswan. And when Egypt nationalized the Suez Canal Company (chapter 6 above), partly as a reprisal and partly to raise the required sum, Britain was provided with a *casus belli*. By 29

---

[1] *Evening Standard*, London, 13 June 1956, p. 1.

October, the armed forces of Israel, acting in collusion with Britain and France, had attacked and penetrated deeply into Egyptian territory. On 1 November, the British Press published communiqués from the Anglo-French forces in Cyprus, announcing a series of air-raids on Egypt. In the Sudan a state of emergency was eventually declared. Khartoum airport was closed to international traffic; and some Sudanese volunteered to join the Egyptian Army in defence of the Nile Valley.

The United Nations, which had acted more leisurely in 1947 when it shelved the Anglo-Egyptian question indefinitely, now acted with full speed and effectiveness. When Britain and France, two of the five permanent members of the United Nations, paralysed the Security Council by their vetoes, the General Assembly met immediately in emergency session. Unlike 1947, the general feeling in the Assembly was now (1956–7) dominated by the new Afro-Asian group of nations, the the Latin-American camp and the Soviet bloc. Their collective feeling was overwhelmingly against the aggressors—Britain, France and Israel. In his momentous book published in July 1957, John Connell—himself a Briton of Conservative leanings—records that 'the proceedings could not be called a debate; so fierce and so embittered was the hostility of the vast majority to Britain and France'.[1]

Britain and her Commonwealth allies—especially India and Canada —disagreed about this attack on Egypt; the British Labour Party, as the official Opposition in Parliament, aroused public opinion against the Government. The United States—Britain's greatest friend and ally —was indignant. Consequently, the Anglo-French and Israeli armed forces had to abandon their campaign to 'cut Nasser down to size'. Thus, though much damage had been done before the cessation of hostilities, the effective intervention of the United Nations and world opinion helped to avert a Third World War. And though the Middle East remained besieged with one form of crisis or another, relative peace and tranquillity reigned over Suez throughout the rest of 1957.

As for the Anglo-Egyptian Suez Agreement of 1954, its immediate effect at that time enabled efforts to be concentrated on the implementation of the 1953 Agreement about self-government and self-determination for the Sudanese, without the fear of the Suez issue being used, by either co-domini, to gain points on the Sudan question. To this process of self-government and self-determination in the Sudan we must now turn our attention in the next chapter.

[1] John Connell, *The Most Important Country: the True Story of the Suez Crisis*, London, 1957, p. 206.

15

THE EMERGENCE OF THE SUDAN AND THE VOICE
OF THE SUDANESE IN THE DISPUTE: 1899-1956

> *The issue in the Nile Valley is this: are we to remain backward*
> *colonial countries—hewers of wood and drawers of water for the*
> *British; or are we to emerge by means of our own concerted*
> *struggle? For the Sudan we desire neither British nor Egyptian*
> *domination—but we can see clearly that the one issue at stake*
> *at present is British rule, not Egyptian.*
>
> ISMAIL EL AZHARI,
> Leader, Sudanese Delegation on the
> Anglo-Egyptian Treaty, 1946[1]

SOME time ago, a play called *Edward My Son* was running in a London theatre. It was all about Edward: his childhood, the pains and pleasures of his growing up; the trouble he brought upon himself, the heartaches and joys he brought to his parents, and the influence—direct or oblique —which he had on the neighbours. But Edward never appeared on the stage: the main and central character of the play was thus conspicuous by his absence. And yet, this apparent absence made his real role more dramatic, more effective. This, in some ways, is applicable to the Sudan, whose voice thus far had seldom been heard in the power politics of the Nile Valley.

Other than the various economic interests of both Egypt and Britain which we have analysed in Part II, the political future of the Sudan was an important cause of differences between the British and the Egyptian Governments. When Egypt appealed to the United Nations in 1947, the Security Council recognized the inherent right of the Sudanese to self-determination and the right to choose their own future political relationship with Britain and Egypt. But members of the Council declared that they did not know the expressed wishes of the Sudanese themselves. We have, here and there in previous chapters, given only glimpses of the Sudan as a third party in the Anglo-Egyptian dispute; we therefore propose to bring the Sudan out on to the stage, and show

---

[1] 'Sudan and Egypt'—a letter published in the *New Statesman and Nation*, Vol. XXXII, No. 822, London, 23 November 1946, p. 379.

in this Chapter the evolution of political consciousness in the Sudan, and the Sùdanese viewpoints on their country as a bone of contention between the co-domini: 1899–1953. In the next chapter we will indicate the expressed wishes and problems of the Sudanese which emerged during their period of transition (self-government) to Self-Determination as a result of the Anglo-Egyptian Agreement (1953–6). This delayed appearance of the Sudan on the stage of power seems to heighten the political drama on the Nile: it is an added proof of the strong–weak relationship in the game of, and the struggle for, power; the relative helplessness of subjugated Sudan in the face of mighty Egypt and mightier Britain.

1. THE EVOLUTION OF POLITICAL CONSCIOUSNESS IN THE SUDAN: 1899–1953

Until a few years ago, political parties—in the Western sense—were non-existent in the Sudan, even during the period of the Mahdi or at the time of Lord Kitchener. Even in 1956, the main political parties in the Sudan, which we will describe below, still had sectarian elements. Technically, Turkey remained a third voice over the Sudan Question; but the declaration of the British Protectorate over Egypt in 1915 (during the First World War) practically ignored Turkey, on whose behalf Egypt had governed the Sudan before the rise of the Mahdia. In 1923, the Treaty of Lausanne decisively abolished Turkish Suzerainty over Egypt and the Sudan: Article 17 of this Treaty of Peace with Turkey declared that: 'The renunciation by Turkey of all rights and titles over Egypt and the Sudan will take effect as from 5 November 1924'.[1] Even then, the Sudanese had to wait till the end of the Second World War before they could begin to emerge as a third force in place of Turkey.

Since the establishment of the Condominium in 1899, the Sudanese have been experiencing, slowly but steadily, economic and social progress together with political consciousness along Western lines. Soon after the First World War, signs of national consciousness began to show themselves in the Sudan, particularly among the British—and American—educated elements (Ismail El Azhari, the first Sudanese Prime Minister, is a product of the American University of Beirut). A number of Societies and leagues came into being between 1921 and 1924 'claiming either independence for the Sudan or a form of unity with Egypt', but, with the exception of the White Flag League, which stood for the freedom and unity of the Nile Valley and which was very active

---

[1] Great Britain, *Treaty Series No. 16* (1923), Cmd. 1929, p. 21.

in 1924, they were 'extremely nebulous and died away afterwards'.[1] However, these political organizations protested and staged public demonstrations; riots in big towns occurred between June and November 1924. The White Flag League was made up, in the main, of young Army officers, ex-students of Gordon College and government employees, and headed by Ali Abd El Latif[2]; its flag was a representation of the Nile on a white ground, with a miniature copy of the Egyptian flag in one corner and the word 'Forward' in Arabic. The publication of the Milner Report on the disorders and the constitutional crisis in the then British Protectorate of Egypt had repercussions in the Sudan. A violent mutiny broke out among the political prisoners in the Central Prison at Khartoum, and there were mutinies by units of Sudanese troops forming part of the Egyptian Army in the Sudan. In his annual report for 1924, the Governor-General had to state that there was a rude interruption 'by political agitation which threatened public security for the first time in the history of the Condominium'.[3]

In 1931, the Sudan Government decided to reduce from £E8 to £E5½ a month the initial rate of pay to new graduates of the Gordon College, without making any reduction in the starting rates of British officials (although some token cuts were made in the higher incomes). This provoked students to go on strike and graduates to appoint an *ad hoc* committee to take up the matter with the Government, and the matter was settled after unnecessarily prolonged negotiations which brought only partial redress. This left a sense of grievance in the minds of the educated class and encouraged them to organize themselves first for self-protection and eventually for political purposes.

In 1936 the Sudan came up for discussion in Anglo-Egyptian negotiations. The Treaty of 1936 caused widespread anger among the politically conscious Sudanese, who considered it too high-handed and humiliating that their own future should be settled by England and Egypt over their head; and they were determined to put an end to it. This situation was a newly-found impetus for the educated elements to mobilize into the Graduates General Congress, which comprised ex-students of Gordon College and other literate Sudanese, imbued with the desire 'to serve the public interest and of the graduates'. The Congress, originally acting under the banner of a cultural society, became a focus of political activity. Anxious to participate in the affairs of the country, they addressed a letter to the Civil Secretary, requesting that, 'in matters of

---

[1] Abbas, Mekki, p. 107.   [2] He died in exile in 1948.
[3] The Governor-General, *Annual Report*, 1925, p. 4.

public interest involving the Government or lying within the scope of its policy and concern', the Government should 'give due consideration to the views and suggestions which we may submit from time to time'.[1] The British Administration gave a reply amounting to a rebuff. They accepted the Congress's request with the express demand that it should seek no recognition as a political body nor claim to speak for any other Sudanese except its own members. But on 3 April 1942, the Congress, under the presidency of Ibrahim Ahmed (later Vice-President of Gordon College and Chairman of Khartoum Municipal Council, and subsequently Minister of Finance in the Coalition Government of 1956), submitted to the Governor-General a memorandum with twelve demands, among which were the issue, at the first possible opportunity, by the British and Egyptian Governments, of a joint declaration granting the Sudan the right of self-determination directly after the War; this right should be safeguarded by guarantees assuring the Sudanese the right of determining their natural rights with Egypt in a special agreement between the Egyptian and the Sudanese nations; the abolition of ordinances on 'closed areas' (the Southern Sudan) and the lifting of restrictions placed on trade and on the movements of the Sudanese within the Sudan;[2] and the setting up of a legislative assembly to enact laws and approve the budget.

Sir Douglas Newbold (the Civil Secretary) and Sir Hubert Huddleston (the Governor-General) returned the memorandum and refused to entertain any political discussion with Congress. Private sympathy and assurances expressed by the Civil Secretary and the Governor-General failed to convince certain members of Congress. In consequence, Congress broke into two independent factions—the Umma Party, made up initially of members willing to trust the Civil Secretary, in 1944; and the Ashigga (Blood Brothers) Party, composed of those who regarded the British Government's attitude, as conveyed in the answer to their memorandum, as unsympathetic. The Ashigga, having won a majority of seats in a Congress general election of officers after the split, resolved to set up 'A Sudanese Democratic Government in Union with Egypt under the Egyptian Crown'.[3] This resolution was forwarded to the Governor-General, asking him to convey it to the Condominium Governments.

By the end of 1945, when the Condominium Governments were

[1] Henderson, K. D. D., *The Making of Modern Sudan*, London, 1953, pp. 536–7.
[2] *Ibid.*, pp. 540–1.
[3] *Sawt el Sudan*, 13 October 1945 and 20 March 1946.

preparing to negotiate on the revision on the 1936 Treaty, the Congress received another political spur. Ismail El Azhari, then Chairman of the Congress, presented a note to the Governor-General containing demands, agreed upon by the various factions within the Congress, for the following: the establishment of a free democratic Government in union with Egypt and in alliance with Great Britain; the appointment of a joint commission to draw up a scheme for transferring the Government to the Sudanese in the shortest time possible. Half of the commission should be members representing Britain and Egypt, and the other half enlightened Sudanese appointed by the Congress; freedom of the Press, public meetings and associations, travel and trading, within public laws conforming to true democratic principles; and the amendment of those laws which restrict these freedoms.[1]

These general awakenings were influenced by the Egyptian national movement in 1919 and after. They were also accelerated by external factors during and after the Second World War. Among these were the acceleration of general development within the Sudan stimulated by the War; the war-time contacts made by the Sudanese who served in Eritrea, Ethiopia, North Africa, etc., with other servicemen from many parts of the world; the force of the political consciousness spurred on by the emergence of dissatisfied educated classes; the rise of a new Liberalism (Socialism) with the emergence of the Labour Party into power after the Second World War, and the fresh outlook on the Empire; and above all, the emergence of fresh political thought and ideals for a new world order, which had improved the attitudes and policies of Britain towards her subject peoples. The United Nations Charter aims to develop mutual friendship, respect and equality among all nations, and 'self-determination of peoples'. As a result, the post-war years were a period of hope and anticipation when peoples everywhere, and especially the growing intelligentsia in subject countries like the Sudan, looked to the new international institution for a 'new deal'. Thus when the Sudan Question was brought before the Security Council in 1947, Ismail El Azhari headed a Sudanese delegation to Lake Success.[2] Miss Margery Perham, Director, Oxford University Institute of Colonial Studies, was sufficiently impressed by the performances of the Sudanese to have captioned her article 'The Sudan Emerges into Nationhood' and to remark in it that 'there were certain dark and fine-looking men

[1] Dr. Rashed El-Barawy, 'Sudan and Egypt' in *India Quarterly Journal of International Affairs*, New Delhi, Oct.–Dec. 1951, pp. 360–1.
[2] Sudanese Govt., Ministry of Social Affairs, *1001 Facts about the Sudan*, Khartoum, April 1955, p. 4.

in Lake Success, speaking excellent English . . . who claimed to represent the Sudanese Nation and to decide its destiny.'[1]

2. THE SUDANESE VIEWPOINTS (POLITICAL PARTIES)

The experiences of the Sudanese delegation and the publicity given to the Sudan Question in the United Nations increased the Sudanese awareness of their own importance; political parties became infused with fresh vitality. These political parties did educate public opinion and indicated the wishes of the Sudanese in regard to their future relationship with the Codomini Governments. To the political parties we must now turn therefore.

The Unionist Party formulated in 1944 a policy which aimed at the establishment of a free and 'democratic' Sudanese Government. They wanted the termination of the Condominium by peaceful means. As for relationship with Egypt, they approved of a status similar to that of a dominion in the British Commonwealth in which different states have equal rights and sovereignty. It was led by Hammad Tawfig from 1948 till 1952 when it became amalgamated with the National Unionist Party.

It was the most outstanding of the 'Unity' parties with membership mainly in the towns and among the intelligentsia.

The Ashigga (Blood Brothers) Party demanded the establishment of a democratic Sudanese Government in union with Egypt. Under the Egyptian Crown 'the Sudanese would enjoy equal rights with the Egyptians in Egypt and would incorporate their armed forces with those of Egypt'.[2] Ismail El Azhari, as leader of a Sudanese Unionist delegation on the Anglo-Egyptian Treaty revision, claimed that, in spite of the intrigues of British officials in Khartoum, the majority of the Sudanese were in favour of the Unity of the Nile Valley:

I am aware [he said] that the present administration has neither encouraged a social intercourse nor the economic relations between Egyptians and Sudanese. But despite the semi-official support given by the administration, the separatists, led by Al Mahdi Pasha, have not succeeded in rallying around them the majority of the Sudanese population. I do not hesitate to affirm today that the greatest part of the enlightened and labouring classes in the Sudan remain loyal to the principle of the Unity of the Nile Valley under the Egyptian Crown.[3]

[1] *Foreign Affairs*: An American quarterly review, New York, July 1949, p. 665.
[2] *Indian Quarterly Journal of International Affairs*, loc cit., p. 361.
[3] Egyptian Embassy, Press Section, *Egypt/Sudan*, p. 53.

The Unity of the Nile Party was organized in 1946, and it aimed at the complete unity of the Nile Valley: that is, the creation of a unified state in which Sudanese and Egyptians would enjoy equal status. 'This unity may be achieved by all means, peaceful or otherwise.' One of the prominent leaders (President) of the Party was Dirdiri Ahmed Ismail, an advocate who was educated at Leeds in England.

The National Unionist Party: These factions were amalgamated in 1952 into the National Unionist Party under Ismail Azhari. The spiritual father of the Unionists has been and still is Sayed Sir Ali El Mirghani. Of Saudi Arabian origin, settled in the Sudan after the conquest, and a member of the Khatmia religious Sect, there was enough to cause a gulf between him and El Mahdi, leader of the Ansar Sect. This religious antagonism eventually spread to the field of politics. The Mahdi, who at one time hoped to become King of the Sudan, championed independence with British help; and the Mirghani leaned towards Egypt as a safeguard against the Mahdist monarchy. Thus the Mahdi headed the Umma Party and the Mirghani the Unionists.

The Umma (Nation) Party, or People's Party started in 1944 as an off-shoot of the Graduates' General Congress; it demanded independence at the end of tutelage under British rule. Dr. Rashed El-Barawy, in his article 'Sudan and Egypt', published in the *Indian Quarterly Journal of International Affairs*, describes the Umma Party as one led by 'feudalistic *landowners*[1] who are given by the British the best positions . . .' in the administration, and are accordingly a party of 'haves', or rich people naturally content with their advantages and averse to 'hasty' reforms.[2] The *Britannia Book of the Year* 1952 stated that the Umma Party was in no way a mere instrument of British interests, but admitted that its 'aspirations coincide with the intention of the British Government'.[3] Reporting on the constitutional crisis in the Sudan, a Khartoum correspondent of the *Observer*,[4] London, remarked in 1951 that relations between the Umma Party and the British authorities were friendly. In 1954 the organ of the Australian Department of Foreign Affairs commented that the Umma had 'British support against Egyptian pressure in their local politics'.[5]

This pro-British tendency of the Umma Party and the support given

---

[1] Apart from the Mahdi and his family, the leaders of the Umma were not strictly landowners but senior government officials.
[2] *Op. cit.*, p. 362.   [3] P. 41.
[4] *Observer*, 11 March 1951.
[5] 'The Sudanese Elections', *Current Notes on International Affairs*, Vol. XXV, No. 1, Canberra, January 1954, p. 52.

to it by the British administration was perhaps due to the anti-Egyptian sentiments of the Mahdi himself and his followers who, it has been alleged, saw in the prospect of a fully independent Sudan a somewhat royal role for himself and a future for his party.

The spiritual father of the Party is Abdel Rahman el Mahdi, the posthumous son of the great Mahdi (whose forces killed General Gordon at Khartoum). For fear that he might possibly revive the nationalism of his father, the British authorities confined his movements in his youth until the outbreak of World War I and even later. For fear of his influence, especially in the west of the Sudan (Kordofan and Darfur Provinces), where the bulk of his followers live, the British confined him to the Gezira Province. But gradually, the British policy of obstruction gave way to co-operation. To a certain extent, his politics of co-operation with the British to gain as much as possible for his country thereby, is comparable to the role once played in Nigeria by the late Sir Adeyemo Alakija. Like Sir Adeyemo Alakija, Sayed Sir Abdel Rahman el Mahdi was often misunderstood and criticized by those nationalists who had reason to distrust the British. As we have indicated, the British also played politics with Mirghani, using him and the Mahdi as counterweights. When the Mahdi began to champion independence as against union with Egypt, the British inclined towards him and away from Mirghani.

The Sudan Party, an offspring of the Umma, aimed at independence and membership of the British Commonwealth.

The Socialist Republican Party, another offshoot of the Umma, also wanted independence, but without monarchy in the Sudan. It was feared that Sayed Sir Abdel Rahman el Mahdi, who dominated the Umma, might revert to a kind of rule somewhat similar to that of the late Mahdi.

Two other parties emerged just before the 1953 elections, one in the south the other in the north of the country. They are the Southern Party and the Front Against Imperialism. Of these, the Southern Party provided a platform for the politically active Southerners of various political allegiances; some endorsed the Northerners' commitment to a unitary state, whilst others advocated a limited autonomy to the North and the South within a federated Sudan. Some supported union with Egypt, others favoured membership of the British Commonwealth, whilst others supported the advocates for complete independence of the Sudan. This heterogeneous nature of the Southern Party reflected the various competing and conflicting forces working on the minds of the Southern Sudanese. (These forces exploded in August 1955, when many Southerners revolted.) However, the Party had nine seats in the first Sudanese Parliament. The Front against Imperialism was supported by Sudanese intellectuals. It ran a journal called *Maidan* (common platform or free forum). So far, its few members have been alert, resourceful and pushful; they possess wide contacts within and outside the Sudan; they are described by a sympathetic Sudanese school-teacher (now in the Foreign Service of the Sudanese Government) as 'incorruptible'. However, they are generally mentioned as Left-wingers or 'Communists'. (But Abdel Rahman Abdel Rahim, its Secretary-General, informed the writer in Khartoum in February 1956, that the Front's members were workers, *intelligentsia*, and merchants; also, Yahiya Abdel Rahman El Mahdi, Assistant Director of the Mahdi's cotton firm, commented that the Front was 'Leftist' but that the allegation that it was 'communistic' had not been substantiated.) They advocated for the complete independence of the Sudan from both Britain and Egypt, and opposed any military pacts with foreign powers. The president of the Party, Mr. Hassan Tahir Zaroug, is an ex-schoolmaster; the secretary also is a teacher; and this partly explains the Party's interest in mass education—they run evening schools for adults. But only one of their members, supported by the 'Graduates' Constituency, was elected to Parliament in 1953. However, the Party struggles for more strength.

A Sudanese newspaper, *The Voice of the Sudan*, advised Egypt to organize a united front of all the pro-Egyptian parties in Egypt and the Sudan, as they all demanded the evacuation of the Nile Valley by Britain and worked for its unity. The bloc thus formed must go to convince the world (the U.N.) that the Sudanese and the Egyptians were decided to have one and the same Fatherland.[1] General Neguib accepted this suggestion, and after coming to terms with all the Sudanese parties in 1952, he decided to unite and thereby strengthen those that supported Egypt's point of view. Until 2 November 1952, the pro-Egyptian elements were divided into no less than eight different segments. Convinced by General Neguib, they 'agreed to unite into a single "National Union Party" that would be strong enough to defeat the pro-British coalition dominated by the Umma'.[2] The National Unionists who were themselves a coalition, agreed to accept the leadership of Ismail El Azhari, then President of the Ashigga.

El Nil (Ansar Organ—Pro-Independence, 20 February 1953) in an

[1] Egyptian Embassy, *Egypt/Sudan*, p. 53. [2] *Egypt's Destiny*, p. 245.

editorial on the issue of the future status of the Sudan said that whatever Britain and Egypt might think, they must both realize that the Sudanese were not a flock of sheep.

They possess a moral code of their own and are capable of deciding the future form of international association best suited to their conditions. They merely wish that both Great Britain and Egypt shall refrain from influencing Sudanese choice by pretending to protect Sudanese interests.[1]

Ibrahim Bedri, Secretary-General of the Socialist Republican Party, also commented that it was premature to speak of the Sudan joining the British Commonwealth or associating with any other state. The Sudanese would be free to consider that question after full independence had been achieved.[2]

Thus since the Anglo-Egyptian dispute had been discussed at the Security Council in 1947, the Sudanese themselves were full of confidence. They felt that they were ready for self-government and political thought had been concentrated almost entirely on that aim. The only real split politically was on the method of achieving it, and after independence, whether to join the British Commonwealth or form a Union with Egypt. John Hyslop was therefore justified to have emphasized in 1952, after a visit to the Sudan, that the Sudanese in high or low places, whatever their job, were learning fast, and that they would soon be in charge of their own affairs.

In the qualities of character such as courage, loyalty, tolerance and perseverance, they lack nothing possessed by the European. . . . Many of the older Sudanese have all the qualities which go to the making of successful Ministers of State. They have a deep sense of the *dignity* of debate and the responsibilities of public service.[3]

Further to the modest measure of constitutional advance unilaterally introduced in 1948 by the British (see chapter 12), another measure of a more real autonomy was introduced and pushed ahead by the British Administration in collaboration with the Umma Party. Under this draft Self-Government Statute, general elections were to be held in November and December 1952. 'If this had been done, Egypt would, in due course, have been deprived of even theoretical control of the Sudan.'[4]

---

[1] P.R.O./1500019: Public Relations Branch, Khartoum, 26 February 1953.
[2] *Sudan News and Features*, No. 203/53, 21 February 1953.
[3] *Sudan Story*, pp. 14, 133.
[4] Sukumar Sen, Indian Chairman of the 1953 Electoral Commission, 'The General Election in the Sudan', in *Parliamentary Affairs*, Vol. VII, No. 3, London, 1954, p. 305,

It was at this stage that the new regime (the *coup d'état*) in Egypt saved the situation by entering into direct negotiations with Britain and the Sudanese political parties for 'immediate autonomy and self-determination after three years or less'.

That was the general picture, the level of political consciousness and maturity in the Sudan before the November–December General Elections, which, to a large extent, indicated the wishes of the Sudanese about their future with Britain and Egypt.

The general election in the Sudan aroused great anxiety in both Britain and Egypt, because their respective economic interests and political prestige were at stake. Britain supported the advocates of 'independence' (i.e. separation from Egypt) in the hope that such 'independence' would keep the Sudan more closely attached to Britain and eventually to the British Commonwealth than unity with Egypt would permit; further, the British were quite proud of their achievements in the Sudan: one of the British Information Services' posters on the Sudan declares, with truth: 'In the last half-century, under British guidance, a sound administration has been built up, in which the Sudanese have gradually taken an increasing share.'[1]

The British, who have consistently maintained, rightly or wrongly, that Egyptian administration in the Sudan at the beginning of the 19th century was corrupt and inefficient, feared that the modern Administration which Britain had helped to build up in the Sudan would deteriorate under Egyptian control or influence, and in consequence many of the British officials in the Sudan, and indeed several Englishmen in Britain, were personally anti-Egyptian.

As we have already suggested (chapter 8), the British who are indisputably adepts in the game of balancing one power against the other, did not wish for an Egyptian–Sudanese state which might eventually become too strong to cope with, politically. And to these we must add all the elements which we have compounded into the British stake in the Sudan (chapter 8). As a result, British feeling leaned towards the Umma Party and other pro-British persons during the general election.

The Egyptians, on the other hand, felt strongly that the British did not mean to grant real independence to the Sudanese; this the Egyptians gathered from their own experience of remaining practically a British Protectorate even after the declaration of 1922; in addition, they had discovered during negotiations with the British Government that

[1] The Development of the Anglo-Egyptian Sudan 1898–1952, Poster No. 4.

Sudan elections in Nuba Mountains of Kordofan.
Candidates draw lots out of a hat to determine the symbols by which
they will be represented

independence for the Sudanese was mere lip-service on the part of the British. Salah Eddin Bey had told Mr. Bevin in 1950:

> You keep reiterating the slogan of self-government and self-determination for the Sudanese, but when we ask you whether you are prepared to agree that a Sudanese democratic government depending on a truly representative assembly be forthwith established, and that the present administration hand over power to this government, you try to find excuses . . . that the Sudanese are not as yet mature enough for self-government.[1]

They feared, too, that a pro-British self-governing Sudan might be a thorn in the flesh of Egypt; although the Egyptians could recognize and accept certain distinctions between Egypt and the Sudan and although they might admit the virtues of the British administrations, they were anxious that Egyptian–Sudanese co-operation should be encouraged, in order that if and when Sudanese nationalism became an active force, it would not take (as in the time of the Mahdi) an anti-Egyptian character. They were anxious that the time, money and other efforts which they had put into the Sudan for many decades should not go to waste in the sense that such efforts brought no acknowledgment and substantial credit to Egypt. In other words, the Egyptians felt that Egypt had supplied the means, and had contributed to the progress of the Sudan, whilst Britain took most of the credit. A Sudanese union with Egypt would, they thought, remedy that situation. They felt that seventy years of British occupation in Egypt had produced anti-British feeling and a protective attitude towards the Sudanese, as from an experienced 'bigger brother' to a little one. They realized in consequence that political hostility must be avoided between the two beneficiaries of the Nile Waters. Should the Sudan decide to unite with Egypt, Egypt would be more able to achieve her economic interests in the Sudan, which we have analysed (chapter 7); such unity of the Nile Valley might be a nucleus for a new Egyptian Empire, envisaged by Mohammed Ali.

Those were some of the speculations in Britain and Egypt when the Sudanese prepared for the elections.

3. THE 1953 ELECTIONS: CHARGES AND COUNTER-CHARGES OF INTER-
FERENCE BY BRITAIN AND EGYPT. THE CAUSES OF THE VICTORY OF THE
PRO-EGYPTIAN PARTY IN THE SUDAN.

Article 7 of the 1953 Agreement provided for a Mixed Electoral Commission. It was announced on 7 April that it had been formed with representatives of India (Mr. Sukumar Sen, Chairman), Britain, the

---

[1] Egypt, Ministry of Foreign Affairs, *op. cit.*, p. 93.

United States, Egypt and the Sudan. The Indian Chairman of the Commission had successfully arranged in India 'the most extensive democratic elections which the world has ever seen'.[1] The Agreement pledged both Britain and Egypt to enable the Sudanese to elect their Parliament and to determine their own future in a 'free and neutral atmosphere'. The main duty of the International Commission was therefore to ensure impartiality first in the race for the control of Parliament between the pro-Egyptian political parties and the pro-British ones, and secondly to ensure non-interference by the British and the Egyptian Governments, through their respective employees in the Sudan.

In spite of these provisions, there were, during the November–December elections to the first all-Sudanese Parliament (the nature of whose membership would ultimately determine the relationship with Britain and Egypt) allegations and counter-allegations of interference in the elections on the part of Britain and Egypt. In a speech in the House of Commons, Mr. Eden accused the Egyptian Government of using the Press and radio of Egypt and other means 'to influence the decision of the Sudanese people in favour of the party which advocates a link with Egypt'.[2]

In reply, Major Salah Salem, Egyptian Minister for National Guidance and Sudanese Affairs stated: 'It is strange that Mr. Eden accuses us of intervening, whereas Egypt has not got any single responsible official in the Sudan who has any power or any influence.'[3] He alleged that the office of the British Trade Commissioner in Khartoum contained thousands of leaflets and pamphlets calling for British colonization and attacking Egypt. He indicated that the British Government had the help of the British Press, the British Broadcasting Corporation, and several other broadcasting stations under British influence, with which they attacked Egypt, supported one section of the Sudan against another and falsely accused the pro-Egyptian party.

Mr. Eden went to Parliament again to repeat his charges[4] of a week earlier and further alleged that the Egyptian Government had tried to influence the elections by spending money 'on gifts for educational and

---

[1] *The Times*, London, 25 August 1953.

[2] The Public Relations Dept., Sudan Govt., *Sudan News and Features*, Feature No. 319, 6 November 1953.

[3] *Ibid.*, Feature No. 320.

[4] On 6 November 1953 *The Times*, London, carried a leading article supporting Mr. Eden in charges of Egyptian interference. Professor H. A. R. Gibb asserted that it had been the policy of *The Times*, in so far as Anglo-Egyptian relations were concerned, to be 'the mouthpiece of the views held in British official circles' (*International Affairs*, Vol. XXVII, No. 4, October 1951, p. 449).

religious purposes'; that there had been, since the election started, 'an influx of other servants of the Egyptian Government of Sudanese origin who were ostensibly on leave' to coincide with elections.[1]

Major Salem attributed the British accusations to Britain's psychological reaction to the battle she was losing in the Sudan, because it was becoming apparent that British supporters would not succeed in the elections and Britain was therefore looking for a scapegoat. He alleged that the British had been silent over the British Governor of Kassala 'who had forbidden meetings of more than five people during the elections, even though they happen to be in one motor-car together; and he who has thrown in prison every human being who does not support the side supported by himself'. He also mentioned another irregularity by a British official whose conduct was being investigated by the Electoral Commission. As for the Sudanese who were home on leave from Egypt he was happy that thousands of Sudanese were earning their daily bread in Egypt (whilst they could not do so in Britain). He charged the British Government with insincerity about granting complete independence to the Sudanese: similar promises had been made, he went on, for example in 'Kenya, the Sudan's neighbour, and you go on slaughtering the sons of Kenya who disagree with you'.[2]

On a complaint that Lt.-Col. de Robeck, a British District Commissioner, had intervened in the election by persuading a pro-Egyptian National Unionist Candidate to withdraw his nomination, the Electoral Commission pronounced that Col. de Robeck had acted improperly by being present when the candidate withdrew his nomination, but the Commission found that he had exercised no personal pressure on the candidate. It, however, recommended to the Government that suitable disciplinary measures be taken against him.[3]

In subsequent articles on 'The General Election in the Sudan', written for the Hansard Society in Britain neither Mr. Sukumar Sen, the Indian Chairman of the Electoral Commission, nor Mr. Mekki Abbas, the Director of the Sudan Gezira Board, categorically declared that Britain or Egypt did in fact interfere. But they do leave one with the impression that there was opportunity for British officials and Egyptian propaganda to interfere. Mr. Sen comments:

> The Electoral Commission had no Field Staff of its own and the existing Governmental machinery had to be used in preparing for and running the

[1] P.R.O. Khartoum, *Sudan Feature*, No. 327, 14 November 1953.
[2] P.R.O. *Sudan Bulletin*, No. 1923, 13 November 1953, pp. 1–3.
[3] Royal Institute of International Affairs, *Chronology of International Events and Documents*, Vol. IX, No. 22, 5–18, November 1953, pp. 738–739.

elections. This had to be done without giving any scope for legitimate criticism that the British Administration was influencing the elections in any way.[1]

While Mekki Abbas declares:

It is undisputable fact that the sentiments of British Officials serving in the Sudan were, and still are (in 1954), with the independence parties. There have therefore been constant allegations by Egypt and by the National Unionist Party (in the Sudan) that some of these officials tried to influence the elections . . . one of the charges is that British Officials have for many years helped the Mahdi to become extremely rich . . . so much so that he is now able to finance the Umma Party from his own funds.[2]

The Chairman of the Electoral Commission made no suggestion about Egyptian interference. But Mr. Abbas, who asked the Hansard Society 'to emphasise that he is himself a Sudanese who believes in the independence of the Sudan' (from Egypt),[3] declared that British and Egyptian 'influence played a very important part': Egypt did all she could to support the National Unionist Party; the Egyptian Press— widely read in the Sudan—and the Egyptian radio attacked the 'independence' groups, and influential personalities from Egypt visited the Sudan before the elections.

In the midst of these Anglo-Egyptian quarrels the Sudanese went to the polls with zest. After the recording of votes, but before the results were declared, the Chairman of the Electoral Commission broadcast an address from Radio Omdurman in which he stated that over 90 per cent of the total electorate voted—a most gratifying and hopeful sign for the future of the country. He considered it the successful and completely peaceful and orderly finish of a great effort.

I have nothing [he added] but sincere admiration for the exemplary way in which the Sudanese people have conducted themselves during these anxious and uncertain months and weeks. The Electoral Commission and the devoted band of election officials who worked with us spared no efforts to enable you to vote freely according to your individual choice, without fear, coercion or intimidation.[4]

Another feature of the end of the polling was a series of published expressions of thanks by Sudanese newspapers to Mr. Sukumar Sen and his Commission for their work. An example was the editorial in *Sawt*

[1] *Parliamentary Affairs*, p. 305.
[2] *Parliamentary Affairs*, loc. cit.
[3] *Ibid.*, p. 303.
[4] P.R.O. Sudan, *News and Features*, Communiqué No. 10, Khartoum, 26 November 1953.

el Sudan (of 29 November), captioned: 'We salute a man who has done his duty.'[1]

As a result of the election, there are two Houses of Parliament in the Sudan, the House of Representatives, with ninety-seven members, and the Senate, having fifty members. The final results of the elections which began on 2 November and concluded on 5 December 1953, indicated that the National Unionist Party—which is an amalgamation of all groups favouring some link between Sudan and Egypt—established a long lead and a parliamentary majority by obtaining more than double the number of seats gained by the Umma Party.[2] The final results of the Senatorial elections were announced on 15 December, showing that the National Unionist Party had won twenty-one of the thirty seats filled by election, the Umma four seats, the Southern Party three, the Independents two and the National Republicans none. Twenty additional members were later appointed by the Governor-General, after consultation with his Commission.[3]

One of the leaders of the successful Unionists, Mirghani Hamza (subsequently Minister of Education) attempted to define the Sudan's future relations with the Co-domini. His Party's Government would push on rapidly with Sudanization of the administration as a means of 'liberation' from British control; after self-determination, the next stage 'would be to determine relations with other countries; the Sudanese would want to be on good terms with Britain but much would depend upon the behaviour, in the transitional period, of the British administration, whose attitude to the National Unionist Party has not been satisfactory and who have advised the British Government on wrong lines'. As for Egypt, he added: 'there was a strong feeling in the Sudan' advocating strong ties with Egypt for certain common interests,

---

[1] Reproduced by P.R.O. *Sudan News and Features*, 19 December 1953, Feature No. 347.
[2] The final results were:

National Unionist	.	.	.	.	50 seats
Umma	.	.	.	.	23 ,,
Independent	.	.	.	.	11 ,,
Southern Party	.	.	.	.	9 ,,
Socialist Republicans.	.	.	.	3 ,,
Front against Imperialism	.	.	.	1 ,,

[3] The details were:

Unionist .	.	.	10 plus 21 elected members = 31
Umma	.	.	4 ,, 4 ,, ,, = 8
The Southern Party .	.	3 ,, 3 ,, ,, = 6
Independents	.	.	2 ,, 2 ,, ,, = 4
Socialist Republicans.	.	1 ,, 0 ,, ,, = 1

Total in Senate   50

but without accepting Egyptian supremacy. He therefore envisaged: 'Our party will advise the constituent Assembly when it is formed to favour close ties with Egypt. Even the Umma admits that a happy relationship with Egypt is necessary.'[1]

In a broadcast address to the Sudanese people the night before the election results were declared, Major Salah Salem announced that the Egyptians, on their part, had decided to forgive the insults levelled against them by the British and the pro-British Sudanese during the elections. He reaffirmed Egypt's neutrality in the internal affairs of the Sudan, but told the Sudanese: 'You are just invited to co-operate with us in putting an end to colonialism which has been shattering the Arabs and Islam, making of Israel a tool of dissension. Egypt sincerely hopes that the Sudan may successfully emerge from seclusion.'[2]

After the results, General Neguib received prominent Sudanese, resident in Egypt, who called on him with congratulations. He issued a statement of good wishes to 'our brothers, the Sudanese'; he appealed to all peoples and parties for unity in the Sudan, where he foresaw that the future might be made more difficult than necessary by various British intrigues such as attempting to turn the South against the North, or finding pretexts for intervention in Sudanese affairs, in such matters as defence or the budget.[3] (About two years later, in August 1955, there was a mutiny and revolt in the Southern Sudan against the North; this we shall fully discuss in the next chapter.)

Sayed Siddiq Abdel Rahman El Mahdi, leader of the Umma Party and the Mahdi's grandson, supported for many years by the British officials in the Sudan, veered from the policy of a link with Britain towards complete independence. The Socialist Republicans 'the only party which could (still) be called in a sense pro-British'[4] scored a negligible vote. Consequently the results caused much surprise in Britain, 'chiefly owing to the belief that as the majority of the Sudanese people did not wish for union with Egypt in any form, the N.U.P. was not likely to win as many seats as the Umma Party'.[5] Certain elements in Britain interpreted the sweeping victory of the pro-Egyptian party as an expression of Sudanese ingratitude for decades of enlightened British administration.[6] We therefore consider it pertinent to indicate some of

---

[1] *The Times*, 1 December 1953.
[2] P.R.O., *Sudan Feature*, No. 346, 5 December 1953.
[3] *The Times*, 30 November 1953.
[4] *New Statesman and Nation*, 5 December 1953.
[5] *The Annual Register* for 1953, London, 1954, p. 265.
[6] *New Statesman and Nation*, 5 December 1953.

the forces behind the complete victory of the Unionists, which advocated a link with Egypt. Some of the causes are immediate or internal, others are remote or external.

Apart from their general principle and some past performances, the Unionists' electioneering campaigns concentrated on a feeling of anti-imperialism. It must be stated, however, that much as British imperial rule was hated, particularly by the intelligentsia, the British, as a people and as individuals, were admired and respected. This distinction between policy and people, often made by subject peoples, must be borne in mind. The British officials in the Sudan were traduced as 'colonizers' whose duty it was to exploit the Sudan in favour of Manchester cotton and to ensure the country's membership of the Commonwealth[1]; the Unionist Party appeared as the chief champion of the Sudanese against British rule, which was resented and bitterly attacked by most Sudanese, like any other subject peoples. On the other hand the Umma Party identified itself with the British Administration in the sense that its leaders thought that the Sudan could achieve independence in the shortest time and easiest way through co-operation with the British. They therefore became ministers under the various Constitutional arrangements and co-operated with the British Administration. Public opinion was, to a certain extent, against their participation in running the 'imperial' constitution boycotted by the Unionists and other parties. Relying on the bitter experience of the past, the Sudanese had evolved a simple test to which they often resorted when in difficulty; the formula was something like: 'friends of British imperialism are no friends to the Sudan.' Nearly everything fostered by British imperialism was *prima facie* bad until the contrary was proved.

The second point is that the Umma Party was supported by Sir Abdel Rahman El Mahdi, whose father established the Mahdia movement in 1885. Although the original Mahdi died without enjoying the fruits of his successful revolt and although he was not at all responsible for the later horrors of his followers, the Sudanese were anxious that history should not repeat itself; they therefore did not vote for the party championed by the late Mahdi's son, who, they thought, might bring the Mahdia back to life.

The third element for the success of the pro-Egyptian Party was the British preliminary attitude towards the Egyptian proposals leading to the 1953 Agreement. As already indicated, the British showed reluctance in signing the Agreement and tried to delay it. Instead of welcoming the

[1] Royal Institute of International Affairs, *The World Today*, Vol. X, 1954, pp. 3–342.

Egyptian plan as soon as it was announced in November 1952, Mr. Eden haggled for three months—trying to amend the proposals in order to give the (British) Governor-General special powers relating to the Southern provinces during the three-year transitional period.[1] Against this, General Neguib appeared enthusiastic; he seized every opportunity to press further the interests of the Sudanese. To many Sudanese, the general effect of the Anglo-Egyptian negotiations was the impression of bad faith on the part of the British as contrasted with General Neguib's apparent sincerity, good faith and friendliness to the Sudan; his offer of independence to the Sudanese, whether in union with Egypt or not, impressed the Sudanese Leaders with whom he negotiated. 'Britain was stalling, and—General Neguib appeared in the guise of a liberator.'[2] Consequently, the Sudanese chose to accept Neguib's friendly gesture, and in turn to lean towards Egypt.

Fourthly, the deposition of King Farouk and the personality of General Neguib must be added. The Revolution destroyed the Crown, which had been a sort of bogy to many Sudanese. The fact that Neguib was himself half-Sudanese had a favourable effect on the votes cast in the Sudan. The Sudanese have a deep feeling of admiration and respect towards him for the sincere and able way in which he tackled the problems of Egypt. 'Neguib and his young associates have certainly brought a new drive and a new integrity into Egyptian life.'[3] General Neguib had given much of his personal interest and attention to the Sudan and its peoples; he says:

> I naturally have a tender feeling for the land in which I was born and in which so much of my family's blood was shed. It gave me great pleasure, therefore, to be able to create the conditions necessary for supplanting the inequitable and unworkable Agreement of 1899 with the equitable and eminently workable Agreement of 1953.[4]

It was not surprising therefore that many Sudanese voted Unionist to enhance the prestige of, and to register their admiration for, this half-Sudanese President of the Republic of Egypt.

Fifthly, one of the strong points of the Unionist Party was that the Sudan, being a country underdeveloped and economically weak, could not, at least for a while, stand on her own feet. They indicated that the country needed sincere co-operation from an external source. They ruled out Britain on account of what they regarded as her imperialistic

---

[1] *New Statesman and Nation*, 5 December 1953.   [2] *Ibid.*
[3] Anthony Greenwood, *Tribune*, London. 8 January 1952.
[4] *Egypt's Destiny*, p. 241.

outlook, and because of the unpleasant part of her past record in the Sudan and other parts of Africa. One other alternative was Egypt, which, the Unionists submitted, had not done much to offend the Sudanese deeply. On the contrary, she had seized every opportunity to develop a friendly and co-operative attitude to the Sudanese. They therefore felt a link with friendly Egypt would create a respectable bloc in North Africa with a strong bargaining power in economic and political matters externally, and with enough internal strength and stability. The Sudan could not bargain effectively on an equal footing with foreign powers, but with Egypt this would be possible.

There are also, what might be called the negative advantages of association with Egypt, as a counter weight against Britain. The Sudanese felt that the British would delay the handing over of Sudanese affairs to the Sudanese, and would not leave the country, but an alliance with Egypt against the British would, they concluded, quicken the journey to self-determination.

These may be called 'The internal causes of the victory of the pro-Egyptian party in the Sudan. There are certain remote or external causes also.

Nineteen-fifty-three, the year of the Sudanese elections, witnessed a succession of crises in British Colonies which undermined British authority and exposed the British Government to certain accusations by the consciences of men. Just south-east of the Sudan, there was unrest in Kenya, where African leaders were imprisoned, and the Kikuyus were being bombed to overcome their insurrection against the Government. The episodes of 1952–3 included the issues on the Central African Federation, opposed by the African community, who saw in it a 'white' unity for 'black' disintegration, but imposed by the British Government. Away to the south-west of the Sudan, a constitutional crisis was precipitated in British-controlled Nigeria.

Further, in 1953 the British Government suspended the Constitution of British Guiana and deposed the elected Government of the Guianese. The last of these episodes in British possessions was the deposition and exile of an African ruler, the Kabaka of Buganda in Uganda, adjoining the Sudan in the South. Although it is true the Kabaka was flown to England in exile the same day as the Sudanese election results were declared, on 30 November 1953, nevertheless the Sudanese had obviously been watching events in Uganda prior to that date.

In the Union of South Africa White supremacy was spreading beyond the Limpopo to the North and the East, which gave rise to the passive resistance on the part of the 'coloured' peoples. South Africa's racialism stirred the conscience of the United Nations, but Britain, the Mother Country, on the Governmental level showed no appreciable signs of disagreement with the Union's policy. This racial policy of South Africa is in fact a continual factor of friction in British relations with every territory in Africa.

The cumulative effect of this series of episodes was a trend to distrust British intentions in Africa. The *Spectator*, which usually supported the Conservative Government commented: 'The whole episode has shown all over again how much distrust there is among Africans of the intentions of the British Government.'[1] Affairs in Africa became such as to lead the Labour Party—the Opposition—to censure the Government by moving in the House of Commons on 16 December 1953: 'That this House expresses its grave disquiet at the handling by Her Majesty's Government of affairs in Africa.'

This 'grave disquiet', the search for security and the sense of 'belonging' all pushed the Sudanese towards the Egyptians.

Finally, the position of Egypt, apart from her physical contiguity, cultural similarities and blood-mixture with the Sudan, must be considered. Her strategic importance as the gateway to the Middle and Far East is significant; and this would increase with the settlement of the Suez Canal Zone. Egypt is also a natural air base. As the most prosperous of the Middle Eastern countries and leader of the growing Arab nations, Egypt holds a key position. It is the geographical capital of the adjacent Mohammedan bloc, and the point of fusion of West and East. Egypt is one of the states on the continent of Africa which are relatively 'young' and hopeful and imbued with something like a sense of 'manifest destiny'. The Sudan would be better able to make, it has been suggested, a greater contribution to world affairs in conjunction with Egypt than with Britain.

But, as we shall show in the next chapter, the Sudan's projected union with Egypt was weakened by certain events between 1954 and 1955.

[1] 4 December 1953.

16

THE PROCESS AND PROBLEMS OF SELF-GOVERN-MENT—UNDER THE NEW AGREEMENT, AND THE CREATION OF THE SUDANESE REPUBLIC: 1954–56

Let us not be bitter about the past but let us keep our eyes firmly on the future. Let us remember that no blessing of God is so sweet as life and liberty. Let us remember that the highest purpose of man is the liberation of man from his bonds of fear, his bonds of human degradation, his bonds of poverty—the liberation of man. from the physical, spiritual and intellectual bonds which have for too long stunted the development of humanity's majority.
And let us remember, Sisters and Brothers, that for the sake of all that, We Asians and Africans must be united.

PRESIDENT SUKARNO,
Asian-African Conference at Bandung, April 1955[1]

HAVING discussed the evolution of political consciousness in the Sudan from 1899, when there was no political party, to 1953 when not less than eight parties contested the General Elections to the first Sudanese Parliament, we shall now discuss the major problems of self-government under the New Anglo-Egyptian Agreement of 1953. These include the Southern revolt of August 1955; the Anglo-Egyptian controversy over the process of self-determination; the deposition of the first Sudanese Government in November 1955. We shall also show how the Sudan finally achieved independence on 1 January 1956; and how she became a member of the Arab League, and of the United Nations Organization.

Parliament was formally opened on 1 January 1954. In accordance with Article 9 of the 1953 Agreement, the transitional period of self-government was to begin on the day designated as 'the Appointed Day' and end in three years from that day or less. By the end of the transitional period the Sudanese would, in accordance with Article 12, either be united with Egypt in some form or be independent. The 'Appointed Day' was 9 January 1954. When elected Prime Minister, El Azhari, President of N.U.P., pledged: 'I undertake to carry out what I think

---

[1] Embassy of the Republic of Indonesia, London, The Information Department: *Indonesian Information*, Asian-African Conference Issue, Volume VI, No. 5, May 1955, p. 4.

is in the Sudan's best interests, progress and development. My aim will be to achieve the Sudan's liberty and to uphold its prestige. I will be influenced by nothing but the Sudan's well-being.' Appealing apparently to both the British officials in the Sudan Administration and the Opposition members in Parliament and also possibly to the British and Egyptian Governments, El Azhari concluded, 'Let us forget our small difficulties and unite to serve this country.' In congratulating the Prime Minister, Mohammed Ahmed Mahgoub, leader of the Opposition, stressed the qualities of a good Government: 'Integrity, character, strength and justice'.[1]

On 9 January 1954, the Governor-General issued a decree certifying that date to be the 'Appointed Day' for the beginning of the period, a maximum of three years—within which the Sudanese must complete the process of self-determination and decide the external relations of their country. But before self-determination certain things had to be done. As set out in the 1953 Agreement, the Sudanization Committee, composed of one British, one Egyptian and three Sudanese, must complete as far as possible the process of replacing foreign officials, British and Egyptian, who might influence the freedom of the Sudanese at the time of self-determination, with Sudanese in the general administration of the country. Following that, the Sudanese Parliament had to pass a resolution requesting that arrangements for self-determination in accordance with Article 9 of the 1953 Agreement, be put in motion; the co-domini would then be informed of the resolution in Parliament asking for self-determination; the Parliament must also pass a law for the election of a constitutional Assembly. That done, Britain and Egypt must then begin withdrawing their military forces from the Sudan within three months, so that elections could be held in a free and neutral atmosphere. They must comply with any recommendation made by the international body which would be set up to supervise the election of the Constituent Assembly and ensure its impartiality—as in the case of the 1953 General Elections. The elected Assembly would then proceed to exercise, on behalf of the country, its choice between complete independence or some link, if any, with Egypt. Both Britain and Egypt bound themselves to act in accordance with the decisions of the Constituent Assembly, whose work would finally bring the Condominium to an end and enable the Sudan to set out on her chosen path.

The transition period upon which the Sudan entered was difficult and delicate. The new Sudanese Ministers became the political superiors

[1] *The Times*, London, 7 January 1954.

of British officials who had until now ruled the country. But the Governor-General of the Sudan, Sir Robert Howe, struck a hopeful note in his speech at the dinner of the Caledonian Society of the Sudan, held at Khartoum on St. Andrew's Night (30 November 1953). Advising the British Civil Servants, he said inspiringly:

> Now we have reached the final stage in the fulfilment of our policy. With it come new problems which call for still higher efforts of faith, skill and example. There is a fresh challenge to us all. . . . But no craftsman worth his salt, lowers his standards or loses heart as he nears the end of his task; so here, we should enter on this last stage of our work to the best of our ability so that it may be said of us that our departure may become us as much as our stay has done.[1]

As for the Sudanese, a practical gesture to Egypt, Britain and other nations was made when the new Cabinet decided on 11 January to invite General Neguib, Sir Winston Churchill and representatives of the United States, India and Pakistan Governments, and those of the Arab States, to attend the re-opening of the Parliament in March. However, the pomp, pageantry and festivities were marred during the re-opening of Parliament, by political riots and mob violence, inspired by the defeated Umma Party, partly as a show of strength and partly against the apparent leaning of the Azhari Cabinet towards Egypt.

But, after one year of self-government in the Sudan, the prospect of union with Egypt began to suffer reverses, especially after December 1954. A very important factor in the victory of the Unionists during the 1953 Sudanese elections and also in the subsequent shift against them is the fact that public opinion in the Sudan was rather sensitive to events in Egypt. Such inflammatory events included the deposition of General Neguib. Signs of serious conflict within the military regime which had secured the Anglo-Egyptian Treaty of Self-Government for the Sudan, began to emerge. 'Abdel Nasser believed, with all the bravado of a man of thirty-six, that we could afford to alienate every segment of Egyptian public opinion, if necessary, in order to achieve our goals.' 'I believe', revealed General Neguib, 'with all the prudence of a man of fifty-three, that we need as much popular support as we could possibly retain.'[2] While Nasser was the Cassius of the Egyptian Revolution, Neguib was the Brutus. This difference in method of approach and the competition for power between popular Neguib and able Nasser led to open friction and General Neguib was relieved of his office on 14 November 1954. The deposition aroused considerable resentment in the Sudan, even

[1] P.R.O., *Sudan Feature*, No. 379, Khartoum, December 1953.
[2] *Egypt's Destiny*, pp. 215-6.

among members of the Umma Party. Sayed Mubarak Zarouk (the Sudanese Minister of Communications) warned Egypt that Neguib's deposition would 'weaken the unity of the Nile Valley'[1]; there were demonstrations in Khartoum involving several hundreds of students. Sudanese students and residents in Egypt protested; an official delegation left Khartoum for Cairo to pour oil on the troubled waters. But General Neguib, the half-Egyptian, half-Sudanese, faded out of public life; his departure deeply wounded the Sudanese mind. Neither Colonel Nasser, though very able, nor Major Salem, though sincere, was able to fill the gap left by the removal of General Neguib, the emblem of Egyptian-Sudanese union, and the source of emotional attraction for the Sudanese.

There was also the suppression of the Muslim Brotherhood. As we have indicated in Chapter 14, certain members of the Muslim Brotherhood made an unsuccessful attempt to assassinate Colonel Nasser on 26 October 1954. Partly for this reason and partly to crush political oppositions, the military regime took coercive measures against the Brotherhood as a whole. The Brotherhood's Secretary—General Abdel Kader Auda, an old friend of Nasser's, was hanged with some of the terrorists; its Supreme Guide, Sheikh Hassan el-Hodeiby, was sent 'in irons to Toura Prison to break stones for the rest of his life'.[2] The shock was too much for the Sudanese who felt that the Egyptian was his brother in Islam.

The personality and policy of Major Salah Salem also had their influence on the Sudanese. 'The dancing major' (chapter 7, section 3 above) had, as the Egyptian Minister of State for Sudan Affairs (he was born in the Sudan), helped General Neguib to build up good relations with the Sudanese; but after the removal of the General, he blatantly over-played his Government's hand in the Sudan. In his over-anxiety to influence the choice of the Sudanese in favour of union with Egypt, he pursued certain policies which alienated the Sudanese; he waged 'a vitriolic campaign against those Sudanese elements which support the idea of complete national independence, as against union with Egypt'.[3]

Again, Azhari's Policy of 'Independence' was one of certain factors in the Sudan itself, which began to emerge against Union with Egypt:

---

[1] Keesing's *Contemporary Archives*, Vol. IX, 1954–55, p. 1392A.
[2] Royal Institute of International Affairs, 'Change of Leadership in Egypt', in *The World Today*, Vol. II, No. 2, February 1955, p. 55.
[3] Extract from *The Times* of 11 August 1955, in *Sudan Weekly*, Khartoum, 16 August 1955, p. 5.

as far back as 1946, Ismail El Azhari had, as leader of a Sudanese delegation on the revision of the Anglo-Egyptian Treaty, declared: 'For the Sudan we desire neither British nor Egyptian domination' (see first page of chapter 13).

It would appear, therefore, that he had, at best, aimed at complete union with Egypt with the utmost cautiousness; at worst, he merely wanted to use Egypt to 'whip' the British out of the Sudan. On becoming Prime Minister in 1953, Azhari's Cabinet was a judicious blend of Ashigga and Khatmia representatives, most of them men of strong views, whether pro-British, anti-Mahdist or anti-British, among whom the Prime Minister had both to lead and mediate. The Unionist Party, which formed the majority in the Government, had to take care not to lose the next general election as a result of the various campaigns by the pro-independence elements against union with Egypt. Any suspicion of subordination to Egypt might lose the Azhari Government the next election. The British Government, advantageously placed, had played their own hand well in the Sudan even to the surprise of members of the Sudan Cabinet, during the period of transition. Efforts had to be made, therefore, not to antagonize those British who had already been incensed by the effects of Sudanization of the administration. The withdrawal of the British administrators from the Sudan, after the beginning of self-government, made the Sudanese feel that they were really free from British rule; that if they chose independence they would be really independent and not under a new form of British control. In addition, most of those negative forces in British Africa, which had helped to push the Sudanese into the hands of the Egyptians during the 1953 elections, had receded: some agreement had been reached about the constitutional crisis in Nigeria: the British had changed their minds about the deposition and exile of the Kabaka of Buganda (his return from exile in October 1955 was warmly received by the Sudanese Press): and the fight of the 'White settlers' against the Mau Mau in Kenya, though still actively in progress, was becoming stale news. For these reasons, the Azhari Cabinet announced themselves committed to the policy of independence, apparently at least till the Sudan would become strong enough to be an effective partner with Egypt. Until there was more faith in the Egyptian Government, the Military Government in Egypt must convincingly demonstrate to the Sudanese, in the words of General Neguib, 'that we had nothing in common with the oppressive regimes that had misruled the Nile Valley in the past'.[1]

[1] *Egypt's Destiny*, p. 190.

Without taking adequate note of the situation in the Sudan as we have attempted to analyse it, the Egyptian Press and radio made concentrated attacks on the Prime Minister of the Sudan for his policy of 'independence'.

Both Colonel Nasser and Mr. Azhari were present at the Afro-Asian Conference held at Bandung in Indonesia in April 1955. There, a kind of 'cold war' developed between the two delegates, and the sons of the Nile Valley got along better with foreign delegates than with one another. Returning from Bandung, Azhari passed through Cairo. In contrast to the good reception accorded him in Asia, he was mocked by hired mobs calling themselves Sudanese. Some of the real Sudanese, mostly students in Cairo, who managed to demonstrate in favour of Mr. Azhari, were later arrested on one charge or another.

This was in great contrast to Azhari's experience when he visited London in 1954; the British behaved shrewdly and with great foresight. At the Royal Institute of International Affairs (Chatham House), academics, British officials who had served in the Sudan, and some of Mr. Azhari's old teachers at Gordon College, gave him an impressive reception. The British saw to it that he was received not only by Sir Winston Churchill, but even by the Queen herself. (The writer is reminded by a British critic that Azhari was then accorded the normal treatment due to a Prime Minister.)

On 5 August 1955—eleven days before the Sudanese Parliament debated the motion that arrangements for self-determination be put into effect—the *Gumhouriya*, regarded as the mouthpiece of the Egyptian Government, commented that Mr. Azhari was elected with the mandate to work for the unity of the Sudan with Egypt; now that he had changed his policy, he should resign and ask the electorate for a new verdict. The Prime Minister and six members of his Cabinet visited Cairo from 23 to 28 July 1955, for the celebrations of the Anniversary of the Egyptian 1952 Revolution. Later, on 13 August, Mr. Azhari announced that he and his ministers had visited Cairo to 'tell the Egyptian Government two things: that our two countries must be friends, and attacks by one against the other must cease; and that the Sudanese people had an ever-increasing desire to cling to their independence'.[1] He added: 'If we had represented a foreign Power, the treatment we received from our hosts would have made us break off diplomatic relations.'[2] The Prime Minister explained that he had formerly supported union of an autonomous Sudan under an Egyptian constitutional monarchy such as

[1] *Sudan Weekly News*, Khartoum, 16 August 1955, p. 5.   [2] *Ibid.*

A Northern merchant and a Southern beauty

the British Commonwealth's, but that subsequent events in Egypt had altered his views.[1]

Thus during the early part of the transitional period of self-government Egypt's prestige was high in the Sudan; but it began to sink from the summer of 1954, while at the same time, British patience and tact paid enormous dividends. However, since the beginning of the autumn of 1955, especially after the dismissal of Major Salem on 28 August, the tide began to rise steadily again in favour of Egypt. The Khartoum daily *Al Ayam* had told Egypt in July that the Sudan's independence did not necessarily exclude co-operation with Egypt, nor would it obstruct unity between Egypt and the Sudan, 'should the two peoples find it necessary for their interests to unite'.[2] Major Salem had been dismissed; the Egyptian Press had reverted to Neguib's policy of granting the choice of independence to the Sudan as a gesture of hope that the Sudanese would of their own accord join hands with Egypt in due course. That was the respective position of Britain and Egypt in the Sudan when, in August 1955, the Sudanese Parliament asked the two Governments to evacuate their forces from the Sudan.

On Tuesday, 16 August 1955, Mr. Azhari remarked in Parliament that the longer a foreign rule persisted in an 'unfortunate' land, the harder was the task of those nationals who took over. He therefore moved that an Address be presented to the Governor-General in the following terms:

We, the Members of the House of Representatives in Parliament assembled, express our desire that arrangements for self-determination should be put in motion forthwith, and request [His] Excellency to notify the two contracting Governments of this Resolution in accordance with Article 9 of the Agreement between the Egyptian Government and the Government of Great Britain. . . . Dated 12th February, 1953, concerning Self-Government and Self-Determination for the Sudan.[3]

The motion was anticipated in Britain and Egypt by Press and radio comments, each country endeavouring to woo the Sudanese.[4] The motion was considered to be of such importance that cine-cameras and flash-bulbs—unusual in the Parliament—were allowed, and the special occasion was recorded both for the Sudanese and for television in Britain and in the United States. The Sudanese, on the other hand, rose to the situation: like a débutante who attempts to be on good terms with all her courtiers, the Sudan Parliament kept both Britain and

[1] *Ibid.*   [2] Press Review, in the *Sudan Weekly News*, 26 July 1955, p. 3.
[3] Text of the Premier's speech in Parliament on evacuation of 'foreign' troops from the Sudan, in *Sudan Weekly News*, 16 August 1955, p. 1.
[4] See *The Times*, 11 August 1955, and the *Economist*, 27 August 1955.

Egypt reasonably hopeful. When the motion was put, it was carried with complete agreement. But Mr. Nur Eddin (N.U.P. Pro-Unity) remarked:

> Foreign forces will evacuate the Sudan according to the people's wish. We should remember Egypt's help to link with her so that we should not be described as ungrateful. We should bow our heads to our martyrs.[1]

To this Mohammed Ahmed Mahgoub (Umma), Leader of the Opposition, replied:

> The Honourable Member for Halfa reminds us not to be ungrateful to Egypt. But we do (should) not repay favour by giving up our freedom but repay it by supporting the Egyptian people until they achieve democratic freedom.[2]

The 16th of August was one of the happiest days in Northern Sudan. Inside Parliament, Members of the Government shook hands and warmly embraced those of the Opposition. Outside, there was a thick, excited crowd. Led by the Prime Minister and Members of Parliament, parties and organizations, including a body of Sudanese women (described as a rare sight on public occasions) in their robes, carried banners and formed a procession towards the square which overlooks the Blue Nile, and where stands the statue of Lord Kitchener, 'the conqueror of the Sudan and leader of the occupying armies of Britain and Egypt'.[3] There, the Prime Minister and the Leader of the Opposition, addressed a crowd of more than thirty-thousand. 'For the first time in recent history of the human race, an evacuation of foreign troops from a conquered land is being effected without bloodshed, without heartaches and I must add with very little ado', said the Prime Minister. But this was before the plot in the Southern Sudan had hatched.

1. THE SOUTHERN REVOLT OF AUGUST 1955

> *You [British Ambassador] mentioned that there were rumours of subventions paid [by Egypt] to the parties [in the Sudan]; but we, too, hear that there are certain British officials who stir up trouble in the South.*
>
> WING-COMMANDER ZULIFICAR to
> SIR RALPH STEVENSON[4]

While the North was in festive mood about self-determination, the South revolted. Almost the entire Southern Corps of the Sudan Defence

---

[1] *Sudan Weekly News*, 16 August 1955—'What They Said in Parliament', p. 2. Mr. Nur Eddin's remark is similar to that made by Alexander Hamilton when, in July 1793, he asked Americans to remember the 'gratitude due to France, for services rendered to us in our revolution' (the American War of Independence). See *The Federalist*, No. IV.

[2] *Ibid.*   [3] *Ibid.*, p. 1.

[4] Republic of Egypt, *The Sudan Under the New Agreement* (Record of a meeting between the British and Egyptian negotiators, held at the Presidency of the Council of Ministers, on 9 December 1952), p. 44.

Force, of 1,770 officers and men and a large part of the police force in the South, mutinied. Those who mutinied at Torit and elsewhere in Equatoria Province were 1,330 officers and men; at the end of three days' fighting, about 260 Northern Army officers, traders, administrators, and wives and children had been killed. About twenty Southern Army officers and men lost their lives, and fifty-five Southern civilians were drowned, in panic, while crossing the Kuiyeli. (For the accuracy of these figures, the writer is indebted to His Worship Judge Tawfik S. Coutran, Chairman of the Commission of Inquiry, who kindly perused this part of the work and checked the 'facts and figures'.) The nature of the mutiny was such as to induce the writer of the chief editorial in *The Times* of 3 January 1956 (entitled 'The Face of Africa'), to consider the mutiny in the Southern Sudan as the first of the two most important events in British Africa during 1955 (the second being the breaking of the industrial colour bar in the Northern Rhodesian copper-belt). Its significance in the Sudan was emphasized by the fact that the Government appointed a Commission of Enquiry in August 1955; it took the Commission not less than fifty-three sittings—in both North and South —and about five months to complete its findings, which were not published until October 1956.

The Causes of the Revolt. The causes and the course of this incident bring into the open part of the intrigues and the poisonous elements in the Sudan Question as a problem between Britain and Egypt even before 1899, and as a case study in power politics or the struggle for men's minds and resources the world over.

Writing under the caption 'African Independence and After', a contributor to *The Round Table* of December 1955 ascribes the current fissiparous trends in the British-controlled parts of Africa to the debatable point that the 'majority of Africans are still tribesmen at heart'.[1] This may be true in the sense that the American from, say, Texas, or the British Islander from Scotland is often tenaciously proud of his native origin. It may not be true in the sense that, contrary to popular opinion in Europe and America, there is nothing inherent in the African 'tribal' ideal which forbids the individual from expanding from the 'tribal' base, or one ethnic group from co-operating with another. The writer of that essay in *The Round Table* seems to forget to add that an imperial power, quite naturally, considers it risky to build up or deliberately support such educational or political programmes as are calculated to foster national consciousness and outlook, or a fellow-feeling of

[1] No. 181, December 1955, p. 19.

common citizenship; for it might quickly lead to a united front against the occupying power. Commenting on the problem of self-government, the Editor of *W.A.S.U.—New-Service*—the organ of the West African Students' Union in Britain and Ireland, suggests another cause of the neo-tribalism or fragmentations:

> Whenever an alien nation imposes her government upon another country, two political parties emerge. One is the Imperialist Party seeking to perpetuate its domination as long as possible; and the other is the Indigenous Party eager to be free from such domination as soon as possible.[1]

Inevitably, these two interests must clash. Broadly speaking, that is what happened in the Sudan in August 1955.

We have, in the introductory chapter of this work, analysed the causes of the friction, more artificial than natural, between the South and the North of the Sudan. They stand as the remote causes of the mutiny of August 1955. The immediate causes, interwoven with the remote ones, were first, sociological, for which the Northerners' superiority complex was partly responsible; the credulous minds of most Southerners contributed to the friction; there were political intrigues on the part of a few Egyptians and certain British subjects in the Sudan; and military and administrative errors on the part of the Sudanese Government all added to the clash of interests.

The North is relatively more developed, urban and sophisticated; the South is under-developed and rural. Its people are less Europeanized or Arabized: and they are more natural in their disposition. There were seventeen secondary schools (eight Government and nine non-Government) in the North, apart from the University College of Khartoum. But for the whole South, there were only two secondary schools, one for liberal education and the other commercial; both were in Equatoria Province. This difference tends to create a superiority complex among most Northerners in their dealings with the Southerners. The writer is reliably informed by a Northern Sudanese friend, that it is practically impossible for a Southern man to marry a Northern woman; but that a Northern male can easily marry a Southern beauty. This appears, on the surface, to contradict the idea of the social superiority complex of the North; but it should be remembered that the Northerner marries the Southern woman, in the first place because he does dominate the woman and can convert her to his own Muslim religion. As regards the Muslim and the Christian convert, each regards

---

[1] 'Quo Vadimus' in *W.A.S.U.*, Vol. No. 1, London, February 1956, p. 2.

the other as being on the wrong road to the true religion. Secondly, as in most other parts of the world, Sudanese society is patriarchal: ancestry is always traced through the man—the female line being ignored. The Southern pagan is therefore prevented from marrying the Northern Muslim. This is, of course, a general Islamic conception. Seen with a dissatisfied Southerner's eyes, it amounts to social exploitation of the South by the North. Added to this grievance is the fact that Christian Missionaries and British administrators had followed a separatist policy, partly by reviving the memory of slavery against the North. Sayed Daud Abdel Latif, former Governor of Bahr El Ghazal, gave evidence before the Court of Enquiry into the Southern disturbances; he said: 'The policy of the past administration and that of the Missions was aimed at forbidding the entry of Islam into the Southern Sudan'.[1]

Here, we must add that the history of the slave trade has been used by different sets of people, each for its own particular purpose. Missionaries (especially in the North–South boundary areas) used the idea as an instrument for easy conversion into Christianity; the British used it as a justification or pretext to preserve a separatist policy; some Southern politicians demanded local autonomy in federation with the North; and party-politicians even in the North who competed to gain the Southerner's vote, found the idea of great service in their propaganda.

Very few people in the South believed in the recurrence of slavery, but it was easy to use the possibility of such recurrence on the untrained minds in the South to arouse their feelings.

Many Southern Sudanese had hoped that with the advent of self-government they would gain total control over their own affairs. This belief was partly owing to rash election promises by Northern politicians during the 1953 campaigns. But in fact, the more educated and experienced Northerners had to replace most of the British administrators in the South. It was therefore easy for the 'mischievous' to make the 'credulous' believe that the Northerners had come as aliens and new imperialists in the South; this propaganda was accepted by many Southerners despite the fact that the policy of Azhari's Government was conspicuously committed to unification, and to programmes of full development calculated to bring about equal opportunity and equal responsibility for all citizens of the country; and in spite of the fact

---

[1] Ministry of Social Affairs, 'Enquiry into the Southern Disturbances', in the *Sudan Weekly News*, No. 56, 20 September 1955, p. 7.

that there were twenty-two representatives of the South in the Sudan Parliament—some in the Government and some in the Opposition. It appears that the Southerners were more interested in local affairs; to them government was what they saw on the spot, not the Parliament in Khartoum. What they saw on the spot were Northern administrators.

At a Press conference held on 5 September 1955, the Prime Minister told foreign and Sudanese pressmen that the experience of India, Pakistan, Indonesia and Palestine had pointed out to the Sudanese Government that some catastrophe often followed the withdrawal of imperial power.

> What happened in the South was therefore the inevitable outcome of the relics and plottings planned many years ago. In the course of the few months we have been in Government, we have made the utmost effort to obliterate the traces of the past, to provide equity between the South and the North by giving the Southerners a share of responsibility on the Governor-General's Commission, in the Cabinet, and in other posts of Government, compatible with their capabilities. Salaries of Army men, Policemen and Warders were also equalled between Southerners and their comrades in the North. Pay of Chiefs and Sheikhs in the South doubled and wages of labour were ameliorated. All these aimed at ensuring equity between countrymen of the same land and raising the standard of living in the South.

There were, we must point out, several Southern Sudanese who were able to see the problems of the South in a clear perspective. For instance, Santino Deng, a Dinka from the Bahr el-Ghazal Province, emphasized that his people wanted progress first and foremost—more educational, health and communicational facilities; and that they were satisfied that the present administration was doing its 'utmost to provide them'. Consequently they had confidence in the Northern Governor of the province and were satisfied that the local administration was acting without bias against Southerners.[2]

In a broadcast on 28 August, Sayed Buth Diu, a leading Southern Member of Parliament, told the mutineers:

> We believe that this action may hamper the social and constitutional developments of our beloved Sudan for years and years and deprive us in the South of all the gains which we have so far achieved. . . .
>
> The Juba Conference of 1947 confirmed that the South and the North should remain as an integral whole and this has been further confirmed by you Southern people who gave us your votes in membership of the present

---

[1] Ministry of Social Affairs, *Sudan Weekly News*, No. 54, Khartoum, 6 September 1955, p. 6.

[2] *The Times* correspondent in Khartoum—*The Times*, 13 August 1955.

Sudanese Parliament in which, by presenting our case, we are able gradually to achieve the many developments which we want.[1]

Since the transitional period of self-government began in the Sudan in 1954, some Egyptian doctors, teachers and especially engineers employed in the Egyptian Irrigation Department in Southern Sudan, took advantage, notably in 1955, of their position to support Cairo Press and radio propaganda (for which Major Salem was subsequently dismissed), against the Azhari Cabinet in Khartoum. These Egyptians in the Sudan tended to follow the British policy of exploiting the artificial differences between the North and the South as part of the campaign against the Azhari Government which, for the reasons we have given, was showing less enthusiasm for Egypt's thesis of the unity of the Nile Valley. The Prime Minister was branded as a 'stooge of British imperialists'. *The Times* in London, a journal knowledgable in the plots and counter-plots in the Nile Valley, alleged in an editorial that Egypt has tried by bribery to build up 'particularly in the Southern Sudan, support for federation with Egypt and the Unification of the Nile Valley'.[2]

Again, the policy of the British Government in London and of the British Governor-General of the Sudan had been to co-operate as much as possible with the Azhari Administration—to win the Sudanese by friendship and devoted guidance. In fact, many British employees of the Sudanese Administration, especially on the top level, were so exemplary in their behaviour and so devoted to their employees as to disarm completely the most anti-British Sudanese. This developed into mutual respect and confidence among British officials and Sudanese in the North. The Sudanization Committee, selected as provided in the Agreement, was appointed on 20 February 1954; it held its first meeting on 7 March. In the course of an address given a year later—on 12 February 1955—the Sudanese Prime Minister said that the beginning of the implementation of the recommendations of the Sudanization Committee

> would have been extremely arduous had it not been for the faithfulness, perseverance and resolute will on the part of the Government and His Excellency the Governor-General, whose gifts and goodness, coupled with his high traits of character, were greatly responsible for the removal of obstacles attached to the initial execution of the Sudanisation decisions. I should like here to display admiration and gratitude to the British officials

[1] *Sudan Weekly News*, No. 53, p. 6.
[2] 'The Sudan's Future', editorial in *The Times*, 11 August 1955.

affected by the process of Sudanisation for the goodwill they showed whilst handing over their functions to their Sudanese colleagues, which caused us to honour their memory on departure.[1]

However, certain British officials, especially those who worked in the South, found it difficult to make the new adjustment. This is evident in a leading article captioned 'The Secrets of Mutiny Movement', published in *El Sudan El Gadid* of 6 October 1955, which commented on the general facts and some of the details revealed during the Commission of Enquiry. The article, *reprinted by the Sudanese Ministry of Social Affairs*, declared:

> The British policy towards the Southern Sudan was formerly based on the separation of the three provinces to annex them to the Crown colonies, but with the recent political developments in the Sudan, leading eventually to the Parliamentary self-Government, the British Foreign Office thought it would be possible to settle all questions with the Sudan through diplomatic means.
> The British administrators, however, did not accept the latter view and continued the previous policy. Messrs. Duke and de Robeck were the most enthusiastic advocates of the separatist policy. They formed a secret organisation with branches in all parts of the Southern Provinces. The movement began to grow and many soldiers from the Equatorial Corps were enrolled.[2]

The article went on to allege that the mutiny was organized and led by a Briton (whose name was not disclosed) who sent to Uganda saying that he had everything under control. But before the Northern forces who were sent to restore order had reached Juba, Mr. 'X' called on the Priest at Torit, and said: 'I have lost control of the situation. My soldiers care only for robbery and I cannot depend on them in facing the Northern troops; tell me, Father, what shall I do?'[3]

According to the evidence of Army officers given before the Commission of Enquiry, most of whose sessions were public, certain documents were discovered at Torit, 'some in English, revealing a plot to kill Northerners. . . . The documents showed that the Secret organization had received funds from outside sources.'[4]

The following factors combine to show the continued reliance of the Southern rebels on British authority or influence; some of the factors would seem to implicate certain British subjects in the revolt. Among

---

[1] Reference Division, Central Office of Information, *Self-Determination in the Sudan* (No. R. 3127), London, 13 September 1955, p. 2.

[2] *Sudan Weekly News*, No. 59 of 11 October 1955, p. 6.

[3] *Ibid.* This question was addressed, apparently, to one of the Roman Catholic Mission Fathers at Torit—see p. 366 below.

[4] *East Africa and Rhodesia*, Vol. XXXII, No. 1615, London, 22 September 1955, p. 92.

these were the Mutineers' request for British troops. When the British Governor-General instructed the mutineers to lay down their arms, the mutineers radioed this reply, in English,[1] to Sir Knox Helm:

> We all heartily thank you most sincerely, and we are now glad for your return from England to end our trouble. Grateful order Northern troops in Juba evacuate Juba to north or to far-off district before we surrender arms. Otherwise please send British troops immediately to safeguard Southern troops.[2]

The British Governor-General informed them, of course, that no British troops would be sent. Again, the comparative safety of British subjects in the South seemed to be evidence of the British attitude. British subjects, arrived in Uganda from Nzara, reported that 'the attitude of the Southern Sudanese to all Europeans was extremely friendly'.[3] Whilst the rebels inflicted a considerable number of casualties and committed atrocities in Juba, none of the British and French missionaries, nor the Greek and Indian traders was molested. The Ven. Archdeacon Paul Gibson, of the Church Missionary Society, reported that all the European members of the Church and their families were undisturbed and were carrying on their normal duties peacefully.[4] *The Times* correspondent, writing from Uganda, reported that the attitude towards all Europeans of any nationality, whether officials, traders or missionaries, was extremely friendly and that they did not seem to be in any direct danger in that area.[5]

The mutiny broke out at Torit, which is situated in the extreme South close to Uganda. When the rebels were overpowered by the Central Sudanese Government, 148 Southern troops and about 3,000 Southern civilians fled to British Uganda.[6] When requested by the Sudanese Government to return these refugees, the British authorities in Uganda were hesitant, maintaining that the mutineers were political refugees who, according to international law, should not be handed back,[7] whilst the Sudanese Government argued that they were not political refugees, but soldiers who had disobeyed orders.[8] At a special meeting of the Uganda Legislature about these Sudanese refugees, Colonel W. H. Gordon suggested that some of the refugees might help to solve labour problems connected with Uganda's development programmes.[9]

---

[1] It is fair to mention that educated Southerners write in English.
[2] *East Africa and Rhodesia*, Vol. XXXI, No. 1612, London, 1 September 1955, p. 1841.
[3] *Ibid.*   [4] *Ibid.*   [5] *The Times*, 25 August 1955.
[6] House of Lords, *Official Reports*, Vol. CXCIV, No. 28, 2 November 1955, p. 261.
[7] Ministry of Social Affairs, *Sudan Weekly News*, No. 59, 11 October 1955, p. 4.
[8] *East Africa and Rhodesia*, Vol. XXXII, No. 1613, 8 September 1955, p. 15.
[9] *Ibid.*

This mass flight, together with British practice in other Territories seemed also to add to the evidence. In India, Nigeria and the Gold Coast, it is often alleged that British artifice tends to encourage the development of separatist movements, the effect of which delays or obstructs independence from British rule. On the eve of Britain's final departure from India in 1947 'Pakistanization' was preceded by a civil war. In Nigeria, a Northern revolt against Southerners (expressed in the Kano riot of 1953), for which Southern politicians held British officials in the North partly responsible, preceded the disunification of Nigeria at the dawn of self-government. During the period of transition to full self-government, separatist movements developed; Nigeria changed from a political 'unity' to a loose 'federation'. In the same way as the Northern Sudan has been the chief architect of self-government, the Southern regions of Nigeria (East and West) have been the pro-tagonists of self-determination. The general tendency of the British has been, it is frequently alleged, to support the political stragglers, whose position has the effect of delaying self-government. Commenting on the possibilities of self-government for Nigeria in 1956, Lord Ogmore wrote in November 1955:

> The probability is that in 1956 the East and West Regions will opt for full self-government whilst the North may decide not to do so at once owing to their present association with the United Kingdom for some time to come.[1]

On the eve of full self-government in the Gold Coast, the National Liberation Movement developed, with the political aim of replacing Dr. Nkrumah's unitary Gold Coast state with a federation; in effect, the movement was demanding five Parliaments for the five million people of the Gold Coast. Certain British subjects supported this movement. Mr. Fenner Brockway, a Member of the British Parliament, revealed in an article in November 1955 (during the Sudanese mutiny) on his return from a visit to the Gold Coast:

> The selfish element in the Opposition is contributed by business interests. I have evidence which cannot yet be revealed that British capitalist circles associated with the mining, gold and other enterprises have been generous in their support of the National Liberation Movement.[2]

---

[1] 'The Centre and the Regions', in *West Africa*, No. 2020, 12 November 1955, p. 1065.
[2] 'Storm Signals on the Gold Coast', in the *New Statesman and Nation*, Vol. I, No. 1288, 12 November 1955, p. 608. In a rejoinder to Mr. Brockway's statement, General E. L. Spears, Chairman of the London Advisory Committee of the Gold Coast Chamber of Mines, scolded him for endeavouring 'to create prejudice against important British in-terests which are making their contribution to the prosperity of the Commonwealth and Empire by hinting at the existence of evidence which the writer is not prepared to reveal' (*ibid.*, 3 December 1955, p. 751).

Similarly with regard to the Sudan, it was being suggested in Britain, even before the Sudanese Government had completed the efforts at restoring tranquillity in the South, that the Sudan (whose population is no larger than London's[1]) should break into two federated states; that a request be made by the Sudanese Government 'for temporary foreign help with administering the southern part of the federation'.[2]

Further, many British journals tended to be partisan and inclined to embarrass the Northern Administration, so much so that Mr. M. Y. Mudawi, a Sudanese judge on study leave in London, had to protest. In a letter to the Editor of *The Times*, he complained that he had been 'greatly perturbed by attacks launched by some of the British papers upon the Sudan judiciary', under whose auspices the Southern mutiny was being investigated. After laying certain 'facts before the right-thinking members of the British public', Mr. Mudawi remarked that although the Sudanese Administration had taken the normal course under the circumstances, 'we must feel a sense of grace and pride when it is known that more advanced countries would meet situations of less seriousness (than that of the Southern mutiny) with "people's courts" and "suspension of the rule of law" if any existed.'[3]

In the House of Lords on 2 November, the Marquess of Reading also blamed certain sections of the Press for gross exaggeration.[4] Mr. H. A. Nicholson, a former British Governor of Equatoria Province, had to request his fellow citizens of Britain to refrain from making the transitional period of self-government and self-determination more difficult for the Sudanese. In a letter to *The Times* he asked the British to bear two points in mind:

> In the first place, however much we dislike and disapprove of the 1953 Agreement, the die is cast and the Sudan Government must now tackle its own problems. Secondly, do not let us forget that though the Northern members are in the majority in the Sudan Parliament, the South too has its representatives and that a great body of educated Sudanese, both in the North and in the South . . . realise that their greatest task is to build up a united country with equal rights and privileges for its peoples.[5]

The Sudan Agent in London made a statement in which he accused the British Press of retarding the self-determination process and of

[1] In defence, an official at the British Embassy in Cairo reminded the writer that the Sudan, though sparsely populated, 'is half the size of Europe' in area. But at the time of writing, most of the area remained uninhabited desert.

[2] *The Economist*, No. 5854, London, 5 November 1955, p. 49.

[3] Letter to the Editor of *The Times*, London; reproduced in *Sudan Weekly News*, No. 62, 1 November 1955, p. 4.

[4] The House of Lords, *Official Reports*, Vol. CXCIV, No. 28, 2 November 1955, p. 262.

[5] *The Times*, 10 November 1955.

contributing to the political instability in the Sudan. He made representations to Sir Anthony Eden advising him that the unfair British Press attacks on the Sudan might affect the future relations between the two countries.[1]

The British attitude towards the South operating before Sudanization, seems to have lingered. In Chapter 9, we quoted Sir Murdoch MacDonald's statement in the House of Commons in July 1924: 'I see no reason why the races in the Northern Sudan should rule over the blacks in the Southern Sudan.' Afraid of the potential strength of a united Sudan in league with Egypt, he went on 'To erect a single kingdom such as happened in the Mahdi's time in the Sudan, I think, would be a mistake.' But he advocated that the Sudanese together with the Egyptians should be ruled by Britain.

We have cited the open declaration of the National Unionist Party in 1952 that:

> We accuse the Governor-General and his Government of having deliberately adopted the policy of keeping the South completely secluded from the North and virtually debarred civilization and progress. The interests of the Southerners will be more secure when the responsibility for them is assumed by the Sudanese Cabinet in which the Southerners themselves are represented.

It is possible that some British subjects who regarded this statement as an affront and a challenge, had encouraged discontent among the Southern Sudanese to show that they were not 'more secure' under the Unionists who were now in power. Lord Raglan, formerly an administrator in the Southern Sudan, said in the British House of Lords:

> The Government were informed that if these people were placed under the domination of the North without adequate precautions there would be trouble; but they chose to ignore this warning completely . . . they proceeded to scuttle without the least regard for the consequences.[2]

During one of the series of Anglo-Egyptian negotiations in 1951, Sir Ralph Stevenson had categorically told Salah Eddin Bey: 'The stipulation for the evacuation of all British officials from the Sudan . . . is utterly impracticable. The Sudan cannot get on without the British officials.'[3] This view was supported, during the mutiny, in an editorial in which the *Manchester Guardian* blamed the mutiny partly on 'the haste with which the Sudanese leaders, on attaining self-government,

---

[1] *Sudan Weekly News*, No. 66, 29 November 1955, p. 2.
[2] House of Lords, *Official Reports*, Vol. CXCIV, No. 28, 2 November 1955, p. 258.
[3] Egypt, Ministry of Foreign Affairs, *op. cit.*, p. 113 (see page above).

disposed of their British civil servants'.[1] Similarly, *The Times*, in a leading article, suggested that much of the resentment which the Southern Sudan felt against the Northern could be removed 'if a fully sovereign Sudanese Government would employ on contract ex-British officials with experience there'.[2]

As we have already indicated, Egypt had pressed Britain, during the negotiations for the 1953 Agreement, to renounce the British Governor-General's special powers over the Southern Sudan; Britain insisted on retaining such powers to protect the Southerners. In the end, she had to yield, but grudgingly. Pressed by Egypt, the British Government agreed in 1954 to evacuate their forces from the Suez Canal by the middle of 1956; under the 1953 Agreement both they and the Egyptians had to withdraw their forces from the Sudan three months after the resolution in Parliament—i.e. before the end of November 1955. 'It is not surprising, therefore,' *The Hindu* commented, 'that the British should have refused to leave the Sudan' immediately and entirely.[3] In reply to the allegation in the Egyptian Press that the British were trying to separate the South from the North in an attempt to maintain British supremacy in the South, *The Times*, London, declared that the British were not aiming at direct control over the South but were 'merely anxious to secure loyalty of the unfettered Southern leaders to balance the wavering affections of the North'.[4] But Lord Birdwood was more frank and direct; in the House of Lords he suggested: 'Cannot the Northern Sudan be persuaded to turn back to Her Majesty's Government and ask us to resume responsibility at least for the Equatoria Province to be administered as a trust?'[5]

At its present stage of evolution international politics is still, in part, a 'dirty game'; with goodwill often goes ill-will; peaceful and friendly diplomacy is often accompanied with espionage and sabotage. This applied to Anglo-Egyptian practice in the Sudan Question; the Sudanese, too, occasionally used this double-faced diplomacy in their struggle for independence.

The Sudan was, on the whole, a peaceful country under British rule. But occasional revolts were part of the features of the political struggle and competition for power in the Nile Valley (as is often the case in other parts of the world). The Sudanese mutiny against the British authorities in 1924 was partly inspired by Egyptian collaboration with

---

[1] 30 August 1955.   [2] 7 November 1955.
[3] *The Hindu*, Madras, 25 August 1955.   [4] *The Times*, 11 August 1955.
[5] House of Lords, *Official Records*, Vol. CXCIV, p. 273.

certain dissatisfied Sudanese (see Chapter 4 above). In 1948, about 4,000 persons were involved and some lives were lost during political demonstrations, organized by the pro-Egyptian Sudanese National Front against the British Administration which promulgated the 1948 Legislative Assembly Ordinance, and against the Umma Party which supported it (see Chapter 12 above). It would seem logical, therefore, for some of the anti-Egyptian and the anti-National Unionists (which included certain Sudanese and most British officials and subjects) to inspire, in 1955, similar insubordination or political rebellion against those who had inspired the use of such devices in the past.

The Commission of Inquiry which the Sudanese Government set up about the revolt was composed of a Christian-Arab Judge (Sayed Tawfik S. Contran, a Syrian graduate of the London School of Economics and Political Science), a Northern Sudanese whose career had been mainly in the police (ex-Police Magistrate under the British Administration) and who was formerly Assistant Agent in London (Khalifa Mahgoub), and a Southern Chief of the Lokoya People in the neighbourhood of Torit where the mutiny occurred (Chief Lolik Lado). Lord Reading described the Commission as appearing to be 'an authoritative and impartial Committee of inquiry'.[1] The Chief Justice of the Sudan gave the assurance, at a Press conference, that justice would take its course in the normal way and that he would see to it that all accused in connection with the disturbances were given a fair trial.[2] It could be said, therefore, that the Sudanese Government endeavoured to be impartial about the trials.

In November 1955, a few British subjects, missionaries of the Church of England and of the Roman Catholic Church, were accused of conspiring (with the mutineers) to overthrow the Government.[3] Some were found not guilty, but a Protestant missionary in Maridi area, and a Catholic Father were sentenced. On appeal, their convictions were quashed by the Chief Justice. However, that these people were brought to trial at all is significant, and suggestive. (In Chapter 1 we analysed the difficulties of missionaries and the ways in which they get involved with administrators in colonial territories.)

The Commission of Enquiry reveals that messages were sent, during the mutiny, to Nairobi asking for British help from East Africa, and

---

[1] House of Lords, *Official Reports, op. cit.*, p. 279.
[2] *Sudan Weekly News*, No. 59, 11 October 1955, p. 7.
[3] *Observer*, 27 November 1955, p. 4.

that the mutineers had, for some reason, expected such help. Whatever might have been the source of this belief and hopeful expectation, one of the messages from the mutineers to British Kenya, intercepted by the Sudanese authorities, reads:

DATE TIME

From: Troops Torit.   2000900
To: Kenya, Nairobi.   T/303

Situation of our troops remain quiet in their defence positions. Expect serious troubles this afternoon or tonight or tomorrow. Please signal your arrival and the sign of Union Jack flag required to enable us to know you.

(*Signed by* M. T. Renaldo Loleya)[1]

When all these pieces of evidence, sifted and set out above, are put together, it may be held that they give ground for the suspicion that some British persons were implicated in the mutiny at Torit in August 1955. They might seem to justify the allegations in the Egyptian as well as in the Sudanese Press that the British had acted under the feeling that the Sudanese had been running too fast; that they had been too sure of themselves and that a situation might usefully be created as a proof that the art of government was in fact as difficult as the Sudanese had been told, repeatedly, by their British political masters. Debates in the British Parliament, too, might have strengthened these suspicions. For, during the debate in Parliament about the mutiny, Lord Killearn said, with an apparent air of fore-knowledge: 'Some of us did tell you so, though perhaps not of so violent a nature.'[2]

But we must observe that these chains of evidence, both against the Egyptians and the British with regard to the Southern rebellion, are not conclusive; though on the whole authentic, relevant, and contributive, they leave much room for doubt. In the first place, although the regime in Egypt was employing all means available to make the Azhari Government pursue a policy of union with Egypt, secession of the South from the North could not have been one of these. At the Security Council, in 1947 and during subsequent Anglo-Egyptian negotiations, the Egyptians had always maintained their stand on the political unity of the Sudan—both North and South. During the Anglo-Egyptian negotiations in Cairo on Monday, 24 November 1952, Dr. Sultan emphasized to Sir Ralph Stevenson: 'We can make no provision which can lead to separating the South from the North.'[3] The British, on

---

[1] Republic of the Sudan, *Southern Sudan Disturbances*, p. 44.
[2] House of Lords, *Debates*, Vol. CXCIV, p. 275.
[3] Republic of Egypt, *The Sudan under the New Agreement*, p. 18.

the other hand, insisted that 'the South ought not to be united with the Arab North because in human terms it belongs to Africa south of it'.[1] To encourage the South to break away from the North would be the antithesis of Egypt's greatest ambition—the Unity of the Nile Valley.

Secondly, it does not seem likely that the British would, on the whole, want to go so far as to devise consciously the breakdown of the administration which they had helped to build up, and so to lose the good-will and respect of the Sudanese, whom they proudly regarded as some of Britain's most promising pupils in Western democracy. In fact, Sir James Robertson, it is often pointed out, helped, when the Northern Sudanese pressed, to bring together the South and the North in the Legislative Assembly of 1948.

Therefore, judgment on this complex issue for the moment can only be made with reservations. For in the case of the Indian Mutiny of 1857, it can be seen that 100 years later, when Britain no longer ruled India and when Indians could look back less in anger but more in humour, the story of the mutiny began to take a fresh perspective. How time can heal! In 1957, we find Dr. Percival Spear was able to broadcast: 'We can now recollect in tranquillity, as we never could before. And so we are looking at the mutiny with a new wonder and an interest short of passion and prejudice, seeking to re-assess it and place it in proper perspective.'[2]

The New Sudanese Government had its own faults in this matter, at least two glaring ones. In their military organization they had followed the British policy of concentrating in the South troops recruited wholly from local men and not from all parts of the country. This encouraged a tribal or provincial outlook within the Southern Corps. Further, in July 1955, a month before the mutiny, Sayed Simplicio Ataxa, an M.P. from the Torit District, telegraphed to the Governor of Juba (a Northerner) and informed the Governor-General and the Prime Minister in Khartoum, about signs of the coming danger. Rather than examine the warning, Sayed Simplicio Ataxa was summarily imprisoned by the Administration for what was then considered as wrong information and defamation of the Administration's character, thus implying its inefficiency. This unfortunate action was taken by the Administration apparently on Simplicio's previous record as a pro-British Southerner.

---

[1] (British Uganda) Fabian Society, *The Sudan: The Road Ahead*, p. 25.
[2] B.B.C., London, 'The Sepoy Rising of 1857 . . .', recorded in London on 28 December 1956, but broadcast several times in early 1957.

But in fact his own Constituency, too, considered him a turncoat, because to them he appeared more and more pro-Northerner since getting into Parliament. Thus Sayed Simplicio was left between 'the devil and the deep blue sea'—suspected by the Northern Administrators and politicians whom he had learnt now to understand and sympathize with, and by his own Constituency in the South who had more contacts with the British officials in the South than with the Northerners, and by the British officials, whose hopes he had shattered. His warning about the pending revolt was ignored at that time. But he was subsequently released from jail on bond to 'keep the peace'.

In any case, and in spite of it all, the Sudanese Administration faced the crisis with dexterity and a humane approach to their rebellious fellow citizens. Ten weeks after it began, Mr. Colin Legum, correspondent of the *Observer*, wrote from Khartoum on 5 November 1955: 'In view of this extraordinarily difficult situation, the achievement of the Northern administrations and troops has been very considerable. The Administration is working again with reasonable efficiency.'[1] The special correspondent of *The Times* also paid tribute: 'So far the Government in Khartoum has acted with patient moderation with a calmness that is impressive to watch at so difficult a moment for a young Government.'[2] The British Foreign Secretary (Mr. Macmillan) stated in the House of Commons on 7 November that, in taking measures to restore order, the Sudanese Government acted 'with restraint and with due regard for legal process'.[3] Also, in his letter dated 3 July 1957, and addressed to the author of this work, Sir James Robertson commented: 'All my present information is that the Sudan is carrying on well, and that the Government and Civil Service are doing good work.'

2. ANGLO-EGYPTIAN CONTROVERSY OVER THE PROCESS OF SELF-DETERMINATION

Simultaneously, the young Government faced another problem, this time from Britain and Egypt about the process of self-determination. Article 10 of the 1953 Agreement provided for an international body to ensure 'impartiality of the elections and any other arrangements designed to secure free and neutral atmosphere' for self-determination. However, difficulties began to emerge between the two co-domini about the nature and the composition of the proposed international body. As we have seen, Egypt's popularity in the Sudan had suffered some

[1] *Observer*, 6 November 1955, p. 1.   [2] *The Times*, London, 29 August 1955.
[3] *Hansard*, 7 November 1955, p. 1471.

decline; consequently, the Egyptians had some qualms lest the prospective elections in the Sudan would this time lead to a less pro-Egyptian result than that of November–December 1953. The British, on the other hand, were anxious to take advantage of their relative popularity in the Sudan at this time. In an editorial comment on the question of self-determination by the Sudan, the *Observer* calculated: 'If a vote were taken now, there is no doubt that the decision would be for independence [from Egypt]. . . . Britain has won considerable influence among the suspicious Sudanese. . . . Our [British] policy has [therefore] been to encourage them to vote on their status with as little delay as possible.'[1] This explains the rapid changes of tactics in Britain, Egypt and the Sudan, which we will now trace.

Anglo-Egyptian negotiations on the nature of the International Commission were initiated by Britain in June 1955, but they ran into deadlock. Britain proposed that the Commission should be composed of representatives of neutral states, which had neither 'connections' with the Sudan nor 'interests' in the outcome of self-determination; and that neither the co-domini nor the Sudanese themselves should sit on the Commission. Egypt pressed for British, Egyptian and Sudanese representations on the Commission, because she was afraid of giving wide and discretionary powers to a commission in which she did not herself have a voice. The Sudanese Government cast its vote in favour of the British formula on 16 July.[2] Egypt maintained that if Britain would not agree to the representation of both Britain and Egypt, the Egyptian Government 'would not accept a commission with a "pro-Western" majority. They accordingly proposed that two members of the Commission should be from the "Eastern bloc", two from the "Western bloc" and that the Chairman should be an Asian. This the Egyptian Government considered could be a well-balanced body.'[3]

But quite suddenly, on 13 August, Egypt proposed that the composition of the Commission be referred to the parliament of the Sudan for a decision. This both Governments undertook to accept. As a result, the Sudanese Parliament passed, on 23 August, three resolutions excluding Britain, Egypt and the Sudan from the Commission, but permitting representatives of Pakistan, India, Switzerland, Sweden, Yugoslavia, Norway and Czechoslovakia to form the Commission. Thus the Sudanese accepted the Egyptian view about the two 'blocs',

---

[1] *Observer*, London, 13 November 1955, p. 6.
[2] British Foreign Office, News Department, *Text of a Note from the British Government to the Governor-General of the Sudan*, No. 7, dated London, 16 August 1955, p. 1.
[3] *Ibid.*, pp. 1–2.

which was rejected by Britain; but they also accepted the British view that neither of the co-domini nor the Sudan should be represented. A week later, the Sudanese Parliament took another decision on direct plebiscite as the best means by which the Sudanese could express their real wishes for the future of their country.[1] *Al Gumhouriya*, which often expressed the views of the Egyptian Government, complained that the British Government was

> endeavouring to gain time, and to avoid reaching agreement with the Egyptian side over the formation of the international Commission. By these manœuvres, British policy aims at carrying out self-determination process in an atmosphere devoid of any security or international supervision, which might unveil the conspiracies being woven in the dark against the Sudanese people.[2]

However, in an interview with the writer, an official at the British Embassy in Cairo put a counter blame on the Egyptian Government's uncertainty and indecision in September and in the first half of October: Colonel Nasser was pre-occupied with an arms deal with the Soviet bloc; Major Salem had been dismissed on 28 August, and his successor had to feel his way and find a fresh policy on the Sudan. In consequence, the Egyptian Government, anxious that the proposed Commission should start work before the British and Egyptian armed forces were evacuated, issued, on 21 October, invitations to the seven countries already mentioned by the Sudanese Parliament. This Egyptian move was immediately followed in London by the publication (also in Khartoum) of a new proposal by the Sudanese Government that self-determination should be decided not by a plebiscite but by a simple vote in the present Sudanese Parliament[3]; and by denunciation of what was regarded as Egypt's unilateral action: whereas the Egyptian Minister of State for Sudan Affairs, had, in a letter dated 19 October, informed the British Ambassador in Cairo: 'I deem it necessary to communicate to the States designated by the Sudanese Government on 22 August 1955 as members of the International Commission, the decision taken by the said Parliament, together with the said terms of reference.'[4] The British objection was interpreted in Cairo as an attempt on the part of Britain to proceed with the process of self-determination without international supervision as provided in the 1953 Agreement. The

---

[1] *Sudan Weekly News*, No. 61, 30 August 1955, p. 3.
[2] Quoted in *The Times*, 22 October 1955.
[3] *The Times*, London, 24 October 1955.
[4] Documents exchanged between the Co-domini on Plebiscite and International Commission, published in the *Sudan Weekly News*, No. 64, 16 November 1955, p. 2.

Egyptian Government formally protested about a statement alleged to have been made by Mr. W. H. T. Luce, the Senior Adviser to the Governor-General of the Sudan, in which he, it was alleged, remarked that Britain would support the Sudanese Parliament if it opted for independence (from Egypt). The protest also charged that: 'Mr. Luce's statement shows that the British Government's policy is clearly aimed at realizing private British interests in the Sudan and is a breach of the 1953 Agreement.'[1]

3. THE OVERTHROW OF THE FIRST SUDANESE GOVERNMENT

At this stage, another political volcano, caused not by simple-minded Southern Sudanese but by the machinations of sophisticated Northerners in Parliament, erupted. Less than a week before the final day on which all British and Egyptian troops were due to have evacuated the Sudan in accordance with the Sudanese Parliament's motion of 16 August 1955, just seven days before a proposed debate on 'self-determination'; the National Unionist Government, elected to Parliament on a pro-Egyptian platform, was overthrown through a 'democratic' process: on a parliamentary vote of confidence engineered by the Opposition during a budget debate, the Cabinet was defeated by 48 votes to 46. Southern members distributed their votes on both sides,[2] whilst four Parliamentary Under-Secretaries voted with the Opposition against the Government.[3] On Thursday 12 November, the Cabinet resigned. Their resignation having been accepted by the Governor-General, the Council of Ministers issued a statement, pointing out that:

> The Government succeeded to office through the people's wish expressed in Parliament and have done all in their power to ensure the people's interests and made it their first duty to liberate the country. They brought to a successful conclusion the Sudanisation and Evacuation—the Officer Commanding British troops left the Sudan when the House was discussing the Budget proposals.[4]

The collapse of the First Sudanese Government had little to do with the Government's budget proposals. While making a statement on the defeat of the Government, the National Unionist Party referred to 'foreign elements [who] instructed their agents to foment sedition,

---

[1] *The Times*, London, 24 October 1955; *Sudan Weekly News*, No. 61, 25 October 1955, p. 5.
[2] *The Times* correspondent in Khartoum: *The Times*, London 11 November 1955, p. 8a.
[3] *Sudan Weekly News*, No. 64, 16 November 1955, p. 2.
[4] 'Statement by Council of Ministers', in *Sudan Weekly News*, No. 64, 16 November 1955, p. 2.

arouse apprehensions and use various devices to overthrow the National Unionist Party Government'; he announced that 'suddenly it became clear that efforts were being made to overthrow the Government under the pretext of forming a national government'.[1]

The Evacuation Day celebrations planned to take place throughout the Sudan on Monday 14 November, were postponed indefinitely; however, Dr. Ali Uro, Sudan Agent in London, celebrated the occasion by giving a reception at the Sudan House in London on 15 November. The 100 guests included members of the British Parliament and Foreign Office, and of the Egyptian Embassy in London. But within the Sudan, both politicians and the general public continued in their anxiety, apprehension and suspense. During this time of uncertainty in the Sudan, on the third day of the fall of the first Sudanese Government, the *Observer* in London advised:

> Those who are asking whether Britain should abdicate her responsibilities before peace and tranquillity, as well as law and order, have been established in the Sudan, [should realise that] the blunt truth is that any attempt to turn the clock back now would only throw the Sudanese into the arms of the Egyptians.[2]

The four days which preceded the sitting of Parliament on Tuesday 15 November—(a week after the fall of the National Unionists)—witnessed political activities, unprecedented in speed and intensity in the Sudan. They evince, on the domestic level, an aspect of the power politics which went on between Britain, Egypt and the Sudan on international level. With scarcely a wink of sleep or a moment of rest the two main rival parties—the Umma and the National Unionists—spent these days in continuous contact with each other or with the rival religious leaders (Sir Abdel Rahman El Mahdi and Sir Ali El Mirghani). Failing to reach agreement, each side started to work hard to strengthen its camp by recruiting more men for the coming battle, which to each camp was either moral death or victory. As with the husband of a wife in labour, there was waiting and anxiety not only in Khartoum but also in Cairo and London. However, the National Unionist Party was somehow relieved when the three out of their four Parliamentary Under-Secretaries who had voted in Parliament against the Cabinet, returned to their camp.

On the arrival of the fateful day, Tuesday, 15 November 1955, Parliament re-assembled. Sayed Abdulla Khalil moved that Sayed

[1] *Sudan Weekly News*, No. 65, 23 November 1955, p. 1.
[2] *Observer*, 13 November 1955, p. 6.

Mirghani Hamza should be elected Prime Minister; he was supported by Sayed Mohammed Ahmed Mahgoub, Leader of the Opposition before the fall of the Government. Sayed Mubarak Zarouk then moved that Sayed Ismail Azhari, the defeated Prime Minister, be elected. Azhari was re-elected by 48 votes against Hamza's 46. The new Cabinet was made up of the former Ministers with the addition of Sayed Buth Diu, a Southerner, as Minister for Animal Resources. In a recorded radio talk, Mr. Azhari, as Prime Minister of the Sudan avowed:

> By the name of God, the King of Kings, I beg to thank the noble people of Sudan for their full support to me and their confidence in me—which they have expressed in many ways—support and confidence which renewed my intention to proceed on the path which I and my colleagues have outlined for the realization of the country's full liberty and complete independence and for freeing it from any foreign influence whether visible, internal or external.[1]

The return of Azhari and his Cabinet to power increased, quite naturally, their prestige and confidence both within and outside Parliament. However, the Unionist Party announced that as they were not over-shaken by their first defeat, they were not over-joyed by their second victory. It would seem that, though victorious, they were haunted by the fear of what might happen next within Parliament or outside it. Otherwise, the prospects of steering the ship of state through few or no storms during the remaining steps towards self-determination appeared relatively bright. Though the problem of the wounds of the southern mutiny remained to be healed and mutual confidence to be achieved, the life in the South was returning to normal.

On 17 November the Rev. Father Fernando, Sister Maria and Father Sembiate, acting on behalf of the Catholic Mission at Torit, the source of the mutiny, cabled the following message to the Prime Minister:

> May your Excellency kindly accept our humble but heartfelt congratulations on your re-election. The policy of understanding magnanimity and moderation enforced by your Excellency in the South and admirably carried on by Government Officials in Torit area will undoubtedly bring the good fruits we all hope and pray for.[2]

A military communiqué, No. 58, issued on the morning of 26 November 1955, reported that 'all is quiet in all districts'.

The Sudanese Parliament requested Britain and Egypt to expedite

---

[1] *Sudan Weekly News*, No. 64, 16 November 1955, p. 1.
[2] *Ibid.*, No. 66, 29 November 1955, p. 4.

arrangements for the proposed plebiscite. Subsequently agreement was reached between Britain and Egypt over the process of self-determination for the Sudan. Dr. Mahmoud Fawzi (the Egyptian Foreign Minister) and Sir Humphrey Trevelyan, (the British Ambassador) signed in Cairo documents which in effect amended the Self-Determination Clause of the 1953 Agreement. The documents consisted of an exchange of Notes agreeing on the plebiscite to determine the Sudan's future status. Agreement was also reached on the terms of reference for the International Commission to supervise the plebiscite and the subsequent assembly. A joint communiqué after the signing ceremony expressed agreement on the seven countries nominated by the Sudanese Parliament and invited by the Egyptian Government as we have indicated above.

By another exchange of Notes, initiated by Egypt, the co-domini agreed that as soon as the results of the plebiscite and of the constituent assembly were known, the two Governments would consult with the Sudanese Government about bringing the process of self-determination and the Condominium to an end. The documents[1] were signed on 3 December 1955. However, the B.B.C. News Service revealed in London that the British Government did not expect the plebiscite to take place before March 1956.

Thus the Sudanese Government would seem to have looked at the future with a sense of relief mingled with apprehension. They were relieved, because most of the obstacles to self-determination had been removed. There was apprehension, because although the Azhari Cabinet had been returned to power, they were returned with a majority of only two votes. Although the last lap appeared short and easy, anything could happen within that short period of time caused either by the Sudanese themselves or by one or both of the co-domini Governments. Though victorious for the second time, the National Unionists were haunted by the ideas of their isolation, a concomitant of enviable power and position.

The Sudanese Council of Ministers quickly dispatched a memorandum of protest, not against the agreement as such, but against the fact that the Sudanese Government, as a third party, was not consulted by the co-domini about the terms of reference of the International Commission for Self-Determination, a vital matter to the Sudanese. The feeling of the Sudanese Government could be understood in the light of the fact that the Council of Ministers had written, on 9 November, to the two

[1] H.M.S.O., *Treaty Series*, No. 90 (1955) Cmd. 9661, London, December 1955.

Governments regarding the necessity of taking the opinion of the Sudanese Government into account before a final agreement about the terms of reference of that Commission. The Egyptian Government in its reply dated 29 November, welcomed Sudanese participation in the talks; the British Government, in its reply conveyed through the Governor-General on 3 December, considered that the talks had reached an advanced stage, and that it was therefore impractical to afford the Sudan the chance of participating in the talks, without delaying the setting up of the International Commission. In their letter of protest the Council of Ministers expressed doubts about the sincerity of Egypt's acceptance of Sudanese participation in the talks, because the Anglo-Egyptian agreement was concluded only a few days after the Egyptian reply was received. The Council also commented that the grounds on which the British Government based its rejection were not convincing, because it was still possible to give the Sudanese the opportunity at least to see what was agreed upon, at any time before the final signature; they observed that the text of the agreement, which was announced both in Britain and Egypt and widely publicized throughout the world by news agencies and the Press, was not officially communicated to the Sudanese Government. In any case, the official statement issued at Khartoum on 11 December claimed that the Sudanese public had expressed collective opposition to the terms of reference granted by the two Governments to the International Commission.[1]

4. RESIGNATION OF THE GOVERNOR-GENERAL AND THE DECLARATION OF THE SUDAN'S INDEPENDENCE, JANUARY 1956

At this stage, the British Government announced in a Press and radio bulletin that Sir Knox Helm, the Governor-General of the Sudan, had expressed a desire to resign for personal reasons; that they were prepared to accept the resignation and that they did not intend to nominate another British candidate in his place. This was on 12 December, the second day after the protest by the Sudanese Council of Ministers. It would be reasonable to suggest that Sir Knox resigned for more than 'personal reasons'; that since the presence of a British Governor-General had exposed Britain to attacks by the Sudanese who seemed to have become agreed on the termination of the Governor-General's mandate immediately on self-determination, which was so imminent, Britain did not want to expose herself to a further campaign of attacks and pressure—whether justified or otherwise—from the Sudanese and

[1] *Sudan Weekly News*, No. 68, 13 December 1955, p. 1.

via the Egyptians. In any case, most of his essential powers had been eroded. He probably thought it wise, therefore, to resign at this juncture and advise his nation that no British Governor-General should succeed him. This done, the British would give the impression of volunteering to leave the Sudan with grace and thus earn the goodwill of the Sudanese.

Whatever the British real reason and objective, the Sudanese received Sir Knox's resignation with mixed feelings of suspicion and opportunism: suspicion, because some Sudanese leaders, like ʻSayed Sorour Ramli (Socialist Republican) suggested first that the resignation constituted a threat to the Sudan since it was not improbable that Britain would play the same part as she did in Palestine when her withdrawal at a certain point left the country at the mercy of Israel; and then that the resignation of the Governor-General might well create such a vacuum as might leave the Sudan at the mercy of either Britain or Egypt because the process of self-determination was not yet completed and because it was difficult to select a new Governor-General (acceptable to all the interested parties) at that time.[1] Others like Sayed Mohammed Nur El Din considered the resignation as a British conspiracy to complicate the political situation in the Sudan, 'to destroy our achievements and delay Self-Determination'.[2]

But after the first shock and on second thoughts, the Sudanese accepted the resignation with gladness and opportunism. The N.U.P.'s Parliamentary Group stated on 13 December that the resignation offered a propitious opportunity for the Sudanese to complete the demonstration of their sovereignty by appointing a small body of Sudanese to replace the Governor-General and exercise all his powers until such time as the Sudanese were able to elect the Head of the Sudanese State through such means as were provided for in the constitution of an independent Sudan. As soon as this interpretation became known and accepted by most of the Sudanese, the British, so the writer was informed by a Sudanese official at the Sudan Agency in London, attempted to make some modification to the effect that Sir Knox's resignation might apply, not forthwith as already announced, but at a future date. According to the Sudanese Ministry of Social Affairs, Sir Knox left the Sudan on 15 December but told Mr. Azhari that he would return immediately if necessary.[3] The British Embassy in Cairo told the writer that Sir Knox merely expressed a desire to resign as soon as a successor could be appointed, and that he went to London 'on leave, intending to return in early January'.

[1] *Ibid.*, p. 6.   [2] *Ibid.*   [3] *Ibid.*, No. 69, 21 December 1955, p. 2.

The Azhari Government immediately seized the propitious opportunity formally to declare the independence of the Sudan on 19 December.

5. MEMBERSHIP OF THE ARAB LEAGUE AND OF THE UNITED NATIONS

Five Sudanese, elected by Parliament, were to constitute the supreme commission to take over the sovereign power surrendered by the British Governor-General. These were Sayed Ahmed Mohammed Yassin, Speaker of the Senate (N.U.P.), Sayed Dardiri Mohammed Osman (Opposition Parties), Member of the Governor-General's Commission, Sayed Siricio Iro (Southern Liberal Party), Member of the Governor-General's Commission, Sayed Ahmed Mohammed Salih (Non-Party), Senator, and Sayed Abdel Fattah El Maghrabi (Non-Party), Assistant Sudan Agent in London.

But the appointment of a body of Sudanese to replace the Governor-General would be constitutionally impracticable before self-determination, because such a body would be representing, *de jure*, the co-domini and therefore owing allegiance to them. But both Britain and Egypt had been cornered. Neither would find it politic to withdraw recognition at this particular stage. Bearing this in mind, the Sudanese worked on the problem with the speed of an opportunist, grappling with a fleeting occasion that might never return. The first goal was to seek and receive from both Britain and Egypt the necessary official recognition of the declared independence, and to install the five new commissioners. Within a few days, arrangements were completed, and the first day of January 1956 was set for the official ceremony of independence. The members of the Senate and of the House of Representatives, sitting in a joint session of the Parliament, solemnly resolved to adopt the provisions of 'The Transitional Constitution of Sudan to be upheld and to be obeyed by the people of Sudan until other provision is, in due course, made.'[1]

On Sunday, 1 January 1956, the 57th anniversary of the signing of the Condominium, a new flag was officially hoisted in Khartoum. On that day, Mr. Azhari handed to the Speaker of the Sudanese Parliament the letters from the British and the Egyptian Governments, granting recognition to the Sovereign, Democratic Republic of the Sudan.

The note of recognition having been read to both Houses of Parliament who were jointly assembled for the occasion, the five members of the supreme commission which were to take over sovereign power from

[1] See the first folio of *The Transitional Constitution of Sudan* (37 pages).

*Flag Day Ceremony, 1 January 1956.   The Sudan flag flown up
over the Palace, Khartoum*

the British Governor-General were sworn in. These new commissioners led a procession of all the Members of Parliament to the palace over-looking the Nile, where about 2,000 notables, officials and foreign guests had assembled. On the palace roof the British and the Egyptian flags, which were first flown in 1899, were still flying. But there also stood, for the first time since 1899, a bare flagstaff; in front of this, the five Supreme Commissioners took their places, the two religious leaders Sir Abdel Rahman El Mahdi and Sir Ali El Mirghani stood on either side of the flag-staff. Then the Prime Minister (Sayed Ismail Azhari), together with the Leader of the Opposition (Sayed Mohammed Ahmed Mahgoub) hoisted the new Sudanese national flag, of blue, yellow and green—symbolizing the Nile, the Desert and Agriculture. Simultan-eously, two Sudanese officers lowered the Union Jack and the Egyptian flag which Mr. Azhari, with great joy, handed back to the representa-tives of Britain and Egypt. A band played the temporary Sudanese national anthem. A gun boomed out, echoing across the controversial Nile. The Condominium ended.

The Queen, the Prime Minister and the new Foreign Secretary (Mr. Selwyn Lloyd) dispatched messages congratulating the Sudan on becoming an independent sovereign state. In a letter to Mr. Azhari on 1 January, Sir Anthony Eden said:

> It gives sincere pleasure to all who know your country to see the Sudan take her place among the free nations of the world. I look forward to the closest ties of friendship between our countries in the years to come.[1]

On the same day Colonel Nasser, as Egypt's Prime Minister, cabled the new Republic:

> The Egyptian Government in accordance with their declared intention and efforts for the achievement of freedom for the Sudanese people, do hereby declare the recognition, forthwith, of the Sudan as a Sovereign State. . . . On behalf of myself and the Egyptian Government, I have the honour to congratulate you on this memorable day in the history of the Sudan and pray to God to help you in your present and future.[2]

Most of the Great and the Smaller Powers in North and South America, in Africa (even the Negrophobe Union of South Africa), in Asia (including both Communist China and Nationalist China), in Australia and in Europe rushed to congratulate and recognize the new Sudan. The Sudanese, too, quickly took advantage of the good mood

---

[1] *Daily Telegraph*, London, 2 January 1956, p. 11.
[2] Texts of Official Communications by Britain and Egypt recognizing Sudan Inde-pendence, in *Sudan Weekly News*, No. 71, of 4 January 1956, p. 3.

of the Powers of the day to push forward their politics of opportunism. On 10 January 1956, Mr. Mubarak Zarouk, Sudan's first Minister for External Affairs, despatched an application for membership of the League of Arab States. Having received from Abdel Khaliq Hassouna, the League's Secretary-General, a written assurance dated 12 January, Zarouk applied immediately for membership of the United Nations Organization.

In his letter of application, dated 12 January 1956, the Minister of External Affairs of the Sudan informed the Secretary-General of the United Nations that the principle of self-determination enshrined in the Charter of the U.N. had borne fruit in the Sudan when, on 1 January 1956, it was recognized as an independent sovereign Republic, first by the two countries who held authority over it for more than half a century, and later by other countries. Confidently he pleaded:

> By this petition, now, this new born Republic request to be accorded the Equal Status promised to all peace-loving nations, both large and small, in the Charter by being elected to sit and deliberate as a member of the United Nations Organisation.[1]

In considering this application, Britain and the United States were eager not to be outdone by the Arab League which had unanimously accepted the Sudan as a member; they were also anxious not to be outbidden by the Soviet Union, who had championed, at the Security Council in 1947, the right of the Sudanese to self-determination; besides, Mr. N. Bulganin, Chairman of the Soviet Council of Ministers, had written to Mr. Ismail Azhari on 3 January 1956, solemnly declaring the Soviet Union's recognition of the Sudan as an independent sovereign state, and expressing the Soviet Union's 'readiness to establish with the Sudan diplomatic, consular and trade relations and to exchange diplomatic representations'.[2]

Finally, there could be no substantial objection against the Sudanese Republic, which had fulfilled all the constitutional canons of achieving self-determination. Therefore, the United Nations representatives of Britain and the United States quickly asked for a special meeting of the Security Council to consider the Sudan's candidature for membership of U.N.O.

On 6 February, the Security Council unanimously recommended to

---

[1] United Nations Security Council: Document marked 'General, No. S/3543', dated 30 January 1956, p. 1. See also *Sudan Weekly News*, No. 73, Khartoum, 19 January 1956, p. 5.
[2] *Soviet News*, London, 9 January 1956, p. 3. See also *Sudan Weekly News*.

the General Assembly that the Sudan be accepted. In their eagerness, they, by agreement, by-passed the usual procedure of referring such an application to a special committee. Within two hours of the Council's sitting under the chairmanship of Mr. Sobolev, of the Soviet Union, the Sudan practically became the seventy-seventh member of the United Nations Organization.[1]

Thus, the Great Powers, like a band of suitors towards a beautiful woman, bowed to the new Republic of the Sudan. They showered favours on her; they caressed her; but only so long as they could still hope to influence her in one way or the other, especially in the ideological struggle for men's minds in Africa and Asia.

[1] *The Times*, London, 7 February 1956, p. 7.

Part Five

SUMMARY AND CONCLUSIONS

17

BRITISH LEGACY TO THE SUDANESE AND THE FUTURE OF THE SUDAN

We may lose all intimate contact with the peoples of Asia (and Africa), unless, as we release political control, we make a conscious and imaginative effort to build a new relationship on the foundation of mutual interest in our respective ways of life and thought and in our cultural achievements.

British Foreign Office, 1947[1]

Britain has an opportunity in the Sudan to transform imperial rule stage by stage into friendly cultural and economic co-operation.

MARGERY PERHAM
(Director, Oxford University Institute of
Colonial Studies), 1948[2]

THE history of nationalism in various parts of the world shows that subject peoples, when newly released, are deeply jealous of their new 'independence'. It is not surprising, therefore, that 'complete independence' is, for the moment, a popular slogan in the Sudan and that the Sudanese Parliament did declare the Sudan as an independent republic on 19 December 1955, and the paraphernalia of sovereignty was officially conferred by the co-dominion on 1 January 1956.

In theory at least if not always in fact, all sovereign states regardless of their size, population and power, are equal. But in the world of today, sovereignty is not actual independence in political, military, economic or technical matters. In a world of adjustment and compromise, it often becomes necessary, as it were, to get one's bearings right. And so if and when passions have become cool; when the Sudanese have become more used to the exercise of power; when they have passed the necessary stage of trying to convince the British and others who question the ability of the Sudanese to govern themselves; certain factors must be taken into account with regard to complete independence. The independence of any country is in part dependent on its

[1] *Report of the Interdepartmental Commission on Oriental, Slavonic, East European and African Studies*, H.M.S.O., London, 1947, p. 25.
[2] 'The Destiny of the Sudan', in *The Times*, 3 May 1948, p. 5.

economic strength. Economically, the Sudan is poor—no oil or mineral wealth, no avenue to industrial trade on a considerable scale has yet been discovered. For years, the cost of administration had been greater than the revenue, and according to a research made by the British Fabian Society, the deficit was paid by Egypt, 'one very good reason for the Egyptian claim to sovereignty over the Sudan'.[1] It is a fact, as Sir James Robertson commented in a letter to the writer, that the Sudan Government, under British guidance, had succeeded in increasing the revenue of the country 'from about £8,000 in 1898 to nearly £30,000,000 in recent years'. But it is also a fact that only gradually had the annual budget figure been raised to give an income total higher than the expenditure. So far, this revenue is precariously dependent upon a fluctuating export trade in primary agricultural commodities, among which cotton holds a dominant position. Partly because of the relative economic weakness of the Sudan, the British have expressed the fear that 'the country might lose all hope of independence and fall a prey again to its rich neighbour Egypt'.[2] But we must observe that no country is absolutely self-sufficient economically; and that a country might be economically dependent without losing its sovereignty. And yet wealth is part of power.

Sudan's total revenue for 1954–5 was estimated at £E32,459,176,[3] compared with Egypt's £E228,000,000 for the same year—about seven times more than the Sudan's.

A country can remain independent when it is strong enough to defend itself against its potential antagonists with its own strength; or when its neutrality suits the power blocs (e.g. Switzerland); or when its geographical location is so remote as to shelter it from the conflict between the present two major power blocs or any other (e.g. Afghanistan).

We have submitted evidence in the preceding chapters to show that none of these basic conditions sufficiently applies to the Sudan—a part of the Middle East which has been a major centre of world politics (see, in particular, chapter 7 in which we discussed the Sudan within the framework of Mediterranean Geo-politics).

Therefore, the force of geographical proximity and the interdependence of Egypt and the Sudan upon the Nile Waters, the common Arabic language (which has been introduced even in the Southern Sudan), the Islamic religion and the general feeling of consanguinity

[1] *The Road Ahead*, p. 18.   [2] *Ibid.*, p. 26.
[3] *Memorandum on the Sudan Government Budget Estimates 1954–5*, p. 5.

—all of which we have already examined in chapter 7 above—make a 'form of link' between Egypt and the Sudan most likely, sooner or later. In addition, the general trend in the world today is towards regional groupings, encouraged by the Charter of the United Nations Organization.[1] With the growing nationalism in the world, goes increasing internationalism.

In fact, the Sudanese Prime Minister revealed in London, during his official visit in 1954, the intention of the Sudan to become a member of the League of Arab States, in due course.[2] Soon after the confirmation of independence in January 1956, the Sudan's first Minister for Foreign Affairs—Mr. Mubarak Zarrouq—an Ashigga ('Blood Brother' with Egypt) member of the Unionist Party, was appointed. On 10 January, nine days after full independence, Mr. Zarouk despatched a significant memorandum, in Arabic, to the Secretary-General of the Arab League at Cairo. It gave reasons why the Sudan wanted to join the League: the Sudan is an Arab country, which in the past had and still has the same feelings as her sister Arab nations; all the hopes of the League of Arab States as expressed in its Pact are the same as those of the Sudanese people; the Sudan desires to fulfil its obligation towards the Arab peoples and to realize all her own aims and noble ideals; the Sudan, having declared her independence and having become an independent sovereign republic since 1 January 1956, was then able to participate actively with the Arab League States. 'Therefore, I hereby submit the Sudan's application for membership to the League in accordance with the second paragraph of the first Article of its Pact. I hereby assure you of the Sudan's willingness to fulfil all her obligations under this Pact. Finally, I would request that you kindly present this application to an extraordinary meeting of the Council of the League and inform me of their decision. . . .'[3]

In his reply dated 12 January, Abdel Khaliq Hassouna, Secretary-General of the League, enthusiastically welcomed the application and expressed the hope that the participation of the Sudan under the 'battle flag of the Arabs' would open a new phase of a more united front, closer association and greater self-confidence.

A week later, the Sudan was unanimously admitted a member of the League at the extraordinary meeting held publicly, and especially for that purpose, at the Bustan Palace in Cairo on 19 January 1956. (The

[1] The Charter, Article 12—'Regional Arrangements'.
[2] *The Times*, London, 15 November 1954, p. 8b.
[3] For the Arabic text see the minutes of the Council of the Arab League, held at its headquarters in Cairo, on 19 January 1956, Annex 2.

writer was in Cairo on that date.) It all happened in the presence of the Sudan Foreign Minister, who flew to Cairo on the same day and immediately after the end of the Sudan Parliament session, at which the Government won a new vote of confidence from the House.[1] Thus, although King Fuad and King Farouk failed to bring the Sudan 'Under the Egyptian Crown', she has now, to all appearances of her own volition, come under the flag of the Arab League.

The Arab League may seem to have impressed the Western Powers more with its weakness than with its collective strength. But, as a member of the United Nations Secretariat has pointed out, the League's 'very survival is a triumph for pan-Arab public opinion, which carried with it the reluctant governments of the Arab countries'.[2] It must also be remembered that the Covenant of the League provides that those member-states desirous of closer collaboration with each other, and stronger ties than those specified by the present arrangement, have a right to 'conclude such arrangements between themselves towards the realization of those objects, as they desire'.[3] Under Article X of the Covenant, Cairo, which is only five hours' flight from Khartoum, shall be the permanent seat of the League.

It seems reasonable, therefore, to suggest that Egypt has the opportunity of eventually bringing the Sudan nearer to a realization of the visionary unity of the Nile Valley. She endeavours to seize the opportunity. We have shown in chapter 7 section 3 Egypt's increasing efforts to combine the championship of Arab rights in the Middle East and French North Africa with the attempted leadership of all the nationalist movements throughout Africa. The Egyptian aspiration in this respect is emphatically expressed by Colonel Abd El-Nasser, in his booklet on the Philosophy of the Egyptian Revolution, published in 1955. After discussing Egypt's role within the Arab League states as the first consideration, he directs attention to the continent of Africa as the second:

We cannot in any way stand aside, even if we wish to, away from the sanguinary and dreadful struggle now raging in the heart of Africa between five million Whites and two hundred million Africans. . . .

There remains the Sudan, our beloved brother, whose boundaries extend deeply into Africa and which is a neighbour to all the sensitive spots in the centre of the continent. (Book 1, pp. 69–70).

[1] *Sudan Weekly News*, No. 74, 25 January 1956, p. 1.
[2] Isawi, Charles: 'The Bases of Arab Unity', in *International Affairs*, Royal Institute of International Affairs, Vol. XXXI, No. 1, London, January 1956, p. 46.
[3] The Covenant of the League of the Arab States, signed on 22 March 1945. Article XI.

On 7 February 1956, just over a month after the Sudan's independence, eight Professors of the Faculty of Medicine at the Egyptian Ein-Shams University, arrived at Khartoum to continue in the Northern and Southern Provinces of the Sudan, the health researches which they had carried out in the Western Oasis in Egypt. The Ein-Shams University sponsored these researches.[1] Of course, these endeavours were mainly academic; but it is reasonable to suggest that they are also indicative of Egyptian general interest in the Sudan, and especially in her population or settlement problems.

The question could be asked: Why cannot the Sudan form a link with any of the other neighbouring states? We have an answer. The Central African Federation (Nyasaland and the Rhodesias) established in 1953, and the proposed federation of East Africa (Uganda, Tanganyika and Kenya) are committed to the practice of 'White supremacy'; French Equatorial Africa and the Belgian Congo pursue political and cultural patterns divergent from those of the Sudan; the relations between Ethiopia and the Sudan are very good, but the Sudan is already a republic, and cannot willingly form a link with Ethiopia under the crown of the 'Lion of Judah'. The situation is such as would imbue the Sudanese with a feeling of loneliness on the Nile. These and similar factors, we venture to suggest, would eventually make many Sudanese more willing partners with the Egyptians, along the lines of the political groupings which are increasingly emergent in the world and in accordance with Egypt's ideology of the Unity of the Nile Valley.

But the Sudan's declared membership of the Arab League and its eventual partnership with Egypt do not mean a total defeat for the British effort at, and hope for, the Sudan's 'link' with Britain and the Commonwealth. The British are leaving behind in the Sudan certain good and enduring values which will continue to influence Anglo-Sudanese relations.

The history of Greece and Rome shows that when a ruling power transfers a particular form of administration to its subjects, certain marks are left by the departing power. Britain is leaving behind in the Sudan, as she did in India, certain essentials which will be absorbed into the life and heritage of the self-governing Sudanese.

We shall now indicate some of those factors, now visible, which will no doubt mould the Sudanese way of life, and influence the Sudan towards economic, cultural and even political co-operation with Britain. The factors are interwoven but they could be arranged conveniently

[1] *Egyptian Gazette*, 9 February 1956, p. 5.

under five main headings; cultural, economical, political, commercial, and personal.

The Sudanese have, after many decades of British influence, absorbed some aspects of the British way of life into their own Afro-Arabic culture. English has been the second lingua franca of the Sudanese. Certain institutions created by the British administration will remain valuable assets to the Sudanese and important factors in future Anglo-Sudanese relations. Among these are educational institutions, the most significant of which is the University of Khartoum.

The Gordon Memorial College, founded as a primary school, and the Kitchener School of Medicine, established in 1924, have evolved into Faculties of Arts, Science, Law, Engineering, Agriculture, Veterinary Science and Medicine. The two institutions became incorporated in 1951 into the University College of Khartoum, which had special relations with the University of London before becoming a full University in 1956. Owing to the educational policy in the past, there are still very few Sudanese academies; consequently, the University College is less affected by Sudanization than are the schools and Government Departments. The majority (about 90 per cent) of the senior staff—the heads of faculties, the lecturers—are British.[1] British thought and influence will remain for a long time to come. The impressive start in self-government already established in the Sudan was made mainly by men who have passed through the institution. It will continue to be a source from which men and women are recruited to man the various services of the Sudan. The American War of Independence forced British political power out of the American colonies in cold blood and bitterness; in spite of this, Harvard and Yale are even today American institutions with British traditions. The British departure from the Sudan is, in comparison, cordial and friendly. Therefore, the chances of the Khartoum University continuing to be a source of British thought and influence in the Sudan appear more likely, even allowing room for competitive influences from the Arabic world.

The British Administration have helped to build up the economy of the country, as we have observed while analysing the British interests in the Sudan (chapter 8). One of the most conspicuous signs of economic development is the famous Gezira Scheme. It is a most successful example of irrigation engineering and agricultural science, somewhat similar to the Tennessee Valley Authority project in the United States.

---

[1] See Staff List, The University College of Khartoum, *Annual Report for 1953*, Khartoum, 1954, pp. 16–23.

Dr. Mohammed Afzal, the Director of Research of the Pakistan Central Cotton Committee, who visited the Gezira in 1946, commended the scheme: 'The Gezira Scheme is one of those outstanding experiments on socio-economic problems of the current century, and its success is so great that it deserves to go down in history as a great romance of creative achievement. . . .'[1] The scheme has, since Dr. Afzal's visit over nine years ago, developed in stature and importance. It is now one of the greatest British 'gifts' to the Sudanese: however, British capital still remains at least till 1974.

The network of railways (built mostly with Egyptian money) which link up the country, and the civil aviation services, which are up to international standards, are also part of the useful marks left by Britain. In 1955 the route mileage of the Sudan railways was 2,138, and the annual revenue exceeded £E9,000,000. The Sudan has ten main-route airports and twenty-two subsidiary landing grounds. The Khartoum Airport, with a revenue of about £E100,000 per annum, 'is one of the best equipped airports of the world'.[2] A Sudan broadcasting service, inaugurated in 1940, connects the country with Britain, the United States, East Africa and other parts of the world. These are assets from the British rule in the country.

At their departure, the Romans left for the British their science of law, the concept of empire, a system of public administration, and Latin. The British, in their turn, have left similar marks behind in the Sudan. The Sudan Civil Service machinery, the political party system and the British parliamentary 'democracy' are actively in operation in the Sudan. The beautiful new buildings of the Sudanese House of Representatives and the Senate were designed after the Westminster model. The Parliamentary languages are English and Arabic.

Critics have commented that the University of Khartoum was established to prevent the Sudanese from going to Egyptian universities and from strengthening Egyptian-Sudanese association thereby; that the Gezira Scheme was established for the benefit of the Lancashire textile industry (as we indicated in chapter 8); and that the communication system was established mainly for British military, economic and imperial interest. These observations are correct in part. But, whatever might be the motives for their origin, they now stand on the credit side of the British rule in the Sudan, and are likely to influence Anglo-Sudanese relations for the good.

[1] Quoted by the Sudan Govt., in *1001 Facts about the Sudan*, Khartoum, 1952, p. 14.
[2] *Ibid.*, 1955, p. 30.

The British are making fresh endeavours to strengthen Anglo-Sudanese relations. As part of these endeavours, the President of the Board of Trade sent, on behalf of the British Government, a Mission to the Sudan early in 1955; the purposes of the mission were to carry a message of goodwill to the people, to study the country's requirements, to report on the ways in which British industry and commerce could 'assist' in the development of the country; and to indicate the opportunities open to the United Kingdom.[1]

The Mission was received by the Prime Minister of the Sudan. They had separate meetings with the Sudanese Ministers, the senior officials and advisers of nearly all the Government Departments.[2] While analysing British stakes in the Sudan (chapter 8), we observed that official documents of non-confidential nature are careful not to reveal Britain's real interests and intentions overseas. But the published Report of this Mission is an exception. 'Throughout our report', they declare, 'we have deliberately attempted to state our arguments in terms of practical self-interest without any appeal to romance or emotion.'[3]

Among other things, they report and recommend, first that British capital would be welcomed in the Sudan, and no restrictions would be placed on its movement or on the transfer of profits; that British firms should make special effort to attract Sudanese to Britain for training and experience, 'and thus continue the close technical affiliation which has hitherto existed between the two countries by reasons of the large numbers of British engineers and others who have been working in the Sudan;'[4] that the Sudanese cultural centre in Khartoum be preserved and that the British Council in London, 'from which the centre receives financial assistance', should do all it can to keep it open, and that the Sudan is a market worth keeping; to this end, the country—now self-governing—must be freshly studied and explored. If this is done, the British 'should be able to hold their own [against Egypt and other competitors]. . . . We found no political prejudice against them [i.e. the British]. Their goods are well-known and liked. Tradition and habit [developed by the British in the Sudan] are on their side.'[5]

It is therefore evident that the British are making new efforts, adapted to the new Sudan, to maintain 'a form of link' with Britain and the Commonwealth. The trade exchange between Britain and the Sudan

---

[1] H.M.S.O., *Report of the United Kingdom Trade Mission to Egypt, the Sudan and Ethiopia*—Terms of appointment—London, 1955, p. 7.
[2] *Ibid.*, p. 70. [3] *Ibid.*, p. 10.
[4] *Ibid.*, p. 88.
[5] *The Report of the Mission to the Sudan, op. cit.*, pp. 71–2,

since 1954 suggests that the British efforts are yielding fruit. The statistical report published by the British Board of Trade shows that Britain's total imports from the Sudan during the first ten months of 1955 (January to October) were valued at £E2,072,165 compared with £E772,720 for the corresponding period in 1954. Britain's exports to the Sudan in October 1955 were valued at £E1,568, 685, which is about double the figure for October 1954.[1]

In spite of the general knowledge that the English are at home very reserved, and the fact that they are much more so in the countries in which they rule, and despite the colour consciousness of the British, there has grown up many genuine individual and private friendships between Britons and influential Sudanese. In the Assembly, in offices, on the playing fields, and as a result of a few social functions on an 'inter-racial' basis, the Briton and the Sudanese have learned to know and to appreciate each other privately if not always officially. In May 1952, Sir James Robertson, the retiring Civil Secretary who had worked in the country for thirty years (he is now Governor-General of Nigeria) said in the Sudan Assembly: 'We have also made many friends, and have learned to appreciate their points of view.'[2] Such contacts have not ceased with the official and political departure of the British from the Sudan; they are continued in fresh forms through the University at Khartoum; through the Sudan Cultural Centre, whose aim is 'providing for the study of the literature of East and West (the Middle East and the Western Nations), strengthening the bonds of friendship and understanding between all members by the development of cultural and sporting interests',[3] and through Sudanese students at British Universities, whose number has been increasing rapidly since self-government in the Sudan. Those sponsored by the Sudan Government to undertake various courses of study in Britain since 1951—two years before and two years after independence—are as follows:

Year	Number of Students
June 1951	93
,, 1952	101
,, 1953	130
,, 1954	136
November 1955	220

[1] *Sudan Weekly News*, 13 December 1955, p. 5.
[2] Full text of the Address is reproduced by John Hyslop, *op. cit.*, pp. 134–6.
[3] Sudanese Govt., *Sudan Almanac, 1955*, p. 222. There are over 4,000 English and 1,500 Arabic volumes in the Centre's library.

These figures[1] exclude the large numbers of private Sudanese students in Britain and Ireland. Such students, Government-sponsored and private, are channels through which Anglo-Sudanese relations will continue to flow in the years to come.

We can therefore conclude that although the 1953 Anglo-Egyptian Agreement about the Sudan constituted a political defeat for the British and although the British officially withdrew from the Sudan, nevertheless the cultural, economic and political legacy bequeathed by the British to the Sudanese, increased by Britain's fresh gestures and by personal contacts in the Sudan and in Britain, may well have left permanent imprints upon Sudanese life and institutions, which will in some degree redress the balance in Anglo-Sudanese relations now and in the future. In a letter to the writer Sir James Robertson concluded confidently in December 1955: 'Of course mistakes were made, and of course we didn't go fast enough for some people in handing over power [to the Sudanese]—but by and large it was a good show.'

Several Sudanese with whom the writer discussed the matter in February 1956, seemed to agree with this appraisal of British efforts. Among them was Mr. M. A. Mahgoub (at present Leader of the Opposition), one of the severest critics of British policy in the Sudan (he resigned from the Legislative Assembly in 1950 and from the Constitution Commission in 1951 because he disagreed with the British viewpoint) who told the writer: 'The little that the British did in the Sudan was well done. . . . I have two sons in England, because English education is good.'

We can therefore conclude that politically the future of the Sudan is, for better or for worse, more with the Arab League and Egypt, than with the British Commonwealth. But in matters of commerce, higher education and technological science, the Republic will continue to be linked with Britain in the foreseeable future—it was not the works of the British that subject peoples resented, it was chiefly the visible presence of Britain's imperial power and dominance.

[1] Figures supplied by courtesy of Miss L. Clayton, of the Sudanese Office, London, in letter No. L.O. 2003.1, dated 25 November 1955, addressed to the writer.

18

SUMMARY AND CONCLUSIONS

1. THE SUDAN QUESTION—A CLASSIC EXAMPLE OF POWER POLITICS

> THIRD FISHERMAN:
> *Master, I marvel how the fishes live in the sea.*
> FIRST FISHERMAN:
> *Why, as men do a-land: the great ones eat up the little ones.*
> SHAKESPEARE, *Pericles*, II, I, 29

> *Even if there were only two men left in the world and both of them were saints, they wouldn't be happy even then. One of them would be bound to try and improve the other.*
> FRANK O'CONNOR, *Songs Without Words*[1]

ANY summary is apt to be something less than the full truth, which usually contains certain exceptions that are difficult to condense into neat sentences and paragraphs. We must remind the reader of the complex nature of international relations in general and of the Sudan Question in particular. Nevertheless, it should be clear from all the evidence we have submitted, that the Sudan situation exemplifies in many ways the kinds of situation and problem which have existed, and still exist, in many parts of the world. The Sudan Question is therefore a classic example of power politics among nations. In the following pages we shall attempt to summarize some of the facts that most merit attention and some of the conclusions established in this context.

Before proceeding, however, we should attempt to define the term 'Power Politics', and indicate the general sense in which we shall use it. The relationship between states, or the interaction of state policies, constitutes 'international politics'. In an international society, where there is yet no over-all state to control effectively the behaviour of states, the possession of power by states appears essential; to achieve and maintain their national rights and interests, states want power, in its broadest sense, just as individuals often feel the need for status in society. The term 'power' is ubiquitous in nearly all theoretical discussions of international politics. By 'power' we mean the total capa-

---

[1] In the *Irish Reader* edited by Diarmuid Russell, New York, 1946, p. 356.

bilities of a state to gain its desired end in relation to other states. Power is a most comprehensive term; it operates in many forms and has many facets—military, economic, cultural, propaganda (power over opinion), ideological, moral, etc. In short, it is the ability to win states as friends and allies; to influence as many people as possible within other states and nations. When states struggle and compete to gain and exercise such power, 'power politics' ensues. When all is said, the story of the Anglo-Egyptian Sudan is that of the struggles for, and interactions of, political power between Egypt, Britain and the Sudan. According to Mr. Martin Wight (of the London School of Economics and Political Science) 'Power politics means the relations between *independent* Powers'.¹ Mr. Wight seems to overlook the fact that subject peoples or dependent states also actively seek power, even if they are hindered from enjoying it in full measure. Movements for 'freedom' in colonial territories, even such as the Mau Mau, are struggles for power between the ruler and the ruled—they, too, constitute power politics. Therefore, power politics means the relations not only between independent states but also between these and the dependent states as well. In the context of our subject, power politics means the struggles between Britain (independent) and Egypt (before and after 'independence') to exercise power over the Sudan (dependent); the Sudanese, too, actively participated in this power politics by struggling for independence—for power to resist power, and for freedom to choose their own future and their political associations. In short, while the British sought to keep their preponderance of power over the Sudan, the Egyptians struggled to increase theirs; and the Sudanese to acquire power from both.

Having attempted to define our terms, we should explain, at the same time, that power is not itself necessarily either good or evil; the multiplicity and the conflict of its drives often make it appear poisonous. Power can be creative as well as destructive. It can be used for physical coercion, as in the series of the British ultimatums (e.g. 1924) and intimidations, some of which we cited in the preceding chapters, and the Egyptian incidents against the British at Ismailia. But it can also be employed for a most moral cause, such as the good in the British legacy to the Sudanese (chapter 17) and the ideals of the British Commonwealth; or the brotherhood of man envisaged in the Egyptian concept of the Unity of the Nile Valley. In this context, we are in agreement with Professor T. V. Smith of Syracuse University, New York, when he says:

¹ *Power Politics* (Royal Institute of International Affairs, Pamphlet No. 8), London and New York, 2nd impression, 1949, p. 7.

'Morality matures (can mature) through politics, since consciences-in-conflict find no resolution save in compromise.'[1] The late Mahatma Gandhi put it in another way: 'The best politics is right action.'[2] The wide powers of governments have been used, as in the Sudan, to dominate, but also to uplift. Social or international progress might end if personal or national ambition and the urge for power were to be eliminated. But in its more extreme forms, the power urge becomes not only a psychological aberration or obsession, but also a plague at home or abroad. However, we cannot here concern ourselves with the devilish-ness or the innocence of power politics. We are restrained partly by the fact that neither have all good men and women as yet been agreed on all questions of goodness, nor all just men upon all questions of justice; even all holy men have not agreed upon all holiness. Furthermore, in power politics one man's food can be another's poison. While power may corrupt, the lack of it may debase. With these general reflections regarding power politics as a background, we may proceed to sum-marize some of the most striking points and conclusions about the Sudan as a focus of power politics.

Throughout history, the major cause of conflict between nations and states has been competition for power over a territory and its peoples or for national jurisdiction. The present conflict between the two major power blocs of the world—the East and the West—for instance, is partly a competition for spheres of influence primarily in Asia and Africa. Similarly, Britain and Egypt have competed for power over the Sudan, an immense plain or plateau in the Nile Valley. Geographically, the Sudan is a part of Africa, situated on the North-eastern quarter of the continent. Culturally, politically and strategically, it has come to be regarded as part of the Middle East. It is more than double the size of Egypt or about eleven times the size of Britain and Northern Ireland. However, a great deal of the country is desert and the population is estimated to be only about nine million—just about the number of people in London or New York City. Broadly speaking, the inhabitants are divided into a Negroid-African South, which the British often consider as part of British Uganda, and an Arabized-African North, where the seat of the Government is, and where greater opportunities for general advancement exist. Partly because of these unbalanced opportunities, the British 'Southern Policy' and the rivalry between the

---

[1] T. V. Smith, 'Power: Its Ubiquity and Legitimacy', in the *American Political Science Review*, Vol. XLV, No. 3, September 1951, p. 697.

[2] Quoted by the American Service Committee in *Speak Truth to Power: A Study of International Conflict*, 1955, p. 55.

Crescent and the Cross, there has been friction between the Muslim North and the semi-Christian South, where christian missionaries work. The Southern policy stemmed, as we have indicated in chapter 1, partly from a genuine British desire to protect the 'weak' South against the 'strong' North. But it was also due to the personal rivalry between the average British official and the educated and ambitious Northerner. A member of the Fabian Society, who has first-hand knowledge of British feelings, declares: 'British serving officials have little time and no great inclination for social contacts with educated Sudanese. They feel far more at ease with tribesmen, whose whole world is utterly different from and does not compete with their own, than with natives wearing European clothes. . . .'[1]

(Incidentally, the same British attitude applies to the more sophisticated Southern Nigerians as to the less politically-conscious Northern Nigerians.) During the change-over to self-government and self-determination in the Sudan, when the British officials had to be replaced mostly by more able Northerners, the influence of local and foreign elements with vested interests contributed to the Southern soldier's incitement to mutiny and the general revolt against the North in August 1953.[2]

Political power over a territory and the control of its people could be acquired by (a) cession, (b) occupation, (c) accretion, (d) subjugation and (e) prescription. The Sudan had belonged to Egypt through its subjugation by Mohammed Ali, who conquered it in 1820; and then by Anglo-Egyptian occupation, which began in 1899. Egyptians had been connected with the Sudanese as early as 2800 B.C., when they traded with the people of Dongola area. In about 2000 B.C. they colonized the Sudan as far as the fourth Cataract of the Nile. But a very effective control does not seem to have been established until 1820, when Mohammed Ali, Turkey's Viceroy of Egypt, began a period of Turko-Egyptian rule in the Sudan; this lasted till about 1885, when the Mahdi —the self-styled Messiah of Islam—successfully led a Sudanese revolt against Egypt. The Sudan remained independent until 1898, when Britain allied herself with Egypt in order to 'smash the Mahdi'. In short, the Sudan had, as a matter of history, been under Turko-Egyptian sovereignty up to 1898, when Britain appeared in decisive strength upon the scene.

[1] Fabian Colonial Bureau, *The Sudan: The Road Ahead*, Research Series No. 99, London, September 1945, p. 23.
[2] See section on the Southern mutiny in chapter 14.

Britain went all out to conquer the Sudan; and this for various reasons, among which were: concern to avenge the death of General Gordon, who had been killed by the Mahdists at Khartoum; the death of the Mahdi, which cleared the way by removing the centre of emotional appeal for Sudanese nationalists and fanatics who had been too dangerous for Britain and Egypt; the decline of Liberalism in Britain and the rise of the European scramble for Africa; and the emergence of the United States of America as a political and commercial competitor on the world scene.

Consequently, an Anglo-Egyptian force, financed by Egypt but led by Kitchener, reconquered the Sudan in 1898: and the Condominium rule of Britain and Egypt was established in 1899. Henceforth, the predominant and effective authority in the Sudan remained in the hands of the British (chapter 3). Britain remained the prime factor in the Anglo-Egyptian Sudan scene, until the Egyptian revolution of 1952, bringing in a government which succeeded in reaching agreement with Britain and the Sudan on a formula for self-government and self-determination for the Sudanese.

2. EGYPT AND BRITAIN: THE DIPLOMACY OF UNREASON

The Condominium Agreements of 1899 established the Anglo-Egyptian Sudan over which each of the co-domini had, in theory, an equal right of control. But, in practice, the partnership was unequal. At the beginning of the issue, Egypt herself was under Turkish suzerainty, and from about 1882 to 1898 Britain gave the impression of acting merely as Egypt's adviser and guardian.

Eventually, under the Condominium Agreement, it became clear that Britain was in fact determined to be permanent master, not only in the Sudan, but even in Egypt as well. Though nominally a Turkish Province, Egypt herself was occupied and administered by Britain. In theory the government of Egypt was in the hands of the Khedive; but in fact the Khedive's authority belonged to the British Agent, who actively interfered in the details of administration; most of the key positions in the military and civil departments of Egyptian Government were manned by British officers. The interests of the other Western Powers (the Capitulations) were opposed to some of the British political objectives in Egypt. However, the exigencies of the First World War provided the opportunity for Britain to declare Egypt a British Protectorate on 18 December 1914. Efforts by Egyptian leaders to secure independence for Egypt soon after the war were frustrated; Zaghlul

Pasha and three other leading members of the Wafd Party were deported to Malta.

Inevitably, the power relationship (the Protectorate status of Egypt) affected the relative influence of each of the co-domini over the Sudan. Egyptians were irritated, Professor Toynbee observes, by the habit into which Englishmen, 'even in high places, had fallen of thinking, and acting as though the Sudan were not subject to an Anglo-Egyptian Condominium, but was an integral part of the British Empire.'[1]

Egyptians tried many devices for increasing their power, as against Britain's, in the Sudan. Boutros Ghali, the Egyptian Minister of Foreign Affairs, who signed the Condominium Agreement with Cromer, was assassinated in 1910; but that failed to affect the situation. Soon after the war, the Egyptians tried various other devices including many direct negotiations: during the Milner Commission, 1919 to 1920; during the negotiations on the Nile Waters, 1921; at the Declaration of Egyptian Independence in 1922, and during the MacDonald–Zaghlul talk in September 1924.

After these negotiations had failed, Sir Lee Stack, the Governor-General of the Sudan, was assassinated in Cairo in November 1924. The Egyptian Government, while accepting no responsibility for the murder, took adequate steps to denounce the action, to punish those guilty and to express official sympathy with the British Government. However, the British Government, turning down the Egyptian apologies, took retaliatory and coercive measures within twenty-four hours after the assassination. By the 1924 Ultimatum, Egypt's military forces were expelled from the Sudan, thus still further reducing Egyptian influence. In sympathy with Egypt, a platoon of Sudanese Infantry mutinied at Khartoum. 'After they had obstinately refused to return to duty', to quote Toynbee, 'British troops opened fire on them . . . and mutineers, who fought to the last man, were annihilated.'

Appeal to the League of Nations was ineffective, mainly because of the comparative superiority of Britain over Egypt, and the former's comparatively great influence among the member states of the League, of which the latter was not a member (chapter 4). Even in 1924, the power relationship between Britain and Egypt was almost as it had been in 1882, when Seymour Keay had commented that: 'England's enormous power is now arrayed against the feeble Egyptian state. . . . The lamb cannot long contend against the lion.'[2]

---

[1] *Survey of International Affairs*, 1925, Vol. I, p. 242.
[2] *Spoiling the Egyptians*, p. 84.

However, during the period between 1925 and 1930, Egypt endeavoured by a series of negotiations with Britain, to restore what had been her position in the Sudan before the British Ultimatum of 1924. Britain's policy at this time was relatively cordial, now that she had won her prizes from the weak. But she was, at the same time, careful not to yield on anything essential to her interests. Egypt, on the other hand, pressed her points, but avoided further open clashes with the strong. This conciliatory attitude on both sides continued until a world crisis was heralded by the Italo-Abyssinian conflict in 1935. Pressed by threats from Fascism and Nazism, which endangered Egypt's national security and Britain's vital interests in the Mediterranean and in Africa, the co-domini sank their differences for the time being, and concluded the 1936 Treaty of Friendship and Alliance. The Treaty recognized Egypt as a sovereign state with all the formal international rights accorded to a free state; it re-affirmed the Condominium Agreement of 1899, and removed the difficulties imposed upon Egypt following the assassination of Sir Lee Stack. Though it made Britain predominant, the Treaty provided steps towards a more even balance of power over the Sudan: Egypt was to have some share in the higher administrative and judicial posts of the Sudan Government. For the first time, the co-domini defined the aim of their joint administration as being the 'welfare of the Sudanese'. Thus, there was a change of mood: Egypt, the dependency, became an ally, the British Residency in Cairo an Embassy; Egyptian students took a long holiday from their habitual demonstrations against British authority, and die-hard Egyptian nationalists became friendly and co-operative with the British (chapter 5).

At the outbreak, and throughout the duration, of the Second World War (1939–45) Egypt took the necessary steps to implement the terms of the Treaty, under Article 7, by which Egypt undertook to come to the aid of Britain, in case of war, as an ally. The Egyptians carried out their obligations, the British admit, 'with a remarkable spirit of loyalty' (chapter 10(1)). But, though the war was won by the Allied Powers, Britain's interests in the Sudan and in the Nile Valley as a whole (the Suez base included) remained vital. For Egypt, the storm of danger had passed away with the defeat of Italy. But for Britain, the storm had not totally subsided, even with the defeat of Germany, Italy and Japan; it re-emerged from another direction—this time from Moscow, the centre of Soviet strength and of the Communist International. Consequently, Britain could not accede to Egyptian demands, though reasonable, soon after the war. Eventually, the Anglo-Egyptian Treaty of Friendship became a source of friction. Frustrated by unsuccessful negotiations with Britain in 1946 (Sidky–Bevin), Egypt appealed to the United Nations in 1947. Though the Security Council was, on the whole, sympathetic to Egypt, and recognized the innate right of the Sudanese to self-determination, it failed to adopt any unanimous resolution. However, it decided to adjourn the consideration of the Anglo-Egyptian question *sine die*—to leave it on the list of matters of which the Security Council was technically 'seized' (chapter 11).

Britain and Egypt having failed at Lake Success to reach agreement about the future political status of the Sudan in relation to the co-domini, the British Government initiated a fresh approach. It was felt in London that, if the two Governments could agree upon the more practical and less loaded question of a constitutional reform in the Sudan, the ultimate decision about the political status of the Condominium might conveniently be left to the future. Besides, such a step, we suggest, would show the Sudanese that the British were as eagerly interested in championing the cause of the Sudanese as the Egyptians. Consequently, the two Governments exchanged constitutional proposals throughout 1947 and 1948. The outcome was the controversial Campbell–Khashaba Protocol of 1948, accepted by Britain but rejected by Egypt. Egyptian leaders reasoned, among other things, that: the proposals were in essence a continuation of the Condominium regime which the Egyptians had repeatedly condemned; they would imply that Egypt had given constitutional power to the British Governor-General and not to 'the King of Egypt and the Sudan'; and they gave only limited, instead of full, electoral rights to the whole population of the Sudan, forthwith.

Consequently, the constitutional proposals were rejected by Egypt, with counter-proposals. The disagreement between the co-domini accentuated the split in the personality of the Sudan. There were physical clashes involving about 4,000 people, between the pro-Egyptian elements and pro-British. However, Britain, supported by the Umma Party, went ahead with the constitutional machinery; the Legislative Assembly and Executive Council Ordinance was promulgated in June 1948, without Egypt's blessing, and boycotted by the Ashigga Party.

Failure to obtain satisfaction from the Security Council of the United Nations in 1947, and the unilateral action of Britain in promulgating the Legislative Assembly Ordinance in the Sudan, brought a hardening of public opinion in Egypt. It became more difficult for any Egyptian

Government to retreat from the position which the Egyptian delegation had taken at the Security Council. Thus, on taking office in 1950, the Wafd Government inevitably aimed: 'To hasten the evacuation of the two parts of the Nile Valley (Egypt and the Sudan) and to protect their unity under the Egyptian Crown against any encroachment of aggression' (chapter 12).

On the initiative of the Wafd Government, fresh negotiations to revise the Treaty of 1936 were resumed in accordance with the recommendation of the Security Council in 1947. But, seeing the issues of the Nile Valley in the light of her own wider world problems and strategy, Britain could not satisfactorily respond to Egyptian overtures. The Egyptian Government, on the other hand, were no longer able to delay the settlement of the Sudan question 'on account of the troubles confronting Britain in other parts of the world'. In consequence, the Egyptian Parliament announced on 8 October 1951, their unilateral abrogation of the Condominium Agreement and the Treaty.

Now, in the relations between states, as between individuals, contracts or agreements are terminated by mutual consent, by lapse of time or expiration of the course of such contracts, by the death of the contracting parties, and by revocation.

Egypt had struggled in vain to obtain Britain's consent to a termination of the Condominium and the Treaty. As for the death of contracting parties, States, unlike individuals, do not necessarily die. Egyptians suspected that Britain would, even after the expiration of the Treaty in 1956, find an excuse to prolong it indefinitely. Egypt was left with the last remaining alternative—abrogation. In abrogating the Agreement and the Treaty, Egypt chose a favourable moment, given by Britain's post-war decline—from a first-class to a third-class power; by the humiliation endured by Britain at the hands of Iran in 1951, over the oil refinery at Abadan: and by Egyptian anxiety to settle the problem while a less high-handed regime (Labour) was still in power at Westminster.

However, as it takes two to make an agreement, it may often take two to bring one to an end. Thus, Egypt failed to achieve, immediately, the end she desired. Her calculations, mentioned above, misfired. In spite of the consequent guerilla incidents at Ismailia and the 'Black Saturday' in Cairo in 1952, the Treaty and the Condominium obligations continued until the emergence, in the middle of 1952, of the Revolution Regime, which succeeded in concluding with Britain first, the 1953 Agreement, granting self-government and promising self-determination to the Sudan (chapter 13), and secondly, the Evacuation Agreement of 1954 (chapter 14).

The Sudan regained independence from the co-domini, not by the emergence of a fresh Mahdi or by the 'cult of the individual', but thanks to a combination of factors. New generations of Sudanese had grown up educated (mostly by the British) to assume a place in the Sudan Service; these had developed into a middle class, with a corresponding political consciousness, who persistently competed (under pro-British and pro-Egyptian Parties) with the co-domini for power over the Sudan.

The rise in the standard of living and general enlightenment (contributed mostly by Britain, partly by Egypt and by the Sudanese themselves) enabled the masses to join with the middle class in their demand for home rule.

The rise of nationalism in Asia and Africa, particularly in Egypt, had resounding echoes in the Sudan, while the emergence of the Soviet Union as the Second World Power, whose Communist ideology competed with the Western Powers' Capitalist doctrine for the conquest of men's minds in the under-developed areas of the world in general, and in the Middle East in particular. Then there were the evolution of imperialism and the development of a new Liberalism (Socialism or Welfare-Statism) in Britain.

We must elaborate on this. The Condominium Constitution of the Sudan was completed by Cromer in 1899, the year in which Kipling completed his political poem of White supremacy—'The White Man's Burden'. In ordinary prose the doctrine of the White Man's Burden (even taking into account Professor Charles Carrington's 'Apologia' published in 1955[1]), was to 'civilize' and govern Africans and Asians —the White Man's 'new-caught, sullen peoples, half-devil and half-child'. Twenty-five years after Kipling's poem, Sir Frederick Lugard published in 1924 the *Dual Mandate*, in which he expressed the idea of the White Man's Burden less crudely: 'We hold these countries [in Africa] because it is the genius of our race to colonise, to trade and to govern' (chapter 8 above). Twenty-five years after Lugard's book, Lord Altrincham, another colonial administrator, had to write: 'Colonialism is dead. [But] we can guide and assist our dark African fellow-subjects: we cannot command them as we have done in the past.'[2]

The rise of socialist philosophy in Britain tends to mould public

---

[1] *Rudyard Kipling: His Life and Work*, London, 1955, pp. 275–6.
[2] *Kenya's Opportunity*, London, 1955, p. 153.

opinion against the old brand of imperialism. The British socialist has begun to see the subject peoples overseas and himself, sometimes, in the light of his own feeling and thinking about the capitalists in Britain—that the economic problems of Britain's under-privileged class at home are in some ways similar to those of her under-developed territories abroad.

Similarly, the Egyptians, who had somewhat pursued the European attitude of a superiority complex, also moved with the times. In the past they were eager to demonstrate that they did not belong to the 'Dark Continent' and were anxious not to be identified with Negroid Africans. Having themselves been victims of the White Man's Burden and discovered some of its fallacies, Egyptians now endeavoured to Africanize themselves, and to express sympathy with African national-ism, often to the embarrassment of the British interests in the Continent (chapter 7(3)). The Revolution Regime abandoned Egypt's traditional claim for the Union of Egypt and the Sudan 'under the Egyptian Crown' and offered instead self-determination for the Sudanese.

Lastly, there were the ideals of the United Nations Charter, which inspired in dependent people the hope for self-determination, and for equality of nations big and small. Thus, the Sudanese applied in January 1956 (and were accepted) for membership, and were accorded the 'equal status' envisaged for all nations.

Neither Britain nor Egypt has ever openly specified her real interests and objectives in the Sudan. Each has carefully couched her official policies and public statements in humanitarian or ideological terms. They each presented, as the goal, political ideals or images of the 'good society' in the Sudan. Such ideals are not, as a rule, susceptible of proof or disproof. Thus in Article II of the Treaty of Friendship and Alliance, they assured the Sudanese and the world that: 'The High Contracting Parties agree that the primary aim of their administration is the welfare of the Sudanese.'

Indeed, the British are among the most humanitarian people of the world; and several of them went to the Sudan urged by altruism. But, on the whole, for the British people to have exposed themselves to the jealousy and even the ill-will of the Egyptians and to the resentment of every politically-conscious Sudanese; for the British officials to have left their kith and kin to sojourn within the borders of the Sahara Desert and Equatorial Africa mainly for 'the welfare of the Sudanese'; to have maintained a military force in the Sudan mainly for the interests of the Sudanese; these possibilities would seem to be more than the nature of man could allow of at this stage of his development. The same applies, of course, to the Egyptian motives in the Sudan.

Egypt's immediate interests in the Sudan included the waters of the Nile, without which there would be no Egypt; a living space (*Lebensraum*) for Egypt's surplus population, and external markets for goods and capital investments.

Her remote interest was the possibility of the Sudan's becoming a buffer state against Egypt's exposure to the dangerous currents of world strategy and politics in the Mediterranean and in the Middle East (chapter 7).

In their international dealings, governments use as tools political formulas or ideological clichés, both to enlist support for their actions and as indispensable props for the execution of political objectives. Thus, as a means to their objectives in the Sudan, Egyptians employ the doctrine of 'The Unity of the Nile Valley'. This is a political pyramid, built as it were with the stones of the Islamic religion, which is dominant in Egypt and Northern Sudan; ethnology; common customs or culture; the Nile as a common means of subsistence, and as a communication link; the common geographical features between Egypt and the Sudan; and the increasing trend towards regional arrangements of solidarity in the world.

Our main criticism of the ideology of the Unity of the Nile Valley is its obfuscation of the real political and economic problems of this most international and controversial valley. Otherwise, it is, on the whole, reasonable (chapter 7(2)).

The British stake in the Sudan can be thought of first as economic. The Sudan was (and still is) a source of raw cotton for the wheels of Lancashire; it was a market for British capital investment and some mining. British shipping and naval interests were involved, and an important part of the trans-African branch of the British Empire Air Mail and Communication Service centred in the Sudan; it was a market for British imports and exports; and the Sudan was a field of employment for British technicians and administrators.

There were also strategic considerations. The Sudan was a British defence outpost in Africa; it was part of the 'Equatoria Line' of defence, stretching from the Gold Coast, through Nigeria and the Sudan, to Kenya and Tanganyika. It was also part of the British Middle East Military Scheme, and a source of man-power for recruitment in time of war, and above all, a British instrument for balancing the Powers in the Nile Valley and in the Middle East.

But British Power in the Sudan was not the repository of egotistical designs only; altruistic elements were also present. The British were often driven by a desire to bring 'civilization', as they know it, or Western values and attitudes of life, to the Sudanese whom they regarded, rightly or wrongly, as culturally more backward than they themselves (chapter 8).

At our present stage of development, no nation is yet genuinely and purely altruistic. Like individuals, states are, on the whole, egocentric. No country, whether imperialistic or nationalistic, is disinterestedly philanthropic to another. Even the United States of America, though possessing natural resources in great abundance within her own national boundaries, and though her citizens are a most hospitable people, actively pursues abroad a policy of 'enlightened self-interest'. It is therefore understandable that Britain, whose local resources are so meagre and whose very existence consequently depends at large on resources from foreign soils, should have been so anxious to retain her power over the Sudan. The natural jealousy between states leads to a rule which is familiar enough—the balance of power. Every annexation of territory and resources by one power compels each of the others to search for a similar extension to redress the balance. Hence, Egypt fought tooth and nail to annex the Sudan.

But it is equally true that, as with individuals within a society, some of the self-interest of the imperial powers often coincides with the interest and welfare of their subject peoples. Thus, the interest and welfare of the Sudanese were often, but not always, promoted through the promotion of the respective British and Egyptian interests in the Nile Valley. However, the crux of the Sudan Question is the conflict of interests between the two co-domini on the one hand, and between them and the Sudanese on the other.

The conflict of interests between the co-domini were mainly over the physical resources of the Sudan and the loyalty of the Sudanese. But frictions also arose because of divergences in the mental pictures which the British and the Egyptians had about the abstract issues involved, and because of the differences in the 'personalities' of the disputing states. Empiricism led the British to insist, with apparent sincerity, that the Sudan was not ripe for self-government; the Egyptians (and the Sudanese) on the other hand, emphatically persisted that the disputed territory was more than ripe. The British philosophy of gradualism derives partly from long habit and old age. With regard to granting self-government to their subject peoples, the British have acquired the habit of reacting rather than acting; of making great and necessary decisions only when they 'have been pushed, prodded and provoked by events beyond immediate control'.[1] Lovat Fraser, in an article on 'Britain's Future in India', calmly but resolutely sets out the aim of this British philosophy of gradualism in their colonies:

> To hold what we have, to make concessions slowly and cautiously, to rule justly and fearlessly, to continue our thankless endeavours to advance the well-being of India without praise and gratitude, and never to do anything to impair the stability of our rule—these things must suffice.[2]

Britain, an old and experienced country, projected her own past into the present of her wards. She falls into the common error of parents everywhere who often fail to realize the fact that their children are growing up in a world of speed, quite different from their own.

While some British officials played, no doubt, for more time to work on the Sudanese mind with a view to their joining the Commonwealth under the British Crown, the Egyptians, too, were eager to strike the iron while it was hot—to bring about the unity of the Nile Valley under the Egyptian Crown (now Republic).

There was another problem. Britain's interests were global, and the Egyptians' regional. In his mind, the British negotiator saw the Anglo-Egyptian Question essentially in terms of imperial strategy of defence, covering the whole Mediterranean and the western half of the Indian Ocean, and also in terms of the whole African continent; in these considerations Egypt and the Sudan formed the pivot. The Egyptian negotiator, on the other hand, saw the problem mainly in the restricted and narrow range of the Nile Valley.

The reactions of each of the co-domini to the problems they faced at conference tables were also influenced by the difference in the climate of their domestic politics. In the British Parliament, foreign policy is practically bi-partisan; the British Press, while often critical, is generally calm and subtle. The British Government could therefore pursue a decisive policy without playing to the gallery. But the Egyptian Government, before the Revolution, was most susceptible to pressures from an inciting and anti-British Press; from incessant riots by the Egyptian mob, which lacks the equivalent of Speakers' Corner at Hyde Park, London, as a dumping ground for their political griefs; and from

---

[1] Lippmann, Walter: in an address at the University of Chicago in November 1955. See 'The American Lead' in the *Manchester Guardian*, 19 November 1955, p. 6.
[2] *The History of 'The Times'*, Vol. IV, Part II, London, 1952, p. 834.

habitual demonstrations by Egyptian University students, whose unions lack the organization and prestige of their British counterparts which are miniatures of the British Parliament.

British Immunity and Egyptian Sensitivity to Crisis was another 'personality' conflict in the Anglo-Egyptian question. With time, the British Foreign or Colonial Office has developed professional immunity to international or colonial crises, whereas the Egyptians are comparatively sensitive. Moreover, Britain, with the greater power and prestige, could afford a long spell of patience as against Egypt's short spell.

A chief psychological conflict was the divergent concepts about race and nationality in the Nile Valley. The British insisted that the peoples of the Southern Sudan were different in race from those in the North, and that both were of a racial stock entirely different from the Egyptians. The Egyptians maintained that the peoples of the Nile Valley were racially the same. This difference in racial attitudes is due to the prominent place which race or colour consciousness occupies in Western European thought and behaviour, and to the ambiguity of the word 'race'. But, on the whole, it was an artifice employed negatively, first by Bonaparte to incite the native Egyptians against those he called 'the impious race of the beys'; later it was used by the British to 'protect' the Southern Sudanese from the Northerners, and both from the Egyptians. Thus the French and the British employed class, race and religion in order to divide and rule. The same artifice was used, positively by the Egyptians (and the Unionists in the Sudan) to achieve political unity and strength for the Nile Valley. In other words, the co-domini used 'race', the British in the partisan and the Egyptians in the scientific sense, to achieve their respective economic, political and strategic objectives in the Nile Valley. As many people know, race is not an absolute criterion of nationality (chapter 9).

The principle of the balance of power—a political formula to maintain the independence or weakness of unit of a state system, so as to prevent any one unit from being so strong as to threaten the rest—has existed since time immemorial as a formulated or unformulated guide in state actions. It has shown itself in many Western States wherein the units have struggled competitively for power.

Machiavelli, writing as far back as 1513, put it cogently: 'The Prince who contributes toward the advancement of another power ruins his own.'[1]

---

[1] *The Prince, ed. cit.,* p. 15.

This principle has become recognized as an integral feature of British policy in Europe and overseas. In pursuit of the policy Britain had waged war on, and raised coalitions against, the Spain of Philip II, France at the time of Louis XIV and of Napoleon I, and against Germany in the reign of Wilhelm II.

This balancing of power is evident in the Sudan Question. Britain struggled against the 'Unity of the Nile Valley' for fear that an Egypto-Sudanese union might create a large political bloc in the Eastern Mediterranean and on the Western flank of the Red Sea; such a bloc would include the 22 million Egyptians and the approximately 9 million Sudanese, whose military potentiality was brought home to the British during the Mahdia, the First World War, the Italo-Abyssinian War, and during the Second World War. Such a bloc would challenge within a short time British interests and authority in the Mediterranean and in Africa. With a natural desire to prevent, or at least delay, the forma-tion of such a bloc, Britain persistently manœuvred to maintain the Sudan under British regime, thereby ensuring some effective influence on Egyptian policy. Also, there appears to have been the motive of keeping the Sudan, Egypt and the Middle East as areas of influence for Britain and the other Western Powers (N.A.T.O.), to counterbalance the growing political power of the Soviet Bloc.

Conversely, Egyptians struggled to achieve a merger of the Sudan with Egypt and to 'form a link with the Arab League States, so as to ensure that Egypt might be strong enough to meet the Great Powers of the day on a footing less unequal. Thus, quite inevitably, a conflict of wills and a clash of interests persisted between Britain and Egypt.

It may be asked: What effect did this competitive struggle have upon the disputed Sudan? Korea and occupied Germany offer illustrations of the effects of dual sovereignty. In Korea the Chinese influence followed by Japanese domination and the governance of Capitalistic and Com-munistic regimes, have caused a split in the political and cultural personality of the country. Koreans are a mixture of their own local ways of life and of the foreign powers which have ruled them at one time or another. Now, in addition to this, they are divided into two sharp groups—the pro-American South with Capitalistic orientation, and the pro-Soviet North with Communistic outlook. The tension thus caused by this split in the personality of Korea led to a civil war, involving the bloody intervention by the United Nations Organization. Germany, too, is now broken into conflicting spheres of influence by the major Powers—the Eastern Zone under Soviet influence, and the

Western Zone under the Western Allies. These two sectors are being developed along divergent lines.

Similarly, the co-domini left various marks on the Sudan; the conflicting external influences from Britain and Egypt accentuated the internal differences. The Mahdia movements destroyed tribalism to a certain degree in the Sudan; but the subsequent British dual system of 'Native Administration', imported from Nigeria in 1920, built up tribal chiefs who became increasingly powerful in prestige and in politics. As Miss Margery Perham describes it, this dual system is 'one in which expediency and principle were fused together'.[1] Thus, the tribal chiefs once formed over half of the members of the Legislative Assembly of the Sudan. On the other hand, the educational developments along Western lines produced an intelligentsia which, under the impact of European ideals of democracy, demanded effective say in the running of their own country, not according to more hereditary rights, but through enlightenment and ability. Consequently, there grew up (as on the Gold Coast) some conflict between the set of illiterate chiefs and the new generations of educated Sudanese; the educated elements were in turn sub-divided sometimes into rival groups of those educated in institutions in the Sudan, in Egypt or Britain, or in the American College at Beirut, etc. There were also religious rivalries between the sect supporting Sayed Sir Rahman El Mahdi, spiritual head of the Umma Party, usually described as pro-British, and the other sect following Sayed Sir Ali El Mirghani, spiritual father of the pro-Egyptian Ashigga (Unionist) Party. This sectionalism was fanned by the conflicting external pressures of the co-domini. El Mahdi was supported by the British Administration in the Sudan and by the British Press; El Mirghani and his party, on the other hand, received the backing of the Egyptian Government and Press. British influence was greater in the South than in the North, where the Egyptian impact was greater.

Consequently, there was a good deal of mistrust between the Sudanese and the co-domini Governments, and lack of mutual confidence amongst the Sudanese themselves; thus many Southerners revolted against the Northerners in August 1955. Before 1953, the dispute between Britain and Egypt made the Sudanese politicians put the question of the future of their country too far above any immediate programme of action calculated to promote the general development of the country. Rather than negotiate with one master, the Sudanese were faced with two; inevitably, they tried to play one off against the other. The Condo-

[1] A radio talk on Lord Lugard, *Listener*, London, 2 June 1955.

minium arrangement put the Sudan in a peculiar position. Politically, the Sudan was neither a colony, a protectorate nor an independent state. In fact, it was governed as a British protectorate; but it was not, in the British official classifications, a member of the British Empire. The British Foreign Secretary, and not the Colonial Secretary, handled Sudanese affairs in the House of Commons, as though the Sudan were a free state or a dominion. Culturally, the Sudanese are now Anglo-Arabic Africans.

However, despite the disintegrating effects, the double sovereignty had its advantages. It accelerated political consciousness among the Sudanese who kept the British and the Egyptians constantly on the move. The rivalry and the incessant criticism of the Sudan Administration from Egyptian quarters made the British officials work with greater care. The British Government had to send out to the Sudan men (and a few women) who were carefully chosen and impeccably trained. Consequently, the Sudan Political Service became the most 'élite' body of its kind in the world. British attempts to 'buy' intellectuals away from the pro-Egyptian tendencies and to satisfy criticisms from Egypt led to the appointment of educated men into the administrative service in increasing numbers and eventually to the appointment of Sudanese as Ministers. While it took India about two centuries to become sovereign after British domination, and whereas the British Colonies and Protectorates of the Gold Coast and Nigeria, though more advanced in political consciousness than the Sudan, were still struggling (in 1956) for self-government, the Anglo-Egyptian Agreement of 1953 led to the creation of the Sovereign Republic of the Sudan in 1956; this is less than sixty years after the Condominium Agreement of 1899.

Thus, despite their wranglings, bickerings and intrigues, Britain and Egypt brought into existence the first Sudanese Parliament in January 1954—a notable achievement, when several of the other parts of British and European-dominated Africa were in crises of varying degrees. This brings us to a conclusion—*the dynamic nature of power*. As the patterns of power change, readjustments in relationships and in natural policies inevitably follow. The Sudan was conquered by Egypt in the name of Turkey, once a world power. When Turkey became 'The Sick Man of Europe', her position in Egypt and the Sudan was taken by Britain— then the Strong Man of Europe who had elbowed France out from the Nile Valley. As the national power in Egypt rose, her ability to bargain effectively with Britain rose accordingly. In the Sudan, along with the rise of political consciousness, there came an increase in the will and the ability of the Sudanese to take from both Britain and Egypt the effective control of their own administration. With the 1953 and 1954 Agreements, a fresh level of relationships began: the three parties to the dispute (aged Britain, regenerated Egypt, and the youthful Sudan) are adjusting, each to the other, in proportion to the content of power possessed.

In the Anglo-Egyptian issue one can readily see the type of relationship that exists in the world today between a big power and a small one; between a Western and an Asiatic or African nation. The Sudan brought Britain and Egypt together in a form of partnership. But this partnership, in practice, was definitely unequal. By a joint conquest (moral or immoral), and by the Condominium Agreement of 1899, supplemented by the Treaty of 1936, Britain and Egypt became co-sovereigns over the Sudan. The British Union Jack and the Egyptian Green Flag flew side by side in Khartoum. The partnership was, however, much more symbolic than real. The instruments of partnership were drawn up between two states, politically and industrially unequal: they were signed when Britannia was strong enough to 'rule the waves', and Egypt was politically under the Porte, militarily weak and economically in low water. This is not to suggest, of course, that treaties must be made only between powers of exactly equal strength; but as a measure of equality is a firm bond of love, so it is essential to faithfulness between one state and another. Had powerful Britain, in spite of the weakness of Egypt, endeavoured to follow and carry out in good faith the principles of true partnership, much of the friction and the cut-throat competition over the Sudan for many years past might perhaps have been avoided.

Under the circumstances which prevailed, however, the inevitable results followed: as Egypt advanced in strength and confidence, Anglo-Egyptian tension grew. Egyptian leaders, annoyed at what they felt to be humiliation unnecessarily imposed by Britain, became possessed by a sense of mission; they carried 'chips on their shoulders' and sought to right, in their own way, the wrongs in the Sudan Question. Egypt's virtual exclusion from actual participation in the affairs of the Sudan led her to intensify her efforts in encouraging Sudanese nationalism; she sought to buy adherents in the Sudan at the expense of Britain. A number of factors made it easy for most Egyptian politicians to stir public feeling against British policy. Amongst these were the British occupation of Egypt for several decades and subsequent penetration into the Sudan; the desire of the Sudanese to govern themselves and the

British resistance; the establishment of neo-Judaism in Palestine, supported by Britain first against Egyptian sentiment and secondly against the terms of the Treaty of 1936; and the injured pride of the Egyptians at the use of British power to dictate policy in the Sudan and to influence domestic politics in Egypt.

Thus, the major concern of nearly every government which came to power in Egypt became the Anglo-Egyptian issue. Most of the thinking in Egypt was driven off sound bases and conditioned to such a degree as hindered sufficiently realistic weighing of the factors involved; in the circumstances, formulation of a policy regarding the Sudan Question, based upon sober judgment, was lacking.

The Egyptian side was quite often swayed by emotion, which sometimes led to violence. Public feeling was quickly excited, bitter, and easily responsive to insinuations and attacks on British policy. Almost every party in office, through policy or conviction, joined in the hue and cry. The result was a tendency to follow instead of guiding public opinion. Consequently, rash attitudes and wrong policies were often adopted; quite often, the extremists resorted to 'hatchet politics': they assassinated the Governor-General of the Sudan, Sir Lee Stack, in Cairo in 1924; incited the mutinies in the Sudan in the same year; rioted and burned British property in Cairo in 1952 and carried on guerrilla war at Ismailia; they boycotted the instruments of constitutional changes in the Sudan in 1948. All these had the effect of turning the distaste of British officials for co-operation with Egyptians into a stronger determination to keep the Egyptians out of the Sudan, permanently.

The humiliating British occupation, the lack of sufficient political power or industrial strength, and Britain's disinclination to treat Egypt as a full sovereign state after the grant of independence in 1922, and even despite the Treaty of 1936, gave rise to politico-psychological tensions. Egyptian feelings of inferiority were expressed in fierce and aggressive bitterness and resentment against Britain. Many Egyptians became obsessed with the conception that, beneath every guileless or even stupid British exterior, there lay an unfathomable cunning. This obsession was an embarrassment and impediment to Anglo-Egyptian negotiations. For instance, Lord Lloyd, when High Commissioner in Egypt, made a speech in 1927, in which he referred to King George's interest in the welfare of the Egyptians and the Sudanese. He obviously was conveying an expression of diplomatic goodwill and formal greeting on behalf of his Sovereign. But it excited a sense of grievance among certain Egyptian and Sudanese leaders, who, hyper-sensitively, regarded the greetings as really meant to assert that the British King held sway over Egypt and the Sudan.[1]

To the British the Egyptians seemed loud, verbose and boastful—all in contrast with the British habits of understatement and mumbling self-restraint. Inevitably, the British saw the Egyptians as conceited and showy, while in Egyptian eyes the British were reserved, cold, hostile and arrogant. Nahas Pasha and his successors had been loyal to the 1936 Treaty in realizing that Egypt's interests lay in the complete fulfilment of its terms. However, owing to the obstacles which we have indicated, it was difficult for them always to act wisely in pursuit of their objectives. Only the 1952 Revolution effectively succeeded in cleansing Egyptian policy of some of its political dust and in controlling its over-passionate elements, and thus it was the Revolutionary Regime which was able to conclude with Britain the Agreements of 1953 and 1954.

But, if Egypt was unreasonable, Britain was even more so. Britain's 'friendship' with Egypt was shallow, if not insincere. With regard to the 1936 Treaty, Professor Gibb, himself a responsible British authority in a position to know, observes that, although it is explicitly declared to be a Treaty of Friendship and Alliance, 'Neither in official circles, nor by mass public opinion in this country [Britain], has the word *friendship* corresponded to any reality whether in action or feeling'.[2]

To the Egyptian, however, the drawing up and signing of a treaty was not so important as the manner in which it would be executed; this meant not only faithfulness to the terms of the agreement, but also 'loyalty and friendliness to the man in the street',[3] who might in the long run be called upon to make some sacrifice towards the implementation of the Treaty's terms. For about fifty years, from the time of the campaign for the reconquest of the Sudan, British officials had maintained that Egypt and the Sudan were one country. But later, beginning after the formal independence of Egypt, many British officials, it is alleged, actively pursued the policy of separating the Sudan from Egypt; and when many Northern Sudanese were becoming politically rather assertive and were showing signs of sympathy with the Egyptian view of the Unity of the Nile Valley, Britain took certain steps which had the effect of driving a wedge between the North and the South of the Sudan as well. Britain saw Egypt and the Sudan mainly in terms of British

[1] George Glasgow, 'An Emotional Bubble in Egypt', *Contemporary Review*, London, July 1927, p. 115.

[2] Gibb, H. A. R.: see *United Empire*, London, April 1952.

[3] Yousef, Amine, Bey, *op. cit.*, p. 4.

domestic and international interests; the Nile Valley must be 'guarded and protected', even though it meant ignoring the vehement objections which Egyptian and Sudanese leaders raised against the restrictions thereby placed upon their freedom and liberty. In face of the swift wave of Egyptian and Sudanese nationalism, the British persisted in their philosophy of gradualism. An Englishman admitted 'We resent being rushed, particularly when it can be represented that it is against our will.'[1]

Thus, while the British pursued their policies, the Egyptians remained uneasy and disillusioned in their partnership; Britain seemed, on the whole, indifferent to the necessity of retaining the goodwill both of the Egyptians and of the Sudanese.

In most of the negotiations and in her broad policy, Britain failed to rid herself of the ideas she inherited from her 19th-century position in the world and particularly in Egypt. As is often the case whenever a Western Power meets an Asiatic or African Power, the British ignored (though they witnessed) the Egyptian consciousness of a great past as a cradle of world civilization. To the Egyptians, on the other hand, the higher morality or political maturity claimed by the Western Powers was superficial. An Egyptian nationalist, the late Mustafa Kamal, expressed little respect for the mechanical civilization of the West, as such:

> To us Orientals material civilization is not a genuine civilization. True civilization is based on moral rectitude and freedom of the peoples. Of what value to us are the telegraph, the telephone, the gramophone, and all Europe's mechanical inventions, if we are oppressed by the inventors of those fine appliances, and if they only serve to hasten our subjection? I would rather a thousand times wander on horseback in the desert and feel free, than fly with the threefold rapidity of the motor car across the country dominated by the English.[2]

In their dealings with Africans and Asiatics, the British have always evinced what Professor Gilbert Murray calls 'signs of excessive faith in ourselves'.[3]

It is tempting to assume that states, in their relations one with another, will be prepared to act as sensible individuals often do, when faced with similar problems. On the individual level, relations between the British, the Egyptians and the Sudanese can be described as reasonable, if not

---

[1] Owen Tweedy, 'Zaad Pasha Zaghlul', in *Fortnightly Review*, Vol. CXXII, October 1927, p. 502.
[2] Quoted by Hans Kohn, *History of Nationalism in the East*, London, 1929, pp. 158–9.
[3] Murray, G., *From the League to the U.N.*, London, 1948, p. 28.

happy. Even in 1951, a most critical year in Anglo-Egyptian relations, there were in British Universities about 350 Egyptian students.[1] In November 1955, there were 220 Government-sponsored Sudanese students, excluding private ones, in British institutions.[2]

Between the individual British and the students from the Nile Valley genuine friendships are often made; in fact there have even been cases of intermarriage. However, contracting parties in international affairs seldom behave as sensible individuals; they are states armed and determined to assert their will and power to the 'extremity of unreason and even of cruelty'.[3] As nations grow in power they become, almost in geometrical progression, more assertive, more determined to be masters not in their own homes only, but also abroad; they grow more and more sensitive about their sovereignty and become more difficult to control by the honest rule of justice and fairplay.

Since no other nation, of such status and strength as Britain, has deliberately and successfully used such power to bring abiding sanity into international politics, perhaps Britain's policy-makers ought not to be seen as solely to blame. As a whole our world is still a place in which might rather than right tends to prevail. We are still in a harsh age in which 'civilization' has yet to develop to such a stage that humanitarian ethics may be the sole determinant in the relations among nations. Moral philosophers in the realms of international relationships are plentiful; but in practice, it is not common—and perhaps it is not possible—for statesmen or diplomats to act, or even to pose, as moralists.

3. CONCLUSION AND BALANCE SHEET OF THE QUESTION

The reader can well appreciate, from the evidence we have submitted from the beginning to the end, the complex nature of this intriguing subject, in respect of which passions still run high and certain implications point forward not only into the future of the African Continent but also, to a certain extent, even of the world. And so, many complex conclusions inevitably emerge; some of these we have already noted. However, the following inter-related points do seem to need making:

(I) That the Sudan Question is a case of power politics—a triangular struggle between the imperialistic British, the ambitious Egyptians, and the subordinated Sudanese, for power over the physical resources, and the human masses of the Sudan.

---

[1] UNESCO: *Study Abroad*, International Handbook of Fellowship, Scholarships Educational Exchange, Vol. V, 1953, p. 19.

[2] See chapter 17 on 'British Legacy to the Sudanese and the Future of the Sudan'.

[3] Jacks, L. P., *Co-operation or Coercion? The League at Crossroads*, London, 1938, p. x.

(II) That this struggle for power emanated from a plurality of conflicting drives—some good, some very bad, and with inevitable effects in both Egypt and the Sudan. The British power and influence were both creative and destructive, tending simultaneously to suppress and to uplift. Hence, power is in itself neither good nor evil—it makes a good man or state better but a bad one worse; British rule was disliked not so much for being so bad, as for being so alien.

(III) That in some ways man is still a beast, influenced in international politics often more by his lower, than by his higher, nature. He employs bickering, incitement (by racial, religious or ideological artifices), fighting and even killing to achieve his political and economic objectives, and to preserve by force of arms what cannot be defended on moral principles.

(IV) That power is dynamic and changeable: a people can be adjusted and can cause others to adjust, in proportion to the content of the actual or potential power they respectively possess.

(V) That international conflicts are due not always to the pursuit of selfish interests and desires as such, but quite often to altruistic intentions and to environmental differences: that is, to distinguishable national psychology built up over the years. In other words, to differences in mental frames of reference.

(VI) That, as shown by the history of the Condominium Agreement and the Treaty, it takes more than the signing of pacts and agreements to bring about genuine international co-operation. The highest forms of friendship are not secured by pacts. However, international pacts are useful to the extent that they may contribute to the stability of the world, since pacts, once signed, are difficult to abrogate unilaterally.

(VII) That, without the acceptance, and the application, of the principles of equality, integrity and mutual respect, justice and fair-play or co-operation between one state and another becomes practically one-sided; it inevitably results in the imposition of the will of the STRONG upon the WEAK, until such time as the Weak has acquired enough power to exact respect and a fair deal.

(VIII) That, in time, a weak and oppressed people can acquire or regain strength and power by constitutional methods and peaceful negotiations—by following studiously the political canons set by the Master States and using such canons to push the Masters to a state where it would be too awkward for them not to yield power to their Wards.

(IX) That as nations grow in power, they commonly become increasingly jealous of their sovereignty, assertive, and difficult to control.

(X) That the Sudanese cannot stand alone on the moody and controversial Nile and amidst the stormy political battle between Black and White in the neighbouring parts of Africa; that sooner or later, the economically weaker Sudan seems likely to become more closely aligned with the economically stronger Egypt, provided, of course, that the Egyptians do not alienate the Sudanese or overplay their hand. And that, at the same time, Britain's legacy to the Sudan, together with her further endeavours since the grant of self-government to the Condominium, will influence for the better, and strengthen, what remains of Anglo-Sudanese relations. What the Sudanese (and other subject peoples) resent is not British enterprise, commerce and technology, but their experience of Britain's imperial power and domination.

The Balance Sheet of the Question.

We must re-emphasize some of the major problems in the Sudan as a case study in power politics. A real obstacle to reasonable and early settlement about the Sudan was the mutual distrust, which each party sought to justify from his own standpoint. Britain felt that her economic, political and strategic interests in the Nile Valley could not be left to depend merely upon Egyptian good faith or collaboration. Egyptian and Sudanese nationalists, on the other hand, suspected that there was a real British intention of allowing the freedom and independence, for which they strove, to be mere shadow and illusion.

Between Egypt and the Sudan there was, and still is, mutual suspicion and anxiety, fanned by the presence of British influence, over the waters of the Nile upon which depend Egyptian and Sudanese agricultural economy and prospective hydro-electric power.

Geographically, the Nile Valley (Egypt with the Sudan) is situated on the edge of a world political volcano, given to incessant and uncertain eruptions. Among the dominant Powers of N.A.T.O., there was, and still is, a deep fear of the Communist danger (real or imaginary) to Western influence and prestige if the control of Western power, represented by Britain, were removed from the Nile Valley and the Mediterranean. (On Monday, 16 April 1956, three and a half months after the withdrawal of British control, the B.B.C. News Service announced, with uneasiness, that the Prime Minister of the Sudan, then attending a conference of the Arab League in Cairo, had confirmed that the Sudan was negotiating an arms deal with Communist Czecho-Slovakia.)

We have shown the great resistance by peoples of the Nile Valley to such a control and the consequent difficulties of maintaining it in a world of nationalism; the world at large is beginning to look askance at the old brand of imperialism and reliance on sheer force; the Charter of the United Nations has encouraged the natural rights and aspirations of dependent peoples.

Thus, as a result of the current conflicts of power blocs, there is still considerable cause of anxiety, in the immediate future, with regard to the problems of the Nile Valley, especially when one considers some of the many explosive factors in international affairs. These include the increasing national aspirations and assertiveness in the Nile Valley and in all of Africa; the possible emergence of power groupings on the African continent, quite apart from the Arab League of which the Sudan is now a member; and the various intrigues and schemes for 'collective security' on both sides of the 'Iron Curtain', and their consequent conflicting effects in the Middle East and Africa.

But having recognized these inflammable factors, it is reasonable to suggest that many of the dangers now apparent or real in Africa and the Middle East, or in the world for that matter, may be removed; some may even take a surprising turn to the benefit of all. Others, not now suspected, may emerge. But, on the whole, the future appears not without hope. More and more people, for whatever reasons, are becoming more and more affected with international-mindedness. Though the Sudan has become a sovereign Republic outside the British Commonwealth, she is by no means isolationist. She is a member of the Arab League, of which Egypt is the head; she has, at the same time, become a member of the United Nations, of which Britain is a leading member. The many decades of triangular relationship between Britain, Egypt and the Sudan; the sensible British habit of eventually coming to terms with reality; and the spirit of compromise which brought the prolonged and explosive controversy to a peaceful end in 1956, should make it not only possible but easy for the two Republics of the Nile Valley to come into close amity with the British Commonwealth, sooner or later.

Moreover, the day may be approaching when the deficiencies, which have left about three-quarters of the human race technologically backward and consequently impotent in the face of Western European domination will have become imperceptible. Asia and Africa are slowly but surely responding to some of the elements which have given Europe and North America their seemingly impregnable mastery of the world. Science brings the world closer together by swift means of communication and transport; technology is levelling off the standards of living; the possibilities of nuclear war with the consequent anxiety in which the citizens of the Great Powers have now to live; all these tend to make men see their security in the oneness of mankind and the fair sharing of the resources of the universe.

Thus, beneath the current diplomacy of threats and terror employed by the Great Powers and the fierce nationalism of the dominated nations, forces are at work towards a closer union, reflected in measures conceived not as expedients improvised to meet a current danger, but as steps towards a future in which the deep-rooted sense of superiority, in Western Europe and North America, will be outgrown with its power of arousing feuds and intense resentment. The relationship between Britain, Egypt, and the Sudan began with Kipling's philosophy of 'The White Man's [and the Arab's] Burden'. It will end, we feel, with Kipling's *Ballad of East and West*:

> But there is neither East nor West,
> Border nor Breed nor Birth,
> When two strong men stand face to face,
> Though they come from the ends of the earth!

APPENDIXES

I. INSTRUMENTS OF POWER FOR THE ADMINISTRATION OF THE SUDAN—1800–1956

APPENDIX 1

Firman granted by Turkey (*the Porte*) to Egypt (*Mohammed Ali*), 13 February 1841.[1]

Translation

TO my Vizier Mehemet Ali Pasha, Governor of Egypt, to whom I now confide the administration of the provinces of Nubia, Darfour, Cordufan, and Sennaar.

O my above-mentioned Vizier! since, as has been said in another Imperial Ordinance, I have thought fit to reinstate you in the government of Egypt, comprehended within its known limits, and to add thereto the hereditary succession upon certain conditions, I have also taken the gracious resolution of granting to you, without the hereditary succession, the government of Nubia, Darfour, Cordufan, and Sennaar, with all their dependencies, that is to say, with all the territories annexed to them situated out of Egypt, and I have issued an Imperial Ordinance upon this subject.

You will then study, by means of your intelligence and of your wisdom, to govern those countries and to make them prosper in conformity with my just intentions, and to ensure the tranquillity and the welfare of their inhabitants. You will, likewise, submit to my Sublime Porte an exact list of the annual revenues of the said provinces.

The incursions which the troops are accustomed to make from time to time into the villages of the above-named countries, and in consequence of which young and vigorous individuals of both sexes are made prisoners and remain in the hands of the soldiers in discharge of their pay, lead necessarily to the ruin and depopulation of those countries, and are contrary to our holy law and to the rules of justice.

As, then, this custom, as well as that of reducing some of the said captives to the condition of eunuchs, is in all respects contrary to my Imperial will, and as in general such acts of cruelty are repugnant to the principles of justice and humanity which I have loudly proclaimed since my accession to the throne:

You will devise with the greatest care the means of rigidly prohibiting them and of abolishing them in a definitive manner.

All the officers, soldiers, and other public servants who are in Egypt, with

[1] *British Parliamentary Papers*, 1841, Vol. VIII, pp. 251–2.

the exception of certain individuals who repaired thither with my fleet, having been graciously pardoned by me, you will have to announce this happy intelligence to all.

According to what is said in the other Imperial Ordinance above-mentioned, the officers employed about you, and whom it may be a question of appointing to a rank superior to that of Kol Aghassi (Major), cannot be appointed until a reference shall have been made to my Sublime Porte.

However those who are actually in service shall be confirmed in their rank; and you will have to submit to my Sublime Porte a list of these officers, in order that their firman of confirmation may be published and sent to them.

It being my Imperial will that all these several points should be executed, you will take pains to act exactly in conformity therewith, and it is to this end that, &c., &c.

APPENDIX 2

Extracts from the Firman addressed by the Sultan to the Viceroy of Egypt, modifying the Order of Succession, and granting certain Privileges, 27 May 1866.[1]

Translation

(After the customary titles)

HAVING taken cognizance of the request which thou hast submitted to me, and in which thou informest me that the modification of the order of succession established by the Firman, addressed under date of the month of Rebiul-Akhir 1257, to thy grandfather, Mehmed Ali Pasha, conferring on him the hereditary Government of the Province of Egypt, and confirmed by my Imperial Hatt, and the transmission of the succession from father to son in a direct line, and in order of primogeniture, would contribute to the good administration of Egypt and to the development of the welfare of the inhabitants of that province.

Appreciating, likewise, to their full extent, the efforts thou hast made with this object since thy nomination to the Governor-Generalship of Egypt, which is one of the most important provinces of my Empire, as well as to the fidelity and devotion of which thou hast always given proof towards me, and wishing to confer on thee a striking proof of the full and entire confidence I repose in thee, I have determined that, henceforth, the Government of Egypt, *with the territories which are annexed to it, and its dependencies, and with the Kaimakamates of Suakin and Massowah, shall be transmitted to the eldest of thy male children, and, in the same manner, to the eldest sons of thy successors.*

That if, in case of vacancy, the Governor-General shall leave no male issue,

---

[1] *Firmans granted by the Sultans to the Viceroys of Egypt*, 1841–73, with Correspondence relating thereto. Presented to both Houses of (British) Parliament by Command of Her Majesty in 1899. See *Egypt No. 4* (1879).

the succession shall be transmitted to the eldest of his brothers, and in default of brothers, to the eldest of the male children of the eldest of his defunct brothers . . .

Thou, on thy part, with the loyalty and zeal which characterize thee, and profiting by the knowledge thou hast acquired of the state of Egypt, shouldst devote thy care to the good administration of that country, shouldst labour to ensure to its population complete tranquillity and security, and, in recognition of the value of the proof I have just given thee of my Imperial favour shouldst carefully observe the conditions above laid down.

Written the 12th day of the month of Moharem, in the year of the Hegira 1283 (27th May, 1866).

APPENDIX 3

Principal Articles of the Anglo-Egyptian Convention regarding the Sudan, 19 January 1899[1]

Whereas certain provinces in the Sudan which were in rebellion against the authority of His Highness the Khedive have now been reconquered by the joint military and financial efforts of Her Britannic Majesty's Government and the Government of His Highness the Khedive; . . .

And whereas it is desired to give effect to the claims which have accrued to Her Britannic Majesty's Government, by right of conquest, to share in the present settlement and future working and development of the said system of administration and legislation; . . .

ARTICLE 1. The word 'Sudan' in this Agreement means all the territories south of the 22nd parallel of latitude, which:

1. Have never been evacuated by Egyptian troops since the year 1882; or
2. Which, having before the late rebellion in the Sudan been administered by the Government of His Highness the Khedive, were temporarily lost to Egypt, and have been reconquered by Her Britannic Majesty's Government and the Egyptian Government, acting in concert; or which may hereinafter be reconquered by the two Governments acting in concert. . . .

ARTICLE 2. The British and Egyptian flags shall be used together, both on land and water, throughout the Sudan, except in the town of Suakin, in which locality the Egyptian flag alone shall be used.

ARTICLE 3. The supreme military and civil command in the Sudan shall be vested in one officer, termed the 'Governor-General of the Sudan'. He shall be appointed by Khedivial Decree on the recommendation of Her Britannic Majesty's Government, and shall be removed only by Khedivial Decree, with the consent of Her Britannic Majesty's Government.

[1] *British and Foreign State Papers*, Vol. XCI, p. 19.

ARTICLE 4. Laws, as also orders and regulations with the full force of law, for the good government of the Sudan, and for regulating the holding, disposal, and devolution of property and every kind therein situate, may from time to time be made, altered, or abrogated by Proclamation of the Governor-General. Such laws, orders, and regulations may apply to the whole or any named part of the Sudan, and may, either explicitly or by necessary implication, alter or abrogate any existing law or regulation.

All such Proclamations shall be forthwith notified to Her Britannic Majesty's Agent and Consul-General in Cairo, and to the President of the Council of Ministers of His Highness the Khedive.

ARTICLE 5. No Egyptian Law, Decree, Ministerial Arrêté, or other enactment hereafter to be made or promulgated, shall apply to the Sudan or any part thereof, save in so far as the same shall be applied by Proclamation of the Governor-General in the manner herein before provided.

ARTICLE 6. In the definition by Proclamation of the conditions under which Europeans, of whatever nationality, shall be at liberty to trade with or reside in the Sudan, or to hold property within its limits, no special privileges shall be accorded to the subjects of any one or more Powers. . . .

ARTICLE 8. The jurisdiction of the Mixed Tribunals shall not extend, nor be recognised for any purpose whatsoever, in any part of the Sudan, except in the town of Suakin.

ARTICLE 9. Until and save so far as it shall be otherwise determined by Proclamation, the Sudan, with the exception of the town of Suakin, shall be and remain under martial law.

ARTICLE 10. No Consuls, Vice-Consuls, or Consular Agents shall be accredited in respect of nor allowed to reside in the Sudan, without the previous consent of Her Britannic Majesty's Government. . . .

Done in Cairo, the 19th January, 1899.

(Signed) CROMER
BOUTROS GHALI

APPENDIX 4

Treaty of Alliance between His Majesty, in respect of the United Kingdom, and His Majesty the King of Egypt

LONDON,
August 26, 1936.

(Ratifications exchanged at Cairo on December 22, 1936)

His Majesty The King of Great Britain, Ireland and the British Dominions beyond the Seas, Emperor of India, and His Majesty the King of Egypt;
Being anxious to consolidate the friendship and the relations of good

understanding between them and to co-operate in the execution of their international obligations in preserving the peace of the world;

And considering that these objects will best be achieved by the conclusion of a treaty of friendship and alliance, which in their common interest will provide for effective co-operation in preserving peace and ensuring the defence of their respective territories, and shall govern their mutual relations in the future;

Have agreed to conclude a treaty for this purpose, and have appointed as their plenipotentiaries:—

His Majesty The King of Great Britain, Ireland and the British Dominions beyond the Seas, Emperor of India (hereinafter referred to as His Majesty The King and Emperor):

For Great Britain and Northern Ireland:

The Rt. Hon. Anthony Eden, M.C., M.P., His Principal Secretary of State for Foreign Affairs.

The Rt. Hon. James Ramsay MacDonald, M.P., Lord President of the Council.

The Rt. Hon. Sir John Simon, G.C.S.I., K.C.V.O., O.B.E., K.C., M.P., His Principal Secretary of State for the Home Department.

The Rt. Hon. Viscount Halifax, K.G., G.C.S.I., G.C.I.E., Lord Privy Seal.

Sir Miles Wedderburn Lampson, K.C.M.G., C.B., M.V.O., His High Commissioner for Egypt and the Sudan.

His Majesty the King of Egypt:

Moustapha El Nahas Pacha, President of the Council of Ministers.

Dr. Ahmed Maher, President of the Chamber of Deputies.

Mohamed Mahmoud Pacha, former President of the Council of Ministers.

Ismail Sedky Pacha, former President of the Council of Ministers.

Abdel Fattah Yehia Pacha, former President of the Council of Ministers.

Wacyf Boutros Ghali Pacha, Minister of Foreign Affairs.

Osman Moharram Pacha, Minister of Public Works.

Makram Ebeid Pacha, Minister of Finance.

Mahmoud Fahmy El-Nokrachi Pacha, Minister of Communications.

Ahmed Hamdi Seif El Nasr Pacha, Minister of Agriculture.

Aly El Chamsi Pacha, former Minister.

Mohamed Helmi Issa Pacha, former Minister.

Hafez Afifi Pacha, former Minister.

Who, having communicated their full powers, found in good and due form, have agreed as follows:—

ARTICLE 1

The military occupation of Egypt by the forces of His Majesty The King and Emperor is terminated.

ARTICLE 2

His Majesty The King and Emperor will henceforth be represented at the Court of His Majesty the King of Egypt and His Majesty the King of Egypt will be represented at the Court of St. James's by Ambassadors duly accredited.

ARTICLE 3

Egypt intends to apply for membership to the League of Nations. His Majesty's Government in the United Kingdom, recognising Egypt as a sovereign independent State, will support any request for admission which the Egyptian Government may present in the conditions prescribed by Article 1 of the Covenant.

ARTICLE 4

An alliance is established between the High Contracting Parties with a view to consolidating their friendship, their cordial understanding and their good relations.

ARTICLE 5

Each of the High Contracting Parties undertakes not to adopt in relation to foreign countries an attitude which is inconsistent with the alliance, nor to conclude political treaties inconsistent with the provisions of the present treaty.

ARTICLE 6

Should any dispute with a third State produce a situation which involves a risk of a rupture with that State, the High Contracting Parties will consult each other with a view to the settlement of the said dispute by peaceful means, in accordance with the provisions of the Covenant of the League of Nations and of any other international obligations which may be applicable to the case.

ARTICLE 7

Should notwithstanding the provisions of Article 6 above, either of the High Contracting Parties become engaged in war, the other High Contracting Party will, subject always to the provisions of Article 10 below, immediately come to his aid in the capacity of an ally.

The aid of His Majesty the King of Egypt in the event of war, imminent menace of war or apprehended international emergency will consist in furnishing to His Majesty The King and Emperor on Egyptian territory, in accordance with the Egyptian system of administration and legislation, all the facilities and assistance in his power, including the use of his ports, aerodromes and means of communication. It will accordingly be for the Egyptian Government to take all the administrative and legislative measures, including the establishment of martial law and an effective censorship, necessary to render these facilities and assistance effective.

ARTICLE 8

In view of the fact that the Suez Canal, whilst being an integral part of Egypt, is a universal means of communication as also an essential means of communication between the different parts of the British Empire, His Majesty the King of Egypt, until such time as the High Contracting Parties agree that the Egyptian Army is in a position to ensure by its own resources the liberty and entire security of navigation of the Canal, authorises His Majesty The King and Emperor to station forces in Egyptian territory in the vicinity of the Canal, in the zone specified in the Annex to this Article, with a view to ensuring in co-operation with the Egyptian forces the defence of the Canal. The detailed arrangements for the carrying into effect of this Article are contained in the Annex hereto. The presence of these forces shall not constitute in any manner an occupation and will in no way prejudice the sovereign rights of Egypt.

It is understood that at the end of the period of twenty years specified in Article 16 of the question whether the presence of British forces is no longer necessary owing to the fact that the Egyptian Army is in a position to ensure by its own resources the liberty and entire security of navigation of the Canal may, if the High Contracting Parties do not agree thereon, be submitted to the Council of the League of Nations for decision in accordance with the provisions of the Covenant in force at the time of signature of the present treaty or to such other person or body of persons for decision in accordance with such other procedure as the High Contracting Parties may agree.

ANNEX TO ARTICLE 8

1. Without prejudice to the provisions of Article 7, the numbers of the forces of His Majesty The King and Emperor to be maintained in the vicinity of the Canal shall not exceed, of the land forces, 10,000 and of the air forces, 400 pilots, together with the necessary ancillary personnel for administrative and technical duties. These numbers do not include civilian personnel, e.g. clerks, artisans and labourers.

2. The British forces to be maintained in the vicinity of the Canal will be distributed (*a*) as regards the land forces, in Moascar and the Geneifa area on the south-west side of the Great Bitter Lake, and (*b*) as regards the air forces, within 5 miles of the Port Said–Suez railway from Kantara in the north, to the junction of the railway Suez–Cairo and Suez–Ismailia in the south, together with an extension along the Ismailia–Cairo railway to include the Royal Air Force Station at Abu Sueir and its satellite landing grounds; together with areas suitable for air firing and bombing ranges, which may have to be placed east of the Canal.

3. In the localities specified above there shall be provided for the British land and air forces of the numbers specified in paragraph 1 above, including 4,000 civilian personnel (but less 2,000 of the land forces, 700 of the air forces

and 450 civilian personnel for whom accommodation already exists), the necessary lands and durable barrack and technical accommodation, including an emergency water supply. The lands, accommodation and water supply shall be suitable according to modern standards. In addition, amenities such as are reasonable, having regard to the character of these localities, will be provided by the planting of trees and the provision of gardens, playing fields, etc., for the troops, and a site for the erection of a convalescent camp on the Mediterranean coast.

4. The Egyptian Government will make available the lands and construct the accommodation, water supplies, amenities and convalescent camp, referred to in the preceding paragraph as being necessary over and above the accommodation already existing in these localities, at its own expense, but His Majesty's Government in the United Kingdom will contribute (1) the actual sum spent by the Egyptian Government before 1914 on the construction of new barracks as alternative accommodation to the Kasr-el-Nil Barracks in Cairo, and (2) the cost of one-fourth of the barrack and technical accommodation for the land forces. The first of these sums shall be paid at the time specified in paragraph 8 below for the withdrawal of the British forces from Cairo and the second at the time for the withdrawal of the British forces from Alexandria under paragraph 18 below. The Egyptian Government may charge a fair rental for the residential accommodation provided for the civilian personnel. The amount of the rent will be agreed between His Majesty's Government in the United Kingdom and the Egyptian Government.

5. The two Governments will each appoint, immediately the present treaty comes into force, two or more persons who shall together form a committee to whom all questions relating to the execution of these works from the time of their commencement to the time of their completion shall be entrusted. Proposals for, or outlines of, plans and specifications put forward by the representatives of His Majesty's Government in the United Kingdom will be accepted, provided they are reasonable and do not fall outside the scope of the obligations of the Egyptian Government under paragraph 4. The plans and specifications of each of the works to be undertaken by the Egyptian Government shall be approved by the representatives of both Governments on this committee before the work is begun. Any member of this Committee, as well as the Commanders of the British forces or their representatives, shall have the right to examine the works at all stages of their construction, and the United Kingdom members of the committee may make suggestions as regards the manner in which the work is carried out. The United Kingdom members shall also have the right to make at any time, while the work is in progress, proposals for modifications or alterations in the plans and specifications. Effect shall be given to suggestions and proposals by the United Kingdom members, subject to the condition that they are reasonable and do not fall outside the scope of the obligations of the Egyptian Government under

paragraph 4. In the case of machinery and other stores, where standardization of type is important, it is agreed that stores of the standard type in general use by the British forces will be obtained and installed. It is, of course, understood that His Majesty's Government in the United Kingdom may, when the barracks and accommodation are being used by the British forces, make at their own expense improvements or alterations thereto and construct new buildings in the areas specified in paragraph 2 above.

6. In pursuance of their programme for the development of road and railway communications in Egypt, and in order to bring the means of communications in Egypt up to modern strategic requirements, the Egyptian Government will construct and maintain the following roads, bridges and railways.

(*Here follow details of* (A) *Roads, and* (B) *Railways.*)

The Egyptian Government will complete the work specified in (*a*), (*b*) and (*c*) above before the expiry of the period of eight years aforesaid. The roads and railway facilities mentioned above will, of course, be maintained by the Egyptian Government.

19. The British forces in or near Cairo shall, until the time for withdrawal under paragraph 8 above, and the British forces in or near Alexandria until the expiry of the time specified in paragraph 18 above, continue to enjoy the same facilities as at present.

ARTICLE 9

The immunities and privileges in jurisdictional and fiscal matters to be enjoyed by the forces of His Majesty The King and Emperor who are in Egypt in accordance with the provisions of the present treaty will be determined in a separate convention to be concluded between the Egyptian Government and His Majesty's Government in the United Kingdom.

ARTICLE 10

Nothing in the present treaty is intended to or shall in any way prejudice the rights and obligations which devolve, or may devolve, upon either of the High Contracting Parties under the Covenant of the League of Nations or the Treaty for the Renunciation of War signed at Paris on the 27th August, 1928.[1]

ARTICLE 11

1. While reserving liberty to conclude new conventions in future, modifying the agreements of the 19th January and the 10th July, 1899, the High Contracting Parties agree that the administration of the Sudan shall continue to be that resulting from the said agreements. The Governor-General shall continue to exercise on the joint behalf of the High Contracting Parties the powers conferred upon him by the said agreements.

[1] *Treaty Series*, No. 29 (1929) (Cmd. 3410).

The High Contracting Parties agree that the primary aim of their administration in the Sudan must be the welfare of the Sudanese.

Nothing in this article prejudices the question of sovereignty over the Sudan.

2. Appointments and promotions of officials in the Sudan will in consequence remain vested in the Governor-General, who, in making new appointments to posts for which qualified Sudanese are not available, will select suitable candidates of British and Egyptian nationality.

3. In addition to Sudanese troops, both British and Egyptian troops shall be placed at the disposal of the Governor-General for the defence of the Sudan.

4. Egyptian immigration into the Sudan shall be unrestricted except for reasons of public order and health.

5. There shall be no discrimination in the Sudan between British subjects and Egyptian nationals in matters of commerce, immigration or the possession of property.

6. The High Contracting Parties are agreed on the provisions set out in the Annex to this Article as regards the method by which international conventions are to be made applicable to the Sudan.

(Here follows Annex to Article 11)

ARTICLE 12

His Majesty The King and Emperor recognises that the responsibility for the lives and property of foreigners in Egypt devolves exclusively upon the Egyptian Government, who will ensure the fulfilment of their obligations in this respect.

ARTICLE 13

His Majesty The King and Emperor recognises that the capitulatory regime now existing in Egypt is no longer in accordance with the spirit of the times and with the present state of Egypt.

His Majesty the King of Egypt desires the abolition of this regime without delay.

Both High Contracting Parties are agreed upon the arrangements with regard to this matter as set forth in the Annex to this Article.

(Here follows Annex to Article 13)

ARTICLE 14

The present treaty abrogates any existing agreements or other instruments whose continued existence is inconsistent with its provisions. Should either High Contracting Party so request, a list of the agreements and instruments thus abrogated shall be drawn up in agreement between them within six months of the coming into force of the present treaty.

ARTICLE 15

The High Contracting Parties agree that any difference on the subject of the application or interpretation of the provisions of the present treaty which they are unable to settle by direct negotiation shall be dealt with in accordance with the provisions of the Covenant of the League of Nations.

ARTICLE 16

At any time after the expiration of a period of twenty years from the coming into force of the treaty, the High Contracting Parties will, at the request of either of them, enter into negotiations with a view to such revision of its terms by agreement between them as may be appropriate in the circumstances as they then exist. In case of the High Contracting Parties being unable to agree upon the terms of the revised treaty, the difference will be submitted to the Council of the League of Nations for decision in accordance with the provisions of the Covenant in force at the time of the signature of the present treaty or to such other person or body of persons for decision in accordance with such procedure as the High Contracting Parties may agree. It is agreed that any revision of this treaty will provide for the continuation of the Alliance between the High Contracting Parties in accordance with the principles contained in Articles 4, 5, 6 and 7. Nevertheless, with the consent of both High Contracting Parties, negotiations may be entered into at any time after the expiration of a period of ten years after the coming into force of the treaty, with a view to such revision as aforesaid.

ARTICLE 17

The present treaty is subject to ratification. Ratifications shall be exchanged in Cairo as soon as possible. The treaty shall come into force on the date of the exchange of ratifications, and shall thereupon be registered with the Secretary-General of the League of Nations.

In witness whereof the above-named plenipotentiaries have signed the present treaty and affixed thereto their seals.

Done at London in duplicate this 26th day of August, 1936.

(*Here follow signatures.*)

AGREED MINUTE

The United Kingdom and Egyptian Delegations desire at the moment of signature to record in a minute certain points of interpretation of the provisions of the Treaty of Alliance upon which they are agreed.

These points are as follows:—

(xiv) With reference to paragraph 1 of Article 11, it is agreed that the Governor-General shall furnish to His Majesty's Government in the United Kingdom and the Egyptian Government an annual report on the administration of the Sudan. Sudan legislation will be notified directly to the President of the Egyptian Council of Ministers.

(xv) With reference to paragraph 2 of Article 11, it is understood that, while the appointment of Egyptian nationals to official posts in the Sudan must necessarily be governed by the number of suitable vacancies, the time of their occurrence and the qualifications of the candidates forthcoming, the provisions of this paragraph will take effect forthwith on the coming into force of the Treaty. The promotion and advancement of members of the Sudan Service shall be irrespective of nationality up to any rank by selection in accordance with individual merits.

It is also understood that these provisions will not prevent the Governor-General occasionally appointing to special posts persons of another nationality when no qualified British subjects, Egyptian nationals or Sudanese are available.

(xvi) With reference to paragraph 3 of Article 11, it is understood that, as the Egyptian Government are willing to send troops to the Sudan, the Governor-General will give immediate consideration to the question of the number of Egyptian troops required for service in the Sudan, the precise places where they will be stationed and the accommodation necessary for them, and that the Egyptian Government will send forthwith, on the coming into force of the Treaty, an Egyptian military officer of high rank whom the Governor-General can consult with regard to these matters.

(xvii) With reference to Article 11, as it has been arranged between the Egyptian Government and His Majesty's Government in the United Kingdom that the question of the indebtedness of the Sudan to Egypt and other financial questions affecting the Sudan shall be discussed between the Egyptian Ministry of Finance and the Treasury of the United Kingdom, and as such discussions have already commenced, it has been considered unnecessary to insert in the Treaty any provision in regard to this question.

(xviii) With regard to paragraph 6 of the Annex to Article 13, it is understood that questions relating to this declaration are not subjects for the appreciation of any Courts in Egypt.

Signed in duplicate at London this 26th day of August, 1936.

> ANTHONY EDEN,
>> His Majesty's Principal Secretary of State for Foreign Affairs.
>
> MOUSTAPHA EL-NAHAS,
>> President of the Egyptian Council of Ministers.

APPENDIX 5

ANNEX 2

Draft Sudan Protocol, October 1946[1]

The policy which the High Contracting Parties undertake to follow in the Sudan within the framework of the unity between the Sudan and Egypt under

---

[1] *Papers regarding the Negotiations for a Revision of the Anglo-Egyptian Treaty of 1936: Egypt No. 2* (1947), Cmd. 7179.

the common Crown of Egypt will have for its essential objectives to assure the well-being of the Sudanese, the development of their interests and their active preparation for self-government and consequently the exercise of the right to choose the future status of the Sudan. Until the High Contracting Parties can in full common agreement realise this latter objective after consultation with the Sudanese, the Agreement of 1899 will continue and Article 11 of the Treaty of 1936, together with its Annex and paragraphs 14 to 16 of the Agreed Minute annexed to the same Treaty, will remain in force notwithstanding the first Article of the present Treaty.

ANNEX 3

Draft Evacuation Protocol

The High Contracting Parties agree that the complete evacuation of Egyptian territory (Egypt) by the British Forces shall be completed by 1st September, 1949.

The towns of Cairo and Alexandria and the Delta shall be evacuated by 31st March, 1947. The evacuation of the remainder of the country shall proceed continuously during the period ending at the date specified in the first paragraph above.

The provisions of the Convention of 26th August, 1936, concerning immunities and privileges will continue provisionally to be applied to the British Forces during the period of their withdrawal from Egypt. Such amendment of the agreement as may be necessary in view of the fact that British troops will after 31st March, 1947, be withdrawn from the Delta and the two cities shall be settled by a subsequent agreement between the two Governments to be negotiated before this date.

APPENDIX 6

Agreement between the Representatives of Sudanese Parties, and a Representative of the Egyptian Government[1]

Representatives of the Sudanese Parties including the Umma Party, the Socialist Republican Party, the National Unionist Party and the National Party held a meeting with Major Salah Salem, who submitted to them the points of difference which have arisen during the talks between the Egyptian and British Governments. They have all agreed to the following resolutions as final and irrevocable:

1. *The Question of the South*

All Parties agreed to the following Egyptian proposal. Paragraph 6 (*c*) of the Egyptian Note shall read as follows:

6(*c*) Any resolution passed by the Commission which the Governor-General might regard as inconsistent with his responsibilities or any

[1] Republic of Egypt, Presidency of the Council of Ministers, *The Sudan Under the New Agreement*, Cairo, 1953, pp. 6–8.

legislation passed by the Parliament which he considers incompatible with the principle of ensuring fair and equitable treatment to all inhabitants of the different provinces of The Sudan. In these cases the two Governments must give answer within one month of the date of formal notice. The Commission's resolution or the legislation passed by the Parliament shall stand unless the two Governments agree to the contrary.

2. *The Governor-General's Commission*

   (a) The Commission shall be set up immediately after the promulgation of the self-government Statute and before holding the elections.
   (b) The appointment of the Commission shall conform to the procedure prescribed in the Egyptian Note.
   (c) The Commission shall collectively act instead of the Governor-General during his absence. It will be presided over by the neutral Indian or Pakistani member.

3. *Sudanisation*

   (a) The following shall be added to Article 12 of the Egyptian Note:
   'When the Sudanese Parliament decides the date for Self-Determination within a period not exceeding three years, the remaining British or Egyptian officials (referred to in Article 10 of the Egyptian Note) shall be replaced by other neutral elements designated by the Sudanese Government if Sudanese elements are not available.'
   (b) Omit from Paragraph 12 the words 'and the ratification by the two liquidating Governments'.
   (c) Delete from Paragraph 13 of the Egyptian Note the words 'On the ratification by the two liquidating Governments of the date on which the transitional period is to be terminated' and replace by 'On the termination of the transitional period'.

4. *Elections*

   Elections shall be direct throughout The Sudan wherever possible and practicable. This shall be decided by the Electoral Commission which will supervise and conduct the elections as set forth in the Egyptian Note.

5. *Withdrawal of Foreign Troops*

   (a) The withdrawal of British and Egyptian military forces from The Sudan shall be completed before holding the elections for the Constituent Assembly which will decide the future of The Sudan as prescribed in the Egyptian Note.
   (b) When the withdrawal of British and Egyptian military forces is completed, security and public order within The Sudan shall be entrusted to the Sudanese Armed Forces. The supreme command and allegiance of these Forces will be to the Parliament and the then existing Sudanese

Government from the date on which the withdrawal is completed until the termination of Self-Determination. The Governor-General shall have no authority over the Sudanese Armed Forces during this period.

The Sudanese Parties signatories to this document have agreed that the aforesaid points shall constitute the basis for the Sudanese Self-Government Statute. Failing this these Parties have unanimously agreed to boycott the elections held under any other Statute.

The Parties have also agreed to meet to arrange and carry out means for boycotting elections in such eventuality.

KHARTOUM,
January 10th, 1953.

FOR THE UMMA PARTY

EL-SAYED SEDDIK ABDUL RAHMAN EL MAHDI
(President of the Umma Party)
Lt.-Gen. ABDULLA KHALIL
(Secretary-General of the Umma Party)
EL-SAYED ABDUL RAHMAN ALI TAHA
(Minister of Education and Member of the Umma Party)

FOR THE NATIONAL UNIONIST PARTY

EL-SAYED ISMAIL EL-AZHARI
(President of the Party)
EL-SAYED MOHAMMED NUR EL-DIN
(Vice-President of the Party)
EL-SAYED EL DARDIRI MOHAMMED OSMAN
(Member of the Executive Committee of the Party)

FOR THE SOCIALIST REPUBLICAN PARTY

EL-SAYED ZEIN EL-ABEDIN SALEH
(Founding Member of the Party)
EL-SAYED EL-DARDIRI MOHAMMED AHMED
(Founding Member of the Party)

FOR THE NATIONAL PARTY

EL-SAYED YAHIA MOHAMMED ABDEL-KADER
(Secretary-General of the Party)
Major SALAH SALEM
(Representing Egypt)

APPENDIX 7

Agreement between the Government of the United Kingdom of Great Britain and Northern Ireland and the Egyptian Government concerning Self-Government and Self-Determination for the Sudan

CAIRO,
February 12, 1953[1]

The Government of the United Kingdom of Great Britain and Northern Ireland (hereinafter called the 'United Kingdom Government') and the Egyptian Government,

Firmly believing in the right of the Sudanese people to Self-Determination and the effective exercise thereof at the proper time and with the necessary safeguards,

Have agreed as follows:—

ARTICLE 1

In order to enable the Sudanese people to exercise Self-Determination in a free and neutral atmosphere, a transitional period providing full self-government for the Sudanese shall begin on the day specified in Article 9 below.

ARTICLE 2

The transitional period, being a preparation for the effective termination of the dual Administration, shall be considered as a liquidation of that Administration. During the transitional period the sovereignty of the Sudan shall be kept in reserve for the Sudanese until Self-Determination is achieved.

ARTICLE 3

The Governor-General shall, during the transitional period, be the supreme constitutional authority within the Sudan. He shall exercise his powers as set out in the Self-Government Statute (2) with the aid of a five-member Commission, to be called the Governor-General's Commission, whose powers are laid down in the terms of reference in Annex I to the present Agreement.

ARTICLE 4

This Commission shall consist of two Sudanese proposed by the two contracting Governments in agreement, one Egyptian citizen, one citizen of the United Kingdom and one Pakistani citizen, each to be proposed by his respective Government. The appointment of the two Sudanese members shall be subject to the subsequent approval of the Sudanese Parliament when it is elected, and the Parliament shall be entitled to nominate alternative candidates in case of disapproval. The Commission hereby set up will be formally appointed by Egyptian Government decree.

[1] *Treaty Series*, No. 47 (1953), Cmd. 8904.
[2] See page 13 of Cmd. 8904 for text of Statute as promulgated.

The two Contracting Governments agree that, it being a fundamental principle of their common policy to maintain the unity of the Sudan as a single territory, the special powers which are vested in the Governor-General by Article 100 of the Self-Government Statute shall not be exercised in any manner which is in conflict with that policy.

The Governor-General shall remain directly responsible to the two Contracting Governments as regards:
- (*a*) external affairs;
- (*b*) any change requested by the Sudanese Parliament under Article 101 (1) of the Statute for Self-Government as regards any part of the Statute;
- (*c*) any resolution passed by the Commission which he regards as inconsistent with his responsibilities.   In this case he will inform the two Contracting Governments, each of which must give an answer within one month of the date of formal notice. The Commission's resolution shall stand unless the two Governments agree to the contrary.

There shall be constituted a Mixed Electoral Commission of seven members. These shall be three Sudanese appointed by the Governor-General with the approval of his Commission, one Egyptian citizen, one citizen of the United Kingdom, one citizen of the United States of America, and one Indian citizen. The non-Sudanese members shall be nominated by their respective Governments. The Indian member shall be Chairman of the Commission. The Commission shall be appointed by the Governor-General on the instructions of the two Contracting Governments. The terms of reference of this Commission are contained in Annex II to this Agreement.

To provide the free and neutral atmosphere requisite for Self-Determination there shall be established a Sudanisation Committee consisting of:
- (*a*) an Egyptian citizen and a citizen of the United Kingdom to be nominated by their respective Governments and subsequently appointed by the Governor-General, together with three Sudanese members to be selected from a list of five names submitted to him by the Prime Minister of the Sudan. The selection and appointment of these Sudanese members shall have the prior approval of the Governor-General's Commission;
- (*b*) one or more members of the Sudan Public Service Commission who will act in a purely advisory capacity without the right to vote;
- (*c*) the function and terms of reference of this Committee are contained in Annex III to this Agreement.

ARTICLE 9

The transitional period shall begin on the day designated as 'the appointed day' in Article 2 of the Self-Government Statute. Subject to the completion of the Sudanisation as outlined in Annex III to this Agreement, the two Contracting Governments undertake to bring the transitional period to an end as soon as possible. In any case this period shall not exceed three years. It shall be brought to an end in the following manner. The Sudanese Parliament shall pass a resolution expressing their desire that arrangements for Self-Determination shall be put in motion and the Governor-General shall notify the two Contracting Governments of this resolution.

ARTICLE 10

When the two Contracting Governments have been formally notified of this resolution, the Sudanese Government, then existing, shall draw up a draft law for the election of the Constituent Assembly which it shall submit to Parliament for approval. The Governor-General shall give his consent to the law with the agreement of his Commission. Detailed preparations for the process of Self-Determination, including safeguards assuring the impartiality of the elections and any other arrangements designed to secure a free and neutral atmosphere, shall be subject to international supervision. The two Contracting Governments will accept the recommendations of any international body which may be set up to this end.

ARTICLE 11

Egyptian and British military forces shall withdraw from the Sudan immediately upon the Sudanese Parliament adopting a resolution expressing its desire that arrangements for Self-Determination be put in motion. The two Contracting Governments undertake to complete the withdrawal of their forces from the Sudan within a period not exceeding three months.

ARTICLE 12

The Constituent Assembly shall have two duties to discharge. The first will be to decide the future of the Sudan as one integral whole. The second will be to draw up a constitution for the Sudan compatible with the decision which shall have been taken in this respect, as well as an electoral law for a permanent Sudanese Parliament. The future of the Sudan shall be decided either:
(a) by the Constituent Assembly choosing to link the Sudan with Egypt in any form, or
(b) by the Constituent Assembly choosing complete independence.

ARTICLE 13

The two Contracting Governments undertake to respect the decision of the Constituent Assembly concerning the future status of the Sudan and each

Government will take all the measures which may be necessary to give effect to its decision.

ARTICLE 14

The two Contracting Governments agree that the Self-Government Statute shall be amended in accordance with Annex IV to this Agreement.

ARTICLE 15

This Agreement together with its attachments shall come into force upon signature.

In witness whereof the undersigned duly authorised thereto have signed the present Agreement and have affixed thereto their Seals.

Done at Cairo this twelfth day of February, 1953.

For the Government of the United Kingdom of Great Britain and Northern Ireland:

RALPH SKRINE STEVENSON (L.S.)

For the Egyptian Government:

MOH^{ed} NAGUIB, Major-General (L.S.)

In two copies, one of which shall remain deposited in the archives of the Government of the United Kingdom of Great Britain and Northern Ireland, and one of which shall remain deposited in the archives of the Egyptian Government.

APPENDIX 8

The Government of the United Kingdom of Great Britain and Northern Ireland and the Government of the Republic of Egypt,

Desiring to establish Anglo-Egyptian relations on a new basis of mutual understanding and firm friendship,

Have agreed as follows[1]:—

ARTICLE 1

Her Majesty's Forces shall be completely withdrawn from Egyptian territory in accordance with the Schedule set forth in Part 'A' of Annex I within a period of twenty months from the date of signature of the present Agreement.

ARTICLE 2

The Government of the United Kingdom declare that the Treaty of Alliance signed in London on the 26th of August, 1936, with the Agreed

[1] Republic of Egypt, Ministry of Foreign Affairs: Agreement between the Government of the Republic of Egypt and The Government of Great Britain and Northern Ireland, signed in Cairo on 19 October 1954.

Minute, Exchanged Notes, Convention concerning the immunities and privileges enjoyed by the British Forces in Egypt and all other subsidiary agreements, is terminated.

ARTICLE 3

Parts of the present Suez Canal Base, which are listed in Appendix A to Annex II, shall be kept in efficient working order and capable of immediate use in accordance with the provisions of Article 4 of the present Agreement. To this end they shall be organised in accordance with the provisions of Annex II.

ARTICLE 4

In the event of an armed attack by an outside power on any country which at the date of signature of the present Agreement is a party to the Treaty of Joint Defence between Arab League States, signed in Cairo on the 13th of April, 1950, or on Turkey, Egypt shall afford to the United Kingdom such facilities as may be necessary in order to place the Base on a war footing and to operate it effectively. These facilities shall include the use of Egyptian ports within the limits of what is strictly indispensable for the above-mentioned purposes.

ARTICLE 5

In the event of the return of British Forces to the Suez Canal Base area in accordance with the provisions of Article 4, these forces shall withdraw immediately upon the cessation of the hostilities referred to in that Article.

ARTICLE 6

In the event of a threat of an armed attack by an outside power on any country which at the date of signature of the present Agreement is a party to the Treaty of Joint Defence between Arab League States or on Turkey, there shall be immediate consultation between Egypt and the United Kingdom.

ARTICLE 7

The Government of the Republic of Egypt shall afford over-flying, landing, and servicing facilities for notified flights of aircraft under Royal Air Force control. For the clearance of any flights of such aircraft, the Government of the Republic of Egypt shall accord treatment no less favourable than that accorded to the aircraft of any other foreign country with the exception of states parties to the Treaty of Joint Defence between Arab League States. The landing and servicing facilities mentioned above shall be afforded at Egyptian Airfields in the Suez Canal Base area.

ARTICLE 8

The two Contracting Governments recognise that the Suez Maritime Canal, which is an integral part of Egypt, is a waterway economically, commercially and strategically of international importance, and express the determination to uphold the Convention guaranteeing the freedom of navigation of the Canal signed at Constantinople on the 29th of October 1888.

ARTICLE 9

(*a*) The United Kingdom is accorded the right to move any British equipment into or out of the Base at its discretion.

(*b*) There shall be no increase above the level of supplies as agreed upon in Part C of Annex II without the consent of the Government of the Republic of Egypt.

ARTICLE 10

The present Agreement does not affect and shall not be interpreted as affecting in any way the rights and obligations of the parties under the Charter of the United Nations.

ARTICLE 11

The Annexes and appendices to the present Agreement shall be considered as an integral part of it.

ARTICLE 12

(*a*) The present Agreement shall remain in force for the period of seven years from the date of its signature.

(*b*) During the last twelve months of that period the two Contracting Governments shall consult together to decide on such arrangements as may be necessary upon the termination of the Agreement.

(*c*) Unless both the Contracting Governments agree upon any extension of the Agreement it shall terminate seven years after the date of signature and the Government of the United Kingdom shall take away or dispose of their property then remaining in the Base.

ARTICLE 13

The present Agreement shall have effect as though it had come into force on the date of signature. Instruments of ratification shall be exchanged in Cairo as soon as possible.

IN WITNESS WHEREOF THE UNDERSIGNED, being duly authorised thereto, have signed the present Agreement and have affixed thereto their seals.

Done at Cairo, this 19th day of October, 1954, in duplicate, in the English and Arabic languages, both texts being equally authentic.

A. Nutting   Gamal Abdel Nasser
R. C. S. Stevenson   Abdel Hakim Amer
E. R. Benson   Abdel Latif Baghdad
                      Saler Salem
                      Mahmoud Fawzi

(II) SELECT BIBLIOGRAPHY

A. GOVERNMENT OFFICIAL SOURCES

BRITAIN (U.K.)

Foreign Office Publications (Despatches):

No. 2, 6 January 1882, Granville to Malet. P.R.O. F.O. 141/152.
No. 387, 30 October 1882, Granville to Barry. P.R.O. F.O. 141/153.
No. 99, 7 May 1883, Granville to Cartwright. P.R.O. F.O. 78/3550.
No. 302, 25 November 1883, Granville to Baring. P.R.O. F.O. 78/3551.
No. 210, 4 January 1884, in Egypt No. 1 (1884).
No. 213, 4 January 1884, Granville to Duffering in Egypt No. 1 (1884).
No. 57, 12 April 1898, Cromer to Salisbury. P.R.O. F.O. 78/4956.
No. 109, 2 August 1898, Salisbury to Cromer. P.R.O. F.O. 78/4955.
No. 96, 7 May 1883, Granville to Malet. P.R.O. F.O. 78/3550.

Public Record Office:

War Office:

32/132/7700/7661.
32/124/346.
32/124/7700/495.
32/124/495.
127/7700/309–20.
32/130/7700/2812.
32/127/7700/1772.
32/131/7700/3463.

British Parliamentary Papers:

Communications with Mohamet Ali, 1833; 1839 (207), Vol. L.
Official Reports by H.M. Agents and Consuls-General on the Finances, Administration and Condition of Egypt and the Sudan in:—
1883 (Egypt No. 13).
1890–1 (Vol. LXXVI; C. 6278).
1899 Provisions of the Condominium.
1898–9 State Papers, Vol. XCI, 1902.
Treaty Series No. 9 (1901), Pacific Settlement of International Disputes.
1902 (Egypt No. 1).
Treaty Series No. 16 (1902), Article III.
1904 (Egypt No. 1).
Treaty Series No. 6 (1905), Egypt and Morocco.
1906 (Egypt No. 3).
1910 (Egypt No. 1).
1914 (Egypt No. 1).
Treaty Series No. 17 (1929), Use of the Water of the Nile for Irrigation Purposes.
Treaty Series No. 6 (1937), Cmd. 5360.
Treaty Series No. 30 (1954). Cmd. 9132.

Report for the Period 1914–19, Cmd. 957:
  1920 (Egypt No. 1).
  1921 (Egypt Nos. 2 and 4).
  1922 (Egypt No. 1).
Papers respecting Negotiations with the Egyptian Delegation:
  (1921) Cmd. 1555.
1924 Despatch to H.M. High Commissioner respecting the position of H.M. Government in regard to Egypt and the Sudan; Cmd. 2269.
Protocol for the Pacific Settlement of International Disputes, 1924.
Papers respecting Negotiations for a Treaty of Alliance with Egypt:
  (1928) Cmd. 3050.
  (1924) Cmd. 2273. Protocol for the Pacific Settlement of International Disputes.
Exchange of Notes on Proposal for an Anglo-Egyptian Settlement:
  (1929–30) Cmd. 3376.
Papers regarding the Negotiations for a Revision of the Anglo-Egyptian Treaty of 1936:
  (1946–7) Cmd. 7179.
  (1949) Cmd. 7695. Royal Commission on Population.
Anglo-Egyptian Conversations on the Defence of the Suez Canal and on the Sudan; Cmd. 8419 (Egypt No. 2, 1951).
Documents concerning Constitutional Development in the Sudan and the Agreement between Britain and Egypt concerning Self-Government and Self-Determination for the Sudan; 17 February 1953 (Egypt No. 2, 1953), Cmd. 8767. See also Egypt No. 1, 1953 (Cmd. 8904).
Exchange of Notes between Britain and Egypt regarding the Construction of the Owen Falls Dam in Uganda. Cairo, 5 January 1953; Cmd. 9132 (Treaty Series No. 30, 1954).
Supplementary Agreement between Britain and Egypt for the Establishment of an International Commission to supervise the process of Self-Determination in the Sudan (with Exchange of Notes, modifying the 1953 Agreement). Cairo, 3 December 1955; Treaty Series No. 90, 1955, or Cmd. 9661.
Report of the British Trade Mission to Egypt, Sudan and Ethiopia, London, 1955.
Central Office of Information, Reference Division, London:
  The Commonwealth in Brief, London, February 1955.
  Owen Falls Scheme, Uganda, Ref. No. R/2811, 8 March 1954.
  Commonwealth Survey, 23 November 1951.
  The Sudan, 1899–1953, July 1953.
  The Gezira Scheme, No. R/1972, June 1950.
  The Nile Waters Development, No. R/2434, July 1952.
  Ministry of Materials: *Raw Cotton Commission Annual Reports*.
  Overseas Economic Survey, Egypt, 1951.
  Parliamentary Debates (various).

House of Commons and House of Lords:

Anglo-Egyptian Relations since the 1936 Treaty, and the Sudan: Bibliography No. 72, London, 26 July 1951; No. 72 (a), 28 October 1954.

EGYPT

Ministry of Foreign Affairs (Department of Information):

The Egyptian Question, 1882–1951, Cairo, 1951.

The Sudan Question—a translation of a report published in French in the bulletin of Agence France-Presse, 'Information et Documentation' in Paris, on 14 and 21 June 1947.

Egypt/Sudan (a compilation of some of the documentary evidence substantiating Egypt's claims), Cairo, 1947.

The Sudan Question based on British Documents (by Abdel-Moneim Omar), Cairo, 1952.

Records of Conversations, Notes and Papers exchanged between the British and the Egyptian Governments (March 1950–November 1951), Cairo, 1951.

Verbatim Records of the Security Council concerning the Anglo-Egyptian Dispute, 1947.

Statement in Parliament (on Abrogation) by Salah Eddin Pasha, Minister for Foreign Affairs on 6 August 1951.

Agreement between the Republic of Egypt and Britain (Suez Agreement), 1954: With agreed Minutes, Exchanges of Notes and Annexes, Cairo, 1955.

Presidency of the Council of Ministers:

The Contribution of Egypt in World War II, Cairo, 1947.

The Sudan Under the New Agreement (with Notes and Papers exchanged), Cairo, 1953.

Documents on the Sudan, 1899–1953 (by the Egyptian Society of International Law), Cairo, March 1953.

Ministry of Social Affairs, Labour Department, *Annual Report*, Cairo, 1951.

National Bank of Egypt: *Report of the 55th Ordinary General Meeting 1954*, Cairo, 1955.

Ministry of Finance and Economy, Statistical Dept.: *Pocket Year Book for 1953*, Cairo, 1954.

Annual Statement of Foreign Trade for 1952, Cairo, 1954.

SUDAN

Sudan Antiquities Service: Museum Pamphlet No. 1—*A Short History of the Sudan* (up to A.D. 1500), by Margaret Shinnie.

Annual Official Reports by the Governor-General
    1921–7 (see index to the Parliamentary Papers 1920–9).
    1928–40 (Papers 1929–43).
    1939–41 (Cmd. 8097).
    1942–4 (Cmd. 8098).
    1948 (Cmd. 8181).
    1949 (Cmd. 8434).
Central Economic Board, *Reports*, Khartoum, 1915, 1916.
Chamber of Commerce Monthly Journal, Khartoum, 1915–17, 1919–20, 1937, etc.
Department of Economics and Trade, *Foreign Trade Report*, Khartoum, 1947.
Ministry of Social Affairs: *1,001 Facts about the Sudan*, Khartoum, May 1955.
Sudan Almanac: An Official Handbook, Khartoum, 1955 and 1956.
The Anglo-Egyptian Sudan from Within (a book published under the auspices of the Sudan Government), London, 1935.
Advisory Council of the North Sudan, *Proceedings of the VI Session*, Khartoum, 1947.
Gezira Board, *Second Annual Report*, 1953.
Laws of the Sudan, Vol. III: The Natives Disposition of Lands Restriction Ordinance of 1918 and 1922.
Gezira Board, *Third Annual Report*, 1953.
Ministry of Irrigation and Hydro-electric Power: *The Nile Waters Question*, Khartoum, 1955.
The Transitional Constitution of the Sudan, Khartoum, December 1955.
Foreign Trade and Internal Statistics, January 1955.
Ministry of Social Affairs: *Sudan Weekly News*, Khartoum, 1953 to February 1956.

REPUBLIC OF THE SUDAN
Southern Disturbances, August 1955, Report of the Commission of Enquiry, Khartoum, 1956.

UNITED NATIONS
Security Council: *Official Records*, 2nd year, No. 70 (The Egyptian Question).
Department of Economic Affairs, Financial Division: *Egypt—Public Financial Information Papers*, New York, 1950.
General Assembly, *Supplement No. 15* (A/2188), 1952.
Verbatim Records, 197th Meeting of the Security Council, 11 August 1947.

UNESCO
What is Race? Paris, 1952.
Race and Society, Paris, 1952.

B. BOOKS

ABBAS, MEKKI: *The Sudan Question*, London, 1952.

BARING, E. (Earl of Cromer), *Modern Egypt*, Vol. II, London, 1908.

BILLINGTON, R. A., *et al.*, The Making of American Democracy: *Readings and Documents*, Vol. II, New York, 1950.

BOUNTY, E., *The English People*, London, 1904.

BOVERIE, M., *Mediterranean Cross Currents*, London, 1938.

BRANSTON, U., *Britain and European Unity*, Conservative Political Centre, London, 1953.

BUELL, R. L., *International Relations*, 1929.

BULLARD, SIR R. W., *Britain and the Middle East*, London, 1951.

CHAMBERLAIN, J., *Political Memoirs*, 1880–92, London, 1953.

CHANDRASEKHAR, S., *Hungry People and Empty Lands*, London, 1954.

CHURCHILL, W. S., *The River War*, London, 1899.

CHURCHILL, W. S., *The Hinge of Fate*, The Second World War, Vol. IV.

Church Missionary Society, *Introducing the Diocese of Sudan*, London, 1946.

CROMER, EARL of, see BARING, E.

DAVIE, M. R., *Negroes in American Society*, New York, 1949.

DUGMORE, A. R., *The Vast Sudan*, London, 1924.

DUNCAN, J. R. S., *The Sudan*, London, 1951.

EL-BARAWY, R., *Egypt, Britain and the Sudan*, Cairo, 1952.

EL-BARAWY, R., *The Military Coup in Egypt*, Cairo, 1952.

ELGOOD, P. G., *The Transit of Egypt*, London, 1928.

FEIS, H., *Europe, the World's Banker, 1870–1915*, New Haven, 1931.

GLASGOW, G., *MacDonald as Diplomatist—The Foreign Policy of the First Labour Government in Britain*, London, 1924.

GRONDONA, L. ST. C., *Commonwealth Stocktaking*, London, 1953.

GUNTHER, J., *Inside Africa*, London and New York, 1955.

HAMILTON, J. DE C., *Anglo-Egyptian Sudan from Within*, London, 1935.

HENDERSON, K. D. D., *The Making of the Sudan*, London, 1952.

HERTZ, F., *Nationality in History and Politics*, London, 1944.

HOBSON, C. K., *The Export of Capital*, London, 1914.

HODGKIN, R. A., *Sudan Geography*, Khartoum, 1936.

HUGHES, P., *A History of the Church*, Vol. I, London, 1948.

HYSLOP, J., *The Sudan Story*, London, 1952.

JAMES, D. H., *The Rise and Fall of the Japanese*, London, 1951.

KANTOROWICZ, H., *The Spirit of British Policy and the Myth of the Encirclement of Germany*, English ed., London, 1931.

KEAY, S. J., *Spoiling the Egyptians: A Tale of Shame*, 4th ed., London, 1882.

KEITH, A. BERRIEDALE, *Wheaton's International Law*, 6th ed., Vol. I, London, 1929.

Appendixes

LANE, W. E., *The Manners and Customs of the Modern Egyptians*, London, 1936. Everyman's Library Edition.

LANGER, W. L., *The Diplomacy of Imperialism, 1890–1902*, Vol. I, New York, 1935.

LANGER, W. L., *European Alliances and Alignments*, 2nd ed., New York, 1950.

LANGLEY, M., *No Woman's Country*, London, 1950.

LAUTERPACHT, H., *Oppenheim's International Law*, Vol. I, 7th ed., London, 1948.

LAWRENCE, T. E., *Seven Pillars of Wisdom*, London, 1935.

LITTLE, K. L., *Negroes in Britain: A Study of the Racial Relations in English Society*, London, 1948.

LLOYD, G. A., *Egypt since Cromer*, Vol. I and Vol. II, 1925.

LUGARD, SIR F. D., *The Dual Mandate in Tropical Africa*, London, 1922.

MACHIAVELLI, N., *The Prince*, The World's Classics Edition, 1952.

MACMICHAEL, H. A., (1) *The Anglo-Egyptian Sudan*, London, 1934; (2) 1954.

MARLOWE, J., *Anglo-Egyptian Relations*, London, 1954.

MIMANT, M., *Les Corporations, 1929*.

MONROE, E., *The Mediterranean in Politics*, London, 1938.

MORGENTHAU, H. J., *Politics Among Nations*, New York, 1954.

MURRAY, T. D., and SILVA, A., *Samuel Baker: A Memoir*, London and New York, 1895.

NEGUIB, M., *Egypt's Destiny*, London, 1955.

NORTHRUP, F. S. C., *The Meeting of East and West*, New York, 1949.

NORWICH, LORD, *Old Men Forget*, London, 1953.

OWEN, F., *Tempestuous Journey: Lloyd George, His Life and Times*, London, 1954.

PARMA, N. T. K., *Deposition of H.M. the Kabaka of Buganda*, London, 1954.

POWELL, G. H., *Reminiscences and Table Talk of Samuel Rogers*, 1903.

QUENNELL, M., and C. H. B., *Everyday Life in Roman Britain*, London.

RANGA, N. G., *The Colonial and Coloured Peoples*, Bombay, 1946.

ROSE, J. H., *et al.*, *Cambridge History of the British Empire*, Vol. I, 1929.

Royal Institute of International Affairs, *Annual Surveys of International Affairs, 1924 to 1952*.

Royal Institute of International Affairs, *Great Britain and Egypt, 1914–51*, London, 1952.

Royal Institute of International Affairs, *The Middle East*; a Political and Economic Survey, 2nd ed., London, 1954.

Royal Institute of International Affairs, *Nationalism*, London, 1939.

Royal Institute of International Affairs, *Political and Strategic Interests of the United Kingdom*, Oxford, 1940.

RUSSELL, B., *Freedom and Organisation, 1814–1914*, London, 1934.

RUSSELL, R. S., *Imperial Preference: Its Development and Effect*, London, 1949.

SCHOLFIELD, H. J., *The Suez Canal in World Affairs*, London, 1952.

SCHUMAN, , F. L., *International Politics*, New York, 1948.

SELIGMAN, S. G., *Races of Africa*, revised ed., London, 1939.

SHIBEIKA, M., *British Policy in the Sudan*, London, 1952.

SIMMONDS, F. H., and BROOKES, E., *The Great Powers in World Politics*, New York, 1939.

SLADEN, D., *Egypt and the English*, London, 1908.

SLOCOMBE, G., *The Dangerous Sea; The Mediterranean and its Future*, London, 1936.

SPYKMAN, N. J., *Geography and Foreign Policy*, New York.

TAYLOR, H., *Public International Law*, Chicago, 1901.

TAYLOR, J. V., *Christianity and Politics in Africa*, London, 1957.

TEMPERLEY, H. W. V., *A History of the Peace of Paris*, London, 1924.

TOYNBEE, A. J., *A Study of History*, Vol. VII, London, 1954.

TRIMINGHAM, J. S., *The Approach to Islam in the Sudan*, 1948.

WAVELL, F.-M. EARL, *Allenby: Soldier and Statesman*, London, 1946.

WILSON, SIR A. T., *The Suez Canal, Its Past, Present and Future*, 2nd ed., London, 1939.

WOODWARD, SIR L., *Some Reflections on British Foreign Policy, 1939–45*, Stevenson Memorial Lecture, London School of Economics and Political Science, 24 May 1955.

WYNDHAM, R., *The Gentle Savage*, 4th ed., London, 1937.

YOUSEF, AMINE, BEY, *Independent Egypt*, London, 1940.

C. NEWSPAPERS AND PERIODICALS

African Affairs, London.

American Journal of International Law, New York, Vol. XXXI, 1937, *et seq.*

Bulletin of International Affairs, London.

Christian Science Monitor, New York.

Colonial Review, London.

Contemporary Review, London.

Daily Express, London.

Daily Worker, London.

East Africa and Rhodesia, 1955.

Economist, London, various dates to 1956.

Egyptian Gazette, Cairo.

Foreign Affairs, New York.

Foreign Policy Bulletin, New York.

Fortnightly Review, London from 1899 onwards.

India Quarterly.

La Bourse Egyptienne, Cairo, various dates up to 1955.

Listener (B.B.C.), London.

Manchester Guardian.

Middle East Monthly Review.

New Statesman and Nation, London, 1946–56

New York Times.
News Chronicle, London.
Nigeria Trade Journal, Lagos, October/December 1954.
Observer, London, various dates to 1956.
Round Table (semi-official), London, 1910–56.
Sawt El Sudan, Khartoum.
Soviet News.
Spectator, London.
Sudan Weekly News (Official), Khartoum, 1953–6.
Sydney Herald, Australia, 11 March 1885.
The Times, London, 1884–1956 (a vital source).
The World Today, Royal Institute of International Affairs, London.
West Africa, 11 December 1954.

D. SPECIAL ARTICLES

ADAMS, B., 'The New Struggle for Life among Nations', *Fortnightly Review*, Vol. LXV, 1899.

AMERY, J., 'Hold on to Suez', *Time and Tide*, 24 July 1954.

BENNETT, E. N., 'After Omdurman', *Contemporary Review*, Vol. LXXV, 1899.

BEY, S. E., 'Why Egypt Broke with Britain', *The U.S. News and World Reports*, 19 October 1951.

DAGHER, I., 'Religious Heritage in Current History', *The Monthly Magazine of World Affairs*, Vol. XXVI, No. 152, April 1954.

DICEY, E., 'Our Route to India', *Nineteenth Century*, Vol. I, June 1877.

FELKIN, R., 'The Sudan Question', *Contemporary Review*, Vol. LXXIV, 1898.

FOLLOWER, F. J., 'Some Problems of Water Distribution Between East and West Punjab', *Geographical Review*, Vol. XL, No. 4, 1950.

GIBB, H. A. R., *Anglo-Egyptian Relations*, Royal Institute of International Affairs, Vol. XXVII, No. 4, October 1951.

GLADSTONE, W. E., 'Aggression on Egypt', *Nineteenth Century*, Vol. II, August 1877.

GLASGOW, G., 'An Emotional Bubble in Egypt', *Contemporary Review*, July 1927.

GLASGOW, G., 'Foreign Affairs', *Contemporary Review*, No. 852, 1936.

GUNTHER, J., 'Inside Egypt', *Readers Digest*, May 1955.

GUSSMAN, B., 'Egypt's Dilemma', *Contemporary Review*, Vol. CLXXII, 1947.

HAMPGOOD, N., 'Mr. Gladstone', *Contemporary Review*, Vol. LXXIV, 1898.

HOSKINS, H. L., 'Some Aspects of the Security Problem in the Middle East', *American Political Science Review*, Vol. XLVII.

LEWIS, H. O. L., 'Race and European Culture', *Negro Year Book*, Department of Records and Research, Tuskegee Institute, Alabama, 1947.

MCLEISH, A., 'The Kashmir Dispute', *World Affairs Journal*, Vol. IV, No. 1, January 1950.

MANNING, C. A. W., 'The Teaching of International Relations', *Listener*, Vol. 51, No. 1317, 27 May 1954.

NICOLSON, SIR H.,'The Origins and Development of the Anglo-French Entente,' *International Affairs*, No. 4, October 1954.

PRICE, P. M.,'Indo-China, Egypt and Persia', *Contemporary Review*, September 1954.

RUSSELL, G. W. E., 'Gladstone's Theology', *Contemporary Review*, Vol. LXXIII, 1898.

SMITH, T. V., 'Power: Its Ubiquity and Legitimacy', *The American Political Science Review*, No. 3, September 1951.

E. MISCELLANEOUS PUBLICATIONS

Annual Register, 1798, 1883, 1885, 1899, 1914, 1921, 1924, 1926 . . . 1953.

The British Society for International Understanding: The British Survey, Popular Series No. 100—*The Anglo-Egyptian Sudan*.

Bulletin of International Affairs, Vol. VI, No. 30, 22 May 1930; Vol. XIII, No. 6, 12 September 1936.

BURKE, E., *Thoughts on the Cause of the Present Discontents*, 1770.

BURNS, E., *British Imperialism in Egypt*, Colonial Series No. 5, 1928.

France: *Revue de Droit International et de Legalisation*, 1924, No. 5.

HILMI, A., 'A Few Words on the Anglo-Egyptian Settlement. . . .'

International Conciliation (Arab League 1945–55), May 1955.

International Cotton Advisory Committee: *Cotton Monthly Review of the World Situation*, Vol. VI, June 1953.

Italy: *Oriente Moderno*, Vol. IV.

Keesing's *Contemporary Archives*, 1935–56 (vital source).

League of Nations Official Journal, Vol. V, 1924.

ROBERTSON, SIR JAMES W., Private Correspondence with the Author (L. A. Fabunmi).

U.K.: Conservative Research Department. 'The Commonwealth, the Colonial Affairs, Central African Federation', London, 31 December 1952.

U.K.: Conservative Research Department. Monthly Survey of Foreign Affairs No. 61: 'Britain in the Middle East—The Anglo-Egyptian Treaty in Perspective', London, January 1954.

U.K.: *The Round Table* (semi-official).

INDEX

Abadan incident, 289–90
Abbas II, Khedive of Egypt, 65; deposition of, 66
Abbas, Mekki, 3, 4, 178, 179, 339, 340; attitude to 'Southern policy', 11–12; on missionary activities in the Sudan, 16; on validity of Anglo-Egyptian 1899 Agreement, 57; on importance of Nile to Egypt, 117
Abdul-Latif, Ali, 80
Abdullahi, father of Mohammed Ahmed, 39
Abuquir Bay, destruction of French fleet at, 27
Abu's-Sa'ud, Zakki, Pasha, 64
Abu Simbel, temple at, 23
Abyssinia: War with Italy, 104; Egypt's sympathy with, 105. *See also* Ethiopia
Acheson, Dean, 286
Adli Pashā, 69, 77, 98; and Nile Waters negotiations, 77–8
Adowa, Battle of, 49
Afifi, Dr. Hafiz, 111
Africa: the scramble for, 46–7, 58; widespread nationalism in, after World War II, 268
Africa, East: as alternative British base to Suez, 322–3; arguments against, 323; proposed Federation of, 388
Africa, French North, 169; insurrection in, 268
Africa, South, Union of, 161; apartheid in, 268, 345–6; and evacuation of Suez base, 317
Africa, West: labour from, in Gezira scheme, 129; Egyptian overtures to, 169; demand for home rule in, 268; British withdrawal from, 324
Afzal, Dr. Mohammed, 390
Ahmed (Mohammed Ahmed's grandson), 40
Ahmed, Ibrahim, 329
Ahmed, Mohammed (The Mahdi), 25, 32–3; character and personality of, 39–40; his descendants, 40; death, 46; desecration of his tomb, 50; his revolt, 32ff., 397
Ahmose II, King of Egypt, 23
Aisha, wife of Mohammed Ahmed, 40
Airports and Airways, Sudanese, 390; importance of, to Britain, 188–9
Akinloye, Mr., of Nigeria, 169

Al Akhbar, 170
Alakija, Sir Adeyemo, 333
Al Ayam, 353
Al-Balagh, 226
Albert, Lake, dam on, 126
Al-Birair, Ali, 233, 235
Alexandria: British troops occupy Customs offices at (1924), 91; British warship at (1927), 99; wartime raids on, 230; demonstrations in (1947), 260
Alexāndroff, I., 163–4
Al Gumhouriya, 371
al-Hilali, Ahmad Nagib, 288
Ali Bey, 116
Ali, Mohammed, Viceroy of Egypt, 23–4, 28, 30, 119, 130, 154, 165, 170, 397
Ali, Mohammed, Premier of Pakistan: and Cairo talks (1953), 309–10
Allen, Charles H., 75n.
Allenby, Field-Marshal Viscount, 64, 66, 70, 74, 79; on Sudan's economic progress, 73; ultimatum after Stack assassination, 84, 87ff.; resignation, 87; exchange of Notes on Nile Waters, 121
Al Misri, 273–4, 275
Altrincham, Lord, 403
'Amalgamate' school of Sudanese ethnology, 7
American Journal of International Law, 110–11
Amery, Julian, 305, 316
Ammer, Dr. Abbas, 156–7
Anglo-Egyptian Agreement (1899). *See* Condominium
Anglo-Egyptian Agreement (1953), 57, 193, 296–8, 437–40; difficulties when worked, 299ff.
Anglo-Egyptian Agreement (1954). *See under* Suez Canal zone
Anglo-Egyptian Committee (1948), 270–1
Anglo-Egyptian Convention (1922): drafted by Egypt, 78–9; deletion of Sudan references, 79
Anglo-Egyptian Conversations (1950–1), 145, 273–82
Anglo-Egyptian negotiations, after World War II, 267ff.
Anglo-Egyptian Treaty of Friendship and Alliance (1936), 103ff., 134, 141,

Index